B.C.	IMPORTANT EVENTS	
1000		ARK STORIES
950	937 Division of the Hebrew Empire.	EARLY SAUL STORIES
	932 Invasion of Shishak.	EARLY DAVID STORIES
900	875–850 Work of Elijah.	
	854–839 Campaigns of Shalmaneser II.	EARLY JUDEAN SAUL
850	850–795 Work of Elisha.	AND DAVID NARRATIVES
	842 Jehu's Tribute to Shalmaneser II.	
	810 Joash's Tribute to Hazael.	
800	781–740 Reign of Jeroboam II.	
750	750–740 Preaching of Amos.	
	745–736 Work of Hosea.	
	737–690 Work of Isaiah.	POPULAR JUDEAN
	722–721 Capture of Samaria.	DAVID STORIES
700	686–641 Reactionary Reign of Manasseh.	LATER EPHRAIMITE
	663 Ashurbanipal's Capture of Thebes.	SAMUEL NARRATIVES
650		VERY LATE PO
	626 Earlier Sermons of Zephaniah and Jeremiah.	PROPHETIC TRA
	621 Great Reformation of Josiah.	
600	597 The First Captivity. Work of Ezekiel.	FIRST EDITION
	586 The Final Captivity.	OF I, II SAMUEL
	560 Expulsion of Foreigners from Egypt.	
550	538 Capture of Babylon by Cyrus.	**FINAL REVISION**
	520–516 Rebuilding of the Temple.	
	520–516 Reorganization of Persian Empire.	
500	490 Battle of Marathon.	
	480 Battles of Thermopylæ and Salamis.	
450	470 Expulsion of Persians from Europe.	
	445 Rebuilding the Walls of Jerusalem.	
	432 Nehemiah's Second Visit.	
400	400 Adoption of the Priestly Law by the Judean Community.	LATE TEMPLE HISTORY (?)
350	346 Devastation of Palestine by Ochus.	MID
	332 Conquest of Syria by Alexander.	THE BOOK
	301 Battle of Ipsus.	OF ISRAE
300	272 Death of Pyrrhus.	
	250 Beginning of Translation of Greek O. T.	**BOOKS OF CHRONICLES } CH**
250	217 Battle of Raphia.	
200	198 Conquest of Palestine by Seleucids.	
	168 Persecution of the Jews.	
	165 Rededication of the Temple.	
150	141 Election of Simon High Priest, General, and Governor of the Jews.	**I MACCABEES**
	139 Renewal of Treaty with Rome.	
100	94 Subjugation of Moab and Ammon.	
	63 Seizure of Judea by Rome.	
50		

KNOWN ONLY THROUGH QUOTATIONS.

EXPLANATION

REFERRED TO B

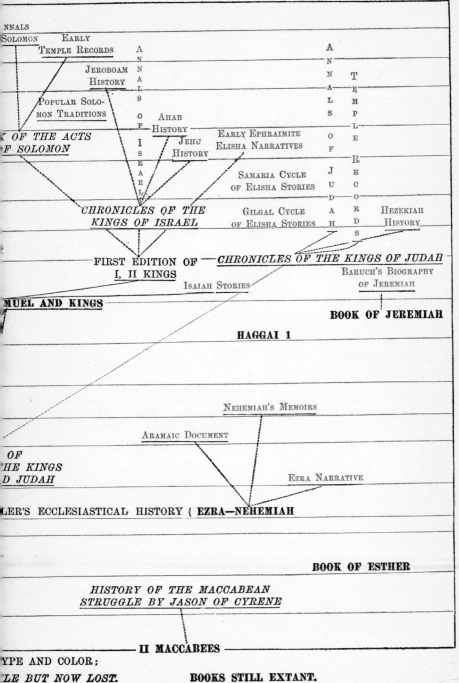

NNALS

SOLOMON EARLY
TEMPLE RECORDS

JEROBOAM
HISTORY

POPULAR SOLO-
MON TRADITIONS

AHAB
HISTORY

EARLY EPHRAIMITE
ELISHA NARRATIVES

K OF THE ACTS
F SOLOMON

JEHU
HISTORY

SAMARIA CYCLE
OF ELISHA STORIES

*CHRONICLES OF THE
KINGS OF ISRAEL*

GILGAL CYCLE
OF ELISHA STORIES

HEZEKIAH
HISTORY

ANNALS OF ISRAEL

ANNALS OF JUDAH

TEMPLE RECORDS

FIRST EDITION OF
I, II KINGS

CHRONICLES OF THE KINGS OF JUDAH

BARUCH'S BIOGRAPHY
OF JEREMIAH

ISAIAH STORIES

MUEL AND KINGS

BOOK OF JEREMIAH

HAGGAI 1

NEHEMIAH'S MEMOIRS

ARAMAIC DOCUMENT

*OF
HE KINGS
D JUDAH*

EZRA NARRATIVE

LER'S ECCLESIASTICAL HISTORY { EZRA—NEHEMIAH

BOOK OF ESTHER

*HISTORY OF THE MACCABEAN
STRUGGLE BY JASON OF CYRENE*

II MACCABEES

YPE AND COLOR:

LE BUT NOW LOST.   **BOOKS STILL EXTANT.**

Charles L. Souvay

The Student's Old Testament

ISRAEL'S
HISTORICAL AND BIOGRAPHICAL
NARRATIVES

THE STUDENT'S OLD TESTAMENT

LOGICALLY AND CHRONOLOGICALLY
ARRANGED AND TRANSLATED

BY

CHARLES FOSTER KENT, Ph.D.

WOOLSEY PROFESSOR OF BIBLICAL LITERATURE IN YALE UNIVERSITY

ARRANGEMENT OF VOLUMES

I. Narratives of the Beginnings of Hebrew History. (*Now Ready.*)

Introduction. The Beginnings cf Human History. Traditional Ancestors of the Hebrews. Deliverance of the Hebrews from Egypt. Life of the Hebrews in the Wilderness and East of the Jordan. Conquest and Settlement of Canaan.

II. Historical and Biographical Narratives. (*Now Ready.*)

Introduction. The United Monarchy. History of Northern Israel. History of Judah. Re-establishment of the Jewish Community in Palestine. The Maccabean Struggle. Life of the Jews of the Dispersion.

III. Prophetic Sermons, Epistles, and Apocalypses

Introduction. The Prophets of the Assyrian Period. Prophets of Judah's Decline. Prophets of the Babylonian Exile. Prophets of the Persian Period. Prophets of the Greek and Maccabean Periods.

IV. Laws and Traditional Precedents

Introduction. Constitutional Laws. Criminal Laws. Private Laws. Humanitarian Laws. Religious Laws. Ceremonial Laws.

V. Songs, Psalms, and Prayers

Introduction. Folk and National Songs. Songs of Love and Marriage. Songs of Lamentation. Imprecatory Psalms. Historical Psalms. Royal and Messianic Psalms. Psalms of Thanksgiving. Psalms of Praise and Adoration. Reflective Psalms. Penitential Psalms. Psalms of Worship. Prayers.

VI. Proverbs and Didactic Poems

Introduction. Practical and Ethical Observations and Precepts. Religious Proverbs. Gnomic Essays. Numerical Enigmas. Discussions of the Problem of Evil. Discussions regarding the Value of Life and its Wise Enjoyment. Poems describing Wisdom.

The Student's Old Testament

ISRAEL'S
HISTORICAL AND BIOGRAPHICAL
NARRATIVES

FROM THE ESTABLISHMENT OF THE HEBREW KINGDOM
TO THE END OF THE MACCABEAN STRUGGLE

BY

CHARLES FOSTER KENT, Ph.D.

Woolsey Professor of Biblical Literature in Yale University

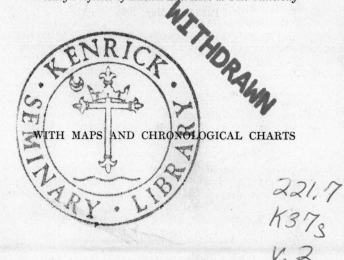

WITH MAPS AND CHRONOLOGICAL CHARTS

NEW YORK
CHARLES SCRIBNER'S SONS
1905

PREFACE

IT is a significant fact that nearly half of the entire Old Testament consists of historical and biographical narratives. These represent the oldest, the simplest, and the most concrete record of God's revelation of Himself "through life to life." That revelation is real and intelligible, and the faith that grew up about it possesses a permanent and universal value, because its foundations were the actual experiences of men who lived and struggled, amid trying circumstances, with the ever-recurring problems of human existence. In a very true sense Israel's unique faith was the substance of things seen and felt. Not in the garden of Eden but in the fiery furnace of adversity were the rude, primitive Hebrew tribes trained and given that divine message which made them Jehovah's chosen people—his witnesses, called to conquer the world, not by the sword but by unselfish service and the compelling power of truth.

Their later historians were inclined to invest the earlier periods and characters with a halo and to ignore the evidence of their elemental barbarity; but embedded in Judges, Samuel, and Kings are found extracts from older narratives that faithfully reflect those conditions which are the true background, and which make clear by contrast the real nature and significance of that marvellous development and revelation, the consummation of which is recorded in the later chapters. Israel's faith and ethical standards gradually unfolded under the divine teaching in the school of national experience, as did its political and social institutions. It is because they were constantly developing that they are significant. Along the same paths each individual must proceed from the comparative ignorance and barbarism of childhood to the maturity and strength of manhood. The Old Testament histories are unique, not merely because they record important events, but because the causes, the meaning, and the consequences of these are constantly interpreted by Israel's inspired historians. Hence the narratives, which begin with Samuel and end with I Maccabees, are the natural gateway through which to enter the broad fields represented by the Bible. Because of their vividness and concreteness the stories of Samuel, of Saul, and of David at once attract and hold the attention of young and old alike. Studied in their logical order—which is the order of events—the historical narratives introduce the student in succession and in their true relations to the significant characters and factors in Israel's remarkable history. Thus a definite, systematic basis is established for all subsequent study. In the light of this knowledge, the noble work and messages of Israel's teachers at once become real and possessed of a vital, personal interest and value.

PREFACE

The remarkable success that has attended the few initial experiments is convincing evidence that the time is not far distant when elementary, as well as advanced, Bible classes will abandon the unsystematic and largely fruitless methods still in vogue and enter upon a graded, unified course of study, which will in the end give a complete and thorough knowledge of the contents of both Testaments. In one year of systematic study it is possible to become acquainted with the essential outlines and facts of Israel's history; in another with the strong personality and noble messages of the prophets; then, intelligently and with greatest profit the fascinating narratives of the beginnings of Hebrew history, which come largely from the pens of the early prophets, can be studied, with the assurance that the intricate problems which they present will vanish when viewed from the vantage-points already gained. Similarly, as in succeeding years the great messages of the psalmists, priests, and sages are considered, they will each yield their wealth of inspiring truth, and in the end the entire Old Testament will be as familiar ground as the Gospel of Luke or the twenty-third psalm. This is not a distant ideal, but an easily attainable goal, provided our Bible teachers will set it definitely before their classes and inspire zeal and enthusiasm in steadily advancing toward it. They will soon find that various parts of the Old Testament are of very different values; but each stage in the study will reveal unsuspected beauties and vital truths which will kindle interest and arouse the sense of definite work and conquest and personal growth. Also, when they pass at times from the Scriptures which Jesus studied so deeply, and from which he and his apostles drew those truths and illustrations and expressions which they wove into all their teachings, to the New Testament, they will find that it has an entirely new meaning and significance.

Modern scholarship furnishes most valuable aid in restoring the original text, in explaining the obscurities and contradictions, in interpreting events in the light of universal history, and in supplementing the often meagre biblical narrative by the testimony of contemporary monumental literature; but modern Old Testament histories, however excellent, should never be substituted for that vivid, clear, dramatic history, written by Israel's own historians. It has been said, with much truth, that the Bible was never more studied and less read than to-day. Knowledge of its history, structure, and contents is essential; but it cannot without great loss take the place of personal acquaintance with the exalted ideas and records of the original writers, expressed in their own unrivalled literary form. The supreme aim, therefore, in this volume, as in the series of which it is a part, has been to facilitate the intelligent reading and personal study of the Bible itself. Introductions and foot-notes are simply intended to indicate the chief reasons for the faith that is rapidly becoming the common possession of all Bible students. Fortunately, while the Hebrew text of Samuel, Kings, and Ezra-Nehemiah is in many places obscure or defective, the Greek and other early versions have preserved a large number of original readings and in some cases long passages, so that it is now possible to place at the disposal of English readers a much more lucid and complete text of these important books. In adding

PREFACE

a new translation of I and II Maccabees, it is also felt that a real and growing need will be met.

Through the generous and efficient co-operation of the publishers it has also been possible to furnish within the compass of this volume an unusually complete equipment for the study of Old Testament history. The debt which I owe to the hundreds of scholars who have made this work possible is too great to acknowledge in detail; the classified list of books of reference in Appendix I gives the titles of those most often used. I am under deep obligation to my colleagues, Professor Torrey for suggestions in connection with chapters V and VI of the Introduction, to the Reverend Frederick Lent, M. A., for important collaboration in the translation of I Maccabees, and to the Reverend George D. Castor, M. A., in the translation of II Maccabees. The Reverend A. A. Madsen, M. A., has also placed at my disposal the valuable results of his detailed investigations in the fields of biblical geography and chronology, while Professor McFadyen, of Knox College, Toronto, has generously contributed at each point his most admirable criticisms. Last of all I wish to acknowledge the large debt which I owe to the members of my biblical and Hebrew seminars, whose practical discussions and sane conclusions have thrown clear light upon many difficult problems.

C. F. K.

YALE COLLEGE,
Easter, 1904.

CONTENTS AND CLASSIFICATION

INTRODUCTION

THE HISTORY OF ISRAEL'S HISTORICAL AND BIOGRAPHICAL NARRATIVES

CONTENTS AND CLASSIFICATION

THE UNITED MONARCHY

* References in parentheses are to later additions to the earlier narratives. Minor additions of a word or short clause are not indicated.

CONTENTS AND CLASSIFICATION

CONTENTS AND CLASSIFICATION

xiii

CONTENTS AND CLASSIFICATION

CONTENTS AND CLASSIFICATION

CONTENTS AND CLASSIFICATION

CONTENTS AND CLASSIFICATION

HISTORY OF JUDAH

CONTENTS AND CLASSIFICATION

CONTENTS AND CLASSIFICATION

CONTENTS AND CLASSIFICATION

CONTENTS AND CLASSIFICATION

THE MACCABEAN STRUGGLE

CONTENTS AND CLASSIFICATION

CONTENTS AND CLASSIFICATION

TABLE OF CONTENTS

APPENDIX

CHRONOLOGICAL CHARTS AND MAPS

INDEX OF BIBLICAL PASSAGES

EXPLANATION OF TYPOGRAPHICAL SYMBOLS AND ABBREVIATIONS

Text in roman type.

Supplemental and editorial additions to an older section in smaller type.

Superscriptions IN SMALL CAPITALS.

Poetical passages are distinguished by smaller type and broken lines.

Explanatory clauses, found in the original, in ( ).

English equivalents of the more significant Hebrew proper names in [ ].

Words implied by the context or supplied to restore the original narratives, where these have been abridged in the process of editorial fusion, *in italics.*

Foot-notes, presenting the reasons for the analysis and classification of the material, significant alternate readings, and explanatory material, in small roman type.

Interpretative side-headings, giving a condensed summary of the accompanying text, on the margins in small roman type.

Chapter numbers in arabic figures. **Verse numbers** in small figures placed above the line. **Successive portions of a verse** indicated by ^{a}, ^{b} or ^{c}, placed after the verse number. Thus, Genesis II. 4 (second part of the verse) to IV. 6 (first half) inclusive is written 2^{4b}–4^{6a}.

Complete stories or literary units (with their parallels, if any) are numbered with arabic numerals successively throughout the entire volume and are referred to as sections. Thus, § 2 refers to § 2, **The Primitive Story of Man's Creation and Fall,** pp. 53–56.

General Abbreviations

AmRV = American Revised Version (1901).
AV = Authorized Version (1611).
Apocr. = Apocrypha or apocryphal.
Aram. = Aramaic.
Assyr. = Assyrian.
Bab. = Babylonian.
cf. = compare.
e. g. = for example.
f. = and following.
Gk. = Greek B (Vatican) text of the O.T.

Gk.A = Alexandrian Gk. text of the O.T.
Gk. א = Sinaitic Gk. text of the O.T.
Heb. = Hebrew.
i. e. = that is.
Jos. = Josephus.
Lat. = Latin (Vulgate) text of Jerome.
Lit. = literally.
Luc. = Lucian's Recension of the Greek O.T.
N.T. = New Testament.

Old Lat. = Old Latin Version of the O.T.
Origen = Reading found in Origen's *Hexapla.*
O.T. = Old Testament.
Pent. = Pentateuch.
RV= Revised Version (1885).
Sam. = Samaritan Version of the Pent.
Sem. = Semitic.
Syr. = Syriac Version of the O.T.
Targ. = Targum.
Vs. = verse.

Abbreviations for the Old Testament and Apocryphal Books

Gen. = Genesis.
Ex. = Exodus.
Lev. = Leviticus.
Num. = Numbers.
Dt. = Deuteronomy.
Josh. = Joshua.
Judg. = Judges.
Sam. = Samuel.
Kgs. = Kings.
Chr. = Chronicles.
Neh. = Nehemiah.
Esth. = Esther.
Ps. = Psalms.
Pr. = Proverbs.
Ecc. = Ecclesiastes.
Sg. of Sgs. = Song of Songs.

Is. = Isaiah.
Jer. = Jeremiah.
Lam. = Lamentations.
Ezek. = Ezekiel.
Dan. = Daniel.
Hos. = Hosea.
Am. = Amos.
Ob. = Obadiah.
Jon. = Jonah.
Mic. = Micah.
Nah. = Nahum.
Hab. = Habakkuk.
Zeph. = Zephaniah.
Hag. = Haggai.
Zech. = Zechariah.
Mal. = Malachi.

Esdr. = Esdras.
Wisd. Sol. = Wisdom of Solomon.
B. Sir. = Ben Sira or Ecclesiasticus.
Bar. = Baruch.
Sg. of Three = Song of the Three Children.
Sus. = Susanna.
Pryr. of Man. = Prayer of Manasses.
Mac. = Maccabees.
Enoch = Book of Enoch.
Ps. of Sol. = Psalms of Solomon.

THE HISTORY OF ISRAEL'S HISTORICAL
AND BIOGRAPHICAL NARRATIVES

INTRODUCTION

I

THE ORIGIN AND PRESENT LITERARY FORM OF THE OLD TESTAMENT HISTORICAL AND BIOGRAPHICAL NARRATIVES

ISRAEL's national and literary history begins with the establishment of the Hebrew monarchy under Saul. Up to this time the only records of the past appear to have been disconnected popular traditions, recounted beside the camp fire, in the secret of the harem, at marriage feasts, at the local sanctuaries, during the annual feasts, at the wells, or beside the city gates, wherever men or women were gathered together and the story-teller could find an audience (cf. Vol. I, p. 13). These early stories, many of which are found in the first eight books of the Old Testament, undoubtedly preserve a great number of significant historical facts, but they do not constitute a national history, for the oldest and most authentic stories originated before the Israelitish tribes had yet crystallized into a nation, and the narratives furnish only occasional pictures of the more important acts and actors in that great drama which later unfolded on the soil of Palestine. They represent rather the prologue to the subsequent history, since they record the movements of the nomadic ancestors of the Hebrews and the early struggles of the individual tribes to secure and maintain possession of the much-contested land of Canaan. Through these varied traditions the historian is able to trace in outline at least the beginnings of Hebrew history.

The beginnings of Israel's national history

Before there can be a history in the generally accepted sense of that term, there must be historians possessed of the facilities for recording their facts and events worthy of record and calculated to inspire them to write. In ancient Israel these two conditions were first met and then fully supplied during the brilliant reigns of David and Solomon. The assimilation of the highly developed civilization of the Canaanites and the diplomatic and commercial relations with other centres of literary culture, such as Egypt, Phœnicia, and Damascus, gave the Hebrew historians their system of writing and also precedents to follow. From the days of David recorders and scribes figure among the court officials. The dramatic, epoch-making events of the reigns of Saul and David gave them themes well worthy of the pen of patriotic historians. The national pride, and splendor, and comparative peace of the reign of Solomon also afforded them the atmosphere and opportunity which undoubtedly gave rise to the earliest Hebrew historical records.

Conditions favorable for the writing of history

3

Literary form of the earliest records
These were either very brief annals of important events, such as the successions of kings, wars, building enterprises, treaties, and alliances, or else oral traditions which recounted the deeds of important religious or military leaders, like Samuel and Saul and David. Both of these very different types of sources underlie the narrative of Samuel and Kings. As the history unfolded, the tendency became marked to weave these various sources into a continuous narrative. Naturally, later historians would also further supplement the older records with current traditions regarding the earlier period. Thus it is that the narratives of Samuel and Kings have all the literary characteristics—absence of technical details, the few characters, the striking contrasts, the vividness, and the dramatic action—of the primitive traditions regarding the beginnings of Hebrew life. The story of David's family history, for example, is presented in II Samuel 9–20 in a literary form that suggests the great tragedies of Greece. The dramatic dialogue is also effectively employed, as in the more primitive traditions, to make the history realistic. The result is that the characters live and move and speak before the awakened imagination of the reader.

The introduction of sermons and addresses
When the Hebrew prophets became preachers and statesmen, swaying public opinion by the power of their voice and by the divine messages which they proclaimed in the form of public addresses, the historians also introduced sermons and long orations into their narratives. This literary form is common to all literature. Mark Antony's famous address in Shakespeare's *Julius Cæsar* is perhaps the most familiar modern example. This effective form of narration was in Hebrew literature but the natural outgrowth of the ancient oracle, as for example Jacob's blessing in Genesis 49, and of the dialogue. It appears first and most prominently in the writings of the later Ephraimite school, which bore the stamp of Hosea's strong, inspiring personality, and was still further developed by its Judean heir, the late prophetic or Deuteronomic school (cf. Vol. I, Introd., pp. 37–42). The most striking examples in the opening books of the Old Testament are the farewell addresses of Moses in Deuteronomy and Joshua in Joshua 23 and 24. In Samuel and Kings there are also many examples: Samuel's long sermons in I Samuel 8 and 12, Nathan's in II Samuel 7, Solomon's speech at the dedication of the temple in I Kings 8, and Ahijah's warnings in 11$^{31-39}$ and 14$^{7-16}$. In each case the language and ideas indicate that these are from the later schools of writers. In the didactic stories in Chronicles, which are based on the earlier narratives of Samuel and Kings, these hortatory addresses are still more common. They are in fact the favorite literary form of the later Jewish writers, as is shown by the long prayers in Ezra 9 and Nehemiah 9, and even by the speeches attributed to Judas and his fellow-leaders in the more strictly historical books of I and II Maccabees.

Prominence of personal biographies
Israel's historians were always more interested in individual men than in movements. Since their chief sources were also current traditions regarding popular heroes, the texture of their histories largely consists of personal biographies, which they have woven together into a larger whole. Remove from the historical books the biographies of Samuel, Saul, David, Solomon, Jeroboam, Ahab, Elijah, Elisha, Jehu, Hezekiah, Isaiah, Jere-

4

miah, Nehemiah, and Ezra, and little besides bare statistics and the record of three or four important events in the history of the temple remain. It is this prominent personal element that constitutes the chief charm of the narratives; while their vital touch with actual men and real life is the main source of their permanent and practical value.

The prominence of the biographical element is likewise due to the fact that the authors of the so-called historical books were not primarily historians, but rather religious teachers seeking apt and familiar illustrations of the spiritual truths which impelled them to write. From Israel's history as a whole they drew many valuable lessons, but even more from the life of a hero like David, or of an intrepid champion of righteousness like Elijah. Hence the Old Testament records lack historic proportion. David's final epoch-making victory over the Philistines is only meagrely described, while to his private family history many chapters are devoted. Omri's important reign is dismissed with a few verses, while four chapters are given to describing the work of the Tishbite prophet. This fact is the basis of the common assertion that there is strictly speaking no real history in Hebrew literature until we reach the Maccabean period. The books which are designated as historical are either collections of historical illustrations, which enforce prophetic principles, or else traditions regarding the temple and the origin of its later ceremonial institutions. *[Dominant aim not historical but religious]*

The amount of authentic data which such books as Samuel, Kings, and Ezra-Nehemiah contain at once place them in the first rank among the historical records coming from antiquity, but the historical facts are nevertheless incidental, although for this reason none the less valuable. It is exceedingly important, therefore, always to remember the higher ethical and religious purpose which determined the form and contents of these books. This, as well as the fact that they consist largely of quotations from earlier works, explains their lack of unity and the presence of occasional contradictions. These are but the guide-posts which point the way back to the original sources and make it possible to trace the complex literary history of these composite books and thus to do the work of reconstruction which is necessary, before they can be fully appreciated as literature, as history, and above all as illustrations of those eternal principles which regulate the life of nations and men. *[Indications that the earlier historical books consist chiefly of quotations]*

The fact that the aim of Samuel and Kings was primarily prophetic rather than historical was recognized by the Jews who formed the Old Testament canon, for they classified them, together with Joshua and Judges, as *The Former Prophets*. In reality the two books of Samuel, together with those of Kings, constitute one continuous narrative, bound together by closest bonds. The Greek translators so treated them, calling them the *Books of the Kingdoms*, dividing them into their present divisions. Jerome gave them the title of *Kings,* and in the case of the second two he has been followed by the English translators, while the first two retain their Hebrew title. *[History of the books of Samuel and Kings]*

The books of Samuel trace the history of the Hebrews from the latter part of the period of the Judges to the accession of Solomon, and therefore represent approximately one century. In the present form they consist of *[Contents of I and II Samuel]* five general divisions: (1) Samuel and Saul narratives, I Samuel 1–15; (2) stories regarding the rise of David and the decline and death of Saul, 16–31; (3) the account of David's rule first over Judah and then over all Israel, II Samuel 1–8; (4) David's family history, 9–20; (5) an appendix, 21–24.

Principle of arrangement in I Samuel In I Samuel the principle of arrangement is in general chronological. In 1–15, however, two very different portraits of Samuel are given: in the one (9, 10) he is the local seer of Ramah, who finds Saul and encourages him to become king, but in the other (7, 8, 12), the prophet-judge, who protestingly at the demand of the people turns over the supreme authority to their first king. In the one also (13, 14), the Philistines are defeated by Saul in a fierce engagement, but in the other (7) they are miraculously smitten in response to Samuel's prayer. The duplicate versions in 16–31 of certain of the more important incidents also indicate that the book is composite throughout, and that its literary unity and chronological arrangement are due to the careful work of the editor.

In II Samuel In II Samuel the material is grouped according to subject matter. In 1–8 the most important political events in David's reign are briefly outlined, beginning with his accession to the throne of Judah and concluding with a summary of his foreign wars. The events recounted in 9–20 are in part contemporary with those recorded in 1–8, but they trace the series of crimes in his family and court which so sadly dimmed the lustre of his reign. Their natural and probably original sequel is found in I Kings 1 and 2. The last division contains a heterogeneous group of narratives, which were evidently taken from various sources, and probably added to the original book of Samuel after it was separated from Kings. It includes an account of the fate of Saul's sons (21$^{1-14}$), which is closely related in theme to 9, a description of the exploits of David's heroes, 21$^{15-22}$, 23$^{8-39}$, into the midst of which at a comparatively late date Psalm 18 and David's traditional "Last Words" were introduced, and finally the record of a census, which appears to belong to the period of David's foreign wars. In the character of its contents, and in their relation to the narratives in the rest of the book this appendix closely resembles that found at the end of Judges (17–20). Unlike Judges and Kings, the books of Samuel have received few editorial additions. Aside from a few chronological notes, the earlier material has simply been grouped without being fitted into an editorial framework.

Contents of the books of Kings In the books of Kings the work of the editor is much more prominent. Beginning with the accession of Solomon and the death of David about 975 B.C., he traces the double thread of Hebrew history to the Babylonian exile and Jehoiachin's liberation in 561 B.C.; the books therefore represent a period of about four centuries. The principle of arrangement is prevailingly chronological, although groups of stories, as for example the Elisha traditions (II Kgs. 2^1–8^{15}), are introduced as a unit. Three general divisions may be distinguished: (1) the records of Solomon's reign, I Kings 1–11; (2) the parallel history of Israel and Judah, I Kings 12–II Kings 17; (3) the history of Judah, II Kings 18–25.

In the first division the editor's contributions appear chiefly in 11, where he condemns Solomon's foreign marriages and the toleration of heathen cults in Israel. Beginning with the history of the two kingdoms after the division, he incorporates his data regarding each reign in a regular framework, consisting of an introductory and concluding formula. The opening one always defines the synchronism with the neighboring kingdom and the length of the reign (cf. Appendix II for a fuller treatment of Hebrew chronology). To this is added in the case of the kings of Judah the name of the queen-mother. It concludes with a general judgment upon each king. Upon the rulers of Israel this is always adverse, for the basis of the condemnation appears to be the ruler's attitude toward the religion of Jehovah, and in the opinion of the editor the northern cult was altogether wrong because it centred about the high places selected by Jeroboam I to rival the temple at Jerusalem (I Kgs. 12²⁶⁻³³). Occasionally detailed reasons for the condemnation are also given (cf. I Kgs. 14²²⁻²⁴, 15¹¹⁻¹⁴, 16³⁰⁻³³). The concluding formula includes a reference to the editor's source and a record of the death of the king and the name of his successor. To this is added, in the case of the kings of Judah who did not come to a violent end, the statement that, *he slept with his fathers.* The editorial framework

Parallel to the narrative of Kings and for the most part simply quoted from it are the historical sections in the book of Isaiah (36–39). Far more important are the corresponding passages in Jeremiah (26, 34, 36–45), for they richly supplement the narrative of Kings, which unfortunately has only a brief account of the events immediately preceding and following the fall of Jerusalem in 586 B.C. These historical sections in Jeremiah are doubly valuable because they appear to be taken from a practically contemporary biography of Jeremiah, probably written by his faithful scribe Baruch. Historical sections in Isaiah and Jeremiah

It is a striking and fortunate fact that with few exceptions the most important events and epochs in the biblical history are recorded in two or more distinct books. The beginnings of Israel's history and the work and teachings of the Founder of Christianity are presented in four parallel strands of narrative. For the period beginning with Saul and extending to the Babylonian exile there are two, and at certain points three distinct records. Parallel records

The second continuous history of Israel is found in the books of Chronicles. They begin with a group of genealogical tables, which goes back to Adam, and carry the history down to the decree of Cyrus permitting the Jews to return after the Babylonian exile. Their dependence upon the older books of Samuel and Kings is clearly shown by the presence of many verbatim quotations. To these are added long sections which give this later history its distinctive form. Although it traces the genealogy of the race back to Adam, the narrative really begins with the death of Saul and henceforth focusses the attention on Judah, the temple, and especially the religious institutions which grew up about it. The books of Chronicles consist of four general divisions: (1) An introduction containing genealogical lists, interspersed with brief narratives, I Chronicles 1–9; (2) the history of David's reign, 10–29; (3) an account of Solomon's reign, II Chronicles 1–9; (4) the history of Judah to the fall of Jerusalem, with an appendix containing the decree of Cyrus, 10–36. Contents of the books of Chronicles

History of Ezra-Nehemiah   The immediate sequel to Chronicles is found in the books of Ezra and Nehemiah. In the original Jewish and Greek canon they form a single book. The separation of the book of Nehemiah under its distinct title was probably the work of Alexandrian scholars, and was adopted by Jerome. This division is not only artificial but also misleading, for as will be shown later (p. 32) parts of the original Ezra narrative are also found in Nehemiah. The original book therefore is best designated as *Ezra-Nehemiah*. It begins with the decree of Cyrus in 538 B.C., and traces the priestly genealogy down to the close of the Persian rule in 332, and therefore represents a period of a little over two centuries.

Its contents   A satisfactory analysis of it in its present form is impossible, for its constituent parts have evidently been disarranged. Thus for example, the conclusion of the Ezra narrative is found in Nehemiah 7^{70}–10^{39} in the midst of Nehemiah's account of the rebuilding of the walls, which begins in 1–6 and is concluded in 12^{27-43}. Nehemiah 12^{1-26} also contains a list *of the priests and Levites who went up with Zerubbabel and Jeshua*, which has no obvious connection with its context. As it now stands Ezra-Nehemiah consists of six general divisions: (1) an account of the events which resulted in the restoration of the temple, Ezra 1–6; (2) a description of the expedition of Ezra and his preliminary reforms, 7–10; (3) Nehemiah's history of his work in rebuilding the walls of Jerusalem and restoring the Judean community, Nehemiah 1^1–7^{69}; (4) an account of the reading of the law by Ezra and the public confession which was followed by the acceptance of the new code by the Jewish community, 7^{70}–10^{39}; (5) a census of the Jews in Palestine, with a list of the priests and Levites, 11^1–12^{26}; (6) Nehemiah's description of the dedication of the walls and of his later reform measures, 12^{27}–13^{31}.

Period covered by I Maccabees   The narrative of Israel's history is taken up where Ezra-Nehemiah leaves it by I Maccabees, which begins with Alexander's Asiatic conquests in 333–332 B.C. and ends with the death of the Hasmonean ruler Simon, in 135 B.C. Like Ezra-Nehemiah it, therefore, represents a period of about two centuries. The events preceding the reign of Antiochus Epiphanes (176 B.C.) are passed over briefly, but from this time on they are recorded in chronological order and with a fulness and historic proportion unsurpassed in any other Jewish narrative.

Its contents   It consists of four general divisions: (1) an introduction briefly describing the origin of the Seleucid empire and the attempt of Antiochus Epiphanes to abolish the Jewish religion, 1; (2) the history of the successful struggle for religious freedom led by Judas Maccabeus, 2–6; (3) the record of the wars and alliances by which the Jews finally secured political independence, 7–12; (4) the history of Simon's benign rule, 13–16.

Period covered by II Maccabees   Second Maccabees is parallel to I Maccabees, but deals with a much briefer period. It begins with the accession of Antiochus Epiphanes and closes with the restoration of the temple service and the death of Nicanor in 161 B.C. It pictures in great detail the horrors of the religious persecution and the bravery of the martyrs for the law. The parallels with I Maccabees are closest in the accounts of the wars of Judas, which occupy the second half of the book (8–15).

8

In its present form it contains five general divisions: (1) two letters purporting to have been sent by the Jews of Palestine to the Jews of Egypt urging them to observe the feast of Dedication, 1^1–2^{18}; (2) the author's preface, 2^{19-32}; (3) a description of the events which led up to the persecution, 3–5; (4) an account of the persecution and the endurance of the faithful, 6, 7; (5) the history of Judas's wars and victories, 8–15. *Its contents*

Although it is a popular story rather than a history, the book of Esther may also be included with Israel's historical and biographical narratives, because it reflects the pride and hatred with which the Jews during the Maccabean period regarded their heathen neighbors, with whom they were constantly brought into close and painful contact. Like the apocryphal book of Tobit, which also belongs to the same class of literature, it throws light indirectly upon the life of the Jews of the dispersion, among whom were probably to be found in the later centuries fully half of the members of that persecuted race. The story is a closely knit literary unit, is vividly told, and abounds in dramatic contrasts and the effective dialogues which constitute the charm of the earlier Old Testament narratives. *Theme and character of the book of Esther*

Viewed as literature, the historical and biographical narratives as a whole constitute an exceedingly attractive and important department of the Old Testament library. They are concrete, vivid, realistic portraits of the complex life of ancient Israel. Their literary forms are almost as varied as their themes. Brief annals, genealogical lists, personal memoirs, impassioned orations, songs of lamentations, popular traditions, didactic stories, and historical romances are all represented. Viewed as the record of nine centuries of Israel's national experiences they are unique among the writings of antiquity because of the relative completeness and exactness of the picture which they present. The important events and epochs are usually portrayed with great fulness, while the unimportant are passed over rapidly or in silence. The duplicate narratives make it possible to study the vital facts from very different points of view. The significant characters in the history and their acts also stand out in clear relief. Intimate acquaintance with the men who made Israelitish history discloses the dominant tendencies of each age and the forces which influenced it. Above all, these Old Testament narratives at every point call attention to the divine guidance and purpose which moulded Israel's history and made it not merely the record of the life of an insignificant race, but a transcendently important chapter in the history of humanity, for through the life of that race God was revealing his character and will to the world. *General character of the Old Testament historical literature*

II

THE EARLIER HISTORIES AND BIOGRAPHIES INCORPORATED IN SAMUEL AND KINGS

The growth of Samuel and Kings

THE historical value of the great prophetic record in the books of Samuel and Kings is due to the fact that it consists for the most part of verbatim quotations from earlier histories and biographies. The determination of their character and date is therefore not only interesting but also absolutely essential before they can be used in reconstructing the true outlines of Israel-itish history. The growth of these books was gradual and the process nearly as complex as in the case of the opening books of the Old Testament. No sharp line of demarcation separates the one group from the other. Contemporaneously and as the result of similar forces, each took form. They drew their data from the same fund of common tradition, and doubtless in many cases the same authors or at least school of authors contributed to each. The following chapter aims simply at giving a clear outline of the conclusions presented in this volume regarding the nature of the sources which underlie Samuel and Kings, and their literary history. The detailed reasons and analyses will be given in connection with the text (for a graphic representation of the different sources and their relations to each other and to the completed book, compare the Frontispiece to this volume).

1. The Early Judean Saul and David Narratives

The ark stories

The original book of Judges closed abruptly in chapters 13–16 with an account of the Philistine advance and Samson's ill-organized and futile counter-attacks. The original sequel to these in the early Judean prophetic narratives appears to be embedded in I Samuel 4, which tells of the repeated defeats of the Israelites by the Philistines and of the loss of the ark. The subsequent fortunes of this sacred palladium, which already has figured most prominently in the Judean narratives (cf. Vol. I, §§ 79, 86), and which found its final resting place in the southern capital and sanctuary, are recounted in 5^2–7^1. Possibly these popular narratives were once taken from a cycle of stories which centred about the ark itself, but their present language, picturesque literary form, and natural representation, reveal their relationship to the products of the early Judean prophetic school.

Saul cycle of stories

From the same point of view and in the same literary style are written the vivid stories in 9^1–10^{16}, $11^{1-11,\ 15b}$, 13^1–14^{46}. They also assume precisely the conditions pictured in 4–6. They tell of the natural steps whereby Saul was made king and wrested from the Philistines the independence lost when the ark fell into the hands of those strong foes. These Saul stories constitute a closely knit literary unit. The character and work of Israel's

10

first king are presented sympathetically and appreciatively. Samuel does not oppose, but rather works earnestly for the establishment of the kingdom. Circumstances force the people to take the successive steps which ultimately led to union and national independence. As in the case of the different groups of the patriarchal stories (Vol. I, pp. 22, 23), these traditions were probably found originally in the form of a Saul cycle and then incorporated in their larger history of Israel by the early Judean historians. They may therefore be appropriately designated as the *early Judean Saul narratives*.

With 16^{14-23} the point of view perceptibly changes. Henceforth David is the central object of interest and Saul suffers by contrast. The facts and conditions, however, presented in the preceding early Judean narratives are assumed. The same vivid style and picturesque words and expressions recur. The representation is natural and the historical motive is prominent. Again the conviction deepens that the group of stories which from this point run through II Kings 2, picturing realistically the fortunes and achievements of David, is the sequel of the preceding Judean narratives, but that originally they were drawn from that largest and most important cycle of stories in the Old Testament, which gathered about the character of Israel's popular hero and conqueror-king. They may therefore be designated as the *early Judean David narratives*.

These narratives are found in I Samuel 16^{14}–$17^{11, 32-40, 42-49, 51-54}$, $18^{6-8, 12-16, 20-29a}$, 19^{1-17}, 20^{1-39}, 21^{1-9}, 22^{1}–23^{14a}, 25^{2}–28^{2}, 29–31, II Samuel $1^{1-4, 11, 12, 17-31, 7}$–$5^{13, 17-24}$, 6, 8^{7-10}, 9^{1}–21^{14}, 23^{8-39}, 24, I Kings 1, 2^{13-45}. Many of them stand alone by themselves as complete stories, and it is possible that, as is maintained by some scholars, those found in II Samuel 9–20 originally constituted an independent group, but the unity of the David stories as a whole is very marked. Not only are they written in the same style and characterized by the same familiar idioms, but the same conceptions of the events of the history and of the chief characters constantly recur. David in his declining years, overshadowed by his great sin, is not so attractive as the hero of the earlier struggles, but he is still the object of the nation's love, the great king whose earlier achievements the people cannot forget (II Sam. 19). The Joab of II Samuel 18 and 20 is identical with the bold, unscrupulous general of II Samuel 3. The unique friendship between David and Jonathan and its dark background, the hatred and jealousy of the house of Saul, run through and bind together all these stories.

Viewed either as literature or as historical sources, the early Judean David narratives are unsurpassed by any others in the Old Testament. The pictures which they give of the actors and events in this epoch-making period in Israel's history are not only interesting and full of life and local color, but they may be accepted as substantially true, even in detail, to the historical facts. They and the related Saul stories probably represent the first extensive Hebrew writings. The impressions which the stirring events recorded made upon the popular mind were exceedingly vivid. It was doubtless because of their great importance and universal interest that the impulse to commit them to writing was first felt by Israel's patriotic his-

Marginal notes: Early David narratives / Their extent and unity / Their character and history

torians. This conclusion is fully confirmed by their character. As the earliest product of the Judean prophetic school, they naturally have certain characteristics peculiar to themselves, partly due to their priority and partly to the nature of the original traditions which they embody. They appear to have shaped the ideas, determined the methods, and given the inspiration to the early Judean writers, which led them subsequently to collect the traditions regarding the period of the Judges and then of each preceding period, until they traced their history back to the first man in the Garden of Eden (cf. Vol. I, pp. 18, 19).

Their date

From their themes and literary character, as well as from their relation to the longer Judean narrative, it may be fairly inferred that the Saul and David histories were written not very long after, if not before, the division of the Hebrew empire at the death of Solomon. There is in them no reflection of the hostility between the North and South which immediately followed that event. The later reign of Jehoshaphat (876–851 B.C.), when the armies of the two kingdoms again fought side by side and when the political, commercial, and probably the intellectual life was very active, furnishes a most natural background for the work of the prophets who gleaned them from the mouth of the people and committed them to writing.

2. The Later Ephraimite Samuel Narratives

Absence of the early Ephraimite narratives in Samuel

In view of the division of the Hebrew empire at the death of Solomon and the bitterness engendered in the North against the house of David, the Northern or Ephraimite historians had little desire or incentive to record the glories of the united kingdom. These belonged in a peculiar sense to the South. Moreover, the Judean records were so complete that there was no necessity for the late prophetic editors to draw from the traditions of the North, which perhaps presented the darker side of these reigns in a manner not altogether agreeable to the conceptions of later Judean editors. Whatever are the real reasons, there is no clear evidence of citations in Samuel and Kings from the early Ephraimite prophetic narratives. With the accounts of the achievements of the northern heroes recounted in Judges, the quotations in the Old Testament from this early source apparently cease, except as the stories of Elijah (corresponding to the Saul and David stories in their relation to the Judean narratives) probably represent the prototype of the writing of this school (cf. p. 18).

The Samuel narratives

Side by side, however, with the Judean account of the establishment of the monarchy is a connected series of narratives which have all the characteristics of the later Ephraimite source. They recount the deeds of a prophet —Samuel of Ramah in the North. In these later narratives he is conceived of as judging the people, as did Moses according to the related tradition of Exodus 18. Like his great predecessor, he rules as Jehovah's regent over all Israel (cf. Vol. I, pp. 38, 39). When the people confess their sin (7[6], 12[10]; cf. Num. 14[40], Judg. 10[10, 15]), Samuel intercedes for them (7[5], 8[6]; cf. Gen. 20[7, 27]; Num. 11[2], 21[7]), and Jehovah miraculously delivers them from their powerful foes.

In the early Judean narratives the kingship is regarded as so desirable Evidence that they are from the Ephraimite school that Samuel persuades Saul to assume the leadership, and in the late prophetic or Deuteronomic as a necessary institution, the abuses of which must be carefully guarded against (Dt. 17$^{14-20}$). In I Samuel 8 and 12, however, it is absolutely condemned in almost the same terms as were the kings of his day by the Ephraimite prophet Hosea (cf. I Sam. 8 and Hos. 8^{4a}, 13^{11}). Many other minor indications, as for example, the reference to a sacred stone or pillar (I Sam. 7^{12}), still regarded as legitimate in the Ephraimite narratives (Vol. I, p. 40), but sternly forbidden in the late prophetic, leave little doubt that this peculiar conception of the history and the work of Samuel originated in the Northern prophetic guilds.

These narratives are found in I Samuel 1^1–5^1, 7^{2b}–8^{22}, 10$^{17-25}$, 12 and 15. Their contents and history The interest throughout is religious rather than political. The purpose is didactic rather than historical. The whole is a popular biography of Samuel rather than a parallel history of the period. It begins with the account of his birth, consecration, early life at Shiloh, and call to be a prophet; but throughout the stories, the attention is focussed on Samuel, the man of God, rather than on Samuel, the individual. That all Israel was led by a prophetic representative of Jehovah, as in the days of Moses, is assumed. The supernatural is prominent. The same peculiar conceptions and point of view reappear in the Elijah and Elisha stories of I Kings 20–II Kings 15. The kinship of these three groups of traditions is clearly very close. They were undoubtedly cherished in the same prophetic circle in the North—probably many of them at the sanctuary of Gilgal near Shiloh, which appears to have become the inheritor of its traditions when the older shrine was destroyed by the Philistines (Jer. 19^3, cf. note § 3).

Some time after the days of Hosea and before Josiah's reformation in Their date 621 B.C. the cycle of Samuel stories, together with kindred products of the later Ephraimite prophetic school, was committed to writing. Whether or not it originally existed independently for a period is a question which can never be absolutely decided, and which is of only secondary importance.

3. Very Late Popular Prophetic Traditions

In I Samuel 15^{35b}–16^{13}, 19^{18}–20^{1a}, I Kings 12^{33}–13^{34}, 20$^{35-43}$, II Kings 1$^{9-16}$ Characteristics and date of the late popular prophetic traditions are found certain stories which are related in many ways to the preceding groups. They illustrate the later belief in the dominant, almost supernatural position assumed by the earlier prophets in the life of the nation. They were evidently retold for generations in prophetic circles. While related, this group evidently reflects a still later conception of the prophets than the Samuel cycle. Their real ethical and religious work is almost forgotten and the men of God are conceived of as mere wonder-workers. Thus for example in I Samuel 19$^{18-24}$ the messengers of Saul, and later the king himself, fall down in ecstasy before Samuel, or in II Kings 1$^{9-16}$ the military companies sent by Ahaziah are consumed by fire from heaven at the command of Elijah. Evidently the popular imagination has contributed much to the stories. They recall the *midrashim* or late Jewish didactic tales (cf. p. 26).

While it cannot be maintained that they are all from the same school or date, they reflect the same very late point of view.

4. Popular Judean David Stories

Contents and history of the popular Judean David stories

From the lips of the people also doubtless came the variant versions of the more important incidents in David's early life, as for example, his contest with Goliath, his marriage with Saul's daughter, the king's futile attempt to kill him, and his magnanimity in sparing Saul's life. A comparison shows that they are clearly duplicates of the corresponding early Judean narratives, but here the stories are told with slight variations; details and names are usually forgotten, the coloring is heightened, and the language illustrates the effects of their having been retold from generation to generation. The same love and admiration for David are revealed, only he has been so completely idealized that his faults and sins have been forgotten. The scenes are most of them laid in Southern Judah. It is difficult to conceive that they originally came from any other source than the memories of his fellow-clansmen in the South. The popular version of the story of his contest with Goliath, which was probably added to the Hebrew text at a very late date, since it is not found in the earliest Greek version, may well have been cherished at Bethlehem in Judah.

Their date and place in the books of Samuel

The popular David stories are found in I Samuel $17^{12-31, 41, 50, 55-58}$, $18^{1-5, 10, 11, 17-19, 29b, 30}$, 21^{10-15}, $23^{16}-24^{22}$, II Samuel 1^{5-10}. Most of these were evidently committed to writing before the late prophetic editor compiled his history of the period—that is before the first capture of Jerusalem in 597 B.C. In his zeal to preserve everything known regarding David, he made the early Judean narratives the basis of his history from I Samuel 16 on, and then supplemented them by the popular traditions, not welding the duplicates closely together as is often done by early editors in the first seven books of the Old Testament, but giving each a different setting. The one exception to this rule is found in I Samuel 17 and 18, and is clearly the work of a still later editor.

5. The Book of the Acts of Solomon

The literary activity in Solomon's reign

With the reign of Solomon a new era in Hebrew history opened. The alliances with neighboring peoples, and especially the Phœnicians, introduced foreign culture. The ambition of the king was to bring his people and kingdom into line with those of contemporary Semitic potentates. The emphasis was placed on the development of his court and capital rather than upon conquest. Literature, as well as art, was probably encouraged by him. In addition to the chancellor or recorder, two scribes were counted among the important officials of his court (I Kgs. 4^3). Their duty was probably primarily to conduct the royal correspondence, but for diplomatic reasons, if for no other, a record of the most important events of each reign would also be needed for reference. Hence from the days of Solomon it appears that the Hebrew historians were not dependent upon popular memory and tradition, but had access to brief contemporary annals for the more important political facts. Here, therefore, the Judean prophetic history properly ends, for the task of its authors was to collect and put in literary form the inherited traditions regarding the period antedating that of contemporary records. At the same time it is clear that the connection was very close between the work of the southern annalists and that of the Judean historians, for the one was the virtual successor of the other.

The compiler of Kings refers his readers for further details to what appears to have been three distinct historical works. They must have been extant and accessible in his day, and, we may infer from the form of his references that they were well known. They are the *Book of the Acts* (or *Events) of Solomon* (I Kgs. 11^{41}), the *Chronicles* (lit., *Book of the Acts of Days) of the Kings of Israel*, and the corresponding *Chronicles of the Kings of Judah*. It is reasonable to conclude that these histories, to which he frequently refers, were also among the chief sources from which he himself drew his political facts regarding the earlier periods. The character and aim of his work and the form of his allusions to them further indicate that he simply quoted from them that which was adapted to his more distinctively religious and pragmatic purpose. References to early Hebrew histories

That these older histories were more than mere annals is clearly indicated. The reference in I Kings 11^{41} is to the point: *Now the rest of the acts of Solomon and all that he did and his wisdom, are they not recorded in the Book of the Acts of Solomon?* The same inference is confirmed by the allusions to the contents of the *Chronicles* (cf. p. 16). The term *Book* in this connection also implies a continuous, more or less expanded history. The *Chronicles* recorded the events of many different centuries. Their historical value depended upon the fact that they were compiled from older sources. The work of other authors appears to have been simply to combine and expand the earlier material. The state annals appear to have been the basis of their work and the expansion at important points to have been accomplished by introducing long quotations from existing histories of important kings and reigns like those of Jeroboam, Ahab, and Jehu. Their character

For the *Book of the Acts of Solomon*, two and possibly three sources appear to have been utilized. The detailed, annalistic material, for example in 4$^{1-19, 22, 23, 26-28}$, 5^{1}–7^{12}, 9$^{10-29}$, 10$^{11, 12}$–11^{25}, was presumably taken from the annals of his reign. Only written records would preserve many of the recondite facts there found. From the same source may have come the detailed data regarding the ornamentation, furnishing, and dedication of the temple in 7^{13}–8^{13}, but they would more naturally be kept in the temple records, citations from which appear later in Kings (cf. p. 17). With these may be compared the Babylonian temple accounts which come from a very early period (cf. Johns, *Bab. and Assyr. Laws, Contracts, and Letters*, p. 295). Finally there are found in I Kings 3$^{4-28}$ and 10$^{1-10, 13}$ certain popular traditions, evidently of early origin, which illustrate Solomon's wisdom. If the reference to the record of the king's wisdom in 11^{41} is original it would strengthen the conclusion that those traditions were found in the *Book of the Acts of Solomon*, although these, like the popular David stories, may well have been added by the late prophetic editor. Earlier sources incorporated in the Acts of Solomon

15

Its
char-
acter
and
date

In I Kings, 3–11 are found also many late prophetic passages evidently not from the *Book of the Acts*, but the original quotations from it suggest its general character. It was a reasonably comprehensive history dealing with the political and religious events of Solomon's reign. Its primary aim was not religious but rather to record facts. The tendency, however, to idealize Solomon and his reign, which became very marked in later generations, is apparent. The author was evidently a Judean and probably lived not earlier than 800 B.C. He may well have belonged to the early Judean prophetic school. His purpose was to carry the Judean history down to the division of the Hebrew kingdom. Repetition of the same notices in different settings further suggests that his work was supplemented and possibly rearranged before it was used by the late prophetic editor.

6. The Israelitish and Judean Royal Chronicles

Char-
acter of
the
royal
chron-
icles

The author of the present book of Kings always refers to the *Chronicles of the Kings of Israel* and the *Chronicles of the Kings of Judah* as if they were distinct books. Their titles also suggest that they were originally independent. This conclusion is confirmed by the fact that the same events, as for example the campaign of Hazael (II Kgs. 10^{32}, 13^3, cf. $12^{17, 18}$), are recorded twice in quotations apparently taken from these histories, each describing the invasion as it affected one of the two Hebrew kingdoms and ignoring its effects upon the other. The character and contents of the *Chronicles* appear to have been very similar to those of the *Book of the Acts of Solomon*. Their exact title, *Book of the Acts of Days of the Kings*, suggests that they were histories containing detailed records of events, arranged in chronological order, and that their chief sources were the older annals of the two kingdoms. The thirty-one references which the editor of Kings makes to them and their contents and the quotations which he evidently cites from them establish their character. In the first place they included a continuous and complete history of all the different reigns. In the case of all the kings except Jehoram, Ahaziah, Hoshea, Jehoahaz, Jehoiachin, and Zedekiah, who met untimely fates, the editor explicitly states that the *Chronicles recorded the deeds of each.*

Their
con-
tents

For twenty-three distinct items the reader is referred for information or fuller details to the *Chronicles*. Some of these facts are: Jeroboam's wars, the mighty deeds of Baasha, the treason of Zimri, Ahab's ivory house, the cities built by Asa, Hezekiah's construction of the pool and conduit, and Manasseh's sin. They deal chiefly with secular subjects, such as the wars, building enterprises, successes, and the material splendors of each reign. Their attitude toward most of the kings appears to have been commendatory—in striking antithesis to the adverse judgment passed upon them for religious reasons by the author of Kings. The implication of his references to these histories is that they contained many more details than he saw fit to introduce in his brief summaries. Like the *Acts of Solomon*, they doubtless contained quotations from older sources. These were, as in the *Acts of Solomon*, the independent annals of the two kingdoms. The citations

16

were probably in most cases transcribed verbatim and, having been again quoted by the editor of Kings, found a place in our present books. They can be recognized by their brief sententious form and by their use of certain expressions, as *then* or *at that time*, and the peculiar use of the personal pronoun (for the corresponding Babylonian synchronistic chronicle, compare Appendix X).

The author of the *Chronicles of the Kings of Judah* appears also to have had access to temple records. Extracts from these are found in II Kings 11, 12, 16$^{10-18}$ and 22^3–23^{23}. In these passages the attention is focussed not on the king and the fortunes of the kingdom, but upon the temple and its ritual. As in ancient Babylonia, many of the priests were probably scribes, and that they would keep a record of the more important events in the temple history was most natural. The desire to expand these brief records into fuller narratives would also later be felt. They represent the antecedents of the much later temple and institutional history found in Chronicles and Ezra-Nehemiah. That quotations from the temple records had already been incorporated in the *Chronicles*, to which the editor of Kings refers as his main source, is at least probable, although not certain. It is also significant that the citations in II Kings 16 are joined immediately to material taken from the state annals, with no trace of the harmonistic or introductory clauses which the editor usually adds when he himself unites quotations from different sources. *{Their sources: temple records}*

The authors of the *Chronicles of the Kings of Israel*, on the other hand, appear to have drawn from the older private histories of important kings like Jeroboam (I Kgs. 11$^{26-31,\ 40}$, 12$^{1-25}$), Ahab (20$^{1-34}$, 22$^{1-37}$), Jehu (II Kgs. 9^1–10^{27}). These personal histories correspond very closely to the early Saul and David histories in Samuel. They were probably not written during the lifetime, but a generation or two after the death of the given king. They give a natural and at the same time sympathetic and favorable portrait of him and the events of his reign. The resulting picture is often in striking contrast to the very different estimates found in the prophetic sources and in the epitomes of the editor of Kings. *{Also private histories}*

Quotations from the *Chronicles* and references to them cease with the reign of Jehoiakim (II Kgs. 24^5). They contain none of the expressions and ideas peculiar to the late prophetic school which dominated the thought of the exile. It would seem, therefore, that they were composed some time not long after 597 B.C., between the first and second captivities. Possibly the work was begun earlier, and the data regarding the later reigns added as appendices by subsequent writers. The *Chronicles of the Kings of Israel* probably attained their final form shortly after the fall of Samaria in 722 B.C. Together they carried the two great histories of the North and South practically down to the final destruction of both kingdoms. *{Period covered by the Chronicles}*

7. The Early Ephraimite Elijah Stories

With I Kings 17 is suddenly introduced a unique form of narrative. The brief quotations and annalistic style of the preceding chapters are supplanted

Char-
acter
and
date of
the
Elijah
stories

by a picturesque, detailed story. Interest is centred not in the kings of Israel, but in Elijah the Tishbite; not in the insurrections and wars, but in the religious and social life of the nation. Towering above the king and dominating the history is the commanding personality of the great prophet of Gilead. As the spokesman of Jehovah, like Moses in the early prophetic or Samuel in the later Ephraimite narratives, he moulds the history. At the same time there is a freshness, a concreteness, a directness in the language, and a naturalness and reserve in the representation which stamp the stories as comparatively early. The worship at the public shrines like Bethel and Dan, with their golden calves, receives no censure, as it does in the sermons of Amos and Hosea. The toleration and popular identification of the Baal-cult with that of Jehovah are the chief objects of attack. They therefore clearly antedate 750 B.C., when Amos appeared at Bethel with his revolutionary message. On the other hand, the character of Elijah has begun to be clothed with a certain mystery. The tone of the narratives suggests that the traditions which they embody were not committed to writing until a generation or two after the great prophet had passed away. Their approximate date may accordingly be fixed not long after 800 B.C.

Their
history

The stories were doubtless treasured in prophetic circles and later kept in written form. The spirit and point of view, as well as the direct reference to Judah in 19³, as a foreign nation, demonstrate that they came from Northern Israel. Occasional expressions, like *after these things* (17¹⁷, 21¹), the designation of the sacred mountain as *Horeb* (19⁸), and above all the commanding rôle attributed to the prophet proclaim the kinship of these with the early Ephraimite prophetic narratives in the opening books of the Old Testament (cf. Vol. I, 37–40). Of the two, however, the Elijah stories seem to be the more primitive. They were probably the nucleus about which gathered the similar narratives which ultimately traced the history of the theocratic people back to the days of Abraham. In their light it is for the first time possible fully to understand why this school conceived of the earliest prophets as clothed with almost omnipotent authority and, like Elijah and Isaiah of a later and very different age, shaping from the first the history of the Israelitish race.

Their
original
extent

In the Greek version the narratives of 17–19 are continued immediately by 21, and in this order they probably stood in the original text. Extracts from the same source appear in II Kings 1. That they are but extracts from a more complete biography of Elijah is clearly shown by the abruptness with which he is introduced in 17—many facts being assumed which are nowhere stated in the fragments which have been preserved—and by the incompleteness of the biography as it stands. Following his usual method only those sections were quoted which conserved the broad purpose of the prophetic editor of Kings.

8. The Gilgal Cycle of Popular Elijah Stories

In II Kings 2¹–8¹⁵, 13¹⁴⁻²¹ is found a collection of narratives which centre about Elisha. They have all the characteristics of stories long transmitted from mouth to mouth. Details regarding the exact setting and the names of the reigning kings have been lost. The supernatural elements are prominent and the ethical motives are often obscured. In these Elisha figures as the man of God, the great wonder-worker. That they are later and modelled after the early Elijah narratives is demonstrated by the fact that the same elements and in some cases almost the identical stories reappear in enlarged proportions. Thus for example, the story of the widow's meal and jar of oil that failed not (I Kgs. 17$^{8-16}$) reappears in the account of the widow's pot of oil which did not fail until she had, at Elisha's command, drawn enough from it to defray all her debts (II Kgs. 4$^{1-7}$). Closely similar to the account of the reviving of the widow's son by Elijah (I Kgs. 17$^{17-24}$) is the story of his resuscitating the Shunammite's son (II Kgs. 4$^{8-37}$). It would seem that just as the same tale of deception regarding his wife was twice told about Abraham in different settings and once about Isaac (cf. Vol. I, §13), so in popular tradition, not only the mantle, but also the reputation of Elijah fell upon his chief disciple. {.margin Dependence of the Elisha stories upon the Elijah group}

The Elisha stories are not as closely knit together as are the Elijah narratives. They are rather a bundle of anecdotes, each complete in itself. Minor inconsistencies also indicate that they were originally taken from at least two distinct groups. Thus for example in 5^{27} Gehazi is a leper and therefore an outcast, but in 8^4 he is introduced conversing with the king and is still the trusted servant of the man of God. There is not the slightest reference to the incurable disease with which, according to 5^{27}, he was afflicted. In one cycle of stories Elisha is represented as residing at Gilgal. This is evidently not the Gilgal near Jericho but the sanctuary southeast of Shiloh (cf. 2$^{1-4}$). There he lives in close association with the guild of the sons of the prophets which was located at that place (4$^{38-44}$). In this cycle there are frequent references to these sons of the prophets and their wives. Furthermore, the stories without exception all relate to the events of private life, and they resemble most those found in the early Elijah group. Evidently they were treasured on the lips of the people living in the West Jordan valley, not far from Elisha's home at Abel-Meholah, and were probably first collected by some member of the prophetic guild at the neighboring town of Gilgal. {.margin The two distinct cycles of Elisha stories}

In the Gilgal cycle may be included II Kings 2, 4$^{1-7,\ 38-44}$, 6$^{1-7}$. It is impossible to fix their date exactly. Several generations have evidently transmitted them orally. They have the Northern Israelitish stamp, but since the fall of Samaria in 722 B.C. did not mean the deportation of the bulk of the inhabitants of Israel, it is possible that they were not put in literary form until after that event. This later date also best accords with their general character. {.margin Date of the Gilgal cycle}

9. The Samaria Cycle of Popular Elisha Stories

In the other cycle, which included the remaining stories in II Kings 3–8^{15}, to which may be added 14$^{8-14}$, Elisha is conceived of as residing at Samaria, the capital (5^3, 6$^{24,\ 32}$), and as being in close touch with the king and court (3^{11}, 4^{13}, 5^8, 6$^{9,\ 32}$). Most of the stories reflect his activity not in private but in public life, and especially in the wars with Moab and Aram. The

Contents and character of the Samaria cycle
Arameans in fact figure in six out of nine stories belonging to this cycle. No references are found to the sons of the prophets, but instead Gehazi is the servant, ever attendant upon the prophet ($4^{12, 14, 25-36}$, 5^{20-27}, 6^{15}, 8^4). Like a king, Elisha is usually represented as simply giving directions or else sending his servant with his potent staff to work the wonders recorded. The earlier stories here reflected are found not only in the Elijah group but also in the early Ahab history. Thus for example the parallel between I Kings 22 and II Kings 3 extends even to similar scenes and language (cf. II Kgs. 3^{7-11} and I Kgs. 22^{4-7}). Close analogies may also be traced with certain of the patriarchal stories, as for example the prediction that the Shunammite woman should have a son before a year had passed (cf. 4^{16} and Gen. 18^{14}).

Its date
It is difficult to determine which of these cycles is the older. They doubtless grew up contemporaneously. The Samaria group, however, clearly embodies more historical data and probably was committed to writing before the fall of that city in 722 B.C. The fact that Samaria was a literary centre would facilitate the process. These two cycles of popular Elisha stories were apparently combined—citations being taken alternately from each—before they were incorporated as II Kings. The fact that they are all introduced together and have received practically no editorial revision probably indicates that they were among the latest additions to the book. It is more than possible that they came into the possession of the late prophetic editor as a result of the conquests and reforming expeditions of Josiah, which, according to II Kings $23^{19, 20}$, extended to the sanctuaries of Samaria.

10. The Isaiah Stories

Contents and character of the Isaiah stories
It was most natural that in later generations among Isaiah's disciples there should also grow up a cycle of stories associated with him and preserving in traditional form the memory of his work. Three stories from such a group are found in II Kings $18^{17}-20^{19}$ (cf. §§ 122, 124). They are again quoted by the editor of the book of Isaiah in 36-39, with the further addition of a psalm which is attributed to Hezekiah (38^{10-20}). The first of these narratives is evidently a duplicate of the extract in II Kings $18^{17}-19^{9a, 36, 37}$, which was apparently taken from a Hezekiah history. In popular transmission the details of the incident have been partially forgotten; while in the expansion of the story in 20^{8-11}, Isaiah like Elisha is conceived of as a wonder-worker. The references to the Babylonian exile in $20^{15, 17}$ indicate that these stories were committed to writing after 586 B.C.

11. The Final Editing of the Books of Samuel and Kings

Work of the pre-exilic editors
This brief study of the sources of Samuel and Kings has sufficed to show that many very early elements enter into these composite books, and that their growth was gradual, representing a period of fully four centuries. Their real author or authors selected the quotations from the older annals, biographies, and temple records, arranged them in their present order and, in the book of Kings, fitted them into a stereotyped framework (cf. p. 7).

EARLIER HISTORIES IN SAMUEL AND KINGS

The language, the expressions, and the distinctively religious ideas of these editorial sections are those of the late prophetic group of writers who were inspired by the book of Deuteronomy and the great reform of Josiah in 621 B.C. (for a detailed list of their words and expressions, cf. Driver, LOT, pp. 200–203, Hast. DB II, pp. 859–861). The original editor of Kings carried his history down to the reign of Jehoiakim, but apparently writes from the point of view of Palestine, and while the Judean state was still standing (cf., *e.g.*, *to this day*, II Kgs. 8[22], 16[6], 17[24-34]).

The exile, which quickly followed, transformed the thought of Israel's religious teachers so completely that a later editor, writing probably in Babylonia not long after 561 B.C., gave to the book of Kings its final form. He likewise belonged to the late prophetic school, so that it is not always easy to distinguish his work from that of his predecessor. He certainly added the account of the final destruction of Jerusalem and the liberation of Jehoiachin in 561 B.C. The conception of Jehovah in I Kings 8[27-30] and of the temple as a place of worship for all peoples is closely akin to that found in Isaiah 40–56. Also [33, 34] seem to imply the point of view of the exile. This is also true of II Kings 21[7-15]. It is probable that in their present form the prophetic addresses in I Kings 8[14]–9[9] and II Kings 21[7-15], as well as certain other minor additions, are from the latest editor. Later priests and scribes added occasional notes, but by 540 B.C. the prophetic historical books of Samuel and Kings were practically complete.

[marginal note:] Work of the final editor

III

THE CHRONICLER'S ECCLESIASTICAL HISTORY OF JUDAH AND THE TEMPLE

Contents of the late ecclesiastical history
EXCEPTING in the three or four quotations from the temple records, the books of Samuel and Kings are throughout national and prophetic in their interests. Their final editors were clearly prophets, and to the same group of religious patriots belonged the authors of most of the older sources which are quoted. It was natural that the other prominent class of Israel's teachers, the priests, whose interests were distinctly ritualistic and ecclesiastical, should also write their own version of the history. Closely corresponding in spirit and purpose to the late priestly narratives in the Pentateuch is the parallel history of Judah found in the books of Chronicles and their direct continuation Ezra-Nehemiah. Identity in literary style and point of view, as well as the repetition of the opening verses of Ezra (1[1-3]) at the close of Chronicles (36[22, 23]), leaves no doubt that the books are all from the same author or editor, and originally constituted one continuous narrative, beginning with Adam and concluding with the account of the great priestly reformation associated with Ezra (about 400 B.C.).

Its date
The fact that the author of this extensive history speaks of the days of Nehemiah and Ezra as though they belonged to the distant past (Neh. 12[26, 47]) and the kings of Persia as though he lived under a different rule (Ezra 1[1, 2, 8], 3[7]) at once suggests that he wrote at least from the point of view of the succeeding Greek period. Nehemiah 12[11, 22] also mentions Jaddua who was high-priest in 332 B.C., when Alexander conquered Palestine. The awkward Hebrew which he used, and the highly developed ceremonial institutions with which he is familiar, as well as his general point of view, indicate that he wrote not earlier than 300 B.C., probably about the middle of the third century.

Method of the author
Again the historical value of the work turns largely upon whether the author depended for his facts merely upon the traditions current in his own day or upon written sources, and also whether he recast the information, which he collected, in his own language, or quoted it practically verbatim from much earlier sources. An examination of his work at once demonstrates that his method, like that of the editors of Samuel and Kings, was primarily compilation. Nearly half of the books of Chronicles consists of exact or slightly variant quotations from the Old Testament books of Samuel and Kings. Variations in style, point of view, and even minor inconsistencies in representation clearly indicate that the greater part of Ezra-Nehemiah, and probably certain of the remaining portions of Chronicles, were taken bodily from older written sources. The real work of the writer of Chronicles and Ezra-Nehemiah was therefore not primarily that of an original author

but of a compiler and editor. An appreciation of this fact is essential to an understanding of his unique history. It also tends to enhance its historical value, for it is obvious that in general the nearer the records stand to the events the greater their accuracy and authenticity.

Since his name is not known, the final editor of this extensive history may be conventionally designated as the *Chronicler*. From his modifications of the older narrative of Samuel-Kings, from his systematic omissions, as well as from the passages which came originally from his pen, it is possible to determine definitely his point of view and distinctive peculiarities. Like the writers of the late priestly school, his interests are ecclesiastical rather than national, ritualistic rather than prophetic, and didactic rather than historical. He was interested in Judah, because in it was the temple, and in the temple, because about it gathered the ceremonial institutions which he regarded as the beginning and end of existence. History was to him important simply because it gave the background and recorded the beginnings of these institutions, and because it furnished apt illustrations of the peculiar ethical and religious principles which were uppermost in his mind. In common with that post-exilic Judaism whose point of view is likewise reflected in the non-canonical writings, which he quotes, he was dominated by the natural and irresistible tendency to idealize the past and project back into it the conditions and institutions existing in his day. Thus a comparison with the older parallel narratives of Samuel and Kings at once shows that numbers are often raised from hundreds to thousands (cf. I Chr. 22^{14}, II Chr. 13$^{3, 17}$, 14$^{8, 9}$, 17$^{14-19}$, 28$^{6, 8}$), gold takes the place of brass, the priest of the warrior, and a miracle of the victory won by the swords in the hands of Israel's gallant defenders. David is regarded by him as the founder of the post-exilic guilds of singers and the organizer of the elaborate temple ritual, even though the sanctuary itself was not built until the days of Solomon and did not attain its dominant religious prestige until centuries later. In I Chronicles 26 he appears even to have forgotten this fact and refers to the gates of the temple (designated by their Persian name) as already existing in the day of David.

The Chronicler lived in an age when zeal for the ritual had almost completely obscured the historical perspective. Certain accepted theories were also regarded as more authoritative than recorded facts. It was therefore doubtless in all honesty that he at times modified his older sources. Thus the later idealization of Solomon led him to invert the testimony of I Kings 9$^{11-14}$ and represent the builder of the temple as receiving certain cities from Hiram of Tyre rather than ceding them to him (II Chr. 8^2). The later conception of Jehovah's rule and the new belief in a personal adversary led him to state that David was influenced by Satan, not by Jehovah, to number the people (cf. II Sam. 24^1 and I Chr. 21^1). To reconcile the story with the more familiar version in I Samuel 17, he represents Elhanan as slaying, not Goliath, as in II Samuel 21^{19}, but the brother of Goliath (I Chr. 20^5). Some of the variations from the narrative in Samuel and Kings are doubtless due to the fact that the Chronicler followed a different tradition, as for example, when he states that Jehoshaphat joined with Ahaziah in a commercial enterprise

Point of view and peculiarities of the Chronicler

Modification of his earlier sources

23

(II Chr. 20³⁵), while according to I Kings 22⁴⁹ he refused to unite with him. Sometimes his quotations from distinct sources introduce absolute contradictions into his narrative, as for example, when he affirms, following Kings, that Asa and Jehoshaphat did not remove the high places (I Kgs. 15¹⁴, 22⁴³, II Chr. 15¹⁷, 20³³), although, quoting from late traditions which idealized these kings, he had already stated that they did remove the high places (II Chr. 14⁵, 17⁶). In every case the reason for the variation is transparent and reveals his peculiar point of view and aim.

Omissions

His omissions are equally suggestive. Those facts which did not suit his purpose or were contrary to his theory of the history were omitted. Thus nothing is said of David's crimes and the national disasters that followed in their train, for in his thought David was the man after God's own heart, to whom was due the conception and organization of the temple. Many references to the primitive idolatry which survived in Judah until the Babylonian exile (e.g., I Kgs. 14²²⁻²⁴, II Kgs. 18⁴) are passed over in silence; no mention is made of Hezekiah's tribute to Assyria (II Kgs. 18¹⁴⁻¹⁶). Most significant of all is the almost complete absence of the Northern Israelitish history which figures so prominently in Kings. Saul is only introduced on the fatal battle-field of Gilboa, and then to be condemned. For the Chronicler the chosen people are those of the South, and *Jehovah is not with Israel* (II Chr. 25⁷). Judah, Benjamin—which he always associates with the southern kingdom—and Levi are the three tribes which command his first attention in the opening genealogies and throughout his history. The northern kingdom has so completely vanished from his vision that *Israel* is frequently used as a designation of Judah (e.g., II Chr. 21², 28¹⁹). The reason for this omission is obvious. According to his retributive philosophy of history the early fall of the northern kingdom was conclusive evidence of its rejection by Jehovah. More important still was the historical fact that the antecedents of the later Judean community and the temple, which alone interested the Chronicler, all went back to Judah, not to Israel.

His aim to write an ecclesiastical history

His aim, however, was not to give an ordinary history of Judah. Many incidents of great political significance are ignored. Nor was it to write the history of Israel's religion, else he would not have passed over without mention the great work of Elijah, Amos, and Hosea. It was rather to record the history of Judah, conceived of from the first as a sacred state centring about the temple, with the priests, the Levites, and earlier the king and his court, as its officials. Although the words, *church* and *ecclesiastical*, are in a sense anachronisms, the Judah which the Chronicler knows and pictures is nothing more than an ecclesiastical state, and his narrative as a whole may best be designated as the *Ecclesiastical History of Judah and the Temple.*

His position in the community

The prominence which he gives to the Levites and the frequency with which he introduces into his quotations from earlier sources detailed descriptions of the temple music and especially of the levitical guilds of singers, strongly suggest that he belongs to one of these. Connection with the ruling class in the Jewish hierarchy put him in possession of the current priestly traditions and doubtless enabled him to consult the then extant histories of his race.

24

THE CHRONICLER'S ECCLESIASTICAL HISTORY

The references of the Chronicler at first glance give the impression that in writing I and II Chronicles he had before him a large number of writings in addition to those now included in the Old Testament. Of these sixteen distinct titles are given. Four of these, the *Book of the Kings of Judah*, the *Book of the Kings of Judah and Israel*, the *Book of the Kings of Israel*, and the *Affairs of the Kings of Israel*, are without much doubt variant titles of the same work. To these may be added in all probability the title *Midrash of the Book of the Kings* (II Chr. 24[27]), for it is referred to in II Chronicles 24 as containing a group of facts kindred to those found in the work bearing the preceding titles. Furthermore, as has been acutely urged, it is difficult to see why, if distinct and yet relating to the reigns of all the kings, it should be referred to but once by the Chronicler. His references to earlier histories

Moreover, as will be shown later, most of his quotations from non-canonical sources evidently came from what might most appropriately be designated a *Midrash* (cf. p. 26). When the Chronicler at the conclusion of a reign does not refer his readers for further information to a book having one of the five titles cited above, he substitutes some special authority, as for example the *Words of the Seer Samuel, the Prophet Nathan and the Seer Gad* (I Chr. 29[29]), or the *Words of Nathan the Prophet* and the *Prophecy of Ahijah the Shilonite* and the *Visions of Iddo the Seer* (II Chr. 9[29]). Each of these titles is connected with the name of some prophet or seer mentioned in the history of the period. The fact that they are always introduced as substitutes for the titles of the more comprehensive work, and never appear with them in connection with the same reign, seems to indicate that they simply refer to sections of the greater *Book of the Kings* in which these prophets figured. This conclusion is strongly confirmed by such passages as II Chronicles 20[34], *Now the other acts of Jehoshaphat, the earlier as well as the later, have already been recorded in the Words of Jehu the son of Hanani, which is inserted in the Book of the Kings of Israel*, and by the Hebrew version of II Chronicles 32[32], *Now the acts of Hezekiah as well as his pious deeds have already been recorded in the Vision of the Prophet Isaiah the son of Amoz, in the Book of the Kings of Judah and Israel*. The natural implication of these statements is that possibly the *Words* and *Vision* were once originally distinct, but that they then constituted a section of the larger work. The remaining title, the *Midrash of the Prophet Iddo* (II Chr. 13[22]), may have been distinct, but it is also possible that the Chronicler employed it as synonym of the work attributed to the same author and in II Chronicles 9[29] and 12[15] refers to it under the variant titles, the *Visions of Iddo the Seer* and the *Words of Iddo the Seer*. Words of the prophets and seers

The contents of the books of Chronicles support in general the inferences drawn from the references to earlier sources. The many verbatim quotations from the canonical books of Samuel and Kings and especially from the sections which came from the late prophetic editor leave little doubt that they, like the earlier pentateuchal books, were before the Chronicler and were made by him the basis of his work. His use of Samuel-Kings

The history of the *Book of the Kings of Judah and Israel*, to which he so often refers, must necessarily remain largely a matter of conjecture. It is

The Book of the Kings of Judah and Israel

certain from the references and probable quotations from it that it was distinct from the Old Testament books of Samuel and Kings. It may possibly have been based on these, but it also contained much else. This additional material may in part have come from the larger *Chronicles of the Kings of Judah* and the *Chronicles of the Kings of Israel*, which the editor of Kings frequently mentions. There are occasionally found in the writings of the Chronicler detailed statistics which are probably authentic and which favor the conclusion that they were ultimately derived from an older source. In levitical and priestly circles the older histories would inevitably be modified and expanded very much as the Chronicler treated the material of Samuel and Kings. Another familiar and instructive illustration of the same transforming process is found by comparing the early Judean prophetic accounts of the exodus, the wilderness wandering, and the conquest of Canaan with the corresponding late priestly versions (cf. Vol. I, §§ 63–116). Soon after the beginning of the Babylonian exile the originally distinct chronicles of the northern and southern kingdoms may have been blended into one work.

The Midrash of the Book of the Kings

It does not seem probable that the Chronicler had before him an exilic *Book of the Kings of Judah and Israel*. Certainly most of his data, other than those from the canonical books of Samuel and Kings, if not, as has been claimed, his own creation, must have been taken from what may properly be called a *Midrash of the Book of the Kings*. The word *midrash* describes a large proportion of the literature of later Judaism. It is derived from the Hebrew word meaning *to search out, explore*. It is applied to an edifying story like Tobit, or to an address or exposition intended to bring out the implied or hidden meaning of a scriptural passage. Its aim is always didactic. If the story is highly embellished, it is to attract the reader and emphasize the moral. As in the modern didactic novel, the leading characters are frequently introduced simply to give expression to the teachings of the author (cf. p. 4). The passages not quoted by the Chronicler from his canonical source are excellent examples of this type of literature. They always relate to prominent historic characters and scenes. They usually start with certain well-authenticated facts. Questions suggested in the older source are answered at length, numbers are multiplied, all the details assume larger and more exalted proportions, right is always richly rewarded and wickedness signally punished, miracles are common, and prophets and kings deliver noble, majestic, spiritual addresses, embodying the best doctrines of later Judaism. Sometimes the story element is more prominent and sometimes the addresses. These didactic stories and addresses constitute the really distinctive element in the books of Chronicles. A few, and possibly all of them, may have been written by the Chronicler, who is imbued with their spirit and aim, but some appear to have been cited by him from an extensive *Midrash of the Book of the Kings* which probably grew up gradually on the basis of the earlier exilic *Book of the Kings of Judah and Israel*. It must, however, be frankly admitted that the evidence which has led the latest commentators, like Benzinger and Kittel, to assign a large part of Chronicles to this source is meagre and not altogether decisive. The presence of the Chronicler's peculiar idioms and ideas throughout all these sections still furnishes a good basis for the thesis of the earlier German critics, who maintained that the Chronicler had but one source, Samuel-Kings, and that all else was the creation of his own active imagination. On the whole, however, the simplest and most satisfactory explanation of all the facts is that he had before him one or two midrashic sources to which he frequently refers under many different titles. In vocabulary and literary style, as well as in point of view, the stories which he takes from them are so closely related to those from the pen of the Chronicler that any detailed analysis is necessarily very uncertain and unsatisfactory. Their theological and moral ideas and their attitude toward the ritual are also closely parallel to those of the Chronicler himself. Some of them so obviously favor the Levites at the expense of the priests that they must have come, like the book of Chronicles, from the pens of Levites.

In general they may be dated in the century of religious and national revival which followed the reformation associated with Nehemiah and Ezra about 400 B.C. When the late priestly law was accepted as the absolute guide of the community, the religious leaders sought not only to conform their lives and those of their own generation to its definite and revolutionary demands, but they also began to rewrite history in order to bring the past into harmony with it. At the same time they were influenced by the desire to find in the precedents of the past, authority for the usages of their day. Thus not only Moses, but also David, Solomon, Jehoshaphat, Hezekiah, and Josiah were represented as being strict upholders of the post-exilic institutions. Since these *midrashim* stand so near in date, as well as point of view and literary style, to the work of the Chronicler, even if they could in each case be definitely distinguished, the analysis would be of little value. *Date of the midrashim in Chronicles*

From the same periods probably come the apparent quotations in I Chronicles $15^{1-15, 25}-16^3$, 21^{1-27}, 22^{2-13}, 28^{1-19}, 29^{1-9}, and possibly the nucleus of 23–26 and II Chronicles 24^{4-14}. They are based upon the briefer narratives of Samuel and Kings. These, however, are revised, so that the priests and Levites figure as the guardians of the ark, and everything is done in accordance with the late priestly law. The Levites are divided into six classes, 15^{3-9}, instead of three as elsewhere by the Chronicler. The theme which binds together these different sections is their interest in the temple. They appear therefore to have been taken from a late priestly temple history, which may have been incorporated in the *Midrash of the Book of the Kings*, but was probably originally distinct. *Late priestly temple history*

Thus the Chronicler's work is the outgrowth of many earlier writings, and represents the culmination of a long process of development. He himself does not stand alone, but is rather the final editor or epitomizer of the work of a school of writers. Their predecessors were the editors of Judges, Samuel, and Kings, who likewise selected their stories to illustrate their religious and ethical doctrines. Their contemporaries were those who wrote the very late priestly stories in the Pentateuch (*e.g.*, the account of the war with Midian, Vol. I, § 101). Their successors were the authors of the later Jewish *midrashim*, who for example in the book of Jubilee rewrote *Point of view of the Chronicler's school* and freely expanded the stories of the patriarchs with a similar didactic aim. Time and circumstance explain their lack of the historical sense. Prolonged subjection to foreign rulers had excluded the Jews from all participation in political life. The shadow of the exile still rested heavily upon them. At this time the future offered little to inspire them. Their chief joy and pride and comfort were the magnificence of their ritual and the glories of their past. Prominent before their eyes were the dazzling splendors of the Persian and Greek empires. These furnished their basis by comparison with which the facts recorded in the primitive sources of Samuel and Kings seemed paltry and insignificant. Idealizing and almost idolizing the leaders and great events in the past history of their nation, it was inevitable that they should readily overlook the sins and the mistakes, and represent its victories and glories on a scale corresponding to that with which they were familiar.

Their noble religious conceptions

Their idealized past also furnished dramatic illustrations of that moral order in the universe in which they firmly believed. Aside from their interest in the ritual, which to their minds represented worship and true religion, their supreme purpose was to proclaim that God is just, that he is merciful, and that he rules directly and personally in human life. The might of armies and nations counts as nothing against him. In the end the right will surely win. Obedience and faith in Jehovah are more effective instruments in the hands of Israel's kings than powerful armies and strong alliances. Thus, although the historical perspective of the Chronicler and his school is often defective, their stories emphasize certain of the most vital spiritual truths.

IV

THE ORIGINAL SOURCES AND HISTORICAL VALUE
OF EZRA-NEHEMIAH

WHILE the Chronicler aims in the first great division of his work (I and II Chr.) to show that the ceremonial institutions of his day could all be traced back to David and Solomon, in the second, Ezra-Nehemiah, his purpose is to demonstrate that these institutions were revived, in connection with the second temple, by the exiles who returned from Babylonia. Unfortunately, the parallel prophetic history of Samuel-Kings stops with the exile, so that the historian is almost entirely dependent upon the Chronicler for information regarding the Jewish community during the Persian period. The sermons of Haggai and Zechariah supplement and correct the Chronicler's portrait at one important epoch (cf. note § 146), and the book of Malachi and the prophecies in the latter part of Isaiah throw light upon social and religious conditions, but otherwise the additional data are few. On the other hand, the Chronicler stands much nearer the events which he records in the second great division of his work, and his testimony is accordingly more valuable.

Importance of Ezra-Nehemiah

Fortunately, his peculiar ideas and tendencies and those of the late priestly and levitical writers whom he quotes, are clearly revealed by comparative study of Samuel, Kings, and Chronicles. These reappear in Ezra-Nehemiah and must be reckoned with in reconstructing the true course of the history. In his mind the priests and Levites are so much more important than the laymen, that only the Babylonian exiles, among whom were found the priests who survived the catastrophe of 586 B.C., were deemed by him eligible to rebuild the temple and reinstitute the rule of the law. The people of the land—those who survived the captivity and under the inspiring teaching of Haggai and Zechariah actually rebuilt the temple in 520 B.C. (cf. note § 146)—were in his eyes ceremonially unclean. The true Israel—like the Jewish community of his own day, ruled by priests and devoted solely to maintaining the temple ritual and fulfilling the insistent demands of the ceremonial law—is the chief actor in his history. As in the *midrashim* of Chronicles, events are the results of direct divine intervention. Jehovah is represented as influencing the most powerful Persian kings to pour upon the returning exiles the wealth of the empire and to issue decrees, the language and purport of which were well calculated to satisfy the strictest priestly patriot. Ezra 1, 3^{1}–4^{5} and 6^{16-22} are excellent illustrations of the Chronicler's conceptions of the revival of the Jewish community. Undoubtedly important historical facts are at the basis, but the idealized character of the narrative is clearly revealed by comparing it with the early record found in Haggai 1 or Ezra 5^{3}–6^{15}.

Chronicler's peculiar conceptions of the post-exilic history

29

His
sources:
the
Aramaic
document

The analysis of Chronicles has demonstrated, however, that the Chronicler was not primarily an author, but a compiler. This fact also determines the great historical value of Ezra-Nehemiah. He makes long, verbal quotations from three or four older sources. The first is the Aramaic document cited in Ezra 5^3–6^{15}. It records an unsuccessful attempt by the local Persian satrap to stop the building of the temple. Not only is the language different, but the vocabulary and literary style are distinct from those of the Chronicler. A Persian monarch like Cyrus is referred to simply as *the king*, implying that the document was at least composed before the Greek period, when he was designated as *the king of Persia*. At the same time the Jewish form of the decree in 6^{3-12} suggests that that idealizing process had begun, which is still more prominent in the sections which come from the Chronicler (cf. Appendix XII for a recently discovered decree of Darius). In general, however, the data, which it presents, may be regarded as authentic. Probably from the same series of documents, which appear to have recorded the official relations between the Persian government and the Judean community, was taken the other Aramaic section in Ezra 4^{7-23}. It is very loosely connected with its context, which relates to the rebuilding of the temple, while it records an independent attempt to restore the walls. Its true setting is to be found in connection with the work of Nehemiah (cf. note § 155). Whether or not these Aramaic documents were more extensive and furnished the Chronicler additional data is an interesting question, which cannot be definitely answered. Ezra 1 appears to be his expansion and idealization of the facts derived from the Aramaic document quoted in 5^3–6^{15}. The continuation of Ezra 1, found in I Esdras 5^{47}–6^5 (cf. § 144), and Ezra 3^1–4^6 may possibly contain some older data derived from his Aramaic source, but there is no conclusive evidence.

Nehemiah's memoirs

The oldest and by far the most important source quoted by the Chronicler is the memoirs of Nehemiah. Written to record the stirring events in which he was the leader, they rank as in many ways the most authentic and valuable historical document in the Old Testament. In a concise, straightforward, vivid narrative this noble Jewish patriot tells of how he accomplished the seemingly impossible task of rebuilding the ruined walls of Jerusalem and of reconstructing fundamentally the moral and religious standards of the degenerate Jewish community. In Nehemiah 1^1–7^{5a}, with the probable exception of chapter 3, the Chronicler quotes bodily from this source. Unless it is found in $11^{1, 2}$, the sequel to 7^{5a} has been lost in the complex process of editorial readjustment, to which the material in Ezra-Nehemiah has been subjected. The conclusion of the account of the rebuilding of the walls is probably to be found in $12^{31, 32, 37-40}$. In 13^{3-31} Nehemiah's energetic reforming spirit again finds expression. Since the section concerns the reform of the ceremonial life of the community, the Chronicler has evidently here departed from his usual custom in quoting from the memoirs of Nehemiah and recast and supplemented his source at several points (cf. note § 158). The references in $3, 6$ also imply that he failed to reproduce that part of the memoirs which probably told of Nehemiah's other acts as governor and of his return to Artaxerxes. Otherwise we appear to be in complete

30

possession of the autobiography of the most important Jew of his age. The preservation of this document, which records the work not of a priest nor of a Levite, but of a layman, must forever be reckoned to the Chronicler's credit. It certainly represents his greatest service to history. Upon a brief but exceedingly important period, which is preceded and followed by centuries of comparative obscurity, it throws the clear light of contemporary testimony.

Nehemiah's memoirs also furnish a definite starting point for the consideration of the complex and difficult problems presented by the remaining chapters of Ezra-Nehemiah. Within the past decade an extensive literature has grown up about them (cf. Appendix I), in which very diverse conclusions have been maintained by different scholars. Basing his deductions upon a careful, exhaustive study of the vocabulary and literary style, Professor Torrey in his *Composition and Historical Value of Ezra-Nehemiah* concludes that they were all originally written by the Chronicler, and that Ezra is but the creation of his imagination. Others maintain that in Ezra 7^{27}–9^{15}, 10, we have verbatim quotations from Ezra's memoirs, and in Nehemiah 7^{70}–10^{39} documents of the time of Ezra (cf., *e.g.*, Guthe, *The Book of Ezra and Neh.* in SBOT). This position naturally carries with it the acceptance of the testimony of these records as substantially historical. These wide variations in opinion are possible from the historical point of view, because Ezra is mentioned nowhere else in the Old Testament outside Ezra-Nehemiah. Even in Ben Sira's list of Israel's immortals (written about 190 B.C.) the name of Ezra is not found beside those of Zerubbabel, Jeshua, and Nehemiah (49^{11-13}). This omission is all the more significant because Ben Sira himself is an intelligent and reverent disciple of the law and of the traditions that gathered about it. Likewise in the still later traditions found in II Maccabees 1^{18-23} Nehemiah, not Ezra, is the one who is represented as coming back from Babylon to Jerusalem to restore the worship. In estimating the work and relative importance of these two men it is significant that outside the writings of the Chronicler the one, a priest and scribe, is ignored and the other, a layman, is honored for the next three or four centuries by Judaism, the chief interest of which nevertheless centred in ceremonialism and the law.

Many of the otherwise insuperable difficulties of Ezra-Nehemiah disappear, when it is recognized that, if at all historical, the work of Ezra must have followed, not preceded that of Nehemiah. If an expedition of the size and importance of the one described in Ezra 8 had gone to Judah only thirteen years before, it is incredible that Nehemiah would have made no reference to it, and also have found conditions in Jerusalem as he did. Not one of the ardent reformers mentioned in Ezra 8 is referred to in Nehemiah's detailed record. The leaders of the community also, instead of being ready to submit to any sacrifice, are even suspicious of the man who comes to help them build their walls. Moreover, after the community had submitted to Ezra's sweeping measures, Nehemiah's mild reforms are meaningless. On the other hand, such an expedition as Ezra is represented as leading back to Judah was a practical impossibility before Nehemiah had fortified Jerusalem,

Various conclusions regarding the origin and value of the Ezra narrative

Priority of Nehemiah's work

31

reorganized the community, and brought the dismembered sections of the Jewish race into sympathetic touch with each other. Likewise his pioneer reforms, enforced by his energy and authority and claim to the gratitude of the Palestinian community, alone make credible the revolutionary changes associated with Ezra and realized in the character of later Judaism. Direct evidence also may be found in Ezra's prayer in Ezra 9, in which he gives thanks that the wall of Jerusalem has been rebuilt and Judah's defences restored (vs. ^{9}). Instead of a defenceless, afflicted city, he found a strong, populous community, ready to follow him to any extreme, even if it involved the severance of all relations with foreigners and the rending asunder of their homes (Ezra 10).

Present order due to the Chronicler
The present impossible order of events in Ezra-Nehemiah is probably due to the Chronicler's desire to give Ezra, the priest and scribe, the precedence over Nehemiah. His free readjustment of his sources is illustrated not only in Chronicles but also repeatedly in Ezra-Nehemiah. Thus for example the account of an attempted interruption of the rebuilding of the walls in the days of Artaxerxes he introduced in 4$^{7-23}$ as an explanation of why the temple was not completed before the days of Darius. In Nehemiah 12^{44}–13^{31} the analogy is even closer. Just before the quotation in 13$^{10-12}$, which tells of Nehemiah's pioneer regulations providing for the income of the Levites and singers, he himself adds a section, 12$^{44-47}$, in which it is stated that this arrangement had already been made and was in force in the days of Zerubbabel and in the days of Nehemiah (§ 158). Possibly the original Ezra tradition read in Ezra 7 the *thirty-* or *forty-seventh year of Artaxerxes,* or the reference may have been to Artaxerxes II or III. It is more probable, however, that the Chronicler simply introduced his favorite number to establish the priority of Ezra. Additional evidence of his desire to give Ezra a prominent position is found in the fact that he also in Nehemiah 12^{36} places Ezra at the head of the procession of priests at the dedication of the walls, although the older sources give no suggestion that this priestly reformer was then at Jerusalem.

Original order of the Ezra narrative
That the similar material in Nehemiah 7^{70}–10^{39}, which is injected into the midst of the quotations from Nehemiah's memoirs, belongs with the dismembered section, Ezra 7–10, was even recognized by the editor of I Esdras, who introduces Nehemiah and immediately after Ezra 10. Of the many attempts to restore the original order, that of Torrey alone gives a connected and consistent narrative: Ezra 7, 8, Nehemiah 7^{70}–8^{18}, Ezra 9, 10, Nehemiah 9, 10. With the exception of the editor's introduction, Ezra 7$^{1-10}$, and a few supplemental passages, the unity of representation and ideas is confirmed by the constant recurrence of the same peculiar words and expressions. It must be admitted that the strenuous efforts of certain scholars to find here the work of several different authors is a failure. Even those sections in which Ezra is represented as speaking in the first person are not exceptions. As Professor Torrey has further demonstrated, nowhere outside that book itself do we find more, if as many, of the literary characteristics that distinguish the book of Chronicles. They are so marked and recur in nearly every verse with such persistency that all possibility is eliminated

SOURCES AND VALUE OF EZRA-NEHEMIAH

that this is due to mere chance. This fact is fully recognized and further
illustrated in great detail by Geissler (in *Die literarischen Beziehungen
der Esramemoiren*), who, however, maintains that the Chronicler was not
the original author of the narrative. Contents and method of representation
also emphasize the close relationship with the narratives of Chronicles. If
a majority of the distinctive passages in that book are from the Chronicler,
he is unquestionably the author of the Ezra narrative. But if, as seems
more probable (cf. pp. 26, 27), he quoted largely from the *midrashim* which
came from the very late priestly school to which he belonged and of which
he was the final editor, he here again figures in his ordinary rôle of editor
and reviser. The arbitrary manner in which he has rearranged the narrative,
dismembering it without adjusting the parts to their new settings, strongly
suggests that he had an older document before him. Certain grammatical
and stylistic peculiarities, as well as characteristic words and idioms, also
distinguish this Ezra narrative from the passages elsewhere assigned to the
Chronicler (cf. Geissler, LBE pp. 22–24). His own additions can also be
detected at several points. As Geissler has shown, the earlier scriptures
most quoted are the pre-exilic and exilic prophets, Deuteronomy, and the
Holiness Code, but not the later sections of the priestly code, which figure
most prominently in the writings of the Chronicler.

The possibility that Ezra himself wrote a memoir and that we have quotations from it is therefore not absolutely precluded, but literary and historical considerations do not support it. The vocabulary and literary structure of what may be called the *Ezra narrative* proclaim that it stands nearer
the Chronicler and the author of Esther than Nehemiah or the late priestly
writers. Its contents support the same inference. The decree of Artaxerxes,
Ezra 7[11-26], the account of the fabulous wealth brought back by the exiles,
8[24-27], and the sudden conversion of the Judean community read much more
like the *midrashim* in Chronicles than Nehemiah's detailed memoirs. The
parallels between the history of Nehemiah and that of Ezra are also many
and striking: the liberal decree of Artaxerxes, the journey to Jerusalem
with a following and unusual authority, the preliminary study of the conditions, the detailed reforms, and finally the recording it all in the form of a
personal memoir. It is significant that practically every element in the covenant recorded in Nehemiah 10 corresponds to a distinct reform instituted
by Nehemiah (13[4-31]). When we add to this the conspicuous absence of
any other references to Ezra in the literature of the next three or four centuries, the conviction deepens that this is partly idealized history, in which
the mantle of Nehemiah has fallen upon Ezra. An instructive analogy might
be drawn between the Nehemiah-Ezra and the Elijah-Elisha stories. Elijah
and Nehemiah were both men who met grave crises with dauntless courage
and energy, and as a result of their achievements set to work forces which
revolutionized the subsequent history of their race. Later schools of writers,
however, manifested a strong tendency to transfer the renown of their work
to two of their successors who represented more perfectly the ideals of the
later school in which the Elisha and Ezra traditions respectively assumed
their final literary form (cf. pp. 18–20).

33

Its
histor-
ical
signifi-
cance
At the same time there is good reason for believing that Ezra, as well as Elisha, actually lived and that he performed an important, although less conspicuous service than tradition attributed to him, in introducing the priestly law to the Judean community. As portrayed, he and his acts faithfully symbolize that fundamental and probably gradual reformation which converted the weak, discouraged people to whom Nehemiah and the author of Malachi spoke into a body of heroes and martyrs, who in the Maccabean struggle won religious and political freedom.

Origin
of the
gene-
alogical
lists
The remaining chapters of Ezra-Nehemiah consist chiefly of genealogical lists in which the Chronicler was deeply interested. The data incorporated in them may in part have been derived from the *Book of the Chronicles*, to which he refers in Nehemiah 12[23], but their setting and present literary form are clearly due to the editor himself. It must be admitted that their historical value is slight, except as they reveal the organization of the Judean community in the days of the Chronicler and in the immediately preceding century. The census of the Jews in Palestine in the latter part of the Persian period (cf. note § 165) has been introduced by the editor into the Nehemiah history and again in Ezra 2, where it purports to give the list of those who returned soon after 538 B.C.

His-
torical
value
of
Ezra-
Nehe-
miah
as a
whole
Thus in its present form, as it comes from the Chronicler, Ezra-Nehemiah gives the reader a confused and misleading conception of the real course of post-exilic history. And yet side by side with the dull and almost valueless genealogical lists, this book contains some of the most detailed and exact historical writings in all the Old Testament. In a fragmentary manner, and yet with vivid flashes of light at critical points, it records the rebuilding of the second temple, the elaborate development of its ritual, the revival of the Judean state, the return of the exiles, the unification of the Jewish race, and the birth of that Judaism which treasured the writings and traditions incorporated in the Old Testament and furnished the background and atmosphere of the New.

V

THE RECORDS OF THE MACCABEAN AGE

THE list of the Jewish high-priests in Nehemiah 12[10, 11] carries the history of the Jewish people down to the conquests of Alexander in 332 B.C. This leaves a period of over three centuries, until the birth of Christ, regarding which the historical records in the present Protestant Bible are absolutely silent. It is, however, one of the most important periods in biblical and Israelitish history. It was during these centuries that several of the books of the Old Testament, such as Chronicles, Ezra, Nehemiah, Daniel, Ecclesiastes, and Esther were written, and many more like Proverbs and Psalms crystallized into their present form. It also witnessed the gradual growth and practical completion of the canon of the Old Testament. These memorable three centuries not only bind the Old Testament to the New, but represent the final development of that Judaism which is the outgrowth of the life recorded in the Old Testament. Without a knowledge of the events and forces of this revolutionizing era, any study of either of the Testaments is necessarily incomplete. It was then that Greek and Jewish ideas and civilization met in mortal combat and later contributed each their peculiar message to Christianity. Out of the fires of persecution came that passionate love for race, for law, for traditions, and for Jerusalem, which fused all the scattered members of the Jewish nation together, and which has kept them practically intact until the present. Then the feud between Jew and Samaritan reached its height of bitterness, and through the conversion of the Idumeans at the edge of the sword, the malign influence of the Herodian house became a potent factor in Jewish history. Then also the Jews of Galilee and Perea were brought into religious union with those of Judea. The same transitional epoch saw the birth and full development of the Pharisaic and Sadducean parties. The brilliant victories under the leadership of Judas Maccabeus and his successors gave the Jews that taste of liberty and conquest which made them so restive under the rule of Rome and so eager to welcome the visions of a temporal Messianic kingdom.

Fortunately, the most important events of this reign are recorded in detail in two books which are still included in the Old Testament canon accepted by the Greek and Roman Catholic churches, and which have only in very recent times been dropped from the Protestant Bible. In the case of several of the so-called Apocryphal Old Testament books the conclusions of the Reformers and the final decision of the Bible Societies, during the earlier part of the last century, are amply justified. But the tendency which is becoming so marked among thoughtful Bible students in this country and in Europe to restore at least in practice such a book as I Maccabees to its rightful place beside Samuel and Kings is sane and thoroughly justified by the facts. Its lateness and the fact that, unlike Ecclesiastes and many Psalms,

Importance of the Greek and Maccabean periods

Value and canonicity of I Maccabees

35

it was not associated with revered names like those of Solomon or David, alone kept it out of the Palestinian Jewish canon. Otherwise its historical title to a place in the Old Testament is well established. Measured by the more fundamental and enduring standards of value and authority, its claim to a place in the Old Testament is well supported. As has just been noted, the events which it records are surpassed in importance and inspiring qualities by none in Israelitish history. Judas and Simon are certainly as brave and noble types as David and Solomon. The deeply patriotic and religious spirit in which it is written compares favorably with that of Samuel, Kings, or Chronicles. As a vivid, faithful record of the events of which it speaks it is equalled by no other Jewish writing.

Value and canonicity of II Maccabees   While its historical title to canonicity is equally valid, II Maccabees does not rank with the first book. Its theme, however, is in general the same, and it supplements the earlier history at many points. Its spirit is also strongly religious, although far less historical. It may be compared with the Chronicler's late ecclesiastical history. In both the primary aim is not merely to record events, but rather to edify and instruct. Nowhere else in pre-Christian Jewish literature does the belief in the resurrection of the dead find such clear expression (cf. 7$^{9, 11, 14, 36}$, 12$^{43-45}$, 14^{46}). In a great variety of ways it effectively aids in bridging the chasm which otherwise yawns between the history and teaching of the Old Testament and that of the New.

Original title of I Maccabees   The present titles to the Maccabean histories were given by the Greek translators on the basis of their contents. The term *Maccabean* was derived from the surname or possibly the original name of the chief hero in the history. The Jews themselves, however, never applied it to the histories nor to the members of his family, but used instead the term *Hasmonean* (or *Asmonean*), the family name of the house of Mattathias. The original Hebrew or Aramaic title of I Maccabees, which was known to Origen (cf. Eusebius, HE 6), was probably *Book* (or *History*) *of the Hasmoneans*. This title is certainly a felicitous designation of the history which records the achievements of the different members of the famous Hasmonean house and the events of their rule.

Its original language and later translations   The independent testimony of Origen and Jerome that it was originally written in Hebrew is completely confirmed by the presence in every verse of characteristic Semitic idioms, and above all by the fact that certain of the obvious errors in the Greek text, which alone survives, are due to the failure of the translator to understand his Hebrew original. Frequently it is possible by restoring the Hebrew to correct the current translation. The original Hebrew version was early lost, probably because it never found a place in the Palestinian canon of the Old Testament, while the Greek, accepted as canonical by the Jews of the dispersion, survived. This translation is exact without being slavishly literal, and was evidently made by a Jew who was well acquainted with the Hebrew and yet master of a good Greek style which was well adapted to the subject matter. Josephus in his history, Jerome in the Vulgate, and the translator of the Syriac version all depended upon the Greek text.

The author of I Maccabees was evidently a Jew and a native of Palestine,

as is shown by his minute acquaintance with its topography and comparative Its
author
ignorance of places and affairs outside Judea. His familiarity with political
events and court intrigues strongly suggests that he was a man of rank and
in close touch with the leaders of his day. His loyalty to each of the Maccabean rulers and evident approval of their policy indicate that, if affiliated
with either of the leading parties of the state, it was with the Sadducean,
rather than the Pharisaic, which soon after the restoration of the temple
began to view askance the political and military ambitions of Judas's successors. It is as a devoted and enthusiastic patriot that he writes his
history. The earlier historical books are his models. The familiar expressions, *to this day* (13^{30}), or, *now the rest of the acts of John and his
wars and his brave deeds—behold they are recorded in the Chronicles of
his high priesthood* ($16^{23, \ 24}$, cf. 9^{22}), indicate that he wrote with the feeling
that he was the true successor of the earlier Hebrew historians. His spirit
is devout, and he is by no means blind to the religious significance of the
stirring deeds that he records, but his first aim is simply historical, that is,
to produce a simple, vivid narrative of events. His own reflections he
keeps for the most part to himself, but his enthusiasm and piety doubtless
find expression in the exalted addresses, usually in the form of poetry, which
are uttered by Mattathias ($2^{7-13, \ 49-60}$), Judas (3^{18-22}, 4^{8-11}), and the people
(3^{50-53}). These and other passages reveal a man zealous for the religious
institutions of his race, assured of its noble destiny, but believing that this
was to be realized not by miracles but through men who combined faith
with courage and action.

The author of I Maccabees records the death of Simon 135 B.C. and refers Its
date
in the epilogue, $16^{23, \ 24}$, to the wars of John Hyrcanus and the rebuilding
of the walls which belong to the earlier part of his reign, between 135 and
125 B.C. The absence of any reference to the later important acts of John's
reign, as for example the conquest of Idumea and the destruction of
Samaria, indicate that the history was probably completed by 125 B.C. It
also reflects throughout the national pride and exultation that reached their
height during the days of Simon and the earlier part of the reign of John
Hyrcanus. There is no suggestion of the clouds that began to gather during
the latter part of John's reign, because of the opposition of the Pharisees,
nor of the storm of civil war which swept over Judea during the reign of
Alexander Jannæus. The Romans, instead of being regarded as the future
conquerors of Judea, are spoken of as distant allies whose friendship is most
desirable. On the other hand there is no positive evidence pointing to a
later date. Instead, the minute details, the marvellous acquaintance with
men and facts and forces are best explained by the conclusion that the author
was reporting events with which he was personally familiar.

The unity of I Maccabees and the absence of abrupt transition and con- Its
sources
and
in-
tegrity
tradiction distinguish it from books like Samuel and Kings, which are com-
pilations from earlier sources. Furthermore, aside from the two stereotyped
formulas, which he introduced in imitation of the earlier historians (9^{22},
16^{24}), the author nowhere gives the slightest suggestion that when he wrote,
earlier sources relating to the period were in existence. The simple, straight-

forward style of the book is most like that of Nehemiah's memoirs, and indicates that popular traditions contributed very little, if anything, to it. From the first it probably took its position as the standard history of the period. It is the only Jewish source quoted by Josephus for this epoch, and he appears to have known it in practically its present form. It has been questioned whether certain of the documents incorporated in the book are not late additions (especially $10^{25\text{-}45}$, $14^{27\text{-}47}$, $15^{15\text{-}24}$). That these are exact copies of the original edicts and letters is not probable, but that the epitomes were made by the author of I Maccabees, who was in a position to be familiar with their conditions, seems on the whole the most natural explanation of the facts.

General character of II Maccabees
In passing from the sober, exact, carefully dated records of I Maccabees to the second book the transition is most marked. In his preface, $2^{19\text{-}32}$, the author of the present book of II Maccabees states that his work was an abridgment of a longer work of five volumes written by Jason of Cyrene. Being a Jew of the dispersion, Jason naturally wrote in Greek. This is further proved by the absence of Semitic idioms, and the flowing and highly ornate Greek style which is the antithesis of that employed in I Maccabees. The vocabulary is also extensive, and many rare words occur. Its faults and its virtues are those of the Alexandrian Greek school of writers.

The history of Jason of Cyrene
The two letters prefixed to the book may be authentic, but they simply relate to the feast of Dedication, and were probably added later to the historical section which begins with 3. The important question is, who was Jason of Cyrene, whose history is the basis of the present book? Unfortunately, the evidence must be derived from the epitome of his work. His knowledge of everything that relates to Syria is far more accurate than in the case of Egypt or Palestine (cf. $4^{27,\ 30}$, 5^{24}, 8^{32}, 12, 14^{12}), which suggests that when he wrote his home was at or near Antioch rather than in Cyrene in northern Africa. His aim in writing, like that of his epitomizer, was probably to edify his readers, the Jews of the dispersion. He differs too often in the order of events, as well as details, from I Maccabees to have been acquainted with that work. From the nature of his material it seems clear that his sources were oral traditions, emanating in some cases at least from eye-witnesses. Regarding the wars of Judas in 164–163 B.C. he has preserved two variant versions, $10^{14\text{-}38}$, $12^{10\text{-}45}$. In $13^{23\text{-}26}$ and $11^{13\text{-}21}$ are what appear to be two confused accounts of the final treaty with Lysias. Further, the evidence that he utilized originally independent traditions is found in the fact that Timotheus, whose death is recorded in 10^{37}, is described in 12 as again leading a campaign.

His date
Depending as he does on the oral testimony of those who were contemporary with the events, it is probable that Jason wrote his history some time between 160 and 140 B.C. The wide variations from I Maccabees do not necessarily point to a considerable lapse of time, but are rather due to the fact that the author of the one was actuated by the historical spirit, and was in personal touch with the events which he recorded, while the other was largely dependent upon oral tradition, which develops with marvellous rapidity in the East.

The epitomizer plainly states that his aim was simply to abridge the larger work. He does not appear to have utilized any other sources. His method seems to have been, as he implies in his preface (2^{24-33}), to quote those passages which seemed to him attractive and edifying, omitting others which dealt with uninteresting details, and briefly to epitomize still others. His work was not known to Josephus, although it was evidently before Philo and the author of Hebrews (cf. $11^{35,\ 36}$), from which it may be inferred that he lived somewhere between 60 and 10 B.C. and wrote at Alexandria. *(margin: Date and work of the epitomizer)*

The historian Niese has recently maintained (in his *Kritik der beiden Makkabaerbücher*) that II Maccabees is equal or superior to I Maccabees at many points. He is undoubtedly right in his contention that the second has preserved valuable historical facts; but unless all evidence regarding the origin and purpose of the two books is to be disregarded, there is no doubt that the first is by far the more reliable in reconstructing the history. External as well as internal evidence supports in general the order of events in I Maccabees, and where it is contradicted by II Maccabees the error is in most cases to be found in the latter. Where II Maccabees is the only witness, its historical testimony may be utilized after due allowance has been made for its well-known tendencies to exaggerate. In general the two histories confirm and supplement each other and together give a remarkably vivid and detailed picture of the Maccabean struggles. *(margin: Relative historical value of I and II Maccabees)*

The book of Esther may be counted as one of the indirect sources for the Maccabean period. In an intensified and far from attractive form it expresses the proud, almost insolent (cf. Mordecai's refusal to recognize the authority of Haman) attitude of the Jews toward the heathen, which was the outgrowth of the Maccabean conflicts and victories. It reflects the same vindictive spirit that led them under John Hyrcanus and Alexander Jannæus to slay by thousands their Idumean, Samaritan, and Philistine foes. The presence of both Aramaic and Persian words and the literary style of the book indicate that it comes from a comparatively late date. The Persian empire lies in the vague past and many of the established usages of its court have been forgotten. The proselyting spirit, which did not appear in Judaism until the Greek and Maccabean periods, is also present (9^{27}). From the nature of its theme it is impossible to determine the exact date of the book. It may be assigned with assurance to the second century B.C. According to the concluding sentence in the Greek translation, this version was known in Egypt by 114 B.C. (if the reference be to Soter II), which points to the first part or middle rather than the second half of the century. *(margin: Date of the book of Esther)*

The improbabilities and impossibilities of the story have long been recognized. That a Persian king would make an Amalekite and then a Jew his prime-minister and a Jewess his queen was contrary to all the firmly established customs of the empire. It is also incredible that he would permit and even decree the slaughter not only of all the Jews but also of thousands of his Persian subjects and that, after eleven months' warning, they would make no resistance. The chronological difficulties are equally great. Thus, for example, Mordecai, transported to Babylon in 597 B.C., in 474 becomes Xerxes's prime-minister. The events of the book are also *(margin: Evidence that it is a romance)* dated at the time when the king was engrossed in his disastrous campaigns in Greece and when Amestris, a cruel and dominating woman, was queen (Herod. 7^{114}, 9^{112}). Above all, the highly dramatic representation and coloring indicate that it is one of the popular stories or *midrashim* with which later Jewish literature abounded.

Its purpose and origin Its obvious purpose was to give the traditional origin, and to encourage the observance of the feast of Purim (9^{17-32}). A German scholar (Jensen, *Elamitische Eigennamen*) has recently called attention to the fact that Hamman was the chief deity of the Elamites, whose capital was Susa (Shushan), while Marduk (from which the name *Mordecai* is derived) was the leading god of the Babylonians. In the same pantheon and related to Marduk was the goddess Ishtar, whose name appears in the later Babylonian as *Estra*, which would be *Esther* in the Hebrew. Similarly Vashti is the name of an Elamite deity. Thus it would seem that the story, like the account of creation in Genesis 1, originated among the Babylonians. It apparently reflected the ancient hostility between them and the Elamites, each people being represented by its chief deities. If so, it has been freely adapted by the Jewish story-teller, who heightens the dramatic interest by making Mordecai a descendant of the family of Saul and Haman of Agag, the Amalekite king captured by Saul (I Sam. 15).

Possible Babylonian origin of the feast of Purim If this is the origin of the story, the feast probably also once commemorated a great victory of the ancient Babylonians over their hereditary foes the Elamites. The non-Hebrew word, *Purim*, seems to be derived from the Babylonian *pur, stone*, which would point to their custom of casting the lot to determine the date of the feast, as they are known to have done in the case of their great New Year's festival; or it may come from the Babylonian *puhru, assembly*. If it was adopted by the Jews of the East from the Babylonians, it retained its secular character and continued to be observed simply as a time of general merry-making. As a modern analogy, attention has been called to the fact that the Jews to-day in many Christian countries celebrate the Christmas festival.

Place of Esther in the canon The interest and aim of the book of Esther are thoroughly secular. Its morality is far removed from that of Israel's noblest prophets. Aside from their commendable courage and loyalty to race, no thoughtful teacher would hold up Esther or Mordecai as examples to be emulated. The spirit that seems to exult in the slaughter of thousands simply because they are heathen is as alien to the better genius of Judaism as to that of Christianity. It is not strange that the place of the book in the Jewish canon was long and hotly contested by the Jewish scribes, and although the Christians adopted the Palestinian canon *in toto*, its position in it has repeatedly been challenged. Certainly no one to-day would maintain that its claim on historical or ethical or religious grounds was superior or equal to those of I and II Maccabees or Ben Sira or the Wisdom of Solomon. If, however, the Old Testament is regarded as the faithful record of the many-sided life and thought of that Israelitish race through which Jehovah gradually revealed his universal purpose, then the book of Esther may still be accorded its traditional place.

VI

THE RECOVERY OF THE ORIGINAL TEXT OF THE HISTORICAL BOOKS

THE oldest existing manuscripts of the Old Testament books, with possibly one or two minor exceptions, come from the tenth and eleventh centuries of the present era. This surprising lack of comparatively ancient texts is due to the fact that the copies were written on perishable papyrus, parchment or leather, and when they became worn they were, because of their sanctity, systematically destroyed by the Jews, that they might not be thrown aside and suffer pollution. When it is recalled that the surviving manuscripts of the earlier historical records were made eighteen hundred years after the originals were written, the marvel grows that they are as well preserved as they are. Their accuracy depends upon the care and fidelity of the hundreds of scribes, who through the centuries have transmitted the original. There is abundant evidence that in general the existing copies reproduce in nearly all important passages the thought of the prophets, priests, and sages who first wrote them. *The marvellous preservation of the Hebrew text*

On the other hand, the evidence that a vast number of minor errors has crept into the surviving Hebrew manuscripts is equally conclusive. This is demonstrated by the differences in the Hebrew texts themselves, by the variations found in the early translations made from manuscripts far older than any which still survive, and by the obviously confused and corrupt character of many passages. The Jews fully recognized that mistakes were inevitable, and ruled that all texts in which there were more than three errors in a column be destroyed or withdrawn from use. Fortunately these textual errors usually affect the literary style and individual words and expressions rather than the vital messages of the Old Testament books. *Evidence of many minor textual errors*

These errors are due to a great variety of causes, all of which are amply illustrated in the historical books. Sometimes the text from which the copy was made was worn or its letters were not clearly written. Certain letters because of similarity of form were easily mistaken for others. The ancients were well aware of this danger. In the Mishna (*Sabb.* 103[b]) the copyists are warned against confusing the Hebrew letter *b* with *k*, *g* with *ç*, *d* with *r*, soft with hard *h*, *w* with *y*, *z* with *n*, *t* with *p*, and *m* with *s*. A great number of errors are clearly traceable to this simple cause. Since the vowel letters were not originally written, a wide difference of reading was possible. Abbreviations were also frequently misunderstood. The consonants, which were at first alone written and without being separated, were sometimes wrongly divided, the last letter or two of one word being read with the following; or when the last letter in one word was the same as that of the following, one letter would be omitted. Transpositions of letters and even clauses were *Their causes*

41

not uncommon. Instead of rewriting a roll, a copyist would insert an over-looked clause or verse at the point at which he discovered his omission. Words and clauses were also frequently repeated by mistake (dittography), and conversely one of two clauses or verses with the same beginning or ending was readily overlooked (homoioteluton).

Scribal changes During the early centuries in which the number of copies of each book was limited and before the integrity of the text was jealously guarded, each copyist, who was also usually a scribe, was at liberty to change the text. These changes are undoubtedly many and can in most cases be readily recognized. They consist of explanatory glosses, first placed in the margin and then by later copyists introduced into the text, not infrequently in a connection different from that originally intended. Still more common are the supplemental additions intended to conform the reading to the point of view of later scribes. It is often very difficult to distinguish these additional notes from those of the earlier editors of the book. In some cases the scribes deliberately altered the text in accordance with their peculiar religious ideas. The later Jewish aversion to using the sacred name *Jahweh* not only led them to substitute the vowels of the Hebrew word for *Lord*, but also elsewhere to introduce *God* (*Elohim*), where the Greek, for example, retains the older name. Interpreting literally the statement in Hosea 2^{16} that Jehovah would *take the names of the Baalim out of their mouth*, they substituted the vowels of *bosheth*, the Hebrew word for *shame*, wherever *Baal* occurred. Thus in II Samuel 2^8 and elsewhere, *Ishbaal* appears as *Ishbosheth*.

History of the Hebrew text The history of the Old Testament books is closely connected with that of the canon. As soon as a book was included in a canon of scripture its integrity was carefully guarded. The first canon to be formed was probably that of the law between 400 and 300 B.C. To this was later added the canon of prophetic writings, which included the books of Samuel and Kings. By the close of the first Christian century the canon of the Old Testament was complete. Thus for four or five centuries at least each historical book was dependent simply upon the care and fidelity of copyists who did not regard them with the deep veneration that filled the hearts of the later scribes. It is clear that during this long period, which in the case of Samuel-Kings and Chronicles-Ezra-Nehemiah included the time of the bitter persecution and the Maccabean wars, the Hebrew text suffered the greatest alterations. This conclusion is not a mere matter of conjecture, but is demonstrated by a comparison with the early Greek versions, which in many cases have undoubtedly retained the original readings. Furthermore, the historical books were never protected by the same exalted reputation for sanctity as the law. The result is that the existing Hebrew versions of these books contain more obvious errors than those of any other Old Testament books excepting possibly Ezekiel.

Basis of the existing Hebrew texts From the first Christian century the strongest efforts were put forth to guard the consonantal text from all possible errors. Many elaborate rules were laid down for the guidance of copyists. The verses and words and even letters in each book were counted. The middle word and letter was

42

determined. A careful census of the frequency of occurrence of many words and phrases was made. All peculiarities in the writing of the text were also recorded. These and other facts point to the conclusion that early in the Christian era a certain Hebrew text was adopted as the standard edition. Probably from that time on, as later, all variant Hebrew manuscripts were destroyed in order to insure one consistent reading. This recension is the basis of the present Hebrew Bible. It is obvious that it cannot represent at every point the original autograph text. If it was a critical recension, as seems probable, it simply represents the judgment of the rabbis who were able to compare the existing variant texts. If not, it is but one—probably the best—of the then existing texts. The extravagant claims made concerning its perfection by later Jewish scholars and at times adopted by the church rest on a dogmatic rather than an historical basis.

At the close of the fourth century A.D. Jerome knew only a consonantal text. From the fifth to the eighth century, however, a group of Jewish scholars devoted themselves to reproducing by the use of signs to represent the vowel sounds and punctuation marks the traditional Hebrew text as it was then recited in the synagogues. The tradition regarding the text was at that time known as the *Masoreth*, and they were therefore called the *Massorites*. Their work also included the division of the original consonants into words and the addition of a large body of critical notes on the margin calling attention to anomalous forms and suggesting traditional readings or conjectural emendations. These are often very valuable and aid materially in restoring the original. The Massorites were the pioneers in Hebrew textual criticism. While they did not always agree among themselves, their work, when completed about the end of the ninth century, became the basis of all later editions of the Hebrew (cf. the modern standard editions of Baer, 1892, Ginsburg, 1894). *[margin: Work of the Massorites]*

This brief outline of the history of the Hebrew text has illustrated the inevitable growth of variant versions and the impossibility of checking their multiplication even by repeatedly adopting a critical recension and guarding it with the most strenuous precautions and jealous care. Since this is so, it is fortunate that translations of the Hebrew scripture were made at an early date. Their history was similar to that of the Hebrew text. Each original translation was soon succeeded by a brood of variant versions, the variations of which were increased because they were constantly being revised by scholars who were familiar with the existing Hebrew manuscripts. While these many variant versions make the task of recovering the original text superlatively complex, they are of the greatest service, for in some one of the many the original has in very many cases been preserved. *[margin: General value of the early translations]*

The first essential in the practical use of any version is acquaintance with its history and characteristics. Jewish and Christian tradition agree in assigning the translation of the law to the reign of Ptolemy Philadelphus (284–247 B.C.). If, as is asserted, it was done under the patronage of Demetrius, the librarian of the Alexandrian library, it was during the earlier part of the reign, before he fell into royal disfavor. The prologue of Ben Sira, written in 132 B.C., speaks of a Greek translation of *the law, the prophets,* *[margin: Date of the original Greek translation] and the other books of the fathers,* which indicates that the books of Samuel and Kings were doubtless translated before that time. The Greek version of Esther appears to have been extant in 114 B.C. The absences of all references to Ezra (cf. p. 31) strongly suggests that Ezra-Nehemiah and perhaps Chronicles were not translated until near the beginning of the Christian era. Otherwise for the early history of the historical books we are entirely dependent upon the internal evidence.

Date of the translation of Samuel-Kings This favors the conclusion that the books of Samuel and probably Kings were translated soon after, and possibly before, the Pentateuch. One of the motives which influenced the Jews to translate their scriptures into Greek was apologetic, that is, to refute the charges that were brought against them by their persecutors especially in Alexandria. These charges aimed to throw discredit upon their past history. The books of Samuel and Kings contained the best answer to this charge and also proclaimed the past glories of their race. From the period which begins with the Babylonian exile, many Jews were found in Egypt, and one of the most powerful influences that maintained their racial integrity and kept alive their faith in Jehovah was the memory of their past triumphs. A strong incentive to translate these books would therefore not be lacking even before the days of Ptolemy Philadelphus. Since they were not then regarded as sacred as the Law, no barrier would deter a patriotic Jew from translating them. Whatever be the historical facts, there is good evidence in the character and relative completeness of the version, that the books of Samuel and probably Kings were translated at a comparatively early date, and that they were based on a Hebrew text superior at a great many points to that found in the Hebrew manuscripts at present available.

Value of the Greek translations of the historical books The Greek versions of Chronicles contribute comparatively little additional data. That of Esther adds practically nothing to the well-preserved Hebrew text. Of Ezra there are two distinct Greek translations, one in I Esdras and the other in chapters 1–10 of Esdras B in the Greek. A careful comparison of these with the Hebrew version leaves little doubt but that the one found in I Esdras, aside from the *Story of the Three Young Men,* which was added later, is the older and is also based upon a text in some respects better and more complete than the one in the present Hebrew of Ezra 1–10. These conclusions of course do not mean that the Greek renderings of Samuel and I Esdras are to be followed in a majority of cases in preference to the Hebrew. A translation is necessarily defective, and the translators of these books often failed fully to understand the original, and were also subject to their own idiosyncrasies. On the whole, however, these books have been translated with unusual fidelity and skill.

Growth of variant Greek texts If we had the original Greek translations of Samuel-Kings and Ezra-Nehemiah, they would be practically equal to a Hebrew manuscript at least one thousand years older than any we now possess. But as in the case of the Hebrew, the surviving Greek manuscripts are copies of copies. The result was that many variant texts soon sprang into existence. Often the Jewish copyists were not well acquainted with the Greek. The mistakes of the original translators also led them astray. The text was not guarded with the same religious zeal as the original Hebrew. The copyists, as well as the translators, were also usually Jews of the dispersion and therefore constantly tempted to make slight alterations where the original did not accord with their own broader views.

Meantime other independent Greek translations had been made which were based upon the then current Hebrew text. These have an independent value of their own, and also because they exercised a strong influence upon the older Greek translations. Of these, that of Aquila of Pontus, a proselyte to Judaism and a disciple of the great Rabbi Akiba, was the oldest. It was made about 140 A.D. Since it was a slavishly literal rendering of the Hebrew, it is exceedingly useful in restoring that original, although it is too literal to be valuable as a Greek translation. Two fragments of the book of Kings (I Kgs. 20⁷⁻¹⁷ and II Kgs. 23¹²⁻²⁷) were discovered in 1897 in the Cairo synagogue (published by F. C. Burkitt). Otherwise the translation is known only through the writings of the Church Fathers. *Version of Aquila*

The translation made about 200 A.D. by the Ebionite Christian Symmachus was the antithesis of that of Aquila, for its aim was to express the thought of the original in clear, idiomatic Greek. It is important to note that both appear to have had before them a Hebrew text almost identical with that edited by the Massorites. Some time before the close of the second Christian century a certain Theodotion, either an Ebionite or a Jewish proselyte, made a thorough revision of the older Greek translation by the aid of the Hebrew. His work is valuable because he appears to have employed an excellent Greek version and to have followed it closely, supplementing it by many transliterations of Hebrew words. It is also probable that in the present accepted Greek Old Testament his work is the basis of the text of Daniel and Esdras B. *Versions of Symmachus and Theodotion*

In time the variations in the Greek versions became so many and distressing that the famous Christian scholar Origen, while living at Cæsarea, in 240 A.D. arranged these four Greek versions, together with the current Hebrew and a Greek transliteration of it, in six parallel columns. This monumental work, consisting of about fifty large volumes, was known as the *Hexapla*. Unfortunately its size rendered it impracticable to copy it. Portions are reproduced in a surviving Syriac translation of the Greek column (the *Syro-Hexaplar*) and in the writings of the Church Fathers, and the extant fragments have been published (*e.g.*, Field, *Origen's Hexapla*, Oxford, 1875). Origen not only prepared the way for a comparative study of these early texts but also revised the older Greek by the use of the Hebrew and the later Greek translations, especially that of Theodotion. Fortunately, he distinguished his later additions by asterisks. While the principles that he followed cannot be accepted to-day, Origen contributed much to the methods as well as to the equipment of the modern textual critic. His recension appears to have been widely used in Palestine. Its effect, however, was to introduce additional variations into the original Greek text. *Origen's Hexapla*

A little later two other recensions appeared. One was prepared by Hesychius, and according to Jerome was current in Alexandria and Egypt. The other was the work of Lucian, who founded a school at Antioch, and in *Other recensions*

311 A.D. died as a martyr. It was accepted in Antioch and Constantinople. It is valuable because it is evidently based on several variant versions, one of which was probably distinct from those found in Origen's *Hexapla*, and upon an older Hebrew text differing from and often superior to the present Massoretic text. Lucian evidently aimed judiciously to eliminate contradictions between the different readings, and to secure a lucid, smooth, complete translation.

The Vatican manuscripts Fortunately, the existing Greek manuscripts are much older than the Hebrew. The four principal ones come from the fourth and fifth centuries. The chief is the *Codex Vaticanus* (B, referred to in the notes as *Gk.*). It represents only a recension, but the one which is supported by the greatest number of the best manuscripts and is therefore generally recognized as on the whole the closest representative of the original Greek translation of the Old Testament. The admirable new edition of this text, prepared by Professor Swete (Cambridge, 1900), inaugurates a new epoch in the history of Old Testament translations.

Other important manuscripts Another important recension is represented by the *Codex Alexandrinus* (A, in the notes, *Gk. A*). Its readings are supported by another group of manuscripts. It appears to have been revised at many points so as to correspond to the accepted Hebrew. Much more important is Lucian's recension because it is based in part upon a Hebrew text older than any we now have. For the legal and historical books this has been tentatively restored by Lagarde on the basis of marginal readings of the *Syro-Hexaplar* and a group of cursive Greek manuscripts (19, 82, 93, 108, 118).

Other translations: Old Latin As Christianity spread through the ancient world, it carried the old as well as the New Testament scriptures, and to meet the needs of foreign peoples translations were made into many different languages. Most of these were prepared on the basis of the Greek versions, since the early Christian scholars were usually not familiar with the Hebrew language. Of these the most ancient is probably the Old Latin version which was made in the second Christian century. It was evidently based on a Greek version older than that used by Origen and was current among the Christians of Northern Africa. Only fragments survive. These and the quotations from Cyprian and other Latin writers indicate that it contained many errors.

Latin Vulgate Jerome's translation of the Old Testament marks a new epoch in the history of the versions, for not only was it made by the leading scholar of his age, but it was based on the then accepted Hebrew text, supplemented in difficult and doubtful passages by the readings of the different Greek versions, especially that of Symmachus. His work on the Old Testament was begun about 390 and completed in 404 A.D. Confronted by a version whose authority rested simply upon its merits and the reputation of the scholar who made it, the Latin Church rejected and opposed it for two centuries, clinging to the defective and corrupt Old Latin. But as is well known, by the seventh century it was generally accepted by the Western Church, became the basis of its later noble missionary activity, and in the end was raised to a position of despotic authority. The best manuscript of Jerome's translation (*Codex Amiatinus*) comes from the seventh century. The chief value of Jerome's

THE RECOVERY OF THE ORIGINAL TEXT

translation to textual criticism is that it aids in establishing the fourth century readings of the Massoretic text. Its admirable renderings are also very suggestive.

The oldest Syriac translation (known as the *Peshitta*, the *Simple*, or popular version) was probably prepared by Jews at Edessa in the second or third Christian centuries. It was made from the Hebrew, which corresponds closely to the accepted Massoretic text, although at many points its readings originally or later have been modified by the influence of the Greek versions. In the sixth and seventh centuries Christian scholars made translations into the Syriac directly from the Greek. The chief critical use of the Syriac version is in restoring the Hebrew, but its usefulness is limited because the published texts do not always represent the oldest manuscripts. Syriac versions

Translations were also made between the third and sixth centuries into Ethiopic, Coptic, Armenian, and Gothic, but only in the case of a few Old Testament books do they possess a critical value. The Targums, or Aramaic paraphrases of the Old Testament, which were used in the synagogues, represent the Jewish exegesis current in the early Christian centuries. Sometimes they assume or give literal translations of a Hebrew text slightly better than the accepted Massoretic edition. The Targums

Thus in recovering the original texts of the Old Testament books we are practically dependent upon two great groups of witnesses. The first group goes back to the original of the accepted Massoretic text of the second century A.D. The chief witnesses are the ninth century Hebrew manuscripts, supplemented by the notes of the Massorites, the early Syriac version, Jerome's Vulgate, and the Targums, together with the independent translations of Aquila, Symmachus, and Theodotion, and the Hebrew column in Origen's *Hexapla*. In general the testimony of the Hebrew manuscripts is strongest, but when these have suffered corruption, some one of the many translations may preserve the original and indicate the nature of the error. Frequently that which points to a sound text, deviating from the present Massoretic, is original, for the later copyists were always inclined to bring all versions into agreement with the Hebrew, and preserved a variant only when it rested on good authority. Recovery of the basis of the Massoretic text

The second group goes back to the original Greek translation, probably made in the case of Samuel and Kings before 200 B.C., and in the case of the other historical books a little later. The chief guide in recovering this is the *Codex Vaticanus*, the reading of which must be tested and corrected by the aid of the Alexandrian and Lucian texts, which may be regarded as separate recensions, and by the fragments of the Old Latin and Origen's *Hexapla*. Due allowance must be made for the influence of the later Hebrew version upon the Alexandrian, and for the tendency in the Lucian version to produce a smooth, complete text. The readings of the cursive manuscripts must also be considered. Recovery of the earlier original pre-Christian Greek translations

In the great majority of cases the Massoretic Hebrew text may be followed unhesitatingly. Where there is practical agreement between the early Greek texts and they differ from the accepted Hebrew, their testimony is exceedingly strong. Even when some agree with the Hebrew, the agreement may be Use of the Greek versions

47

due to a later harmonizer, and the variant Greek text may contain the original reading. In general the briefer text represents the earlier, for the tendency of later scribes was to expand. The Greek variant must also be retranslated into Hebrew and tested in the light of the context. Where the Massoretic text has obviously suffered corruption from any of the usual causes, or when it is not supported by its group of witnesses and the Greek on the other hand has a well-authenticated, consistent reading, the latter may be accepted as representing the pre-Christian and probably the original text. If it is confirmed by the corrected Massoretic reading, the evidence is conclusive. In some cases the data are not so decisive. Then the reading adopted must be the result of a careful judgment, based upon a consideration of all the possibilities of error and a weighing of the testimony of each of the important versions and the evidence of the parallels and context. The tendencies of each individual translation must also be noted. When all has been done, many passages remain in which absolute certainty is impossible. The time, however, has passed when any one text or version can be blindly followed and all others disregarded. The great foundations of faith, as established in the Bible, will not be moved, but patient, exact scholarship, careful judgment, better editing and deeper study of the existing texts, and the discovery of new manuscripts will give each succeeding generation a translation which will represent more and more exactly the original books written by Israel's inspired teachers more than two thousand years ago. With the aid of the printing press and photography critical scholars are rapidly putting into imperishable form the best that the past has given us. The future holds out the assured possibility of valuable discoveries. Thus, instead of leaving farther behind, each decade brings much nearer to the present the long-lost autograph copies.

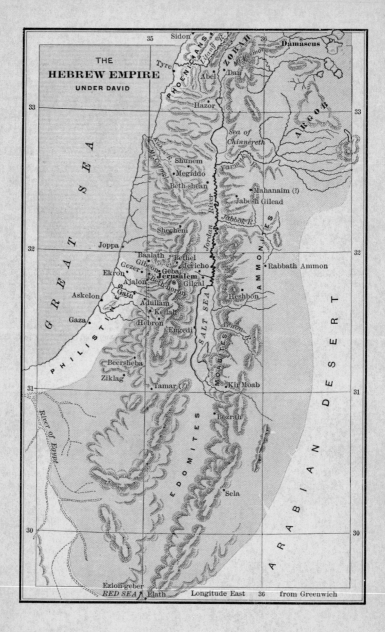

THE
HEBREW EMPIRE
UNDER DAVID

Sidon

Tyre

PHOENICIANS

ZOBAH

Damascus

Abel

Dan

ARGOB

Hazor

33

Sea of
Chinnereth

Shunem

Megiddo

Beth-shean

Mahanaim (?)

Jabesh Gilead

AMMONITES

Shechem

32

Joppa

Baalath

Bethel

Gezer

Gibeon

Jericho

Ekron

Geba

Jerusalem

Ajalon

Beth-horon

Gilgal

Rabbath Ammon

Askelon

Gath

Adullam

Keilah

Heshbon

Gaza

Hebron

Engedi

SALT SEA

MOABITES

Beersheba

Ziklag

Tamar (?)

Kir Moab

31

River of Egypt

Bozrah

EDOMITES

Sela

ARABIAN DESERT

30

Ezion-geber

RED SEA Elath

GREAT SEA

PHILISTINES

Jordan River

Longitude East   36   from Greenwich

HISTORY OF THE UNITED MONARCHY

I Sam. 1–I Kgs. 11, I Chr. 10–II Chr. 9

HISTORY OF THE UNITED MONARCHY

I

THE WORK OF SAMUEL AND THE ESTABLISHMENT OF THE HEBREW KINGDOM, I Sam. 1–15

§ 1. The Birth and Consecration of Samuel, 1, 2¹¹, ¹⁸⁻²¹

Later Ephraimite Samuel Narratives

I Sam. 1 ¹Now there was a certain man of Ramah, a Zuphite[a] of the hill-country of Ephraim, and his name was Elkanah the son of Jeroham, the son of Elihu, the son of Tohu, the son of Zuph, an Ephraimite. ²And he had two wives: the name of the one was Hannah, and the name of the other Peninnah; and Peninnah had children, but Hannah had none. *(Samuel's home and tribe)*

³And this man used to go up from his city year by year to worship and to sacrifice to Jehovah of hosts in Shiloh. And Eli and his two sons,[b] Hophni and Phinehas, were there priests unto Jehovah. ⁴And it came to pass on one occasion that Elkanah sacrificed. Now he used to give portions to Peninnah his wife and to all her sons and daughters, ⁵but to Hannah he used to give one[c] portion, although he loved Hannah; but Jehovah had shut up her womb. ⁶And her rival used to vex her bitterly in order to make her angry, be- *(The yearly pilgrimage)*

The Work of Samuel and the Establishment of the Kingdom.—The first fifteen chapters of I Sam. record the important events which resulted in the election of Saul and the union of the leading Hebrew tribes under one head. The history centres about two individuals. In the opening chapters and in 7, 8, 12, and 15 the personality of Samuel overshadows all other men and events. He is conceived of as ruling over all the Hebrew tribes, and the history unfolds under the influence not of natural but supernatural forces. Later prophetic ideas and ideals have evidently here been projected back into this important early period. To understand the real course of Hebrew history, as well as the very different representation in the remaining chapters of I Sam. 1–15, it is absolutely necessary to appreciate the fact that the opening chapters embody the traditions regarding the character and work of Samuel which were current in later prophetic circles. Cf. Introd., pp. 12, 13.

In the remaining chapters Saul is the central figure and Samuel is the patriotic seer of Ramah. Literary style and representation indicate that they were originally taken from an old and very valuable cycle of Saul traditions. Cf. Introd., pp. 10–12. Recognizing these two very different points of view, the perplexing difficulties which confront the careful student of I Sam. entirely disappear.

§ 1 Tradition rarely begins with the childhood of the heroes. Jacob, Moses, and Samuel are the conspicuous O.T. exceptions. Furthermore, stories regarding the childhood of a great man in antiquity were not appreciated and therefore recounted until long after he had ceased to live. In their origin they are, therefore, usually much later than those which record his life work. The Samuel stories, however, in the first part of I Sam. constitute a closely knit literary unit. Samuel's connection with Eli, the ark, and the sanctuary at Shiloh is the link which binds the new era, inaugurated by the establishment of the kingdom, with the earlier period of the Judges. In the opening chapters he appears as the champion of the

---

[a] 1¹ The Heb. is untranslatable. The Gk. indicates the nature of error which has crept into the text and suggests the true reading.
[b] 1³ So Gk. and demanded by ⁹. Heb. simply, *the two sons of Eli*, but Eli and not his two sons figure in this part of the story.
[c] 1⁵ The current translation, *double portion*, is impossible. Making a slight correction suggested by the Gk., the passage reads consistently as above.

51

Later Ephraimite Samuel Narratives

cause Jehovah had shut up her womb.ᵈ ⁷And thus he did year by year, as often as she went up to the house of Jehovah, she used to vex her; therefore she wept and would not eat. ⁸But Elkanah her husband said to her, Hannah, why do you weep and not eat, and why is your heart sad?ᵉ Am not I better to you than ten sons?

Han- nah's vow
⁹So Hannah rose up, after they had eaten in Shilohᶠ, and stood before Jehovah. Now Eli the priest was sitting at his seat at the door-posts of the temple of Jehovah. ¹⁰And she was greatly distressedᵍ and prayed fervently to Jehovah and wept bitterly. ¹¹And she vowed a vow, saying,

> O Jehovah of hosts!
> If thou wilt indeed look on the affliction of thy maid-servant,
> And remember me and not forget thy maid-servant,
> But wilt give to thy maid-servant a man child,
> Then I will give him to Jehovah all the days of his life,
> And a razor shall not come upon his head.ʰ

Eli's reproof and blessing
¹²And while she continued praying before Jehovah, Eli observed her mouth. ¹³Now Hannah was speaking to herself; only her lips moved, but her voice was not heard; therefore Eli took her for a drunken woman. ¹⁴So Eli said to her, How long will you act like a drunken woman? Put away the effects of your wine and go from the presence of Jehovah.ⁱ ¹⁵But Hannah answered and said, No, my lord, an unfortunate womanʲ am I; I have drunk neither wine nor intoxicating drink, but I have been pouring out my soul before Jehovah. ¹⁶Do not take your maid-servant to be a vile woman, for because of the greatness of my grief and vexationᵏ have I continued speaking until now. ¹⁷Then Eli answered and said, Go in peace, and the God of Israel grant your petition that you have asked of him. ¹⁸And she said, Let your maid-servant find favor in your sight. So the woman went her way and ate, and her countenance was no more sad.ˡ

---

older order, while in 9 and 10 he is the herald of the new. With the exception of a few minor additions, it seems certain that 1–3 were taken from the Samuel history which was based in turn on prophetic traditions committed to writing by the later representatives of the Ephraimite school. Cf. Introd., pp. 12, 13.

ᵈ ¹⁶ The original and sufficient reason for Hannah's tears and refusal to eat, ⁷ᶜ, when her husband came up to offer his sacrifice, ⁴ᵃ, is that she had no children and therefore received only one portion. This alone is assumed in the rest of the story. The additional reason in ⁶ and ⁷ᵇ is not found in the Gk. The anguage in which it is expressed is awkward (cf. ⁷) and it does not fit the context, which is complete without it. It appears, therefore, to be a very late addition, based on common oriental experience in connection with the institution of polygamy.

ᵉ ¹⁸ Gk., *why does your heart reproach you?* This is evidently based on a slightly different Heb. text.

ᶠ ¹⁹ So Gk. The Heb. adds, *and after they had drunk.* In the original text attention is fixed almost exclusively upon Hannah, but in the later recensions of the Heb. and Gk. the tendency is to give Elkanah a more prominent rôle.

ᵍ ¹¹⁰ Heb., *bitter of soul.* The Gk. appears to have preserved the original text.

ʰ ¹¹¹ This last clause may be a later explanatory addition by a scribe who regarded Samuel as a Nazirite. The Gk. adds, *and wine and fermented liquor he shall not drink.* Cf. Num. 3⁹, 18⁶. The Heb. version has the balanced poetic parallelism which appears in vows and oracles.

ⁱ ¹¹⁴ The last clause is found only in the Gk.

ʲ ¹¹⁵ Heb., *hard of spirit.* This idiom elsewhere means obstinate. Cf. Ez. 3⁷. The Gk. has, *hard of day, i.e.,* unfortunate. Cf. Job 30²⁵.

ᵏ ¹¹⁶ᵇ Not found in the Gk. Evidently added by some later redactor who introduced ⁶, ⁷ᵇ.

ˡ ¹¹⁸ᵇ Gk., *so the woman went her way and entered her lodging place, and ate with her husband and drank.*

Later Ephraimite Samuel Narratives

[19]And they rose up in the morning early, and worshipped before Jehovah, Samuel's birth and returned and came to their house at Ramah. And Elkanah knew Hannah his wife; and Jehovah remembered her. [20]And Hannah conceived[m], and it came to pass at the coming around of the new year[n] that she bore a son, and called his name Samuel [Asked of God],[o] saying, For I have asked him of Jehovah.

[21]And the man Elkanah and all his household went up to offer to Jehovah Presentation the yearly sacrifice and his vow. [22]But Hannah did not go up; for she said to Jehovah to her husband, When the child is weaned then I will bring him and he shall appear in the presence of Jehovah and shall dwell there forever. [23]And Elkanah her husband said to her, Do what seems good to you: wait until you have weaned him; only may Jehovah establish your[p] word. So the woman waited and nursed her son until she weaned him. [24]And when she had weaned him, she took him up with her, together with a three-year-old[q] bullock and a bushel[r] of flour and a skin of wine, and brought him to the house of Jehovah in Shiloh.[s] [25]And they[t] slew the bullock and Hannah[u] brought the lad to Eli. [26]And she said, Oh, sir, by your life, I am the woman who stood near you here, praying fervently to Jehovah. [27]This is the lad regarding whom I was fervently praying, and Jehovah has granted me my petition which I asked of him. [28]Now, I on my part have given him to Jehovah; as long as he lives he is given to Jehovah.[v]

2 [11]So she left him there before Jehovah and went to Ramah. But the Life at lad was ministering to Jehovah in the presence of Eli the priest.[w] Shiloh

[18]And Samuel continued ministering before Jehovah—a lad girded with a linen ephod. [19]And his mother used to make him a little robe and bring it to him from year to year, when she came up with her husband to offer the yearly sacrifice. [20]And Eli blessed Elkanah and his wife and said, Jehovah repay[x] you with offspring from this woman for the gift which she

---

m 1[20a] Following the Gk. order, which is logical.

n 1[20] Heb., *at the coming around of days i.e.*, when the feast of ingathering was again observed.

o 1[20] This was evidently the popular etymology, based on a certain similarity of sound. The true etymology appears to be, *Name of God*, although the meaning, *Heard of God*, is not impossible.

p 1[23] So Gk. and Syr. Heb., *his*. The meaning is: may Jehovah enable you to carry out your promise.

q 1[24] So Gk. and Syr. and demanded by [25]. The Heb. text is evidently corrupt.

r 1[24] Heb., *ephah*.

s 1[24] The Heb. adds, *the lad was a lad*, which is an un-Hebraic expression and adds nothing to the story. It is also unsupported by the Gk.

t 1[25] Referring to the attendants who had charge of the details of the offering.

u 1[25] Gk., *and Hannah the mother of the child brought him to Eli*.

v 1[28] The Heb. adds, *And he worshipped Jehovah there*.

w 2[11] The close connection of the thought demonstrates that 2[11] is the immediate sequel of 1[28]. The so-called song of Hannah in 2[1-10] is a psalm of praise to Jehovah for victory over Israel's foes and for his wise rule. The reference in [5] to *the barren having borne seven* probably explains why a later editor introduced it here. The expression, however, only embodies an illustration of Jehovah's benign rule over mankind. The psalm as a whole is far more appropriate on the lips of the post-exilic Jewish community than in the mouth of Hannah. Cf. Vol. V *in loco*.

x 2[20] Heb., *put*. A copyist has apparently left out a letter which, when restored, gives the original reading preserved by the Gk.

Later Ephraimite Samuel Narratives

gave to Jehovah.ᵃ Then they returned to theirᵇ own home. ²¹And Jehovah visited Hannah so that she conceived and bore three sons and two daughters. And the child Samuel grew up before Jehovah.

§ 2. The Doom of the House of Eli and the Call of Samuel, I Sam.
2 ¹²⁻¹⁷, ²²⁻³⁶, 3, 4¹ᵃ

Later Ephraimite Samuel Narratives

Crimes of the sons of Eli

I Sam. 2 ¹²Now the sons of Eli were base scoundrels; they had no regard forᶜ Jehovah, ¹³nor for what was justly due the priest from the people.ᵈ Whenever a man offered a sacrifice, the priest's servant would come, while the flesh was boiling, with a three-pronged fork in his hand, ¹⁴and would strike into the pot or the kettle or the basin or the dish. All that the fork brought up the priest would take for himself.ᵉ So they did to all the Israelites who came to sacrifice to Jehovah in Shiloh.ᶠ ¹⁵Moreover before they burned the fat, the priest's servant used to come and say to the man who was making the offering, Give flesh to roast for the priest; for he will not take from you boiled flesh, but raw. ¹⁶Should the man, however, say to him, First you should burn the fat, then take as much as you desire, he would reply, No, you must give it at once or else I will take it by force. ¹⁷Thus the sin of the young men was very great before Jehovah; for the men despised the offering of Jehovah.

Eli's ineffectual reproof

²²But Eli was very old; and whenever he heardᵍ what his sons were doing to all Israel, how they lay with the women who did service at the door of the tent of meeting,ʰ ²³he said to them, Why do you do such things as these, which I hear from the mouth of all the people.ⁱ ²⁴No, my sons; for it is no good report that I hear the people of Jehovah spreading abroad. ²⁵If one man sin against another, Godʲ will mediate for him ; but if a man sin against Jehovah, who shall act as mediator for him? Notwithstanding they did not listen to the voice of their father, because Jehovah desired to slay them. ²⁶But the lad Samuel kept on growing larger and better in the estimation both of Jehovah and of men.

ᵃ 2²⁰ Heb., *that which was borrowed by Jehovah.* Gk., *for the loan which you loaned to Jehovah.* But cf. 1²⁸. where Hannah is the one who gives the child to Jehovah. A slight emendation of the Heb. gives this harmonious reading.
ᵇ 2²⁰ Heb., *they went to his place.* Many Heb. codices and Syr. read, *their place.* The impossible *for,* which is found in the accepted Heb. text at the beginning of the next verse may represent the final missing letter of ²⁰.
§ 2 Cf. notes §§ 1 and 6.
ᶜ 2¹² Heb., *knew not,* in the sense of paying heed to, regarding.
ᵈ 2¹³ So Gk., Syr., Targ., and nine Heb. MSS. Lat., *not knowing God nor the duty of the priest toward the people. I.e.,* what the priest had a right to demand from the people. The verse division has obscured the original meaning.
ᵉ 2¹⁴ Heb., *with it.* Gk., Syr., and Targ. have the better reading followed above.
ᶠ 2¹⁴ So Gk. Heb., *came there in Shiloh.* But this is tautological and the Heb. idiom awkward.
ᵍ 2²² The Heb. adds, *all,* but this is not found in the Gk.
ʰ 2²² This clause is also not found in the Gk. It appears to be a very late addition to the Heb., based on the priestly passage Ex. 38⁸ᵇ. This crime is referred to nowhere else in the story.
ⁱ 2²³ So Gk. The Heb. has, *for I am hearing of your evil deeds from all the people, even these,* but the construction is ungrammatical. The last word is probably due to dittography.
ʲ 2²⁵ As in Ex. 21⁶, 22⁸, *God* appears to be equivalent to *judges,* those who represented God in the judicial capacity.

Later Ephraimite Samuel Narratives

Announcement of divine judgment upon the house of Eli

[27]And there came a man of God to Eli and said to him, Thus saith
Jehovah, 'I revealed myself to thy father's house,[k] when they were in Egypt
servants[l] to Pharaoh's house, [28]and I chose him from all the tribes of Israel
to be my priest to go up to mine altar to burn sacrifices, to bear an ephod
before me,[m] and I gave to thy father's house for food[n] all the offerings of
the Israelites made by fire. [29]Why dost thou look with envious eyes upon
my sacrifices and offerings,[o] and honorest thy sons above me in fattening
yourselves with the first-fruits of all the offerings which the Israelites bring
me?' [30]Therefore Jehovah the God of Israel saith, 'I had indeed thought
that thy house and the house of thy father would walk before me forever;'
but now saith Jehovah, 'Far be it from me; for them that honor me I will
honor, and they that despise me shall be lightly esteemed. [31]The days
are quickly coming when I will cut off thine arm and the arm of thy father's
house.[p] [32]And thou shalt look in affliction and enviously upon all the prosperity
which I[q] will give Israel; and there shall not be an old man in thy house forever.
[33]And the man of thine whom I do not cut off from mine altar shall be spared to consume
his[r] eyes and to wear out his soul, and all the increase of thy house shall
die by the sword of men.[s] [34]And this shall be the sign to thee that shall
come upon thy two sons, Hophni and Phinehas: on the same day both
shall die. [35]And I will raise up for myself a faithful priest who shall do
according to that which is in my heart and in my desire; and I will build him
an enduring house; and he shall walk before mine anointed forever. [36]And it shall
come to pass that every one who is left in thy house shall come to do him obeisance
for a piece of money or a loaf of bread, and shall say, "Put me, I beg, in one of the
priests' offices, that I may eat a morsel of bread."'[t]

The revelation to Samuel

3 [1]And the child Samuel continued ministering before Jehovah in the
presence of Eli. And the word of Jehovah was rare in those days; there
was no frequent vision. [2]Now once at that time, when Eli was lying in his
place—his eyes had begun to grow dim, so that he could not see—[3]and
while the lamp of God was still burning, and Samuel was lying in the temple
of Jehovah where the ark of God was, [4]Jehovah called, Samuel! Samuel![u]

---

k 2[27] So Gk. The Heb. makes the sentence a question calling for the answer, *No*, which is unintelligible. Dittography explains the presence of the interrogative.

l 2[27] So Gk. The Heb. simply implies the word, *servants*.

m 2[28] *I.e.*, Take charge of the oracle. Cf. § 14.

n 2[28] Added by the Gk.

o 2[29] The current translations are untenable and do not give an idea in harmony with the context. The Gk. which is followed above is evidently based on an original text of which the present Heb. is probably a corruption.

p 2[31] Vs. [32a] is evidently a later insertion anticipating subsequent conditions, and when it was inserted the original phrase, *there shall not be an old man in thy house*, was repeated, so that it is found in the present Heb. both in [31b] and [32b].

q 2[32a] Heb., *he will give*. The context requires either the first person or *Jehovah* as the subject. The Gk. omits [31b, 32a].

r 2[33] The Heb. has, *thy;* but the Gk., *his*. The first half of the vs. is not consistent with the latter half and also anticipates much later events.

s 2[33] Required by context and found in the Gk. The Heb. without the expression, *by the sword of*, is unintelligible and the current translations unwarranted.

t 2[35b, 36] Apparently the original oracle simply contemplated the destruction of Eli's descendants at Aphek, § 3, and Nob, § 13, and the succession of Samuel to the position of religious leadership. Vss. [35b, 36] clearly refer to the later elevation of the house of Zadok, and the language reflects the provision in Dt. for the priests of the high places outside Jerusalem. Hence they must be late prophetic or priestly additions to the original Samuel history.

u 3[4] Heb., *to Samuel*. The Gk. has the direct address and repeats the name as in [10]. This is in harmony with the literary style of the Ephraimite source.

Later Ephraimite Samuel Narratives

And he said, Here am I.   ⁵And he ran to Eli, and said, Here am I; for you called me.   But he said, I did not call, lie down again.   So he went and lay down.   ⁶Then Jehovah called yet again, Samuel! Samuel! And Samuel arose and went to Eli and said, Here am I; for you called me.   But he answered, I did not call, my son; lie down again.   ⁷Now Samuel did not yet knowᵛ Jehovah neither had the word of Jehovah yet been revealed to him.   ⁸So when Jehovah called Samuel again the third time, he arose and went to Eli, and said, Here am I; for you called me.   Then Eli perceived that Jehovah was calling the child.   ⁹Therefore Eli said to Samuel, Go, lie down; and if you are called, say, ' Speak, Jehovah; for thy servant is listening.'   So Samuel went and lay down in his place.

Message regarding Eli   ¹⁰Then Jehovah came, and stood, and called as at other times, Samuel! Samuel!   And Samuel said, Speak; for thy servant is listening.   ¹¹And Jehovah said to Samuel, See, I am about to do such a thing in Israel, that the ears of every one who hears it shall ring.   ¹²In that day I will perform toward Eli all that I have spoken against his house from beginning to end.   ¹³For I have told him that I will judge his house forever, for the guilt which he knew, in that his sons were blaspheming Godʷ and he did not rebuke them.   ¹⁴And therefore I have sworn to the house of Eli that the guilt of Eli's house shall not be expiated with sacrifice nor offering forever.

Announcement of the message to Eli   ¹⁵And Samuel lay until the morning; then he rose early in the morningˣ and opened the doors of the house of Jehovah.   And Samuel feared to make known the vision to Eli.   ¹⁶But Eli called Samuel and said, Samuel, my son.   And he said, Here am I.   ¹⁷And he said, What is the thing that Jehovah hath spoken to you?   I pray, conceal nothing from me; may God do to you whatever he will, if you conceal from me a word of all that he spoke to you.   ¹⁸So Samuel told him everything; and concealed nothing from him.   And he said, It is Jehovah; let him do what seems good to him.

Samuel's establishment as a prophet   ¹⁹And Samuel grew, and Jehovah was with him and let none of his words fall to the ground.ᵃ   ²⁰And all Israel from Dan even to Beersheba knew that Samuel was established as a prophet of Jehovah.   ²¹And Jehovah again appeared in Shiloh, for Jehovah revealed himself to Samuel.ᵇ   4 ¹ᵃThus the word of Samuel came to all Israel.ᶜ

ᵛ 3⁷ᵃ *I.e.*, as the prophets knew Jehovah through a special revelation, cf. ⁷ᵇ.

ʷ 3¹³ The Heb. is ungrammatical and untranslatable.   The Gk. has clearly preserved the original reading.

ˣ 3¹⁵ This clause is preserved in the Gk. and was evidently omitted in the Heb. as the result of a common copyist's error.

ᵃ 3¹⁹ The Gk. and Luc. possibly have the original reading, *none of his words fell to the ground*.

ᵇ 3²¹ So Gk.   The Heb. contains a late tautological addition, *in Shiloh by the word of Jehovah*.   The Gk. also repeats and adds what may have been found in the original text, *but Eli was exceedingly old and his sons kept on doing worse and worse before Jehovah*.

ᶜ 4¹ᵃ Clearly a late editorial *résumé*, not found in the Gk.

§ 3. The Capture of the Ark and the Fall of the House of Eli, I Sam. 4¹ᵇ–5¹

Early Judean Prophetic	Later Ephraimite Samuel Narratives

Israel's defeat by the Philistines

I Sam. 4 ¹ᵇNow in those days the Philistines assembled to make war against Israel,ᵈ ²ᵇand the battle was hard fought f and they slew in the ranks on the field about four thousand men.

4 ¹ᶜNow Israel went out against the Philistines to battle, and encamped at Ebenezer;ᵉ and the Philistines encamped in Aphek. ²ᵃAnd the Philistines put themselves in array against Israel, and Israel was smitten before the Philistines.

The second defeat and the loss of the ark

³ᵃBut when the people returned to the camp, ⁴ᵃthe people sent to Shiloh and took from there the ark of Jehovah of hosts who sits enthroned above the cherubim. ⁵ᵃ·ᶜAnd when the ark of

³ᵇThen the elders of Israel said, Why hath Jehovah smitten us to-day before the Philistines? Let us bring to us the ark of our Godᵍ out of Shiloh, that it may come among us and save us from the hand of our enemies.ʰ ⁴ᵇSo they sent to Shiloh; and the two sons of Eli, Hophni and Phinehas, were there with the ark of God. ⁵ᵇAnd when the ark of God came to

---

§ 3 The fate which overtook the house of Eli is recorded in 4. The account is closely connected with the doom predicted in the preceding chapter. Although Samuel is not mentioned, it is obvious that one of the reasons why the story is introduced here is because it recounts those revolutionizing changes which opened the way for his activity recorded in the following chapters. Characteristic expressions also confirm the conclusion that most of the chapter is from the Ephraimite school of writers. It is probably from an older stratum than the citations in 1–3, 7, 8, 12, 15, but it has been so woven into the later series of stories that it may be classified with them.

Recent commentators on the book of Samuel have recognized that this chapter is composite. Thus in the original passage ¹ᵇ (which has been preserved in the Gk.) the Philistines are represented as having assumed the aggressive, while in ¹ᶜ the Israelites do so. In one series of passages the term *ark of Jehovah* and in another *ark of God* occurs. Duplicates are also found in which the synonyms characteristic respectively of the Judean and Ephraimite narratives appear. Thus cf. ⁷ᵇ and ⁷ᵃ; ⁷ᵇ and ⁸ᵃ; ⁹ᵇ and ⁹ᵃ; ¹⁰ᵃ and ¹⁰ᵇ. These duplicates, when classified, are found to contain two brief but complete and consistent accounts of the defeat of the Israelites and the loss of the ark. They were so closely parallel that certain expressions appear to have been common to both and at one or two points the analysis is uncertain.

The importance of the event also leads us from analogies in the preceding books of the O.T. to anticipate two versions. They are the natural sequels to the Judean and Ephraimite narratives in Judg. 11–16. The Judean Samson stories suggest the increasing aggressions of the Philistines, and the primitive account of the anointing of Saul by Samuel and Saul's initial wars against the Philistines assume the facts stated in the brief Judean version in 4. Its brevity is probably due to the natural reluctance which a patriotic historian felt in recounting the disasters which overtook his people. Many linguistic indications confirm the analysis given above.

If originally recorded, the account of the destruction of the sanctuary at Shiloh, which apparently occurred at this time, has been lost. The absence of any subsequent references to the sanctuary as existing (cf. I Kgs. 12²⁹, Am. 5⁵), and the definite statements in Jer. 19³ and II Kgs. 21¹², ¹³ practically establish the fact. From I Sam. 10⁵, 13³ and the subsequent records, it is also clear that the Philistines from this time on made the Israelites tributary to them.

ᵈ 4¹ᵇ These introductory words are not found in the Heb., but in all Gk. MSS., and are required by the context.

ᵉ 4¹ᶜ Heb., *Eben-ha-ezer*, so 5¹.

f 4²ᵇ The Heb. gives no sense. The Gk. translators evidently had difficulty with it, *the battle inclined.* A change of one letter (suggested by Smith, *Sam.*, p. 32) gives the above reading. Cf. II Sam. 2¹⁷, where the idiom occurs in a similar Judean passage.

ᵍ 4³ᵇ A later scribe, who preferred the Deuteronomic designation, *ark of the covenant of Jehovah*, has introduced it in the Heb. here and through ⁵, but no further. The absence of the words, *of the covenant*, in the Gk. indicate that the addition was very late. The scribe substituted the more familiar designation for the above which is preserved in the Gk.

ʰ 4³ᵇ The ancient war-cry used in connection with the ark, Num. 10³⁵.

Early Judean Prophetic	Later Ephraimite Samuel Narratives

Jehovah came to the camp, the earth resounded. ⁶ᵇAnd when [the Philistines] knew that the ark of Jehovah had come to the camp, ⁷ᵇthey said, Woe to us! for it has not been thus before; ⁹ᵇbut be men and fight.

¹⁰ᵃˑᶜSo the Philistines fought and there was a great slaughter.

the camp, all Israel shouted a great shout. ⁶ᵃAnd when the Philistines heard the noise of the shout, they said, What is this noise of great shouting in the camp of the Hebrews? ⁷ᵃ'The Philistines were afraid, for they said, These are their gods; they have come to them to the camp.ⁱ ⁸Woe to us! Who shall deliver us out of the hand of these mighty gods? These are the gods who smote the Egyptians with every sort of plague and pestilence.ʲ ⁹ᵃBe courageous and be men, O Philistines, that you may not be slaves to the Hebrews, as they have been slaves to you. ¹⁰ᵇAnd Israel was defeated and fled each to his tent. And there fell of Israel thirty thousand footmen. ¹¹And the ark of God was taken, and the two sons of Eli, Hophni and Phinehas, perished.

Death of Eli   ¹²And a Benjamite ran from the ranks and came to Shiloh the same day with his garments torn and with earth on his head. ¹³And just as he came, Eli was sitting upon his seat beside the gate watching the road,ᵏ for his heart was trembling for the ark of God. And when the man came to the city to inform it, all the city cried out. ¹⁴And when Eli heard the noise of the crying he said, What is this tumultuous noise? And the man came quickly and told Eli. ¹⁵(Now Eli was ninety-eight years old, and his eyes were set, so that he could not see).ˡ ¹⁶And the man said to Eli, I am he who came from the ranks, for I fled to-day from the ranks. And he said, How went the matter, my son? ¹⁷And he that brought the tidings answered and said, Israel fled before the Philistines, and there was also a great slaughter among the people, and your two sons also, Hophni and Phinehas, are dead, and the ark of God has been captured. ¹⁸And it came to pass when he mentioned the ark of God, that Eli fell from his seat backward by the side of the gate; and his neck was broken and he died, for he was old and heavy. And he had judged Israel forty years.

Circumstances attending the birth of Ichabod   ¹⁹And his daughter-in-law, Phinehas's wife, was with child, about to be delivered. And when she heard the report regarding the capture of the ark of God, and that her father-in-law and her husband were dead, she bowed herself and gave birth to a child; for her birth-pains came upon her.

ⁱ 4⁷ᵃ Heb. and Lat., *God is come to the camp.* Gk., *These gods have come to them to the camp.* Lucian, *This is their God.* The fuller reading and the plural seem to be demanded by the context. Cf. especially ⁸.

ʲ 4⁸ Heb. and Lat., *with every sort of plague in the wilderness.* Gk., *plague and in the wilderness.* None of the Heb. traditions represents the Egyptians as having been smitten in the wilderness. The different readings are probably due to the mistake of a copyist who mistook the Heb. word for *pestilence* for the very similar word meaning *wilderness.*

ᵏ 4¹³ So Gk. The gate is evidently that of the sanctuary. Heb., *by the side of the road watching.* But this is inconsistent with the subsequent context, for, if he was by the road, the messenger would come to him first.

ˡ 4¹⁵ This verse interrupts the narrative in ¹⁴, which is continued in ¹⁶, and its representation is contrary to that of ¹³ which states that Eli *was watching the road.* It appears to be a later embellishment of the story. The Gk. expands still further, *And Eli said to the men who were standing about him, What is this resounding noise?*

Later Ephraimite Samuel Narratives

^{20}And about the time of her death the women who stood by her said to her, Fear not for you have given birth to a son. But she neither answered nor heeded. ^{21}Therefore they named the child Ichabod [No glory], saying, The glory is taken away from Israel, because of the capture of the ark of God, and because of her father-in-law and her husband.[m] **5** ^{1}And the Philistines took the ark of God and brought it from Ebenezer to Ashdod.

§ 4. The Fortunes of the Ark Among the Philistines, I Sam. 5^{2}–7^{2a}

Early Judean Narratives

The ark in the temple of Dagon

I Sam. 5 ^{2}Then the Philistines took the ark of Jehovah[n] and brought it to the house of Dagon and set it up by the side of Dagon. ^{3}And when the Ashdodites arose early the next day and came to the house of Dagon,[o] behold there was Dagon fallen upon his face to the ground before the ark of Jehovah. And they raised up[p] Dagon and set him in his place again. ^{4}But when they arose early on the following morning, behold there was Dagon fallen upon his face to the ground before the ark of Jehovah. And the head of Dagon and both his hands were cut off upon the threshold, and only the body[q] of Dagon was left. ^{5}Therefore the priests of Dagon and all who enter the house of Dagon do not tread on the threshold of Dagon in Ashdod to this day, but leap over it.[r]

Plagues attending the ark

^{6}And the hand of Jehovah was heavy upon the Ashdodites, and he destroyed them, and smote them with boils, even Ashdod and its borders.

---

m 4^{21} The Heb. adds, ^{22}, *And she said, The glory is taken away from Israel; for the ark of God has been captured.* This is simply a repetition of ^{21} and is probably a scribal note added to call attention to the proverb, *The glory is taken away from Israel,* which reappears in Hos. 10^{5}. Vs. ^{21b} may also be a later addition based on ^{19a}.

§ 4 This tradition is one which would naturally be preserved at the Jerusalem temple, where the ark found its final resting-place. The prominence of the ark in the early Judean narratives (cf. Vol. I, notes § 79, 86) also leads us to anticipate that this story was treasured in the southern kingdom. Furthermore, its account of the return of the ark and the fact that it was left in the care of Abinadab, 7^{1}, are assumed as the basis of the early Judean David traditions regarding its transfer to Jerusalem, II Sam. 6$^{1-4}$, § 29. On the other hand the subsequent Ephraimite passages contain no allusion to the ark. With the partial fulfilment of the doom upon the house of Eli, the aim of this school of writers in introducing the tradition was realized. There are a few suggestions of duplication in these chapters, but they may be simply due to editorial expansion. Cf. notes [s, t, v]. If they are composite, no satisfactory analysis has yet been found.

Possibly the account of the fall of Dagon, 5$^{2-5}$, was originally distinct from the rest of the narrative. If so, 5$^{2-5}$ is probably secondary and the original story, as usually in the early Judean narratives, simply records a natural event, namely, the spread of a fearful pestilence wherever the ark was carried. That this was spread by the ark itself is shown by the fact that it bears the contagion to the Hebrews as well as to the Philistines, 6^{19}. This conclusion is confirmed by the nature of the objects sent to propitiate Jehovah. Mice among the Egyptians, and therefore in all probability among the Philistines, who had long been absorbing Egyptian civilization, were the symbols of the plague. The golden boils, prepared in accordance with the primitive belief that a cure could be effected by making a representation of the disease, as well as the details of the story, leave little doubt that the pestilence was the terrible bubonic plague. The story throughout contains the popular, primitive explanation of this dread scourge, the physical causes of which were entirely unknown, and which was universally regarded as a direct judgment from God. The Judean plague stories in Ex. and the description of the pestilence recorded by the same school in II Sam. 24 present very close analogies.

n 5^{2} So Gk. The Heb. has, *ark of God.* Later Jewish scribes manifest a strong tendency to substitute *God* for *Jehovah.*

o 5^{3} So Gk. The Heb. has an abbreviated text.

p 5^{3} The Gk. and Luc. have, *raised up.* But cf. for Heb. idiom 7^{12}.

q 5^{4} A word appears to have dropped out of the Heb., which reads, *only Dagon was left of him.* This makes no sense.

r 5^{5} The last clause is from the Gk., but it appears to be original. Cf. Zeph. 1^{9}.

Early Judean Narratives

⁷And when the men of Ashdod saw that it was so, they said, the ark of the God of Israel shall not remain with us; for his hand is severe upon us and Dagon our god.ˢ ⁸So they sent and gathered all the tyrants of the Philistines to them, and said, What shall we do with the ark of the God of Israel ? And they answered, Let the ark of the God of Israel be brought around to Gath. So they brought the ark of the God of Israel around. ⁹But after they had brought it around, the hand of Jehovah was against the city— there was a very great panic—and he smote the men of the city, both young and old, so that boils broke out upon them. ¹⁰Therefore they sent the ark of God to Ekron. But when the ark of God came to Ekron, the Ekronites cried out, saying, They have brought around the ark of the God of Israel to us, to slay us and our people. ¹¹They sent therefore and gathered together all the tyrants of the Philistines and said, Send away the ark of the God of Israel, that it may go back to its own place and not kill us and our people. For a deadly panic had seized the entire city; the hand of God was very heavy there. ¹²And the men who did not die were smitten with the boils; and the cry of lamentation from the city went up to heaven.ᵗ

Plans for returning the ark 6 ¹And the ark of Jehovah was in the country of the Philistines seven months.ᵘ ²Then the Philistines summoned the priests and the diviners, saying, What shall we do with the ark of Jehovah? Show us how we shall send it to its place. ³And they said, If you are sending the ark of the God of Israel, you must not send it away empty; but you must return to him a trespass-offering. Then you will be healed and it shall be made known to you why his hand is not removed from you. ⁴Then said they, What shall be the trespass-offering which we shall return to him? And they said, Five golden boils, and five golden mice,ᵛ corresponding to the number of the tyrants of the Philistines; for one plague was upon you as well as upon your tyrants. ⁵Therefore you shall make images of your boils, and images of your mice that mar the land; and you shall give glory to the God of Israel; perhaps he will lighten his hand from upon you and your gods and your land.ʷ ⁶Why then will you make your hearts stubborn, as the Egyptians and Pharaoh made their hearts stubborn? Was it not after he had made sport of them that they let them go so that they departed?ˣ ⁷Now therefore take and prepare a new cart, and two milch cows upon which the yoke has not come; and fasten the cows to the cart, but you shall leave their calves behind them at home. ⁸And take the ark of Jehovah and place it on the cart and put the golden objects

---

ˢ 5⁷ This verse may be due to editorial expansion, for instead of the *Ashdodites* of ³, ⁶ the term *men of Ashdod* is used. A different verb is also employed in the familiar idiom, *the hand of God was heavy*. Vs. ⁸ very naturally continues ⁶, although ⁷ is not absolutely inconsistent with its context.

ᵗ 5¹¹ᵇ⁻¹² Evidently from another source or more probably an editorial expansion. Cf. *hand of God* and the variant idiom, *deadly panic* (in ⁹, *great panic*). The peculiar idiom, *the cry went up*, in ¹²ᵇ is found elsewhere in the priestly passage, Ex. 2²³. The Heb. word is different from that translated *cry* in ¹⁰. The continuation of 5¹¹ᵃ is 6².

ᵘ 6¹ The Gk. adds, *and their land swarmed with mice.*

ᵛ 6⁴ The Gk. omits, *five golden mice*, here but retains them in ⁵ and omits the mention of the boils. The evidence seems to indicate that both were found in the original: the boils as symbols of the bubonic plague, and the mice as symbols of pestilence in general. Cf. note § 4.

ʷ 6⁵ Evidently an explanatory note added by an editor who did not understand the symbolism of the mice and who wished to glorify Israel's God by the testimony of the hated Philistines.

ˣ 6⁶ Possibly also an editorial expansion with a religious purpose. The references are to passages found not in the Ephraimite but Judean sources, Ex. 7¹⁴, 8¹¹, ²⁸, 9⁷, ³⁴, 10².

Early Judean Narratives

which you are returning to him as a trespass-offering, in a box at its side.
Then send it away that it may depart. ⁹And see, if it goes on the way to
its own border to Bethshemesh, then it is he who hath done us this great
harm, but if not, then we shall know that it was not his hand that smote
us; it was an accident that befell us.

¹⁰And the men did so, and took two milch cows and fastened them to
the cart, and shut up their calves at home. ¹¹And they placed the ark of
Jehovah on the cart, and the box with the golden mice and the images of their
boils.ᵃ ¹²And the cows took a straight course in the direction of Bethshemesh; they went along the highway, lowing as they went, and did not
turn aside to the right hand or to the left. And the tyrants of the Philistines went after them to the border of Bethshemesh. ¹³And the inhabitants
of Bethshemesh were harvesting their wheat in the valley. And they lifted
up their eyes and saw the ark, and came rejoicing to meet it.ᵇ ¹⁴And when
the cart came into the field of Joshua the Bethshemeshite, it stood still there.
And a great stone was there. So they split up the wood of the cart and
offered the cows as a burnt-offering to Jehovah. ¹⁵But the Levites took down
the ark of Jehovah and the box that was with it, in which were the golden objects,
and placed them on the great stone; and the men of Bethshemesh offered to Jehovah
on that day burnt-offerings and ordinary sacrifices.ᶜ ¹⁶And when the five tyrants
of the Philistines saw it, they returned to Ekron on that day.

¹⁷And these are the golden boils which the Philistines returned as a trespass-offering
to Jehovah: for Ashdod one, for Gaza one, for Ashkelon one, for Gath one, for Ekron
one. ¹⁸But the golden mice correspond to the number of all the cities of the Philistines belonging to the five tyrants, both of fortified cities and of country villages.ᵈ
And a witness is the great stone,ᵉ by which they set down the ark of
Jehovah. To this day it is in the field of Joshua of Bethshemesh.

¹⁹The sons of Jechoniah, however, did not rejoice with the men of Bethshemesh, when they looked upon the ark of Jehovah.ᶠ So he smote among
them seventy men;ᵍ and the people mourned because Jehovah had smitten
the people with a great slaughter. ²⁰And the men of Bethshemesh said,
Who is able to stand before Jehovah this holy God? And to whom shall
he go up from us? ²¹Then they sent messengers to the inhabitants of
Kiriath-jearim, saying, The Philistines have brought back the ark of Jehovah. Come down and bring it up to you. 7 ¹So the men of Kiriath-
jearim came, and brought up the ark of Jehovah, and carried it into the

Its res-
tora-
tion to
the He-
brews

Confir-
mation
of the
story

The
ark at
Beth-
shem-
esh and
Kir-
iath-
jearim

ᵃ 6¹¹ The Gk. omits, *and the images of their boils.*
ᵇ 6¹³ So Gk. and Luc. Heb., *to see it.*
ᶜ 6¹⁵ Probably from a priestly editor who felt the lack of proper attendance and service
in connection with the ark. Vs. ¹⁴ records the original sacrifice, while ¹⁵ reflects the point of
view of later Judaism.
ᵈ 6¹⁷, ¹⁸ᵃ A recapitulation in the spirit and language of the late Jewish scribes. It also
seeks to explain the double symbolism of the golden tumors and mice.
ᵉ 6¹⁸ᵇ Heb., *even to the great meadow.* But this translation is doubtful and gives no
sense. A change of one letter gives the original reading, *stone,* preserved by the Gk. and Targ.
A slight correction in the traditional vocalization of the Heb. also gives the above intelligible
and consonant reading.
ᶠ 6¹⁹ So Gk. Heb., *and he smote of the men of Bethshemesh, because they had looked
at the ark of Jehovah, and he smote,* etc. Not only does this contain an awkward repetition
but also an idea foreign to the prophetic narratives. It seems probable, therefore, that the
Heb. simply represents the clumsy attempt of a scribe to correct a corrupt text. The Gk.
reading is consistent and original.
ᵍ 6¹⁹ Fifty thousand is added and is evidently an awkward gloss, suggested by the statement that there was a great slaughter.

Early Judean Narratives

house of Abinadab on the hill, and consecrated Eleazar his son to guard the ark of Jehovah. [2a]From the time the ark began to abide in Kiriath-jearim, many years passed, and it was twenty years. [h]

§ 5. The Secret Anointing of Saul by Samuel, I Sam. 9[1]–10[7, 9-16]

Early Judean Saul Narratives

Saul's family and appearance

I Sam. 9 [1]Now there was a man of Gibeah[i], whose name was Kish the son of Abiel, the son of Zeror, the son of Becorath, the son of Aphiah, a Benjamite, a man well to do.[j] [2]And he had a son whose name was Saul, a man in the prime of life and handsome; and there was not one among the Israelites more handsome than he. From his shoulders and upwards he was higher than any of the people.[k]

His search for the lost asses

[3]Now the she-asses of Kish, Saul's father, were lost. And Kish said to Saul his son, Take now one of the servants with you and arise and go seek the asses. [4]And they[l] passed through the hill-country of Ephraim, and the land of Shalishah, but did not find them. Then they passed through the land of Shaalim, but they were not there. And they passed through the land of the Benjamites but did not find them.

Appeal to Samuel

[5]When they were come into the land of Zuph, Saul said to his servant who was with him, Come, let us return, lest my father cease thinking of the asses and become anxious for us. [6]And he answered him, Behold now, there is in this city a man of God, and the man is held in honor; all that he says is sure to come true. Now let us go thither; perhaps he can give us

---

[h] 7[2a] All of [2a] may be from a later editor who wished to introduce the account of the deliverance which follows. If so, the last clause is a still later insertion.

§ 5 Chap. 4 records a sweeping victory of the Philistines over the Hebrews, who were completely vanquished and left without leaders or defenders. Chaps. 9[1]–10[16], 11, 13, 14 reflect precisely the same conditions. Samuel himself at Jehovah's command is seeking for a leader *who shall save his people out of the hand of the Philistines; for Jehovah has seen the affliction of his people and their cry for deliverance has come up to him,* 9[16b]. The whole land and people were held in abject bondage to the Philistines. Cf. especially 13[3, 16-23]. Not until Saul and Jonathan finally succeeded in rallying the people to successful resistance were they relieved of the intolerable burden. Hence it is perfectly obvious, that if the overwhelming victory, recorded in 7[3-14], as a result of which it is stated that *the Philistines were subdued and came no more within the border of Israel, and the cities which the Philistines had taken from Israel were restored to Israel from Ekron even to Gath,* [13, 14], has any historical basis, it has been introduced by a later editor into a wrong setting, where it obscures the real course of history. In note § 7 the reason of this transposition and the evidence that it is the later prophetic version of the victory recorded in 13, 14 will be indicated.

The citation in 9[1]–10[16] from the early Judean Saul narratives (cf. Introd., pp. 10, 11) at once puts the reader into touch with the problems and leaders of the period. Like a clear mirror it reflects conditions as they actually were, without doctrinal or traditional bias. The interest centres in the sturdy young warrior Saul, while Samuel is the patriotic seer of Ramah, intent upon finding the man to deliver the people from the Philistine yoke. The literary style is vivid, concise, dramatic, abounding in dialogues, realistic—the style of the oldest stories in Judges and the Hexateuch. So complete and consistent is the narrative that the original editor who quoted it and his successors found little occasion to supplement it. To the student of history and literature it, and the citations from the same source which follow, are among the inestimable treasures of the O.T.

[i] 9[1] I Sam. 11[4], 10[26], assume that Saul is from Gibeah. This word has probably fallen out of the text, for the latter part of the verse states the fact that Kish was a Benjamite.

[j] 9[1] *I.e.*, a man of wealth and standing in the community. Cf. Ruth 2[1], but also I Kgs. 11[28], I Chr. 9[13].

[k] 9[2] Cf. 10[23]. This may here be an editorial addition to complete the portrait.

[l] 9[4] So Gk. In the Heb. some of the verbs are in the singular.

Early Judean Saul Narratives

information regarding the mission on which we are going. [7]Then Saul said to his servant, But, suppose we go, what shall we take to the man? for the bread is gone from our sacks, and there is no present to take to the man of God. What have we? [8]And the servant answered Saul again, and said, See I have with me a fourth part of a silver shekel, and you[m] shall give it to the man of God that he may furnish us information regarding our mission. [9](Formerly in Israel, when a man went to inquire of God, thus he said, Come let us go to the seer; for he who is now called a prophet was previously called a seer).[n] [10]Then Saul said to his servant, Your advice is good; come, let us go. So they went to the city where the man of God was.

[11]As they were going up the ascent to the city, they met young maidens going out to draw water and said to them, Is the seer here? [12]And they answered them and said, He is; behold he is before you. Make haste now, for he is come to-day into the city; for the people have a sacrifice to-day on the high place. [13]As soon as you come to the city, you will at once find him before he goes up to the high place to eat; for the people will not eat until he come, for he is to bless the sacrifice; and afterwards the guests eat. Now therefore go up; for at this time you will meet him. [14]So they went up to the city. When they came within the city gate,[o] Samuel was just coming out toward them, to go up to the high place. [15]Now Jehovah had given to Samuel, a day before Saul came, the following revelation,[p] [16]At this time to-morrow I will send thee a man out of the land of Benjamin and thou shalt anoint him to be a prince over my people Israel. And he shall save my people out of the hand of the Philistines; for I have seen the affliction[q] of my people and their cry has come to me. [17]And when Samuel saw Saul, Jehovah indicated to him, This is the man of whom I spoke to thee! He it is who shall rule over my people. [18]Then Saul drew near to Samuel in the gate, and said, Tell me, if you will, where the seer's house is. [19]And Samuel answered Saul and said, I am the seer; go up before me to the high place, for you shall eat with me to-day; and in the morning I will let you go, and will tell you all that is in your heart. [20]And as for your asses that were lost three days ago, do not trouble yourself[r] about them for they have been found. And to whom belongs all that is desirable in Israel? Does it not to you, and to your[s] father's house? [21]And Saul answered and said, Am I not a Benjamite, of the smallest of the tribes of Israel, and is not my family the least of all the families of the tribe of Benjamin? Why then do you speak thus to me?

[22]And Samuel took Saul and his servant and brought them into the hall and made them sit at the head of the guests (who were about thirty persons).

[margin notes: Meeting with the seer; At the sacrificial meal]

---

m 9⁸ So Gk. and Luc. Heb., *I wil' give.* Syr., Lat., Targs., *we.* These changes seem later. Cf. for a similar change in Gk. v. ¹⁹.

n 9⁹ Apparently a later explanatory note. It fits the context very awkwardly, for the seer is first introduced in ¹¹.

o 9¹⁴ Heb., *city,* but ¹⁸ favors *gate.* Gk., *as they were proceeding into the midst of the city.*

p 9¹⁵ Heb., *uncovered the ear.*

q 9¹⁶ So Gk., Luc., and Targs. Heb. omits *affliction.*

r 9²⁰ Heb., *put your mind on.*

s 9²⁰ So Gk. The Heb. adds, *all.*

Early Judean Saul Narratives

²³And Samuel said to the cook, Bring the portion I gave you, which I told you to put aside. ²⁴And the cook took up the leg[t] and placed it before Saul. And Samuel said, See, the meat is served! eat! for it was kept for you until the appointed time, that you might eat with those whom I have invited.[u] So Saul ate with Samuel that day.

Public
anoint-
ing by
Samuel ²⁵And after they came down from the high place into the city, they spread a bed for Saul on the roof, and he lay down. ²⁶Then at daybreak Samuel called to Saul on the roof, saying, Up, that I may send you away.[v] So Saul arose, and he and Samuel[w] went out into the street. ²⁷As they were going down at the outskirts of the city, Samuel said to Saul, Bid the servant pass on before us,[x] but you stand here that I may make known to you the word of God. 10 ¹Then Samuel took the vial of oil, and poured it on his head, and kissed him and said, Hath not Jehovah anointed you to be a prince over his people Israel? And you shall reign over the people of Jehovah and deliver them from the power of their enemies around about. And this shall be the sign that Jehovah has anointed you to be a prince over his heritage:[a] ²when you go from me to-day you shall find two men at Rachel's tomb,[b] in the boundary of Benjamin at Zelzah; and they will say to you, ' The asses which you went to seek are found, and now your father has dismissed the matter of the asses and is anxious for you, saying, " What shall I do for my son?"' ³Then you shall go on from there and come to the oak of Tabor; and there three men going up to God to Bethel will meet you, one carrying three kids, and another carrying three loaves of bread, and another carrying a skin of wine. ⁴And they will salute you and give you two loaves of bread which you shall take from their hand. ⁵After that you shall come to Gibeah, where is the garrison[c] of the Philistines; and furthermore when you come thither to the city, you shall meet a band of prophets coming down from the high place with a lyre, a tambourine, a flute, and a harp before them; and they will be prophesying. ⁶And the spirit of Jehovah will rush upon you, and you shall prophesy with them and shall be turned into another man. ⁷And when these signs come to you, you shall do as the occasion offers;[d] for God is with you.[e]

---

[t] 9²⁴ So Gk. The Heb. adds, *and brought it (the leg) up.*
[u] 9²⁴ The present Heb. text has suffered so much in transmission that it is impossible to translate it as it stands. The above reconstruction (which incorporates suggestions of Gk., Budde and Smith) at least represents the sense of the passage.
[v] 9²⁵, ²⁶ᵃ So Gk., Luc., and Lat. When two minor errors are corrected in the Heb. it gives the same reading.
[w] 9²⁶ So Gk. The Heb. adds, *both of them.*
[x] 9²⁷ So Gk. and Syr. The Heb. adds, *and he passed on,* which seriously interrupts the context.
[a] 10¹ᵇ So Gk., Luc., and Lat. A later copyist, possibly by mistake or else because he regarded it as not fulfilled in the work of Saul and especially inharmonious with 8, left it out in the Heb.
[b] 10² Evidently not identical with the tomb of Rachel of later tradition which was found near Bethlehem.
[c] 10⁵ The Heb. word is variously translated. Gk., *pillar;* Targs., *soldiers;* Lat. and Syr., *post* or *garrison.* In 13³ the same word occurs.
[d] 10⁷ Heb., *what there your hand finds.*
[e] 10⁷ Vs. ⁸ has no connection with its context and anticipates the corresponding later addition to the story in 13⁷⁻¹⁵. Cf. note § 8.

Early Judean Saul Narratives

⁹Accordingly when he turned his back to go from Samuel, God gave him another heart,[f] and all those signs came to pass that day. ¹⁰And just as he came thence to Gibeah, a band of prophets met him, and he prophesied among them. ¹¹And when every one who knew him saw him in the act of prophesying with the prophets, the people said to one another, What is this that has come upon the son of Kish? Is Saul also among the prophets? ¹²And one of the bystanders answered and said, And who is their[g] father? Therefore it became a proverb, Is Saul also among the prophets? ¹³And when he had made an end of prophesying, he went to the high place.

Meeting with the band of prophets

¹⁴And Saul's cousin said to him and to his servant, Where did you go? And he said, To seek the asses; and when we saw that they were not found, we went to Samuel. ¹⁵And Saul's cousin said, Tell me, I pray, what Samuel said to you. ¹⁶And Saul said to his cousin, He told us definitely that the asses were found. But concerning the matter of the kingdom, of which Samuel had spoken, he told him nothing.[h]

Return home

§ 6. Events Connected with Saul's Election as King, I Sam. 7¹⁵–8²², 10¹⁷–12²⁵

Early Judean Saul Narratives	Later Ephraimite Samuel Narratives	
I Sam. 10 ²⁷ᵇNow it came to pass after about a month **11** ¹that Na-	**7** ¹⁵Now Samuel judged Israel all the days of his life. ¹⁶And he used to go around from year to year in succession to Bethel, Gilgal, and Miz-	*Samuel's judgeship*

ava- on nd erms ffered y Na- he m- onite

---

f 10⁹ This clause may be secondary; the latter part of the verse tells of the fulfilment of the sign.

g 10¹² Gk., *his father*.

h 10¹⁶ᵇ This may be a later note, the contents of which is implied by ¹²ᵃ. The word *kingdom* is found only in the later passages, 10²⁵, 11¹⁴.

§ 6 The establishment of the Hebrew kingdom under Saul was an event of such far-reaching significance that succeeding generations inevitably estimated it very differently. The oldest account is evidently that in 11¹⁻¹⁵. It reflects the same conditions as are presented in 9¹⁻10¹⁶. The Israelites are the prey of their hostile neighbors and have no leader until Saul, already encouraged by Samuel, like the champions whose deeds are recorded in the corresponding stories in Judg., challenges the warriors to follow him against the insolent Ammonites. When he returns victorious, he is, like Gideon (Judg. 8), asked to be their king and leader. The simplicity of the narrative and its consistency with actual conditions establish its priority and historical accuracy.

Very different were the traditions cherished by the later prophets. The figure of an Elijah, an Elisha, or an Isaiah dictating in the name of Jehovah to king and people was on the one hand prominently before them. On the other the evils of the kingship, as exemplified in the despotic, luxurious, and—to their enlightened point of view—apostate reigns of such kings as Solomon and Ahab, were uppermost in the minds. To them the kingship seemed a step not forward from anarchy and oppression, as it actually was, but backward from that ideal theocracy which their imagination had unconsciously projected on the canvas of their early past. All Israel was conceived of as enjoying the benign guidance of the great prophet-judge, Samuel. To him they are represented as coming with the demand for a king, and he, voicing in 8 the mature experiences and conclusions of prophets like Hosea, seeks to dissuade them by pointing out the baneful consequences. Since they persist, he at last reluctantly consents, referring the choice through the lot, directly to Jehovah, 10¹⁷⁻²⁴. Then follows a long and noble address, full of historical illustrations, recalling the traditional farewells of Moses in Dt. and Joshua in Josh. 23, 24 (cf. Vol. I, §§ 104, 128), in which Samuel preaches to the people, as would the prophetic successors of Hosea and Isaiah in the presence of the audience and conditions which they, through the dim light of tradition, seemed to see confronting him.

As has already been shown, Introd., pp. 12, 13, the relationship of these sections to the later Ephraimite narratives seems well established. So widely divergent are the style, point of view, and representation of the primitive and later prophetic sources that the analysis is comparatively easy. While the historian naturally follows the one and may almost ignore the other, the religious and ethical teacher finds in the latter, valuable prophetic teachings and principles, possessing a perennial value entirely independent of their setting.

Early Judean Saul Nar-
ratives

Later Ephraimite Samuel Narratives

hash the Ammonite came up and besieged Jabesh in Gilead;¹ and all the men of Jabesh said to Nahash, Make terms with us and we will serve you. ²But Nahash the Ammonite said to them, On this condition will I make terms with you: that I bore out the right eye of each of you and thereby bring a reproach upon all Israel. ³And the elders of Jabesh said to him, Give us seven days respite, that we may send messengers through all the territory of Israel. Then if there be none to save us we will come to you.

Reception of the news by Saul

⁴So the messengers came to Gibeah of Saul and recounted the facts in the hearing of the people, and all the people wept aloud. ⁵And Saul was just coming from the field after the oxen. And Saul said, What is the trouble with the people that they are weeping? Then they told him the words of the men of Jabesh. ⁶And the spirit of Jehovah^m rushed upon Saul when he heard these words, and

pah; and he used to judge Israel in all those places. ¹⁷And his return was to Ramah, for there was his home; and there he judged Israel. And there he built an altar to Jehovah.

8 ¹But when Samuel was old he appointed his sons judges over Israel. ²And the name of his eldest was Joel, and the name of his second, Abijah; they were judges in Beersheba.^j ³However his sons walked not in his ways, but turned aside after unjust gain and took bribes and perverted justice.

Crimes of his sons

⁴Then all the elders of Israel assembled and came to Samuel at Ramah, ⁵and they said to him, See, you have become old and your sons walk not in your ways. Now appoint for us a king to judge us like all the nations. ⁶But the statement displeased Samuel, when they said, Give us a king to judge us. And Samuel prayed to Jehovah. ⁷And Jehovah said to Samuel, Listen to the voice of the people according to all that they say to thee; for they have not rejected thee, but they have rejected me from being king over them. ⁸Like all the deeds which they have done to me since the day that I brought them up out of Egypt even to this day, in that they have forsaken me and served other gods, so also are they doing to thee.^k ⁹Now therefore hearken to their voice, except that thou shalt solemnly warn them, and shalt show them the prerogative of the king who shall reign over them.

Popular demand for a king and Jehovah's response

¹⁰And Samuel told all the words of Jehovah to the people who were asking of him a king. ¹¹And he said, This will be the prerogative of the king who shall reign over you: he will take your sons and appoint them for himself over his chariots and horsemen; and they shall run before his chariots; ¹²and he shall appoint them for himself as commanders of thousands and commanders of hundreds,¹ and some to plow his ground and to

Samuel's warning regarding a king

ⁱ 10²⁷ᵇ, 11¹ So Gk. and Luc. and a slightly corrected Heb. text. Present Heb., *and he was like me holding his peace.*

ʲ 8² Jos., *Ant.*, VI, 32, *one in Bethel and one in Beersheba.* This vs. may be a later insertion.

ᵏ 8⁸ The direction continuation of ⁷ is ⁹. The language of ⁸ is that of the late prophetic writers. It also contradicts ⁷.

ˡ 8¹² So Gk., Luc., and Lat. Heb., *fifties.* Cf. Ex. 18²¹˒ ²⁵, and I Sam. 22⁷, which supposes the reading given above.

ᵐ 11⁶ So Gk., Targs., and certain Heb. MSS. and the prevailing usage in the chapter. Received Heb. text, *God.*

Early Judean Saul Nar-   *Later Ephraimite Samuel Narratives*
ratives

his anger was greatly aroused. ⁷And he took a yoke of oxen, and cut them in pieces, and sent them throughout all the territory of Israel by the hand of messengers, saying, Whoever does not come forth after Saul and after Samuel, so shall it be done to his oxen.

he de-
ver-
nce by
he
srael-
es un-
er
aul

Then a terror from Jehovah fell upon the people, and they rallied as one man. ⁸And he mustered them in Bezek; and the Israelites were three hundred thousand, and the men of Judah thirty thousand.ᵒ
⁹And they said to the messengers who came, Thus say to the men of Jabesh in Gilead, ' To-morrow, by the time the sun becomes hot, deliverance shall come to you.' So the messengers came and told the men of Jabesh, and they were glad. ¹⁰Therefore the men of Jabesh said, To-morrow we will come out to you, and you shall do to us whatever you please. ¹¹Accordingly on the following day, Saul divided the people into three divisions; and they came into the midst of the camp in the morning watch, and smote the Ammonites

reap his harvest and to make his implements of war and the furnishings for his chariots. ¹³And he will take your daughters to be perfumers and to be cooks and to be bakers. ¹⁴And of your fields and your vineyards and your oliveyards, he will take the best and give them to his servants. ¹⁵And he will take the tithe of your grain fields and of your vineyards and give to his eunuchs and to his servants. ¹⁶And he will take your men-servants and your maid-servants, and the best of your cattleⁿ and your asses, and use them for his work. ¹⁷He will take the tithe of your flocks; and you shall become his servants. ¹⁸Then you will cry out in that day on account of your king whom you will have chosen for yourselves; but Jehovah will not answer you in that day.

¹⁹But the people refused to listen to the voice of Samuel, and said, Nay, but a king shall be over us, ²⁰that we also may be like all the nations, and that our king may judge us and go out before us and fight our battles. ²¹And Samuel heard all the words of the people and repeated them to Jehovah. ²²And Jehovah said to Samuel, Listen to their voice and make them a king. And Samuel said to the men of Israel, Go every man to his city.ᴾ

Persist-
ent de-
mand
of the
people

10 ¹⁷And Samuel called the people together to Jehovah to Mizpah; ¹⁸and he said to the Israelites, Thus saith Jehovah the God of Israel, ' I brought up Israel out of Egypt, and I delivered you out of the hand of the Egyptians, and out of the hand of all the kingdoms that were oppressing you. ¹⁹But you yourselves have this day rejected your God, who himself has been saving you from all your calamities and your distresses, and you have said to him, ' Nay, but a king shalt thou set over us.' Now therefore present yourselves before Jehovah by your tribes and by your thousands.

Denun-
ciation
of their
ingrati-
tude

ⁿ 8¹⁶ So Gk. and Luc. Heb., *young men,* but those have already been alluded to in ¹¹.
ᵒ 11⁸ᵇ Numbers are not usually given in the earliest stories and their size in this case is good evidence that they have been supplied by an editor.
ᴾ 8²²ᵇ This may have been added by an editor in order to introduce the narrative in 9¹⁻10¹⁶, but it is also demanded by 10¹⁷. For a similar assembly at Mizpah cf. 7⁶.

Early Judean Saul Narratives

until the heat of the day. And then they who remained scattered, so that no two of them were left together.

His election as king

¹²And the people said to Samuel, Who is he that says, 'Saul shall not*s* reign over us?' Bring the men that we may put them to death. ¹³And Saul said, To-day not a man shall be put to death, for to-day Jehovah hath wrought deliverance in Israel. ¹⁴Then said Samuel to the people, Come, and let us go to Gilgal, and renew the kingdom there*t*. ¹⁵And all the people went to Gilgal; and there they made Saul king before Jehovah in Gilgal; and there they sacrificed peace-offerings before Jehovah; and there Saul and all the men of Israel rejoiced exceedingly.

Later Ephraimite Samuel Narratives

Choice of Saul by lot

²⁰So Samuel brought all the tribes of Israel near, and the tribe of Benjamin was taken. ²¹And he brought the tribe of Benjamin near by their clans; and the clan of the Matrites was taken; and he brought near the clan of Matri man by man*q* and Saul the son of Kish was taken; but when they sought him he could not be found. ²²Therefore they asked of Jehovah further, Did the man come hither?*r* And Jehovah answered, Behold, he hath hid himself among the baggage. ²³And one ran and brought him from there. And as he stood among the people, he was taller than any of the people from his shoulders upward. ²⁴And Samuel said to all the people, Have you seen him whom Jehovah hath chosen? for there is none like him among all the people. And all the people shouted loudly, May the king live!*u*

Samuel's resignation and farewell

12 ¹Then Samuel said to all Israel, See, I have hearkened to your voice in all that you have said to me and have appointed a king over you. ²And from now on, behold the king who will go before you; but as for me, I am old and gray, and my sons are with you: and I have walked before you from my youth to this day. ³Here am I! Testify against me before Jehovah, and before his anointed: whose ox have I taken? or whose ass have I taken? or whom have I oppressed? whom have I defrauded? or from whose hand have I taken a ransom, or a sandal?*v* Testify and I will restore it to you. ⁴And they said, You have not oppressed us, nor defrauded us, nor have you taken anything from any man's hand. ⁵Therefore he said to them, Jehovah is witness against you, and his anointed is witness this day, that you have not found anything in my hand. And they*w* said, He is witness. ⁶Then

---

q 10²¹ᵇ Gk. has retained this clause, which is wanting in the Heb. but demanded by the sense.

r 10²² So Gk. It is in harmony with the answer of Jehovah which follows.

s 11¹² So Gk., Syr., and Targs. The Heb. omits the negative.

t 11¹²⁻¹⁴ Vss. 12 and 14ᵇ contain clear allusions to the secondary tradition in 10¹⁷⁻²⁷ and 13 is dependent upon 12. These verses therefore appear to have been introduced to harmonize the two variant traditions and to give Samuel the commanding position. The original narrative probably here recorded the fact that the people asked Saul, who had proved himself their deliverer, to become their king.

u 10²⁴ Samuel's address in 12 naturally follows the public choice of the king and precedes the formal dismissal of the people recorded in 10²⁵⁻²⁷. The transposition was doubtless made by the editor who brought in the account in 11 of Saul's victory over the Ammonites, which in the early narratives led to his being chosen by the people.

v 12³ So Gk., confirmed by Ben Sira 46¹⁹. Minor corruptions in the Heb. have given the very different reading. As in Ruth 4⁸, ⁹ the sandal may well represent the transfer of title to property offered to the judge as a bribe.

w 12⁵ So Gk. Heb., *he said.*

Later Ephraimite Samuel Narratives

Samuel said to the people, Jehovah is witness, who appointed Moses and Aaron[x] and who brought your fathers up out of the land of Egypt.

[7]Now therefore take your stand that I may declare to you before Jehovah all the righteous acts of Jehovah, which he did to you and to your fathers. [8]When Jacob[y] came to Egypt, and your fathers cried to Jehovah, then Jehovah sent Moses and Aaron to bring your fathers out of Egypt, and made[a] them dwell in this place. [9]But they forgot Jehovah their God, and he sold them into the hand of Sisera, commander of the army of Hazor, and into the hand of the Philistines and into the hand of the king of Moab; and they fought against them. [10]And they cried to Jehovah and said, We have sinned because we have forsaken Jehovah and served the Baalim and the Ashtartes. But now deliver us out of the hand of our enemies, and we will serve thee. [11]And Jehovah sent Jerubbaal, and Barak,[b] and Jephthah, and Samuel, and delivered you out of the hand of your enemies round about you so that you dwelt in safety.[c] [12]And you saw that Nahash the king of the Ammonites came against you[d]. And you said to me, ' Nay, but a king shall reign over us,' although Jehovah your God was your king. *(margin: The historical retrospect)*

[13]Now therefore see the king whom you have chosen,[e] for Jehovah has now set a king over you. [14]If you will fear Jehovah and serve him and listen to his voice, and not rebel against the commandment of Jehovah, and both you and the king who reigns over you follow Jehovah your God, well. [15]But if you will not hearken to the voice of Jehovah, but rebel against the commandment of Jehovah, then shall the hand of Jehovah be against you and your king.[f] [16]Now therefore take your stand and see this great thing, which Jehovah is about to do before your eyes. [17]Is it not wheat harvest to-day? I will call upon Jehovah, to send thunder and rain; and you shall know and see that your wickedness is great, which you have done in the sight of Jehovah in asking you a king. [18]So Samuel called upon Jehovah, and Jehovah sent thunder and rain that day; and all the people were greatly afraid of Jehovah and Samuel. *(margin: The solemn warning)*

[19]Then all the people said to Samuel, Intercede with Jehovah your God in behalf of your servants that we die not; for we have added to all our sins the crime of asking a king. [20]But Samuel said to the people, Fear not; you have indeed done all this evil, yet do not turn aside from following Jehovah, but serve Jehovah with all your heart; [21]and do not turn aside after vain things which cannot profit or deliver, for they are vain. [22]For Jehovah because of his great name will not cast away his people, for Jehovah has undertaken to make you a people for himself. [23]Moreover, as for me, far be it from me *(margin: Confession of the people and Samuel's final exhortation)*

---

[x] 12⁶ The Heb. is corrupt. The Gk. and Luc. have preserved the text followed above.

[y] 12⁸ *And his sons* is added in the Gk.

[a] 12⁸ Heb., *they* (*i.e.*, Moses and Aaron) *made them dwell;* but this is contrary to all the early traditions. The Gk. again has a consonant reading which is here followed.

[b] 12¹¹ Heb., *Bedan;* evidently a corruption for *Barak,* which is preserved in Gk., Luc., and Syr.

[c] 12⁷ᵇ⁻¹¹ This entire retrospect may be from the late prophetic editor.

[d] 12¹² The reference to Nahash is apparently based upon the early Judean narrative in 11, and, if so, is from a later editor familiar with both sources.

[e] 12¹³ So Gk. Heb. adds pleonastically, *and whom you have asked.*

[f] 12¹⁵ So Gk. and demanded by ¹⁴ᵇ. The Heb., *and against your fathers,* is an obvious error.

Later Ephraimite Samuel Narratives

that I should sin against Jehovah in ceasing to intercede for you; but I will instruct you in the good and the right way. ²⁴Only fear Jehovah and serve him in truth with all your heart, for you see what a great thing he hath done in your presence. ²⁵But if you persist in doing wrong, both you and your king shall be destroyed.

Dismissal of the people

10 ²⁶Thus Samuel revealed to the people the manner of the kingdom, and wrote it in a book, and laid it up before Jehovah. And Samuel sent all the people away, each man to his home. ²⁶And Saul also went to his home at Gibeah; and there went with him the brave men ᵍ whose hearts God had touched. ²⁷ᵃBut there were base scoundrels who said, How shall this man save us? And they despised him, and brought him no present. ʰ

§ 7. The Great Deliverance from the Philistines, I Sam. 7²⁻¹⁴, 13¹⁻⁴ᵃ, ⁶, ⁷ᵃ, ¹⁵ᵇ—14⁴⁶, ⁵²

Early Judean Saul Narratives

Outbreak of the war and the advance of the Philistines

I Sam. 13 ²Saul chose him three thousand men of Israel:ⁱ two thousand were with Saul in Michmash and on the mountain of Bethel and a thousand were with Jonathan his sonʲ in Gibeah of Benjamin. But the rest of the people he had sent each to his home.

Later Ephraimite Samuel Narratives

7 ²ᵇThen all the nation Israel turned to Jehovah. ³And Samuel spoke to all the nation Israel,

Confession of the people

ᵍ 10²⁶ So Gk. Heb., army or *fighting force*.
ʰ 10²⁵⁻²⁷ᵃ These verses appear to be simply editorial, and are intended to explain Saul's appearance in the rôle of a private citizen in 11.
§ 7 Originally in the early Judean Saul history 13, 14 immediately followed 11. The *garrison of the Philistines*, peculiar to this source, again figures prominently in the story. Cf. 13³, ⁴. To the original narrative in 13, however, there was closely joined at an early period a secondary tradition which represents Saul as rallying his forces not at Gibeah, the seat of the battle, but at the ancient sanctuary of Gilgal, far down in the Jordan valley, where he waits seven days for Samuel to appear and offer a sacrifice. Its interest is not in the war, but in the reason why Saul's family was rejected by Jehovah and forfeited the throne to David. Cf. § 8. This story is found in ⁴ᵇ, ⁵, ⁷ᵇ⁻¹⁵ᵃ. Vs. ⁷ᵃ appears to be common to the older and later narratives. The exaggerated numbers in ⁵ᵇ probably belong to the later. The fact that *the Philistines encamped in Michmash* is first stated in the earlier narrative in ¹⁶ᵇ. Removing these later editions, a remarkably complete and consistent record remains of the epoch-making deliverance of the Hebrews from their Philistine oppressors.
Of the manner in which the great victory was wrought a very different tradition was current in the later Ephraimite prophetic circles. Since the deliverance took place while Samuel was still alive (cf. 15), it was an inevitable result of their peculiar conception of the history of the period (cf. note § 6) that they should think of him as the leading agent in accomplishing it, and of the method as direct supernatural intervention. Their version is found in 7³⁻¹⁴. It has been supplemented at many points by a late prophetic editor, but the language and the point of view are those which characterize the later Ephraimite prophetic school.
The points of contact between the primitive and late tradition are suggestive: not Gibeah of Saul, but Mizpah, the place where according to the later source Samuel gathered the people to elect Saul king, 10¹⁷, is where he again assembles them, 7⁵⁻⁷, ¹¹. Thither the Philistines come, when they hear of the rally of the Israelites, 7, just as in the early Judean they advance after Jonathan's attack on the garrison at Gibeah, 13³, ⁴ᵃ, ¹⁶. In both the Hebrews were seized with terror. In the older account Jonathan precipitates the battle by attacking the Philistine stronghold, in the later Samuel offered a sacrifice and prayed to Jehovah for deliverance. One records that *the earth quaked*, 14¹⁵, the other that *Jehovah thundered with a loud voice;* both that the Philistines retreated in confusion, pursued by the Israelites. The older source states that there was bitter war with the Philistines all the days of Saul, 14⁵², while the later, losing the historical perspective and reflecting conditions first realized in the days of David,

---

ⁱ 13² The Gk. which begins the chapter with ² ᵃhas here been followed. The Heb. has the impossible reading in ¹, *Saul was a year old when he began to reign and he reigned two years over Israel*. The fact that it is lacking in the Gk. strongly suggests that it is a very late addition by a scribe who felt that the framework of Sam.-Kgs. demanded some such introduction. Cf. II Sam. 2¹⁰, 5⁴, 14²¹, etc.
ʲ 13² In the Heb. the designation, *his son*, which is required here where Jonathan is first introduced, is lacking, but is retained in the Syr.

70

Early Judean Saul Narratives | *Later Ephraimite Samuel Narratives*

³Then Jonathan smote the garrison of the Philistines that was in Gibeah.ᵏ And the Philistines heard the report, The Hebrews have revolted. But Saul had meantime caused the trumpet to be blown throughout all the land.ˡ ⁴ᵃAnd all Israel heard the report, Saul has smitten the garrison of the Philistines, and also Israel has brought itself into ill odor with the Philistines. ⁵ᵃAnd the Philistines were gathered together to fight with Israel. ⁶When the men of Israel saw that they were in a strait (for the people were hard pressed),ⁿ the people hid themselves in caves, in holes,ᵒ in rocks, in tombs, and in pits. ⁷ᵃAlso many peopleᵖ went over the Jordan to the land of Gad and Gilead. ¹⁵ᵇAnd Saul numbered the people who were with him, about six hundred men. ¹⁶And Saul and Jonathan his son, together with the people who were with them, were staying in Gibeahᑫ of Benjamin, while the Philistines encamped in Michmash. ¹⁷And the plunderers came out of the camp of the Philistines in three divisions: one division turned in the direction of Ophrah in the land of Shual, ¹⁸and another division turned in the direction of Bethhoron, and another division turned in the direction of the hillʳ that looks down over the valley of Zeboim toward the wilderness.

Lack of arms in Israel

¹⁹Now there was no smith found throughout all the land of Israel, for the Philistines said, Lest the Hebrews make sword or spear; ²⁰but all the Israelites went down to the Philistines

saying, If with all your heart you are returning to Jehovah, then put away the foreign gods and the Ashtartesᵐ from among you and direct your hearts towards Jehovah and serve him alone that he may deliver you out of the hand of the Philistines. ⁴Then the Israelites put away the Baalim and the Ashtartes, and served Jehovah only.

⁵And Samuel said, Assemble all Israel at Mizpah and I will intercede for you with Jehovah. ⁶So they assembled at Mizpah, and drew water and poured

Victory over the Philistines

asserts that they *were subdued and came no more within the border of Israel* and that all the cities from Ekron to Gath fell into the hands of the Israelites, 7¹³, ¹⁴.

The evidence in the light of the oldest sources that the Philistine encroachments continued without interruption from the days of Samson to those of Saul, has already been noted (cf. note § 5). That 7³⁻¹⁴ represents in reality the later version of the events recorded in 13, 14 is also obvious. The reason why the later tradition is given its early position in I Sam. is primarily because the later prophets naturally assigned the great deliverance to that early idealized period, when they conceived of Samuel as ruling as a theocratic judge over all Israel. Cf. note § 6. Later editors also retained it in this early position, for nowhere else in the history could a place be found for it where the striking inconsistencies with the other narratives would not be obvious even in an uncritical age. It is chiefly valuable to-day because it vividly illustrates the growth of tradition and expresses that absolute faith in Jehovah's direct leadership and protection of his people which was one of the noblest messages of the Hebrew prophets.

ᵏ 13³ So certain versions and demanded by 10⁵ and supported by 14¹⁶, and by the Gk. in 13¹⁶. Heb., *Geba;* but in the original they are easily confused as the variant readings of the versions testify.

ˡ 13³ As it now stands the Heb. reads, *and Saul blew the trumpet throughout all the land, saying, Let the Hebrews hear.* But the designation *Hebrews* in the mouth of an Israelite is unprecedented. It is appropriate rather on the lips of the Philistines. Instead of *hear* the Gk. has *revolted.* Following this reading and transposing this clause, we have what was the original text.

ᵐ 7³ Gk., *groves.* Cf. Judg. 2¹³, where Gk. has the Phœnician form, *Ashtartes.*

ⁿ 13⁶ Or following a suggestion of the Gk., the repetition is eliminated by reading, *on all sides.* Or the Heb. may mean, *for the army of the Philistines drew near for battle.*

ᵒ 13⁶ Heb., *thickets.* A slight emendation gives the above more consistent reading. Gk., *enclosed spaces* or *folds.*

ᵖ 13⁷ᵃ The Heb. and Gk. make no sense. The simple transposition of two letters gives the above reading.

ᑫ 13¹⁶ So Gk. Cf. 14¹⁶ and note ᵏ. Heb., *Geba.*

ʳ 13¹⁸ So Gk. Heb., *border.*

Early Judean Saul Narratives

*Later Ephraimite
Samuel Narratives*

to sharpen each his plowshare and his coulter and his ax and his mattock; ²¹yet they had a file for the mattocks, and for the coulters and for the forks and for the axes and to set the ox-goads.ˢ ²²So it came to pass on the day of Michmash that none of the people with Saul and Jonathan had either sword or spear; but Saul and Jonathan his son had them.ᵗ

Jona-
than's
pro-
posal

²³And the garrison of the Philistines went out to the pass of Michmash. **14** ¹Now on that day Jonathan the son of Saul said to the young man who bore his armor, Come and let us go over to the Philistines' garrison, that is on the other side. But he did not tell his father. ²And Saul was sitting in the outskirts of Gibeah under the pomegranate tree which is by the threshing-floor,ᵘ and the people who were with him numbered about six hundred men. ³And Ahijah the son of Ahitub, Ichabod's brother, the son of Phinehas, the son of Eli, the priest of Jehovah at Shiloh, was in charge ofᵛ an ephod. And the people did not know that Jonathan had gone. ⁴And between the passes by which Jonathan sought to go over to the Philistines' garrison there was a rocky crag on the one side, and a rocky crag on the other side; and the name of the one was Bozez [the Shining], and the name of the other Seneh [the Thorny]. ⁵The one crag rose up on the north in front of Michmash, and the other on the south in front of Geba. ⁶And Jonathan said to the young man who bore his armor, Come, let us go over to the garrison of these uncircumcised Philistinesʷ; perhaps Jehovah will act for us, for there is nothing that can prevent Jehovah from saving by many or by few. ⁷And his armorbearer said to him, Do whatever your judgment dictatesˣ; see I am with you; your wish is mine. ⁸Then Jonathan said, See, we will pass over to the men and show ourselves to them. ⁹If they say to us, 'Stand still until we can reach you,' then we will stand still in our place, and will not go up to them. ¹⁰But if they say, 'Come up to us,' then we will go up; for Jehovah has given them into our hand; and this shall be the sign to us.ᵃ

it out before Jehovah, and fasted on that day and said, We have s i n n e d against Jehovah. And Samuel judged t h e Israelites i n Mizpah. ⁷And when the Philistines heard that the Israelites had assembled at Mizpah, the tyrants of the Philistines went up against Israel. And when the Israelites heard it they were afraid of the Philistines.

⁸And the Israelites said to Samuel, Cease not to cry to Jehovah our God for us, that he will save us out of the power of the Philistines. ⁹And Samuel took a sucking lamb, and offered it as a whole burnt-offering to Jehovah; and Samuel cried to Jehovah in behalf of Israel, and Jehovah a n s w e r e d h i m. ¹⁰And while Samuel

---

ˢ 13²¹ Only a conjectural translation of this verse is possible.
ᵗ 13¹⁹⁻²² These verses appear to be a later explanatory note. Not only are they not demanded by the context, but they also are not entirely consistent with the representation elsewhere. Cf. the account of the armed pursuit of the Philistines in 14.
ᵘ 14² Heb., *Migron*. But this town was located north of Michmash. The Heb. word is translated by Syr. as above.
ᵛ 14³ Lit., *bearing*.
ʷ 14⁶ Heb., *uncircumcised*, a contemptuous designation of the Philistines.
ˣ 14⁷ So Gk. lit., *all to which your heart* (or mind) *inclines*, which appears to have preserved the original reading, of which the present awkward Heb., *Do all that is in your heart: turn, behold, I am with you according to your heart*, is the corruption.
ᵃ 14¹⁰ For a similar sign cf. Gen. 24¹⁴, where Abraham's servant thus appeals to Jehovah for a decision.

Early Judean Saul Narratives

*Later Ephraimite
Samuel Narratives*

¹¹Now when both of them showed themselves to the garrison of the Philistines, the Philistines said, There are Hebrews coming out of the holes where they have hidden themselves. ¹²And the men of the garrison cried out to Jonathan and his armorbearer, saying, Come up to us that we may tell you something. Then Jonathan said to his armorbearer, Come up after me; for Jehovah has given them into the hand of Israel. ¹³And Jonathan climbed up on his hands and feet, and his armorbearer after him. And they fell before[b] Jonathan, and his armorbearer kept despatching them after him. ¹⁴And in the first attack Jonathan and his armorbearer slew about twenty men with javelins and rocks from the field.[c] ¹⁵And there was a trembling in the camp, in the field, and among all the people; the garrison, and even the raiders also trembled; and the earth quaked so that it produced a supernatural[d] panic.

¹⁶And the watchmen of Saul in Gibeah of Benjamin looked, and saw a tumult surging hither and thither.[e] ¹⁷Then said Saul to the people who were with him, Investigate now and see who is gone from us. And when they had investigated they found that Jonathan and his armorbearer were not there. ¹⁸And Saul said to Ahijah, Bring hither the ephod;[f] for at that time he had charge of the ephod before Israel. ¹⁹And while Saul was yet speaking to the priest, the tumult in the camp of the Philistines kept on increasing. Therefore Saul said to the priest, Draw back your hand. ²⁰And Saul and all the people that were with him responded to the call, and came to the battle; and thereupon every man's sword was turned upon his fellow and there was very great confusion. ²¹And the Hebrews,[i] who were

was offering the burnt-offering, the Philistines drew near to fight against Israel; but Jehovah thundered with a loud voice on that day against the Philistines, and threw them into confusion, and they were defeated before Israel. ¹¹And the men of Israel went forth from Mizpah and pursued the Philistines and smote them until they were below Bethcar.

¹²Then Samuel took a stone and set it between Mizpah and Yeshana[g] and called its name Ebenezer,[h] saying, Hitherto hath Jehovah helped us. ¹³So the Philistines were subdued and came no more within the border of Israel. And the hand of Je-

b 14¹³ Gk. and Luc., *they looked upon, i.e.,* were seized with terror at the sight of.
c 14¹⁴b The Heb. is untranslatable. The questionable rendering, *within as it were half a furrow's length in an acre of land,* gives no satisfactory sense. The Gk. interprets it as referring to the weapons used by the armorbearer. The Syr. reading, *like bearers of stone* or *like drivers of a yoke of oxen in the field,* is intelligible, but seems to be only a heroic endeavor to translate certain of the words. A radical revision of the text gives the possible rendering, *part from the garrison and part from the field,* which would refer to the Philistines slain.
d 14¹⁵ Gk., Luc., and Syr., *of Jehovah.* Heb., *God.*
e 14¹⁶ Making a slight correction required in the Heb., and suggested by the Gk.
f 14¹⁸ The Gk. has undoubtedly here preserved the original reading. A later scribe evidently substituted, for theological reasons, *the ark of God* for *ephod,* forgetting that the ark was still at Kirjath-jearim and that according to the oldest narratives it never appears to have been used as an oracle. According to ³ Ahijah *was in charge of the ephod.*
g 7¹² So Gk., Luc., and Syr. Heb., *Shen.* Yeshana is mentioned in II Chr. 13¹⁹ among the Benjamite towns and was probably located north of Bethel.
h 7¹² Heb., Eben-ha-ezer as in 4 and 5.
i 14²¹ Gk., *slaves, i.e.,* of the Philistines.

73

Early Judean Saul Narratives

Later Ephraimite Samuel Narratives

with the Philistines heretofore, who had come up into the camp,ᵏ also turned to be with the Israelites who were with Saul and Jonathan.   ²²Likewise all the men of Israel, who were in hiding in the hill-country of Ephraim, when they heard that the Philistines fled, also pursued close after them in the battle.   ²³So Jehovah saved Israel that day, and the battle passed over beyond Bethhoron.ˡ

hovah was against the Philistines all the days of Samuel.ʲ   ¹⁴And the cities which the Philistines had taken from Israel were restored to Israel from Ekron even to Gath; and their territory Israel delivered from the power of the Philistines. And there was peace between Israel and the Amorites.

Saul's rash vow and Jonathan's violation of it   And all the people were with Saul, about ten thousand men; and the fighting was scattered over all the hill-country of Ephraim.   ²⁴Then Saul committed a great act of folly that day,ᵐ for he laid an oath on the people, saying, Cursed is the man who shall eat any food until evening and until I avenge myself on my enemies.   So none of the people tasted food.   ²⁵Now there was honey on the surface of the ground,ⁿ ²⁶and when the people came to the honeycomb,ᵒ the bees had just flown away, but no one put his hand to his mouth, for the people feared the oath.   ²⁷But Jonathan had not heard when his father adjured the people; therefore he put forth the end of the rod that was in his hand and dipped it in the honeycomb and put his hand to his mouth, and his eyes were lightened.   ²⁸Then spoke up one of the people and said, Your father adjured the people saying, ' Cursed be the man who eats food this day.'   But the people were exhausted.ᵖ ²⁹Then said Jonathan, My father has brought disaster on the land.   See how I have been refreshed,ᑫ because I tasted a little of this honey.   ³⁰If only the people had eaten freely to-day of the spoil of their enemies which they found, how much greater would have been the slaughter of the Philistines !ʳ

ʲ 7¹³ Characteristic late prophetic expressions.   Cf. Judg. 3⁸⁻¹¹, and Dt. 9.
ᵏ 14²¹ Making a correction in the Heb. which is supported by the Gk.
ˡ 14²³ So Gk. and Luc.   Heb., *Bethaven.*
ᵐ 14²³ᵇ, ²⁴ᵃ So Gk. and Luc. with a necessary emendation.
ⁿ 14²⁵ The first part of the verse in the Heb. is untranslatable.   The original meaning may have been, *all the land flowed with honey,* cf. Gk., *all the land dined,* but 25a is more probably but a repetition of 25a through the error of a copyist (*the land* being equivalent to *the people* as in 29).
ᵒ 14²⁶ Emending the Heb. to conform with the Gk.
ᵖ 14²⁸ᵇ Apparently a scribal comment.   It awkwardly disturbs the context.   It would be more harmonious after 30.   Various emendations have been proposed of which the more probable are, *and he strictly warned the people,* or, joining to the next verse in accordance with a suggestion of Josephus, *and he (Jonathan) left off eating.*
ᑫ 14²⁹ Heb., *my eyes have been enlightened.*
ʳ 14³⁰ So Gk. and Luc. and one possible reading of the Heb.

Early Judean Saul Narratives

³¹But they smote the Philistines that day from Michmash to Aijalon,ˢ Saul's
and the people were very faint. ³²Then the people rushed upon the spoil ceremo-
and took sheep and oxen and calves and struck them to the earth, and the precau-
people ate them with the blood. ³³When they told Saul, saying, See, the tions
people are sinning against Jehovah in eating with the blood, he said to
those who told him,ᵗ Roll hitherᵘ to me a great stone. ³⁴And Saul said,
Go out among the people and say to them, ' Let each man bring to me his
ox and his sheep, and slay it here and eat; but do not sin against Jehovah in
eating the flesh together with the blood. And all the people brought that
night, each what he had in his hand,ᵛ and slew them there. ³⁵So Saul
built an altar to Jehovah; that was the first altar that he built to Jehovah.

³⁶And Saul said, Let us go down after the Philistines by night and plunder Penalty
amongʷ them until daybreak, and let us not leave a man of them. And of the
broken
they said, Do whatever you think best. Then said the priest, Let us here vow
draw near to God. ³⁷And Saul asked of God, Shall I go down after the Philistines? Wilt thou deliver them into the hand of Israel? But he did not
answer him that day. ³⁸And Saul said, Come hither, all you chiefsˣ of the
people and know and see in whom is this guilt to-day. ³⁹For as Jehovah
liveth, who delivereth Israel, though it be in Jonathan my son, he shall surely
die. But no one of all the people answered him. ⁴⁰Then he said to all
Israel; You be on one side, and I and Jonathan my son will be on the other
side. And the people said to Saul, Do what seems good to you. ⁴¹Therefore Saul said, Jehovah, God of Israel, why hast thou not answered thy
servant this day? If the guilt be in me or in Jonathan my son, Jehovah,
God of Israel, give Urim; but if the guilt is in thy people Israel, give Thum-
mim.ᵃ Then Jonathan and Saul were taken and the people escaped. ⁴²And
Saul said, Cast the lot between me and Jonathan my son. He whom Jehovah
shall take, must die. And the people said to Saul, It shall not be so! But
Saul overruled the people and they cast the lot between him and Jonathan
his son.ᵇ And Jonathan was taken.

⁴³Then Saul said to Jonathan, Tell me what you have done. And Jona- Jonathan told him saying, I did indeed taste a little honey with the end of the than's
confes-
staff that was in my hand; and here I am! I am ready to die.ᶜ ⁴⁴And sion
Saul said, May God do to me whatever he pleases, you shall surely die, Jona- and de-
liver-
ance

ˢ 14³¹ The Gk. reads, *in Michmash*, and omits, *to Aijalon*. Smith would join this clause
to the preceding speech of Jonathan, omitting, *that day*. Of the proposed emendation the
most plausible is, *from midday until evening.*
ᵗ 14³³ Heb., *You deal treacherously;* Gk., *Gittaim;* but a probable correction in the text
gives the above reading.
ᵘ 14³³ So Gk. and Luc. A minor corruption in Heb. gives the meaningless reading, *this day.*
ᵛ 14³⁴ So Gk. and Luc. Heb., *each his oxen his hand.*
ʷ 14³⁶ Or possibly emending the text to accord with 11¹¹, *let us smite them.*
ˣ 14³⁸ Heb., *corner-stones.*
ᵃ 14⁴¹ Fortunately the Gk. and especially Luc. have preserved what bears on its face the
evidence of being the original reading. The occurrence of the same word led the Heb. scribe
to overlook the omitted material.
ᵇ 14⁴² A similar mistake or deliberate purpose appears to have here resulted in a similar
omission in the Heb. as in ⁴¹. Again the Gk. has preserved what seems to be an original element in the narrative.
ᶜ 14⁴³ Cf. Josephus, Antiq. VI, 6⁵.

Early Judean Saul Narratives

than !d   45But the people said to Saul, Shall Jonathan die who has wrought this great deliverance in Israel? Far from it! As Jehovah liveth, there shall not one hair of his head fall to the ground, for he has wrought with God this day. Therefore the people redeemed Jonathan, so that he did not die.. 46Then Saul went up from pursuing the Philistines; and the Philistines went to their own country.

Saul's military policy 52But the war against the Philistines was severe all the days of Saul. And whenever Saul saw any valiant or efficient man, he would attach him to himself.

§ 8. Saul's Disobedience and Rejection, I Sam. 10⁸, 13⁴ᵇ, ⁵, ⁷ᵇ⁻¹⁵ᵇ, 15¹⁻³⁸ₐ

Later Judean Prophetic Narratives	*Later Ephraimite Samuel Narratives*
Samuel's command to Saul **I Sam. 10** ⁸*Now when Samuel anointed Saul, he commanded him, saying,* You shall go down before me to Gilgal, and then I will come down to you, to offer burnt-offerings and to sacrifice peace-	**15** ¹And Samuel said to Saul, Jehovah sent me to anoint you to be king over his people Israel.ᵉ Now therefore listen to the words of Jehovah.f ²Thus saith Jehovah of hosts, ' I have determined to punish that which Amalek did to Israel, in that he opposed him in the way, when he came up out of Egypt. ³Now go and smite Amalek and utterly destroyᵍ him and all that he has, and spare him **Command to slay the Amalekites**

---

d 14⁴⁴ Gk. and Syr. add, *to me.* Cf. 3¹⁷. The usual condition is not given, but instead the sentence is interrupted, thus vividly expressing the intensity of Saul's feeling.

§ 8 The untimely death of Saul and the misfortune which pursued his family until his kingdom passed completely under the rule of another, presented a moral problem to later generations akin to that which confronted the friends of Job. That like later kings, he had sinned against Jehovah in disobeying the divine command proclaimed by his prophet, was universally believed; but regarding the exact nature of that sin traditions differed. The oldest is found in 13⁷ᵇ⁻¹⁵ᵇ. References in ¹¹ indicate that ⁵ belongs to the same. The unexplained change of geographical background from Geba in ³ to Gilgal (beside the Jordan) in ⁴ᵇ is best explained on the basis that ⁴ᵇ is also from this secondary section. The strange command in 10⁸ *to go down to Gilgal,* etc., which has no connection with its context finds its true place and meaning as the introduction to this secondary tradition of Saul's rejection. The fact that this story has been so closely grafted on to the early Judean account of the Philistine war suggests that it comes from a later stratum of the same narratives. This is strongly confirmed by the linguistic similarity and by the fact that it is assumed that it was quite right for Saul to offer sacrifices; his sin is simply failure to obey the divine command, ¹⁴.

Parallel to this tradition, but associating the rejection with an entirely different occasion, is the slightly later version in 15. The points in common are many. Gilgal is in both the place of the rejection; the reason in each is that Saul has failed to comply with a distinct command of Samuel: in each he forfeits the kingdom to another. The occasion alone is different. In 15 Samuel has handed over his responsibilities as judge to Saul, but otherwise he is portrayed in precisely the same commanding prophetic rôle as in 7, 8, and 12.

The political situation revealed in the early Saul narratives and the necessity of repelling foreign attacks are entirely ignored. The one vital question is whether or not Saul will obey the divine command proclaimed by Jehovah's prophet. Many expressions peculiar to the preceding Ephraimite narratives also recur. The story is the culmination of that group of narratives found in 7, 8, 10¹⁷⁻²⁷ and 12, which starts with certain outstanding historical facts, like the victories over the Philistines and Amalekites and the downfall of the house of Saul, and with these as a basis develops an objective philosophy of history in which the religious teachings of Amos and Isaiah and especially those of the great prophet of the north, Hosea, are concretely illustrated.

In ⁵⁻⁹ the later prophetic writer has apparently quoted from an older tradition which like the early Judean narratives of 9-11, 13, 14, tells in a natural, circumstantial manner of Saul's campaign against the Amalekites. The same primitive sources may have also recorded the fact that Agag was slain by the hand of the stern, patriotic seer of Ramah.

e 15¹ These words were probably added by a scribe familiar with 9¹⁻10¹⁶.

f 15¹ So Gk. The Heb. combines two forms of expression, *listen to the voice of* the words of Jehovah.

g 15³ Heb., *devote, place under the ban.* So throughout the chapter.

Later Judean Prophetic Narratives

offerings. Wait seven days until I come to you and show you what you shall do.

13 ⁴ᵇTherefore, *when he had been made king*, the people were assembled together after Saul at Gilgal. ⁵ᵇAnd the Philistines were gathered together to fight with Israel — thirty thousand chariots and six thousand horsemen and people,⁶ as numerous as the sand on the sea. And they came up and encamped in Michmash, east of Bethaven.ʰ ⁷ᵇBut Saul was still in Gilgal, and all the people followed him trembling.ⁱ

⁸And he waited seven days for the appointed time which Samuel had set; but Samuel did not come to Gilgal, and the people scattered away from him. ⁹Therefore Saul said, Bring here to me the burnt-offering and the peace-offerings. And he offered the burnt-offering. ¹⁰And then, just as he had finished offering the burnt-offering, Samuel came; and Saul went out to greet him.ʲ ¹¹But Samuel said, What have you done? And Saul said, Because I saw that

Later Ephraimite Samuel Narratives

not, but slay both man and woman, child and infant, ox and sheep, camel and ass.'

⁴And Saul summoned the people and mustered them in Telaim, two hundred thousand footmen and ten thousand men of Judah. ⁵And when Saul came to the city of Amalek, he lay in wait in the valley. ⁶And Saul said to the Kenites, Go away, withdraw from among the Amalekites, lest I destroy you with them, for you showed kindness to all the Israelites when they came up from Egypt. So the Kenites departed from among the Amalekites. ⁷And Saul smote the Amalekites from Havilah as far as Shur, which is before Egypt. ⁸And he took Agag the king of Amalek alive and completely destroyed all the people with the sword. ⁹But Saul and the people spared Agag and the best of the sheep, the oxen, the fatlings, the lambs, and all that was good, and would not completely destroy them; but everything that was worthless and despised, that they completely destroyed.

¹⁰Then the word of Jehovah came to Samuel saying, ¹¹I repent that I have made Saul king, for he has turned from following me and has not carried out my commands. And Samuel was angry and cried to Jehovah all night. ¹²And early in the morning Samuel rose to meet Saul. Then Samuel was told, Saul came to Carmel and has just set up a monument and has turned and passed on and gone down to Gilgal. ¹³And when Samuel came to Saul, Saul said to him, Blessed be thou of Jehovah! I have fulfilled the command of Jehovah. ¹⁴And Samuel said, What then is this bleating of the sheep in my ears and the lowing of the cattle which I hear? ¹⁵And Saul said, They have brought them from the Amalekites, for the people spared the best of the sheep and of the oxen to sacrifice to Jehovah your God; and the rest we have completely destroyed. ¹⁶Then Samuel said to Saul, Stop! and let me tell you what Jehovah hath said to me

Marginal notes (left): ne :ua- :n at ilgal

aul's .sobe- .ence nd :jec- :on

Marginal notes (right): The war and Saul's disobe- dience

Sam- uel's rebuke

ʰ 13⁶ *I.e., Bethel.* So Syr. Gk., *Bethhoron.*
ⁱ 13⁷ᵇ The Heb. is difficult. Luc. reads, *trembled from after him*, i.e., because of fright had deserted him.
ʲ 13¹⁰ Heb., *to bless him*, i.e., to greet him with the customary salutation, *May you be blessed*, cf. II Kgs. 4²⁹.

Later Judean Prophetic Narratives

the people were scattering away from me and you did not come within the appointed time, and the Philistines were gathering together at Michmash, ¹²I said, ' Now will the Philistines come down to me at Gilgal, and I shall not have appeased Jehovah.'ᵏ So I constrained myself and offered the burnt-offering. ¹³Then Samuel said to Saul, You have acted foolishly. If you had kept the command of Jehovah your God,¹ which he commanded you, then would Jehovah have established your kingdom over Israel forever. ¹⁴But now your kingdom shall not continue. Jehovah hath sought out a man after his own heart, and Jehovah hath appointed him a leader over his people, because you have not kept that which Jehovah commanded you. ¹⁵ᵃThen Samuel arose and went up from Gilgal and proceeded on his way to Gibeah of Benjamin.ᵒ

Later Ephraimite Samuel Narratives

this night. And he said to him, Speak. ¹⁷And Samuel said, Though you are little in your own sight, are you not the head of the tribes of Israel ? And Jehovah anointed you king over Israel, ¹⁸and Jehovah sent you on an expedition and said, ' Go, and completely destroy the sinners of Amalek and fight against them until they are consumed.' ¹⁹Why then did you not obey the voice of Jehovah and why did you swoop upon the spoil and displease Jehovah ? ²⁰And Saul said to Samuel, I have obeyed the voice of Jehovah and have gone on the expedition upon which Jehovah sent me and have brought back Agag the king of the Amalekites and have completely destroyed the Amalekites. ²¹But the people took of the spoil, sheep and oxen, the best of the things which were placed under the ban to sacrifice to Jehovah your God in Gilgal. ²²And Samuel said,

Does Jehovah delight in burnt-offerings and sacrifices
  As in obedience to the voice of Jehovah ?
Behold to obey is better than sacrifice,
  And to hearken than the fat of rams.
²³For rebellion is as bad as the sin of divination,
  And obstinacy as the iniquity of the teraphim.ᵐ
Because you have rejected the word of Jehovah,
  He hath rejected you from being king.ⁿ

²⁴And Saul said to Samuel, I have sinned, for I have transgressed the command of Jehovah and your words because I feared the people and listened to their voice. ²⁵Now therefore pardon my sin and turn back with me, that I may worship Jehovah. ²⁶But Samuel said to Saul, I will not turn back with you, for you have rejected the word of Jehovah and Jehovah hath rejected you from being king over Israel. ²⁷And as Samuel turned to go away, Saul seized the skirt of his robe, but it tore. ²⁸Then Samuel said to him, Jehovah hath to-day torn the kingdom of Israel from you and hath given it to your neighbor who is better than you.

Saul's confession and petition for mercy

ᵏ 13¹² Heb., *mollify the face of Jehovah.*
¹ 13¹³ Making a slight change in the Heb. to conform to the context.
ᵐ 15²³ The Heb. is confused. The above conforms to the parallelism and the reading of Symmachus. *The teraphim* is an allusion to the early use of household gods for divination.
ⁿ 15²³ Gk. adds, *over Israel;* but this may be taken from ²⁶ and it disarranges the rhythm. The words of Samuel are cast in rhythmical form, as are most of the sermons of the prophets.
ᵒ 13¹⁵ᵃ So Gk. Some copyist evidently mistook the second Gilgal for the first with the result that the intervening clauses have been omitted.

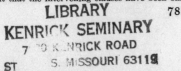

Later Ephraimite Samuel Narratives

[29]Moreover the Glory[p] of Israel will not lie nor repent; for he is not a man that he should repent.[q]   [30]Then he said, I have sinned, yet honor me now at least before the elders of my people and before Israel, and turn back with me, that I may worship Jehovah your God.   [31]So Samuel turned back and followed Saul, while Saul worshipped Jehovah.

[32]Then Samuel said, Bring here to me Agag the king of the Amalekites. And Agag came to him trembling.   And Agag said, Surely death is bitter.[r]   [33]And Samuel said, As your sword has bereaved women, so shall your mother be the most bereaved of women.   Thereupon Samuel hewed Agag in pieces before Jehovah in Gilgal.   [34]Then Samuel went to Ramah, but Saul went up to his house to Gibeah of Saul.   [35a]And Samuel saw Saul no more until the day of his death, for Samuel grieved over Saul.

Fate of Agag and Samuel's departure

§ 9. Summary of Saul's Reign, I Sam. 14[47-51]

Early Editorial Epitome

I Sam. 14 [47]Now when Saul had taken the kingdom over Israel, he fought against all his enemies on every side: against Moab and the Ammonites and Edom and Beth-rehob,[s] the king of Zobah and the Philistines; and wherever he turned he was victorious.[t]   [48]And he did mighty deeds and smote the Amalekites and delivered Israel out of the hands of its plunderers.

Saul's wars

[49]Now the sons of Saul were: Jonathan, Ishbaal,[u] and Malchishua.   And these are the names of his two daughters: the eldest, Merab, the youngest, Michal.   [50]And the name of Saul's wife was Ahinoam the daughter of Ahimaaz.   The name of the commander of his army was Abner the son of Ner, Saul's cousin.   [51]And Kish the father of Saul and Ner the father of Abner were sons of Abiel.

His family

---

[p] 15[29] The exact meaning of the Heb. word is doubtful.   *The Faithful One* (Syr. following context) and *the Victor* have been suggested.

[q] 15[29] For the older expression of this idea cf. Num. 23[19], from whence a later editor may have derived this verse.   Cf. also [11] of this chapter.   Originally [28], [29] were probably poetical in form.

[r] 15[32] Following Gk. and Luc.   The Heb. text has probably suffered from dittography. The current translation is not justified even by the Heb.

§ 9 The conclusion of the account of the great deliverance from the Philistines is interrupted by the insertion between [46] and [52] of a summary of Saul's wars and of the names of the important members of his family.   It corresponds to the summary of Samuel's activity in 7[15-17], of David's in II Sam. 8, and of Solomon's in I Kgs. 4[1]-5[14].   Its attitude toward Saul is sympathetic not critical, and there are none of the chronological data which are usually found in the corresponding epitomes from the hand of the late prophetic editor.   Its connection with the early Judean Saul narratives is evidently close.   The citations from them cease in 14 and it may have been their original conclusion, but more probably it is an editorial epitome based upon them.   A few of the facts, as for example, the references to the wars of the Moabites and Arameans and the name of Saul's wife are given only here, indicating that the editor probably had a fuller narrative before him.   It is difficult to determine its date.   The reference to the Amalekite war seems to be quite independent of 15.   It would appear, therefore, that his work antedated that of the editor who added the later Ephraimite narratives, for their contents are completely ignored.

[s] 14[47] Following the Gk. and Luc., *Edom* may be a mistaken reading for *Aram*.   Budde maintains that these references to Israel's foes are derived from the account of David's wars, II Sam. 8[3, 14].   The present record of Saul's reign is, however, too incomplete to justify such a negative conclusion.   Excepting in the three citations from his history, the tendency is to minimize the importance of his rule.

[t] 14[47] Gk. lit., *was delivered* by Jehovah.   The Heb., *acted impiously*, is evidently corrupt or else has been deliberately changed by a later scribe who had no sympathy with Saul.

[u] 14[49] So many Gk. MSS. and elsewhere, *e.g.*, II Sam. 2[8] and Introd., p. 42.   The name, because it contains the name of the heathen deity, *Baal*, is usually mutilated by later scribes. The word here translated *Ishvi* is for *Ish-Jahweh, man of Jehovah* instead of *man of Baal*.

II

THE DECLINE OF SAUL AND THE RISE OF DAVID,
I Sam. 15³⁵ᵇ–31¹³, I Chr. 10, 12¹⁻²²

§ 10. David's Introduction to Public Life, I Sam. 15³⁵ᵇ–17⁵⁴

Early Judean David Narratives | *Very Late Popular Prophetic Tradition*

David's introduction to the court of Saul

I Sam. 16 ¹⁴Now the spirit of Jehovah had departed from Saul and an evil spirit from Jehovah tormented him. ¹⁵And Saul's servants said to him, See now, an evil spirit from Jehovahª is tormenting you. ¹⁶Let your servants who are before you speak and they will seek for our lordᵇ a man skilful in playing the lyre. Then whenever the evil spiritᶜ comes upon you he shall play with his hand, and you will be better. ¹⁷Then Saul said to his servants,

15 ³⁵ᵇNow Jehovah repented that he had made Saul king over Israel, 16 ¹and Jehovah said to Samuel, How long wilt thou grieve over Saul, when I have rejected him from being king over Israel? Fill thy horn with oil and go. I will send thee to Jesse the Bethlehemite; for I have provided me a king among his sons. ²And Samuel said, How can I go, since Saul will hear of it and kill me? But Jehovah said, Take a calf with thee and say, ' To sacrifice to Jehovah am I come! ' ³And invite Jesse to the sacrifice, and I will show thee what thou shalt do, and anoint him whom I name to thee. ⁴And Samuel did that which Jehovah had commanded. And when he came to Bethlehem, the elders of the city came trembling to meet him and said, Does

The anointing of David by Samuel

The Decline of Saul and Rise of David.—Beginning with the sixteenth chapter of I Sam. and throughout II Sam. the interest of the narratives centres in David. Most of the material is evidently derived from the early Judean David history. Cf. Introd., pp. 10–12. With one or two exceptions, these extracts appear to stand in their original order. They have been supplemented, however, by variant versions of the more important incidents and by two or three additional stories. The interest in the variant versions is still focussed on David; but many details have been forgotten, while the element of the marvellous is more prominent than in the corresponding early narratives. Evidently they have been subject to a longer period of oral transmission. They represent the popular David traditions, probably current and first committed to writing in the southern kingdom. Cf. Introd., p. 14. From the large and varied cycle of David traditions the editors have selected and combined their material so effectively that the result is a remarkably vivid, sympathetic, and on the whole, consecutive account of David's life and deeds.

§ 10 The difficulties and contradictions in 16 and 17 have long been recognized. Thus, for example, in 16¹⁴⁻²³, David has already won fame as a warrior and has been appointed an armorbearer by Saul; but in 17¹²⁻³¹ he is but a lad, and in 17⁵⁵ not even his name is known to Saul and Abner. The explanation of the wide variations in representation is that these chapters contain at least three different accounts of David's introduction to public life. 16¹⁴⁻²³ is evidently the oldest and is the original continuation of the Judean narrative in 14. David the young shepherd, attractive, athletic, and skilled in the use of the sling, is brought to Saul's court, to soothe the king by his playing, whenever the latter was seized with what appears from the symptoms to have been attacks of either acute melancholia or epilepsy. There he quickly wins Saul's favor and is made his armorbearer.

Although not recognized as such by the majority of scholars, it seems probable that the sections of 17 found in both the Heb. and Gk. represent the original sequel of the preceding.

ª 16¹⁵ So Gk., Luc., and Targ. A later scribe, as in many other places, has substituted *God* in the Heb.

ᵇ 16¹⁶ So Gk. and Luc. Heb., *Let our Lord now command your servants, who are before you to seek, etc.*

ᶜ 16¹⁶ So Gk. The Heb. adds, *from God.*

Early Judean David Nar-
ratives

Very Late Popular Prophetic Tradition

Provide me now a man who plays well, and bring him to me. ^{18}Thereupon one of the young men answered and said, Behold, I have seen a son of Jesse the Bethlehemite who is skilful in playing and a valiant man, a soldier, judicious in speech, a man of good appearance, and Jehovah is with him. ^{19}Therefore Saul sent messengers to Jesse and said, Send me David your son, who is with the flock. ^{20}And Jesse took ten loaves^g of bread, and a skin of wine, and a kid, and sent them to Saul by David his son. ^{21}So David came to Saul and entered his ser-

your coming betoken good? ^{5}And he said Yes, to sacrifice to Jehovah am I come. Purify yourselves and rejoice^d with me in the sacrifice. And he purified Jesse and his sons and invited them to the sacrifice. ^{6}And when they came and he saw Eliab, he said, Surely in Jehovah's presence is his anointed.^{e} ^{7}But Jehovah said to Samuel, Look not on his appearance or on the height of his stature, since I have rejected him; for Jehovah doth not see^f as man sees, for man looks on the outward appearance, but Jehovah looks at the heart. ^{8}Then Jesse called Abinadab, and brought him before Samuel. But he said, Neither hath Jehovah chosen this one. ^{9}Then Jesse brought forward Shammah. But he said, Neither hath Jehovah chosen this one. ^{10}Then Jesse brought his seven sons before Samuel. But Samuel said to Jesse, Jehovah hath not chosen these. ^{11}And Samuel said to Jesse, Are these

---

David is already in the army, ^{54}, attendant upon Saul, ^{32}, and feels the responsibility of his new position. While he is a youth, as in 16$^{14-23}$, he is also more than the mere lad of the parallel version, otherwise the king would not have confidence in his ability to vanquish the Philistine, ^{37}, and have tried the experiment of putting upon him his own giant's armor, $^{38, 39}$. As might have been anticipated, it proves but a hindrance, *for he had not tried it.* Consequently he goes forth and wins his victory with the weapons natural to a peasant warrior, cf. Judg. 20^{16}. The point of view throughout is Judean, and the achievement is referred to subsequently in the Judean narratives, cf. 18^6, 19^5, 21^9, 22^{10}. The slaying of Goliath also best explains David's sudden leap into public favor and Saul's bitter jealousy. The fact that in II Sam. 21^{19} it is attributed to Elhanan the Bethlehemite does not absolutely invalidate the preceding conclusion, for II Sam. 21 evidently contains extracts from a popular cycle of traditions. Cf. § 34. Whatever be the historic fact, it seems clear that in two distinct traditions—one of which is the early Judean—David figured as the slayer of Goliath.

The second account of David's introduction to public life is found only in the Heb. version of 17. That it represents a recension distinct from the Gk. is demonstrated by analogies (cf. Introd., p. 14), by the fact that it was originally lacking in both of the leading Gk. texts, and because it is complete in itself and presents many variations from the older parallel. These are perfectly obvious: in ^{12} David is introduced as for the first time, he is but a stripling, and is unknown to Saul. It was probably the popular idealized version of the story preserved, like certain others in the appendix to Judges and II Sam. and in the book of Ruth, at Bethlehem in Judah and still later introduced into the O.T.

The third account is found in 16$^{1-13}$ and is closely related to the second, but yet it is distinct. In 17$^{17-29}$ the brothers know nothing of David's public anointing, recorded in 16$^{1-13}$. Three, rather than seven, brothers are mentioned. The introduction in 17^{12} would also be unnecessary after 16$^{1-13}$. The point of view of this latter section is also similar in many ways to that of the later Ephraimite Samuel narratives, but the prophet's fear of Saul in ^{2} is very different from his attitude in 15. That the story is very late and that it is modelled after the Judean account of the anointing of Saul in 9, 10 seem obvious. Its aim is to make clear David's divine call to the kingship. It was probably current in very late prophetic circles and by an exilic or post-exilic editor placed where it now stands. Cf. Introd., p. 13.

^{d} 16^5 So Gk. and old Lat. Heb. simply, *come.* The rejoicing was a prominent element in the ancient sacrificial feasts but was viewed askance by later Jewish scribes, who probably changed the Heb. text.

^{e} 16^6 Or, *Surely he is the prince of Jehovah, his anointed.*

^{f} 16^7 So Gk. and Luc. The Heb. omits, *doth Jehovah see.*

^{g} 16^{20} Cf. the parallel 17^{17}, *ten loaves.* The expression, lit., *an ass of bread,* is unprecedented. The text followed by the Gk. was unintelligible, but favors the correction adopted above. The corruption was due to a very slight error in the Heb.

Early Judean David Narratives

Very Late Popular Prophetic Tradition

vice;[h] and he loved him so much that he became one of his armorbearers. ²²And Saul sent to Jesse, saying, Let David enter my service, for he has found favor in my sight. ²³And whenever the evil spirit from God came upon Saul, David would take the lyre and play with his hand and Saul would breathe freely and would feel better and the evil spirit would depart from him.

all the young men? And he said, There is still the youngest, and he is a shepherd with the flock. Therefore Samuel said to Jesse, Send and bring him, for we will not sit down until he is brought here. ¹²So he sent and brought him in. Now he was ruddy, a youth with beautiful eyes and attractive appearance. And Jehovah said, Arise, anoint him, for he it is. ¹³Then Samuel took the horn of oil and anointed him in the midst of his brothers. And the spirit of Jehovah came with power upon David from that day forward. And Samuel arose and went to Ramah.

Popular Judean David Stories

Goliath's challenge to the Hebrews 17 ¹Now the Philistines mustered together their forces for war, and they were gathered together at Socoh, which belongs to Judah, and encamped between Socoh and Azekah, in Ephesdammim. ²And Saul and the men of Israel were gathered together and encamped in the valley of Elah; and they drew up in battle-array against the Philistines. ³And the Philistines were standing on the mountain on the one side, and the Israelites were standing on the mountain on the other side, and the valley was between them. ⁴And there came out a champion from the camp of the Philistines, named Goliath of Gath, whose height was about ten feet. ⁵And he had a helmet of bronze upon his head, and he was clad with a bronze breastplate of scales, the weight of which was about two hundred pounds.[i] ⁶And he had greaves

17 ¹²Now David was the son of an Ephrathite of Bethlehem in Judah, whose name was Jesse, and he had eight sons. And the man was old in the days of Saul, advanced in years among men. ¹³And the three eldest sons of Jesse had gone after Saul to the war; and the names of his three sons who went to the war were Eliab the eldest, his second Abinadab, and the third Shammah. ¹⁴But David was the youngest; and the three eldest had followed Saul. ¹⁵Now David went to and fro from Saul to feed his father's sheep at Bethlehem. ¹⁶And the Philistine drew near morning and evening and took his stand forty days. ¹⁷And Jesse said to David his son, Take now for your brothers a bushel of this parched grain and these ten loaves and carry them quickly to the camp to your brothers. ¹⁸But bring these ten cheeses to the commander of the thousand and look after your brothers' welfare and take a definite assurance from them. ¹⁹Now Saul and they and all the men of Israel are in the valley of Elah fighting with the Philistines.

Dav mis to t cam of S

---

[h] 16²¹, ²² Lit., *stand before me. I. e.*, became a trusted attendant. Cf. Gen. 41⁴⁶, I Kgs. 12⁸.

[i] 17⁴, ⁵, ⁷ According to the Heb. Goliath's height was six cubits and a span, and his breastplate weighed five thousand shekels, and his spear six hundred shekels. To make the picture definite the approximate modern equivalents are given.

Early Judean David Narratives | *Popular Judean David Stories*

of bronze upon his legs and a javelin of bronze between his shoulders. [7]And the shaft of his spear was like a weaver's beam, and the head of his iron spear weighed twenty-four pounds;[i] and his shield-bearer went before him. [8]And he stood and cried out to the ranks of Israel and said to them, Why have you come out to draw up the line of battle? Am not I a Philistine and you Saul's servants? Choose a man for yourselves and let him come down to me. [9]If he be able to fight with me and kill me, then will we be your servants; but if I prevail against him and kill him, then shall you be our servants and serve us. [10]And the Philistine said, I have insulted the ranks of Israel to-day; give me a man that we may fight together. [11]And when Saul and all Israel heard these words of the Philistine, they were terrified and greatly afraid.

[32]But David said to Saul, Let not my lord's courage[k] fail him; your servant will go and fight with this Philistine. [33]And Saul said to David, you are not able to go against this Philistine to fight with him, for you are only a youth and he has been a warrior from his youth. [34]But David said to Saul, Your servant was a shepherd with his father's flock; and when a lion, or a bear would come and take a lamb out of the flock, [35]I would go out after him and smite him and deliver it from his mouth; and if he rose up against me, I would seize him

[20]So David rose up early in the morning and left the flock with a keeper and took and went, as Jesse had commanded him. And he came to the entrenchment[j] just as the army was going forth to the battle-array, shouting the war cry. [21]And Israel and the Philistines drew up the line of battle, army confronting army. [22]And David left his vessels in the charge of the keeper of the baggage and ran to the line of battle and came and asked for the welfare of his brothers. [23]And just as he was talking with them, the champion, the Philistine of Gath, Goliath by name, came up out of the ranks of the Philistines and spoke the same words as before; and David heard them. [24]And all the men of Israel, when they saw the man, fled from him and were greatly afraid. [25]And the men of Israel said, Have you seen this man who has come up? Surely to insult Israel has he come up. Whoever smites him, the king will greatly enrich and will give him his daughter also and will make his father's house free in Israel.

[26]Then David spoke to the men who stood by him, saying, What shall be done to the man who smites that Philistine and takes away the reproach from Israel? For who is this uncircumcised Philistine, that he has dared to insult the armies of the living God? [27]And the people answered him in the words just given, saying, Thus shall it be done to the man who smites him. [28]But Eliab his eldest brother heard when he spoke to the men; and

[right margin: Goliath's challenge]

[left margin: David's offer to fight the Philistine]

i 17 ⁷ See note on previous page.
j 17²⁰ The word apparently means a barricade made of wagons. But there are no references to wagons in this early period. Budde acutely suggests that it is a later embellishment of this popular version of the story.
k 17³² So Gk. and Luc. Heb., *Let no man's courage*. But the context and other parallels favor the above.

Early Judean David Narratives

by his beard, and slay him with a blow.
[36]Your servant smote both lion and
bear. Now this uncircumcised Philistine shall be like one of them, since he
has insulted the armies of the living
God. [37]David also said, Jehovah who
delivered me from the paw of the lion,
and from the paw of the bear, will deliver me from the hand of this Philistine. Therefore Saul said to David,
Go, and may Jehovah be with you.
[38]And Saul clothed David with his garments, and put a helmet of bronze on
his head and clad him with a coat of
mail.[m] [39]And David girded his sword
over his coat and made a vain attempt
to go, for he had not tried them.[n] Then
David said to Saul, I cannot go with
these, for I have not tried them. And
David put them off him.

The duel

[40]And he took his club in his hand, and chose five
smooth stones out of the brook and put them in his
bag,[p] and took his sling in his hand, and he drew
near to the Philistine. [42]And when the Philistine
looked and saw David, he despised him, for he was
but a youth and ruddy, a young man of attractive appearance.[q] [43]And the Philistine said to David, Am
I a dog that you come to me with a club? And
the Philistine cursed David by his gods. [44]And the
Philistine said to David, Come to me that I may
give your flesh to the birds of the heavens and to
the beasts of the field. [45]Then David answered the
Philistine,

You come to me with a sword and a spear and a javelin,
But I come to you in the name of Jehovah of hosts,
And the God of the ranks of Israel whom you have insulted.
[46]To-day Jehovah will deliver you into my hands,
That I may smite you and cut off your head;

Popular Judean David Stories

Eliab's anger was kindled against
David, and he said, Why have you
come down? And with whom have
you left those few sheep[l] in the
wilderness? I know you well and
the wickedness of your heart; for
to see the battle you have come
down. [29]And David said, What
have I now done? Is it not a
matter of importance? [30]And
turning away from him to another, he spoke as before; and the
people answered him again as at
the first time. [31]And when the
words were heard which David
spoke, they reported them to Saul.
And they[o] took him and brought
him before Saul.

The duel

[41]But the Philistine
kept coming nearer to
David, and the man
who was bearing the
shield went before
him. [48b]Then David
quickly ran toward the
line of battle to meet
the Philistine. [50]And
David prevailed over
the Philistine with a
sling and with a stone
and smote the Philis-
tine, and slew him,
although there was no
sword in David's
hand. [55]And when
Saul saw David going
out against the Philis-

[l] 17[28] Lit., *morsel of a flock*. The tone of contempt is clear.
[m] 17[38] The last clause is not found in the Gk.
[n] 17[39] So Gk. and on the basis of a slight correction of the Heb.
[o] 17[31] So Luc. Heb., *and he took him*. Probably at this point a part of the secondary version has been lost, but it is nearly complete as it is, and Saul's ignorance of David's name and identity, revealed in [55], suggests that no conversation was recorded here as in the other account.
[p] 17[40] So Gk. A scribe has added the explanatory note, *in the shepherd's bag which he had*, and this has been incorporated in the Heb.
[q] 17[42] Apparently a gloss taken from 16[12].

Early Judean David Narratives

And I will this day give the dead of the army of the Philistines
To the birds of the heavens and to the wild beasts of the earth,
That all the world may know that there is a God in Israel,
⁴⁷And that all this assembly may know
That not with the sword and spear doth Jehovah save,
For the battle is Jehovah's and he will give you into our hand.ʳ

⁴⁸ᵃThen when the Philistine arose and came and drew near to meet David, ⁴⁹David put his hand in his bag and took from it a stone and slung it and smote the Philistine on his forehead; and the stone sank into his forehead, so that he fell on his face to the earth. ⁵¹Then David ran and stood over the Philistine, and took his sword, and drew it out of its sheath,ˢ and slew him, and cut off his head with it. And when the Philistines saw that their champion was dead, they fled. ⁵²And the men of Israel and Judah arose and raised the battle cry and pursued the Philistines to the entrance to Gath and to the gates of Ekron, so that the wounded of the Philistines fell down on the way from Shaaraim, even to Gath and Ekron. ⁵³And when the Israelites returned from pursuing the Philistines, they plundered their camp, ⁵⁴but David took the head of the Philistine and brought it to Jerusalem; and he put his armor in his tent.

Popular Judean David Stories

tine, he said to Abner, the commander of the army, Abner, whose son is this lad? And Abner said, As you live, O king, I cannot tell. ⁵⁶And the king said, Inquire whose son the young man is. ⁵⁷And when David returned from smiting the Philistine, Abner took him, and brought him before Saul with the Philistine's head in his hand. ⁵⁸And Saul said to him, Whose son are you, my lad? And David answered, I am the son of your servant Jesse the Bethlehemite.

§ 11. David's Growing Popularity and Saul's Insane Jealousy, I Sam. 18¹–19¹⁷

Early Judean David Narratives

avid's pu-rity d ul's ar of m

I Sam. 18 ⁶Now when they came back, as David returned from slaying the Philistine, the women came out dancing from all the cities of Israel to meet Saul the king with tambourines, with cries of rejoicing, and with cymbals.ᵗ ⁷And

Popular Judean David Stories

18 ¹Now when [David] had ceased speaking with Saul the soul of Jonathan was knit to the soul of David, and Jonathan loved

Jonathan's cove-nant with David and his great popularity

ʳ 17⁴⁵ᵇ⁻⁴⁷ Like most of the longer speeches in the historical books, the words of David are here expressed in poetry—the five-beat measure prevailing.
ˢ 17⁵¹ Not found in the Gk.
§ 11 Again the Gk. has a much briefer (18⁶⁻⁹, ¹²ᵃ, ¹³⁻¹⁶, ²⁰, ²¹ᵃ, ²²⁻²⁹ᵃ, 19) and yet complete and consistent text. Its contents, as well as the literary style, indicate that it is the original sequel of the early Judean David narratives in 16 and 17. The Heb. in 18 as in 17 evidently represents a different text which has been supplemented by extracts from a secondary source. They introduce inevitable confusion and contradictions into text. Thus in 18²⁰, ²¹ᵃ, consistent with the representation elsewhere, David is given Saul's daughter Michal as wife, but in ¹⁷⁻¹⁹ it is not Michal but Merab. The account in ¹⁰, ¹¹ of Saul's attempt to kill David, is a duplicate

ᵗ 18⁶ So Gk. The Heb. text has become slightly confused.

Early Judean David Narratives	Popular Judean David Stories

Early Judean David Narratives

the women sang to each other as they danced,ᵘ and said,

> Saul has slain his thousands,
> But David his ten thousands.ᵛ

⁸And it made Saul very angry, and this saying displeased him and he said, They ascribed to David ten thousands, while to me they ascribed but thousands, and what can he have more but the kingdom?ʷ ⁹And Saul kept his eye on David from that day forward. ¹²And Saul was afraid of David, because Jehovah was with him and had departed from Saul.ˣ ¹³Therefore Saul removed him from him, and made him his commander over a thousand; and he went out and came in at the head of the people. ¹⁴And David acted wisely and prosperedᵃ in all his ways, for Jehovah was with him. ¹⁵And when Saul saw that he acted wisely and prospered, he stood in dread of him. ¹⁶But all Israel and Judah loved David, for he went out and came in at their head.

His marriage with Michal

²⁰Michal, Saul's daughter, also loved David. And when they told Saul, he was pleased. ²¹And Saul said I will give her to him, that she

Popular Judean David Stories

him as his own life. ²And Saul took him that day and would not let him return to his father's house. ³And Jonathan made a covenant with David, because he loved him as his own life. ⁴And Jonathan stripped himself of the cloak which he had on and gave it to David and his military coat, even to his sword and to his bow and to his girdle. ⁵And David went out; in all for which Saul sent him, he acted wisely and with success, so that Saul appointed him over the warriors. And he was beloved alike by all the people and by the servants of Saul.

¹⁷And Saul said to David, See, my oldest daughter, Merab, her will

His promised marriage with Mera

---

almost word for word of the version in 19⁹, ¹⁰. Of these two, the one in 19⁹, ¹⁰ is evidently the older and in its true setting; while the secondary one in 18¹⁰, ¹¹ fits very awkwardly in its context, no sufficient motive being given for Saul's act; while the events recorded in 18¹⁷⁻¹⁹⁷ are hardly consistent with a previous open attempt upon David's life. It would seem that the later editor, who collected and introduced the secondary popular versions of the events, recognized the close resemblance between the two duplicates and therefore placed the later version as early in the narrative as possible. An analogous editorial treatment of duplicates has already been noted in 7–14 and in the pentateuchal books cf. Vol. I, § 18. The introductory formula in 18¹⁰, *now on the next day*, confirms the conclusion that originally it stood in a different context, part of which has been lost in the process of combination. The result is that the late popular version of David's experiences in Saul's court is not nearly as coherent as the early Judean.

19¹⁻¹⁷ appears to be the immediate sequel of the early Judean narrative in 18. It records the growing jealousy of Saul and its ever more active and open expression. The successive stages are vividly portrayed, until finally Saul flings the spear and then, in his anger, does not even regard the sanctity of David's home. The references to the killing of Goliath in ⁵ and to Michal in ¹¹⁻¹⁷ still further confirm the relationship to the older sections in 17 and 18. The statement regarding Jonathan's affection for David in 19¹ᵇ would have been quite unnecessary if it was originally a part of the secondary narratives in 18¹⁻⁴. 19², ³ alone seem to be editorial additions, for they are but a reflection of 20. Vs. ⁴ is also the natural sequel of ¹.

ᵘ 18⁷ *I.e.*, sang antiphonally accompanying their words by the dance as in the ancient ballad.

ᵛ 18⁷ The song of the women, like the riddles of Samson, has rhyme as well as rhythm and parallelism.

ʷ 18⁸ᵇ This last cause is lacking in the Gk. and has the characteristics of a late editorial addition.

ˣ 18¹²ᵇ This is not found in the Gk. and appears to be a late explanatory note, probably introduced from ¹⁴ᵇ.

ᵃ 18¹⁴, ¹⁵ The Heb. verb has the double meaning of acting wisely and of enjoying the success which results from such action.

Early Judean David Narratives

Popular Judean David Stories

may be a snare to him and that the hand of the Philistines may be upon him. Therefore Saul said to David, you shall this day be my son-in-law a second time.ᵇ ²²So Saul commanded his servants, saying, Communicate with David secretly and say, 'See, the king is pleased with you and all his servants love you; now therefore become the king's son-in-law.' ²³And Saul's servants spoke these words in the ears of David. And David said, Is it an easy thing in your opinion to become the king's son-in-law, when I am a poor man and of no reputation? ²⁴And the servants of Saul told him saying, David spoke thus. ²⁵And Saul said, Thus shall you say to David, 'The king desires no bride-price, but a hundred foreskins of the Philistines, in order to take vengeance on the king's enemies.' But Saul thought to make David fall by the hand of the Philistines. ²⁶And when his servants told David these words, David was well pleased with the prospect of being the king's son-in-law. And the days were not yet expired;ᵈ ²⁷and David arose and went together with his men and slew of the Philistines a hundredᶠ men; and David brought their foreskins and paid them in full to the king, in order to become the king's son-in-law. Therefore Saul gave him Michal his daughter as wife. ²⁸And when Saul saw and knew that Jehovah was with David and that all Israelᵍ loved him, ²⁹ᵃSaul feared David still more.

I give to you as wife; only be a valiant champion and fight Jehovah's battles. For Saul said to himself, Let not my hand be upon him, but let the hand of the Philistines be upon him. ¹⁸And David replied to Saul, Who am I, and what is my father's clan in Israel, that I should be the king's son-in-law? ¹⁹But when the time came that Merab, Saul's daughter, should have been given to David, she was given as wife to Adrielᶜ the Meholathite. ²⁹ᵇBut Saul remained hostile to David. ³⁰And the princes of the Philistines went forth; and as often as they went forth, David acted more wisely and with greater success than all the servants of Saul, so that his name was held in high repute.ᵉ

19 ¹And Saul commanded Jonathan his son and all his servants to put David to death. But Jonathan, Saul's son, was very fond of David. ²And Jonathan told David, saying, Saul my father is seeking to put you to death; now therefore, I pray you, take care in the morning and stay in concealment and hide yourself. ³And I will go out and stand beside my father in the field where you are, and I will converse regarding you with my father, and whatever I see I will tell you. ⁴And Jonathan spoke well of David to Saul his father,

¹⁰Now on the next day the evil spirit from God rushed upon Saul, and he became frenzied within the house,

Saul's insane attempt to kill David

ᵇ 18²¹ᵇ Not found in the Gk. and evidently an interpolation which anticipates what is stated subsequently. The reading of the last word is very doubtful. It may mean, *on two conditions*, but these are not expressed.

ᶜ 18¹⁹ Aram. form of the name. The Heb. is, *Esdriel*, cf. Jer. 36²⁶. Cf. II Sam. 21⁸ (Gk.). The Heb. makes him the husband of Michal.

ᵈ 18²⁶ᵇ Lacking in the Gk. and not supported by the context which suggests no time limit.

ᵉ 18³⁰ Heb., *was very precious*.

ᶠ 18²⁷ So Gk. Heb., *two hundred*. The change was doubtless due to the later tendency to idealize David's acts.

ᵍ 18²⁸ So Gk. Heb., *Michal, Saul's daughter*, repeated from ²⁰.

Early Judean David Narratives

Popular Judean David Stories

and said to him, Let not the king sin against his servant David, because he has not sinned against you and because his conduct toward you has been exceedingly good; [5]for he took his life in his hand and smote the Philistine, and Jehovah wrought a great deliverance for Israel. You saw it and rejoiced. Why then will you sin against innocent blood, in slaying David without a cause? [6]And Saul harkened to the voice of Jonathan; and Saul gave an oath, As Jehovah liveth, he shall not be put to death. [7]And Jonathan called David, and Jonathan made known to him all these words. And Jonathan brought David to Saul, so that he was again in his presence as formerly. [8]But when there was war again, David went out and fought against the Philistines, and slew great numbers of them, so that they fled before him. [9]Then an evil spirit from Jehovah came upon Saul, while he was sitting in his house with his spear in his hand, and David was playing on the lyre. [10]And Saul sought to pin David to the wall with the spear, but he slipped away out of Saul's presence, so that he smote the spear into the wall, and David fled and escaped.

while David was playing on the lyre[h] as he did each day. And Saul had his spear in his hand; [11]and he lifted up[i] the spear, saying to himself, I will pin David to the wall.[j] But David escaped from his presence twice.[k]

David's escape [11]And that night[l] Saul sent messengers to David's house to watch him, so as to kill him in the morning. But Michal, David's wife, told him, saying, If you do not save your life to-night, to-morrow you will be slain. [12]So Michal let David down through the window; and he fled away and escaped. [13]And Michal took the household god[m] and laid it in the bed, and put a cloth of goat's hair for its head and covered it with the garment. [14]And when Saul sent messengers to take David, she[n] said, He is sick. [15]Then Saul sent the messengers to see David, saying, Bring him up to me in the bed, that I may put him to death. [16]And when the messengers came in, there the household god was in the bed, with the cloth of goat's hair for its pillow. [17]And Saul said to Michal, Why have you deceived me thus, and let my enemy go, so that he has escaped? And Michal answered Saul, He said to me, ' Let me go; why should I kill you? '[o]

---

[h] 18¹⁰ Heb., *with his hand.*
[i] 18¹¹ So Gk. A, Luc., Targ. and a possible reading of the Heb.
[j] 18¹¹ Heb., *I will smite David and the wall.*
[k] 18¹¹ The meaning of the Heb. is exceedingly doubtful. It may have been added by an editor who recalled the parallel incident in 19⁹, ¹⁰ and wished to harmonize them. Possibly it also indicates that this duplicate once followed rather than preceded 19⁹, ¹⁰.
[l] 19¹¹ So Gk. and Luc. The present division of verses joins the clause, *that night*, to ¹⁰.
[m] 19¹³ Heb., *teraphim.* Cf. Vol. I, p. 115, note j.
[n] 19¹⁴ Gk., *they.*
[o] 19¹⁷ A common form of threat.

§ 12. **David as a Fugitive,** I Sam. 19^{18}–21^9, 22$^{1-5}$, 23$^{15-18}$

Early Judean David Narratives

I Sam. 20 ^{1b}Then [David] came and said before Jonathan, What have I done? What is my guilt? And what is my sin before your father, that he is seeking my life? ^{2}And he replied to him, Far be it! You shall not die. See, my father does nothing great or small, but that he discloses it to me; and why should my father hide this from me? Not so. ^{3}And David answered^p and said, Your father well knows that I have found favor in your eyes, and he is saying to himself, ' Let not Jonathan know this lest he be pained.' Nevertheless as surely as Jehovah liveth, and as you live, there is but a step between me and death. ^{4}Then Jonathan said to David, What do you desire to have me do for you? ^{5}And David answered Jonathan, Behold, to-morrow is the new moon and I should not fail to sit^q at the table with the king; therefore let me go and I will hide myself in the field^r until evening. ^{6}If your father misses me, then say, ' David urgently asked leave of me to run to Bethlehem his city; for the yearly sacrifice is there for all the family.' ^{7}If he says ' Good,' then it is well with your servant; but if it arouses his anger, then know that evil is determined upon by him. ^{8}Now

(marginal notes:) David's interview with Jonathan

---

§ 12 The events in 20$^{1-39}$ evidently followed immediately those recorded in 19$^{1-17}$. Before finally fleeing from the court of Saul, David, through Jonathan, whose friendship is attested in all the traditions, seeks to ascertain whether or not a reconciliation with the half-insane king is not still possible. Contents and literary style both indicate that the passage is from the early Judean David narratives. Its theme, however, lent itself readily to expansion and the story is told with unusual fulness. Certain scholars regard 4-17 as a later addition, but the evidence is not conclusive. The story may have been expanded, while still in the oral stage, and therefore have been recorded in its present form (excepting a few textual errors) in the early Judean David history.

The contents of 40-42, however, contradict the implication of the preceding verses, namely, that it was exceedingly dangerous for the two friends in the circumstances to speak directly with each other. If they could thus meet, the elaborate method of communicating recorded in the preceding verses was entirely needless. Their solemn covenant had already been made, 12-17, and farewells said. The passage, therefore, appears to be either an editorial expansion or else an extract from a later form of the tradition.

Still another popular version of the covenant between the two friends is found in 23$^{15-18}$. Vs. 15 is probably simply its editorial introduction intended to adjust it to its context with which, as a matter of fact, it has no real connection. The same elements of the tradition reappear here in somewhat magnified and idealized proportion. That David will be king is in 17 plainly assumed. This fourfold version of the covenant between David and Jonathan, 20$^{12, 17}$, 18$^{3, 4}$, 20$^{40-42}$, 23$^{15-18}$, recalls the fivefold version of the covenant with Abraham, in Gen. Cf. Vol. I, § 13.

That the account of David's flight to Samuel, recorded in 19^{18}–20^{1a}, is secondary is perfectly obvious. Not only does it contain a tradition regarding the proverb, *Is Saul among the prophets?* distinct from that given in the early Judean narratives of 10$^{11, 12}$, but it has no connection with the sober Judean history of David, which represents him as fleeing southward, 21$^{1-9}$, simply stopping to get food for himself and his followers at the sanctuary at Nob. The conception of Samuel and of the prophets as a class is clearly that of a much later period. Its point of view resembles that of the Ephraimite prophetic narratives, but 15^{35a} is contradicted by 19^{23}. Like the story in 16$^{1-13}$, it probably represents a tradition current in very late prophetic circles.

The early Judean narratives trace each step in the fortunes of David. After leaving Nob he found refuge in the stronghold at Adullam, probably located in the southeastern border of Judah, where his family joins him. For the classification of 21$^{10-15}$, cf. § 16. That he placed his father and mother under the protection of the neighboring Moabites is no more unusual than that he himself later sought refuge among Israel's enemies, the Philistines, so that there is no conclusive ground for regarding 22$^{3, 4}$ as secondary. The sudden introduction of the prophet Gad, however, in 5 in a rôle akin to that of Samuel in 8, 12, and 15, strongly suggests that the verse is from an editor, who thus brings David back from heathen soil at the command of a prophet.

p 20^3 So Gk. and Luc. The Heb. is corrupt and reads, *David swore again.*

q 20^5 The Gk. and Origen insert a negative and read, *and certainly will not sit, etc.* The new moon, like the sabbath, was observed by abstaining from all work. Cf. Am. 8^5, II Kgs. 4^{23}.

r 20^5 So Gk. and Luc. Heb. adds, *until the third day,* but this is not supported by the context and is in form ungrammatical.

Early Judean David Narratives

deal kindly with your servant, for you have brought your servant into a sacred[s] covenant with yourself; but if there be guilt in me, slay me myself, for why should you bring me to your father? ⁹And Jonathan said, Far be it from you! for if I should learn that my father had determined that evil should come upon you, I would tell you. ¹⁰Then David said to Jonathan, Who will tell me, if your father answers me harshly? ¹¹And Jonathan replied to David, Come, and let us go out into the field. So the two of them went out into the field.

The covenant between them

¹²And Jonathan said to David, Jehovah, the God of Israel, be witness that I will sound my father about this time to-morrow and if he be well disposed toward David, then I will send and disclose it to you.[t] ¹³God do to Jonathan whatever he will,[u] should my father be disposed to do you evil, and I disclose it not to you and send you away that you may go in peace. And may Jehovah be with you, as he has been with my father. ¹⁴And if I am yet alive, O may you show me the kindness of Jehovah! But if I should die, ¹⁵may you never withdraw your kindness from my house. And if, when Jehovah hath cut off the enemies of David, every one from the face of the earth, ¹⁶the name of Jonathan should be cut off by the house of David, may Jehovah require it at the hand of David's enemies.[v] ¹⁷So Jonathan took oath again to David,[w] because of his love to him; for with all his heart he loved him.

Their plan for communicating

¹⁸Then Jonathan said to him, To-morrow is the new moon and you will be missed, because your seat will be empty. ¹⁹And on the third day you will be greatly missed.[x] Then you shall come to the place where you hid yourself on the day of the affair,[a] and you shall sit down there beside the heap of stones.[b] ²⁰And on the third day I will shoot arrows on one side of it, as though I shot at a mark. ²¹Then, I will send the lad, saying, ' Go, find the arrows.' If I say to the lad, ' See, the arrows are on this side of you; pick them up!'—then come; for it is well for you, and, as Jehovah liveth, there is nothing the matter. ²²But if I say to the boy, 'See, the arrows are beyond you,' go, for then Jehovah sends you away. ²³And as to the word which you and I have spoken, behold, Jehovah is witness between you and me forever.

Discovery of Saul's feeling toward David

²⁴So David hid himself in the field; and when the new moon came, the king sat down at the table to eat. ²⁵And the king sat upon his seat as usual, even on the seat by the wall, and Jonathan sat opposite,[c] and Abner sat by Saul's side; but David's place was empty. ²⁶Nevertheless Saul did not say

---

[s] 20⁸ Heb., *covenant of Jehovah, i.e.*, sanctified and confirmed by Jehovah.
[t] 20¹² The Heb. is very obscure and the Gk. much simpler. The above reconstruction probably represents the thought of the original.
[u] 20¹³ So Gk. which follows the ancient formula of swearing. Cf. 3¹⁷, 23⁹. Heb., *Jehovah do so to Jonathan and more also.*
[v] 20¹⁶ Another exceedingly difficult passage. It seems to be the direct continuation of ¹⁵. Again the Gk. appears to have retained the original reading and has been followed. *Enemies*, in the last clause may be a later insertion. The sense is better without it.
[w] 20¹⁷ So Gk.
[x] 20¹⁹ The Heb. is corrupt. The Gk. has evidently retained a better reading.
[a] 20¹⁹ The event alluded to is unknown.
[b] 20¹⁹ Following the Gk. Heb., *by the stone of Ezel.*
[c] 20²⁵ So Gk. and Luc. Heb., *stood up.*

DAVID AS A FUGITIVE [I SAM. 20²⁶]

Early Judean David Narratives

anything that day, for he thought, It is an accident, he is not ceremonially clean, for he has not been cleansed.ᵈ ²⁷But when on the day following the new moon, David's place was empty, Saul said to Jonathan his son, Why has not the son of Jesse come to the meal, either yesterday or to-day? ²⁸And Jonathan answered Saul, David urgently asked leave of me to go to Bethlehem, ²⁹for he said, ' Let me go, since our family has a sacrifice in the city; and my brothersᵉ have commanded me. Now if I have found favor in your sight, let me slip away and see my kinsmen.' Hence he has not come to the king's table. ³⁰Then Saul's anger was kindled against Jonathan, and he said to him, Son of a depraved woman!ᶠ Do I not know that you are associated withᵍ the son of Jesse to your own shame and to the shame of your mother's nakedness? ³¹For as long as the son of Jesse lives on the earth, neither you nor your kingdom will be established. Therefore now send and bring him to me, for he is doomed to die.ʰ ³²Then Jonathan answered Saul his father and said to him, Why should he be put to death? What has he done? ³³But Saul lifted up his spear at him to smite him. So Jonathan knew that his father had determined to put David to death. ³⁴Therefore Jonathan rose from the table in hot anger and ate no food the second day of the month, for he was grieved for David,ⁱ because his father reviled him.

Popular Judean David Stories

The warning and secret interview

³⁵But in the morning Jonathan went out into the field at the time appointed with David, and a little lad with him. ³⁶And he said to his lad, Run, find now the arrows which I shoot. And as the lad ran, he shot an arrow beyond him. ³⁷And when the lad came to the place where the arrow which Jonathan had shot lay, Jonathan cried after the lad, and said, Is not the arrow beyond you? ³⁸And Jonathan cried after the lad, Hurry, quick, do not stop! So Jonathan's lad gathered up the arrows, and brought them to his master. ³⁹But the lad had no knowledge of anything; only Jonathan and David understood the matter. ⁴⁰And Jonathan gave his weapons to his lad, and said to him, Go, carry them to the city. ⁴¹And as soon as the lad had gone, David rose from beside the stone heap,ʲ and fell on his face to the ground and prostrated himself three times, and they kissed each other and wept at length

I Sam. 23 ¹⁵Now David feared because Saul had come out to seek his life; and David was in the Wilderness of Ziph in Horesha. ¹⁶And Jonathan, Saul's son, arose, and went to David in Horesha and strengthened his hand in God. ¹⁷And he said to him, Fear not, for the hand of Saul my father shall not find you, and you shall be king over Israel and I shall be

ᵈ 20²⁶ So Gk. The Heb. is a mere repetition.
ᵉ 20²⁹ So Gk. and Luc. Heb., *my brother.*
ᶠ 20³⁰ The Heb. is doubtful. It may mean, *son of depravity,* or *perverseness,* or, after the Gk., *son of an escaped slave girl.* It is not intended, however, to reflect at all on the mother, but only on the person addressed.
ᵍ 20³⁰ So Gk. and Luc. Owing to the transposition of one letter the Heb. reads, *You have chosen.*
ʰ 20³¹ Heb., *he is a son of death.*
ⁱ 20³⁴ The Gk. omits, *for he was grieved for David.* It may be a later addition.
ʲ 20⁴¹ So Gk. and the corrected Heb. text.

91

Early Judean David Narratives

Popular Judean David Stories

with each other.[k] [42]Then Jonathan said to David, Go in peace! As to what we two have sworn in the name of Jehovah—Jehovah will be between me and you and between my descendants and your descendants forever. Then David rose and departed and Jonathan went into the city.

next to you; and that also Saul my father well knows. [18]And they two made a covenant before Jehovah; and David abode in Horesha, and Jonathan returned home.

Very Late Popular Prophetic Tradition

David's flight to the priests at Nob

21 [1]And David came to Nob, to Ahimelech the priest. And Ahimelech came trembling to meet David and said to him, Why are you alone and no one with you? [2]And David answered Ahimelech the priest, The king has entrusted me with a matter and has said to me, ' Let no one know anything about the matter upon which I am sending you and which I have commanded you;' and I have directed the young men to meet me at a certain place. [3]Now, therefore, if you have five loaves of bread at hand, or whatever can be found,[m] give it to me. [4]And the priest answered David, saying, There is no ordinary bread at hand, but there is holy bread, if only the young men have kept themselves from women.[n] [5]And David answered the priest and said to him, Of a truth women have been kept from us; as always when I set out on an expedition, the weapons[o] of the young men were consecrated, though it is but an ordinary journey; how much more then to-day shall their weapons be holy![p] [6]So the priest gave him holy bread, for there was no bread there but the showbread,[r]

I Sam. 19 [18]Now David fled and escaped and came to Samuel to Ramah and told him all that Saul had done to him. And he and Samuel went and remained in Naioth.[l] [19]And when it was told Saul, saying, David is there at Naioth in Ramah, [20]Saul sent messengers to take David. But when they saw the company of the prophets prophesying with Samuel standing as head over them, the spirit of God came upon the messengers of Saul, so that they also prophesied. [21]And when it was told Saul, he sent other messengers, and they also prophesied. And Saul sent messengers again the third time, and they also prophesied. [22]Then Saul's anger was aroused[q] and he himself went to Ramah. And when he came to the cistern of the

David flight to Samuel at Ramah

---

[k] 20⁴¹ RV, *until David exceeded, i.e.*, came out ahead in the weeping contest. The idea is, to say the least, peculiar. The Gk. omits *David*, and suggests the above reading.

[l] 19¹⁸ The meaning of this word is unknown. It may come from the root, *to dwell*.

[m] 21³ Heb., *What is under your hand? give me five loaves of bread in my hand or whatever is found.*

[n] 21⁴ The Heb. omits, as frequently, the apodosis; Gk. and Luc. add, *that they might eat.*

[o] 21⁵ Or, *bodies*. Gk., *all of the young men.*

[p] 21⁵ The passage is exceedingly difficult, although the general sense is clear.

[q] 19²² So Gk. The clause, *Saul's anger was aroused*, has apparently dropped out of our present Heb. text.

[r] 21⁶ *I.e.*, the bread set before Jehovah in the sanctuary. Lit., *bread of the presence.*

Early Judean David Narratives

Very Late Popular Prophetic Tradition

that was taken from before Jehovah in order to put hot bread there the day it was taken away. ⁷Now one of the servants of Saul was there that day, detained before Jehovah,ᵗ by the name of Doeg, an Edomite, the chief of Saul's herdsmen.ᵘ ⁸And David said to Ahimelech, Have you not here at hand a spear or sword? For I brought neither my sword nor my weapons with me, because the king's matter required haste. ⁹And the priest said, The sword of Goliath the Philistine, whom you slew in the valley of Elah, there it is wrapped in a garment behind the ephod. If you wish to take that, take it, for there is no other except that here. And David said, There is none like that, give it to me.

threshing floor, which is on the bare height,ˢ he asked, saying, Where are Samuel and David? And one said, There they are at Naioth in Ramah. ²³But when he went thither to Naioth in Ramah, the spirit of God also came upon him, and he went along prophesying, until he came to Naioth in Ramah. ²⁴And he also stripped off his clothes and prophesied before Samuel, and lay naked all that day and all that night. Therefore they say, Is Saul also among the prophets?ᵛ 20 ¹ªThen David fled from Naioth in Ramah.ʷ

22 ¹David therefore departed thence and escaped to the strongholdˣ of Adullam. And when his brethren and all his father's clan heard it, they went down there to him. ²And every one who was in distress, and every one who was in debt, and every one who was embittered gathered about him, and he became their leader.ª And there were with him about four hundred men.

³And David went from there to Mizpeh in Moab; and he said to the king of Moab, Let my father and my mother dwell withᵇ you, until I know what God will do for me. ⁴And he left them in the presenceᶜ of the king of Moab; and they dwelt with him all the while that David was in the stronghold. ⁵And the prophet Gad said to David, Do not remain in Mizpeh;ᵈ depart and come into the land of Judah. Then David departed and came into the forest of Hereth.

David as an outlaw leader

His parents with the king of Moab

ˢ 19²² So Gk. and Luc. Heb., *to the great cistern which is in Secu.*
ᵗ 21⁷ Because of some ceremonial obligation.
ᵘ 21⁷ Gk., *muleherd.*
ᵛ 19²⁴ For the older tradition regarding the origin of the proverb, cf. 10¹⁰, § 6.
ʷ 20¹ª Evidently from the editor and intended to introduce the narrative which follows in 20.
ˣ 22¹ Heb., *cave;* but the parallels in II Sam. 23¹³, I Chr. 11¹⁵, and the reference in ⁴ demand the very similar Heb. word meaning, *stronghold.*
ª 22² Cf. the similar band of outlaws who gathered about Jephthah, Judg. 11³.
ᵇ 22³ So Syr. and Lat. Gk., *be.* A scribal error in the Heb. gives the unnatural reading, *come forth.*
ᶜ 22⁴ So Syr., Lat., Targ., and a slightly modified reading of the Heb.
ᵈ 22⁵ So Syr. Heb., *stronghold*, but according to 23³ the stronghold of Adullam was in Judah. The change of one letter gives the harmonious reading followed above.

§ 13. Saul's Vengeance upon the Priests of Nob, I Sam. 22⁶⁻²³

Early Judean David Narratives

Doeg's malicious testimony

I Sam. 22 ⁶Now when Saul heard that David and the men with him were discovered (Saul was sitting in Gibeah, under the tamarisk-tree on the high place,ᵉ with his spear in his hand, and all his servants were standing about him),ᶠ ⁷Saul said to his servants who were standing before him, Hear O Benjamites! Will the son of Jesse likewise give you all fields and vineyards? Will he make you all commanders of thousands and commanders of hundreds, ⁸that all of you have conspired against me, and no one discloses to me that my son has made a covenant with the son of Jesse, and none of you has pityᵍ upon me or discloses to me that my son has stirred up my servant to be an enemy against me,ʰ as is now the case? ⁹Then Doeg the Edomite, who was standing by the servants of Saul, answered and said, I saw the son of Jesse coming to Nob, to Ahimelech the son of Ahitub. ¹⁰And he inquired of Godⁱ for him and gave him provisions and the sword of Goliath the Philistine.

Slaughter of the priests

¹¹Then the king summoned Ahimelech the priest, the son of Ahitub, and all his father's house, the priests who were in Nob, and they came all of them to the king. ¹²And Saul said, Hear now, O son of Ahitub! And he answered, Here am I, my lord! ¹³And Saul said to him, Why have you, together with the son of Jesse, conspired against me, in that you have given him bread and a sword and have inquired of God for him, that he should rise against me as an enemy,ʰ as is now the case? ¹⁴Then Ahimelech answered the king and said, But who among all your servants is like David, trusted and the king's son-in-law and captain over your retainersʲ and honored in your household? ¹⁵Is this the first time I have inquired of God for him? Far be it from me! Let not the king impute anything to his servant nor to any one of my clan, for your servant did not know the slightest thing about all this. ¹⁶But the king said, You shall surely die, Ahimelech, together with all your clan. ¹⁷And the king said to the runners who stood before him, Turn about and slay the priests of Jehovah, for their hand also was with David, and, although they knew that he was fleeing, they did not disclose it to me. But the servants of the king would not put forth their hands to strike down the priests of Jehovah. ¹⁸Then the king said to Doeg, Turn and strike down the priests. And Doeg the Edomite turned and himself

---

§ 13 While one or two new facts, as, for example, that Ahimelech inquired of Jehovah for David, ¹⁰, are found in 22⁶⁻²³, and not in 21¹⁻⁹, the points of correspondence are so many and close between the two sections that it is difficult to believe, as has sometimes been maintained, that they are not from the same source; the former indeed is the immediate sequel of the latter. The *sword of Goliath* also figures in both, 21⁹ and 22¹³. Abiathar likewise reappears in the subsequent early Judean David narratives, *e.g.*, 23⁶, II Sam. 15²⁹, ³⁵, ³⁶. The natural representation and the vivid style strongly confirm the conclusion that it was taken from the early Judean David narratives.

ᵉ 22⁶ So Gk. and Luc. It was the place of public assembly. Cf. 9¹². The Heb. has the impossible reading, *Ramah*.

ᶠ 22⁶ A long interjected descriptive clause, not uncommon in Heb.

ᵍ 22⁸ Heb., *is sick for.*

ʰ 22⁸, ¹³ So Gk. Heb., *to be in wait.*

ⁱ 22¹⁰ So Syr., Gk., and Luc., and in ¹³, ¹⁵ᶠᶠ. Heb., *Jehovah.*

ʲ 22¹⁴ So Gk., Luc., and Targ. The current translation, *is taken into thy councils*, is hardly tenable.

Early Judean David Narratives

struck down the priests. So he slew on that day eighty-five men who wore the ephod.[k] [19]And the priestly city Nob he put to the sword, both men and women, children and infants, oxen and asses and sheep.[l]

[20]And one of the sons of Ahitub the son of Ahimelech, named Abiathar, escaped and fled to David.[m] [21]And Abiathar told David that Saul had slain the priests of Jehovah. [22]And David said to Abiathar, I knew that day, because Doeg the Edomite was there, that he would surely tell Saul. I myself am guilty[n] of all the lives of your clan. [23]Remain with me, fear not; for whoever seeks your life must also seek mine,[o] since you are placed in my charge.

Abiathar's escape

§ 14. Saul's Pursuit and David's Magnanimity, I Sam. 23[1-14, 19-29], 24, 26

Early Judean David Narratives

Disclosure of David's hiding-place to Saul

I Sam. 23 [1]Now when David was told, The Philistines are fighting against Keilah and are robbing the threshing floors, [2]David inquired of Jehovah, saying, Shall I go and attack these Philistines? And Jehovah said to David, Go, attack the Philistines, and save Keilah. [3]But David's men said to him, Behold we are afraid here in Judah; how much more

Popular Judean David Stories

23 [19]Then the Ziphites came up to Saul to Gibeah, saying, Is not David hiding himself with us in the strongholds in Horesha, in the hill of Hachilah, which is to the south of the desert?[p] [20]Now therefore, O king, according to all your heart's desire come down, and it shall be our part to

---

[k] 22[18] So Gk. and Luc. The Heb. adds, *linen*.

[l] 22[19] Probably an editorial expansion of the story. The language is closely parallel to that of 15[3], which is a late account of the destruction of the Amalekites. The early narratives contain no references to the complete destruction of an Israelite town.

[m] 22[20] The original probably added, *and brought the ephod with him*. Cf. the omission of all reference to the ephod in 14[18].

[n] 22[22] So Gk., Luc., and Syr. One letter in the Heb. has evidently been changed through a copyist's error, so that at present it is untranslatable.

[o] 22[23] Restoring that which must have been the original order in this sentence.

§ 14 23[1-14a] is the direct continuation of the Judean narrative in 22. Abiathar the priest, who alone escaped from the slaughter of the priests at Nob, is present in David's camp, [9]. The language and spirit are characteristic of the early David stories.

Chaps. 23[19]-24[23] and 26 contain what appear clearly to be variant versions of the same incident. In both the Ziphites offer to betray David to Saul, and the geographical background is the same. In each, Saul, while pursuing him, is at the mercy of David, who spares the life of the king because of his regard for the anointed of Jehovah. Both recount much the same conversation between the two which results in their temporary reconciliation. The variations are no more striking than appear in the different versions of events found in Gen.-Judg.

Both versions have many of the expressions and ideas characteristic of the Judean school. Chap. 26 appears to be the older and 23[19]-24[23] the later popular version of the story. Thus in 23[19]-24[23] the tradition has been expanded at several points: 23[19-24] tell at length, and with much repetition, of the preliminary negotiations between the Ziphites and Saul, and 24[8-22] has a long account of the conversation between Saul and David in which ideas peculiar to later Hebrew thought (cf. especially [20, 21]) are prominent. On the other hand, the shorter narrative in 26 is much more circumstantial and individual names are preserved. Cf., for example, 26[6, 8] and 24[5, 7]; 26[5, 14] and 24[4, 6]. David's daring visit to Saul's camp is much more natural; while the version in 24, which represents Saul as falling completely into David's power, exalts the magnanimity of the Judean hero and again strongly suggests a popular tradition. The expression and representation in 23[19]-24[23] are also much less refined. Cf. 24[3, 15]. The religious conceptions of 26 are the more primitive. Cf., *e.g.*, 26[19, 20] and 24[21, 22].

Chap. 26 probably once followed immediately after 23[14a] and was removed from this position by a later editor who preferred the fuller version, and who was, perhaps, also influenced by the prominent mention of Maon in both 23[24-28] and 25. As often in Gen. and Sam. the older parallel was preserved by assigning it to another setting.

[p] 23[19] In 26[1] the hill of Hachilah is east of the desert of Judah (Jeshimmon). The variation and tautology suggest that the second part of this verse is from a late editor.

Early Judean David Narratives

then if we go to Keilah against the armies of the Philistines. [4]Then David inquired of Jehovah yet again. And Jehovah answered him, saying, Arise, go down to Keilah, for I will deliver the Philistines into thy hand. [5]So David and his men went to Keilah, and fought with the Philistines and drove away their cattle and slew a great many of them. Thus David delivered the inhabitants of Keilah. [6]Now when Abiathar the son of Ahimelech fled to David to Keilah, he came down with the ephod in his hand.[q] [7]And when it was told Saul that David had come to Keilah, Saul said, God has sold him into my hand; for he has entrapped himself[s] in entering into a town that has doors and bars.

David's escape

[8]And Saul summoned all the people to war, to go down to Keilah, to besiege David and his men. [9]And when David knew that Saul was devising evil against him, he said to Abiathar the priest, Bring here the ephod. [10]And David said, O Jehovah, the God of Israel, thy servant hath surely heard that Saul is seeking to come to Keilah, to destroy the city because of me. [11]Will Saul come down, as thy servant hath heard?[u] O Jehovah, God of Israel, I beseech thee, tell thy servant. And Jehovah said, He will come down. [12]Then David said, Will the men of Keilah deliver me and my men into the hand of Saul? And Jehovah said, They will deliver thee up. [13]Then David and his men, who were about six hundred, arose and departed from Keilah, and wandered hither and thither. And when it was reported to Saul that David had escaped from Keilah, he abandoned his expedition. [14]So David dwelt in the wilderness

Popular Judean David Stories

deliver him into the king's hand. [21]Then Saul said, Blessed may you be of Jehovah, for you have had compassion on me. [22]Go, I pray, make yet more sure, and know and see the place where his haunt is and who has seen him there; for I am told that he is very cunning. [23]See therefore, and gain knowledge of all the lurking-places where he hides, and return to me, with sure information, and I will go with you, and, if he be in the land, I will search him out of all the thousands of Judah.[r]

[24]So they arose and went to Ziph before Saul. But David and his men were in the Wilderness of Maon, in the Arabah to the south of the desert. [25]And when Saul and his men went to seek him, they told David and he went down to the rock which is in the Wilderness of Maon. And when Saul heard, he pursued after[t] David in the Wilderness of Maon. [26]And Saul went on the one side of the mountain and David and his men on the other side of the mountain; and David was anxiously trying to escape from Saul, for Saul and his men were about to surround David and his men, to seize them, [27]when a messenger came to Saul, saying, Come quickly, for the Philistines have made a raid upon the land. [28]So Saul returned from pursu-

[q] 23[6] Following the order of the Gk. and Luc. The verse was probably inserted in its present position by a later editor who recognized the omission in 22[20] and wished to prepare the reader for the introduction of Abiathar with the ephod in [9].

[r] 23[23] The verse has probably been expanded by a scribe. The Gk. has a much briefer text.

[s] 23[7] So Gk. and the restored Heb. text.

[t] 23[25] Following the Gk., the Heb. text has been slightly changed, so that it reads, *and dwelt in*.

[u] 23[11] A scribe by mistake introduced the question in [12], also at the beginning of [11]. It is not found in the Gk. and has been omitted in the translation.

Early Judean David Narratives   *Popular Judean David Stories*

in the strongholds and remained in the hill-country in the Wilderness of Ziph. And Saul sought him continually, but Jehovah[w] did not deliver him into his hand. [x]

ing after David and went against the Philistines; therefore they called that place, Rock of the Divisions.[v] ²⁹And David went up thence, and dwelt in the strongholds of Engedi.

---

ul's
ursuit
Da-
d in
e wil-
rness

26 ¹Then the Ziphites came to Saul at Gibeah, saying, Is not David hiding in the hill of Hachilah, which is east of the desert? ²Accordingly Saul arose, and went down to the Wilderness of Ziph, having three thousand men of Israel with him, to seek David in the Wilderness of Ziph. ³And Saul encamped in the hill of Hachilah, which is east of the desert on the way. But David remained in the wilderness. And when he saw that Saul was pursuing him into the wilderness, ⁴David sent out spies and learned that Saul had come from Keilah.[a] ⁵And David arose and came to the place where Saul had encamped. And David saw the place where Saul with Abner the son of Ner, the commander of his army lay, and Saul lay within the barricade,[b] and the people were encamped around about him.

avid's
gard
̄
ul's
e

⁶Then David spoke and said to Ahimelech the Hittite and to Abishai the son of Zeruiah, Joab's brother, saying, Who will go down with me to Saul to the camp? And Abishai said, I will go down with you. ⁷So David and Abishai came to the people by night; and Saul was lying there asleep within the barricade, with his spear stuck into the earth at his head, with Abner and the people lying around about him. ⁸Then Abishai said to David, God has delivered your enemy into your hand to-day. Now therefore let me smite him with his spear to the earth at one stroke, and I will not need to smite him twice!

24 ¹And when Saul returned from following the Philistines, it was told him, saying, See, David is in the Wilderness of Engedi. ²Then Saul took three thousand men chosen from all Israel and went to seek David and his men upon the Wild Goats' Crags. ³And he came to the sheepfolds by the way, and there was a cave. And Saul went in to cover his feet, while David and his men were staying in the recesses of the cave.

⁴ᵃAnd the men of David said to him, See this is the day of which Jehovah said to you, ' Behold, I give thine enemy into thy hand and thou shalt do to him as thou pleasest.'[c] ⁶And he said to his men, Jehovah forbid that I should do this thing to my lord, Jehovah's anointed, to put forth my hand against him, since

---

[v] 23²⁸ The implication is that it was so called because the two forces separated from each other at this point. In connection with this rock the story was probably preserved, because, like many of the traditions of Gen., it gave the popular derivation of its name.

[w] 23¹⁴ So Gk. Heb., *God.*

[x] 23¹⁴ᵇ The direct continuation of 14ᵃ is found in 26¹. Vs. ¹⁴ᵇ appears to be a general explanatory gloss.

[a] 26⁴ So Gk. The preceding verb demands the name of some place. The Heb. is evidently corrupt and gives no help.

[b] 26⁵ Cf. 17²⁰, § 10, note ʲ.

[c] 24⁴ᵃ⁻⁷ The original order has evidently been disarranged in transmission, or else ⁴ᵇ, ⁵ represent a later marginal expansion of the story which has been introduced in the wrong place.

Early Judean David Narratives

Popular Judean David Stories

⁹But David said to Abishai, Destroy him not; for who can lay his hand upon Jehovah's anointed and be innocent? ¹⁰And David said, As Jehovah liveth, either Jehovah shall smite him, or his day shall come to die, or he shall go down into battle and be destroyed. ¹¹Jehovah forbid that I should put forth my hand against Jehovah's anointed; but now take the spear that is at his head and the jug of water and let us go. ¹²So David took the spear and the jug of water from Saul's head and they departed. And no man saw it or knew it neither did any awake, for they were all asleep because a deep sleep from Jehovah had fallen upon them.

he is Jehovah's anointed. ⁷ᵃSo David upbraidedᵈ his men with these words, and did not permit them to attack Saul. ⁴ᵇThen David arose, and secretly cut off the skirt of Saul's mantle. ⁵But afterward David was seized with remorse because he had cut off Saul's skirt.

His words to Saul

¹³Then David went over to the other side and stood on the top of a mountain at a distance, a great space being between them. ¹⁴And David cried to the people and to Abner, the son of Ner, saying, Do you make no answer Abner? Then Abner answered and said, Who are you that calls?ᵉ ¹⁵And David said to Abner, Are you not a man? And who is like you in Israel? Why then have you not kept guard over your lord the king? For one of the people came to destroy your lord. ¹⁶This that you have done is not good. As Jehovah liveth, you are deserving of death,ʰ because you have

⁷ᵇAnd when Saul rose from the cave and went on his way, ⁸David also rose after him and went from the cave and cried after Saul, saying, My lord the king. And when Saul looked behind him, David bowed his face to the earth, and did obeisance. ⁹And David said to Saul, Why did you listen to the words of the men who said, 'See, David seeks your hurt?' ¹⁰To-day your eyes see that Jehovah gave you into my hand in the cave, but I refused to kill youᶠ and had pity on you, and I said, 'I will not put forth my hand against my lord, for he is Jehovah's anointed.' ¹¹Moreover, my father, see the skirt of your mantle in my hand, for in that I cut off the skirt of your mantle and did not kill you, know and see that there is neither evil nor guilt on my hands, and I have not sinned against you, though you are aiming to take my life. ¹²Jehovah judge between me and you; but my hand shall not be upon you. ¹³As runs the proverb of the ancients,

Out of the wicked cometh forth wickedness.ᵍ

But my hand shall not be raised against you. ¹⁴After whom is the king of Israel come out? After whom are you pursuing? After a dead

---

ᵈ 24⁷ᵃ Heb., *tear, rend.* Gk., *persuaded.*
ᵉ 26¹⁴ So Gk. The Heb. adds, *to the king,* but this is not supported by the context.
ᶠ 24¹⁰ Following the suggestion of the Gk. in restoring the otherwise incorrect Heb. Lat., *and I thought to kill you.*
ᵍ 24¹³ The infelicitous introduction of the proverb is further evidence of the popular embellishment of the story.
ʰ 26¹⁶ Heb., *children of death.*

Early Judean David Narratives | *Popular Judean David Stories*

not kept watch over your lord, Jehovah's anointed. And now see where the king's spear is and the jug of water that was at his head.

[17]Then Saul recognized David's voice and said, Is this your voice, my son David? And David said, It is my voice, my lord, O king. [18]And he said, Why is my lord pursuing his servant? For what have I done? Or of what kind of evil have I been guilty? [19]Now therefore let my lord the king hear the words of his servant. If Jehovah hath stirred you up against me, let him accept an offering;[j] but if they be men, cursed be they before Jehovah, for they have driven me out to-day, so that I have no part in the inheritance of Jehovah, saying, ' Go serve other gods.' [20]Now therefore, may my blood not fall to the earth far away from the presence of Jehovah, for the king of Israel has come out to seek my life, as one hunts a partridge[k] on the mountains. [21]Then Saul said, I have done wrong; return, my son David, for I will do you no more harm, because my life was regarded as sacred by you[m] to-day. I have acted foolishly and have erred exceedingly. [22]And David answered and said, There is the king's spear! Let one of the young men come over and take it. [23]And Jehovah will reward each man's righteousness and fidelity; for Jehovah delivered you into my hand to-day, but I would not raise my hand against Jehovah's anointed. [24]And just as your life was to-day of great value in my sight, so may my life be of great value in Jehovah's sight, and let him deliver me out of all affliction. [25]Then Saul said to David, Be blessed, my son David; you shall do great things and

dog? After a flea? [15]Jehovah therefore be judge and decide between me and you and see and plead my cause and obtain justice for me from you.

[16]Now when David had finished speaking these words to Saul, Saul said, Is this not your voice, my son David? Then Saul lifted up his voice and wept. [17]And he said to David, You are more righteous than I, for you have done to me that which is good, while I have done to you that which is evil. [18]And you have done great good to me in that to-day,[i] when Jehovah had shut me up in your hand, you did not kill me. [19]For when a man finds his enemy, does he send him on his way safe and sound?[l] Therefore may Jehovah reward you richly for what you have done to me this day. [20]And now see, I know that you will surely be king, and that through you the kingdom of Israel shall be established. [21]Swear now therefore to me by Jehovah, that you will not cut off my descendants after me and that you will not destroy my name from my father's house. [22]So David took oath to Saul.

[margin: aul's ply]

---

i 24[18] Heb., *And you have declared to-day.* A slight emendation gives the above reading, which is much more intelligible and consonant with the context.

j 26[19] Lit., *inhale, i.e.,* be appeased by an offering.

k 26[20] So Gk. texts. Heb. has, *a flea,* which hardly fits the context here. It was probably introduced from 24[15]. Or, making a slight change in the text, *as the eagle hunts the partridge.*

l 24[19] Heb., *on a good way.*

m 26[21] Heb., *was precious in your eyes.*

99

Early Judean David Narratives	*Popular Judean David Stories*
shall surely succeed! So David went his way, but Saul returned to his place.	And Saul went to his home; but David and his men went up to the stronghold.

§ 15. David and Abigail, I Sam. 25[1b-44]

Early Judean David Narratives

Nabal the Calebite

I Sam. 25 [1b]Then David arose and went into the Wilderness of Maon.[n] [2]And there was a man in Maon, whose business was in Carmel. And the man was very rich, and he had three thousand sheep and a thousand goats, and he was shearing his sheep in Carmel. [3]Now the man's name was Nabal; and his wife's name was Abigail; and the woman was sensible and comely, but the man was rough and ill-mannered; and he was a Calebite.

David's message to him

[4]And David heard in the wilderness that Nabal was shearing his sheep. [5]And David sent ten young men, and David said to the young men, Go up to Carmel and enter Nabal's house and greet him in my name; [6]and you shall say to him and to his clan,[o] 'Peace be to you and your house and all that you have. [7]And now I have heard that you have shearers. Your shepherds were with us, and we did not jeer at them, and nothing of theirs was missing all the while they were in Carmel. [8]Ask your young men and they will tell you. Therefore let the young men find favor in your eyes, for we have come on a feast day. Give, therefore, whatever you have at hand to your servants and to your son David.' [9]And when David's young men came, they spoke to Nabal in the name of David and waited as directed.

Nabal's insulting reply and David's plans for vengeance

[10]Then Nabal answered[p] David's servants, and said, Who is David? And who is the son of Jesse? Many are the slaves these days who break away, each from his master! [11]Should I then take my bread and my water[q] and my meat that I have slain for my shearers, and give it to men of whom I know not whence they are? [12]So David's young men turned back on their way, and came and reported all these words to him. [13]And David said to his men, Let every man gird on his sword. And they girded on each man his sword. And David also girded on his sword; and there went up after David about four hundred men; and two hundred remained with the baggage.

Abigail's prompt action

[14]But one of the young men had told Abigail, Nabal's wife, saying, David has just sent messengers from the wilderness to salute our master, and he

§ 15 This account of how David acquired a wife and possessions is one of the most characteristic products of the early Judean school. It gives an exceedingly realistic picture of David's life during his outlaw period. Excepting the opening words, which were evidently intended by the editor of I Sam. to connect it with the preceding editorial note regarding the death of Samuel, [1a], the story has apparently received little, if any, additions.

[n] 25[1b] So Gk. Heb., *Paran*.

[o] 25[6] Restoring the otherwise unintelligible Heb. in accordance with the exceedingly plausible suggestions of Smith (*Sam.*, 223).

[p] 25[9, 10] The Gk. and Luc. translate, possibly preserving an original text, *Nabal jumped up and answered*.

[q] 25[11] Gk., *wine*. But this was probably introduced by the translators from [18], because they did not appreciate the value of water in the wilderness of southern Judah.

Early Judean David Narratives

railed at them. ¹⁵But the men have been very good to us and we have not been jeered at nor have we missed anything, as long as we went with them, when we were in the fields. ¹⁶They were a wall about us both by night and by day all the while we were with them keeping the sheep. ¹⁷Now therefore know and consider what you will do, for evil is determined against our master and against all his house, for he is such a base scoundrel that no one can speak to him. ¹⁸Then Abigail quickly took two hundred loaves of bread and two skins of wine and five roasted sheep and three and a third bushelsʳ of parched grain and a hundred bunches of raisins and two hundred cakes of figs and laid them on asses. ¹⁹And she said to her young men, Go on before me; see, I am coming after you. But she said nothing about it to her husband Nabal. ²⁰And just as she was riding on the ass and coming down under cover of the mountain, David and his men were also coming down toward her, so that she met them. ²¹Now David had said, Surely for nothing did I guard all that belongs to this fellow in the wilderness, so that nothing of all that belongs to him was missing, for he has returned me evil for good. ²²God do whatever he will to David,ˢ if I leave by daybreak of all who belong to him as much as a single man.

²³And when Abigail saw David, she alighted quickly from her ass and fell on her face before David and bowed to the ground. ²⁴And she fell at his feet and said, Upon me, my lord, upon me be the guilt. Only let your maid-servant speak in your ears, and heed the words of your maid-servant. ²⁵Let not my lord pay any attention to that base scoundrel, Nabal, for as his name is, so is he; "Reckless Fool," is his name and folly is his master; but your maid-servant saw not the young men of my lord, whom you sent. ²⁶Now my lord, as Jehovah liveth and as you live, since Jehovah has kept you from committingᵗ an act of bloodshed and from delivering yourself by your own hand—and may your enemies and those who seek to do evil to my lord be as Nabalᵘ—²⁷let this present,ᵛ which your servant has brought to my lord, be given to the young men who follow my lord. ²⁸Forgive, I pray the trespass of your maid-servant, for Jehovah will certainly make for my lord a secure house, for my lord is fighting the wars of Jehovah, and no evil shall be found in you as long as you live. ²⁹And should a man rise up to pursue you and to seek your life, the life of my lord shall be bound in the bundle of the livingʷ in the care of Jehovah your God, but the lives of your enemies will he sling out as from the hollow of a sling. ³⁰And when Jehovah has done to my lord all the good that he has promised you and has made you prince over Israel, ³¹then this shall not be a qualm or a burden on the conscienceˣ of my lord, that you have shed blood without cause

Her wise counsel to David

---

r 25¹⁸ Heb., *five measures.*
s 25²² So Gk. The Heb. adds, *to the enemies of.* But this clause seems to have been inserted by a scribe to deliver David from the charge of forswearing himself.
t 25²⁶ Heb., *from entering into.*
u 25²⁶b This half verse anticipates the judgment which has not yet overtaken Nabal. The entire verse is probably an editorial addition.
v 25²⁷ Cf. Gen. 33¹¹, Judg. 1¹⁵. It was a gift brought for the purpose of securing a blessing.
w 25²⁹ Cf. the later figure, *the book of the living,* Ps. 69²⁹, Ex. 32³², ³³.
x 25³¹ Heb., *cause of stumbling of the heart.*

Early Judean David Narratives ·

or that my lord has delivered himself by his own hand.   And when Jehovah shall give prosperity to my lord, then remember your maid-servant.

David's grateful response   ³²And David said to Abigail, Blessed be Jehovah, the God of Israel, who sent you this day to meet me, ³³and blessed be your discretion, and blessed be you yourself, who have kept me this day from committing an act of bloodshed and from delivering myself by my own hand.   ³⁴For as sure as Jehovah, the God of Israel, liveth, who hath kept me from doing you harm, except you had quickly come to meet me, surely there would not have been left to Nabal by daybreak so much as one man.   ³⁵So David received from her hand that which she had brought him; and to her he said, Go up in peace to your house. See, I have heeded your advice,ᵃ and granted your request.

Death of Nabal   ³⁶But when Abigail came to Nabal, he was just having a banquet in his house, like a king.   And Nabal's heart was merry within him, for he was very drunk, so that she did not tell him anything at all until daybreak.   ³⁷But then in the morning when the effects of the wine were gone from Nabal, his wife told him these things, and his heart died within himᵇ and he became a stone.   ³⁸And at the end of about ten days Jehovah smote Nabal, so that he died.

David's marriage with Abigail   ³ʳNow when David heard that Nabal was dead, he said, Blessed be Jehovah who hath avenged the case of my insult at the hand of Nabal and hath kept back his servant from evil; and the evil-doing of Nabal hath Jehovah brought back upon his own head.   Thereupon David sent and wooed Abigail to take her to him to be his wife.   ⁴⁰And when the servants of David came to Abigail at Carmel and said to her, David has sent us to you to take you to him to be his wife, ⁴¹she arose and bowed with her face to the earth and said, See, your slave is willing to be a maid-servant to wash the feet of my lord's servants.   ⁴²Thereupon Abigail quickly arose and mounted an ass, and five maidens followed as servants.   So she accompanied the messengers of David and became his wife.

His other wives   ⁴³David also took Ahinoam of Jezreel, and they both became his wives. ⁴⁴But Saul had given Michal his daughter, David's wife, to Palti the son of Laish of Gallim.

§ 16. David among the Philistines, I Sam. 21¹⁰⁻¹⁵, 27, I Chr. 12¹⁻²²

Early Judean David Narratives | *Popular Judean David Stories*

David a refugee at the court of Achish   **I Sam. 27** ¹Then David said to himself, I shall be destroyed some day by the hand of Saul.   There is | **21** ¹⁰Then David arose and fled that day from before Saul, and went to Achish the king of Gath.   ¹¹And

---

ᵃ 25³⁵ Lit., *lifted up your countenance, i.e., relieved your gloom or anxiety by granting your request.* Cf. Gen. 19²¹, Job 42⁸, ⁹.
ᵇ 25³⁷ The graphic description points to a stroke of paralysis, the result of his debauchery and the sudden news.
§ 16 Chap. 27 is the natural sequel to the preceding sections and introduces the events recorded in §§ 18 and 19.   A brave, warlike people, like the Philistines, naturally attracted David and his followers and offered the asylum and protection which they desired.   Like the foreigners who later figure prominently in David's court, the outlaw chief became a *gēr* or alien resident in the Philistine territory and, as such, enjoyed the rights and privileges which Semitic

Early Judean David Narratives

nothing better for me than that I should escape into the land of the Philistines. Then Saul will despair of seeking me longer in all the territory of Israel, and I will escape from his hand. ²So David arose and went over, together with the six hundred men who were with him, to Achish the son of Maoch, king of Gath. ³And David dwelt with Achish at Gath, together with his men, each with his household, David with his two wives, Ahinoam the Jezreelitess and Abigail the Carmelitess, Nabal's wife. ⁴And when Saul was informed that David had fled to Gath, he sought him no more.

Popular Judean David Stories

the servants of Achish said to him, Is not this David the king of the land? Was it not of him that they used to sing responsively in the dances, saying,

Saul has slain his thousands,
But David his ten thousands?

¹²And David took these words to his heart and was greatly afraid of Achish the king of Gath. ¹³And he pretended to be insane^c before them, and raved in their hands and drummed^d on the doors and let his spittle run down upon his beard. ¹⁴Then said Achish to his servants, You see plainly that the man is mad; why do you bring him to me? ¹⁵Do I lack madmen that you have brought this fellow to act the madman in my presence? Should this one come into my house?

Chronicler's Ecclesiastical History

Life as a feudal lord at Ziklag

⁵But David said to Achish, If now I have found favor in your sight, let a place in one of the towns in the open country be given me, that I may dwell there; for why should your servant dwell in the royal city with you? ⁶Then Achish gave him Ziklag at that time; therefore Ziklag belongs to the kings of

I Chr. 12 ¹Now these are they who came to David at Ziklag, while he still kept at a distance from Saul the son of Kish; and they were among the mighty heroes, his helpers in war. ²They were armed with bows and could use both the right hand and the left in slinging stones and in shooting arrows from the bow; they were of Saul's tribesmen of Benjamin. ³The chief was Ahiezer; then Joash, the sons of Shemaah the Gibeathite, Jeziel, and Pelet, the sons of Azmaveth, Beracah, Jehu the Anathothite, ⁴Ishmaiah the Gibeonite, a mighty warrior among the Thirty and at the head of the Thirty, Jeremiah, Jahaziel, Johanan, Jozabad the Gederathite, ⁵Eluzai, Jerimoth, Bealiah, Shemariah, Shephatiah the Haruphite, ⁶Elkanah, Isshiah, Azarel, Joezer, Jashobeam, the Ko-

custom confirms to one who puts himself under the protection of a foreign chief or race. Cf. Vol. V *in loco* for the detailed Israelitish laws regarding the *gēr*.

The brief parallel in 21¹⁰⁻¹⁵ has no real connection with its context. It is also inconsistent with the representation of 27, for it is inconceivable that after such an experience, as is recorded in 21¹⁰⁻¹⁵, David would seek or find protection at Gath. The fact that he is called, *king of the land* in ¹¹ and the naïve picture of the way in which he effected his escape by deception indicate that this is evidently the late popular version of his sojourn under the protection of Achish. The Jews appeared to have preserved it because it was more in accord with their views than the older version in 27 which represented David's relations with the Philistines as friendly.

^c 21¹³ Lit., *changed his character* or *understanding*, as in 25³³. The word literally means, *taste.*
^d 21¹³ Interpreting this doubtful Heb. word with the aid of the Gk.

Early Judean David Narratives

Chronicler's Ecclesiastical History

Judah to this day. ⁷And the length of the time that David dwelt in the open country of the Philistines was a year and four months.ᵉ ⁸And David and his men went up, and made a raid upon the Geshurites, the Girzites,ᶠ and the Amalekites; for these tribes dwell in the land which extends from Telemᵍ as far as Shur, even to the land of Egypt. ⁹And as often as David smote the land, he did not leave alive man or woman, but taking the sheep, the oxen, the asses, the camels, and the clothing, he returned and came to Achish. ¹⁰Then when Achish said, Whereⁱ have you made a raid to-day? David answered, Against the South Country of Judah, or against the South Country of the Jerahmeelites and against the South Country of the Ken-

rahites, ⁷Joelah, and Zebadiah, the sons of Jeroham of Gedor. ⁸And of the Gadites there went over to David to the stronghold in the wilderness,

Brave warriors,
Men trained for war,
Who could handle shield and spear,
Whose faces were like the faces of lions,
And they were as swift as the gazelles upon the mountains.

⁹Ezer the first, Obadiah the second, Eliab the third, ¹⁰Mishmannah the fourth, Jeremiah the fifth, ¹¹Attai the sixth, Eliel the seventh, ¹²Johanan the eighth, Elzabad the ninth, ¹³Jeremiah the tenth, Machbannai the eleventh. ¹⁴These of the sons of Gad were commanders of the army.

The least was equal to a hundred,ʰ
And the greatest to a thousand.

¹⁵These are they who went over the Jordan in the first month, when it had overflowed all its banks, and they put to flight all those who dwelt in the valleys, both toward the east and toward the west. ¹⁶And once there came some of the Benjamites and Judahites to the stronghold to David. ¹⁷And David went out to meet them and spoke and said to them, If you come peaceably to me to help me, my heart shall be knit to you; but if to betray me to my adversaries, since there is no wrong in my hands, the God of our fathers look down and rebuke it. ¹⁸Then the spirit came upon Abishai,ʲ the chief of the Thirty:

Thine we are, O David,
And on thy side, O son of Jesse!
Peace, peace to thee,
And peace to thy helpers!
For thy God helpeth thee!

ᵉ I Sam. 27⁷ This verse is regarded by many as a later addition, but the *two years* of 29³ included the period of residence at Gath.

ᶠ I Sam. 27⁸ The identification of these peoples is very doubtful.

ᵍ I Sam. 27⁸ Following certain Gk. manuscripts, Telem is mentioned in 15⁴ as the place where Saul rallied his forces to attack the Amalekites. A change of one letter gives the inconsequential reading, *from of old.*

ʰ I Chr. 12¹⁴ Or, *commander over a hundred.* But cf. Is. 30¹⁷, Lev. 28⁸.

ⁱ I Sam. 27¹⁰ So Syr., Targ., and certain Heb. texts. Gk., *against whom.*

ʲ I Chr. 12¹⁸ Heb., *Amasai;* but he is not mentioned among David's heroes. According to 11²⁰ Abishai was chief of the Three.

Early Judean David Narratives

Chronicler's Ecclesiastical History

ites. ¹¹But David never left alive man or woman, to bring them to Gath, for he thought, They might g i v e information against us and say, 'Thus has David done.' And such was his custom all the while he dwelt in the open country of the Philistines. ¹²And Achish trusted David, saying, He has brought himself into ill odor with his people Israel; therefore he shall be my servant forever.

Then David received them and made them commanders of the guerilla band.

¹⁹Of Manasseh also some went over to David, when he came with the Philistines against Saul to battle; but they helped them not, for the tyrants of the Philistines after consultation sent him away, saying, he will fall away to his master Saul to the jeopardy of our heads. ²⁰As he went to Ziklag, there came over to him of Manasseh, Adnah, Jozabad, Jediael, Michael, Jozabad, Elihu, and Zillethai, commanders of thousands, who were of Manasseh. ²¹And they helped David against the guerilla bands, for they were all brave, valiant warriors and were commanders in the army. ²²Thus from day to day men came to David to help him, until there was a great army, like the army of God.

§ 17. David and the Philistine Invasion, I Sam. 28¹, ², 29

Early Judean David Narratives

I Sam. 28 ¹Now in those days the Philistines assembled their forces to make a campaign against Israel. And Achish said to David, Be assured that you, together with your men, must go with me along with the forces. ²And David said to Achish, Therefore you shall now^k know what your servant can do. And Achish said to David, Therefore I make you my bodyguard^l from this time on. *[David's summons to fight against Israel]*

29 ¹And the Philistines had assembled their forces at Aphek; and the Israelites encamped by the fountain in Jezreel. ²And the tyrants of the Philistines were marching past, with hundreds and with thousands; and David and his men marched in the rear guard with Achish. ³Then the commanders of the Philistines said, What are these Hebrews? And Achish said to the commanders of the Philistines, This is David, the servant of Saul the king of Israel, who has now already been with me two years,^{m} and I have found *[Protest of the Philistine commanders]*

---

§ 17 The continuation of 27 is found in 28¹, ², 29, and 30. Not only does 28³⁻²⁵ interrupt the story, but it also introduces a different theme and contains references to data not found in the early Judean David narratives. Cf. note § 19. Its insertion here is evidently the work of a later editor. Restoring the original order, the early narrative continues the vivid recital of David's experience at this crisis in his life. The popular account of David's experiences at the court of Achish, 21¹⁰⁻¹⁵, § 16, also reflects certain elements found in the present story.

k 28² So Gk., Luc., and Lat.

l 28² Heb., *keeper of my head.*

m 29³ Heb., *these days* or *these years,* is evidently corrupt. All the Gk. texts make the time two years and facilitate the correction of the Heb.

Early Judean David Narratives

no fault in him from the time that he came over to me to the present. ⁴But the commanders of the Philistines were enraged against him, andⁿ said to him, Send back the man that he may return to the place where you have stationed him. Let him not go down with us to battle and let him not be in the campᵒ an adversary to us; for with what could this fellow better ingratiate himself with his master than with the heads of these men? ⁵Is not this David of whom they sang responsively in the dances, saying,

> Saul has slain his thousands,
> But David his ten thousands?

David's dismissal ⁶Then Achish called to David and said to him, As Jehovah liveth, you are upright, and it is my desire that you should go out and in with me in the camp; for I have found no evil in you from the time that you came to me to the present, but you are not regarded favorably by the tyrants. ⁷Therefore now return and go in peace, that you may do nothing to displease the tyrants of the Philistines. ⁸And David said to Achish, But what have I done? And what have you found in your servant from the day that I entered into your service to this day, that I may not go and fight against the enemies of my lord the king? ⁹And Achish answered and said to David, I know that you are as good in my sight as a Messenger of God, but the commanders of the Philistines have said, ' He shall not go up with us to the battle.' ¹⁰Therefore now rise early in the morning, with the servants of your lord who came with you, and go to the place where I have stationed you, and do not entertain any evil design in your heart, for you are good in my sight,ᵖ but rise early in the morning and as soon as it is light, depart. ¹¹So David rose early, together with his men, to depart in the morning to return to the land of the Philistines. And the Philistines went up to Jezreel.

§ 18. David's Pursuit and Defeat of the Amalekites, I Sam. 30

Early Judean David Narratives

The Amalekite raid on Ziklag **I Sam. 30** ¹Now when David and his men on the third day came to Ziklag, the Amalekites had made a raid on the South Country and upon Ziklag, and had smitten Ziklag and burnt it with fire, ²and had carried away captive the women and all who were in it, both small and great, without slaying any, and had carried them off and gone on their way. ³And when David and his men came to the city, there it was burned down, and their wives and their sons and their daughters had been taken captive. ⁴Then David and the people who were with him wept aloud until they were no

---

ⁿ 29⁴ So Gk., Syr., and Lat. The Heb. repeats, *commanders of the Philistines*.
ᵒ 29⁴ So Gk. and Luc.
ᵖ 29¹⁰ A line has apparently dropped out of the Heb. which the Gk. and Luc. retain, relieving the verse of its awkward repetition in immediately succeeding sentences. The current English translations are only artificial attempts to eliminate the tautology.
§ 18 Vss. ⁵, ¹⁸ᵇ fit awkwardly in their respective contexts and appear to have been added later by an editor or scribe especially interested in David's family history. Otherwise the chapter is all from the earliest source.

Early Judean David Narratives

longer able to weep. [5]And David's two wives had been taken captive, Ahinoam the Jezreelitess, and Abigail the wife of Nabal the Carmelite.

The divine command to pursue the marauders

[6]And David was in great straits, for the people spoke of stoning him, because the soul of all the people was embittered, each for his sons and for his daughters; but David strengthened himself in reliance on Jehovah his God. [7]And David said to Abiathar the priest, the son of Ahimelech, Bring here to me the ephod. And Abiathar brought thither the ephod to David. [8]And David inquired of Jehovah, saying,

> Shall I pursue this marauding band?
> Shall I overtake them?

And he answered him,

> Pursue,
> For thou shalt surely overtake,
> And thou shalt surely rescue.[q]

The pursuit

[9]So David went, together with the six hundred men who were with him, and came to the Brook Besor, where those who were left behind remained. [10]But David pursued together with four hundred men; while two hundred remained behind, who were too faint to cross the Brook Besor. [11]And they found an Egyptian in the field and brought him to David and gave him food to eat and water to drink; [12]and they gave him a piece of a cake of figs, and two clusters of raisins.[r] And when he had eaten, his spirit revived,[s] for he had eaten no bread and drunk no water for three days and nights. [13]And David said to him, To whom do you belong? And whence are you? And he said I am an Egyptian lad, an Amalekite's servant, and my master abandoned me because three days ago I fell sick. [14]We made a raid upon the South Country of the Cherethites and upon that which belongs to Judah and upon the South Country of Caleb, and Ziklag we burned with fire. [15]And David said to him, Will you bring me down to this band? And he said, Swear to me by God, that you will neither kill me nor deliver me into the hands of my master, and I will bring you down to this band.

The attack and recovery of the plunder

[16]And when he had brought him down, there they were spread over all the land, eating and drinking and dancing, on account of all the great spoil that they had taken from the land of the Philistines and from the land of Judah. [17]And David smote them from twilight to evening in order to destroy them completely.[t] And none escaped except four hundred young men, who rode upon the camels and fled. [18]And David recovered all the persons whom the Amalekites had taken; and David rescued his two wives. [19]And

---

[q] 30[8] The brief, sententious, poetic form of the question and the oracle is strikingly apparent.

[r] 30[12] The Gk. does not have the *two clusters of raisins.*

[s] 30[12] Heb., *his spirit returned to him.*

[t] 30[17] The Heb. is untranslatable, and all the versions found difficulties with the passage. The current English translations seem to follow a conjecture of Jerome. The above reading is based upon the reconstruction, which does least violence to the text and which is most consistent with early Heb. usage. Cf. Josh. 6[21], 8[2].

Early Judean David Narratives

there was nothing of them missing either small or great, sons or daughters, spoil or anything that they had taken to themselves—David brought back all. ²⁰And he took all the flocks and the herds and drove those animals before the people, and they[u] said, This is David's spoil.

The precedent regarding the division of spoil ²¹Now when David came to the two hundred men, who had been too faint to follow him, so that he[v] had to leave them behind at the Brook Besor, they went out to meet David, and the people who were with him. And when they came near to the people, they saluted them.[w] ²²Then all the wicked and base scoundrels among the men who went with David began to say, Because they did not go with us, we will not give them any of the spoil that we have recovered, except to each, his wife and his children, that he may take them away and depart. ²³But David said, Do not so, after that which Jehovah hath given us[x] and after he hath preserved us and delivered the marauding band that came against us into our hand. ²⁴And who will give heed to you in this matter? For:

> As is the share of him who goes down into battle,
> So is the share of him who remains with the baggage.
> They shall share alike.

²⁵And from that time on he made it a statute and precedent in Israel[a] to this day.

Presents sent to the southern chieftains ²⁶And when David came to Ziklag, he sent some of the spoil to the elders of Judah, his friends,[b] saying, See! a present for you from the spoil of the enemies of Jehovah, ²⁷to them who were in Bethel,[c] in Ramoth in the South Country, in Jattir, ²⁸in Aroer, in Siphmoth, and them who were in Eshtemoa, ²⁹in Carmel,[d] in the cities of Jerahmeelites, in the cities of the Kenites, ³⁰in Hormah, Beersheba,[e] in Athach, ³¹in Hebron, and to those in all the places where David and his men had sojourned.

---

u 30²⁰ The Heb. is unintelligible, if translated literally. As it stands, the first verb is in the singular, but the rest in the plural with no suggestion as to what is their antecedent. Gk. and Luc. have all three in the singular and with the Lat. agree in omitting the *David* inserted in the Heb. in the first part of the verse. In the Lat. the first two verbs are in the singular and the last in the plural. The texts are clearly corrupt. The above reading involves only minor corrections and fairly represents the thought of the original. It was natural that David should take the initiative in dividing the spoil and that to him should fall the animals, while the people shared the booty secured in the camp.

v 30²¹ Heb., *they;* but Gk., Syr., and Lat. and certain manuscripts have, *he.*

w 30²¹ Heb., *David came near to the people and saluted them;* but the consistent reading suggested by Gk., Syr., and certain manuscripts has been followed above.

x 30²³ Restoring the Heb. with the aid of the Gk., otherwise the Heb. gives no sense.

a 30²⁵ In Num. 31²⁷ the late priestly writers, following their usual custom, attribute the origin of this institution to Moses. The present tradition is undoubtedly by far the older and well illustrates the origin of many of Israel's early laws. Cf. Introd., Vol. IV.

b 30²⁶ Gk., Luc., and Syr., *and to his friends* or *kinsmen.*

c 30²⁷ Not the Bethel north of Jerusalem but probably the Bethuel of I Chr. 4³⁰, near Ziklag.

d 30²⁹ So Gk. Heb., *Racal.*

e 30³⁰ So Gk. and Luc. The Heb. has, *Bor-ashan.*

§ 19. Saul's Visit to the Medium of Endor, I Sam. 25¹ᵃ, 28³⁻²⁵

Late Popular Prophetic Narratives

I Sam. 28 ³Now Samuel had died and all Israel had lamented for him and buried him in Ramah, his own city. And Saul had put the mediums and the wizards out of the land.ᶠ ⁴And when the Philistines assembled and came and encamped in Shunem, Saul assembled all Israel, and they encamped in Gilboa. ⁵And when Saul saw the army of the Philistines, he was afraid and his heart was filled with apprehension. ⁶And Saul inquired of Jehovah, but Jehovah did not answer him either by dreams or by Urim or by prophets. ⁷Then Saul said to his servants, Find for me a medium who has a talisman that I may go to her and inquire of her. And his servants said to him, Behold, there is at Endor a medium who has a talisman.

⁸Therefore Saul disguised himself and put on other clothes and went, taking two men with him, and they came to the woman by night. And he said, Divine for me by the talisman and bring up for me the one whom I shall name to you. ⁹And the woman said to him, Behold, you know what Saul has done, how he has cut off the mediums and the wizards from the land. Why then are you laying a snare for my life, to put me to death? ¹⁰And Saul swore to her by Jehovah, saying, As Jehovah liveth, no guilt shall come upon you for this thing. ¹¹Then the woman said, Whom shall I bring up to you? And he said, Bring up Samuel. ¹²And when the woman saw Samuel, she screamed. And the woman said to Saul, Why have you deceived me, for you are Saul? ¹³And the king said to her, Do not be afraid! What do you see? And the woman said to Saul, I see a god coming up out of the earth. ¹⁴And he said to her, What is his appearance? And she said, An old man is coming up, and he is wrapped in a mantle. Then Saul knew that it was Samuel, and he bowed with his face to the earth and worshipped.

(margin notes: Saul's desire for a supernatural revelation. The midnight scene in the hut at Endor.)*

---

§19 The natural sequel of the early Judean narrative in 28¹, ², 29 (and the account of David's fortunes in 30), is the description of the final battle found in 31. In 29¹¹ the Philistines have already advanced to Jezreel at the foot of Mount Gilboa. It is difficult to find a place for the present story, which represents them as encamped at Shunem, ⁴, to the north of the plain of Esdraelon. This fact only confirms the other indications that it is from a different cycle of traditions. Its theme and representation, as well as its style, strongly suggest that it was a story long cherished in the minds of the people, whose beliefs it vividly reflects. It also has many points in common with the account of Saul's rejection by Samuel in 15.

A later editor has further brought the two chapters into close connection by inserting in ¹⁷, ¹⁸ an allusion to and paraphrase of the prediction in 15²³. In both, not Saul, but Samuel is the dominant figure and the king is under the shadow of the divine displeasure. Samuel, however, is not the prophetic judge as in the later Ephraimite prophetic narratives, but the seer whom Saul consults to secure an oracle much as in the early Judean story of 9⁶⁻²⁰. Samuel is still conceived of as the friend of Saul, cf.¹⁵ The pathetic picture whic'. it gives of Saul also tends to support the conclusion that the tradition took written form in some later Judean rather than Ephraimite prophetic school at a period not long before the exile. The linguistic evidence also on the whole favors this conclusion. At the same time it is evident that the story, like 15, embodies some much earlier material and may well rest on a firm historical basis.

ᶠ 28³ Smith has a valuable note on this passage (*Sam.*, 239), in which he adduces many references (cf. especially II Kgs. 21⁶, 23²⁴, Dt. 18¹⁰ and Lev. 20²⁷) to demonstrate that the reference here is not to necromancers and wizards, but to the paraphernalia used in consulting spirits of the dead. From Dt. 18¹⁰, ¹¹ and Lev. 20²⁷, as well as the present story, it is evident that they were something through which an answer could be secured and supposed connection with the dead established. The woman of Endor, who possesses one, corresponds to the modern medium. The Gk. translation, *ventriloquists*, suggests the manner in which the deception was practised. The fact that, according to the story, not Saul but only the woman claims to see Samuel is likewise suggestive.

Late Popular Prophetic Narratives

The message of doom

¹⁵And Samuel said to Saul, Why have you disturbed me by bringing me up? And Saul answered, I am in great straits, for the Philistines are making war against me and God has turned from me and answers me no more, either by prophets or by dreams; so I have called you to tell me what I shall do. ¹⁶And Samuel said, Why do you ask of me when Jehovah hath turned from you and become your adversary? ¹⁷And Jehovah hath done to you as he declared by me; and Jehovah hath rent the kingdom out of your hand, and given it to your associate (David). ¹⁸Because you did not heed the voice of Jehovah, and did not execute his fierce wrath upon Amalek, therefore Jehovah hath done this thing to you to-day. ¹⁹And[g] to-morrow you and your sons with you[h] shall fall; Jehovah will deliver the army of Israel also into the power of the Philistines.

Effect upon Saul

²⁰Then Saul fell at once at full length upon the earth and was greatly afraid, because of the words of Samuel; also he had no strength in him, for he had not eaten bread during all the day and all the night. ²¹And when the woman came to Saul and saw that he was greatly troubled, she said to him, See, your maid-servant has heeded your voice, and I have taken my life in my hand and have listened to your words which you spoke to me. ²²Now therefore, listen also to the advice of your maid-servant and let me set before you a morsel of meat, and eat that you may have strength when you go on your way. ²³But he refused, and said, I will not eat. But his servants, together with the woman urged him, until he listened to their advice. So he rose from the earth and sat upon the couch. ²⁴And the woman had a fatted calf in the house; and she quickly killed it, and took flour and kneaded it and baked from it unleavened bread. ²⁵And she set it before Saul and his servants, and they ate. Then they rose up and went away that night.

§ 20. The Defeat and Death of Saul and Jonathan, I Sam. 31, I Chr. 10

Early Judean David Narratives

Defeat of the Israelites and death of Saul

I Sam. 31 ¹Now the Philistines fought against Israel, and the Israelites fled from before the Philistines and fell down slain on Mount Gilboa. ²And the Philistines followed close after Saul and his sons; and the Philistines slew Jonathan and Abinadab and Malchishua, the sons of Saul. ³And they pressed hard upon Saul, and the archers found him out, and he was wounded by the archers. ⁴Then said Saul to his armorbearer, Draw your sword and run me through with it, lest these uncircumcised Philistines come and make sport of me.[i] But his armorbearer would not, for he was greatly afraid. Therefore Saul took his own sword and fell upon it. ⁵And when

---

[g] 28¹⁹ A scribe has repeated by mistake at the beginning the clause found in the latter part of the vs., *And Jehovah will deliver Israel also with you into the power of the Philistines.* It has been omitted in the above translation.

[h] 28¹⁹ So Gk. The Heb. has simply, *with me,* and no verb. The *with me* of the Heb. probably represents the *with you* of the Gk. which has retained the original.

§ 20 Chap. 31 resumes the early Judean account of the Philistine invasion. The author of Chr. quoted this chapter practically verbatim, doubtless because he recognized in Saul's fall the event which opened the way for the accession of the king whom he regarded as the virtual founder of the temple. At the end of the quotation he adds a moral reflection which indicates that he had before him the fuller Saul history in I Sam.

[i] 31⁴ So Chr. The Heb. repeats, *run me through,* which was not what Saul feared but rather that the enemy would torture and abuse him.

Early Judean David Narratives

his armorbearer saw that Saul was dead, he likewise fell upon his sword and died with him. [6]So Saul and his three sons and his armorbearer[j] died together on the same day.

[7]And when the Israelites who were in the cities of the valley[k] and in the cities of the Jordan saw that the Israelites had fled and that Saul and his sons were dead, they also left the cities and fled, and the Philistines came and remained in them. [8]But when on the following day the Philistines came to strip the slain, they found Saul and his three sons fallen on Mount Gilboa. [9]And they cut off his head and stripped off his armor and sent throughout the land of the Philistines to bring good news to their idols[l] and to the people. [10]And they put his armor in the temple of Ashtarte,[m] and they fastened his body on the wall of Bethshan.[n] [11]And when the inhabitants of Jabesh in Gilead[o] heard what the Philistines had done to Saul, [12]all the valiant men arose and marched all night and took the bodies of Saul and his sons from the wall of Bethshan; and they came to Jabesh and lamented over them there.[p] [13]And they took their bones and buried them under the tamarisk tree in Jabesh, and they fasted seven days.

Fate of Saul's body

Chronicler's Ecclesiastical History

I Chr. 10 [13]So Saul died for his faithlessness to Jehovah, because he did not faithfully observe the word of Jehovah, and also in that he inquired of a talisman, resorting to it [14]instead of to Jehovah.[q] Therefore he put him to death and turned the kingdom over to David the son of Jesse.

An explanation of Saul's sad fate

---

[j] 31⁶ The Heb. adds, *and all his men,* which is not found in Chr. and Gk. Chr. changes, *armorbearer,* to, *all his house.*

[k] 31⁷ The text is difficult. The Heb. makes little sense. Chr. has simply, *and when the men of Israel, who were in the valley, saw.* The simple reconstruction followed above gives an intelligible reading.

[l] 31⁹ So I Chr. 10⁹, Gk., and Luc. The Heb. reading, *to the house of their idols,* is due to an obvious scribal error.

[m] 31¹⁰ So Gk. and Luc. Chr., *of their gods.* The Heb., *Ashtaroth,* as in Judg. 2¹³, is clearly due to a deliberate scribal change.

[n] 31¹⁰ I Chr. 10¹⁰ has for the second half of the verse, *and they stuck up his skull in the house of Dagon.* In [12] the reference to taking the body from the wall of Bethshan is also omitted.

[o] 31¹¹ The loyalty of the men of Jabesh was doubtless due to Saul's act of deliverance recorded in 11¹⁻¹¹.

[p] 31¹² Heb., *and burn them there;* but this is inconsistent with Heb. usage according to which only the bodies of culprits were burned, Lev. 20¹⁴, 21⁹, Josh. 7²⁵, and the statement in the next verse that *they buried their bones.* The clause is also not found in I Chr. 10¹². The mistake probably resulted from an error in the reading of a very similar Heb. word, *to lament for the dead.*

[q] I Chr. 10¹³ᵇ, ¹⁴ᵃ But cf. I Sam. 28⁶, ¹⁶, ¹⁹ which hardly justify the sweeping judgment of the later Jewish traditions which the Chronicler voices. Cf. Introd., p. 23.

III

DAVID'S REIGN AS KING OVER JUDAH AND OVER ALL ISRAEL, II Sam. 1–21, 23⁸–24²⁵, I Kgs. 1¹–2¹¹, I Chr. 11, 12²³–29³⁰

§ 21. David's Reception of the News of the Death of Saul and Jonathan, II Sam. 1

Early Judean David Narratives

Arrival of the messenger

1 ¹Now, after the death of Saul,ᵃ when David had returned from smiting the Amalekites, David remained two days in Ziklag. ²Then on the third day there came a man out of the camp from Saul, with his clothes torn and with earth upon his head. And as soon as he came to David, he fell to the earth and did obeisance. ³And David said to him, Whence do you come? And he answered him, From the camp of Israel have I escaped. ⁴And David said to him, How was the affair? Tell me. And he answered, The people fled from the battle, and many of the people fell,ᵇ and also Saul and Jonathan his son are dead.

His account of Saul's death

⁵Then David said to the young man who told him, How do you know that Saul and Jonathan his son are dead? ⁶And the young man who told him said, I happened to be on Mount Gilboa, just as Saul was leaning on his spear, and as the chariots and horsemen were following close after him. ⁷And when he looked behind him, he saw me and called to me. And I answered, 'Here am I.' ⁸And he said to me, 'Who are

---

David's Reign as King over Judah and over all Israel.—The record of this thrilling epoch in Israel's history is drawn almost entirely from the early Judean David stories. The political events are presented in II Sam. 1–7, concluding in 8¹⁻¹⁴ with an editorial review of David's wars and conquests. To this original book of Samuel apparently a later editor first added the long realistic narratives of 9¹⁻²⁰²², which present in detail the tragedy of David's family and court life. Supplements to the record of political events in 1–8 are found in 21, 23, and 24; while the account of David's family history in 9¹⁻²⁰²² is directly continued in I Kgs. 1¹⁻²¹¹, which was evidently derived from the same early David narratives. Restored to what was approximately their original order, the different stories furnish a remarkably consistent and complete record of David's important reign.

§ 21 The account of David's lamentation on receiving the news of the death of Saul and Jonathan is in perfect harmony with the early Judean David narratives which precede and follow. There is every reason to believe that the beautiful elegy in 18⁻²⁷ first came from the lips of the former shepherd from Bethlehem, whose skill as a minstrel was universally recognized by his own and later generations. The feeling in the poem is strong and genuine and the thought is in keeping with the situation and the spirit of the age. For a study of the literary form of this and kindred poems cf. Vol. V *in loco*. The text has been printed so as to indicate the number of beats or measures in each line.

Not only is the story complete without the details found in ⁵⁻¹⁰, ¹³⁻¹⁶, but they evidently embody a different version of Saul's death from that in I Sam. 31. Thus for example in 31¹³ he is pursued by *the archers*, but in 1⁶ *by the chariots and horsemen;* in 31³ he is represented as wounded, but in 1⁹ dizziness seizes him so that he cannot stand; in 31⁴ he falls upon his sword, but in 1¹⁰ the Amalekite slays him; in 31⁹ the Philistines strip Saul's body, but in 1¹⁰ the Amalekite. On the other hand, there is no evidence in the words or acts of David to indicate that he or the historian regarded the story of the Amalekite as false. Furthermore, there are inconsistencies between 1¹⁻⁴ and ⁵⁻¹⁰, ¹³⁻¹⁶. In ² the messenger is spoken of as a man, presumably an Israelitish soldier, who came as a mourner directly from the camp of Saul, but according to ¹³ he was a *young man, an Amalekite*, who *happened to be on Mount Gilboa* just as the battle was in progress, and instead of mourning for Saul, he comes with gory proofs of his crime to claim a reward from David. The question in ¹³ is a repetition of that in ³. That ⁵⁻¹⁰, ¹³⁻¹⁶ are secondary seems perfectly clear. Expressions like, *Here am I*, in ⁷ and *be afraid* and *destroy* in ¹⁴ are characteristic of the Northern Israelitish group of narratives. This version also saves Saul from the charge of taking his own life. The probabilities are that it was the popular account of Saul's death, current in Northern Israel and introduced here by some editor.

ᵃ 1¹ The fulness and awkwardness of this verse strongly suggests that the editor has at least added the opening clause to join the story to that which immediately precedes.

ᵇ 1⁴ So Luc. and Syr. The Heb. adds, *are dead.*

Early Judean David Narratives

you?' And I replied, 'I am an Amalekite.' ⁹And he said to me, 'Stand, I pray, before me and slay me, for dizziness has seized me, because my life is yet whole in me.'ᶜ ¹⁰So I stood before him and slew him, because I was sure that he could not live after he had fallen; and I took the crown that was upon his head, and the armlet that was on his arm, and have brought them here to my lord.

¹¹Then David took hold of his clothes and tore them; and all the men who were with him did likewise. ¹²And they mourned and wept and fasted until evening for Saul and for Jonathan his son and for the people of Jehovah and for the house of Israel, because they had fallen by the sword.

Lamentation over the fallen

¹³And David said to the young man who told him, Whence do you come? And he answered, I am the son of an Amalekite sojourner. ¹⁴And David said to him, How is it that you were not afraid to put forth your hand to destroy Jehovah's anointed? ¹⁶And David said to him, Your blood be upon your head, for your own mouth testified against you, when you said, 'I have slain Jehovah's anointed.'ᵈ ¹⁵Then David called one of the young men, and said, Go near and strike him down. Accordingly he smote him, so that he died.

Execution of the messenger

¹⁷Then David sang this dirge over Saul and Jonathan his son ¹⁸(behold, it is written in the Book of Jashar), and said,ᵉ

David's dirge

Weep, O Judah!
¹⁹Grieve, O Israel!
On thy heights are the slain'
How have the mighty fallen!

The greatness of the calamity

²⁰Tell it not in Gath,
Declare it not in the streets of Askelon;
Lest the daughters of the Philistines rejoice,
Lest the daughters of the uncircumcised exult.

²¹Ye mountains of Gilboa, may no dew descend,
Nor rain upon you, O ye fields of death!ᶠ
For there was the shield of the mighty cast away,
The shield of Saul, not anointed with oil.

²²From the blood of the slain,
From the fat of the mighty,
The bow of Jonathan turned not back,
The sword of Saul returned not empty.

Bravery and attractiveness of the fallen

²³Saul and Jonathan, the beloved and the lovely!
In life and in death they were not parted;
They were swifter than eagles,
They were stronger than lions.

ᶜ 1⁹ Heb., *for yet my life is whole in me.* Gk., *for all my life is in me.* Luc., as above. Saul's dizziness may have been due to the approach of one of the epileptic attacks to which he appears to have been subject. Cf. the symptoms in I Sam. 16¹⁴⁻²³, 18¹⁰, ¹¹, 19⁸⁻¹⁰, 22⁶⁻¹⁹. If so, *life* would refer to his physical vigor.

ᵈ 1¹⁶ This verse has evidently been introduced, probably through the mistake of a copyist, after ¹⁵ instead of before it, as the sense demands.

ᵉ 1¹⁸ The difficulties presented by this verse are many and the reconstructions suggested equally numerous. The reading adopted above is practically that of Smith (*Sam.*, 259, 260). The statement, *behold it is written in the Book of Jashar*, appears to be an early editorial note, probably first introduced into the margin and subsequently into the latter part of the verse, rather than the first part, where it fits more naturally. Cf. for the character of Book of Jashar, Vol. I, Introd., p. 16. All analogies lead us to expect that the initial words, *and said*, originally introduced the dirge itself. Vs. ¹⁹ with its two lines seem also to be abrupt and incomplete, for practically without exception the following stanzas contain four lines. The Heb. text as it stands is not only ungrammatical but also unintelligible. The word, *bow*, is not found in the Gk. and Luc. Slight corrections in the remaining text give the above consistent reading.

ᶠ 1²¹ So Gk. and Luc. The Heb., *fields of offerings*, is evidently a corruption and makes no sense.

113

Early Judean David Narratives

Saul's services to Israel

²⁴Daughters of Israel, weep over Saul,
Who clothed you daintily in fine linen,
Who put golden ornaments on your garments, [and say]:
²⁵ How have the mighty fallen in the midst of battle!'ᵍ

David's love for Jonathan

Jonathan, in thy death hast thou wounded me!ʰ
²⁶I am distressed for thee, my brother Jonathan!
Thou wert surpassingly dear to me,
Thy love to me was far more than the love of woman!

How have the mighty fallen,
And the weapons of war perished!

§ 22. David King at Hebron and Ishbaal at Mahanaim, II Sam. 2¹⁻¹¹

Early Judean David Narratives

David's establishment as king at Hebron

II Sam. 2 ¹Now after this David inquired of Jehovah, saying, Shall I go up to one of the cities of Judah? And Jehovah answered him, Go up. And when David said, Whither shall I go up, he said, To Hebron. ²So David went up with his two wives, Ahinoam, the Jezreelitess, and Abigail, the wife of Nabal the Carmelite. ³And David brought up the men who were with him, each with his household, and they dwelt in the towns of Hebron. ⁴And the men of Judah came and there anointed David king over the house of Judah.

His message to the Gileadites

And when they told David about the men of Jabesh in Gilead who had buried Saul, ⁵David sent messengers to the men of Jabesh in Gilead and said to them, May you be blest of Jehovah, because you have shown this kindness to your lord Saul and have buried him. ⁶Even so may Jehovah show kindness and truth to you; and I also will do well by you, because you have done this thing. ⁷Now therefore be courageous and valiant; for Saul your lord is dead, and the house of Judah have anointed me king over them.

Ishbaal's kingdom

⁸Now Abner the son of Ner, commander of Saul's army, had taken Ishbaalⁱ the son of Saul, and brought him over to Mahanaim. ⁹And he made

---

g 1²⁵ᵃ Evidently these are the words of lament which the poet would put in the mouths of the wailing women. It is a variation of the refrain in ¹⁹ᵇ, ᶜ.

h 1²⁵ᵇ Heb., *Jonathan on thy heights are the slain.* This gives no sense. The confusion in the text appears here to be due to the fact that the scribe had in mind the rest of the refrain of ¹⁹. The parallelism imperatively demands here a line synonymous with ²⁶ᵃ. Following a suggestion of the Gk. text that the original read not, *on thy heights,* but *in thy death,* the above reading may be conjecturally restored after Budde.

§ 22 This section has all the characteristics of the early Judean David narratives. The chronological notices in ¹⁰ᵃ and ¹¹ are evidently a part of the chronological scheme of the editor. *Forty* is a round number frequently employed by the same editor in Judg. The early narratives imply that Saul was not old at his accession. In I Sam. 14⁴⁹ it is stated and elsewhere implied that Jonathan was the eldest son. Hence unless Saul's reign was much longer than is suggested by the sources, Ishbaal was very young at his accession. This conclusion also explains his inefficiency and folly and the dominant position held by Abner. The reign of David at Hebron was practically synchronous with that of Ishbaal, so that either the *two years* in ¹⁰ᵃ or the *seven and a half* in ¹¹ is a mistake.

There is no indication that David severed his relation of vassalage to the Philistines. The transfer of Israel's capital to Mahanaim, east of the Jordan, is evidence that they held central Canaan. It is not improbable that they also exacted tribute and fealty from Ishbaal.

i 2⁸ Heb., *Ishbosheth, the man of shame.* Evidently this, like *Ashtaroth,* I Sam. 31¹⁰, Judg. 2¹³, represents simply the repugnance of later scribes to repeat the names of the heathen deities. The most striking illustration is in Num. 32²⁸, where the name Meon-baal is followed by a note stating that it is *to be changed in name.* In I Chr. 8³³, 9³⁹, and in some Gk. manuscripts of this passage in the Old Lat. the original form *Ishbaal* is preserved.

Early Judean David Narratives

him king over Gilead and the Ashurites^j and Jezreel and Ephraim and
Benjamin and all Israel.   ¹⁰(Ishbaal, Saul's son, was forty years old when he became king over Israel, and he reigned two years).   But the house of Judah followed David.   ¹¹And the time that David was king in Hebron over the house of
Judah, was seven years and six months.

§ 23. **Hostilities between the Two Kingdoms, II Sam. 2¹²⁻³¹**

Early Judean David Narratives

II Sam. 2 ¹²Now Abner the son of Ner and the servants of Ishbaal the Battle
son of Saul went out from Mahanaim to Gibeon.   ¹³And Joab the son of of Gibeon
Zeruiah and the servants of David went out and met them at the pool of
Gibeon.   And they sat down, the one on the one side of the pool and the
other on the other side of the pool.   ¹⁴Then Abner said to Joab, Let the
young men arise and play before us.   And Joab said, Let them arise.
¹⁵Then they arose and went over by number:^k twelve for Benjamin and
Ishbaal the son of Saul, and twelve of the servants of David.   ¹⁶And they
each caught his opponent by the head and thrust his sword into his side, so
they fell down together.   Therefore that place was called, Field of the Enemies (which is in Gibeon).   ¹⁷And the battle was very fierce that day, and
Abner and the men of Israel were vanquished before the servants of David.

¹⁸And the three sons of Zeruiah were there, Joab, Abishai, and Asahel; Death
and Asahel was as swift of foot as one of the gazelles which are in the field. of Asa-
¹⁹And Asahel pursued Abner; and as he went he turned neither to the right hel
nor to the left from the pursuit of Abner.   ²⁰Then Abner looked behind
him and said, Is it you, Asahel?   And he answered, It is I.   ²¹Therefore
Abner said to him, Turn aside to your right or to your left and seize one of
the young men and take his spoil.^l   But Asahel would not turn aside from
pursuing him.   ²²Therefore Abner said again to Asahel, Turn aside from
following me.   Why should I smite you to the ground?   How then could
I look Joab your brother in the face?^m   ²³But he refused to turn aside.
Therefore Abner smote him with a backward stroke^n in the body, so that
the spear came out at his back; and he fell there and died in his place.   Then
all who came to the place where Asahel had fallen and died, stood still.^o

²⁴But Joab and Abishai, pursued after Abner.   And as the sun was set- Abner's
ting, they came to the hill of Ammah, which is before Giah^p on the highway escape
in the Wilderness of Gibeon.   ²⁵And the Benjamites assembled behind

---

j 2⁹ Probably located immediately north of the plain of Esdraelon.   Cf. Judg. 1³¹, ³² and
Vol. I, map opp. p. 71.   Syr. and Lat. read, *Geshurite* which would include a territory near
Gilead, but Geshur appears to have been independent at this time.   Cf. 3³.
§ 23 The *résumé* in 3¹ may be from the editor, but otherwise the section as a whole appears
to be the original continuation of the preceding.
k 2¹⁵ *I.e.*, were counted off by passing before the teller.
l 2²¹ *I.e.*, the armor and whatever might be stripped from the fallen warrior.
m 2²² Heb. idiom, *hold up my face to Joab.*
n 2²³ Slightly emending the text.   The current translation, *with the hinder end of the spear*,
is very doubtful.
o 2²³b This may be an editorial gloss introduced from 20¹².
p 2²⁴ Giah is unidentified and the text doubtful.

115

Early Judean David Narratives

Abner and formed a solid phalanx, and stood on the top of a hill. [26]Then Abner called to Joab and said, Shall the sword devour forever? Do you not know that the end will be bitterness?[q] How long then will it be before you command the people to turn from pursuing their kinsmen? [27]And Joab said, As Jehovah[r] liveth, if you had not spoken, then assuredly not until morning would the people have ceased each from pursuing his brother. [28]So Joab blew the trumpet; and all the people stood still and pursued Israel no more, nor did they fight any more. [29]But Abner and his men marched all that night through the Arabah and crossed the Jordan and went through the whole Bithron[s] and came to Mahanaim.

Losses in the battle

[30]And Joab returned from the pursuit of Abner. And when he had gathered all the people together, nineteen of David's servants beside Asahel were missing; [31]while the servants of David had smitten of Benjamin and of Abner's men three hundred and sixty.[t] [32]And they took up Asahel and buried him in his father's sepulchre, which was in Bethlehem. And Joab and his men marched all night, and day dawned upon them at Hebron.

Results of the war

3 [1]And the war between the house of Saul and the house of David was prolonged; but David kept growing stronger, while the house of Saul grew gradually weaker.

§ 24. Abner's Disaffection and Death, II Sam. 3[6-39]

Early Judean David Narratives

Abner's quarrel with Ish-baal

II Sam. 3 [6]Now, while there was war between the house of Saul and the house of David,[u] Abner made himself strong in the house of Saul. [7]And Saul had a concubine, whose name was Rizpah, the daughter of Aiah. And Ishbaal the son of Saul[v] said to Abner, Why do you go in unto my father's concubine? [8]Then Abner was very angry because of the words of Ishbaal and said, Am I a dog's head,[w] who am at this time showing kindness to the house of Saul your father, to his kinsmen, and to his friends, and have not delivered you into the hand of David, that you now charge me with guilt in connection with a woman? [9]God do to Abner whatever he pleases, if, as Jehovah hath sworn to David, I do not even so to him, [10]by transferring the kingdom from the house of Saul and by establishing the throne of David over Israel and over Judah from Dan to Beersheba. [11]And he did not dare to make Abner any answer, for he feared him.

---

[q] 2[26] Lit., *bitterness will be the end;* evidently a popular proverb.

[r] 2[27] Heb., *the God,* but Gk. and Luc., *Jehovah.*

[s] 2[29] Or, *Ravine.*

[t] 2[31] So Luc. and Syr. Heb. adds, *they died.*

§ 24 This section is evidently from the original Judean David narratives. It is held by some that [12-19] are secondary, but the grounds are far from conclusive and the references to Michal in [12-16] relate them to the older source in I Sam. 18[20], 19[12-17], § 11. Vss. [17-19], however, introduce a later conception and seem to represent an expansion of the original narrative. Furthermore they awkwardly interrupt the story, for [20] is the immediate continuation of [16].

[u] 3[6a] This repetition of [1] was introduced by the editor who inserted the list of David's sons [2-5].

[v] 3[7] So Gk. The Heb. omits, *Ishbaal the son of Saul,* which is required by the context.

[w] 3[8] So Gk. The Heb. also contains a later explanatory note, *which belongs to Judah.*

Early Judean David Narratives

¹²So Abner sent messengers to David to Hebron,ˣ saying, Make your league with me, then I will co-operate with you in bringing over all Israel to you. ¹³And he said, Good, I will make a league with you, but one thing I require of you, that is, you shall not see my face unless you bring Michal, Saul's daughter, when you come to see me. ¹⁴Then David sent messengers to Ishbaal, Saul's son, saying, Give me my wife Michal, whom I bought for a hundred foreskins of the Philistines. ¹⁵And Ishbaal sent and took her from her husband, Paltiel the son of Laish. ¹⁶But her husband followed her, weeping as he went, to Bahurim. Then Abner said to him, Go, return; and he returned. *Negotiations between Abner and David*

¹⁷Now Abner had entered into communication with the elders of Israel, saying, Already for a long time you have been desirous of having David king over you. ¹⁸Now do it, for Jehovah hath spoken of David, saying, 'By the hand of my servant David will I save my people Israel out of the hand of the Philistines and out of the hand of all their enemies?' ¹⁹Abner also spoke in the ears of Benjamin and went to communicate directly to David in Hebron all that seemed good to Israel and to the whole house of Benjamin. *Abner's advice to the Israelites*

²⁰And when Abner came to David at Hebron, accompanied by twenty men, David gave Abner and the men who were with him a feast. ²¹And Abner said to David, I will arise and go and will gather all Israel to my lord the king, that they may make a covenant with you and that you may be king over all which you desire. Then David sent Abner away, and he went in peace. *His visit to David*

²²Just then the servants of David and Joab came from a raid, and brought in with them great spoil; but Abner was not with David in Hebron, for he had sent him away and he had gone in peace. ²³So when Joab and all the band that was with him came home, they told Joab, saying, Abner the son of Ner came to the king, and he has sent him away, and he has gone in peace. ²⁴Then Joab went to the king and said, What have you done? Behold, Abner came to you; why have you now sent him away, so that he is gone? ²⁵Do you not know that Abner the son of Ner came to deceive you and to note your going out and your coming in and to know all that you are doing?ᵃ ²⁶And when Joab came out from David, he sent messengers after Abner and they brought him back from the Cistern of Sirah without David's knowing it. ²⁷And when Abner returned to Hebron, Joab took him apart to the side ofᵇ the gate to speak with him quietly and smote him there in the body. So he died for the blood of Asahel Joab's brother. *His murder by Joab*

²⁸But afterward when David heard it, he said, I and my kingdom are forever guiltless before Jehovah of the blood of Abner the son of Ner. ²⁹May it fall upon the head of Joab and upon all his father's house, and may there not fail from the house of Joab one who has an issue, or who is a leper, or who is effeminate,ᶜ or who falls by the sword, or who lacks bread. ³⁰But *David's condemnation of the act*

ˣ 3¹² So Luc. Heb., *on his behalf, saying, Whose is the land?* The repetition of, *saying*, and the lack of sense confirm the conclusion that the confusion is due to a copyist and that Luc. retains the original text.
ᵃ 3²⁵ So Gk. and Syr.
ᵇ 3²⁷ So Gk. Heb., *the midst.*
ᶜ 3²⁹ Heb., *holds the spindle, i.e.,* is like a woman. The current translation, *leans on a staff*, follows the Gk.

Early Judean David Narratives

Joab and Abishai his brother slew Abner, because he had killed their brother Asahel at Gibeon in the battle.ᵈ

His lamentation over Abner

³¹And David said to Joab, and to all the people who were with him, Tear your clothes, and gird yourselves with sackcloth, and mourn before Abner! And King David followed the bier. ³²And when they buried Abner in Hebron, the king wept with a loud voice at the grave of Abner, and all the people wept. ³³And the king sang a dirge for Abner and said,

> Must Abner die as dies the impious fool?
> ³⁴Thy hands were not bound,
> Thy feet were not put into fetters;
> As one falls before ruthless men, thou didst fall.

Then all the people wept still more over him. ³⁵Afterwards all the people came to urge David to eat bread while it was yet day; but David took oath, saying, God do to me whatever he will, if I taste bread or anything else before the sun goes down. ³⁶And when all the people observed it, they were pleased; forᵉ everything that the king did pleased all the people. ³⁷So all the people and all Israel understood that day that the king had nothing to do with the slaying of Abner the son of Ner. ³⁸And the king said to his servants, Do you not know that a prince and a great man has fallen to-day in Israel? ³⁹And I am this day weak, though anointed king, for these men, the sons of Zeruiah, are too strong for me.ᶠ May Jehovah requite the evil-doer according to his wickedness!

§ 25. Assassination of Ishbaal, II Sam. 4¹⁻³, ⁵⁻¹²

Early Judean David Narratives

The crime

II Sam. 4 ¹Now when Ishbaal, Saul's son, heard that Abner was dead in Hebron, his hands became limpᵍ and all the Israelites were thrown into confusion. ²And Ishbaal, Saul's son, had two men who were captains of guerilla bands: the name of the one was Baanah, and the name of the other Rechab, sons of Rimmon the Beerothite, of the Benjamites (for Beeroth is also reckoned to Benjamin, ³and the Beerothites fled to Gittaim and have been sojourners there until this day). ⁵And the sons of Rimmon the Beerothite, Rechab and Baanah, went and came about mid-day to the house of Ishbaal, as he was taking his rest at noon. ⁶And just then the doorkeeper of the palace was cleaning wheat, and she became drowsy and slept. So Rechab and Baanah his brother slipt in and thus entered the house, while [the king] was lying

---

ᵈ 3³⁰ The repetitious element and the strange introduction of Abishai indicate that this verse is a scribal addition; intended to excuse Joab's action.

ᵉ 3³⁶ Slightly correcting the Heb. with the aid of the Gk.

ᶠ 3³⁹ The meaning of the Heb. is somewhat doubtful.   Luc. makes Abner the subject and reads, *though he had been a relative and officer of the king, yet these sons of Zeruiah were too strong for them.*

§ 25 Chap. 4 continues the preceding narrative. The awkward explanatory note in ²ᵇ, ³ is probably from a later hand. Some editor has also inserted in ⁴ a brief account of the accident that befell Jonathan's son whereby he became a cripple and therefore ineligible for the throne. It belongs more properly with 9, § 32, which tells of David's treatment of him. Vs. ⁵ is the immediate sequel of ²ᵃ.

ᵍ 4¹ *I.e., he lost courage.*

Early Judean David Narratives

on his bed in his sleeping room, and they smote and killed him and cut off his head.[h]

⁷Then they took his head and went all night by the way of the Arabah. ⁸And they brought the head of Ishbaal to David to Hebron and said to the king, Here is the head of Ishbaal, the son of Saul your enemy, who sought your life. But Jehovah hath avenged my lord the king this day on Saul and his descendants. ⁹Then David answered Rechab and Baanah his brother, the sons of Rimmon the Beerothite, and said to them, As Jehovah liveth, who hath delivered my life out of all adversity, ¹⁰when one told me, saying, ' Behold, Saul is dead,' thinking to have brought good news, I took hold of him, and slew him in Ziklag, to give him the reward for his news.[i] ¹¹How much more, when wicked men have slain a righteous person in his own house upon his own bed, shall I not now require his blood from you and destroy you from the earth? ¹²Then David commanded his young men, and they slew them and cut off their hands and their feet, and hanged them up beside the pool in Hebron. But the head of Ishbaal they took and buried in the grave of Abner at Hebron.

David's attitude toward it [margin note]

§ 26. David's Election as King of All Israel, II Sam. 5¹⁻⁵, I Chr. 11¹⁻³, 12²³⁻⁴⁰

Early Judean David Narratives

II Sam. 5 ¹Then all the tribes of Israel came to David to Hebron and said, See, we are your bone and your flesh. ²In times past when Saul was king over us, it was you who led out and brought in Israel, and Jehovah hath said to you, 'Thou shalt be shepherd of my people Israel, and thou shalt be prince over Israel.' ³And all the elders of Israel came to the king to Hebron, and King David made a covenant with them in Hebron before Jehovah, and they anointed David king over Israel.

The public election [margin note]

⁴David was thirty years old when he became king, and he reigned forty years. ⁵In Hebron he reigned over Judah seven years and six months, and in Jerusalem he reigned thirty-three years over all Israel and Judah.

Length of David's reign [margin note]

Chronicler's Ecclesiastical History

I Chr. 12 ²³And these are the numbers of the leaders of the warriors who came to David to Hebron, to turn over to him the kingdom of Saul, in accordance with the word of Jehovah. ²⁴The Judahites who bore shield

Later tradition regarding the rally of the tribes [margin note]

---

h 4⁶, ⁷ᵃ The Heb. text is untranslatable and the Gk. has here apparently preserved the original.

i 4¹⁰ Following a slightly revised text. The present Heb. reads, *which was the reward I gave him for the good news.*

§ 26 In the original David narratives this important event appears to have been recorded in one verse, ³. Compelled by necessity and believing in David's sincerity and superior ability, the elders of the North ratified with him at Hebron the compact which made him their king. The same is stated in ¹, ² in language which reveals its later origin and point of view. The chronological note in ⁴ is probably from the late prophetic editor.

The Chronicler in I Chr. 11¹⁻³, quotes II Sam. 5¹⁻³ practically verbatim. In 12²³⁻⁴⁰, however, he gives a detailed and much embellished account of the event. The numbers of those represented as having been present have reached incredible proportions: *e.g.*, 120,000 came from across the Jordan. The distinction between the priests and Levites, which was first made in the days of Josiah, is here assumed. The account has all the characteristics of a late Jewish midrash or didactic story, which reflects the magnified conceptions current in the days of the Chronicler regarding this event, the importance of which became more apparent in the light of subsequent ages.

Chronicler's Ecclesiastical History

and spear were six thousand, eight hundred armed warriors. ²⁵Of the Simeonites seven thousand, one hundred brave, able warriors. ²⁶Of the Levites four thousand, six hundred. ²⁷And Jehoiada was the prince of the house of Aaron, and with him were three thousand, seven hundred, ²⁸and Zadok a brave, able young man, together with his father's house: twenty-two commanders. ²⁹And of the Benjamites, the kinsmen of Saul, three thousand; for hitherto the majority of them had maintained their allegiance to the house of Saul. ³⁰And of the Ephraimites twenty thousand, eight hundred brave, able warriors, famous men in their families. ³¹And of the half tribe of Manasseh eighteen thousand who were mentioned by name to come and make David king. ³²And of the Issacharites, men who thoroughly understood the times, so that they knew what Israel ought to do—their two hundred leaders and all their clansmen were under their command. ³³Of Zebulun, there took the field, ready for battle and fully armed with all the weapons of war, fifty thousand—a band united by a common purpose.ʲ ³⁴And of Naphtali a thousand commanders, and with them thirty-seven thousand with shield and spear. ⸱³⁵And of the Danites twenty-eight thousand, six hundred ready for battle. ³⁶And of Asher, there took the field, forty thousand ready for battle. ³⁷And from the other side of the Jordan, of the Reubenites and the Gadites and of the half tribe of Manasseh, a hundred and twenty thousand fully equipped with all the weapons of war. ³⁸All these warriors, united by a single purpose,ᵏ came to Hebron to make David king over all Israel. And all the rest of Israel also had the one purpose of making David king.

The great feast ³⁹And they were with David three days, eating and drinking, for their kinsmen had made preparation for them. ⁴⁰Moreover those who were near them, as far as Issachar and Zebulun and Naphtali, brought food on asses, camels, mules, and oxen—provisions consisting of meal, cakes of figs, bunches of raisins, wine, oil, oxen, and sheep in abundance; for joy reigned in Israel.

§ 27. The War with the Philistines, II Sam. 5¹⁷⁻²⁵, 8¹, 21¹⁵⁻²², 23¹³⁻¹⁷
I Chr. 11¹⁵⁻¹⁹, 14⁸⁻¹⁷, 18¹, 20⁴⁻⁸

Early Judean David Narratives

The Philistine advance **II Sam 5** ¹⁷Now when the Philistines heard that they had anointed David king over Israel, all the Philistines went up to seek David; and when David heard of this he went down to the stronghold.¹

ʲ I Chr. 12³³ Heb., *not with a heart and a heart.*

ᵏ I Chr. 12³⁸ Heb., *by a perfect heart* or *mind.* Cf. ³³.

§ 27 The opening verse states that the events recorded in this section immediately followed David's election as king by all Israel. Jebus does not figure in this contest and its capture in all probability followed later. The statements in ¹⁰⁻¹² cover a considerable period and imply that David is at least master of central Canaan. His anointing as king over all Israel is interpreted by the Philistines as a declaration of war, 5¹⁷. The incidents recorded indicate that the Philistine attack found him unprepared for war. He makes not Jebus but Adullam, which

---

¹ 5¹⁷ *I.e.,* Adullam. Cf. I Sam. 22⁵, II Sam. 23¹³⋅ ¹⁴ and the expression, *went down.* If it had been Jerusalem, *went up* would have been used.

Early Popular David Stories

23 ¹³And three of the Thirty[m] went down, and came to the rock[n] to David to the stronghold[o] of Adullam, while a force of the Philistines was encamped in the valley of Rephaim.[p] ¹⁴And David was then in the stronghold, and the garrison of the Philistines was in Bethlehem. ¹⁵And David longed and said, O that one would give me water to drink from the well of Bethlehem, which is by the gate ! ¹⁶And the three famous warriors broke through the camp of the Philistines and drew water out of the well of Bethlehem, that was by the gate, and took and brought it to David; he would not drink of it, however, but poured it out to Jehovah. ¹⁷And he said, Jehovah forbid that I should do this. It is the blood of the men who went at the risk of their lives.[q] Therefore he would not drink it.[r] These things did the three mighty men.[s]

Brave deed of the three warriors at Bethlehem

Early Judean David Narratives

5 ¹⁸Now the Philistines had come and spread themselves out in the valley of Rephaim. ¹⁹And David inquired of Jehovah, saying, Shall I go up against the Philistines ? Wilt thou deliver them into my hand ? And Jehovah said to David, Go up; for I will certainly deliver the Philistines into thy hand. ²⁰And David came to Baal-perazim, and David smote them there; and he said, Jehovah hath broken down mine enemies before me, like the breaking of waters.[t] Therefore he called the name of that place Baal-perazim [Lord of the breakings through]. ²¹And they left their gods[u] there, and David and his men carried them away.

The first victory in the valley of Rephaim

²²And the Philistines came up yet again and spread themselves out in the valley of Rephaim. ²³And when David inquired of Jehovah, he said,

The second victory

---

was his refuge in the outlaw period, his rallying point. The narratives in 5 are each distinct. It is impossible to determine absolutely the original order of events, but it appears to have been, (1) a long war for independence from the Philistines; (2) establishment of Jebus as the capital of the free and united Hebrew tribes; (3) establishment of the ark at Jerusalem.

The account of the first of these events in 5¹⁷⁻²⁵ is surprisingly brief and vague, considering its great importance in Israel's history. It appears to have been taken from the early Judean David narratives, but may for some reason have been abridged by the editor. It is supplemented, however, by certain anecdotes preserved in the appendix to the book of Sam. These are very loosely connected with their immediate context. Apparently the editor has taken them from some other source and introduced them as apt illustrations. Thus, *e.g.*, 23¹³ refers to the Thirty as though they had already been described, although in the present context that description is first found in ¹⁸. Their background and general atmosphere are the same as in 5¹⁷⁻²⁵, but unlike the latter they recount not national movements but the personal deeds of individual heroes. The stories are undoubtedly very ancient, but their character, contents, and position in Sam. strongly suggest that they are popular traditions associated with David and his heroes. This conclusion is also supported by the fact that in 21¹⁵⁻²¹ Elhanan the Bethlehemite is represented as slaying Goliath, which is in absolute contradiction to the testimony of the parallel traditions of I Sam. 17. Here a very ancient popular story may have preserved the more historical data. The variant of the Chronicler (cf. note[e], p. 122) appears to be simply an attempt to harmonize the two very different popular traditions about Goliath the Gittite.

m 23¹³ Cf. note § 34.

n 23¹³ The Heb. currently translated, *in the harvest time*, is ungrammatical. The parallel, I Chr. 11¹⁵, reads, *to the rock*. A slight emendation to the Heb. brings the text into accord with Luc., which is followed above.

o 23¹³ Heb., *cave*, but the next verse makes a slight correction necessary.

p 23¹³ Southwest of Jerusalem.

q 23¹⁷ So Luc., Syr., and Chr.

r 23¹³⁻¹⁷ A similar story is told of Alexander the Great (Arrian VI, 262).

s 23¹⁷ Probably this is an editorial note, intended to ascribe the deeds recorded in ⁸⁻¹² and ¹³⁻¹⁷ to the same three men. It is more appropriate after ¹².

t 5²⁰ *I.e., through a dam.*

u 5²¹ So Gk. and the parallel I Chr. 14¹².

Early Judean David Narratives

Thou shalt not go up; go about to their rear and come upon them opposite the balsam trees. ²⁴And when thou hearest the sound of marching in the tops of the balsam trees,ᵛ make haste, for then Jehovah has gone out before thee to smite the camp of the Philistines. ²⁵And David did as Jehovah commanded him, and smote the Philistines from Gibeon as far as Gezer.ʷ

Early Popular David Stories

The brave deed of Abishai

21 ¹⁵Now when the Philistines were again at war with Israel, David went down together with his servants and encamped in Gobˣ and fought against the Philistines. ¹⁶Then there arose Dodo, who was one of the descendants of the giants,ᵃ the weight of whose bronze spear was about twelve pounds of brass,ᵇ being girded with the sword, and thought to slay David.ᶜ ¹⁷But Abishai the son of Zeruiah succored him and smote and killed the Philistine. Then the men of David swore, saying, You shall go out no more with us to battle, that you may not quench the lamp of Israel.

Of Sibbecai

¹⁸Now when after this there was again war with the Philistines at Gob,ᵈ Sibbecai the Hushathite slew Saph, who was one of the descendants of the giants.

Of Elhanan

¹⁹And when there was again war with the Philistines at Gob, Elhanan the son of Jair the Bethlehemite,ᵉ slew Goliath the Gittite, the shaft of whose spear was like a weaver's beam.

Of Jonathan

²⁰And there was again war at Gath, where was a man of gigantic stature, who had on each hand six fingers and on each foot six toes; and he also was descended from the giants. ²¹And when he defied Israel, Jonathan the son of Shimei,ᶠ David's brother, slew him. ²²These four were descended from the giants in Gath; and they fell by the hand of David and by the hand of his servants.

David's complete victory

8 ¹And after this David smote the Philistines, and subdued them; and David took the bridle of the mother cityᵍ out of the hand of the Philistines.ʰ

ᵛ 5²⁴ The belief that the Deity resides in trees and speaks through the rustling of the winds in the branches is very ancient. Cf. Gen. 12⁶, Dt. 11³⁰, Judg. 9³⁷.

ʷ 5²⁵ So Gk. and I Chr. 14¹⁶. Cf. Is. 28²¹. In A.D. 66 the Romans retreated before the Jews by the same route. Cf. Jos., Wars, XIX.

ˣ 21¹⁵ The text is obscure and has evidently suffered in transmission. Vs. ¹⁶ begins with, *and they dwelt (encamped) in Nob*. But ¹⁸ suggests that the original read *Gob*. The transposition gives a more natural text.

ᵃ 21¹⁶ Heb., *Raphah*, a collective term for the prehistoric inhabitants of the land. Cf. Dt. 2¹¹, ²⁰, 3¹¹, ¹³. It appears to have been the popular designation of giants.

ᵇ 21¹⁶ Heb., *three hundred shekels*. According to I Sam. 17⁷ the head of Goliath's spear was twice as heavy.

ᶜ 21¹⁶ Reading only conjectural, being based upon a suggestion of Luc. The entire verse is obscure.

ᵈ 21¹⁸ Gk. and Syr., *Gath*. The Chr. parallel, *Gezer*. At least it seems probable that the events recorded in this passage are to be localized in Philistine rather than Israelitish territory, and that they therefore follow the victories recorded in 5.

ᵉ 21¹⁹ So I Chr. 20⁵, the Chr. parallel, reads *Elhanan the son of Jair slew Lahmi the brother of Goliath*. Other late Jewish writings eliminate the conflict with I Sam. 17 by substituting *David* for *Elhanan*.

ᶠ 21²¹ In 13³, *Shimea*; I Sam. 16⁹, *Shammah*; I Chr. 2¹³, 20⁷, *Shimea*.

ᵍ 8¹ The parallel in I Chr. 18¹ reads, *took Gath and its towns*. The Heb. of Sam. is obscure. It may mean the citadel which commanded the city, or more probably the authority over Gath.

ʰ 8¹ An editorial epitome.

§ 28. Capture and Establishment of Jerusalem as the Capital, II Sam. 5^{6-12}, I Chr. 11^{4-9}, $14^{1, 2}$

Early Judean David Narratives

he d- ance gainst ebus

II Sam. 5 6Then the king and his men went to Jerusalem against the Jebusites, the inhabitants of the land, who spoke to David, saying, You shall not come in here, but the blind and the lame shall turn you away,[i] thinking, David cannot come in here.[j]

ts apture nd for- fica- on

7Nevertheless David took the stronghold of Zion[k] (that is the city of David).[l] 8And David said on that day, Whoever smites the Jebusites, let him get up through the watercourse and smite the lame and the blind, whom David's soul hates.[m] Therefore it is said, The blind and the lame cannot come into the temple.[n] 9Then David dwelt in the stronghold, and called it the City of David. And David constructed an encircling wall from Millo[o] and inwards.[p]

David's row- ng res- ge

10And David kept on growing greater, for Jehovah[q] of hosts was with him. 11And Hiram king of Tyre sent messengers to David, and cedar trees and carpenters and masons and they built David a palace. 12Thus David perceived that Jehovah

Chronicler's Ecclesiastical History

I Chr. 11 4Then David and all Israel went to Jerusalem (that is Jebus); and the Jebusites, the inhabitants of the land, were there. 5And the inhabitants of Jebus said to David, You shall not come in here.

Nevertheless David took the stronghold of Zion (that is the city of David). 6And David said, Whoever smites the Jebusites first shall be commander-in-chief. And Joab the son of Zeruiah went up first, and was made chief. 7Then David dwelt in the stronghold; therefore they called it the city of David. 8And he constructed an encircling wall from Millo even round about; and Joab built up[r] the rest of the city.

9And David kept on growing greater, for Jehovah of hosts was with him. **14** 1And Hiram king of Tyre sent messengers to David, and cedar trees and masons and carpenters to build him a palace. 2Thus David perceived that Jehovah had established him king over Israel, for his

---

§ 28 For the probable order of events cf. note § 27. The capture of Jerusalem marks the final downfall of Canaanitish independence in central Palestine. Cf. Josh. 15^{63}, Judg. 1^{21}. It also gave David an almost impregnable capital, more centrally located than Hebron and the common possession of all the tribes. Above all it opened what later proved to be one of the most important chapters in the religious history of mankind.

The original narrative was taken from the early Judean David source. Unfortunately it early became obscure at several points. The Chronicler accordingly gives a rather free paraphrase of the version in II Sam.

[i] II Sam. 5^{6} Or, *except you remove the blind and the lame.*

[j] II Sam. 5^{6} A later gloss to explain the meaning of the Heb. text of the preceding.

[k] II Sam. 5^{7} The southeast hill of the city.

[l] II Sam. 5^{7} A later addition.

[m] II Sam. 5^{8} Or, *whosoever smites the Jebusites brings his own neck into danger; the lame and the blind David's soul hates not.* Either translation is exceedingly doubtful, for the text is almost hopelessly corrupt. The Chronicler substituted an intelligible reading for the baffling original.

[n] II Sam. 5^{8} Apparently a later note, connecting the law regarding the lame and blind (Lev. 21^{18}) with this incident.

[o] II Sam. 5^{9} The encircling wall mentioned in I Kgs. 9^{15} and II Chr. 32^{5}.

[p] II Sam. 5^{9} Or, *towards the house, i.e., palace* or *sanctuary.* The corresponding words in I Chr. are lacking in the Gk.

[q] II Sam. 5^{10} So Gk. and the parallel in Chr. Heb. adds, *God of.*

[r] I Chr. 11^{8} Heb., *gave life to.*

Early Judean David Narratives	Chronicler's Ecclesiastical History
had established him king over Israel, for his kingdom had been exalted[s] for the sake of his people Israel.	kingdom had been exalted on high for the sake of his people Israel.

§ 29. Establishment of the Ark and the Davidic Dynasty at Jerusalem, II Sam. 6, 7, I Chr. 13, 15¹–16⁷, ³⁷–17²⁷

Early Judean David Narratives

The first attempt to bring up the ark, and the death of Uzzah

II Sam. 6 ¹Then David again assembled all the chosen men of Israel, thirty thousand. ²And David arose and went with all the people who were with him, to Baal-Judah,[t] to bring up from there the ark of God which is called by the name of Jehovah of hosts who sits enthroned upon the cherubim.[u] ³And they set the ark of God upon a new cart, and brought it out of the house of Abinadab, that was on the hill,[v] with Uzzah and Ahio the sons of Abinadab guiding the cart: Uzzah went with the ark of God,

Chronicler's Ecclesiastical History

I Chr. 13 ¹Then David consulted with the commanders of thousands and of hundreds, even with all the leaders. ²And David said to all the assembly of Israel. If it is satisfactory to you and pleasing to Jehovah, our God, we will send to all our remaining countrymen in the land of Israel, since the priests and Levites are with them in their cities which have common pasture lands, that they may be gathered to us, ³in order that we may bring back the ark of

---

[s] II Sam. 15¹² So Chr., Gk., and Syr.   Heb., *that he had exalted.*

§ 29 It was natural that after making Jerusalem his capital, David should desire to transfer thither the ark.   The act was prompted by both religious and diplomatic motives.   It was the palladium with which was associated Israel's early experiences and victories.   Undoubtedly it was very popular with the people.   Like Gideon before him and Jeroboam later.   § 60, David also wisely sought to make his new capital a religious as well as a political centre.   The transfer of the ark facilitated the realization of this aim.   The story reflects the same primitive ideas as appear in the other early Judean narratives.   It is closely connected with the account of the ark among the Philistines in I Sam. 5 and 6, § 4.

The parallel in I Chr. 13, 15, 16 represents a very different conception of the events.   In 13 the Sam. narrative is the basis, but it has been abbreviated at points and expanded at others, in the spirit and according to the well-known methods of the Chronicler.   Cf. Introd., pp. 22–24.   Conformably to the strict ceremonial ideas of his age, the priests and Levites are introduced as the guardians of the ark.   In 15¹⁻¹⁵, ²⁵⁻¹⁶³, however, he may have drawn from a late priestly temple history.   Cf. Introd., p. 27.   The basis is still the narrative of II Sam. but the Levites are divided into six classes, 15³⁻¹⁰, not into three as by the Chronicler, 23¹ᶠᶠ.   Many late prophetic ideas and expressions also abound.   The original narrative is recast so that everything is done in accordance with the late priestly law of Lev.   It is still further transformed by the Chronicler, who introduces in 15¹⁵⁻²⁴ and 16⁴⁻⁷, ³⁷⁻⁴³, the guilds of temple singers, which sprang up about the second temple and in which he was especially interested.   Cf. Introd., p. 24.   Finally this highly composite version has been further supplemented by the insertion in 16⁸⁻³⁶ of a psalm compiled from Pss. 105¹⁻¹⁵, 96, 106.

There is no suggestion in the early David narratives that he contemplated building a temple beyond the fact that he transferred the ark to Jerusalem.   The implication of this act doubtless gave rise to the later traditions which trace back to him the plan to rear the sanctuary that subsequently became the centre of Israel's religious life.   II Sam. 7 is clearly from a later hand than 6.   Ideas and experiences are reflected which first came to the Heb. race in the seventh century B.C.   The messianic hope based on the long-continued rule of the house of David, is prominent.   Except possibly in ¹⁰, there are no traces of the influence of the Babylonian exile.   The conception of the kingship is distinct from that of the Ephraimite school, and the ideas and expressions of the late prophetic writers are not much in evidence.   It appears rather to come from some later Judean prophet, imbued with a strong love for the Judean royal house.

[t] II Sam. 6² In Josh. 15²⁻¹¹ and I Chr. 13⁶ this is identified with Kirjath-jearim.

[u] II Sam. 6² As in I Sam. 4⁴ this description of Jehovah is from a later scribe.

[v] II Sam. 6³ Owing to a scribal error part of ³ᵃ in the Heb. has been repeated in ⁴.   The Gk. and the Chr. parallel facilitate the restoration of the original.   The phrase, *that was on the hill,* is not found in Chr. and was probably added by a scribe familiar with I Sam. 7¹.

Early Judean David Narratives	*Chronicler's Ecclesiastical History*
⁴while Ahio went before the ark.ʷ ⁵And David and all the house of Israel were dancing before Jehovah with all their might and with songs and harps and lyres and cymbals. ⁶And when they came to the threshing-floor of Nacon, Uzzah stretched out his hand to the ark of God to hold it, for the oxen slipped. ⁷Then the anger of Jehovah was aroused against Uzzah and God smote him there because he had stretched out his hand to the ark,ᵇ so that he died there in the presence of God. ⁸And David was angry because he had broken forth upon Uzzah. Therefore that place is called Perez-uzzah [Breach of Uzzah] to this day. ⁹And David was afraid of Jehovah that day so that he said, How can the ark of Jehovah come to me? ¹⁰And David was unwilling to remove the ark of Jehovah to the city of David, but carried it aside into the house of Obed-edom the Gittite. ¹¹So the ark remained in the house of Obed-edom the Gittite three months. And Jehovah blessed Obed-edom and all his house.	our God to us, for we sought it not in the days of Saul. ⁴Then all the assembly voted to do so, for the thing seemed right in the eyes of all the people. ⁵So David assembled all Israel from the River of Egyptˣ to the entrance of Hamath,ᵃ to bring the ark from Kiriath-jearim. ⁶Then David with all Israel went up to Baalah, to Kiriath-jearim which belongs to Judah, to bring from there the ark of God which is called by the name of Jehovah, who sits enthroned on the cherubim. ⁷And they carried the ark of God upon a new cart from the house of Abinadab with Uzzah and Ahio guiding the cart. ⁸And David and all Israel played before God with all their might and with songs and harps and lyres and tambourines and with cymbals and with trumpets. ⁹But when they came to the threshing-floor of Chidon, Uzzah stretched out his hand to hold the ark, for the oxen stumbled. ¹⁰And the anger of Jehovah was aroused against Uzzah and he smote him because he had stretched out his hand to hold the ark, so he died there in the presence of God. ¹¹And

David was angry because Jehovah had broken forth upon Uzzah; therefore that place is called Perez-uzzah to this day. ¹²And David was afraid of God that day saying, How can I bring the ark of God home to me? ¹³So David was not willing to remove the ark to the city of David, but carried it aside into the house of Obed-edom the Gittite. ¹⁴Therefore the ark of God remained with the family of Obed-edom near his house three months. And Jehovah blessed the house of Obed-edom and all that he had.

ʷ II Sam. 6⁴ Restoring by the Chr. parallel. The Heb. makes no sense and is evidently corrupt.

ˣ I Chr. 13⁵ Heb., *Nile,* but this is probably a scribal error for, *the River of Egypt,* which was the southwest boundary of Israel.

ᵃ I Chr. 13⁵ *I.e.,* Coelesyria, where the roads leading to Hamath converge.

ᵇ II Sam. 6⁷ Again restoring the corrupt Heb. by the aid of I Chr. 13¹⁰.

Early Judean David Narratives | *Chronicler's Ecclesiastical History*

Its final transfer to Jerusalem

6 ¹²And when the report came to King David: Jehovah hath blessed Obededom and all his house because of the ark of God, David went and brought up with joy the ark of God from the house of Obededom to the city of David.[c] ¹³And when the bearers of the ark of Jehovah had gone six paces, he sacrificed an ox and a fatling. ¹⁴And David was dancing[d] before Jehovah with all his might, and David was girded with a linen ephod.[e] ¹⁵So David and all the house of Israel brought up the ark of Jehovah with shouting, and the sound of the trumpet.

15 ¹Then David made him houses in the city of David and prepared a place for the ark of God and pitched for it a tent. ²Then David said, None ought to carry the ark of God but the Levites: for them hath Jehovah chosen to carry the ark of God and to minister to him forever. ³And David assembled all Israel at Jerusalem, to bring up the ark of Jehovah to its place, which he had prepared for it. ⁴And David gathered together the sons of Aaron, as well as the Levites. ⁵Of the sons of Kohath, Uriel the chief, with his kinsmen, a hundred and twenty; ⁶of the sons of Merari, Asaiah the chief with his kinsmen, two hundred and twenty; ⁷of the sons Gershom, Joel the chief with his kinsmen, one hundred and thirty; ⁸of the sons of Elizaphan, Shemaiah the chief with his kinsmen, two hundred; ⁹of the sons of Hebron, Eliel the chief, eighty; ¹⁰of the sons of Uzziel, Amminadab the chief, with his kinsmen, one hundred and twelve. ¹¹And David called for Zadok and Abiathar the priests and for the Levites, Uriel, Asaiah, Joel, Shemaiah, and Eliel, and Amminadab, ¹²and said to them, You are the heads of the families of the Levites; sanctify yourselves, both you and your kinsmen, that you may bring up the ark of Jehovah, the God of Israel, to the place that I have prepared for it. ¹³Because you were not ready at the first, Jehovah our God broke out upon us, for we sought him not as we should. ¹⁴So the priests and the Levites sanctified themselves to bring up the ark of Jehovah, the God of Israel. ¹⁵And the members[f] of the Levitical guilds bore the ark of God with the staves on their shoulders, as Moses directed according to the command of Jehovah.[g] ¹⁶David also commanded the chief of the Levites to appoint their kinsmen the singers, with instruments of music, lyres, harps, and cymbals, who should raise loud sounds of rejoicing. ¹⁷So the Levites appointed Heman the son of Joel; and of his kinsmen, Asaph the son of Berechiah and of the sons of Merari their kinsmen, Ethan the son of Kushaiah, ¹⁸and with them their kinsmen of the second rank, Zechariah, Uzziel,[h] Shemiramoth, Jehiel, Unni, Eliab, Benaiah, and Maaseiah, Mattithiah, Eliphelehu, Mikneiah, Obed-edom, Jeiel, the door-

---

c II Sam. 6¹² Luc. adds, *and David said, I will turn the blessing to my house.*
d II Sam. 6¹⁴ The word probably means, *whirling*, as the dervishes do to-day.
e II Sam. 6¹⁴ The garment of a priest, I Sam. 2¹⁸.
f I Chr. 15¹⁵ Heb., *sons of the Levites.* Cf. the corresponding expressions, *sons of the prophets*, or the modern Arabic designation of a traveller, *a son of the way.*
g I Chr. 15¹⁵ So Gk. and Luc. The Heb. is so corrupt that it is untranslatable.
h I Chr. 15¹⁸ So Gk. and in ²⁰. In the Heb. the name is variously written, in ¹⁸ *Joaziel*, in ²⁰ *Aziel*, in 16⁵ *Jeiel*, although this name occurs again in the same verse.

Chronicler's Ecclesiastical History

keepers. [19]So the singers, Heman, Asaph, and Ethan were to sound aloud on cymbals of brass, [20]while Zechariah, Uzziel, Shemiramoth, Jehiel, Unni, Eliab, Maaseiah, and Benaiah played with lyres set to Alamoth[i] [21]and with Mattithiah, Eliphelehu, Mikneiah, Obed-edom, Jeiel, and Azaziah, with harps set to the octave, to lead. [22]And Chenaniah, chief of the Levites,[j] was in charge of the ark; he directed the carrying of it, for he was skilful. [23]And Berechiah and Elkanah were doorkeepers for the ark. [24]And Shebaniah, and Jehoshaphat, and Nathanel, and Amasai, and Zechariah, and Benaiah, and Eliezer, the priests, blew the trumpet before the ark of God; Obed-edom and Jehiah were also doorkeepers for the ark. [25]So David with the elders of Israel and the commanders of thousands went to bring up with rejoicing the ark of the covenant of Jehovah out of the house of Obed-edom. [26]And because God was gracious to the Levites who bore the ark of the covenant of Jehovah, they sacrificed seven bullocks and seven rams. [27]And David was clothed with a robe of fine linen, and all the Levites, who bore the ark, and the singers and Chenaniah, who was in charge[k] of the transportation of the ark, and David had on an ephod of linen. [28]Thus all Israel brought up the ark of the covenant of Jehovah with loud shouting and with the sound of the cornet and trumpet and cymbals, sounding aloud with lyres and harps.

Early Judean David Narratives

6 [16]Now when the ark of Jehovah was coming into the city of David, Michal the daughter of Saul looked out of the window, and when she saw King David l e a p i n g and dancing before Jehovah, she despised him in her heart. [17]And when they

[29]But while the ark of the covenant of Jehovah was coming to the city of David, Michal the daughter of Saul looked out at the window and saw King David[l] dancing and sporting. And she despised him in her heart. **16** [1]And when they had brought in the ark of God, they set it in the midst of the tent that David had pitched for it, and they offered burnt-offerings and peace-offerings before God. [2]And when David had finished sacrificing the burnt-offering and peace-offerings, he blessed the people in the name of Jehovah. [3]And he distributed to every one in Israel, both man and woman, a loaf of bread, and a portion of meat, and a bunch of raisins. [4]And he appointed certain of the Levites to minister before the ark of Jehovah and to celebrate, thank, and praise Jehovah, the God of Israel: [5]Asaph the chief, and second to him Zechariah, then Uzziel, Shemiramoth, Jehiel, Matti-

---

[i] I Chr. 15[20] Probably a musical direction. It occurs in the superscription to Pss. 6 and 12. The meaning, *maiden's voices, i.e., soprano* has been conjectured. For a full discussion of Hebrew music and the different musical orders, cf. Introd., Vol. V.
[j] I Chr. 15[22] Gk., *chief of the singing.*
[k] I Chr. 15[27] A scribe has taken the Heb. word to mean, *song,* and added, *singers. Singers* in the first part of the verse is also probably a later insertion.
[l] II Chr. 15[29] According to early Hebrew ideas the king was the chief-priest of the nation. Cf. I Kgs. 9[25].

Early Judean David Narratives	*Chronicler's Ecclesiastical History*
brought in the ark of Jehovah and set it in its p l a c e in the midst of the tent that David had pitched for it, David o f f e r e d burnt - offerings and peace-offerings before Jehovah. ¹⁸A n d when David had finished sacrificing the burnt-offering and the peace-offerings, he blessed the people in the name of Jehovah of hosts. ¹⁹And he distributed to all the people even a m o n g t h e	thiah, Eliab, Benaiah, Obed-edom, and Jeiel, with lyres and harps; while Asaph played loudly with cymbals, ⁶and Benaiah and Jahaziel the priests with trumpets continually before the ark of the covenant of God. ⁷Also on that day David for the first time entrusted to Asaph and his clansmen the giving of thanks to Jehovah. ³⁷So he left there before the ark of the covenant of Jehovah, Asaph and his brethren to minister before the ark continually, as every day's work required ; ³⁸and Obed-edom the son of Jeduthun and Hosah, with their clansmen, sixty-eight,ᵐ to be doorkeepers, ³⁹and Zadok the priest, and his clansmen the priests, before the dwelling of Jehovah in the high place that was at Gibeon, ⁴⁰to offer burnt-offerings to Jehovah upon the altar of burnt-offering continually morning and evening, according to all that is written in the law of Jehovah, which he commanded Israel; ⁴¹and with them Heman and Jeduthun, and the rest of those who were mentioned by name to give thanks to Jehovah, because his kindness endures forever; ⁴²and with them (Heman and Jeduthun) trumpets and cymbals for the musicians and instruments for the songs of God; and the sons of Jeduthun to stand in the gate. ⁴³Then all the people went each to his house, and David returned to greet his family.

whole multitude of Israel, both men and women, to each a cake of bread, a portion of meat,ⁿ and a bunch of raisins. Then all the people departed each to his home.

David and Michal   ²⁰But when David returned to greet his family, Michal the daughter of Saul came out to meet David and said, How glorious was the king of Israel as he exposed himself to the eyes of his servants' maids, as one of the vain fellows shamelessly exposes himself ! ²¹And David said to Michal, It was before Jehovah that I was dancing. Blessed be Jehovah,º who chose me rather than your father and rather than any of his family to appoint me as prince over the people of Jehovah, over Israel. Therefore I will sport before Jehovah ²²and I will be yet more lightly esteemed than this and I will be despised by you.ᵖ But of the maids of whom you have spoken I shall indeed be held in honor. ²³And Michal the daughter of Saul had no child to the day of her death.

ᵐ II Chr. 16³⁸ As the result of a scribal error, *Obed-edom* is repeated.
ⁿ II Sam. 6¹⁹ The Heb. word occurs only here and its exact meaning is not known. The reading given above is only a conjecture based on the probability that meat formed a part of the feast provided.
º II Sam. 6²¹ These initial words in David's speech are preserved in the Gk., but have been omitted in the Heb. through a scribal error.
ᵖ II Sam. 6²² So Gk. The Heb., *in my eyes*, does not fit the context.

Later Judean Prophetic Narratives

7 ¹Now when David had taken possession of his palace,q Jehovah having given him rest around about from all his enemies,r ²the king said to Nathan the prophet, See now, I dwell in a house of cedar, but the ark of God dwells within tent-curtains. ³And Nathan said to the king, Go, do all that you purpose for Jehovah is with you.

⁴But during the same night the word of Jehovah came to Nathan, saying, ⁵Go and tell my servant David, ' Thus saith Jehovah, " Shouldst thou build a temple for me to dwell in ?s ⁶I have not dwelt in a temple since the day that I brought up the Israelites from Egypt, even to this day, but have gone about in a tent-dwelling. ⁷As long as I went about with all the Israelites, did I say anything to one of Israel's judges,t whom I commanded to be a shepherd to my people Israel, saying: Why have ye not built me a house of cedar ?" ' ⁸Now therefore thus shalt thou say to my servant David, " Thus saith Jehovah of hosts, I took thee from the pasture, from after the sheep, that thou shouldest be prince over my people, over Israel;u ⁹and I have been with thee wherever thou didst go, to destroy all thine enemies from before thee, and I will make thee a name,v like the name of the great in the earth. ¹⁰And I will appoint a place for my people Israel, and will plant them, that they may dwell in their own place, and be moved no more, and the wicked shall no more afflict them as formerly, ¹¹from the day that I appointed judges over my people Israel.

> And I will give thee rest from all thine enemies,
> And make thee great and build thee a house.w
> ¹²And when thy days are complete,
> And thou shalt lie down with thy fathers,
> I will raise up thy descendants after thee,
> Who shall come forth from thy body;
> And I will establish their kingdom.
> ¹³He shall build a home for my name,
> And I will establish his royal throne forever.x

> ¹⁴I will be to him a father,
> And he shall be to me a son;
> When he commits iniquity,
> I will correct him with the rod of men,y
> And with the stripes of the sons of Adam.
> ¹⁵And my kindness will I not withdraw from him,

Side notes: David's desire to build a temple; Jehovah's promise to David and his descendants.

q II Sam. 7¹ I Chr. 17 reproduces this chapter practically verbatim.
r II Sam. 7¹ This circumstantial clause is not found in the Chr. parallel and may be a secondary addition. It does not, however, anticipate the subsequent wars of conquest.
s II Sam. 7⁵ The parallel in I Chr. 17⁴ reproduces this as a negative sentence. The negative force is implied in the Heb.
t II Sam. 7⁷ So I Chr. 17⁶. Heb., *tribes*, owing to a scribal error.
u II Sam. 7⁸ There are traces of a metrical structure in this and the following verses but it cannot be restored without fundamentally reconstructing the text.
v II Sam. 7⁹ *I.e.*, reputation. So I Chr. 17⁸. Heb. adds, *great*.
w II Sam. 7¹¹ The scribe evidently mistook a letter so that the Heb. read, *letteth thee* and then added *Jehovah*, as the subject. The Gk. of I Chr. 17¹⁰ has preserved the original which reveals the metre and parallelism so that from this point on the original poetical structure is apparent. The poem is really a messianic psalm.
x II Sam. 7¹³ This verse is an interpolation, for ¹³b repeats ¹² (cf. ¹⁶) and the antecedent is Solomon, while in ¹² it is the dynasty of David.
y *I.e.*, humanely.

Later Judean Prophetic Narratives

As I withdrew it from him who was before thee.[a]
[16]Thy house and kingdom shall always stand firm before me ;
Thy throne shall be established forever."

[17]According to all these words and according to all this vision, Nathan spoke to David.

David's prayer

[18]Then King David went in and sat before Jehovah and said, Who am I, O Lord Jehovah, and what is my house, that thou hast brought me thus far ?   [19]And this was too small a thing in thine eyes, O Lord Jehovah, that thou hast spoken also concerning thy servant's house for distant times, and hast let me see the generations of men for all times to come ![b]   [20]And what shall David say more to thee, for thou knowest thy servant, O Lord Jehovah ? [21]For thy servant's sake and according to thine heart hast thou done it to show thy servant all this greatness.[c]   [22]Therefore thou art great, O Jehovah my God,[d] for there is none like thee, neither is there any God besides thee, according to all that we have heard with our ears.   [23]And what other nation in the earth is like thy people Israel, whom a God went to redeem for himself as a people, to make him a name and to do for them great and terrible things in driving a people and its god before his people ?[e]   [24]But thou didst establish thy people Israel as thine own people forever, and thou, Jehovah, hast become their God.   [25]And now, O Lord Jehovah, confirm forever the promise that thou hast made concerning thy servant and concerning his house, and do as thou hast promised, [26]that thy name be great forever, in that it will be said, ' Jehovah of hosts is God over Israel; and the house of thy servant David shall be established before thee.'   [27]For thou, O Jehovah of hosts, the God of Israel, hast revealed to thy servant, saying, ' I will build thee a house;' therefore hath thy servant found courage to pray this prayer to thee.   [28]And now, O Lord Jehovah, thou art God, and thy words are truth, and thou hast promised this good thing to thy servant; [29]now therefore may it please thee to bless the house of thy servant that it may continue forever before thee !   For thou, O Lord Jehovah, hast spoken it, and with thy blessing will the house of thy servant be forever blessed.

---

[a] II Sam. 7[15] Following Gk., Syr., Lat., and I Chr. 17[13].
[b] II Sam. 7[19] Heb., *and this is the law of men.* The Chronicler and the translators evidently had great difficulty with the text. The above translation is based on a free reconstruction and is supported by the parallelism.
[c] II Sam. 7[21] Reconstructing the text with the aid of the Gk. parallel. Cf. I Chr. 17[19].
[d] II Sam. 7[22] So Luc. Heb. simply, *God.*
[e] II Sam. 7[23] Again the Heb. is obscure and corrupt, but can be restored with the aid of the Chr. parallel, Gk. and Luc.

§ 30. **David's Family and Court,** II Sam. 3²⁻⁵, 5¹³⁻¹⁶, 8¹⁵⁻¹⁸, 20²³⁻²⁶, I Chr. 3¹⁻⁹, 14³⁻⁷, 18¹⁴⁻¹⁷, 27²⁵⁻³⁴

Late Prophetic Editorial Summary

II Sam. 3 ²Now in Hebron sons were born to David: his eldest was David's Amnon the son of Ahinoam the Jezreelitess; ³and his second, Chileab the chil-dren son of Abigail, the wife of Nabal the Carmelite; and the third, Absalom born in the son of Maacah, the daughter of Talmai king of Geshur; ⁴and the fourth, bron He- Adonijah the son of Haggith; and the fifth, Shephatiah the son of Abital; ⁵and the sixth, Ithream the son of Eglah, David's wife. These were born to David in Hebron.

5 ¹³And in Jerusalem David took for himself more concubines and wives, In Jer- after he came there from Hebron; and more sons and daughters were born usalem to David. ¹⁴And these are the names of those who were born to him in Jerusalem: Shammua, Shobab, Nathan, Solomon, ¹⁵Ibhar, Elishua, Nepheg, Japhia, ¹⁶Elishama, Baaliada,ᶠ and Eliphelet.

8 ¹⁵And David was king over all Israel. And David administered justice His and righteousness to all his people. ¹⁶And Joab the son of Zeruiah was in state officials command of the army, and Jehoshaphat the son of Ahilud was chancellor, ¹⁷and Zadok and Abiatharᵍ the son of Ahimelech were priests, and Shoushaʰ was scribe, ¹⁸and Benaiah the son of Jehoiada was in command of the Cherethites and the Pelethites, and David's sons were priests; **20** ²⁶Ira the Jairiteⁱ was also a priest of David, ²⁴ᵃand Adoniramʲ was in charge of the forced labor.

The Chronicler's Summary

I Chr. 27 ²⁵And over the king's treasures was Azmaveth the son of Admin- Adiel, and over the treasures in the fields, in the cities, and in the villages, istra- tors of and in the castles was Jonathan the son of Uzziah, ²⁶and over those who did the the work of the field to cultivate the ground was Ezri the son of Chelub, royal estates ²⁷and over the vineyards was Shimei the Ramathite, and over the increase of the vineyards for the stores of wine was Zabdi the Shipmite, ²⁸and over

---

§ 30 These summaries, inserted often awkwardly and without any close connection with their context, appear to be from the late prophetic editor. They may have been transcribed bodily from the earlier source—probably the early David narratives—but their character sug- gests that they are summaries, perhaps compiled in part by the editor himself and embodying all the facts at his command. II Sam. 20²⁵⁻²⁶ is probably the original, while 8¹⁵⁻¹⁸, which dupli- cates it for the most part, was probably added as a conclusion to the summaries of David's reign in 8.

This material is repeated by the Chronicler, who adds in I Chr. 27²⁵⁻³⁴ a list of twelve offi- cials who had charge of the royal estates and herds. The number twelve suggests that the whole is the creation of a late age, and the language and point of view of the section indicate that it is probably from the pen of the Chronicler himself. David, however, possessed lands and herds, and the names may have been derived from an older source.

ᶠ II Sam. 5¹⁶ The parallel in I Chr. 14⁷ shows that a later scribe substituted here, *Eli* (my God) for the detested name *Baal.* Cf. the similar scribal changes into *Ethbaal* and *Meribaal.*

ᵍ II Sam. 8¹⁷ Heb., *Zadok the son of Ahitub and Ahimelech the son of Abiathar.* But ac- cording to I Sam. 22⁹ Ahimelech was a son of Ahitub and in 22²⁰ Abiathar was priest. Cf. I Kgs. 1²⁵, 2²⁶, where Zadok and Abiathar are priests. Evidently the original text must be restored as above.

ʰ II Sam. 8¹⁷ Heb., *Seriah,* but in 20¹⁵, *Sheiva;* Luc., *Sousa;* I Chr. 18¹⁶, *Shousha.* The latter appears to have been the original form.

ⁱ II Sam. 20²⁶ Luc. and Syr., *Jattivite.*

ʲ II Sam. 20²⁴ᵃ Heb., *Adoram;* but Gk., Luc., and II Chr. 10¹⁸ as above.

The Chronicler's Summary

the olive and the sycamore trees in the Shephelah was Baalhanan the Gederite, and over the stores of oil was Joash, ²⁹and over the herds that fed in Sharon was Shitrai the Sharonite, and over the herds that were in the valleys was Shaphat the son of Adlai, ³⁰and over the camels was Obil the Ishmaelite, and over the asses was Jehdeiah the Meronothite, and over the flocks was Jaziz the Hagrite. ³¹All these were in charge of the property which King David possessed.

Royal counsellors

³²Also Jonathan, David's kinsman, was a counsellor, a man of insight and learning,ᵏ and Jehiel the son of Hachmoni was with the king's sons, ³³and Ahithophel was the king's counsellor, and Hushai the Archite was the king's friend; ³⁴and after Ahithophel was Jehoiada, the son of Benaiah, and Abiathar; and the commander of the king's army was Joab.

§ 31. Public Execution of the Sons of Saul, II Sam. 21¹⁻¹⁴

Early Judean David Narratives

Demand of the Gibeonites

II Sam. 21 ¹Now in the days of David there was a famine three years, year after year. And when David sought the face of Jehovah, Jehovah said, Upon Saul and upon his house there is blood-guilt,ˡ because he put to death the Gibeonites, ²(now the Gibeonites were not of the Israelites, but of the remnant of the Amorites; nevertheless the Israelites had sworn to them; and Saul sought to slay them in his zeal for the Isrealites and the Judahites),ᵐ ³and David said to the Gibeonites, What shall I do for you? And wherewith shall I make the expiation, that you may bless the heritage of Jehovah? ⁴And the Gibeonites said to him, It is not a matter of silver and gold between us and Saul or his house; neither is it for us to put any man to death in Israel. And he said, What do you say that I shall do for you? ⁵And they said to the king, The man who consumed us, and who planned to destroy us that we should not remain in any of the borders of Israelⁿ—⁶let seven men of his sons be given to us, and we will hangᵒ them up to Jehovah in Gibeon in the mount of Jehovah. And the king said I will give them.

ᵏ I Chr. 27³² Heb., *and a scribe.*

§ 31 Again the literary style and primitive conceptions reflected in this story reveal its early date and probable relationship with the early David narratives. It represents David as subject to the firmly established ancient belief that the Deity could best be appeased by human sacrifice. To more enlightened later editors the idea was justly repulsive. They therefore did not quote it in the original edition of the book of Sam. Among the later gleanings from the David narratives it fortunately found a place in the final work, for it makes evident how crude were the religious ideas of the age. It is closely connected with 9. David's words, 9¹, and the representation in this section indicate that it originally preceded that chapter. They both record events which belong to the beginning of David's reign as king over all Israel. Cf. 16, § 42.

ˡ 21¹ The Gk. and Luc. seem to have preserved the original idea and aid in the reconstruction of the Heb.

ᵐ 21²ᵇ This long and awkward explanatory note is clearly a late gloss that has been introduced into the text. The original author would have naturally placed it after ¹. The one who introduced it also repeated in ³ the words in ²ᵃ. Cf. Josh. 9.

ⁿ 21⁵ Slightly correcting the text.

ᵒ 21⁶ The exact meaning of the Heb. verb is not known. The general significance of the Gk. and Targ. favors the above. Cf. Num. 25⁴ and I Sam. 31¹⁰. From ⁹ and the reading of certain Gk. texts, it seems probable that the original read as above. Heb., *in Gibeah of Saul, the chosen of Jehovah.*

132

Early Judean David Narratives

[7]But the king spared Meribaal,[p] the son of Jonathan, the son of Saul, because of Jehovah's oath which was between David and Jonathan the son of Saul.[q] [8]So the king took the two sons of Rizpah the daughter of Aiah, whom she bore to Saul, Armoni and Meribaal, and the five sons of Merab[r] the daughter of Saul, whom she bore to Adriel the son of Barzillai the Meholathite. [9]And he delivered them over to the Gibeonites, and they hung them in the mountain before Jehovah, so that the seven of them fell together; and they were put to death in the first days of harvest.

Execution of the sons of Saul and Rizpah

[10]Then Rizpah the daughter of Aiah took sackcloth, and spread it for her upon the rock, from the beginning of the barley harvest[s] until water was poured upon them from heaven; and she did not permit the birds of the heavens to settle down upon them by day nor the wild beasts by night. [11]And when it was reported to David what Rizpah the daughter of Aiah, the concubine of Saul, had done, [12]David went and took the bones of Saul and the bones of Jonathan his son from the men of Jabesh in Gilead, who had stolen them from the citizens of Bethshan, where the Philistines had hanged them, on the day that the Philistines slew Saul in Gilboa. [13]And he brought up from there the bones of Saul and the bones of Jonathan his son and they gathered the bones of those who were hanged. [14]And they buried the bones of Saul and the bones of Jonathan his son in the territory of Benjamin in Zela in the sepulchre[t] of Kish his father, and they did all that the king commanded. And after this God was propitiated toward the land.

Rizpah's devotion to the dead

§ 32. David's Treatment of the Son of Jonathan, II Sam. 4[4], 9

Early Judean David Narratives

II Sam. 4 [4]Now Jonathan, Saul's son, had a son who was lame in his feet. He was five years old when the news came from Jezreel regarding Saul and Jonathan. And his nurse took him up and fled, and while she was hastily fleeing, he fell and became lame. And his name was Meribaal.

Meribaal's lameness

9 [1]And David said, Is there left of the house of Saul any to whom I may show kindness for Jonathan's sake? [2]Now there was of the house of Saul a servant whose name was Ziba, and they called him to David. And the king said to him, Are you Ziba? And he said, Your servant am I. [3]The king said, is there no one else belonging to the house of Saul to whom I may

David's search for the remaining descendants of Saul

---

p 21[7] Later scribes have changed the name, as in the case of Ethbaal, cf. § 22 note[i], to *Mephibosheth* so that instead of *Baal the warrior*, it means, *who puffs at the shameful thing.* Luc. retains the original form.

q 21[7] The verse is probably a later note intended to harmonize this narrative with that in 9. Cf. note § 32.

r 21[8] So Luc., Targ., and the Heb. codices. Cf. I Sam. 18[19]. In the accepted text the name of Michal has been substituted by a scribe.

s 21[9, 10] At the close of [9] is found the repetitious phrase, *at the beginning of the barley harvest,* suggesting that the transposition was due to some copyist.

t 21[14] Or following certain Gk. codices, *in a chamber of the sepulchre.*

§ 32 Chap. 9 contains the sequel of the preceding story, which is further continued in 16. The note in 4[4] also finds here its natural connection. In its setting it appears to be but an explanatory addition from the hand of the editor, but the facts were doubtless derived from the older source, and it may be a verbatim quotation from the narrative from which 9 was taken. The story vividly presents that rare combination of tact and magnanimity which was one of the chief elements of David's greatness.

Early Judean David Narratives

show the kindness of God? And Ziba said to the king, Jonathan has still a son, who is lame in his feet. ⁴And the king said to him, Where is he? And Ziba said to the king, Behold he is in the house of Machir the son of Ammiel, in Lodebar.ᵘ ⁵Then King David sent and brought him from the house of Machir the son of Ammiel, from Lodebar. ⁶And when Meribaal the son of Jonathan, the son of Saul, came to David, he fell on his face and did obeisance. David said, Meribaal! And he answered, Behold your servant! ⁷Then David said to him, Fear not for I will surely show you kindness for the sake of Jonathan your father and will restore to you all the land of Saul your ancestor; and you shall eat at my table continually. ⁸And he did obeisance and said, What is your servant that you should look favorably upon such a dead dog as I am?

His provision for Meribaal

⁹Then the king called to Ziba, Saul's servant, and said to him, All that belongs to Saul and all his house have I given to your master's son. ¹⁰And you shall cultivate the land for him, together with your sons and servants, and bring in the fruits that your master's son may have food to eat; but Meribaal your master's son shall always eat bread at my table. Now Ziba had fifteen sons and twenty servants. ¹¹Then said Ziba to the king, Just as my lord the king commands his servant, so will your servant do. So Meribaal ateᵛ at David's table like one of the sons of the king. ¹²And Meribaal had a young son, whose name was Mica. And all who dwelt in the house of Ziba were Meribaal's servants. ¹³So Meribaal dwelt in Jerusalem, for he ate continually at the king's table, being lame in both feet.

§ 33. **The Census and Preparations for the Temple, II Sam. 24, I Chr. 21, 22**

Early Judean David Narratives

The taking of the census

II Sam. 24 ¹Then Jehovah's anger was again aroused against Israel, and he instigated David against them, saying, Go number Israel and Judah! ²So the king said to Joab and the commandersʷ of the army who were with him, Go now about among all the tribes of Israel, from Dan even to Beersheba,

Chronicler's Ecclesiastical History

I Chr. 21 ¹Then Satan stood up against Israel and moved David to number Israel. ²So David said to Joab and to the commanders of the people, Go, number Israel from Beersheba

ᵘ 9⁴ Cf. 17²⁷.
ᵛ 9¹¹ So Gk. and Luc. The Heb. puts these two words in the mouth of Ziba, but without revision they are unintelligible.
§ 33 II Sam. 24, like 21¹⁻¹⁴, appears to be a citation from the early David narratives which was added last to the book of Sam. It reflects the primitive belief that a census was displeasing to the Deity, as well as the other popular dogma that calamity was a sure index of Jehovah's condemnation. It probably originally followed 21¹⁻¹⁴. The latter tells of a famine and 24 of a pestilence which Jehovah was believed to have sent as a punishment. The census also belongs naturally in the opening years of David's rule over all Israel, for it was made by Joab and the military commanders and was intended to ascertain the number of men who could be counted upon for enrolment in the militia. Cf. ⁹. The fact that a Jebusite is still in possession of the threshing-floor in Jerusalem also suggests that the event followed not long after David's capture of Jebus.
The importance of the story is of course due to the fact that it records the purchase of what

ʷ II Sam. 24² So Gk., Luc., and in ⁴. Heb., *commander*.

Early Judean David Narratives

Chronicler's Ecclesiastical History

and muster the people that I may know the number of the people. ³Then Joab answered the king, May Jehovah your God add to the people, a hundred times as many as they are, while the eyes of my lord the king are looking on! But why has my lord the king a desire for such a thing? ⁴But the king's command prevailed against Joab and the commanders of the army. And Joab and the commanders of the army went out from the presence of the king to muster the people of Israel. ⁵And they crossed the Jordan, and began from Aroer and from the city that is in the midst of the torrent valley, towards Gad and on to Jazer.ˣ ⁶Then they came to Gilead and to the land of the Hittites, towards Kadesh;ᵃ and they came to Dan, and from Dan they went around to Sidon, ⁷and came to the fortress of Tyre and all the cities of the Hivites, and of the Canaanites; and they went out to the South Country of Judah at Beersheba. ⁸So when they had gone about through all the land, they came to Jerusalem at the end of nine months and twenty days. ⁹And Joab gave to the king the number of the people who had been mustered, and there were in Israel eight hundred thousand able-bodied, fighting men;ᵇ and the men of Judah were five hundred thousand.

to Dan; and bring me word, that I may know their number. ³Then Joab said, Jehovah make his people a hundred times as many as they are; but, my lord the king, are they not all my lord's servants? Why does my lord desire this thing? Why should he be a cause of guilt to Israel? ⁴But the king's word prevailed against Joab. Therefore Joab departed and went throughout all Israel and came to Jerusalem. ⁵And Joab gave to David the number of the people who had been mustered. And all they of Israel were one million, one hundred thousand fighting men; and Judah was four hundred and seventy thousand fighting men. ⁶But he did not include Levi and Benjamin in the muster, for the king's command was abominable to Joab.

David's remorse

¹⁰Then David's conscience smote him after he had numbered the people. And David said to Jehovah, I have sinned greatly in what I have done. But now, O Jehovah, pardon,

⁷And God was displeased with this thing so that he smote Israel. ⁸And David said to God, I have sinned greatly, in that I have done this thing. But now, pardon, I beseech thee, the

probably later became the site of Solomon's temple. It is thus distinctly interpreted in the Chr. parallel, I Chr. 21. The variations in Chr. are so marked and the unity of the parallel is so perfect that it is possible that the Chronicler here and in 22–26 quoted (cf. note § 29) from a late priestly temple history which was based on traditions in II Sam., but freely revising and at some points contradicting and at others expanding the older version. Late prophetic expressions and ideas abound. However, the Chronicler's work is readily recognized in 21²⁸⁻³⁰ and 22¹⁴⁻¹⁹, and the whole may be from his pen. Cf. Introd., p. 27. The tendency to project everything as far backward as possible is here prominent. To David is attributed the collection of the material for the temple. In 23–26, which relate to the priests, Levites, singers, and porters, and therefore belong with the legal material in Vol. IV, the institution of the later religious orders is also assigned to him.
ˣ II Sam. 24⁵ So Gk., Luc., and the restored Heb. text.
ᵃ II Sam. 24⁶ The present Heb. text, which has suffered at several points in transmission, may be restored as above with the aid of the Gk. and Luc. Possibly instead of *Kadesh* on the Orontes, the original read, *Hermon.*
ᵇ II Sam. 24⁹ Heb., *who drew the sword.*

Early Judean David Narratives | *Chronicler's Ecclesiastical History*

I beseech thee, the iniquity of thy servant, for I have done very foolishly.

iniquity of thy servant, for I have done very foolishly.

The divine condemnation and David's choice of the punishment

[11b]Then the word of Jehovah came to the prophet Gad, David's seer, saying, [12]Go and speak to David, ' Thus saith Jehovah, " Three things I offer thee; choose one of them, that I may do it to thee." ' [11a]So when David rose up in the morning,[c] [13]Gad came to David and told him, and said to him, Shall three[d] years of famine come over your land? Or will you flee three months before your foes, while they pursue you? Or shall there be three days' pestilence in your land? Now take counsel and consider what answer I shall return to him who sent me. [14]And David said to Gad, I am in a great strait. We would rather fall into the hand of Jehovah, for his mercy is great, but let me not fall into the hand of man.

[9]And Jehovah spoke to Gad, David's seer, saying, [10]Go and speak to David, saying, ' Thus saith Jehovah, "Three things I offer thee; choose one of them that I may do it to thee." ' [11]So Gad came to David, and said to him, Thus saith Jehovah, ' Choose [12]either three years of famine or that for three months you must flee before your foes and the sword of your enemies;[e] or else that for three days the sword of Jehovah and pestilence be in the land, and the Messenger of Jehovah destroying throughout all the territory of Israel.' Now therefore consider what answer I shall return to him who sent me. [13]And David said to Gad, I am in a great strait. I would rather fall into the hand of Jehovah, for his mercy is very great; let me not fall into the hand of man.

The pestilence

[15]So David chose the pestilence. And when it was the time of wheat harvest, the plague began among the people and slew of the people from Dan to Beersheba seventy thousand men.[f] [16]And when the Messenger stretched out his hand toward Jerusalem to destroy it, Jehovah repented of the evil, and said to the Messenger who was destroying the people, Enough, now stay thy hand! and the Messenger of Jehovah was by the threshing-floor of Araunah

[14]So Jehovah sent a pestilence upon Israel; and there fell of Israel seventy thousand men. [15]And God sent a Messenger to Jerusalem to destroy it; but as he was about to destroy, Jehovah saw it and repented of the evil, so that he said to the destroying Messenger, Enough, now stay thy hand! And the Messenger of Jehovah was standing by the threshing-floor of Ornan the Jebusite. [16]And when David lifted up his eyes and saw the Messenger of Jehovah standing between earth and heaven, having a drawn sword in his hand stretched out over Jerusalem, then David and the elders, clothed in sackcloth, fell upon their faces. [17]And David said to God, Is it not I who

---

[c] II Sam. 24[11a] This has apparently been transposed by a copyist. It is not found in Chr.
[d] II Sam. 24[13] So the parallel in Chr., favored by the symmetrical use of the number three in the passage. Heb., *seven*, probably because *seven years of famine* was a proverbial expression.
[e] I Chr. 21[12] Correcting the Heb. text with the aid of the parallel in Sam.
[f] II Sam. 24[15] The Gk. has a duplicate version of this text, the one reproducing the Heb., *So Jehovah sent a pestilence upon Israel from the morning until the appointed time.* This, however, is indefinite. The other Gk. duplicate followed above is more graphic and accords best with the context.

Early Judean David Narratives | *Chronicler's Ecclesiastical History*

the Jebusite. ¹⁷And David spoke to Jehovah when he saw the Messenger who smote the people, and said, See I have sinned and have acted wickedly; but these sheep, what have they done? Let thy hand, I pray, be against me, and my father's house.ᵍ

thought to number the people? I am the one who has sinned and acted very wickedly; but these sheep what have they done? Let thy hand I pray, O Jehovah my God, be against me and my father's house ; but not against thy people that they should be affected with the plague.

¹⁸And Gad came that day to David, and said to him, Go up, rear an altar to Jehovah on the threshing-floor of Araunah the Jebusite. ¹⁹So David went up at the command of Gad, as Jehovah commanded. ²⁰And when Araunah looked down and saw the king and his servants crossing over to him, Araunah went out and bowed before the king with his face to the ground. ²¹And Araunah said, Why has my lord the king come to his servant? And David said, To buy the threshing-floor of you, to build an altar to Jehovah, that the plague may be averted from the people. ²²And Araunah said to David, Let my lord the king take and offer what he pleases, the oxen for the burnt-offering, and the threshing-sledges and the implements of the oxen for the wood. ²³All this has your servant,ʰ my lord the king, given to the king. And Araunah said to the king, Jehovah your God accept you ! ²⁴And the king answered Araunah, No, but I will surely buy it of you at a price. I must not offer burnt-offerings to Jehovah my God which cost me nothing. So David bought the threshing-floor and the oxen for fifty shekels of silver. ²⁵Then David built there an altar to Jehovah, and offered burnt-offerings and peace-offerings. So

¹⁸Then the Messenger of Jehovah commanded Gad to say to David, that David should go up in order to rear an altar to Jehovah in the threshing-floor of Ornan the Jebusite. ¹⁹So David went up at the command of Gad, which he gave in the name of Jehovah. ²⁰And when Ornan turned about he saw the Messenger, and his four sons who were with him hid themselves. Now Ornan was threshing wheat. ²¹And as David came to Ornan, Ornan looked up and saw David, and went out of the threshing-floor, and bowed before David with his face to the ground. ²²Then David said to Ornan, Give me the place of this threshing-floor, that I may build on it an altar to Jehovah, For the full price shall you give it me, that the plague may be averted from the people. ²³And Ornan said to David, Take it as yours and let my lord the king do what he pleases. See, I give you the oxen for burnt-offerings and the threshing-sledges for wood and the wheat for the cereal-offering —I give it all. ²⁴But King David said to Ornan, No, but I will surely buy it for the full price, for I will not take that which is yours for Jehovah, nor will I offer a burnt-offering which cost me nothing. ²⁵So David gave to Ornan for the place six hundred shek-

(margin: he tar uilt the resh-g-or of rau-ah)

ᵍ II Sam. 24¹⁷ Vs. ¹⁸ is the direct sequel of ¹⁶. Vs. ¹⁷ introduces a note of individual penitence and confession that, like David's confession of his sin to Nathan, § 37, breathed the spirit of a later and more enlightened age.

ʰ II Sam. 24²³ Heb., *Araunah*, which was evidently read by some scribe for the more customary and, in the Heb., very similar word, *servant*.

Early Judean David Narratives | *Chronicler's Ecclesiastical History*

Jehovah was entreated for the land and the plague was averted from Israel.

els of gold by weight. ²⁶Then David built there an altar to Jehovah and offered burnt-offerings and peace-offerings. And when he called upon Jehovah, he answered him from heaven by fire upon the altar of burnt-offering. ²⁷And Jehovah commanded the Messenger to put his sword again into its sheath.

Place of the dwelling of Jehovah ²⁸At that time, after David saw that Jehovah had answered him in the threshing-floor of Ornan the Jebusite, he sacrificed there. ²⁹But the dwelling of Jehovah, which Moses made in the wilderness, and the altar of burnt-offering were at that time in the high place at Gibeon, ³⁰but David could not go before it to inquire of God, for he was afraid because of the sword of the Messenger of Jehovah.

David's preparations for the temple 22 ¹Then David said, This must be the temple of Jehovah God and this the altar of burnt-offering for Israel. ²And David commanded to gather together the foreigners who were resident in the land of Israel, and he set masons to hewing cut stones to build the house of God. ³And David prepared iron in abundance for the nails of the doors of the gates and for the couplings, and brass in abundance without weight; ⁴and innumerable cedar trees, for the Sidonians and the Tyrians brought cedar trees in abundance to David. ⁵Then David said, Solomon my son is young and inexperienced and the temple that is to be built for Jehovah must be exceeding magnificent, far-famed and glorious throughout all lands. I will therefore prepare for it. So David prepared abundantly before his death.

His directions to Solomon ⁶Then he called for Solomon his son and commanded him to build a temple for Jehovah the God of Israel. ⁷And David said to Solomon, My son, I myself had in mind to build a temple to the name of Jehovah my God. ⁸But the word of Jehovah came to me saying, 'Thou hast shed blood abundantly and hast carried on great wars; thou shalt not build a temple to my name, because thou hast shed much blood before me upon the earth. ⁹Behold, a son shall be born to thee, who shall be a man who shall have rest from all his enemies round about, for his name shall be Solomon [Peace], and I will give peace and quietness to Israel in his days. ¹⁰He shall build a temple for my name and he shall be my son and I will be his father; and I will establish his royal throne over Israel forever.' ¹¹Now, my son, Jehovah be with you, that you may prosper and build the temple of Jehovah your God, as he has spoken concerning you. ¹²Only may Jehovah give you discretion and insight, if he gives you charge of Israel, that thus you may keep the law of Jehovah your God. ¹³Then will you prosper, if you faithfully observe the statutes and the ordinances with which Jehovah charged Moses concerning Israel. Be firm and strong, fear not, neither be tempted. ¹⁴Now, see, with much trouble I have prepared for the house of Jehovah a hundred thousand talents of gold, and a million talents of silver, and brass and iron so abundant that they cannot be weighed; timber also and stone have I prepared, and you may add thereto. ¹⁵Moreover there are workmen with you in abundance, hewers and workers of stone and timber and all who are

Chronicler's Ecclesiastical History

skilful in every kind of work. ¹⁶Of the gold, the silver, and the brass and the iron, there is no limit. Arise, and go to work! and may Jehovah be with you.ⁱ

¹⁷David also commanded all the princes to help Solomon his son, saying, To the ¹⁸Is not Jehovah your God with you? And hath he not given you rest on _{princes} every side? for he hath delivered the inhabitants of the land into my hand; and the land is subdued before Jehovah and before his people. ¹⁹Now set your heart and your soul to seek Jehovah your God; arise therefore, and build the sanctuary of Jehovah God, that you may bring the ark of the covenant of Jehovah and the holy vessels of God into the temple that is to be built to the name of Jehovah.

§ 34. David's Illustrious Warriors, II Sam. 23⁸⁻¹², ¹⁸⁻³⁹, I Chr. 11¹⁰⁻¹⁴, ²⁰⁻⁴⁷, 27¹⁻²⁴

Early Judean David Narratives

II Sam. 23 ⁸These are the names of David's mighty heroes: Ishbaal The three the Hachmonite, leader of the Three;ʲ he swung his spear over eight hundred _{famous:} slain at one time.ᵏ _{Ishbaal}

⁹And next to him among the three mighty heroes was Eleazar the son of Elea- Dodo, the Ahohite. He was with David at Pasdammim when the Philis- _{zar} tines gathered there for battle. But when the Israelites retreated,ˡ ¹⁰he stood up and smote the Philistines until his hand was weary and clave fast to the sword. Thus Jehovah brought about a great deliverance that day; and the people returned after him only to take spoil.

¹¹And next to him was Shammah the son of Agee, a Hararite. And the Sham- Philistines gathered together at Lehi. And there was a plot of ground full _{mah} of lentils. But when the people fled from the Philistines, ¹²he stood in the

---

ⁱ I Chr. 22¹⁴⁻¹⁶ If the rest of the section is a quotation, the Chronicler has himself added these verses, for his interest in details and tendency to exaggerate are very prominent.
§ 34 The nucleus of the military organization whereby David built up his empire was an experienced body of warriors who by their bravery and personal achievements had each attained individual distinction. Some of them were foreigners. Most of them had probably followed him in his outlaw days. They were divided into two groups: the three most distinguished, and another band of thirty knights of the second rank. The list of the names given indicates that the number of *the Thirty* was extended so as to include thirty-three. They were classified not according to their ability as leaders, but on the basis of their individual acts of bravery. The brave deeds of some of them are recounted, and reveal a spirit of chivalry which was very like that which inspired the knights of Arthur's round table. The record was probably kept in connection with the other early David stories. Its rude literary form suggests great antiquity. The story in II Sam. 23¹³⁻¹⁷, as has already been noted, § 27, breaks the continuity of the present narrative and is probably a later insertion.
The names have suffered much corruption in transmission. The Chronicler has often preserved a better reading, but in certain cases it is impossible to be sure of the original. The Chronicler adds sixteen more names in 11⁴¹ᵇ⁻⁴⁷. It is difficult to determine whence these were derived. Budde suggests that they belong after I Chr. 12⁷. The majority have the same form as those in the preceding list and it is at least possible that the Chronicler reproduced a fuller version of the original source. In 27¹⁻²⁴, however, he makes the Thirty commanders of army corps with a total force of 288,000 men under them. Even Asahel, Joab's brother, who was early killed by Abner, ⁷, is resurrected, to command one corps!
ʲ 23⁸ I Chr. 11¹¹, chief of the Thirty.
ᵏ 23⁸ So Luc. The Heb. and the parallel in I Chr. 11¹¹ have widely variant readings.
ˡ 23⁹ Following the Chr. parallel, 11¹³, which appears to have preserved the more original meaning. So two Heb. manuscripts. In most of the texts the *Three* and the *Thirty* have apparently been confused, so that they read here, *Three;* but cf. ⁸, where Ishbaal is *leader of the Three.* So also in 14²².

Early Judean David Narratives

The Thirty: their leader

middle of the plot and defended it and slew the Philistines. Thus Jehovah brought about a great deliverance. [18]And Abishai, the brother of Joab the son of Zeruiah, was leader of the Thirty. And he swung his spear over three hundred slain, so that he was renowned among the Thirty. [19]He was honored more than the Thirty, so that he became their commander, but he did not attain to the Three.

Deeds of Benaiah

[20]And Benaiah the son of Jehoiada was a valiant man of Kabzeel, who had done great deeds; he slew the two sons of Ariel of Moab. He also went down and slew a lion in the midst of a pit in time of snow. [21]And he slew a tall[m] Egyptian, who had a spear in his hand, but he went down to him with a club and snatched the spear out of the Egyptian's hand and slew him with his own spear. [22]These things did Benaiah the son of Jehoiada, and he was renowned among the thirty mighty heroes. [23]He was honored more than the Thirty, but he did not attain to the Three. And David set him over his body-guard.

The remaining heroes

[24]Asahel the brother of Joab was one of the Thirty; Elhanan the son of Dodo of Bethlehem, [25]Shammah the Harodite, Elika the Harodite, [26]Helez the Paltite, Ira the son of Ikkesh, the Tekoite, [27]Abiezer the Anathothite, Sibbecai[n] the Hushathite, [28]Zalmon the Ahohite, Maharai the Netophathite, [29]Heled[o] the son of Baanah, the Netophathite, Ittai the son of Ribai of Gibeah of the Benjamites, [30]Benaiah a Pirathonite, Hurai[p] of the brooks of Gaash, [31]Abibaal[q] the Arbathite, Azmaveth the Barhumite, [32]Eliahba the Shaalbonite, Jashen the Gunite,[r] Jonathan, [33]the son of[s] Shammah, the Hararite, Ahiam the son of Sharar the Ararite, [34]Eliphelet the son of Ahasbai, the Maacathite, Eliam the son of Ahithophel, the Gilonite, [35]Hezro the Carmelite, Paarai the Arbite, [36]Igal the son of Nathan of Zobah, Bani the Gadite, [37]Zelek the Ammonite, Naharai the Beerothite, the armor bearers of Joab the son of Zeruiah, [38]Ira the Ithrite, Gareb the Ithrite, [39]Uriah the Hittite—in all thirty-seven.[t]

Chronicler's Ecclesiastical History

The Chronicler's additions

I Chr. 11 [41b]Zabad the son of Ahlai, [42]Adina the son of Shiza the Reubenite, a chief of the Reubenites, and thirty with him, [43]Hanan the son of Maacah, and Joshaphat the Mithnite, [44]Uzzia the Ashterathite, Shama and Jeiel the sons of Hotham the Aroerite, [45]Jedial the son of Shimri, and Joha his brother the Tizite, [46]Eliel the Mahavite, and Jeribai and Joshaviah the sons of Elnaam, and Ithmah the Moabite, [47]Eliel, and Obed and Jaasiel the Mezobaite.

---

m 23²¹ Correcting the Heb. by the parallel in I Chr. 11²³, which adds, *five cubits high.*
n 23²⁷ So Luc. and I Chr. 11²⁹.
o 23²⁹ So twenty-one codices, Targ. and I Chr. 11³⁰.
p 23³⁰ So I Chr. 11³² and certain Gk. codices.
q 23³¹ Correcting by the aid of the Chr. parallel.
r 23³² So Luc. Gk., *Gounite.* I Chr. 11³⁴, *Gizonite.*
s 23³³ So I Chr. 11³⁴. In Heb., *the son of,* has been displaced.
t 23³⁹ In the Heb. not thirty-seven but thirty-three are given under the head of *the Thirty.* To this may have been added *the Three* and Joab the commander of the army, making the thirty-seven.

Chronicler's Ecclesiastical History

27 ¹Now the Israelites after their number, the heads of fathers' *houses* Organ-
and the commanders of thousands and of hundreds, and their officers who ization
served the king in any matter of the corps, which came in and went out month and
by month throughout all the months of the year, were in each corps twenty- of the
four thousand.   ²Over the first corps for the first month was Ishbaal[u] the differ-
son of Zabdiel; and in his corps were twenty-four thousand.   ³*He was* of ent
the children of Perez, the chief of all the captains of the army for the first army
month.   ⁴And over the corps of the second month was Eleazar the son of[v] corps
Dodai the Ahohite,[w] and in his course were twenty-four thousand.   ⁵The
third commander of the army for the third month was Benaiah, the son of
Jehoiada the chief priest; and in his course were twenty-four thousand.
⁶This is that Benaiah, who was the mighty hero of the Thirty, and over the
Thirty; and of his corps was Ammizabad his son.   ⁷The fourth commander
for the fourth month was Asahel the brother of Joab, and Zebadiah his son
after him; and in his corps were twenty-four thousand.   ⁸The fifth commander for the fifth month was Shamhuth the Izrahite; and in his corps
were twenty-four thousand.   ⁹The sixth for the sixth month was Ira the son
of Ikkesh the Tekoite; and in his corps were twenty-four thousand.   ¹⁰The
seventh for the seventh month was Helez the Pelonite, of the children of Ephraim; and in his corps were twenty-four thousand.   ¹¹The eighth for the eighth
month was Sibbecai the Hushathite, of the Zerahites; and in his corps were
twenty thousand.   ¹²The ninth for the ninth month was Abiezer the Anathothite, of the Benjamites; and in his corps were twenty-four thousand.   ¹³The
tenth for the tenth month was Maharai the Netophathite, of the Zerahites; and
in his corps were twenty-four thousand.   ¹⁴The eleventh for the eleventh month
was Benaiah the Pirathonite, of the Ephraimites; and in his corps were
twenty-four thousand.   ¹⁵The twelfth for the twelfth month was Heled the
Netophathite, of Othniel; and in his corps were twenty-four thousand.

¹⁶Furthermore over the tribes of Israel: as prince of the Reubenites, Eliezer The
the son of Zichri; of the Simeonites, Shephatiah the son of Maacah; ¹⁷of tribal
Levi, Hashabiah the son of Kemuel; of Aaron, Zadok ; ¹⁸of Judah, Eliab,[x] mand-
one of the brothers of David; of Issachar, Omri the son of Michael ; ¹⁹of ers
Zebulun, Ishmaiah the son of Obadiah; of Naphtali, Jeremoth the son of
Ezriel; ²⁰of the Ephraimites, Hoshea the son of Azaziah; of the half-tribe of
Manasseh, Joel the son of Pedaiah; ²¹of the half-tribe of Manasseh in Gilead,
Iddo the son of Zechariah; of Benjamin, Jaasiel the son of Abner; ²²of Dan,
Azarel the son of Jeroham.   These were the commanders of the tribes of
Israel.   ²³But David had not taken the number of them from twenty years
old and under, because Jehovah had said he would make Israel as numerous
as the stars of heaven.   ²⁴Joab the son of Zeruiah had begun to number, but
did not finish; and there came wrath for this upon Israel, so that the number
was not put into the account in the Chronicles of King David.

---

u I Chr. 27² Cf. 11¹¹ and the parallel in II Sam. 23⁸.
   v I Chr. 27⁴ Heb., *Dodai*, but according to 11¹² and II Sam. 23⁹, the original must have
read as above.
   w I Chr. 27⁴ Restoring the text which here seems to have suffered through dittography.
   x I Chr. 27¹⁸ Heb. by mistake, *Elihu*.

§ 35. **David's Wars of Conquest, II Sam.** 8²⁻¹⁴, 10¹⁻11¹, 12²⁶·³⁴
I Chr. 18²⁻¹³, 19¹⁻20³

Early Judean David Narratives

Conquest of Moab

II Sam. 8 ²Then David smote Moab and measured them off with a line, making them lie down on the ground; and he measured two lines: one full line to put to death and one full line to save alive.ᵃ And thus the Moabites became subject to David, and brought a present.ᵇ

Cause of the war with the Ammonites

10 ¹Now it came to pass after this, that the king of the Ammonites died and Hanun his son became king in his place. ²And David said, I will show kindness to Hanun the son of Nahash as his father showed kindness to me. So David sent by his servants to condole with him concerning his father. But when David's servants came to the land of the Ammonites, ³the princes of the Ammonites said to Hanun their lord, Do you suppose that David is honoring your father in sending comforters to you? Has not David sent his servants to you to search the city and to spy it out and to overthrow it? ⁴So Hanun took David's servants, and shaved off the one half of their beards, cut their robes in two, even to their hips, and sent them away. ⁵When David was informed regarding the men,ᶜ he sent to meet them, for the men were greatly ashamed. And the king said, Stay at Jericho until your beards are grown and then return.

First victory of the Israelites under Joab

⁶Now when the Ammonites saw that they had become odious to David, the Ammonites sent and hired the Arameans of Beth-rehob, and the Arameans of Zobah, twenty thousand footmen, and the king of Maacah and of Ishtobᵈ with twelve thousand men. ⁷And when David heard of it, he sent Joab and all the army and the trained warriors.ᵉ ⁸And the Ammonites came out, and drew up in battle-array at the entrance of the city. And the Arameans of Zobah and Rehob, and Ishtob and Maacah, were by themselves

---

§ 35 The epitome of David's wars in II Sam. 8¹⁻¹⁴ correspond to the similar review of Saul's wars in I Sam. 14⁴⁷⁻⁵¹. In the original book, II Sam. 8 appears to have been immediately followed by 21 as is shown by the repetitions in parts of 8¹⁵⁻¹⁸ and 22²³⁻²⁶. The family history of David in 9¹⁻20²² was later introduced into the book. This older and fuller history of David was, however, evidently before the editor of the original book of Sam. His brief *résumé* of the Aramean wars in 8³⁻⁶⁰ was clearly based on the more detailed narrative in 10⁶⁻¹⁹, which, together with 10¹⁻⁵, 11¹⁻¹², ²⁶⁻⁵², gives the setting of David's great sin. General character and contents connect these older and fuller narratives with the early Judean Saul story in I Sam. 11.

The editor probably drew the rest of the data in 8 from the Judean David narratives. In 8⁷⁻¹⁰, ¹³, ¹⁴ᵃ, and possibly in 8²², he appears to have introduced quotations from the same source. The account in ¹¹, ¹² of the dedication of all his spoil to Jehovah reflects the ideas of a later age. The earlier usage is best represented in the description of the distribution of the spoil of the vanquished Amalekites in I Sam. 30²²⁻³¹.

The Chronicler follows the narrative in Sam. very closely. He omits the reference in 8² to the wholesale slaughter of the Moabites and the account of David's sin. The result is that, as in the present reconstruction, the contents of II Sam. 11 are brought into immediate conjunction with those of 12²⁶⁻³⁴.

ᵃ 8² So Syr. and Lat. Heb., *two lines to put to death and one full line to keep alive, i.e.,* two out of every three lines he condemned to die. But the Gk. translators in attempting to restore a better reading tacitly suggest an error in the Heb., for they read two lines in both cases. Owing to a common scribal error the full line was in one instance omitted. Cf. I Kgs. 11¹⁵.

ᵇ 8² The euphemistic manner of stating that they paid tribute.

ᶜ 10⁵ So Gk. supported by Chr. and demanded by the context, although the Heb. omits, *regarding the men.*

ᵈ 10⁶ The corrected parallel in I Chr. 19⁷, reads, *so they hired for themselves thirty-two thousand chariots and horsemen, and the Ammonites assembled from their cities and came to fight the Hebrews.* After *Maacah* it reads *with a thousand men and the men of Tob,* but this should make the force twenty-three thousand. The error probably arose from a confusion of the proper name, *Ishtob,* which is retained in the Gk.

ᵉ 10⁷ The trained warriors are distinct from the array which was made up of the militia. Either the last word is a gloss or, as some of the parallels suggest, *and* should be inserted.

Early Judean David Narratives

in the open country. [9]But when Joab saw that he was being attacked both in front and in the rear, he selected the picked men of Israel, and put them in array against the Arameans. [10]And the rest of the people he placed under the command of Abishai his brother; and he put them in array against the Ammonites. [11]And he said, If the Arameans should be too strong for me, then you shall help me, but if the Ammonites should be too strong for you, then I will come to your aid. [12]Be courageous and let us show ourselves men for the sake of our people and for the cities of our God; and may Jehovah do that which seems good to him. [13]Now when Joab and the people who were with him drew near for battle against the Arameans, they fled before him. [14]And when the Ammonites saw that the Arameans had fled, they likewise fled before Abishai, and entered into the city. Then Joab returned from the Ammonites, and came to Jerusalem.

[15]But when the Arameans saw that they had been defeated by the Israelites, they gathered themselves together, [16]and Hadadezer[f] sent, and brought out the Arameans who were beyond the River [Euphrates], and they came to Helam with Shobach, the commander of the army of Hadadezer, at their head. [17]And when it was reported to David, he gathered all Israel together and crossed over the Jordan and came to Helam. And the Arameans set themselves in array against David and fought with him. [18]And the Arameans fled before Israel; and David slew of the Arameans seven hundred horsemen and forty thousand footmen[g] and smote Shobach the commander of their army, so that he died there. [19]And when all the kings who were subject to Hadadezer saw that they were defeated by Israel, they made peace with Israel and were subject to them. So the Arameans feared to help the Ammonites any more.

The second campaign and victory over the Arameans

8 [3]Thus David smote Hadadezer the son of Rehob, the king of Zobah, as he went to establish his rule at the River Euphrates. [4]And David took from him a thousand chariots and seven thousand horsemen,[h] and twenty thousand footmen: and David hamstrung all the chariot horses leaving only a hundred of them. [5]And when the Arameans of Damascus came to help Hadadezer king of Zobah, David smote of the Arameans twenty thousand men. [6]Then David put garrisons in Aram of Damascus, and the Arameans became subject to David and brought a present. And Jehovah helped David wherever he went.

Subjugation of Hadadezer and the Arameans

[7]And David took the shields of gold that were on the servants of Hadadezer, and brought them to Jerusalem. [8]And from Tibhath[i] and from Berothai, cities of Hadadezer, King David took a great amount of brass.

The spoil

[9]And when Tou[j] king of Hamath heard that David had smitten all the army of Hadadezer, [10]Tou sent Hadoram[k] his son to King David, to greet him and to wish him good fortune, because he had fought against Hadadezer and smitten him, for Hadadezer was Tou's military antagonist. And he

Gifts of Tou, king of Hamath

---

[f] 10[16] As the result of a common error, *Hadarezer* is used in the Heb. of this chapter instead of the correct spelling, *Hadadezer*, as in 8[3, 5, 7-10].

[g] 10[18] The Heb., *slew seven hundred chariots*, is impossible and the *forty thousand horsemen*, with no reference to footmen, is, to say the least, extraordinary, cf. 8[4] below. The parallel in I Chr. 19[18] reads, *seven thousand chariots and forty thousand footmen*. The above probably represents the original.

[h] 8[4] So Gk. and I Chr. 18[4]. Heb., *seventeen hundred horsemen*.

[i] 8[8] So Gk. and the parallel in I Chr. 18[8]. Cf. Gen. 22[24].

[j] 8[9] Heb., *Toi*. Gk., Luc., and the parallel in I Chr. 18[9], *Tou*.

[k] 8[10] So Gk. and Chr. Heb., *Joram*.

Early Judean David Narratives

brought with him vessels of silver, of gold, and of brass. [11]These also King David dedicated to Jehovah, with the silver and gold that he dedicated from all the nations that he subdued—[12]from Edom,[l] Moab, the Ammonites, the Philistines, and Amalek, and from the spoil of Hadadezer son of Rehob, king of Zobah.

Defeat of the Edomites

[13]Then David made a reputation for himself. On his return, he smote of the Edomites in the Valley of Salt,[m] eighteen thousand men. [14]And he put garrisons in all Edom;[n] and all the Edomites became subject to David. And Jehovah helped David wherever he went.

Victorious conclusion of the war with the Ammonites

11 [1]Now, a year later,[o] at the time when kings are accustomed to go forth,[p] David sent Joab and his servants with him, even all Israel; and they destroyed the Ammonites, and besieged Rabbah. But David remained at Jerusalem. **12** [26]And Joab fought against Rabbah of the Ammonites and took the water city.[q] [27]Then Joab sent messengers to David, saying, I have fought against Rabbah; also I have taken the water city. [28]Now therefore gather the rest of the people together, and encamp against the city, and take it, lest I take the city and it should be called by my name. [29]So David gathered all the people together and went to Rabbah and fought against it and took it. [30]And he took the crown of Milcom[r] from his head; and its weight was about one hundred and forty pounds[s] of gold, and in it was a precious stone; and it was set on David's head.[t] And he brought away the great amount of spoil that was in the city. [31]And he brought away the people who were in it, and put them at the saws[u] and picks and axes of iron and made them work at the brickmoulds.[v] Even thus he did to all the cities of the Ammonites. Then David and all the people returned to Jerusalem.

§ 36. David's Double Crime, II Sam. 11[2-27]

Early Judean David Narratives

David's sin with Bathsheba

II Sam. 11 [2]Now once at eventide, while Joab was besieging Rabbath-Ammon, David arose from his bed, and walked upon the roof of the king's palace; and from the roof he saw a woman bathing. And the woman was

---

[l] 8[12] So Gk., Syr., eleven Heb. manuscripts, and I Chr. 18[11]. Heb., *Aram.*

[m] 8[13a] The Gk. connects this clause with the preceding paragraph and reads the remainder of the verse as above. The same text was probably before the Chronicler as the basis of his strange reading, I Chr. 18[12], *And Abishai the son of Zeruiah smote the Edomites.* Cf. I Kgs. 11[15a].

[n] 8[14] In the Heb., through an awkward scribal error, this clause is repeated, but I Chr. 18[13] does not have it.

[o] 11[1] Heb., *at the return of the year.*

[p] 11[1] So the parallel in I Chr. 20[1] and all the other versions. Heb., *when the messenger (of David first) went forth.* This may represent the idea of the original author.

[q] 12[26] Heb., *city of kings*, but this is clearly due to a slight scribal error and should read as in [27]. The *water city* was probably an outlying fortress, which protected the water supply of the capital.

[r] 12[30] The idol of the Ammonite god.

[s] 12[30] Heb., *a talent of gold.* Its weight indicating that it could have been placed only upon an idol.

[t] 12[30] *I.e.*, the precious stone was probably set in David's diadem.

[u] 12[31] The Chronicler, I Chr. 20[3], interpreted this to mean *cut with saw, i.e.*, sawed them; and he has been followed by many interpreters.

[v] 12[31] The misreading of one letter in the Heb. gives, *pass through the brickmoulds.* But this is meaningless. The statement that he brought away the people, as he did the spoil, confirms the conclusion that it was not to put them to death, but to enslave them.

§ 36 This faithful record of David's heinous sin plainly belongs to the earliest stratum of the Judean narratives. Although David was the popular hero of his race, the historian unsparingly lays bare the despicable motives and methods whereby he gratified his lust. Through-

Early Judean David Narratives

very beautiful. ³And David sent to inquire concerning the woman. And one said, Is not this Bathsheba, the wife of Uriah the Hittite? ⁴Then David sent messengers to take her; and she came to him, and he lay with her— she having been purified from her uncleanness. Then she returned to her house. ⁵And the woman conceived; and she sent to tell David, saying, I am with child.

⁶Then David said to Joab, Send me Uriah the Hittite. And Joab sent Uriah to David. ⁷And when Uriah had come to him, David asked him concerning the welfare of Joab and the people and the progress of the war. ⁸Then David said to Uriah, Go down to your house and wash your feet. And Uriah departed from the king's house, and there followed him a portion from the king. ⁹But Uriah slept at the door of the king's house with the servants of his lord and did not go down to his house. ¹⁰Now when it was told David, Uriah did not go down to his house, David said to Uriah, have you not come from a journey? Why did you not go down to your house? ¹¹But Uriah said to David, The ark and Israel and Judah are abiding in huts, and my master Joab, and the servants of my lord are camping in the open fields; shall I then go to my house to eat and drink and to lie with my wife! As Jehovah liveth and you live,ʷ I cannot do this. ¹²Then David said to Uriah, Stay here to-day also, and to-morrow I will let you go. So Uriah remained in Jerusalem that day. But on the next dayˣ ¹³David invited him and he ate and drank before him, so that he made him drunk. Then in the evening he went out to lie on his couch with the servants of his lord, but went not down to his house.

His attempt to conceal it

¹⁴And in the morning, David wrote a letter to Joab, and sent it by Uriah. ¹⁵And he wrote in the letter saying, Set Uriah in the face of the fiercest fighting, then retreat from behind him, that he may be smitten and die. ¹⁶So in keeping guard over the city, Joab assigned Uriah to the place where he knew valiant men were. ¹⁷And when the city went out to fight with Joab, there fell some of the soldiers of David, and Uriah the Hittite fell also. ¹⁸Then Joab sent to tell David all the facts concerning the war. ¹⁹And he instructed the messenger, saying, When you have finished telling all the facts concerning the war to the king, ²⁰then if the king's wrath is aroused, and he say to you, 'Why did you go so near to the city to fight? Did you not know that they would shoot from the wall? ²¹Who smote Abimelech the son of Jerubbaal?ʸ Did not a woman cast an upper mill-stone upon him from the wall, so that he died at Thebez? Why did you go near the wall?' Then shall you say, 'Your servant Uriah the Hittite is dead also.'

His murder of Uriah

---

out these stories of his family history the earnest ethical purpose of the prophetic teacher completely overshadows the natural tendency to idealize the character of the great conquering king. In the days of the Chronicler, however, the idealization has advanced so far that he refrains from all references to David's crimes and their consequences.

ʷ 11¹¹ Heb., *as you live and as your soul lives*, is a tautological and unprecedented form of oath. It is probably due to a scribal error. The ordinary idiom has been restored above.

ˣ 11¹² So Luc. and Syr. The Heb. does not join this with the following verse.

ʸ 11²¹ So Luc. The Heb. and Gk. have a corrupt form of the name. Cf. Judg. 9⁵³, Vol. I, § 142.

Early Judean David Narratives

Joab's report

²²ᵃSo the messenger of Joab went to the king at Jerusalem and came and told David all that Joab commanded him concerning the war. ²³Then the messenger said to David, The men boldly attacked us and came out to us in the open field, and so we drove them backᵃ even to the entrance of the gate. ²⁴ᵃAnd the archers shot at your servants from the wall; and some of the king's servants are dead. ²²ᵇThen David was very angry with Joab, and he said to the messenger, Why did you go near the city to fight? Did you not know they would shoot you from the wall? Who smote Abimelech, the son of Jerubbaal? Did not a woman cast an upper millstone upon him from the wall, so that he died in Thebez? Why did you go near the wall?ᵇ ²⁴ᵇBut the messenger said, Your servant Uriah the Hittite is dead also. ²⁵Thereupon David said to the messenger, Thus shall you say to Joab, ' Let not this thing displease you, for the sword devours one as well as another; persist in your attack uponᶜ the city, and overthrow it,' and encourage him.

David's marriage with Bathsheba

²⁶Now when the wife of Uriah heard that Uriah her husband was dead, she made lamentation for her husband. ²⁷But when the mourning was over, David sent and took her home to his house, and she became his wife and bore him a son. But the thing that David had done displeased Jehovah.

§ 37. David's Condemnation and Punishment, II Sam. 12¹⁻²³

Later Popular Prophetic Narratives

Nathan's parable

II Sam. 12 ¹Then Jehovah sent the prophetᵈ Nathan to David. And he came to him, and said to him, There were two men in one city, the one rich, the other poor. ²The rich man had very many flocks and herds. ³But the poor man had nothing, except one little ewe lamb, which he had bought. And he nourished it and it grew up with him and with his children. It used to eat of his own morsel, and drink out of his own cup, and lay in

---

ᵃ 11²³ Heb., *we were upon them.*
ᵇ 11²²ᵇ Following the Gk. which has here preserved the fuller and probably original text, but the instructions in ¹⁹⁻²¹ and the reference to the facts stated in ²³ indicate that this passage belongs after ²⁴ᵃ.
ᶜ 11²⁵ Heb., *strengthen your battle against.*
§ 37 The natural sequel of 11²⁷ᵇ is 12¹⁵ᵇ. *The thing that David had done was displeasing to Jehovah, and Jehovah smote the child which Uriah's wife bore to David.* This reflects the primitive conception of divine retribution. On the other hand the rôle of Nathan in 12¹⁻¹⁵ᵃ is that of a later Isaiah or Jeremiah. Elsewhere in the oldest sources Nathan figures rather as the effective supporter of Bathsheba's son Solomon, I Kgs. 1. The judgment pronounced by Nathan in ¹⁰⁻¹² anticipates the rebellion of Solomon and moves along still different lines and may be from a third hand. David's guilt was a subject that naturally aroused the moral sense of the prophets. His fasting and weeping in 16²¹⁻²³, the object of which was not forgiveness but the life of the child, were in harmony with his character in the early records and with the spirit of his age; but they did not satisfy the more exalted standards of the later prophets. In the thought of their age David was conceived of as the man after God's own heart. It was inevitable that they should also think of him as confessing his sin, as he doubtless would, had he enjoyed the benefit of the noble teachings of Hosea or Isaiah. In this later tradition he is the classic example of the royal penitent. Powerfully and effectively the dramatic story conveys the universal truths regarding the duty and beauty of frank confession. It only remained for a still later Psalmist to voice the passionate cry for forgiveness which rings through the fifty-first psalm.
The parable of the poor man with his one ewe lamb is characterized throughout by a marked poetic parallelism, although the metrical structure is so irregular that it is not practicable to print it as a poem.
ᵈ 12¹ So certain Heb. MSS., Gk., and Syr.

146

Later Popular Prophetic Narratives

his bosom, and was to him as a daughter. ⁴But there came a traveller to
the rich man, and he spared his own flock and did not take from it nor from
his own herd to make ready for the traveller who had come to him, but took
the poor man's lamb and prepared it for the man who had come to him.
⁵Then David's anger was greatly aroused against the man, and he said to
Nathan, As Jehovah liveth, the man who has done this is worthy of death,
⁶and he shall restore the lamb sevenfold,ᵉ because he showed no pity.

⁷Therefore Nathan said to David, You are the man! Thus saith Je- Con-
hovah, the God of Israel, ' I anointed thee king over Israel and I delivered demna-tion of
thee out of the hand of Saul, ⁸and I gave thee thy master's house and thy David
master's wives into thy bosom, and gave thee the house of Israel and of
Judah, and if that were too little, I would add to you as much again.'ᶠ
⁹Why have you despised the word of Jehovah by doing that which is evil?
You have smitten Uriah the Hittite with the sword, and have taken his
wife to be your wife, and have slain him with the sword of the Ammonites.
¹⁰Now therefore the sword shall never depart from your house, because
you have despised me and have taken the wife of Uriah the Hittite to be your
wife. ¹¹Thus saith Jehovah, ' Behold, I will raise up evil against thee out
of thine own house, and I will take thy wives from before thine eyes and
give them to thy neighbor, and he shall lie with thy wives in the sight of
this sun, ¹²for thou didst it secretly; but I will do this thing before all Israel,
and before the sun.' ¹³Then David said to Nathan, I have sinned against
Jehovah. And Nathan said to David, Jehovah also put away your sin;
you shall not die. ¹⁴Yet, because by this deed you have scornedᵍ Jehovah,
the child also that is born to you shall surely die. ¹⁵And Nathan departed
to his house.

Early Judean David Narratives

And Jehovah smote the child which Uriah's wife bore to David, so that Death
it fell sick. ¹⁶Then David besought God for the child, and fasted and went of David's
in and lay all night in sacklothʰ upon the earth. ¹⁷And the elders of his first son
house stood over him in order to raise him up from the earth; but he would by
not arise, neither would he eat bread with them. ¹⁸But on the seventh day Bath-sheba
the child died. And the servants of David feared to tell him that the child
was dead, for they said, Behold while the child was yet alive, we spoke to
him, and he hearkened not to our voice; how can we say the child is dead,
for he will do some harm! ¹⁹But when David saw that his servants were
whispering together, David perceived that the child was dead, and David
said to his servants, Is the child dead? And they said, He is dead. ²⁰Then
David arose from the earth, and washed and anointed himself, and changed

ᵉ 12⁶ So Gk. Heb., *fourfold.* The change was probably made to harmonize it with the
law of Ex. 22¹.
ᶠ 12⁸ Or, *in this or that way.*
ᵍ 12¹⁴ A later scribe has inserted, *enemies* after *scorned* in order to relieve the offensive
expression.
ʰ 12¹⁶ *In sackcloth* is found only in Luc. Cf. ²⁰.

Early Judean David Narratives

his garments; and he came into the house of Jehovah and worshipped. Then he went to his own house; and he asked for bread and they set it before him and he ate. ²¹Then said his servants to him, What is this you have done? You fasted and wept for the child, while it was alive, but when the child died, you arose and ate bread. ²²And he said, While the child was yet alive, I fasted and wept; for I said, ' Who knows whether Jehovah will have mercy, so that the child will live? ' ²³But now he is dead; why should I fast? Can I bring him back again? I am going to him, but he will not come back to me.

§ 38. Birth of Solomon, II Sam. 12²⁴, ²⁵

Early Judean David Narratives

Birth and name of the second son

II Sam. 12 ²⁴Then David comforted Bathsheba his wife, and went in unto her and lay with her and she conceived[i] and bore a son whose name he called Solomon. And Jehovah loved him, ²⁵and sent a message through[j] Nathan the prophet; and he called his name Jedidiah [The Beloved of Jehovah], according to the command of Jehovah.[k]

§ 39. The Crime of Amnon and Absalom's Revenge, II Sam. 13¹⁻²²

Early Judean David Narratives

Amnon's base passion for Tamar

II Sam. 13 ¹Now afterwards it came to pass that Absalom the son of David had a beautiful sister, whose name was Tamar; and Amnon the son of David loved her. ²And Amnon was so distressed that he became sick because of his sister Tamar—for she was a virgin—and it seemed to Amnon impossible to do anything to her. ³But Amnon had a friend whose name was Jonadab the son of Shimeah, David's brother, and Jonadab was a very shrewd man. ⁴And he said to him, Why are you, a king's son, so ill every morning? Will you not tell me? And Amnon said to him, I love Tamar, my brother Absalom's sister. ⁵And Jonadab said to him, Lie down on your bed, and pretend to be sick. Then when your father comes to see you, say to him, ' Let my sister Tamar come and give me bread to eat, and prepare the food in my sight, that I may see it and eat from her hand.' ⁶So Amnon lay down and pretended to be sick. And when the king came to see him, Amnon said to the king, Let my sister Tamar come and make a few[l] heart-shaped cakes in my sight, that I may eat from her hand.

---

i 12²⁴ So Gk., but omitted in the Heb.
j 12²⁵ Heb., *sent by the hand of*. A slight emendation of the text gives a reading consistent with Nathan's prominent position in I Kgs. 1, *and he was given over to Nathan*.
k 12²⁵ So Luc. and one Heb. text. Accepted Heb., *for Jehovah's sake*.
   § 39 The familiar story of the sins of David's sons and the train of disasters that resulted from them is taken from the ancient David narratives. All the different sections are closely connected, each constituting a scene in the stupendous tragedy which portrays not merely the anguish of the king but also the temporary dismemberment of the nation. With only slight additions, later editors and copyists have given us the story practically as it came from the pen of the original prophet historian.
l 13⁶ Heb. idiom, *two*.

Early Judean David Narratives

[7]So David sent home to Tamar, saying, Go now to your brother Amnon's house, and prepare food for him. [8]So Tamar went to her brother Amnon's house while he lay in bed. And she took dough and kneaded it and made cakes as he looked on, and baked the cakes. [9]And she took the pan and poured them out before him, but he refused to eat. And Amnon said, Let all go out from me. And they all went out from him.[m] [10]And Amnon said to Tamar, Bring the food into the inner room, that I may take from your hand. And Tamar took the cakes which she had made, and brought them into the inner room to Amnon her brother. [11]And when she had brought them to him to eat, he took hold of her and said to her, Come, lie with me, my sister. [12]And she answered him, No, my brother, do not force me, for it is not so done in Israel; do not commit this impious act of folly. [13]And as for me, whither could I carry my shame? and as for you, you would become one of the impious fools in Israel. Now therefore, I beg you, speak to the king, for he will not withhold me from you. [14]But he would not hearken to her, but being stronger than she, he violated her and lay with her.

His treacherous assault

[15]Then Amnon hated her with great hatred, for the hatred with which he hated her was greater than the love with which he had loved her. And Amnon said to her, Arise, be gone! [16]But she said to him, No, my brother; far greater is the second wrong in sending me away than the first that you did to me.[n] And he would not listen to her, [17]but called his servant who was standing in front of the house[o] and said, Put this woman out from my presence, and bolt the door after her. [18]And she wore a long-sleeved tunic, for thus the royal maidens were formerly wont to be clad.[p] Then his servant put her out and bolted the door after her. [19]And Tamar put ashes on her head, and rent her long-sleeved tunic which she wore; and she put her hand on her head, and went her way, crying aloud as she went.

His refusal to make amends for his crime

[20]And Absalom her own brother said to her, Has Amnon your brother been with you? But now, my sister, be silent, for he is your brother; do not take this thing to heart. So Tamar dwelt desolate in her brother Absalom's house. [21]But when King David heard of all these things, he was very angry, but he did not discipline[q] Amnon his son, for he loved him, because he was his eldest.[r] [22]And Absalom spoke to Amnon neither good nor bad; for Absalom hated Amnon, because he had violated his sister Tamar.

David's inaction and Absalom's secret hatred

---

[m] 13[9] This verse breaks the continuity of the story and is out of harmony with its context. Possibly [10] is also a later addition.

[n] 13[16] The Heb. text is obscure. Luc., which is here followed, has probably retained the original.

[o] 13[17] So Gk. Heb., *who ministered to him.*

[p] 13[18] This is evidently an explanatory gloss, intended to explain [19], but awkwardly introduced into the present context.

[q] 13[21] Heb., *vex the soul of.*

[r] 13[21] So Gk. The verse is incomplete in the Heb.

§ 40. **Absalom's Revenge,** II Sam. 13²³⁻³⁹

Early Judean David Narratives

Absa-
lom's
revenge

II Sam. 13 ²³Now it happened after two years, that Absalom had sheep-shearers in Baal Hazor near Ephraim, and Absalom invited all the king's sons. ²⁴And Absalom came to the king and said, See your servant has sheep-shearers; let the king, I pray, and his servants go with your servant. ²⁵But the king said to Absalom, No my son, let us not all go, lest we be burden-some to you. And he pressed him; however, he would not go but bade him farewell. ²⁶Then Absalom said, If not, then let my brother Amnon go with us. And the king said, Why should he go with you? ²⁷But when Absalom pressed him, he let Amnon and all the king's sons go with him. ²⁸Then Absalom commanded his servants, saying, See to it, when Amnon's heart is merry with wine, and when I say to you, 'Smite Amnon,' then kill him. Fear not; have not I commanded you? Be brave and show your-selves valiant men!ˢ ²⁹And the servants of Absalom did to Amnon as Absa-lom had commanded. Then all the king's sons arose and each mounted his mule and fled.

David's
recep-
tion of
the
news
of
Am-
non's
death

³⁰And while they were on the way, the news came to David: Absalom has slain all the king's sons so that there is not one of them left. ³¹Then the king arose and tore his clothes and lay on the earth; and all his servants who were standing by him tore their clothesᵗ and stood with torn clothes. ³²And Jonadab the son of Shimeah, David's brother, answered and said, Let not my lord suppose that they have killed all the young men, the king's sons, for Amnon only is dead, since by the statement of Absalom this was decided from the day of the violation of his sister Tamar. ³³Now therefore let not my lord the king take this thing to heart, to think that all the king's sons are dead; for Amnon only is dead. ³⁴And when the watchman lifted up his eyes and looked, there were many people coming down the descent on the Bethhoron road. And the watchman came and told the king, saying, I have seen people coming down from the Bethhoron road by the side of the hill.ᵘ ³⁵And Jonadab said to the king, There the king's sons are coming, as your servant said so it has come to pass. ³⁶As soon as he had finished speaking, the king's sons came and lifted up their voices and wept; and the king also and all his servants wept loudly.

Absa-
lom's
flight

³⁷ᵇAnd David mourned continually for his son. ³⁷ᵃBut Absalom fledᵛ and went to Talmai the son of Amihud, king of Geshur, ³⁸and remained there three years. ³⁹And the spiritʷ of King David longed to go out to Absalom, for he was comforted for the death of Amnon.

ˢ 13²⁸ So Gk., but omitted by a mistake in Heb.
ᵗ 13³¹ So Gk.
ᵘ 13³⁴ So Gk. Owing to a common scribal error half of the verse has been lost from the Heb.
ᵛ 13³⁷ᵃ The clause, *Absalom fled*, has been repeated three times in the Heb., ³⁴, ³⁷ᵃ, ³⁸ᵃ. Its original position was probably in ³⁸ᵃ. A scribe has also apparently introduced ³⁸ᵃ before ³⁷ᵇ. The result is repetition and confusion. The original reading has been restored above.
ʷ 13³⁹ So Luc.

§ 41. Pardon and Return of Absalom, II Sam. 14

Early Judean David Narratives

II Sam. 14 [1]Now when Joab the son of Zeruiah perceived that the king's heart was favorable towards Absalom, [2]Joab sent to Tekoa and brought from there a wise woman and said to her, Pretend to be a mourner and put on mourning garments and do not anoint yourself with oil, but become like a woman who has been many days mourning for one dead, [3]and go to the king and speak thus with him. So Joab put the words in her mouth.

[margin: Joab's intrigue to secure Absalom's pardon]

[4]And the Tekoite woman came to the king, and prostrated herself upon the ground and did obeisance, crying, Help, O king, help ![x] [5]And the king said to her, What is wrong with you? And she said, Verily, I am a widow and my husband is dead. [6]And your maid-servant had two sons, and these two quarrelled in the field when there was no one to part them, and one smote the other and killed him. [7]And now the whole clan has risen up against your maid-servant and say, ' Deliver up the slayer of his brother, that we may put him to death for the life of his brother whom he has killed, and we will destroy the heir.' Thus they will quench my remaining coal so as to leave to my husband neither name nor remnant on the face of the earth.

[margin: Fictitious petition of the Tekoite woman]

[8]Then the king said to the woman, Go to your house and I will give orders regarding you. [9]And the woman of Tekoa said to the king, My lord, O king, the guilt be on me and on my father's house; and the king and his throne be innocent. [10]And the king said, Whoever saith anything to you bring him to me and he shall not touch you again. [11]Then she said, I pray, let the king swear by Jehovah thy God, not to let the avenger of blood destroy and not to let them exterminate my son. And he said, As Jehovah liveth, not one hair of your son shall fall to the ground.

[margin: David's decision]

[12]Then the woman said, Let your maid-servant, I pray you, speak a word to my lord the king. And he said, Speak. [13]And the woman said, Why then do you devise such a thing against the people of God? For in rendering this decision the king is as one that is guilty, in that the king does not bring back his banished one. [14]For we die and are as water spilt on the ground, which cannot be gathered up again; and God will not take away the life of him who devises means not to keep in banishment one who is banished.[a] [15]Now the reason why I have come to speak this word to my lord the king is because the people made me afraid, and your maid-servant said, ' I will now speak to the king; it may be that the king will perform the request of his servant.' [16]For the king will hear, to deliver his servant out of the hand of the man who seeks to destroy me and my son from the heritage of Jehovah.[b] [17]Then your maid-servant said, ' Let the word of my lord the king be a comfort, for like the Messenger of God is my lord the king to hear good and evil.' And Jehovah thy God be with you.

[margin: Application of the principle to the royal judge]

---

[x] 14[4] So Gk. The second *help* is omitted in the Heb.
[a] 14[14b] The latter part of this verse is obscure. The above reading is based upon a slight correction of the text. The Heb. reads, *God will not take away life but desireth means.*
[b] 14[16] Following the suggestion of Luc. and Targ. Heb., *God.*

Early Judean David Narratives

His appreciation of Joab's purpose

¹⁸Then the king answered and said to the woman, Do not conceal from me, I pray, anything that I may ask you. And the woman said, Let my lord the king now speak. ¹⁹And the king said, Was the hand of Joab with you in all this? And the woman answered and said, As sure as you live, my lord the king, I cannot turn to the right hand or to the left from all that my lord the king has spoken, for your servant Joab bade me put all these words in the mouth of your maid-servant; ²⁰in order to change the face of affairs has your servant done this thing. But my lord is wise, according to the wisdom of the Messenger of God, so that he knows all things that are in the earth.

Return of Absalom

²¹And the king said to Joab, See now, I have granted this request; go therefore, bring the young man Absalom back. ²²Then Joab fell to the ground on his face and did obeisance and blessed the king. And Joab said, To-day your servant knows that I have found favor in your sight, my lord, O king, in that the king has granted the request of his servant. ²³So Joab arose and went to Geshur, and brought Absalom back to Jerusalem. ²⁴And the king said, Let him live apart in his own house, but my face he shall not see. So Absalom lived apart to his own house, but he did not see the king's face.

His personal beauty

²⁵Now no man in Israel was so praiseworthy for his beauty as Absalom: from the sole of his foot even to the crown of his head there was no blemish in him.[c] ²⁶And when he shaved his head—at the end every year he cut it, because it was heavy on him, therefore he cut it—he would weigh his hair, about six pounds[d] according to the royal standard of weight. ²⁷And to Absalom there were born three sons and one daughter, whose name was Tamar—she was a beautiful woman.

Restoration to royal favor

²⁸And Absalom dwelt two years in Jerusalem, without seeing the king's face. ²⁹Then Absalom sent for Joab to send him to the king; but he would not come to him. Then he sent again a second time, but he would not come. ³⁰Therefore he said to his servants, See Joab's field is near mine, where he has barley; go and set it on fire.[e] ³¹Then Joab arose, and came to Absalom at his house and said to him, Why have your servants set my field on fire? ³²And Absalom answered Joab, Behold, I sent to you, saying, 'Come here that I may send you to the king, to say, "Why have I come from Geshur? It were better for me to be there still."' Now therefore let me see the king's face, and if there be guilt in me, let him kill me. ³³And when Joab went to the king and told him, he called Absalom. And he came to the king and bowed himself with his face to the ground before the king. Then the king kissed Absalom.

---

[c] 14²⁵⁻²⁷ The statement in 18¹⁸ that Absalom had no children indicates that ²⁷ was drawn from a source distinct from the early David narratives. The reference in ²⁶ to the royal standard of weight also implies that, as in later times, two systems were then in use. This description of Absalom is clearly a later addition to the original narrative which is found in ²⁴ and its immediate sequel ²⁸.

[d] 14²⁶ Heb., *two hundred shekels*, probably according to the Babylonian standard. Gk., *one hundred*.

[e] 14³⁰ Gk. adds with some probability of originality, *And the servants of Joab came to him with torn clothes and said, The servants of Absalom have set the field on fire.*

§ 42. Absalom's Rebellion, II Sam. 15¹–18³²

Early Judean David Narratives

II Sam. 15 ¹Now later Absalom prepared a chariot and horses and Absa-
fifty men to run before him. ²And Absalom used to rise early and stand lom's
beside the way which led to the gate, and every man who had a suit to come trigues
before the king for judgment, Absalom would call to himself and say, Of for popular
what city are you? And when he replied, Your servant is of one of the favor
tribes of Israel, ³Absalom said to him, Evidently your claims are good and
right; but there is no man deputed by the king to hear you. ⁴Absalom said
moreover, O that someone would make me judge in the land, that to me
might come every man who has any suit or cause, and I would give him
justice! ⁵And whenever man came near to do obeisance, he would put out
his hand and take hold of him and kiss him. ⁶And in this way Absalom
did to all the Israelites who came to the king for judgment. So Absalom
stole the hearts of the men of Israel.

⁷And at the end of four^f years, Absalom said to the king, I would like to The
go and pay my vow, which I have vowed to Jehovah, in Hebron. ⁸For your usurpation
servant vowed the following vow^g while I abode at Geshur in Aram, 'If
Jehovah shall indeed bring me back to Jerusalem, I will serve Jehovah in
Hebron.'^h ⁹Then the king said to him, Go in peace. So he arose, and went
to Hebron. ¹⁰But Absalom sent emissaries into all the tribes of Israel,
saying, As soon as you hear the sound of the trumpet, then say, ' Absalom
has become king in Hebron.' ¹¹And with Absalom went two hundred men
from Jerusalem, who were invited and went in their innocence and knew
nothing at all. ¹²And Absalom sent and called^i Ahithophel the Gilonite,
David's counsellor, from his city Giloh, while he was offering the sacrifices.
And the conspiracy was strong, for the people with Absalom kept increasing.

¹³And when a messenger came to David, saying, The heart of the men of David's
Israel has gone after Absalom, ¹⁴David said to all his servants who were flight
from
with him at Jerusalem, Up, let us flee; for otherwise there will be for us no Jerusalem
escape from Absalom. Make haste to depart, lest he quickly overtake us
and bring down evil upon us and put the city to the edge of the sword. ¹⁵Then
the king's servants said to the king, Just as our lord the king decides, we are
your servants. ¹⁶So the king went out, and all his household with him.
And the king left behind ten concubines to keep the palace. ¹⁷And the king
and all the people who followed him went out and stood at the last house,
¹⁸while all his officers passed beside him, and all the Cherethites and all the
Pelethites and all the men of Ittai the Gittite,^j six hundred who had followed
him from Gath passed on before the king.

---

§ 42 The unity of this remarkably well-told narrative and its kinship with those which
precede and follow are obvious. David's character, like that of many other men, is much
stronger and attractive in adversity than in prosperity.
  f 15⁷ So Luc., Theod., and Josephus. Heb., *forty.*
  g 15⁸ For a similar vow, cf. Judg. 11³⁰, ³¹.
  h 15⁸ So Luc. Heb. omits, *in Hebron.*
  i 15¹² So Luc. Heb., *sent.*
  j 15¹⁸ Vs. ¹⁹ implies that Ittai the Gittite has been mentioned in ¹⁸. The relative clause
in ¹⁸ᵇ also clearly applies to him. *The Gittite* of the Heb. should therefore read, *the men of Ittai
the Gittite.*

Early Judean David Narratives

Loyalty of Ittai the Gittite

¹⁹Then said the king to Ittai the Gittite, Why will you also go with us? Return and stay with the king; for you are a foreigner and an exile from your own land. ²⁰Yesterday you came and to-day shall I make you wander with us, while I go whither I may? Return, and take your fellow country-men back with you; and Jehovah will show you kindness and faithfulness.[k] ²¹But Ittai answered the king, and said, As Jehovah liveth and as my lord the king liveth, wherever my lord the king shall be—whether for death or for life—there will your servant be. ²²And David said to Ittai, Well then, go, and pass on. So Ittai the Gittite passed on with all his men and all the little ones that were with him.

David's directions to the priests

²³And all the inhabitants of the land were weeping loudly as all the people passed on. While the king stood[l] in the Kidron valley, the people were passing by before him toward the olive tree[m] in the wilderness. ²⁴And there was Zadok and Abiathar[n] with him, bearing the ark of the covenant of God, until all the people had all passed out of the city. ²⁵And the king said to Zadok and Abiathar, Carry back the ark of God into the city. If I shall find favor in the eyes of Jehovah, he will bring me back, and show me both it and his dwelling. ²⁶But if he say, ' I have no delight in thee'; then here am I, let him do to me as seemeth good to him. ²⁷The king also said to Zadok and Abiathar[o] the priests, Behold, return to the city in peace and your two sons with you, Ahimaaz your son and Jonathan the son of Abia-thar. ²⁸See, I am going to delay at the fords of the wilderness, until word comes from you to inform me. ²⁹Therefore Zadok and Abiathar carried the ark of God again to Jerusalem, and they remained there.

To his friend Hushai

³⁰But David went up the ascent to the Mount of Olives, weeping as he went, and with his head covered and his feet bare. All the people who were with him also covered each his head, and also went up, weeping as they went. ³¹And when David was told, Ahithophel is among the conspirators with Absalom, David said, O Jehovah, I pray, turn the counsel of Ahithophel to foolishness. ³²And when David came to the summit, where one worships God,[p] there came to meet him Hushai the Archite with his garment rent and earth upon his head. ³³And David said to him, If you go on with me you will be a burden to me. ³⁴But if you return to the city, and say to Ab-salom, ' Your brothers have gone away and the king your father has gone away after them, I will be thy servant, O king; I have been your father's servant in the past, so now I will be your servant,' thus you can defeat for me

---

[k] 15²⁰ So Gk. Part of the last clause has fallen out of the Heb.

[l] 15²³ Heb., *was passing over*, but a slight correction gives the above rendering, which is consistent with the subsequent implication that the king remained standing.

[m] 15²³ So Luc. The Heb. is untranslatable.

[n] 15²⁴ The present Heb. text reads, *Zadok and all the Levites with them.* But the Levites are unknown to the original author of these narratives, and the subsequent context in ²⁹, indi-cates that Abiathar was with Zadok. The scribe, who, influenced by the ideas of a later age, substituted *the Levites*, apparently preserved the name in the latter part of the verse, *Abiathar went up.* The subsequent banishment of Abiathar and the prominence of Zadok explain why the name of the former was also left out of ²⁵, and even ²⁷, where its original presence is clearly indicated.

[o] 15²⁷ So Gk. Cf. ²⁹.

[p] 15³² So the original Gk.

Early Judean David Narratives

the counsel of Ahithophel. 35And have you not there with you Zadok and Abiathar the priests? Everything that you hear from the king's palace tell it to Zadok and Abiathar the priests. 36See, they have there with them their two sons, Ahimaaz, Zadok's son, and Jonathan, Abiathar's son; and by them you shall send to me everything that you shall hear. 37So Hushai, David's friend, came into the city, when Absalom came to Jerusalem.

16 1And David was a little past the summit, when Ziba the servant of Meribaal met him with a pair of asses saddled, and on them two hundred loaves of bread, and a hundred bunches of raisins, and a hundred cakes of preserved fruits,[q] and a skin of wine. 2And the king said to Ziba, Why do you have these?[r] And Ziba answered, The asses are for the king's household to ride on, and the bread and the preserved fruit for the young men to eat, and the wine, that those who are faint in the wilderness may drink. 3And the king said, And where is thy master's son? And Ziba answered the king, He remains there at Jerusalem, for he thinks, 'To-day will the house of Israel give me back my father's kingdom.' 4Then said the king to Ziba, All is now yours that belongs to Meribaal. And Ziba said, I do obeisance. Let me find further favor in your sight, my lord, the king.

Ziba's protestations of loyalty

5And when King David came to Bahurim, there came out from there a man of the family of the house of Saul, whose name was Shimei the son of Gera, constantly cursing as he came. 6And he cast stones at David and all the officers of King David and at all the people and all the mighty warriors at his right hand and at his left. 7And thus Shimei said as he cursed, Begone, begone, bloody and vile scoundrel! 8Jehovah has brought back upon you all the blood of the house of Saul, in whose place you have reigned; and Jehovah hath delivered the kingdom into the hand of Absalom your son; and behold now you are in your misfortune, for you are a bloody man!

Shimei's curses

9Then Abishai the son of Zeruiah said to the king, Why should this dead dog curse my lord the king? Let me go over now and take off his head. 10But the king said, What have I in common with you, you sons of Zeruiah? If he curses when Jehovah hath said to him, 'Curse David!' then who shall say, 'Why have you done so?' 11And David said to Abishai and to all his officers, See, my son who came from my bowels seeks my life; how much more this Benjamite! Let him curse, for Jehovah hath bidden him. 12Perhaps Jehovah will look on my affliction and repay me good instead of this cursing that he hath sent to-day. 13So David and his men went along the way; but Shimei went along on the hillside parallel with him, cursing as he went, and threw stones and continually cast dust at him. 14Then the king and all the people who were with him, arrived weary at the Jordan[s] and he refreshed himself there.

David's humility

---

q 16[1] Gk., *dates*, but Luc., *cakes of preserved fruit*, usually figs. The latter was probably intended.

r 16[2] So Gk. and the corrected Heb. text.

s 16[14] So Luc. In the Heb. the name of the place has dropped out. Lucian's reading is supported by 17[16, 22], where it is clear that David had arrived at the fords of the Jordan.

Early Judean David Narratives

¹⁵And Absalom with all the men of Israel,^t came to Jerusalem, and Ahithophel was with him.   ¹⁶Now when Hushai the Archite, David's friend, came to Absalom, Hushai said to Absalom, May the king live, may the king live!   ¹⁷But Absalom said to Hushai, Is this your love for your friend?   Why did you not go with your friend?   ¹⁸Then Hushai answered Absalom, No! for whom Jehovah and his people and all the men of Israel have chosen, to him will I belong, and with him will I remain.   ¹⁹And in the second place, whom should I serve?   Should it not be his son?   As I have served your father, so will I serve you.

²⁰Then Absalom said to Ahithophel, Give your counsel as to what we shall do.   ²¹And Ahithophel said to Absalom, Go in unto your father's concubines whom he has left to keep the palace; and all Israel will hear that you have made yourself abhorrent to your father, and the hands of all who are on your side will be strengthened.   ²²So they pitched for Absalom the tent^u on the top of the house; and Absalom went in unto his father's concubines in the sight of all Israel.   ²³And the counsel of Ahithophel, which he gave in those days, was regarded as if one inquired of the word of God— so was all the counsel of Ahithophel regarded by David and Absalom.

17 ¹Moreover Ahithophel said to Absalom, Let me now choose out twelve thousand men, and I will arise and pursue after David to-night; ²thus I will come upon him when he is tired and weak and will storm him into a panic and all the people who are with him will flee; and I will smite the king alone, ³and I will bring back all the people to you as the bride returns to her husband. You seek only the life of one man,^v and all the people shall be at peace.   ⁴And the advice pleased Absalom, and all the elders of Israel.

⁵Then Absalom said, Call now Hushai the Archite also, and let us hear likewise what he has to say.   ⁶And when Hushai came to Absalom, Absalom spoke to him, saying, Thus Ahithophel has spoken; shall we act upon his advice?   If not, you give advice.   ⁷Then Hushai said to Absalom, The counsel that Ahithophel has given this time is not good.   ⁸Hushai said moreover, You know your father and his men, that they are mighty warriors and of angry temper, like a bear robbed of her cubs in the field.   Furthermore your father is a man of war and will not remain at night with the people. ⁹Even now he has hidden himself in one of the caves or in some other place. And in case some of the people^w fall at the first, whoever hears it will say, ' There is a slaughter among the people who follow Absalom.'   ¹⁰Then even he that is valiant, whose heart is like the heart of a lion, will completely lose courage;^x for all Israel knows that your father is a mighty warrior, and they who are with him are valiant men.   ¹¹But I counsel, Let all Israel be gathered to you, from Dan to Beersheba, as many as the sand that is by the sea, with you yourself marching in the midst of them.   ¹²So shall we come upon him in some place where he has been discovered, and we will light

Marginal notes:

Hushai's protestations of loyalty to Absalom

Absalom's formal usurpation of his father's rights

Ahithophel's advice to pursue at once

Hushai's advice first to rally all Israel

---

^t 16¹⁵ So Gk.
^u 16²² I.e., the bridal tent.
^v 17³ The Gk., which has been followed, undoubtedly here presents the original text.
^w 17⁹ So Luc.   Heb. simply, *some of them.*
^x 17¹⁰ Heb., *completely melt away.*

Early Judean David Narratives

upon him as the dew falls on the ground; and of him and of all the men who are with him there shall not be left even one. ¹³But if he has withdrawn into a city, then all Israel will bring ropes to that city, and we will draw it to the valley, until not even a small stone is found there. ¹⁴And Absalom and all the men of Israel said, The counsel of Hushai the Archite is better than the counsel of Ahithophel. For Jehovah had ordained to defeat the good counsel of Ahithophel, in order that Jehovah might bring evil upon Absalom.

¹⁵Then Hushai said to Zadok and to Abiathar the priests, Thus and thus did Ahithophel counsel Absalom and the elders of Israel; and thus and thus have I counselled. ¹⁶Now therefore send quickly and tell David, saying, Do not spend this night at the fords of the wilderness, but by all means cross over, lest the king and all the people with him be swallowed up. ¹⁷Now Jonathan and Ahimaaz were staying at Enrogel; and a maid-servant was to go[a] and bring them news, and they were to go[a] and tell King David, for they must not be seen to come into the city. ¹⁸But a lad saw them, and told Absalom. Then they both went away quickly and entered into the house of a man in Bahurim, who had a well in his court into which they descended. ¹⁹And the woman took and spread the covering over the mouth of the well, and strewed dried fruit[b] upon it, so that nothing was known. ²⁰And when Absalom's servants came to the woman to the house and said, Where are Ahimaaz and Jonathan? the woman answered them, They are gone over the water brook.[c] And when they had sought and could find nothing, they returned to Jerusalem. ²¹But as soon as they had gone away they came up out of the well, and went and told King David and said to David, Arise, cross quickly over the water for thus has Ahithophel counselled in regard to you. ²²Then David and all the people who were with him arose and they crossed over the Jordan. By daybreak there was not one left behind who had not gone over the Jordan.

²³But when Ahithophel saw that his counsel had not been carried out, he saddled his ass and arose, and went to his house, to his city. And when he had given command concerning his house, he strangled himself, and he died and was buried in his father's sepulchre.

²⁴Then David came to Mahanaim. And Absalom passed over the Jordan, together with all the men of Israel. ²⁵And Absalom set Amasa over the army in the place of Joab. Now Amasa was the son of an Ishmaelite by the name of Jether,[d] who had come in marriage to Jesse's[e] daughter Abigail,

[margin notes: His secret message to David by the priests; Suicide of Ahithophel; David's reception at Mahanaim]

a 17¹⁷ The verbs are frequentative, but the narrative relates simply to the events of a day so that their peculiar significance may be brought out as above.
b 17¹⁹ The exact meaning of the original is unknown. In the current translations, the Lat., *crushed grain*, is followed; but Luc. and Targ., as well as the probabilities in the case, support the above.
c 17²⁰ This word occurs only here and its meaning is doubtful.
d 17²⁵ Heb., *son of a man whose name was Ithra the Israelite*, but I Kgs. 2⁵, ³² confirms I Chr. 2¹⁷ in the reading *Jether* not *Ithra*. For the unnecessary *Israelite* the Chronicler has also undoubtedly retained the original, *Ishmaelite*. The rest of the verse seems to state that, like Samson, Jether consummated a *çadiqa* marriage in accordance with which the wife and the children remained with her clan instead of going to that of the husband.
e 17²⁵ Again the Chronicler is clearly right in reading, *Jesse*, instead of *Nahash*. Absalom, like Saul and David, appointed a kinsman as his military leader.

Early Judean David Narratives

the sister of Zeruiah, Joab's mother.   ²⁶And Israel and Absalom encamped in the land of Gilead.   ²⁷But when David came to Mahanaim, Shobi the son of Nahash of the Ammonite Rabbah, and Machir the son of Ammiel of Lodebar, and Barzillai the Gileadite of Rogelim, ²⁸brought couches, rugs, bowls, and earthen vessels, and wheat, barley, meal, parched grain, beans, lentils, ²⁹honey, curds, sheep, and calvesᶠ for David, and for the people who were with him, to eat; for they thought, The people are hungry and weary and thirsty in the wilderness.

The battle   **18** ¹Then David mustered the people who were with him, and appointed over them commanders of thousands and of hundreds.   ²And David dividedᵍ the people into three divisions, one third was under the command of Joab, another third under Abishai the son of Zeruiah, Joab's brother, and another third under the command of Ittai the Gittite.   And the king said to the people, I also will surely go out with you.   ³But the people said, You shall not go out; for if we flee away, no one will care for us, or if half of us die, no one will care for us, for you are equal toʰ ten thousand of us.   Also it is now better for you to be ready to help us from the city.   ⁴And the king said to them, I will do what you think best!   So the king stood by the side of the gate, while all the people went out by hundreds and by thousands. ⁵And the king commanded Joab, and Abishai, and Ittai, saying, Deal gently for my sake with the young man, with Absalom!   And all the people heard when the king gave all the commanders the order regarding Absalom. ⁶So the people went out into the field against Israel.   And the battle was in the forest of Ephraim.   ⁷And the people of Israel were smitten there before the servants of David, so that the slaughter on that day was great—twenty thousand men.   ⁸And the battle was spread out over the whole country; and the forest devoured more that day than the sword.

Absalom's death   ⁹And Absalom happened to meet the servants of David.   And Absalom was riding upon his mule, and the mule went under the thick boughs of a great oak and his head caught fast in the oak, and he was hungⁱ between heaven and earth, while the mule that was under him went on.   ¹⁰And when a certain man saw it, he told Joab and said, Behold, I saw Absalom hanging in an oak.   ¹¹Then Joab said to the man who told him, So you saw him!   Why did you not smite him there to the ground?   And my part would have been to give you ten shekels of silver and a girdle.   ¹²But the man said to Joab, If I were to feel the weight of a thousand shekels of silver in my hand, I would not put forth my hand against the king's son, for in our hearing the king charged you and Abishai and Ittai, saying, 'Take care of the young man Absalom.'   ¹³Or if I had treacherously taken his life, nothing would have been hidden from the king, and you yourself would have stood aloof. ¹⁴Then Joab answered, I will not tarry thus with you.ʲ   And he took three

---

f 17²⁹ So Luc. and Lat.   The Heb. is obscure.   Syr., *cheese.*
g 18² So Luc. which has apparently preserved the original reading.   Heb., *sent out.*
h 18³ So Gk., Symmachus, and Lat.   The Heb. makes no sense.
i 18⁹ So Luc., Syr., and Targ.   This is more natural than the Heb., *was given.*
j 18¹⁴ Luc. and one form of the Gk., *therefore I will begin before you.*   The variant doubtless arose because the Heb. verb has two distinct meanings.

Early Judean David Narratives

spears[k] in his hand, and thrust them into Absalom's heart, while he was still alive in the midst of the oak. [15]And ten young men who bore Joab's armor gathered about and smote Absalom and put him to death.

[16]Then Joab blew the trumpet, and the people returned from pursuing Israel; for Joab held back the people. [17]And they took Absalom and cast him into the great pit in the forest, and raised over him a heap of stones. And all Israel fled each to his home. [18]But Absalom had already in his lifetime taken and reared up for himself the pillar which is in the King's Dale; for he said, I have no son to keep my name in remembrance; and he named the pillar after his own name. Therefore it is called 'Absalom's Monument,' to this day.

Burial of Absalom

[19]But when Ahimaaz the son of Zadok said, Let me now run and bring the news to the king that Jehovah has pronounced judgment for him against his enemies. [20]Joab said to him, You are not the man to bring news to-day. On another day you may bring news, but not to-day, for the king's son is dead. [21]Then said Joab to the Cushite, Go, tell the king what you have seen. And the Cushite bowed before Joab and ran off. [22]But Ahimaaz the son of Zadok said yet again to Joab, However it may be, I would like also to run after the Cushite. And Joab said, Why is it that you would run, my son, seeing that no reward will be paid out? [23]And he said, However it may be, I would like to run. So he said to him, Run. Then Ahimaaz ran by the way of the Plain of the Jordan and outran the Cushite.

Ahimaaz's eagerness to bear the news

[24]Now David was sitting between the two gates; and the watchman had gone up to the roof of the gate by the wall. And when he lifted up his eyes and looked, he saw there a man running alone. [25]Then the watchman cried and told the king. And the king said, If he be alone, good news are in his mouth. And he kept coming and was drawing near, [26]when the watchman saw another man running; and the watchman called toward the gate,[1] and said, See, another man running alone! And the king said, He also is bringing good news. [27]And the watchman said, I see that the running of the first is like the running of Ahimaaz the son of Zadok. And the king said, He is a good man and comes with good news. [28]Then Ahimaaz drew near and said to the king, All is well. And he bowed before the king with his face to the earth, and said, Blessed be Jehovah your God, who hath delivered up the men who lifted up their hand against my lord the king. [29]And the king said, Is it well with the young man Absalom? And Ahimaaz answered, When Joab sent your servant,[m] I saw a great tumult, but I did not learn what it was. [30]And the king said, Turn aside and stand here, and he turned aside and stood still. [31]And, just then, the Cushite said, Let my lord the king receive the good news that Jehovah hath pronounced judgment for you this day upon all those who rose up against you. [32]And the king said to the Cushite, Is it well with the young man Absalom? And the Cushite answered, may the enemies of my lord the king and all who rise up against you for evil be as that young man!

David's reception of the news

---

[k] 18[14] So Gk. Heb., *clubs*.
[1] 18[26] So Luc., Syr., and Lat.
[m] 18[29] The Heb. also contains the awkward repetition, *the king's servant*.

§ 43. David's Return, II Sam. 18³³–19⁴³

Early Judean David Narratives

David's sorrow for Absalom

II Sam. 18 ³³Then the king was greatly moved and went up to the chamber over the gate and wept. And thus he said, as he kept on weeping, My son Absalom, my son, my son Absalom! O that I had died instead of you, Absalom, my son, my son! **19** ¹And it was told Joab, The king is weeping and lamenting for Absalom. ²So for all the people the victory that day was turned to mourning, since the people heard that day, The king is grieving for his son. ³Therefore the people stole away into the city, as people who are ashamed when they have fled in battle steal away. ⁴But the king covered his face, and cried aloud, My son Absalom, Absalom, my son, my son!

Joab's rebuke

⁵Then Joab came to the king in the palace and said, You have to-day shamed the face of all your servants, who have saved your life and the lives of your sons, your daughters, your wives, and your concubines, ⁶by loving them who hate you and hating them who love you. For you declared to-day that princes and brave officers are nothing to you, for now I know if Absalom had lived and all of us had died to-day, then you would be pleased. ⁷Now therefore come, go forth, and reassure your followers; for I swear by Jehovah, if you do not go forth, not a man will remain to you, and that will be worse for you than all the evil that has befallen you from your youth until now. ⁸Then the king arose, and sat in the gate. And the rumor spread among all the people, See the king is sitting in the gate; and all the people came before the king.

Uncertainty of the people

Now Israel had fled every man to his tent. ⁹And all the people were at strife throughout all the tribes of Israel, saying, The king delivered us out of the hand of our enemies, he saved us out of the hand of the Philistines, but now he has fled out of the land from Absalom. ¹⁰And Absalom, whom we anointed over us, has fallen in battle. Now therefore why do you say nothing about bringing the king back? ¹¹ᵇAnd the word of all Israel came to the king.ⁿ

David's liberal overtures to the elders of Judah

¹¹ᵃThen King David commanded Zadok and Abiathar the priests, Speak to the elders of Judah, saying, ' Why are you the last to bring the king back to his palace? ¹²You are my bone and my flesh, why then are you the last to bring back the king?' ¹³Say to Amasa, ' Are you not my bone and my flesh? God do to me whatever he will, if you shall not henceforth be commander of the army before me in the place of Joab.' ¹⁴And heᵒ turned the heart of all the men of Judah as one man, so that they sent to the king, saying, Return with all your servants. ¹⁵So the king returned, and arrived at the Jordan. And Judah came to Gilgal to meet the king and bring him across the Jordan.

His pardon of Shimei

¹⁶And Shimei the son of Gera the Benjamite, who was of Bahurim, hastened down with the men of Judah to meet King David, ¹⁷with a thousand men of Benjamin; and with him was Ziba the servant of the house of Saul, with

---

§ 43 This is the direct continuation of the preceding early Judean David narrative.
ⁿ 19¹¹ᵇ This clause has evidently been transposed and, *to his place*, has been repeated by mistake from the preceding line.
ᵒ 19¹⁴ Luc. probably rightly inserts *Amasa*, as the subject.

Early Judean David Narratives

his fifteen sons and his twenty servants; and they dashed into the Jordan before the king. ¹⁸And they kept crossing the ford to bring over the king's household[p] and to do what would please him. Meanwhile Shimei the son of Gera prostrated himself before the king, when he was about to cross the Jordan. ¹⁹And he said to the king, Let not my lord consider me guilty nor remember what your servant did perversely the day that my lord the king went out of Jerusalem, that the king should take it to heart. ²⁰For your servant knows that I have sinned; therefore, see, I have come down first of all the house of Joseph to meet my lord the king. ²¹But Abishai the son of Zeruiah spoke and said, Should not Shimei be put to death for this, because he cursed Jehovah's anointed? ²²But David said, What have I to do with you, you sons of Zeruiah, that you should this day oppose me? Should anyone be put to death to-day in Israel? ²³And the king said to Shimei, You shall not die. And the king swore it to him.

²⁴And Meribaal the son of Saul came down to meet the king; and he had neither dressed his feet nor trimmed his beard nor washed his clothes from the day the king departed until the day he came home safe and sound.[q] ²⁵And so when he came to Jerusalem to meet the king, the king said to him, Why did you not go out with me, Meribaal? ²⁶And he answered, My lord, O king, my servant deceived me: for your servant said, 'Saddle me an ass, on which I may ride and accompany the king, because your servant is lame.' ²⁷But he has slandered your servant to my lord the king. My lord the king is as a Messenger of God; do therefore what seems good to you. ²⁸For though all my father's house were only deserving of death before my lord, the king set your servant among those who eat at your table. What right have I now, that I should continue to cry to the king?[r] ²⁹And the king said to him, Why do you continue to speak? I say, you and Ziba divide the land. ³⁰And Meribaal said to the king, rather let him take all, inasmuch as my lord the king has come home safe and sound. *Concessions to Meribaal*

³¹Then Barzillai the Gileadite came down from Rogelim, and he went over the Jordan with the king to bid him good-by at the Jordan.[s] ³²Now Barzillai was a very aged man, eighty years old, and he had provided the king with food while he remained at Mahanaim; for he was a very great man. ³³And the king had said to Barzillai, Come over with me, and I will support you during your old age[t] with me in Jerusalem. ³⁴But Barzillai said to the king, How many years have I still to live, that I should go up with the king to Jerusalem? ³⁵I am now eighty years old. Can I distinguish good from evil? Can your servant taste what I eat or what I drink? Can I hear any more the voice of singing men and singing women? Why then should your servant be a burden to my lord the king? ³⁶Your servant would merely go *Parting with the aged Barzillai*

---

p 19¹⁸ So Gk. and slightly revised Heb. text. The current translation, *there went over a ferry-boat*, is extremely doubtful.
q 19²⁴ Heb., *in peace*.
r 19²⁸ Luc., *And from whose hand shall I receive justice? And he continued to cry to the king*.
s 19³¹ Following a suggestion of Luc. The Heb. is untranslatable.
t 19³³ So Gk. Heb. omits, *during your old age*.

Early Judean David Narratives

over the Jordan with the king, and why should the king give me this recompense? ³⁷Only let your servant return, I pray you, that I may die in my own city, by the grave of my father and my mother. But there is your servant Chimham; let him go over with my lord the king; and treat him as shall seem good to you. ³⁸And the king answered, Chimham shall go over with me, and I will do to him as you would desire; and whatever you shall request of me, that will I do for you. ³⁹Then all the people went over the Jordan. The king also went over[u] after he had kissed Barzillai, and blessed him; so he returned to his home.

Strife between Israel and Judah

⁴⁰And the king passed by[v] Gilgal, Chimham being with him; and all the people of Judah were escorting the king, and also half the people of Israel. ⁴¹Therefore all the men of Israel came to the king, and said to the king, Why have our clansmen, the men of Judah, stolen you away, and brought the king and his household over the Jordan, when all of David's men are his people? ⁴²Then all the men of Judah answered the men of Israel, Because the king is near of kin to us. Why are you angry at this thing? Have we eaten anything at the king's cost? or has he been carried away by us?[w] ⁴³And the men of Israel answered the men of Judah, and said, I have ten shares in the king, furthermore I am the first-born rather than you;[x] why then did you despise me? And was not our advice first to bring back the king? But the words of the men of Judah were fiercer than the words of the men of Israel.

§ 44. Sheba's Rebellion and the Murder of Amasa, II Sam. 20¹⁻²²

Early Judean David Narratives

Rebellion of the northern tribes

II Sam. 20 ¹Now there chanced to be there a vile scoundrel, whose name was Sheba, the son of Bichri, a Benjamite. He blew on a trumpet and cried,

> We have no share in David,
> And we have no claim in the son of Jesse!
> Each to his tents, O Israel![a]

²So all the men of Israel ceased to follow David, and followed Sheba the son of Bichri; but the men of Judah remained loyal to their king, from the Jordan even to Jerusalem.

---

u 19³⁹ Luc. possibly has preserved the original reading, *But the king stood still*. The current translation makes Barzillai cross and then immediately recross the river.
v 19⁴⁰ So Gk.
w 19⁴² Or, *has anything been carried away by us*. The meaning is doubtful. The Gk. translates it in two ways.
x 19⁴³ So Gk., which has clearly retained the original reading.
§ 44 From 21¹ and I Sam. 9¹ it appears that Sheba like Shimei, II Sam. 16⁵, belonged, as did Saul, to the tribe of Becher. Cf. Gen. 46²¹. All Saul's descendants with the exception of the cripple Meribaal being dead, Sheba evidently assumed the rôle of a claimant to the throne of Northern Israel. The story which is the immediate sequel of the preceding clearly reveals the bitter jealousy which still existed between the North and the South and the rival houses of David and Saul.
a 20¹ Like all the ancient Hebrew war-cries, poetical in form. It was the cry of the Northerners, which was again heard after the death of Solomon, I Kgs. 12¹⁶.

Early Judean David Narratives

³And when David came to his palace at Jerusalem, he took care of his ten Fate of David's concubines concubines, whom he had left to take charge of the palace, and put them in a guarded house and supported them, but went not in unto them. So they were shut in until the day of their death, living as widows.[b]

⁴Then the king said to Amasa, Summon in my name the men of Judah Reinstatement of Joab and the death of Amasa within three days, and also be present yourself. ⁵So Amasa went to summon Judah. But when he delayed longer than the time which David had appointed him, ⁶David said to Abishai, Now will Sheba the son of Bichri do us more harm than did Absalom; take your lord's servants, and pursue after him, lest he find for himself fortified cities and escape out of our sight. ⁷So there went out after Abishai,[c] Joab and the Cherethites and the Pelethites, and all the mighty heroes. They set out from Jerusalem to pursue Sheba the son of Bichri. ⁸When they were at the great stone which is in Gibeon, Amasa came to meet them.[d] And Joab was girt with a sword under his warrior's cloak, and also over it was a girdle with a sword fastened upon his loins in its sheath; and as he went forth it fell out.[e] ⁹And Joab said to Amasa, Is it well with you, my brother? And Joab took Amasa by the beard with his right hand to kiss him. ¹⁰But Amasa did not notice the sword that was in Joab's hand; so he smote him with it in the body, and shed his bowels to the ground, and he did not strike a second blow; but he died. And Joab and Abishai his brother pursued Sheba the son of Bichri. ¹¹And one of Joab's young men stood by him and said, Whoever favors Joab and is for David, let him follow Joab. ¹²But Amasa lay wallowing in his blood in the middle of the highway. And when the man saw that all the people stood still, he carried Amasa out of the highway into the field, and cast a garment over him, inasmuch as he saw that every one who came to him stood still. ¹³When he was removed out of the highway, all the people went on after Joab, to pursue Sheba the son of Bichri.

¹⁴But he passed through all the tribes of Israel to Abel-beth-maacah. And Pursuit of Sheba and the counsel of the wise woman of Abel all the Bichrites[f] gathered together, and entered also after him. ¹⁵And they came and besieged him in Abel-beth-maacah, and they cast up a mound against the city, and it stood even with the wall; and all the people with Joab were devising how to throw down the wall. ¹⁶Then a wise woman out of the city, cried, Hear, hear! Say, I pray, to Joab, ' Come near that I may speak with you.' ¹⁷And he came near her; and the woman said, Are you Joab? And he answered, I am. Then she said to him, Hear the words of your maid-servant. And he said, I am listening. ¹⁸Then she spoke, saying, They used to say formerly, ' Let them ask in Abel and Dan whether what the faithful in Israel have established has ceased to be.'[g] ¹⁹I

---

[b] 20³ So Gk. The Heb. is obscure, lit., *as living widows.*
[c] 20⁷ So Gk. Heb. omits, *Abishai.*
[d] 20⁸ Or, making a slight correction, *leading the people.*
[e] 20⁸ This description is exceedingly obscure. The present Heb. makes no sense and the other versions give little help. Vs. ¹⁰ aids in the restoration. The idea appears to be that Joab concealed an extra sword under his warrior's cloak, while he purposely caused his ordinary sword on the outside to fall, as he approached Amasa, in order to disarm suspicion.
[f] 20¹⁴ Heb., *Birtes;* but Gk. and Lat. favor the above reading, which would mean that Sheba was supported by the members of his own clan.

Early Judean David Narratives

am of those who are peaceful and faithful in Israel. You seek to destroy
a city and a mother in Israel; why will you consume the inheritance of
Jehovah?

Death of Sheba and the end of the rebellion

²⁰And Joab answered and said, Far be it, far be it from me, that I should
consume or destroy. ²¹That is not at all our errand. But a man of the
hill-country of Ephraim, Sheba the son of Bichri by name, has lifted up his
hand against the king, even against David; only deliver him, and I will
leave the city. And the woman said to Joab, Behold his head shall be
thrown to you over the wall. ²²Then the woman went and advised all
the people[h] in her wisdom. And they cut off the head of Sheba the son of
Bichri and threw it out to Joab. So he blew the trumpet, and they were
dispersed from the city, each to his home. And Joab returned to the king
at Jerusalem.

§ 45. Adonijah's Attempted Usurpation and Solomon's Establishment on the Throne, I Kgs. 1, I Chr. 23¹

Early Judean David Narratives

The aged king intrusted to the care of Abishag

I Kgs. 1 ¹Now King David was advanced in years,[i] and although they
covered him with clothes, he was not warm. ²Therefore his servants said
to him, Let there be sought for my lord the king a young virgin and let her
attend the king and constantly take care of him; and let her lie in your
bosom, that the lord my king may be warm. ³So they sought for a beautiful maiden throughout all the territory of Israel and found Abishag the
Shunammite[j] and brought her to the king. ⁴And the maiden was surpassingly beautiful; and she took care of the king and ministered to him; but
the king knew her not.

Adonijah's conspiracy

⁵Then Adonijah the son of Haggith exalted himself, saying, I will be
king. Therefore he prepared for himself chariots and horsemen and fifty
men to run before him as runners. ⁶And his father had never in his life
troubled him by saying, Why have you done so? And he was also an exceedingly good-looking man, and he was by birth next after Absalom. ⁷And
he entered into negotiations with Joab the son of Zeruiah and with Abiathar the priest, so that they espoused Adonijah's cause.[k] ⁸But Zadok the
priest and Benaiah the son of Jehoiada and Nathan the prophet and Shimei
and Rei and David's famous heroes were not with Adonijah. ⁹And Adoni-

---

g 20¹⁸ Heb., *Let them ask in Abel and so they are at an end.* But the Gk. reading which is
followed above, seems to be demanded by the succeeding context. It means that Abel was
famous as a conserver of Israelite custom and tradition.

h 20²² So Gk.

§ 45. Contents and literary style indicate that I Kgs. 1 is the direct continuation of II Sam.
9–20. With graphic details the early Judean David narratives record the circumstances which
led to Solomon's accession. Since the given facts did not appeal to the Chronicler, he simply
states I Chr. 23¹, that, *When David was old and advanced in years, he made Solomon his son
king over Israel.*

i 1¹ According to the editor David at this time was about seventy years old, II Sam. 5⁴, ⁵,
I Kgs. 2¹¹.

j 1³ From the town of Sunem opposite Gilboa on the northern side of the plain of Esdraelon.
Cf. I Sam. 28⁴ and II Kgs. 4⁸.

k 1⁷ Lit., *his words were with* . . . *so that they helped him, following Adonijah.*

Early Judean David Narratives

jah slew[1] sheep and oxen and fatlings by the Serpent's Stone, which is beside the Fuller's Spring, and he invited all his brothers, the king's sons, together with all the royal officials of Judah; [10]but the prophet Nathan and Benaiah and the famous heroes and Solomon his brother, he did not invite.

[11]Then Nathan said to Bathsheba the mother of Solomon, Have you not heard that Adonijah the son of Haggith has been made king without David our lord knowing it? [12]Now therefore come, let me counsel you that you may save your own life and the life of your son Solomon. [13]Go at once to King David and say to him, ' Did you not, my lord, the king, swear to your maid-servant, saying, "Solomon your son shall be king after me, and he shall sit on my throne? Why then has Adonijah been made king?" ' [14]Just as you are talking with the king, I also will come in after you, and confirm your words.

Nathan's plan to insure Solomon's succession

[15]And Bathsheba went in to the king into his apartment; and the king was very old, and Abishag the Shunammite was ministering to the king. [16]And Bathsheba bowed and did obeisance to the king. And the king said, What do you wish? [17]And she said to him, My lord, you swore to your maid-servant by Jehovah God, ' Solomon your son shall be king after me and he shall sit upon my throne.' [18]And now, see, Adonijah has been made king, without my lord, the king, knowing it. [19]And he has slain oxen and fatlings and sheep in abundance, and has invited all the sons of the king and Abiathar the priest and Joab the commander of the army; but Solomon your servant he has not invited. [20]And now, my lord, the king, the eyes of all Israel are on you, that you should tell them who shall sit on the throne of my lord the king after him.[m] [21]Otherwise the result will be, when my lord the king shall sleep with his fathers, that I and my son Solomon will be regarded as criminals.

Bathsheba's message to David

[22]And, while she was still talking with the king, Nathan the prophet came in. [23]And they told the king, saying, Nathan the prophet is here. And he came in before the king and did obeisance before the king with his face to the ground. [24]And Nathan said, My lord the king, have you said, ' Adonijah shall be king after me and shall sit on my throne? ' [25]For he has gone down this day and slain oxen and fatlings and sheep in abundance, and has called all the king's sons and the commanders of the army[n] and Abiathar the priest; and there they are eating and drinking before him, and saying, ' May King Adonijah live! ' [26]But me, even me, your servant, and Zadok the priest, Benaiah the son of Jehoiada, and your servant[o] Solomon, has he not invited. [27]Has this been brought about by my lord the king,[p] and have you not showed your servants who should sit on the throne of my lord the king after him?

Nathan's confirmatory words

---

[1] 1[9] The word ordinarily means, *to sacrifice*. The implication is that it was a sacrificial meal in honor of his accession.

[m] 1[20] So Targ. and certain Heb. MSS. Accepted Heb., *you*.

[n] 1[25] Luc., *the commander-in-chief Joab*. This may well be original.

[o] 1[26] Luc., *son*.

[p] 1[27] The Heb. form of the question implies the negative answer.

Early Judean David Narratives

David's reassertion that Solomon should be king

[28]Then King David answered and said, Call Bathsheba to me. And
she came into the king's presence and stood before the king. [29]Then the
king took an oath and said, As Jehovah liveth, who hath redeemed me out
of all adversity, [30]as I have sworn to you by Jehovah, the God of Israel,
saying, 'Solomon your son shall be king after me and he shall sit on my
throne in my place;' verily so will I do to-day. [31]Then Bathsheba bowed
her face to the earth, and did obeisance to the king and said, May my lord
King David live forever.

Command to proclaim him king

[32]Then King David said, Call to me Zadok the priest, Nathan the prophet,
and Benaiah the son of Jehoiada. And when they came before the king
[33]the king said to them, Take with you the servants of your lord, let Solomon
my son ride upon my own mule, bring him down to Gihon,[q] [34]and there
let Zadok the priest and Nathan the prophet anoint him king over Israel;
and blow the trumpet, and say, May King Solomon live! [35]Then you shall
go up after him, and he shall enter in and sit upon my throne, for he shall
be king in my place; and I have appointed him to be leader over Israel and
Judah. [36]And Benaiah the son of Jehoiada answered the king and said,
So may it be! thus may Jehovah establish the words of my lord the king.[r]
[37]As Jehovah has been with my lord the king, even so may he be with Solomon, and make his throne greater than the throne of my lord King David!

Public anointing and acceptance of Solomon as king

[38]Then Zadok the priest, Nathan the prophet, and Benaiah the son of
Jehoiada, together with the Cherethites and the Pelethites, went down and
set Solomon on King David's mule, and brought him to Gihon. [39]And
Zadok the priest took the horn of oil out of the tent and anointed Solomon.
Thereupon they blew the trumpet; and all the people said, May Solomon
live! [40]Then all the people went up after him and the people played on
flutes and rejoiced so loudly that the earth seemed to be rent with their voice.

Announcement of the fact to the conspirators

[41]Now Adonijah and all the guests who were with him heard it just as
they had finished eating. And when Joab heard the sound of the trumpet,
he said, Why is there the noise of the city in an uproar? [42]While he was still
speaking, Jonathan the son of Abiathar the priest came. And Adonijah
said, Come in, for you are a valiant man and bring good news.[s] [43]And
Jonathan answered and said to Adonijah, Nay, but our lord King David
has made Solomon king. [44]And the king has sent with him Zadok the priest,
Nathan the prophet, and Benaiah the son of Jehoiada, together with the
Cherethites and the Pelethites, and they have set him on the king's mule,
[45]and Zadok the priest and Nathan the prophet have anointed him king in
Gihon, and they have come up from there rejoicing, so that the city is thrown
into an uproar. That is the noise which you heard. [46]And Solomon also
has taken his seat on the royal throne! [47]And moreover the king's servants
have already come to congratulate[t] our lord King David, saying, 'May God[u]

---

[q] 1[33] Probably to be identified with Virgin's Fount, the intermittent spring south of the temple hill.

[r] 1[36] So practically Gk. and Luc. Heb., *thus may Jehovah the God of my lord the king say.*

[s] 1[42] Jonathan figures as a messenger in II Sam. 15[27] and 17[17].

[t] 1[47] Lit., *bless.*

[u] 1[47] So Gk., Lat., Luc., and Targ. Heb., *thy God.*

Early Judean David Narratives

make the name of Solomon better than your name, and his throne greater than your throne!' and the king bowed himself on his bed. ⁴⁸And furthermore thus said the king, ' Blessed be Jehovah the God of Israel, who hath given one of my descendants^v to sit on my throne this day, my eyes even seeing it.'

⁴⁹Then all the guests of Adonijah were seized with terror and rose up and each went his way. ⁵⁰But Adonijah in his fear of Solomon arose, and went and caught hold of the horns of the altar. ⁵¹And it was reported to Solomon, See, Adonijah fears King Solomon, for behold he has caught hold of the horns of the altar, saying, Let King Solomon swear to me first that he will not slay his servant with the sword. ⁵²Solomon said, If he shall show himself a worthy man, not a hair of him shall fall to the earth, but if wickedness be found in him he must die. ⁵³So King Solomon sent to bring him away from the altar. And he came and did obeisance to King Solomon. And Solomon said to him, Go to your house.

Pardon of the conspirators

§ 46. David's Final Injunctions and Death, I Kgs. 2¹⁻¹¹, I Chr. 28¹–29³⁰

Popular Solomon Traditions	*Chronicler's Ecclesiastical History*	
David's exhortation to Solomon	**I Kgs. 2** ¹Now when the time drew near that David must die, he charged Solomon his son, saying, ²I am going the way of all the earth. Be strong therefore, and show yourself a man; ³and faithfully discharge your duty to	**I Chr. 28** ¹Then David assembled all the princes of Israel, the princes of the tribes, and the commanders of the divisions that served the king, and the commanders of thousands, and of hundreds, and the rulers over all the possessions and cattle of the king and of his sons, together with the chamberlains and the mighty heroes—every valiant man—to Jerusalem. ²Then David the king stood up on his feet and said, Hear me, my brothers and my people. I myself had in mind to build a house of rest for the ark of the covenant of Jehovah, and for the footstool of our God;	*David's address to the leaders and people*

---

v 1⁴⁸ So Gk. and Luc. Heb. omits the important expression, *of my descendants*.

§ 46 In I Kgs. 2²ᵇ⁻⁴, ¹⁰, ¹¹ the language and ideas of the prophetic editor are readily recognized. Regarding the origin of the remaining verses, however, there is some doubt. The reason urged in ²⁸ for the execution of Joab is not the command of David but Joab's complicity in Adonijah's conspiracy. The motive in ³⁶⁻⁴⁶ appears to be Solomon's purpose to remove all opponents; at least there is no reference in ¹³⁻⁴⁶ (which evidently came from the early David source) to the king's commands in ¹⁻⁹. Certain Gk. texts also introduce the account of David's death immediately after 1, suggesting that ¹⁻⁹ was not found in the text upon which they are based. The bloodthirsty feeling is also not in harmony with the character of David portrayed elsewhere. Leniency and regard for human life distinguished him in a marked degree from his contemporaries. On the whole, therefore, it seems probable that this parting testament was derived from a later narrative. In the early David narratives, Solomon puts Shimei and Joab to death to prepare the way for his absolute rule. This was undoubtedly the real motive. In ⁵⁻⁹, however, the responsibility for the act is transferred to David and thus Solomon is exculpated. This fact suggests that 2⁵⁻⁹ was based on a popular Solomon tradition.

The traditional last words of David become in the I Chr. 28 and 29 explicit directions for Solomon regarding the building of the temple. The presence of late prophetic expressions and many ideas and idioms, which are not exactly characteristic of the Chronicler, suggest that they may originally have been taken from an earlier source. If so, it was the late priestly history of the temple. Cf. note § 33. The noble prayer in 29¹⁰⁻¹⁹, as well as ²⁰⁻³⁰, is, however, from the pen of the Chronicler, and possibly the entire section.

Popular Solomon Traditions

Jehovah your God, by walking in his ways, by keeping his statutes, his commands, his judgments, and his testimonies, as it is written in the law of Moses, that you may act wisely and prosper in all that you do and in all that you undertake; ⁴that Jehovah may redeem his promise which he made to me, saying, 'If your sons take heed to walk before me in truth with all their heart and with all their soul, there shall not fail you' (said he) 'a man on the throne of Israel.'

Injunction to put to death his foes ⁵And you also know what Joab the son of Zeruiah did to me, how he did to the two commanders of the armies of Israel, Abner the son of Ner, and Amasa the son of Jether, how that he slew them and thus in time of peace avenged blood shed in war,ʷ and put innocent bloodˣ upon his girdle that was about his loins, and in his shoes that were on his feet. ⁶Act therefore according to your wisdom, so that you will not let his hoary head go down

Chronicler's Ecclesiastical History

and had made ready for the building. ³But God said to me, 'Thou shalt not build a temple for my name, because thou art a man of war, and hast shed blood.' ⁴However Jehovah, the God of Israel, chose me out of all the house of my father to be king over Israel forever; for he hath chosen Judah to be prince; and in the house of Judah, the house of my father, and among the sons of my father, he took pleasure in me to make me king over all Israel. ⁵And of all my sons (for Jehovah hath given me many sons), he hath chosen Solomon my son to sit on the throne of Jehovah's rule over Israel. ⁶And he said to me, 'Solomon thy son shall build my temple and my courts; for I have chosen him to be my son, and I will be his father. ⁷And I will establish his kingdom forever, if he will faithfully execute my commands and my ordinances as at present.' ⁸Now therefore, in the sight of all Israel, the assembly of Jehovah, and in the audience of our God, observe and seek to know all the commands of Jehovah your God, that ye may possess this good land, and leave it for an inheritance to your children after you forever.

⁹And thou, Solomon my son, know thou the God of thy father, and serve him with a whole heart, and with a willing mind; for Jehovah searcheth all hearts, and perceiveth every impulse of the thoughts; if thou seek him he will be found of thee; but if thou forsake him he will cast thee off forever. ¹⁰Take heed now; for Jehovah hath chosen thee to build a temple as a sanctuary; faithfully do it. **Exhortation to Solomon**

¹¹Then David gave to Solomon his son the model of the porch, and the buildings belonging to it: the treasuries, the upper rooms, the inner chambers, and the place of the mercy seat; ¹²and the plan of all that he had in mind regarding the courts of the temple of Jehovah, and all the surrounding chambers for the treasures of the house of God, and for the treasures of consecrated objects, ¹³as well as for the courses of the priests and the Levites, and for all the work of the service of the temple of Jehovah, and for all the vessels for use in the temple of Jehovah; ¹⁴regarding **Plan and organization of the temple**

ʷ I Kgs. 2⁵ So Luc. Heb., *put the blood of war on peace*, which is, to say the least, extremely awkward.

ˣ I Kgs. 2⁵ So Gk. and Luc. The Heb., *blood of war*, is probably due to a scribal repetition of the expression in the preceding sentence.

*Popular Solomon
Traditions*

to Sheol in peace. ⁷But show kindness to the sons of Barzillai the Gileadite that they may be among those who eat at your table; for so they came to me when I fled from Absalom your brother. ⁸Furthermore you have with you the Benjamite, Shimei the son of Gera of Bahurim, who uttered a grievous curse against me on the day when I went to Mahanaim. But when he came down to meet me at the Jordan, I swore to him by Jehovah, saying, 'I will not put you to d e a t h w i t h t h e sword.' ⁹But now do not let him go unpunished; you are a wise man and know what to do in order to bring his hoary head down with blood to Sheol.

Chronicler's Ecclesiastical History

the gold by weight of gold for each kind of vessel used in the service, regarding all the vessels of silver by weight for each kind of vessel used in the service, ¹⁵by weight also for the golden candlesticks, and for its golden lamps by weight for each candlestick, and for its lamps and for the silver candlesticks by weight for each candlestick, and for its lamps according to the use of each candlestick, ¹⁶and the gold by weight for the tables of showbread, for each table, and silver for the tables of silver, ¹⁷and the flesh-hooks, and the basins, and the cups of pure gold, and for the golden bowls by weight for each bowl, and for the silver bowls by weight for each bowl, ¹⁸and for the altar of incense refined gold by weight, and gold for the model of the chariot, the golden cherubim, that spread out their wings and covered the ark of the covenant of Jehovah.ᵃ ¹⁹Regarding all this—even all the execution of the plan—he has given me instruction by a writing from the hand of Jehovah.

²⁰And David said to Solomon his son, execute it faithfully and courageously! Fear not nor be dismayed, for Jehovah God, my God, is with you! He will not fail you, nor forsake you, until all the work for the service of the temple of Jehovah is finished. ²¹And there are the courses of the priests and of the Levites for all the service of the house of God, and there shall be with you in every work whoever has skill for any kind of service; also the leaders and all the people for all your undertakings.ᵇ

Command to Solomon to complete the work

29 ¹Then David the king said to all the assembly, Solomon my son, whom alone God hath chosen, is yet young and tender, and the work is great; for the palace is not for man, but for Jehovah God. ²Now I have prepared as far as I have been able for the house of my God the gold for the things of gold, and the silver for the things of silver, and the brass for the things of brass, the iron for the things of iron, and wood for the things of wood, onyx and stones for setting, and dark-colored stones and of divers colors, and all

David's provisions for the temple

ᵃ I Chr. 28¹³⁻¹⁸ Their awkward literary form and the minute details mark these verses as undoubtedly from the Chronicler.
ᵇ I Chr. 28²⁰, ²¹ These also clearly originated with the Chronicler, ²⁰ being a repetition of ¹⁰, and ²¹ being based on ²³⁻²⁶.

Chronicler's Ecclesiastical History

kinds of precious stones, and marble in abundance. ³Moreover also because I have set my affection on the house of my God, since I have a treasure of my own of gold and silver, I give it to the house of my God, over and above all that I have prepared for the holy house: ⁴three thousand talents of gold, of the gold of Ophir, and seven thousand talents of refined silver, with which to overlay the walls of the houses,—⁵the things of gold with gold, and the things of silver with silver, and also all kinds of work made by the hands of artificers. Who then is now willing to give with free hand to Jehovah?

Response of the people by word and gift
⁶Then the head of the families, and the princes of the tribes of Israel, and the commanders of thousands and hundreds, with the officers over the king's work, announced themselves as willing. ⁷And they gave for the service of the house of God in gold, five thousand talents and ten thousand darics, and in silver, ten thousand talents, and of brass, eighteen thousand talents, and of iron, a hundred thousand talents. ⁸And those who had precious stones gave them to the treasure of the temple of Jehovah, into the charge of Jehiel the Gershonite. ⁹Then the people rejoiced in that they offered willingly, with a whole heart they offered willingly to Jehovah; and David the king also rejoiced greatly.

David's prayer
¹⁰Then David blessed Jehovah before all the assembly; and David said, Blessed be thou, O Jehovah, the God of Israel our father, for ever and ever. ¹¹Thine, O Jehovah, is the greatness, and the might, and the glory, and the eminence, and the majesty, for all that is in the heavens and in the earth is thine. Thine is the kingdom, O Jehovah, and thou art exalted as head above all. ¹²Riches and honor come from thee, and thou rulest over all, and in thy hand is might and strength, and in thy hand it is the power to make every one great and strong. ¹³Now therefore, our God, we thank thee and praise thy glorious name. ¹⁴But who am I, and what is my people that we should be able to offer such voluntary gifts, for all things come of thee, and from thine own hand have we given to thee. ¹⁵For we are only guests before thee and sojourners, as all our fathers were. Our days on the earth are as a shadow, and there is no hope. ¹⁶O Jehovah, our God, all this store of things that we have prepared in order to build thee a temple for thy holy name comes from thy hand, and all belongs to thee. ¹⁷I know also, my God, that thou triest the heart and hast pleasure in uprightness. As for me, in the uprightness of my heart I have willingly offered all these things; and now have I seen with joy thy people, who are present here, offer willingly to thee. ¹⁸O Jehovah, the God of Abraham, of Isaac, and of Israel, our fathers, keep this forever as the purpose in the thoughts of the hearts of thy people, and direct their hearts toward thee, ¹⁹and grant to Solomon my son that he may with whole heart keep thy commands, thy testimonies, and thy statutes, and do all these things, and build the palace for which I have made provision.

Response of the people
²⁰And David said to all the assembly, Now bless Jehovah your God. Then all the assembly blessed Jehovah, the God of their fathers, and bowed down their heads, and did homage to Jehovah and their king. ²¹And they offered sacrifices to Jehovah, and on the next day they offered burnt-offerings

170

Chronicler's Ecclesiastical History

to Jehovah, a thousand bullocks, a thousand rams, and a thousand lambs, with their accompanying libations, and sacrifices in abundance for all Israel. ²²Then they ate and drank before Jehovah on that day with great gladness.

Then they made Solomon the son of David king the second time,ᵉ and anointed him to be Jehovah's prince and Zadok to be priest. ²³So Solomon sat on the throne of Jehovah as king in the place of David his father. And he prospered, and all Israel obeyed him; ²⁴and all the princes, and the mighty heroes as well, all the sons of King David paid homage to Solomon the king. ²⁵And Jehovah exalted Solomon greatly in the sight of all Israel and bestowed upon him such royal majesty as no other king before him in Israel had possessed.

Establishment of Solomon on the throne of Israel

Late Prophetic Summary

ᵃth
avid

¹⁰Then David slept with his fathers and was buried in the city of David. ¹¹And the period that David reigned over Israel was forty years: seven years in Hebron, and thirty-three years he reigned in Jerusalem.

²⁶Thus David the son of Jesse was king over all Israel. ²⁷And the time during which he reigned over Israel was forty years: seven years he reigned in Hebron, and thirty-three years he reigned in Jerusalem. ²⁸And he died in a good old age, satisfied with living, with riches, and with honor; and Solomon his son reigned in his place. ²⁹Now the acts of David the king from beginning to end are already described in the history of Samuel the seer, ³⁰together with all his reign and his brave deeds, and the fortunes that befell himᵈ and Israel and all the kingdoms of the countries.

Reign and death of David

IV

THE SPLENDORS AND BUILDING ENTERPRISES OF SOLOMON'S REIGN, I Kgs. 2¹²–11⁴³, II Chr. 1–11

§ 47. Removal of Solomon's Opponents, I Kgs. 2¹²⁻⁴⁶, II Chr. 1¹

Early Judean David Narratives

I Kgs. 2 ¹²Now Solomon sat upon the throne of David his father and his kingdom was firmly established. ¹³Then Adonijah the son of Haggith came to Bathsheba the mother of Solomon and bowed before her. And she said, Do you

Adonijah's solicitations for Abishag

ᵉ I Chr. 29²² Not found in Gk. Evidently it is a harmonizing scribal gloss.
ᵈ I Chr. 29³⁰ Heb., *times that went over.*
The Splendors and Building Enterprises of Solomon's Reign.—I Kgs. 2¹²⁻⁴⁶ is really the conclusion of the David history. The citations from the Solomon history begin with 3 which contains certain popular stories illustrating his wisdom and furnishing a fitting introduction to that which follows. The kernel of the Solomon history is the record of his building enterprises. The list of his officers which precedes and the account of his wealth and income which follows

§ 47. This account of the initial acts of Solomon's reign is related not to the following, but to the preceding passages. There is no tendency to idealize the policy of the king, but the grim facts are presented with the directness and naturalness, as well as picturesqueness, that characterize the early Judean David narratives of which this section is the conclusion. The story was objectionable to the Chronicler, who in common with his age idealized the character and history of the builder of his beloved temple. Accordingly he omits it altogether, simply stating (II Chr. 1¹) that *Solomon the son of David was strongly established in his kingdom and Jehovah his God was with him and made him exceedingly powerful.*

Early Judean David Narratives

come in a friendly manner?ᵃ And he replied, Yes, ¹⁴and added, I have something to say to you. And she said, Speak. ¹⁵And he said, You know that the kingdom was mine and that all Israel regarded me as the coming king, but now the kingdom has been taken away from me and has become my brother's, for it was his from Jehovah. ¹⁶Now, however, I would ask one thing of you; do not refuse me. And she said to him, Speak. ¹⁷And he said, Then request Solomon the king—he will not refuse you—to give me Abishag the Shunammite as wife. ¹⁸And Bathsheba said, Good, I will speak for you to the king.

Solo-
mon's
indig-
nation
and
speedy
execu-
tion of
Adoni-
jah

¹⁹Bathsheba went therefore to King Solomon to speak to him for Adonijah. And the king rose up to meet her and bowed before her, and sat down on his throne, and a seat was placedᵇ for the king's mother, and she sat on his right. ²⁰Then she said, I would make a small request of you; do not refuse me. And the king said to her, Make your request, my mother, for I will not refuse you. ²¹And she said, Let Abishag the Shunammite be given to Adonijah your brother as wife. ²²Then King Solomon answered and said to his mother, Why then do you ask Abishag the Shunammite for Adonijah? Ask for him the kingdom also! for he is my elder brother,ᶜ and on his sideᵈ are Abiathar the priest and Joab the son of Zeruiah. ²³Thereupon King Solomon swore by Jehovah, saying, God do to me whatever he pleaseth if Adonijah has not spoken this word against his own life. ²⁴Now therefore as Jehovah liveth, who hath established me and caused me to mount the throne of David my father, and who hath, as he promised, given me posterity,ᵉ Adonijah shall surely be put to death this day. ²⁵Then King Solomon sent Benaiah the son of Jehoiada; and he struck him down, so that he died.

Banish-
ment
of
Abia-
thar the
priest

²⁶And to Abiathar the priest the king said, Go to Anathoth to your estate; for you are to-day condemned to die,ᶠ but I will not put you to death, because you bore the ark of Jehovahᵍ before David my father and because you shared all the afflictions which my father experienced. ²⁷Thus Solomon ejected Abiathar, so that he was no longer Jehovah's priest, that he might fulfil the word of Jehovah which he spoke concerning the house of Eli in Shiloh.ʰ

Joab's
bloody
end

²⁸But when the report came to Joab—for Joab had supported Adonijah, although he had not supported Absalomⁱ—Joab fled to the tent of Jehovah, and caught hold of the horns of the altar. ²⁹And it was told King Solomon,

---

are clearly connected with this major theme. Chap. 11 alone reflects the deep shadow which hung over Solomon's reign as a consequence of his selfish despotic policy. By subsequent generations the shadow was forgotten and the builder shared the veneration and glory that centred about the temple. The tendency to idealize the comparatively small and modest structure originally reared by Solomon, as one of his palace buildings, is well illustrated by the great number of supplemental notes which have been added to the older accounts and the tendency to overlay it profusely with gold and precious woods.

ᵃ 2¹³ Lit., *Is your coming peace?* The last clause is found in Gk. and Luc. and is probably original.

ᵇ 2¹⁹ So Gk. and Syr. Heb., *caused to be placed.*

ᶜ 2²² Heb. adds through a scribal error, *and for him.*

ᵈ 2²² So Gk., Luc., Syr., and Lat. The Heb. omits, *on his side.*

ᵉ 2²⁴ Heb., *made me a house.*

ᶠ 2²⁶ Heb., *a man of death.*

ᵍ 2²⁶ So Gk. and Syr. The Heb. adds by mistake before *Jehovah* the word, *Lord.*

ʰ 2²⁷ Evidently this is a later note, added by an editor familiar with the later Ephraimite passage, II Sam. 2³¹⁻³⁶.

ⁱ 2²⁸ So Heb., Gk., and Targ. Luc. and Syr., *Solomon.*

Early Judean David Narratives

Joab has fled to the tent of Jehovah and is there beside the altar. Thereupon Solomon sent to Joab, saying, How comes it that you have fled to the altar? Joab replied, Because I was afraid of you and so I fled to Jehovah.ʲ Then Solomon sent Benaiah the son of Jehoiada, saying, Go, strike him down. ³⁰And Benaiah went to the tent of Jehovah and said to him, The king commands, 'Come forth.' But he said, No; I will rather die here. And Benaiah brought the king word again, saying, Thus said Joab and thus he answered me. ³¹And the king said to him, Do as he has said: strike him down and bury him, that you may take away the innocent blood which Joab shed from me and from my father's clan. ³²And Jehovah will requite his bloody act upon his own head, because he struck down two men more honorable and better than he, and slew them with the sword without the knowledge of my father David: Abner the son of Ner, commander of the army of Israel, and Amasa the son of Jether, commander of the army of Judah. ³³So shall their blood come back upon the head of Joab and the head of his descendants forever; but to David, and to his descendants, and to his house, and to his throne may there be peace forever from Jehovah. ³⁴Then Benaiah the son of Jehoiada went up and struck him down and slew him; and he was buried in his own house in the wilderness. ³⁵And the king put Benaiah the son of Jehoiada in his place over the army, and the king put Zadok the priest in the place of Abiathar.

³⁶Then the king summoned Shimei and said to him, Build a house in Jerusalem, there you may live, but you shall not go forth from there to any place whatever. ³⁷For as soon as you go away and cross the Brook Kidron, know for certain that you shall surely die; your blood shall be upon your own head. ³⁸And Shimei said to the king, The statement is fair; Your servant will do as my lord the king has said. And Shimei lived in Jerusalem a long time. *[The conditions imposed upon Shimei]*

³⁹But at the end of three years, two of Shimei's slaves ran away to Achish son of Maacah king of Gath. And when it was reported to Shimei, Your slaves are in Gath, ⁴⁰Shimei rose and saddled his ass and went to Gath to Achish to seek his slaves. And Shimei went and brought his slaves from Gath. ⁴¹And it was told Solomon that Shimei had gone from Jerusalem to Gath and had come back again. ⁴²Then the king summoned Shimei, and said to him, Did I not cause you to take an oath by Jehovah and solemnly admonish you, saying, 'Know for certain that as soon as you go away to any place whatever, you shall surely die'? And you said to me, 'The statement is fair.' ⁴³Why then have you not kept the oath of Jehovah and the command that I laid upon you? ⁴⁴The king also said to Shimei, You are aware of all the wickedness which you yourself alone know, that you did to David my father; now Jehovah hath brought your wickedness upon your own head. ⁴⁵But King Solomon shall be blessed and the throne of David shall be established before Jehovah forever. ⁴⁶So the king gave command to Benaiah the son of Jehoiada, and he went out and struck him down, and thus he died. So the kingdom was brought completely under the control of Solomon. *[Shimei's fate]*

ʲ 2²⁹ The entire clause, *Thereupon Solomon sent . . . to Jehovah*, has fallen out of the Heb., but is retained in the Gk. and Luc.

§ 48. Solomon's Wisdom, I Kgs. 3²⁻²⁸, 4²⁹⁻³⁴, II Chr. 1²⁻¹³

Popular Solomon Tradi- | *Chronicler's Ecclesiastical History*
tions

Solomon's sacrifice at Gibeon

I Kgs. 3 ³Now Solomon loved Jehovah so that he walked in the statutes of David his father; only he sacrificed and burnt offeringsᵏ on the high places. ²The people likewise sacrificed on the high places because up to that time no temple had been built for Jehovah.¹ ⁴And the king went to Gibeon to sacrifice there; for that was the great high place; a thousand burnt offerings did Solomon offer upon that altar.

II Chr. 1 ²And Solomon summoned all Israel, the commanders of thousands and of hundreds, and the judges and every prince in all Israel, the heads of the clans. ³So Solomon, and all the assembly with him, went to the high place that was at Gibeon; for there was the tent of meeting of God, which Moses the servant of Jehovah had made in the wilderness. ⁴But the ark of God David had brought up from Kiriathjearim to the place that David had prepared for it; for he had pitched for it a tent at Jerusalem. ⁵Moreover the brazen altar, that Bezalel the son of Uri, the son of Hur, had made, was there before the dwelling of Jehovah. And Solomon and the assembly sought it. ⁶And Solomon made an offering there before Jehovah on the brazen altar which was at the tent of meeting, and sacrificed upon it a thousand burnt-offerings.

His request for wisdom to rule justly

⁵In Gibeon Jehovah appeared to Solomon in a dream by night. And God said, Ask what I shall give thee. ⁶And Solomon said, Thou hast showed to thy servant David my father great kindness, according as he walked before thee in truth, in righteousness, and in uprightness of heart with thee; and thou hast reserved for him this great kindness, in that thou hast given him a son who sits on his throne this day. ⁷And now, O Jehovah my God, thou hast made thy servant king in the place of David my father, although I am but a child, not knowing how to go out or come in.

⁷In that night God appeared to Solomon and said to him, Ask what I shall give thee. ⁸And Solomon said to God, Thou hast showed great kindness to David my father, and hast made me king in his place. ⁹Now, O Jehovah God, let thy promise to David my father be established; for thou hast made me king over a people as numerous as the dust of the

---

§ 48 In the Gk. 3¹ follows 4 and is also connected with 9¹⁶ with which it naturally belongs. Vss. ², ³ are clearly from late prophetic editors, ² having been inserted last. In the passage beginning with ⁴, the worship at high places is assumed as perfectly natural, but the later editors felt it necessary to excuse Solomon's act. These stories appear to have been taken from the popular cycle which grew up about the name of Solomon, as about those of Saul and David. Cf. Introd., p. 15. The Chronicler in the parallel passages explains his going to Gibeon by stating that the tent of meeting was there, ¹³. The narrative in I Kgs. 3⁴⁻²⁸ is as a whole prophetic in character, and is based no doubt on popular tradition. It has been supplemented at many points, however, by the late prophetic editor, whose work is clearly revealed by the presence of his characteristic phrases.

ᵏ I Kgs. 3³ The Heb. here and elsewhere is correctly translated, *burn incense;* but it is very doubtful whether or not incense was ever employed in the pre-exilic Heb. ritual. The original meaning of the verb is, *to cause the savor of the sacrifice to rise.* In II Kgs. 16¹³, ¹⁵ it is used to describe the burning of the burnt-offering and the cereal-offering. It is employed elsewhere in connection with the burning of the fat or vegetable sacrifices. Ordinarily in pre-exilic literature it simply means, *offer sacrifice.*

¹ I Kgs. 3² So Gk. Heb., *for the name of Jehovah.* The introduction of *the name* is probably a later scribal refinement.

Popular Solomon Traditions

⁸And thy servant is in the midst of thy people which thou hast chosen, a great people too numerous to be numbered or counted. ⁹Give thy servant therefore an understanding mind to judge thy people, that I may discern between good and evil; for who is able to judge this thy great people? ¹⁰And it pleased the Lord that Solomon had asked this thing. ¹¹And God said to him, Because thou hast asked this thing and hast not asked for thyself long life nor riches nor the life of thy enemies, but hast asked for thyself insight to discern justice; ¹²behold, I have done according to thy request: I have given thee a wise and discerning mind, so that there hath been none like thee before thee, neither after thee shall any arise like thee. ¹³And I have also given thee that which thou hast not asked: both riches and honor, so that, as long as thou livest, there shall not be any among the kings like thee. ¹⁴And if thou wilt walk in my ways, so that thou wilt keep my statutes and my commands, as did thy father David, then will I give thee long life. ¹⁵And when Solomon awoke, behold it was a dream. Then he returned to Jerusalem, and stood before the ark of the covenant of Jehovah and offered up burnt-offerings and sacrificed peace-offerings and made a feast for all his servants.ᵐ

Chronicler's Ecclesiastical History

earth. ¹⁰Give me now wisdom and knowledge, that I may go out and come in before this people; for who can judge this thy great people? ¹¹Then God said to Solomon, Because this was in thy heart and thou hast not asked riches, wealth, nor the life of those who hate thee, neither hast thou asked long life, but hast asked wisdom and knowledge for thyself, that thou mayest judge my people over whom I have made thee king, ¹²wisdom and knowledge is granted to thee; and I will give thee riches and wealth and honor, such as none of the kings has had who have been before thee, neither shall there any after thee have the like. ¹³So Solomon came from the high place that was at Gibeon, from before the tent of meeting, to Jerusalem. And he reigned over Israel.

¹⁶Then two harlots came to the king and stood before him. ¹⁷And the one woman said, O, my lord, this woman and I dwell in the same house; and I was delivered of a child in her presence within the house. ¹⁸Now on the third day after I was delivered, this woman was also delivered and we were together, there being no one else with us in the house: we two being alone in the house. ¹⁹And this woman's child died in the night, because she lay upon it. ²⁰And she arose at midnight and took my son from beside me, while your maid-servant slept, and laid it in her bosom and laid her dead child in my bosom. ²¹And when I rose in the morning to nurse my child, there it was dead; but when I looked at it in the morning, behold, it was not my son whom I had borne. ²²Then the other woman said, No; but the living is my son, and the dead child is your son. And the first woman was saying, No; but the dead is your son and the living child is my son. Thus they contended before the king.

ᵐ I Kgs. 3¹⁵ The inconsistency of Solomon's first going to Gibeon to sacrifice, if he was accustomed to do so before the ark, did not occur to the late prophetic editor, who added this half-verse in order to bring Solomon's conduct into harmony with later usage and ideas.

Popular Solomon Traditions

His
saga-
cious
decision
²³Then the king said, This one says, 'This is my son, the living, and your son is the dead.' And the other says, 'No; but your son is the dead, and my son is the living!' ²⁴Thereupon the king said, Bring me a sword. And they brought a sword before the king. ²⁵And the king said, Divide the living child in two and give half to the one and half to the other. ²⁶Then the woman to whom the living child belonged, spoke to the king—for her heart yearned over her son—and she said, O, my lord, give her the living child and on no account put it to death. But the other said, It shall be neither mine nor yours! Divide it! ²⁷Then the king answered and said, Give her the living child, and on no account put it to death; she is his mother. ²⁸And when all Israel heard of the judgment which the king had rendered, they revered the king, for they saw that divine wisdom to execute justice was in him.

His
reputa-
tion for
wis-
dom
4 ²⁹And God gave Solomon wisdom and insight in plentiful measure, and breadth of mind, even as the sand that is on the sea-shore, ³⁰so that Solomon's wisdom surpassed the wisdom of all the eastern Arabians[n] and all the wisdom of Egypt. ³¹For he was wiser than all men: than Ethan the Ezrahite, and Heman, Calcol, Darda, the sons of Mahol, and his fame was in all the surrounding nations. ³²And he uttered three thousand proverbs, and his songs were five thousand.[o] ³³And he spoke of different varieties of trees from the cedar that is in Lebanon even to the hyssop that springs out of the wall; he spoke also of beasts, of birds, of creeping things, and of fishes.[p] ³⁴And there came some from among all peoples to hear the wisdom of Solomon, deputed by all kings of the earth, who had heard of his wisdom.[q]

§ 49. Organization and Glories of Solomon's Kingdom, I Kgs. 3¹. 4¹⁻²⁵, ²⁷, ²⁸, 9¹⁶, ¹⁷ᵃ, II Chr. 1¹⁴⁻¹⁹

Annals of Solomon

Solo-
mon's
court
officials
I Kgs. 4 ¹Now Solomon was king over all Israel. ²And these were the princes whom he had: Azariah the son of Zadok was priest; ³Elihoreph and Ahijah, the sons of Shisha, were scribes; Jehoshaphat the son of Ahilud was chancellor;[r] ⁴and Benaiah the son of Jehoiada was at the head of the

---

[n] 4³⁰ Lit., *children of the East.* But this is used in Judg. 6³, ³³, 7¹², Is. 11¹⁴, Jer. 49²⁸, and elsewhere to designate the nomadic Arabian tribes east of Israel in northern Arabia, the home of the popular proverb.

[o] 4³² So Gk. and Luc. and certain Lat. MSS. Heb., *one thousand and five,* but by analogy the round number is probably original.

[p] 4³³ Cf. for an example, Pr. 6⁶. The habits of plants and animals were frequently used by ancient proverb-makers to illustrate their teachings.

[q] 4²⁹⁻³⁴ A part of these verses in the Gk. follow 2²⁵. They embody the late prophetic tradition regarding the wisdom of Solomon, which is here magnified and conceived of as ethical as well as mere keenness of wit, as in the previous early tradition cited as an illustration. The author appears to have in mind proverbs similar to those found in the early collection in Pr. 10¹⁻16²².

§ 49 I Kgs. 4 marks a new beginning independent of the preceding chapter. The flowing, picturesque style of the popular story is suddenly exchanged for the repetitious verbiage of the state annals which appear here to have been quoted verbatim. The Gk. seems to have preserved the original order. Since it is also much more logical than the Heb. it has been followed for the most part. Vss. ²⁰, ²¹, ²⁴⁻²⁵ however, are awkwardly introduced in the Gk. after 2²⁶. They appear to be later insertions which, as is frequently the case with similar additions, have found a different place in the two versions. Vs. ²⁶ in the Gk. is combined with 10²⁶, where it probably belonged in the original text.

The older sections vividly present that system of organization, taxation, and forced labor, which was the source of Solomon's wealth and glory and at the same time the cause of the ultimate division of the empire.

[r] 4³ *The one who called to remembrance, i.e.,* laid important questions before the king, doubtless advising him. He probably also kept records of important events, so that the meaning *recorder* is not misleading, but this did not apparently represent all his functions.

Annals of Solomon

army; and Zadok and Abiathar were priests;ˢ ⁵and Azariah the son of Nathan was at the head of the officers; and Zabud the son of Nathan was a priestᵗ and the king's friend; ⁶and Ahishar was prefect of the palace; and Adoniram the son of Abda was in charge of the forced levy.

⁷And Solomon had twelve officers over all Israel, who provided food for the king and his household: each man had to make provision for a month in the year. ⁸And these are their names: Ben-hur,ᵘ in the hill-country of Ephraim; ⁹Ben-deker, in Makaz, Shaalbim, Bethshemesh, and Elonbethhanan: ¹⁰Ben-hesed, in Arubboth; to him belonged Socoh and all the land of Hepher; ¹¹Ben-abinadab, in all the highland of Dor (he had Tapath the daughter of Solomon as wife); ¹²Baana the son of Ahilud, in Taanach and Megiddo and all Bethshean, which is beside Zarethan, beneath Jezreel, from Bethshean to Abel-meholah, as far as the other side of Jokneam; ¹³Ben-geber in Ramoth in Gilead; to him belonged the towns of Jair the son of Manasseh, which are in Gilead;ᵛ to him belonged the region of Argob, which is in Bashan,ʷ sixty great cities with walls and brazen bars; ¹⁴Ahinadab the son of Iddo in Mahanaim; ¹⁵Ahimaaz, in Naphtali (he also took Basemath the daughter of Solomon as wife); ¹⁶Baana the son of Hushai, in Asher and Bealoth;ˣ ¹⁷Jehoshaphat the son of Paruah, in Issachar; ¹⁸Shimei the son of Ela, in Benjamin; ¹⁹Geber the son of Uri, in the land of Gad,ᵃ the country of Sihon king of the Amorites and of Og king of Bashan; and one officer was over all the officials who were in the land.ᵇ

²⁷And these officers provided food for King Solomon and for all who came to King Solomon's table, each in his month. They let nothing be lacking. ²⁸Barley also and straw for the horses and swift steeds they brought to the proper place—each according to his individual responsibility. ²²And Solomon's provision for one day was about six hundred bushelsᶜ of fine flour, and about one thousand, two hundred bushelsᵈ of meal, ²³ten fat, and twenty meadow-fed oxen, and a hundred sheep, besides harts, gazelles, roebucks, and fatted fowls.

²⁴For he had dominion over everything on the other side the River Euphrates, from Tiphsah even to Gaza, over all the kings on the other side the River. And he had

Marginal notes: Officers intrusted with the collection of food for the court — Amount of the provisions — Extent of Solomon's rule

---

ˢ 4⁴ Evidently a later insertion. In 1 Zadok's son has succeeded him and in 2²⁶⁻²⁷ Abiathar's banishment is recorded.

ᵗ 4⁵ Possibly the word means, *an official*, but the priests were early regarded as members of the court.

ᵘ 4⁸ *Ben-hur*, and the names, compounded with *ben, son of*, are not surnames, but unfortunately five of these names have been lost in all texts. Probably the original text was annalistic in part, each line beginning with a name (cf. Josh. 12⁹⁻²⁴), and the words next to the margin suffered a common fate.

ᵛ 4¹³ The Gk. and Luc. omit. It was probably added by a late editor from Dt. 3¹⁴.

ʷ 4¹³ This last descriptive clause may also have been added from Dt. 3⁴. It is found, however, in the Gk.

ˣ 4¹⁶ This place has not been identified. *Zebulon* has been suggested with much plausibility.

ᵃ 4¹⁹ So Gk. and Luc. Heb., *Gilead*.

ᵇ 4¹⁹ Not only is the current translation, *he was the only officer who was in the land*, unwarranted by the Heb., but it is also contradicted by ¹³, ¹⁴. A more than probable reconstruction, suggested by the Lat., gives the above consistent reading. The Gk., which has lost one of the preceding names, completes the twelve by reading, *in the land of Judah*.

ᶜ 4²² Heb., *20 cor*. The cor = the homer = about 80 gallons.

ᵈ 4²² Heb., *60 cor*.

Annals of Solomon

peace on all sides of him,[e] [25]so that Judah and Israel from Dan to Beersheba dwelt in safety, every man under his own vine and fig tree, as long as Solomon lived. [20]Judah and Israel were as numerous as the sand which is by the sea; they were ever eating and drinking and making merry. [21]And Solomon was the ruler from the River to the land of the Philistines, and to the border of Egypt. They brought tribute and were subject to Solomon as long as he lived.

Alliance with Egypt

3 [1]And Solomon allied himself by marriage with Pharaoh king of Egypt, and took Pharaoh's daughter, and brought her into the city of David, until he had completed the building of his own palace and the temple of Jehovah and the wall around Jerusalem.

Capture of Gezer

9 [16]Then Pharaoh king of Egypt went up, captured Gezer, and burnt it with fire, slew the Canaanites who dwelt in the city, and gave it as a portion to his daughter, Solomon's wife. [17a]And Solomon rebuilt Gezer.

§ 50. Solomon's Preparations for his Building Enterprises, I Kgs. 5, II Chr. 2

Annals of Solomon

Solomon's request that Hiram send workmen and materials

I Kgs. 5 [1]And Hiram king of Tyre sent his servants to Solomon because he had heard that they had anointed him king in the place of his father; for Hiram had loved David. [2]And Solomon sent to Hiram, saying, [3]You yourself know that David my father was not able to build a temple for the name of Jehovah his God on account of the warlike foes[f] who were about him on every side, until Jehovah brought

Chronicler's Ecclesiastical History

II Chr. 2 [1]Now Solomon purposed to build a temple for the name of Jehovah, and a temple for his kingdom. [2]And Solomon counted out seventy thousand burden-bearers and eighty thousand hewers of stone in the mountains and three thousand six hundred to oversee them. [3]And Solomon sent to Huram king of Tyre, saying, As you dealt with David my father, in that you sent him cedars to build himself a palace in which to dwell, [4]so I now am about to build a temple for the name of Jehovah my God, to dedicate it to him, and to burn before him incense of sweet spices, and for regular presentation of the bread of the presence, for the burnt-offerings morning and evening, on the sabbaths and on the new moons

[e] 4[24] Evidently, like kindred passages in the post-exilic writers, e.g., Ezra 4[10, 11, 16], 7[21, 25], Neh. 2[7, 9], written from the point of view of Babylon and therefore a late insertion. From *Tiphsah* . . . *the River* is not found in Gk.A and Luc. The verse as a whole is a later duplicate of [21].
    § 50 I Kgs. 5 appears to be a continuation of the quotation from the annals, although somewhat more expanded, as the subject-matter required. To the original narrative the late prophetic editor has evidently also made certain additions in order to harmonize it with his representations elsewhere and to bring into prominence the religious motives which most concerned him. Thus [3, 4, 5b] depend on II Sam. 7. Cf. Dt. 12[9, 10]. The late religious conception of Solomon's wisdom is reflected in [7, 12]. Vss. [15, 16] do not appear to be in complete harmony with [13, 14]. Not only may the large numbers be questioned, but [15, 16] seem after [13, 14] to be superfluous, even though they do not refer to the same people. From their position, *in the mountains* would naturally refer to the Lebanons, but the reference is ambiguous, as well as the question whether the workmen were Israelites or not. Cf. 9[22]. It is significant that the Chronicler reproduces these verses and ignores [13, 14], which give a different picture of the levy and one in harmony with the extracts from the annals. Removing these secondary passages, the remaining narrative has all the characteristics of a primitive source of the highest historical value.
    [f] I Kgs. 5[3] The Heb. has the abstract noun, *warfare*, although it contains the plural antecedent of the following verb. Targ., *enemies*.

Annals of Solomon

them into subjection to him.ᵍ ⁴But now Jehovah my God hath given me rest on every side: there is neither adversary nor misfortune. ⁵Now I purpose to build a temple for the name of Jehovah my God, as Jehovah spoke to David my father, saying, 'Thy son, whom I will set on thy throne in thy place, he shall build the temple for my name.' ⁶Therefore command that they cut for me cedar timber from Lebanon; and my servants will go with your servants, and I will give you wages for your servants just as you shall say; for you know that there is no one among us who knows how to cut timber as the Sidonians.

⁷Now when Hiram heard the words of Solomon, he rejoiced exceedingly and said, Blessed be Jehovah this day, who hath given to David a wise son over this great people. ⁸So Hiram sent to Solomon, saying, I have heard your message to me; I, on my part will fulfil all your wishes in regard to cedar and cypress timber. ⁹My servants shall bring them down from Lebanon to the sea, and I will make them into rafts to go by sea to the place that you shall appoint, and will have them broken up there, and you shall receive them. You also shall fulfil my wish by providing food for my household. ¹⁰So Hiram

Chronicler's Ecclesiastical History

and on the set feasts of Jehovah our God (which is the constant practice of Israel). ⁵And the temple which I am about to build is great, for our God is greater than all gods. ⁶But who is able to build him a temple, since heaven and the heaven of heavens cannot contain him? Who am I then, that I should build him a temple? It is fitting only to offer sacrifice before him. ⁷Now therefore send me a man skilful in working in gold, silver and in purple, crimson and violet stuffs, and who knows how to engrave stone in conjunction with the skilful men who are with me in Judah and in Jerusalem, whom David my father provided. ⁸Send me also cedar, cypress, and sandalwood from Lebanon; for I know that your servants understand how to cut timber in Lebanon; and, behold, my servants will unite with your servants, ⁹even to prepare me timber in abundance; for the temple which I am about to build should be great and wonderful. ¹⁰And I will now give to your servants, the hewers that cut timber, four hundred thousand bushelsʰ of beaten wheat and four hundred thousand bushelsʰ of barley, and one hundred and sixty thousand gallonsⁱ of wine and one hundred and sixty thousand gallons of oil.

¹²And Huram said, Blessed be Jehovah, the God of Israel, who hath made heaven and earth, who hath given to David the king a wise son, endued with discretion and understanding enough to build a temple for Jehovah and a temple for his kingdom. ¹¹And Huram the king of Tyre sent to Solomon the following reply in writing, Because Jehovah loveth his people, he hath made you king over them. ¹³And now I have sent a skilful man, endued with understanding, Huram-abi, ¹⁴the son of a Danite woman; and his father was a man of Tyre, who knows how to work in gold, silver, brass, iron, stone, and timber, and in purple, violet, and fine

ᵍ I Kgs. 5³ Heb., *put them under the soles of the feet.*
ʰ II Chr. 2¹⁰ Heb., *20,000 cor.*
ⁱ II Chr. 2¹⁰ Heb., *20,000 baths.*

179

Annals of Solomon

furnished Solomon cypress timber, as much as he wished. ¹¹And Solomon gave Hiram four hundred thousand bushels[j] of wheat for food for his household, and one hundred and sixty thousand gallons[k] of oil from the beaten olives. This much Solomon gave to Hiram year by year. ¹²And Jehovah gave Solomon wisdom, as he promised him; and there was peace between Hiram and Solomon, and they made an alliance with each other.

Chronicler's Ecclesiastical History

linen, and in crimson; also to do all kinds of engraving and to plan any artistic work which may be assigned to him, together with your skilled workmen and with the skilled workmen of my lord David your father. ¹⁵Now therefore the wheat and the barley, the oil and the wine, of which my lord has spoken, let him send to his servants; ¹⁶and we will cut wood out of Lebanon, as much as you need, and we will bring it to you in floats by sea to Joppa, and you shall carry it up to Jerusalem.

Solomon's forced levy of workmen

¹³And King Solomon raised a forced levy out of all Israel; and the levy consisted of thirty thousand men. ¹⁴And he sent them to Lebanon, ten thousand a month in relays; a month they were in Lebanon, and two months at home; and Adoniram was in charge of the forced levy. ¹⁵And Solomon had seventy thousand burden-bearers and eighty thousand hewers of stone in the mountains; ¹⁶besides Solomon's chief officers who were in charge of the work, three thousand, three hundred, who superintended the people who did the work. ¹⁷And the king commanded that they should hew out great, costly stones, to lay the foundation of the temple with cut stone. ¹⁸And Solomon's builders and Hiram's builders and especially the Gebalites[l] shaped them and prepared the timber and the stones to build the temple.

¹⁷And Solomon took a census of all the resident aliens who were in the land of Israel, according to the census which his father had instituted. And there were found a hundred and fifty-three thousand, six hundred. ¹⁸And he made seventy thousand of them burden-bearers, and eighty thousand hewers of stone in the mountains, and three thousand, six hundred overseers to make the people serve.

§ 51. Building the Temple, I Kgs. 6, II Chr. 3¹⁻¹⁴

Annals of Solomon

Dimensions of the temple

I Kgs. 6 ¹Now in the four hundred and eightieth year after the departure of the Israelites from the land of Egypt, in

Chronicler's Ecclesiastical History

II Chr. 3 ¹Then Solomon began to build the temple of Jehovah at Jerusalem on Mount Moriah where

---

j I Kgs. 5¹¹ Heb., *20,000 cor.*
k I Kgs. 5¹¹ So Gk. and II Chr. 2¹⁰ and Josephus, *20,000 baths.* Heb., *20,000 cor.* But the *cor* was a dry measure.
l I Kgs. 5¹⁸ The prominent place given to the workmen from Gebal is not explained here or in any previous reference. The Gk. takes the word as a verb. If this be the true rendering, the corresponding verb would mean, *and they bordered them with grooved edges.*
§ 51. The importance of the subject explains why this section has been supplemented by many editorial and scribal additions. I Kgs. 6¹ᵃ was evidently a later note which in abbreviated form appears in the Gk. and Luc. before 5¹⁷, and its place is taken by 6³⁷, ³⁸ᵃ. The somewhat more logical order of the Gk. is probably due to the translators, although it may possibly represent the original text. That 6¹ᵃ is a late note is demonstrated by its use of a late Heb. word for month, instead of the earlier synonym, and by the fact that it outlines the general chronological scheme which is followed by the late editor of the book, *i.e.*, 480 (40x12) years from

Annals of Solomon	*Chronicler's Ecclesiastical History*
the fourth year of Solomon's reign over Israel, in the month Ziv, that is the second month, he built the temple of Jehovah. 2And the length of the temple which King Solomon built for Jehovah was sixty and its breadth twenty cubits, and its height thirty cubits. 3And the porch before the large room[m] of the temple was twenty cubits wide, corresponding to the breadth of the temple, ten cubits deep before the temple. 4And for the temple he made windows with narrowed frames.[n]	Jehovah had appeared to David his father in the place which David had prepared, on the threshing-floor of Ornan the Jebusite. 2And he began to build in the second day of the second month, in the fourth year of his reign. 3And these are the foundations which Solomon laid for the building of the house of God. The length by cubits, according to the old measure, was sixty cubits, and the breadth twenty cubits. 4And the porch that was before the temple— its length before the front of the temple was twenty cubits, and the height a hundred and twenty; and he overlaid it within with pure gold.

5And around against the wall of the temple he built wings,[o] both around the larger room and the inner room,[p] and made side chambers round about.   6The lower side-chamber[q] was five cubits broad, and the middle six cubits broad, and the third seven cubits broad; for on the outside he made offsets around about the temple in order not to make an inset into the walls of the temple.[r]   7In building the temple it was built with stone which had been made ready at the quarry:[s] neither hammer nor chisel nor any iron tool was heard while the temple was building.   8The entrance into the lower[t] side-chambers was on the south side of the temple. And one could go up by winding

(margin note: The side-chambers)

---

the exodus to the building of Solomon's temple, and 480 years from the latter event to the close of the Babylonian exile.   6¹ᵃ is also not found in the parallel passage in Chr.

The statements that all the walls of the outer and inner rooms, 20ᵇ, 21ᵃ, were overlaid with gold seem to be from later scribes who sought thereby to enhance the glories of the temple. When it was later plundered, there is no reference to this gold. Special decorations might be expected in the case of the cherubim (cf. the golden calves of Jeroboam I) and the doors leading into the sanctuary, although these may also be only the ideas of the scribes. The decision really turns upon whether or not the Hebrew or the Phœnician workmen were at this time acquainted with a process of thin gilding with liquid gold. Cf. Pr. 26²³.

The remaining passages have been taken from the annals of Solomon's reign. With 10, 9 the briefer description ends, so that the more detailed account beginning with 15 is probably from the temple records. The Chronicler has a briefer narrative, heightened at certain points. Cf. 3⁴, ⁹. For the probable form and structure of the temple, cf. the accompanying plans. The cubit in Kgs. was probably equivalent to about twenty inches.

m I Kgs. 6³ Lit., *great house*. It is the technical designation of the large central hall, or *Holy Place*. It corresponded to the audience-room of a palace.

n I Kgs. 6⁴ *I.e.*, smaller on the outside than on the inside of the wall, as in an ancient fortress. So Lat. and Syr., *oblique narrowed*. Otherwise, following the Gk., it means, *windows with frames closed, i.e.*, with grating or lattice-work.

o 1 Kgs. 6⁵ Heb. contains what is probably simply a later scribal note, *around the walls of the temple*. Gk. and Luc. omit it. It appears to be an explanatory duplicate of the immediately following clause.

p I Kgs. 6⁵ *The most holy place*, behind the large room, where the ark was placed. Cf. 19.

q I Kgs. 6⁶ Heb., *wing*, but this is probably due to a scribal confusion with the similar Heb. word, *side-chamber*. This is also suggested by Gk. and Targ. and is confirmed by 8.

r I Kgs. 6⁶ *I.e.*, that the beams which supported the side-chambers might not be set into the exterior walls, but rather rest on the rebatements.

s I Kgs. 6⁷ So Gk. The Heb. makes no sense.

t I Kgs. 6⁸ So Gk. and Luc. Heb., *middle*.

Annals of Solomon

stairs[u] into the middle story, and from the middle into the third. ¹⁰And he built the wings against all the temple, each story five cubits high; and they rested on the temple with timbers of cedar.[v] ⁹So he built the temple and finished it; and he covered the temple with cedar.[w]

Temple Records

The interior decorations

¹⁵And he built the walls of the temple within with boards of cedar: from the floor of the temple to the rafters of the ceiling, overlaying them on the inside with wood; and he covered the floor of the temple with boards of cypress.[x] ¹⁶And he built off the back twenty cubits from the innermost part of the temple with boards of cedar from the floor to the rafters:[a] he built it within for an inner room, even for the most holy place.[b] ¹⁷And the temple, that is the large room before the inner room[c] was forty cubits long. ¹⁸And there was cedar in the interior of the temple, carving in the form of gourds and open flowers; all was cedar, no stone was seen.[d] ¹⁹And he prepared an inner room in the interior of the temple in order to place there the ark of the covenant of Jehovah.[e] ²⁰And the inner room[f] was twenty cubits long and twenty cubits broad and twenty cubits high. And he overlaid it with pure gold. And he made[g] an altar of cedar wood ²¹before the inner room, and he overlaid it with gold.[h] ²²And the whole temple he overlaid with gold, until all the temple was finished.[i] ²⁹And he carved all the walls

⁵And the chief structure he ceiled with cypress wood, which he overlaid with fine gold, and wrought thereon palm trees and chains. ⁶And he beautified the temple with precious stones; and the gold was gold of Parvaim. ⁷He also overlaid the temple, the beams, the thresholds, and the walls, and the doors with gold; and engraved cherubim on the walls. ⁸And he constructed the most holy room: its length, corresponding to the breadth of the temple, was twenty cubits, and its breadth twenty cubits. And he overlaid it with fine gold, amounting to six hundred talents. ⁹And the weight of the nails was fifty shekels of gold. And he

---

u I Kgs. 6⁸ So Syr. and Targs. Gk. and Luc., *winding stairs*. But these are probably inventions peculiar to the Greek age.

v I Kgs. 6¹⁰ Vss. ⁹, ¹⁰ have apparently been transposed by mistake. Restoring them to what appears to have been their original order the sense is clear.

w I Kgs. 6⁹ So Gk., Luc., and Syr. Heb. has a gloss before cedar, *beams and planks*, which was probably a marginal note. The resulting Heb. sentence is also ungrammatical.

x I Kgs. 6¹⁵ Omitted by Gk. and Luc.

a I Kgs. 6¹⁶ Again reading with Gk. and Luc. Heb., *walls*.

b I Kgs. 6¹⁶ A very late explanatory note, introducing the terminology of the post-exilic priestly writers, cf., *e.g.*, Ex. 26³³, ³⁴, Num. 4⁴.

c I Kgs. 6¹⁷ This explanatory note was apparently added after the Gk. translation was made.

d I Kgs. 6¹⁸ This descriptive verse was also added after the Gk. translation was made.

e I Kgs. 6¹⁹ The phrase, *ark of the covenant*, indicates that this was added by a late prophetic editor. It is unnecessary after ¹⁶.

f I Kgs. 6²⁰ Heb., *before the inner room*. Evidently this is due to a dittography of the same phrase in ¹⁷.

g I Kgs. 6²⁰ So Gk. and Luc. The Heb., through a scribal error, repeats the preceding, *covered*.

h I Kgs. 6²¹ So Gk. and Luc. A very late and confusing gloss has crept into the Heb. which is really only an anticipation of ²²ᵃ.

i I Kgs. 6²²ᵇ So Gk. and Luc. The Heb. here has a duplicate of the original ²¹.

Temple Records

of the house round about with carved figures of cherubim and palm trees and opening flowers, both in the inner and outer rooms. ³⁰And the floor of the temple he overlaid with gold.ʲ

²³ᵃAnd in the inner room he made two cherubim of olive wood. ²⁶The height of the one cherub was ten cubits, and so was that of the otherˡ—²³ᵇeach ten cubits high. ²⁴And one wing of the cherub measured five cubits, and the other wing of the cherub also five cubits—ten cubits from the extremity of one wing to the extremity of the other. ²⁵And the other cherub also measured ten cubits: both the cherubim were of the same measurement and form. ²⁷And he set up the cherubim in the inner room of the temple, and the wings of the cherubim were stretched forth, so that the wing of the one touched the one wall, while the wing of the other cherub touched the other wall, and their wings touched each other in the middle of the temple; and he overlaid the cherubim with gold.

overlaid the upper chambers with gold.

¹⁰And in the most holy room he made two cherubim of imageᵏ work; and they were overlaid with gold. ¹¹And the wings of the cherubim were twenty cubits long; the wing of the one cherub measured five cubits, reaching to the wall of the temple, and the other wing likewise measured five cubits, reaching to the wing of the other cherub. ¹²And the wing of the other cherub measured five cubits reaching to the wall of the temple; and the other wing measured five cubits also, joining to the wing of the other cherub. ¹³The wings of these cherubim spread themselves forth twenty cubits. And they stood on their feet, and their faces were toward the temple.

³¹And the door of the inner room he made with folding doors of olive wood: the pilastersᵐ formed a pentagonal. ³²And on the two doors of olive wood he carved carvings of cherubim and palm trees and opening flowers, and he spread the gold over the cherubim and the palm trees.

¹⁴And he made a veil of violet, purple, crimson, and fine linen, and he wrought cherubim thereon.

³³So also he made for the door of the large roomⁿ posts of olive wood, four square, ³⁴and two folding leaves of cypress-wood: the two leaves of the one door were folding, and the two leaves of the other door were folding. ³⁵And he carved cherubim and palm trees and opening flowers, and overlaid them with gold applied evenly to the carving. ³⁶And he built the inner court with three courses of hewn stone and a course of cedar beams.

ʲ I Kgs. 6²⁹, ³⁰ So Gk. Heb., *within and without,* but *without* would have no meaning in ³⁰. A slight revision gives the reading followed above.
ᵏ II Chr. 3¹⁰ The meaning of the word translated, *image,* is very doubtful.
ˡ I Kgs. 6²⁶ The obscurities of ²⁶ are removed by the restoration of the verse to what was clearly its original position.
ᵐ I Kgs. 6³¹ An exceedingly difficult passage. The current translation, *lintel,* is untenable in the light of the usage of the term in Ezek. 41³ and 40⁹. *Posts* seems to have been added in Heb. as an explanatory gloss, or from ³³. The door appears to have been of this shape: ⊓
ⁿ I Kgs. 6³³ So Gk. and restored Heb.

183

Temple Records

Completion of the temple

[11]And the word of Jehovah came to Solomon, saying, [12]Concerning this temple which thou art building, if thou wilt walk in my statutes, and execute my judgments, and keep all my commandments by walking in accordance with them, then will I redeem with thee my promise, which I gave to David thy father. [13]And I will dwell among the Israelites and will not forsake my people Israel. [14]So Solomon completed the building of the temple.[o] [37]In the fourth year was the foundation of the temple of Jehovah laid, in the month Ziv.[p] [38]And in the eleventh year, in the month Bul[p] (that is the eighth month), was the temple completed in all its parts, and according to all the specifications. Thus he was seven years in building it.

§ 52. Ornamentations and Furnishings of the Temple, I Kgs. 7^{13-51}, II Chr. 3^{15}–5^{1}, Jer. 52^{21-23}

Temple Records

The pillars at the entrance made by Hiram-abi

I Kgs. 7 [13]Then King Solomon sent and brought Hiram-abi from Tyre. [14]He was the son of a widow of the tribe of Naphtali, an Aramean worker in brass;[q] and he was gifted with skill, understanding, and knowledge to carry on all kinds of work in brass. And he came to King Solomon and did all his work. [15]For he cast[r] the two pillars of brass for the porch of the temple.[s] Eighteen cubits was the height of one pillar, and its circumference measured twelve cubits; the thickness of the pillar was four fingers—it was hollow. And the second pillar was similar.[t] [16]And he made two capitals of molten brass, to set upon the tops of the pillars; the height of the one capital was five cubits, and the height of the other capital was five cubits. [17]And he made[u] two nets (woven work, festoons, chain-work)[v] for the capitals which were on the top of the pillars; a net[w] for the one capital, and a net[w] for the other capital. [18b]And he made the pomegranates;[x] and two

---

[o] I Kgs. 6^{11-14} These verses are not found in Gk. and Luc. They have no real connection with their context and their language and thought, as well as their absence in the Gk. and Luc., confirm the conclusion that they were added to the Heb. by a late priestly editor.

[p] I Kgs. $6^{37, 38}$ The foundation therefore was laid in Apr.-May and the work was completed in Oct.-Nov. The names of the months are those of the old Canaanitish calendar. Cf. Appendix XIII.

§ 52 The prominence given in I Kgs. 7^{13-51} to the temple in comparison with the brief description in 7^{1-12} of the building of Solomon's palace and other extensive buildings strongly suggests that the latter was taken from the annals, while the more detailed account of the ornamentation and furnishings of the sanctuary came from the temple records. The nature of the subject-matter also confirms this inference.

Again the Chronicler has a briefer and somewhat magnified parallel version. Thus according to him the pillars in front of the temple were thirty-five, 3^{15}, instead of eighteen cubits in height, as in I Kgs. 7^{15}. Also probably having in mind the furnishings of the second temple, he introduces a brazen altar and golden candlesticks not found in the parallel passage in Kgs. and probably not known to the Hebrews until after their contact with the Assyrians and Babylonians. Cf. the brazen altar erected by Ahaz after paying homage to Tiglath-Pileser at Damascus, II Kgs. 16^{7-18}, § 119.

[q] $7^{13, 14a}$ According to II Chr. $2^{12, 13}$ the workman's name was *Huram-abi* and he was the son of a Danite mother. Vs. ^{14a} seems to have been added, like the variant reading in Chr., to make him of part Israelitish origin. The original text probably read, *Hiram-abi, an Aramean worker in brass*.

[r] 7^{15} So Gk. and Luc. An apparent error in Heb. gives the reading, *fashioned*.

[s] 7^{15} So Gk. and Luc. Heb. omits, *for the porch of the temple*.

[t] 7^{15} So Gk., confirmed by Jer. 52^{21}, Luc., and in part by the Syr. The last three clauses have been almost entirely lost in the Heb.

[u] 7^{17} So Gk. and Luc.

[v] 7^{17} This explanatory note is found in none of the versions and parallel passages.

[w] 7^{17} So Gk. and Luc. in accord with ^{17a}. Heb., *seven*.

[x] 7^{18b} So certain Heb. manuscripts confirmed by the parallel passage, Jer. 52^{22}. Other Heb. manuscripts read, *pillars*.

Temple Records

rows of pomegranates in brass were upon the one network,[a] [20b]and there were two hundred pomegranates—two rows around about the one capital. [18c]And he did the same to the other capital. [19]And the capitals that were upon the top of the pillars in the porch were of lily-work—four cubits. [20a]And there were capitals above also upon the two pillars, in connection with the bowl-shaped[b] part of the pillar which was beside the network.[c] [21]And he set up the pillars at the porch of the temple: and he set up the pillar at the right and called it Jachin;[d] and he set up the pillar at the left and called it Boaz. [22]And upon the top of the pillars was lily-work. So was the work of the pillars finished.

[23]And he made the molten sea ten cubits in diameter from brim to brim, and five cubits high, and its circumference measured thirty cubits. [24]And under its brim on the outside were gourds which encircled it, for thirty[e] cubits, encircling the sea on the outside;[f] the gourds were in two rows, cast when it was cast. [26]And it was a handbreadth thick;[g] and its brim was wrought like the brim of a cup, similar to the flower of a lily. It held about sixteen thousand gallons.[h] [25]It stood upon twelve oxen, three looking toward the north, and three looking toward the west, and three looking toward the south, and three looking toward the east; and the sea was set down upon them, and all their hinder parts were turned inward.

[27]And he made the ten stands of brass: each stand was four cubits long, four cubits broad, and three cubits high.[i] [28]And the stands were made as follows: they had border-frames, and the border-frames were between the upright supports; [29]and on the border-frames that were between the upright supports were lions, oxen, and cherubim; and upon the upright supports likewise; and above and beneath the lions and oxen and cherubim was bevelled work.[j] [30a]And every stand had four wheels of brass and axles of brass.[k] [32]And the four wheels were underneath the border-frames; and the axles and the wheels were cast as a part of the stand. And the height of

(marginal notes: Molten sea; Movable brazen stands)

---

[a] 7[18b] The Syr. order, which is probably original, has been followed. In Heb., [20b] has been transposed.

[b] 7[20a] Lit., *belly*. The exact meaning is not entirely clear.

[c] 7[19, 20a] The account of the construction of the pillars is apparently completed in [18b] to which [21] is the natural sequel. This is the order in the Gk. and Luc. The additional notes regarding the appearance of the pillars in [19, 20, 22] are evidently from a later hand and were introduced into the text differently in the Gk. and Heb. versions. Furthermore in the recapitulation in [41, 42] there is no reference to the lily-work and bowl-shaped part of the pillars. It may well have been suggested to a later scribe by the Egyptian temples in which the *motif* was common.

[d] 7[21] The meanings of the names is obscure. *Jachin* may mean, *he (Jehovah) establishes.* They probably represented the sacred pillars which were set up before every ancient Canaanite sanctuary.

[e] 7[24] Heb., *ten*, but this must be the mistake of a scribe who confused the diameter and the circumference.

[f] 7[24] Probably a gloss, as is indicated by the use of a different word for *encircling.*

[g] 7[26] Gk. order [26, 25]. This is undoubtedly original.

[h] 7[26] Heb., *two thousand baths.*

[i] 7[27] Gk. and Luc. make the entire dimensions including the stand, 5x4x6.

[j] 7[29] Following Gk. and Luc.

[k] 7[30a] From this point on the description of the stands is confusing. Those recently discovered in Cyprus at Larnaka and Enkomi were probably used for the same purpose and were of similar construction. Cf. Murray in *Journ. of Royal Inst. of Brit. Architects*, 1899, VII, pp. 20 ff.; Stade in *ZATW.*, 1901, pp. 145 ff. In [30b, 33] the top of the stand is described, and these vss. logically follow [35, 36]. Transposing them, the accounts of the wheels beginning in [30a] is continued in [32, 34]. The resulting order in which the stands are described is (1) their bases with the engravings of lions, oxen, and cherubim on the outside framework, (2) the wheels and axles beneath, and (3) the opening at the top (into which were set the pots [39]) and the ornamentation of the outside framework.

Temple Records

each wheel was a cubit and a half. [33]And the construction of the wheels was like that of a chariot wheel: their axles, their felloes, their spokes, and their hubs, were all cast. [34]And at the four corners of each stand were four shoulder-pieces; the shoulder-pieces were cast as part of the stand. [35]And in the top of the stand was a round opening,[1] half a cubit high, and on the top of the stand were its stays and its border-frames. [36]And on the flat surface of the stays and border-frames, he engraved cherubim, lions, and palm trees, according to the space on each, with wreaths round about. [30b]And the four corners[m] had shoulder-pieces: beneath the bowl the shoulder-pieces were cast, with wreaths at the side of each. [31]And its opening within the shoulder-pieces[n] was a cubit and more: and its opening was round after the form of a pedestal (a cubit and a half) and also upon its opening were gravings, and its[o] border-frames were square, not round. [37]Thus he made the ten stands: all of them had one casting, and were of the same measure and form.

Position of the stands with their lavers [38]And he made ten lavers of brass: one laver contained three hundred and twenty gallons,[p] and each laver measured four cubits; and on each one of the ten stands was a laver. [39]And he set the stands, five on the right side of the temple and five on the left side of the temple: and he set the sea on the right side of the temple eastward toward the south.

Altar of brass **II Chr. 4** [1]Moreover he made an altar of brass—twenty cubits long, and twenty cubits broad, and ten cubits high.

Candlesticks [7]And he made the ten candlesticks of gold according to the directions concerning them; and he set them in the temple, five on the right hand and five on the left. [8]He made also ten tables, and placed them in the temple, five on the right side and five on the left. And he made a hundred golden bowls.

Completion of the work **I Kgs. 7** [40]And Hiram[q] made the lavers and the shovels, and the bowls. So Hiram completed all the work that he wrought for King Solomon in the temple of Jehovah: [41]the two pillars and the two bowl-shaped capitals that were on the top of the pillars, [42]and the four hundred pomegranates for the two networks to cover the two bowl-shaped capitals that were on the top of the pillars, [43]and the ten stands and the ten lavers on the stands, [44]and the one sea with the twelve oxen under the sea.

Vast amount of brass required [45]And the pots, the shovels, and the bowls, and all these vessels which Hiram made for King Solomon in the temple of Jehovah, were of burnished brass. [47]There was no weighing the brass from which he made all these vessels, because it was so very much, the weight of the brass could not be determined.[r] [46]In the Plain of the Jordan he cast them, in the clay ground between Succoth and Zarethan.

Arrangement of the vessels in the temple [48]And Solomon placed all the vessels which he had made in the temple of Jehovah: the golden altar and the golden table on which was the showbread; [49]and the candlesticks, five on the right side, and five on the left before the inner

---

1 7[35] Unfortunately the subject has fallen out of the text. It must be supplied from [30].
m 7[30b] Heb., *feet*, but this is probably a scribal error for, *corners*.
n 7[31] Again some Heb. scribe apparently misread a letter giving, *capital*, instead of *shoulder-pieces*.
o 7[31] Heb., *their*.
p 7[38] Heb., *forty baths*.
q 7[40] So Gk., Luc., and Lat., confirmed by the summary in [45] and the parallel in II Chr. 4[11].
r 7[46-48a] So Gk. and Luc., which introduce [46] in its natural place after [47] and preserve a much better reading for [47] and [46a].

Temple Records

room, of pure gold; and the flowers, the lamps, and the golden tongs; [50]and the cups, the snuffers, basins, bowls, and fire-pans, of pure gold; and the golden hinges, both for the folding doors of the inner room (the most holy place) and for the folding doors of the temple (the large room).[s]   [51]Thus all the work that King Solomon wrought in the temple of Jehovah was finished. And Solomon brought in the things which David his father had dedicated, even the silver and the gold and the vessels, placing them in the treasuries of the temple of Jehovah.

§ 53. Dedication of the Temple, I Kgs. 8, 9[1-9, 25], II Chr. 5[2]-7[10], 8[12-16]

Temple Records

I Kgs. 8 [1]Then Solomon assembled the elders of Israel, and all the heads of the tribes, the princes of the fathers' houses of the Israelites in Jerusalem to bring up the ark of the covenant of Jehovah out of the city of David, which is in Zion.   [2]And all the men of Israel assembled about King Solomon at the feast, in the month of Ethanim, which is the seventh month.[t]   [3]And all the elders of Israel came, and the priests took up the ark.   [4]And they brought up the ark of Jehovah, and the tent of meeting, and all the holy vessels that were in the tent; even these did the priests and Levites bring up.   [5]Then King Solomon and all the congregation of Israel, who were assembled to him, were with him before the ark sacrificing so many sheep and oxen, that they could neither be counted nor numbered. [6]So the priests brought in the ark of the covenant of Jehovah to its place in the inner room of the temple (in the most holy place) under the wings of the cherubim.   [7]For the cherubim spread forth their wings over the place of the ark, so that the cherubim formed a covering above the ark and its staves. [8]And the staves were so long that the ends of the staves were seen from the place before the inner room;[u] but further out they could not be seen. And there they are to this day.   [9]There was nothing in the ark except the two tables of stone which Moses put there at Horeb, when Jehovah made a covenant with the Israelites as they came from the land of Egypt.   [10]And when the priests

(margin: Transfer of the ark into the temple*)*

---

[s] 7[48b-50] These verses by their awkward constructions, late terms (such as *most holy place*), and contents are clearly marked as later additions. The golden altar and candlesticks are not mentioned in the original narrative and first appear in the writings of the Chronicler. Cf. the introd. note to this section.

§ 53 The temple records, and probably also the annals of Solomon, had an account of the dedication of the temple. It was, however, a theme which lent itself readily to later expansion. Succeeding generations pictured the act as it would have been performed in their own day. The original kernel of the narrative is represented by the much briefer version of 8[1-5], preserved by the Gk. and Luc. This appears in the Heb., supplemented by the expressions and ceremonial usages characteristic of the priestly writers who flourished during and after the Babylonian exile.

Beginning with [14], a very late prophetic editor, who evidently lived in the shadow of the exile, adds a majestic, spiritual address, prayer, and blessing, embodying the lofty sentiments which seemed appropriate at the dedication of the temple, which was regarded by him and his contemporaries as the one legitimate sanctuary. Cf. [16]. The prayer in [22-53] was clearly suggested by the curses in Dt. 28[15-68]. The peculiar expressions and ideas are those of the late prophetic school. Such passages as 8[46-53] and 9[6-9] reflect the exilic background. In the account of the festival in [62-66] he perhaps incorporates earlier material.

The Chronicler for the most part reproduces the address in I Kgs., but at certain points he introduces the singers and other data calculated further to adapt it to the peculiar views of his own age.

[t] 8[2] The seventh month (Bab., *Tishri*), Sept.-Oct.

[u] 8[8] Heb., *holy place.*

Temple Records

had come from the sanctuary,ᵛ the cloud filled the temple of Jehovah, ¹¹so that the priests could not stand to minister because of the cloud, for the glory of Jehovah filled the temple of Jehovah.

Solomon's hymn of dedication
¹²Then Solomon said,

> Jehovah hath set the sun in the heavens,
> But he hath himself determined to dwell in thick darkness.
> ¹³So I have built thee a temple as a place of abode,
> A dwelling for thee to abide in forever.

Is it not written in the Book of Jashar?ʷ

Later Prophetic (Exilic) Addition

His address to the people
¹⁴Then the king turned about and blessed all the assembly of Israel; and all the assembly of Israel stood up. ¹⁵He said, Blessed be Jehovah, the God of Israel, who has with his own hand fulfilled what he spoke with his mouth to David my father, saying, ¹⁶'Since the day that I brought forth my people Israel from Egypt, I chose no [other] city out of all the tribes of Israel to build a temple, that my name might be there;ˣ but I have chosen Jerusalem that my name might be there, and I have chosen David to be over my people Israel.' ¹⁷Now it was in the heart of David my father to build a temple for the name of Jehovah, the God of Israel. ¹⁸But Jehovah said to David my father, 'Whereas it was in thy heart to build a temple for my name, thou didst well that it was in thy heart; ¹⁹nevertheless thou shalt not build the temple; but thy son, who shall come forth out of thy loins, he shall build the temple for my name.' ²⁰Now Jehovah has fulfilled his promise that he made: for I have risen up in the place of David my father and sit on the throne of Israel, as Jehovah promised, and have built the temple for the name of Jehovah, the God of Israel. ²¹And there have I set a place for the ark in which is the covenant of Jehovah, which he made with our fathers, when he brought them out of the land of Egypt.

His dedicatory prayer for the reigning house
²²Then Solomon stood before the altar of Jehovah in the presence of all the assembly of Israel and spread forth his handsʸ toward heaven, ²³and said, O Jehovah, the God of Israel, there is no God like thee in heaven above or on earth beneath, who keepest the covenant and showest kindness to thy servants who walk before thee with all their heart, ²⁴who hast kept with

---

ᵛ 8¹⁰ᵃ, II Chr. 5¹¹ᵇ In the following long parenthesis, here inserted by the Chronicler into the older source, the musicians in which he was so deeply interested were made to have a part in the dedication of the temple: ¹¹ᵇ (*for all the priests that were present had sanctified themselves, it being impossible to arrange them in divisions;* ¹²*and all the Levites who were singers, even Asaph, Heman, Jeduthun, and their sons and their clansmen, arrayed in fine linen, with cymbals and lyres and harps, stood at the east end of the altar, and with them a hundred and twenty priests blowing on trumpets;* ¹³*and the trumpeters and singers united in one harmonious sound of praise and thanksgiving to Jehovah, and they lifted up their voice with the trumpets and cymbals and musical instruments and praised Jehovah, saying, For he is good, for his loving-kindness endureth forever*).

ʷ 8¹², ¹³ Restoring on the basis of Gk. and Luc., which, however, place the quotation later in the context (8⁵³).   *Book of Jashar, i.e.*, the Righteous One (Israel). Cf. Vol. I, p. 16.

ˣ 8¹⁶ So Gk. and II Chr. 6⁶.   The abbreviation of the Heb. is due to a scribal error.

ʸ 8²² II Chr. 6¹³ adds the characteristic parenthetic note: (*for Solomon had made a brazen scaffold, five cubits long and five cubits broad and three cubits high, and had set it in the midst of the court; and upon it he stood and kneeled down upon his knees before all the assembly of Israel and spread forth his hands toward heaven*).

Later Prophetic (Exilic) Addition

thy servant David my father the promise that thou didst make to him; yea,
thou spakest with thy mouth and hast fulfilled it with thy hand, as it is this
day. ²⁵Now therefore, O Jehovah, the God of Israel, keep with thy servant
David my father the promise that thou hast made to him, saying, 'There
shall not fail thee a man in my sight to sit on the throne of Israel, if only
thy children take heed to their way, to walk before me as thou hast walked
before me.' ²⁶Now therefore, O God of Israel, let thy word, I pray thee,
be verified, which thou hast spoken to thy servant David my father.

²⁷But can God actually dwell with men[a] on the earth? Indeed heaven
and the highest heaven cannot contain thee; how much less this temple that
I have built! ²⁸Yet have respect to the prayer of thy servant and to his
supplication, O Jehovah, my God, listening to the cry and to the prayer
which thy servant offereth before thee this day, ²⁹that thine eyes may be
open toward this temple night and day, even toward the place of which
thou hast said, 'My name shall be there,' to listen to the prayer which thy
servant shall offer toward this place. ³⁰And hear thou the supplication of
thy servant and of thy people Israel, when they shall pray toward this place;
yea, hear thou in heaven thy dwelling place; and when thou hearest forgive.

For-
give-
ness
of the
sins

³¹If a man sin against his neighbor, and an oath be laid upon him to cause
him to swear, and he come and swear before thine altar in this temple,[b]
³²then hear thou in heaven, and act and judge thy servants, condemning
the wicked, to bring the consequences of his conduct upon his own head
and justifying the righteous, to recompense him according to his righteousness.

Of the
indi-
vidual

³³When thy people Israel are smitten down before the enemy because
they have sinned against thee, if they turn again to thee and confess thy
name and pray and make supplication to thee in this temple, ³⁴then hear
thou in heaven and forgive the sin of thy people Israel and bring them
again to the land which thou gavest to their fathers. ³⁵When heaven is
shut up and there is no rain, because they have sinned against thee; if they
pray toward this place and confess thy name and turn from their sin, when
thou doest humble them, ³⁶then hear thou in heaven and forgive the sin of
thy servants and of thy people Israel, when thou teachest them the good
way in which they should walk, and send rain upon thy land, which thou
hast given to thy people for an inheritance. ³⁷If there be in the land famine,
if there be pestilence, if there be blasting or mildew, locust or caterpillar, if
their enemy besiege them in any of their gates;[c] whatever plague, whatever
sickness there be, ³⁸whatever prayer and supplication be made by any man,[d]
who knows his own personal affliction,[e] and spreads forth his hands toward
this temple, ³⁹then hear thou in heaven thy dwelling place and forgive and
act and render to every man according to all his ways, whose heart thou
knowest (for thou, even thou only, knowest the hearts of all the children of

Of the
nation

---

a 8²⁷ Supported by Gk., Luc., and Targ.
b 8³¹ Cf. Ex. 22¹⁻¹¹.
c 8³⁷ Supported by Gk., Luc., and Syr. Heb., *in the land of their cities.*
d 8³⁸ So Gk. and Luc.
e 8³⁸ Heb. lit., *who shall know each the plague of his own heart.* The Gk. and Luc. suggest
the rendering given above.

Later Prophetic (Exilic) Addition

men), ⁴⁰that they may fear thee all the days that they live in the land which thou gavest to our fathers.

Of the repentant alien

⁴¹Also to the alien, who is not of thy people Israel, but comes from a far country for thy name's sake—⁴²for they shall hear of thy great name and of thy mighty hand and of thine outstretched arm—when he shall come and pray toward this temple, ⁴³wilt thou listen in heaven thy dwelling place, and do all things as the alien requests of thee, that all the peoples of the earth may know thy name, to fear thee, as doth thy people Israel, and that they may know that this temple which I have built is called by thy name.

For success in battle

⁴⁴If thy people go out to battle against their enemy, by whatever way thou shalt send them, and they pray to thee[f] in the direction of the city which thou hast chosen and the temple which I have built for thy name, ⁴⁵then hear thou in heaven their prayer and their supplication and uphold their cause.

For deliverance from captivity, if the people repent

⁴⁶If they sin against thee—for there is no man that sinneth not—and thou be angry with them and deliver them to their enemy, so that they carry them away captive to the land of the enemy, far off or near; ⁴⁷yet if they shall be converted in the land to which they are carried captive and turn again and make supplication to thee in the land of their captivity,[g] saying, 'We have sinned, and have acted perversely and wickedly;' ⁴⁸if they return to thee with all their heart and with all their soul while yet in the land of their enemies, who carried them captive, and pray to thee in the direction of their land, which thou hast chosen and the temple which I have built for thy name, ⁴⁹then hear thou their prayer and their supplication in heaven thy dwelling place, and uphold their cause,[h] ⁵⁰and forgive thy people who have sinned against thee, and all their transgressions with which they have transgressed against thee, and give them compassion with those who carried them captive, that they may have compassion on them—⁵¹for they are thy people, and thine inheritance, which thou broughtest forth out of Egypt, from the midst of the iron furnace—⁵²that thine eyes may be open to the supplication of thy servant and to the supplication of thy people Israel, to listen to them whenever they cry to thee. ⁵³For thou didst separate them from all the peoples of the earth to be thine inheritance, as thou spakest by Moses thy servant, when thou broughtest our fathers out of Egypt, O Lord Jehovah.

Concluding blessing and exhortation

⁵⁴After Solomon had finished praying all this prayer and supplication to Jehovah, he arose from kneeling on his knees before the altar of Jehovah with his hands spread forth toward heaven, ⁵⁵and stood, and with a loud voice blessed all the assembly of Israel, saying, ⁵⁶Blessed be Jehovah who hath given rest to his people Israel, according to àll that he promised. One word hath not failed of all his good promise, which he made by Moses his servant. ⁵⁷Jehovah our God be with us, as he was with our fathers; let him not leave us nor forsake us, ⁵⁸that he may incline our hearts to him,

---

f 8⁴⁴ Heb., *to Jehovah*, probably due to a copyist's error.
g 8⁴⁷ So Gk., Luc. and II Chr. 6³⁷.
h 8⁴⁹ᵇ Gk. and Luc. omit, perhaps correctly.

Later Prophetic (Exilic) Addition

to walk in all his ways and to keep his commands and his statutes and his ordinances, which he commanded our fathers. ⁵⁹And let these my words, wherewith I have made supplication before Jehovah, be near to Jehovah, our God, day and night, that he uphold the cause of his servant and the cause of his people Israel, as each day shall require, ⁶⁰that all the peoples of the earth may know that Jehovah is God alone. ⁶¹Let your heart therefore be perfect with Jehovah our God, to walk in his statutes and to keep his commandments, as at this day.

II Chr. 7 ¹Now when Solomon had made an end of praying, the fire came down from heaven, and consumed the burnt-offering and the sacrifices. And the glory of Jehovah filled the temple, ²so that the priests could not enter into the temple of Jehovah, because the glory of Jehovah filled Jehovah's temple. ³Also all the Israelites looked on, when the fire came down, and the glory of Jehovah was upon the temple. And they bowed themselves with their faces to the ground upon the pavement and worshipped and gave thanks to Jehovah, saying, For he is good; for his lovingkindness endureth forever. *The divine response*

I Kgs. 8 ⁶²Both the king and all Israel offered sacrifice before Jehovah. ⁶³Solomon offered for the sacrifice of peace-offerings, which he offered to Jehovah, twenty-two thousand oxen, and a hundred and twenty thousand sheep. So the king and all the Israelites dedicated the temple of Jehovah.ⁱ ⁶⁴The same day the king hallowed the middle of the court that was before the temple of Jehovah; for there he offered the burnt-offering and the cereal-offering and the fat pieces of the peace-offerings, because the brazen altar that was before Jehovah was too small to receive the burnt-offering and the cereal-offering and the fat of the peace-offerings. ⁶⁵So Solomon held the feast at that time and all Israel with him—a great assembly, from the entrance to Hamath to the brook of Egypt—before Jehovah our God, seven days.ʲ ⁶⁶But on the eighth day he sent the people away; and receiving a blessing from the king,ᵏ they went to their homes, joyful and glad of heart for all the goodness that Jehovah had showed to David his servant, and to Israel his people. *Feast and sacrifices of dedication*

9 ¹Now when Solomon had finished the building of the temple of Jehovah, and the royal palace, and all Solomon's plansˡ which he wished to carry out, ²Jehovah appeared to Solomon the second time, as he had appeared to him at Gibeon. ³And Jehovah said to him, I have heard thy prayer and thy supplication, that thou hast made before me.ᵐ I have hallowed this temple which thou hast built to put my name there forever; and mine eyes and my heart shall be there perpetually. ⁴If indeed thou wilt walk before me, as *Jehovah's promises and warnings in response to Solomon's prayer*

ⁱ 8⁶³ᵇ This is lacking in Gk. The Chronicler in II Chr. 7⁶ furthermore adds, *And the priests stood, according to their offices; the Levites also with instruments for the music of Jehovah, which David the king had made to give thanks to Jehovah (for his lovingkindness endureth forever), by means of whom David gave praise. And the priests sounded trumpets before them; and all Israel stood up.*

ʲ 8⁶⁵ The shorter text is supported by the Gk., and required by the introductory conjunction of ⁶⁶, *And on the eighth day.* So Gk., Luc., and Lat. Heb. adds, *and seven days, even fourteen days.*

ᵏ 8⁶⁶ The present Heb. is due to an early scribe who mistook the singular suffix for the plural ending. It then became necessary to supply an object. The Gk. translators support as original the above reading, though not understanding it.

ˡ 9¹ A slight change in the Heb. gives the above rendering which is supported by the Gk. and Luc.

ᵐ 9³ᵃ Gk. and Luc. add, *I have acted in accordance with all thy prayer,* which may be original.

Later Prophetic (Exilic) Addition

David thy father walked, in integrity of heart and in uprightness, to do according to all that I have commanded thee, and wilt keep my statutes and mine ordinances, [5]then I will establish the throne of thy kingdom over Israel forever, as I promised to David thy father, saying, 'There shall not fail thee a man upon the throne of Israel.' [6]But if ye shall turn away from following me, ye or your children, and shall not keep my commands and my statutes which I have set before you, but shall go and serve other gods, and worship them; [7]then I will take away Israel from the land, which I have given them; and this temple which I have hallowed for my name, will I cast away from me, and Israel shall be a proverb and a byword among all peoples. [8]Moreover this temple shall become ruins,[n] every one that passeth by it shall be astonished and shall hiss, and they shall say, 'Why hath Jehovah done thus to this land and to this people?' [9]And they shall answer, 'Because they forsook Jehovah their God, who brought forth their fathers from the land of Egypt, and took up with other gods, worshipping and serving them; therefore Jehovah hath brought all this evil upon them.'

Chronicler's Ecclesiastical History

Institution of the regular service of the temple

[25]And three times in the year Solomon used to offer burnt-offerings and peace - offerings upon the altar which he built to Jehovah, and he used to cause the savor of the sacrifice to rise before Jehovah.[o] So he finished the temple.

II Chr. 8 [12]Then Solomon offered burnt-offerings to Jehovah on the altar of Jehovah, which he had built before the porch, [13]even as the service of each day required, offering according to the command of Moses, on the sabbaths, on the new moons, and on the set feasts, three times in the year, even at the feast of unleavened bread and at the feast of weeks and at the feast of tabernacles. [14]And he appointed, according to the ordinance of David his father, the courses of the priests to their service and the Levites to their offices, to praise and minister before the priests, as the service of each day required; the doorkeepers also by their courses at every gate, for so had David the man of God commanded. [15]And they departed not from the king's command to the priests and Levites concerning any matter or concerning the treasures. [16]Now all the work of Solomon was completed to the day of the foundation of the temple of Jehovah and until it was finished. So the temple of Jehovah was completed.

---

[n] 9⁸ Heb. lit., *And this house shall be most high,* which is contrary to the idea of the context. Gk. and Luc. seem to have had the present Heb. Lat., *And this house shall be for an example.* A slight change in Heb. gives the above rendering, which the Syr. supports.
[o] 9²⁵ The present Heb., by inserting *it which,* has become meaningless. The shorter reading is supported by Gk., Luc., and Lat.

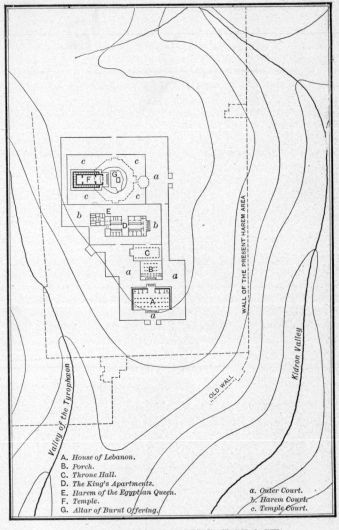

Valley of the Tyrophœon

WALL OF THE PRESENT HAREM AREA

Kidron Valley

OLD WALL

A. House of Lebanon.
B. Porch.
C. Throne Hall.
D. The King's Apartments.
E. Harem of the Egyptian Queen.
F. Temple.
G. Altar of Burnt Offering.

a. Outer Court.
b. Harem Court.
c. Temple Court.

PLAN OF SOLOMON'S PALACE

(ACCORDING TO STADE)

§ 54. Solomon's Palace, I Kgs. 7^{1-12}, 9^{24a}, II Chr. 8^{11}

Annals of Solomon

House of Lebanon and Hall of Judgment

I Kgs. 7 [1]And Solomon was building his palace thirteen years, until he
had completely finished his palace. [2]There also he built the Forest of
Lebanon;[p] its length was a hundred cubits, and its breadth fifty cubits, and
its height thirty cubits, upon three[q] rows of cedar pillars, with cedar beams[r]
upon the pillars. [3]And it was covered with cedar above over the forty-five
beams, that were upon the pillars; and the number of the pillars[s] was fifteen
in a row. [4]And there were window-frames in three rows, and window was
over against window in three tiers. [5]And all the doors and windows were
made with square frames: and door was over against door in three tiers.[t]
[6]And the hall of pillars he made fifty cubits long and thirty cubits broad;
and a porch before them and pillars and a threshold[u] before them. [7]And
he made the throne-hall where he was to judge, even the Hall of Judgment;
and it was covered with cedar from floor to ceiling.

Private palace of Solomon and his Egyptian queen

[8]And his palace, where he was to dwell, in another court farther in from
the Hall of Judgment, was of the same workmanship. He also made a
palace for Pharaoh's daughter (whom Solomon had taken as wife), similar to
his hall. **9** [24a]And Pharaoh's daughter came up out of the city of David
to her palace which Solomon had built for her.

Materials used in constructing the palace

7 [9]All these were of costly stones, hewn according to measurements, sawed
with saws, both on the interior and on the exterior, even from the foundation
to the coping, and from the exterior to the great court. [10]And the foundation
was of costly great stones—stones of ten cubits and stones of eight cubits.
[11]And above were costly stones, hewn according to measurements, and cedar
wood. [12]And the great encircling court had three courses of hewn stone
and a course of cedar beams; even so it was round about the inner court of
the temple of Jehovah and the court of the porch of the palace.[v]

§ 55. Solomon's Resources and Wealth, I Kgs. $9^{10-15,\ 17b-23,\ 26-28}$, $10^{11,\ 12,\ 14-29}$, II Chr. $8^{1-10,\ 17,\ 18}$, $9^{10,\ 11,\ 13-28}$.

Annals of Solomon

Solomon's payment for the material furnished by Hiram

I Kgs. 9 [10]Now at the end of twenty years, during which Solomon had built the
two buildings: the temple of Jehovah and the king's palace, [11]Hiram the king of Tyre
having furnished Solomon with cedar and cypress wood and with gold as much as he

---

§ 54 This narrative appears to have been the conclusion of the original account of Solomon's building enterprises. In the Gk. text it stands at the end of 7, but the fact that [12b] has been left behind indicates that it was the work of a later editor. The description is so brief that it is at points scarcely intelligible and the statistical element is prominent. It has all the characteristics of a passage taken directly from the original annals of Solomon. With this the detached passage, 9^{24a}, logically belongs. Cf. 7^{8}. For the plan of Solomon's palace, cf. accompanying diagram.

[p] 7^{2} Doubtless so named because the four rows of supporting cedar of Lebanon pillars gave the effect of a forest or else because the wood came from Lebanon.

[q] 7^{2} So Gk. and Luc. Heb., *four*.

[r] 7^{2} Gk. and Luc., *shoulder-pieces*.

[s] 7^{3} So Gk. Heb. omits, *and the number of the pillars*.

[t] 7^{5b} So Gk. and Luc. The Heb. is but a dittography of [4b].

[u] 7^{6} The meaning of this word is doubtful. *Projecting roof* and *cornice* have been suggested, but all are only conjectural.

[v] 7^{12} Incorporating two words which have been preserved in the Gk. and Luc.

§ 55 Following the account of Solomon's building enterprises are a series of miscellaneous notices intended further to illustrate his resources, wealth, and wisdom. The order is far from logical. The Gk. and Chr. each differ from the Heb. The Gk. on the whole has the best order

Annals of Solomon

wished, King Solomon gave Hiram twenty cities in the land of Galilee.ʷ ¹²But when Hiram came from Tyre to see the cities which Solomon had given him, he was displeased with them. ¹³And he said, What sort of cities are these which you have given me, my brother? So they are called the land of Cabul [Good for nothing]ˣ even to the present day. ¹⁴But Hiram sent to the king one hundred and twenty talents of gold.

His additional building enterprises and forced levies

¹⁵And this is the way it was with the levy which King Solomon raised to build the temple of Jehovah, his own palace, Millo, the wall of Jerusalem, Hazor, Meggido, Gezer, ¹⁷ᵇlower Bethhoron,ʸ ¹⁸Baalath, and Tamar in the wilderness in the land of Judah, ¹⁹and all the store-cities that Solomon had, and the cities for his chariots, and the cities for his horsemen, and that which Solomon was pleased to build for his pleasure in Jerusalem, in Lebanon, and in all the land over which he ruled. ²⁰All the people who were left of the Amorites, the Hittites, the Perizzites, the Hivites, and the Jebusites, who were not of the Israelites, ²¹their children who were left after them in the land, whom the Israelites were not able utterly to destroy, of them did Solomon raise a forced levy of bondmen, even to this day. ²²But of the Israelites Solomon made no bondmen, for they were the warriors and his servants, his generals, his captains,ᵃ his officers over his chariots, and his horsemen.

Officials over the levy

²³These were the chief officers who were over Solomon's work, five hundred and fifty, who directed the people who did the work.

His Red Sea fleet

²⁶And King Solomon made a fleet of ships in Ezion-geber, which is near Elath on the shore of the Red Sea in the land of Edom. ²⁷And Hiram sent with the fleet his subjects—seamen, who had knowledge of the sea, together with the servants of Solomon. ²⁸And they went to Ophir, and took from there gold, four hundred and twenty talents, and brought it to King Solomon.

Products brought by Hiram's fleet

10 ¹¹And Hiram's fleet of ships, that bore gold from Ophir, also brought a great amount of red sandal woodᵇ and precious stones. ¹²And the king made of the sandal wood from Ophir pilastersᶜ for the temple of Jehovah, and for the royal palace, and lyres and harps for the singers. There came no other such sandal wood nor has the like been seen to the present day.

Solomon's income in gold

¹⁴Now the weight of gold that came to Solomon in one year was six hundred and sixty-six talents of gold, ¹⁵besides what came from the traffic of the merchantsᵈ and from all the kings of the Arabiansᵉ and from the governors of the country.

---

and this has been followed, except in one or two cases where a more logical arrangement is possible. Like the notices in 4, 5, most of these appear to have been taken from the annals of Solomon. They have, however, been supplemented by later notes embodying current traditions and intended still further to glorify Solomon's reign. With the exception of 10²³, ²⁷, which are clearly late generalizations, these supplementary notices seem to embody earlier data, drawn from the annals, so that it is difficult to distinguish with assurance between the original and the later expansions; but a later hand is clearly discernible in the introductory words, 9¹⁰, ¹¹ᵃ and in ²⁰⁻²² (where the theory is expressed that only the older inhabitants were enlisted in the forced levy), and perhaps in 10¹⁴, ¹⁵, ²¹.

ʷ 9¹⁰, ¹¹ The Chronicler could not be reconciled to the idea of Solomon's having ceded Israelitish territory, so he has, 8², *But the cities which Huram had ceded to Solomon, Solomon fortified and settled Israelites there.*

ˣ 9¹³ A popular etymology based simply on the sound of the word.

ʸ 9¹⁵⁻¹⁸ Cf. map opp. p. 49 and Ezek. 47¹⁹, 48²⁸.

ᵃ 9²² The exact meaning of this word is not known. Lat. as above.

ᵇ 10¹¹ Heb., *almug wood*. The exact meaning of the word has not been determined.

ᶜ 10¹² The meaning is doubtful. The above is suggested by the Gk., Luc., and Lat.

ᵈ 10¹⁵ Emending what is otherwise untranslatable.

ᵉ 10¹⁵ So II Chr. 9¹⁹ and many Gk. texts.

Annals of Solomon

^16And King Solomon made two hundred bucklers of beaten gold—six   His
hundred shekels^f of gold went on one buckler—^17and three hundred shields   buck-
of beaten gold—three minahs^g of gold went on one shield—and the king   shields,
put them in the House of the Forest of Lebanon.   ^18The king also made a   throne
great throne of ivory, and overlaid it with the finest gold.   ^19The throne had   of gold
six steps and behind the throne were heads of calves, and on both sides of
the seat were arms, and beside the arms stood two lions, ^20on the six steps
stood twelve lions on each side.   The like was not made in any kingdom.

^21And all King Solomon's drinking vessels were of gold: none were of   His
silver; it was accounted of no value in the days of Solomon.   ^22For the king   royal
had at sea a fleet of Tarshish ships with the fleet of Hiram.   Once every   income
three years the fleet of Tarshish ships came bringing gold, silver, ivory,
apes, and peacocks.   ^23So King Solomon exceeded all the kings of the earth in
riches and in wisdom.   ^24And all the earth sought the presence of Solomon, to hear his
wisdom, with which God had endowed his mind.   ^25And they brought each a present: vessels of silver and gold, clothing, weapons, spices, horses, and mules,
year by year.

^26And Solomon gathered together chariots and horsemen; and he had   His
one thousand four hundred chariots and twelve thousand horsemen that   chariots
he stationed in the chariot cities and with the king at Jerusalem.   ^27And the   trade
king made silver in Jerusalem as common as stones, and cedars he made as plentiful   in
as the sycamore trees that are in the lowland.   ^28Solomon's import of horses   horses
was from Muçri^h and Kuë; the king's traders received them from Kuë at
a price, ^29so that a chariot could be imported from Muçri for six hundred
shekels of silver and a horse for a hundred and fifty.   Even so through their
agency these were exported to all the kings of the Hittites and the Arameans.

§ 56. **Visit of the Queen of Sheba, I Kgs. 10^1-10, 13, II Chr. 9^1-9, 12**

Popular Solomon Traditions

I Kgs. 10 ^1Now when the queen of Sheba heard of the fame of Solomon   Impres-
through the name of Jehovah,^i she came to test him with riddles.   ^2So she   sion
came to Jerusalem with a very great retinue, with camels that bore spices   by Solo-
and very much gold and precious stones.   And as soon as she came to Solo-   wealth
mon, she told him all that was on her mind.   ^3And Solomon answered all   and
her questions; there was nothing hid from the king which he could not   dom
answer her.   ^4And when the queen of Sheba had seen all the wisdom of   the
Solomon, the house that he had built, ^5the food of his table, the seating^j   queen
of his courtiers, the attendance of his waiters, their clothing, his cup-   Sheba

---

^f 10^16 Probably between twenty and twenty-five pounds.
^g 10^17 About three and one-half pounds.
^h 10^28 The horse does not seem to have been known in Egypt until about 1600 B.C. and
after that time was probably imported rather than exported, so that the current translation,
Egypt, has little probability.   Muçri, however, in Northern Syria had fine pasture lands, and
Ezek. 27^14 refers to the importation of horses into Israel from that region.   Dt. 17^16, however,
indicates that Egypt was also later regarded as a source of supply for horses.   Kuë is identified
with the plain of Cilicia, cf. Appendix V, note ^b.
^i 10^1 Many emend so as to read, *and the report of the house which he had built to the name
of Jehovah.*
^j 10^5 *I.e.*, at his royal table.   The context does not favor the other possible meaning,
dwellings.

Popular Solomon Traditions

bearers, and his burnt-offering which he used to offer at the temple of
Jehovah, there was no more spirit in her.[k]　[6]And she said to the king, True
was the report that I heard in my own land of your acts and of your wisdom.
[7]But I would not believe the words until I came and saw with my own eyes;
the half was not told me; you exceed in wisdom and prosperity the report
which I heard.　[8]Happy are your wives![l]　Happy are these your courtiers
who stand continually before you and hear your wisdom!　[9]Blessed be
Jehovah your God who delighted in you and has set you on the throne of
Israel!　Because Jehovah loved Israel forever, he has made you king that
you may do justice and righteousness.　[10]Then she gave the king a hundred
and twenty talents of gold and a very great store of spices and precious
stones; never again came so many spices as these which the queen of Sheba
gave to King Solomon.

His
gifts
to her
[13]And King Solomon gave to the queen all that she wished and asked,
aside from that which she had brought to Solomon, according to his royal
bounty.　So she returned and went to her own land, together with her
servants.

§ 57. Solomon's Idolatry, I Kgs. 11¹⁻¹³

Annals of Solomon

Solomon's
foreign
marriages
I Kgs. 11 [1a]Now King Solomon was a lover of women; and he took many
foreign wives—Moabites, Canaanites, Edomites, Sidonians, Hittites,
and Ammonites—[2]From the nations concerning which Jehovah had said to the Israelites,
ye shall not go among them, neither shall they come among you; for otherwise they
will turn away your heart after their gods; Solomon clung to these in love.

His
apostasy
in worshipping
the
gods of
his
wives
[3]And he had seven hundred wives, princesses, and three hundred concubines; and his wives turned away his heart.[m]　[4]Now when Solomon was old
his heart was not perfect with Jehovah his God, as was the heart of David
his father; and his wives turned away his heart after their gods.　[7]But Solomon
built a high place for Chemosh the god of Moab, in the mount that is before Jerusalem, and for Milcom the god of the Ammonites,[n] [5]and also for
Ashtarte the goddess of the Sidonians.[o]　[8]And so he did for all his foreign
wives, burning incense and sacrificing to their gods.[p]

---

[k] 10⁵ *I.e.*, she was completely overwhelmed.
[l] 10⁸ So Gk., Luc., Syr., and II Chr. 9⁷. Heb., *men*.
§ 57 At least two distinct stages are represented in the literary history of this passage.
The original is represented by the brief extracts from the annals to the effect that Solomon made
many alliances, sealed by marriages with foreign princesses, and that, as the international law of
his day demanded, he reared shrines in Jerusalem in honor of the gods of the allied peoples.
These acts the original annalist doubtless regarded as only further evidence of Solomon's glory.
　The late prophetic editor, whose peculiar ideas and expression are found in a majority of
the verses, enjoyed much greater religious enlightenment and therefore found in these foreign
marriages and the toleration of heathen worships the direct cause of the rebellions which darkened the closing years of Solomon's reign.
　The section has been much recast and supplemented.　The Gk., which has a briefer, more
logical, and doubtless more original reading, has been followed in most cases.
[m] 11³ So Gk. and Luc.　The Heb. awkwardly transposes the order of the clauses.
[n] 11⁷ With the aid of the Heb. in ⁵ and the Gk., it is possible to reconstruct the original.
For *god*, the latter scribes have in the Heb. substituted, *abomination*.　Cf. ³³ where the Heb. has
retained, *god*, while the Gk. has in one case, *abomination*.
[o] 11⁵ So Gk. and Luc.　The Heb. reads, *And Solomon went after Ashtoreth the goddess of
the Sidonians and Milcom the abomination of the Ammonites.*
[p] 11⁸ So Luc.　The present Heb. text delivers Solomon from the curse of idolatry by
making his wives perform the heathen sacrifices.

Annals of Solomon

⁶And Solomon did that which displeased Jehovah and did not faithfully follow Jehovah, as did David his father. ⁹And Jehovah was angry with Solomon, because his heart was turned away from Jehovah, the God of Israel, who had appeared to him twice, ¹⁰and had commanded him concerning this thing, that he should not go after other gods; but he did not take care to doᵠ that which Jehovah had commanded.

¹¹Therefore Jehovah said to Solomon, Inasmuch as this is thy character and thou hast not kept my statutes, which I have commanded thee, I will surely rendʳ the kingdom from thee, and will give it to thy servant.ˢ ¹²Notwithstanding in thy days I will not do it, for David thy father's sake; but I will rend it out of the hand of thy son. ¹³However I will not rend away all the kingdom; but I will give one tribe to thy son, for the sake of David my servant and for the sake of Jerusalem which I have chosen.

Jehovah's condemnation

§ 58. Solomon's Adversaries and Death, I Kgs. 11¹⁴⁻⁴³, II Chr. 9²⁹⁻³¹

Annals of Solomon

I Kgs. 11 ¹⁴Then Jehovah raised up against Solomon an adversary, the Edomite Hadad, of the race of Edomite kings; ¹⁵ᵃ· ᶜfor when David smote the Edomites, he smote every male in Edom. ¹⁷ᵇBut Hadad being a child, one of his father's servants brought him to Egypt. ¹⁹ᵃAnd he found great favor in the eyes of Pharaoh, so that he gave him to his chief wife, ²⁰ᵇand she brought him up in Pharaoh's palace among the sons of Pharaoh. ²¹But when Hadad heard in Egypt that David slept with his fathers, he said to Pharaoh, Let me depart that I may go to my own country. ²²Then Pharaoh said to him, What do you lack with me that you are now seeking to go to your own country? And he said to him, Nevertheless you must let me go. . . . ²⁵ᵇThis is the evil that Hadad did; and he abhorred Israel and ruled in Edom.

Hadad, the Edomite

¹⁵ᵇAlso when Joab the commander of the army went up to bury the slain— ¹⁶for Joab and all Israel remained there six months—¹⁷ᵃAdad fled and certain Edomites with him. ¹⁸And they set out from Midian and came to Paran and took men with them out of Paran and came to Egypt to Pharaoh king of Egypt, who gave him a house and land. ¹⁹ᵇHe also gave him as

Adad, the Midianite

ᵠ 11¹⁰ So Gk. and Luc. Heb., *kept.*
ʳ 11¹¹, ¹³ Gk. and Luc., *take.* So also in Heb. ³⁴, ³⁵, but cf. ³¹.
ˢ 11¹¹ Lat., *with thee.*
§ 58 Four distinct rebellions against the authority of Solomon appear to have been originally recorded. The history and state of the accounts favor the conclusion that the first three were found in the annals of Solomon, where they would naturally belong. Probably because of the similarity of the names of the chief actors and because they both found refuge in Egypt, two of these accounts have been closely combined, as is frequently the case with the parallel stories in Gen., Ex., Num., and Judg. The resulting confusion is apparent in 11¹⁴⁻²². Two names, *Hadad* and *Adad*, recur. As the narrative reads in Kgs., Hadad, a little child, being carried as a refugee to Egypt, is at once given an Egyptian princess as wife and his son Genubath is reared in the palace as a son of Pharaoh. The original character of the two stories is revealed by the analysis, and with this the inconsistencies disappear. One tells of an Edomite prince, Hadad, who as a child was brought to Egypt and adopted by Pharaoh's queen; the other of Adad, a Midianite chief, who, as a refugee in Egypt, was given as wife an Egyptian princess, who in turn bore to him a son named Genubath.
The brief account of Rezon in ²³⁻²⁵ᵃ is not found in the Gk. and was probably introduced at a very late date into the Heb. text. It clearly comes, however, from an early source, which may originally have been the annals of Solomon.
Finally in ²⁶ᶠᶠ appears the first extract from what was probably once an independent Jeroboam history. In ³²ᵇ⁻³⁹ the oracle of Ahijah is expanded by a late prophetic editor. A somewhat briefer version is preserved in the Gk., while in 12²⁴ᵃ⁻ᶠ (Swete) the apparently later and widely variant version is found. In this there is no mention of Ahijah, suggesting that possibly this was not found in the original story. In ⁴¹⁻⁴³ appears the late prophetic editor's regular formulas.

Annals of Solomon

wife the sister of Tahpenes.ᵗ ²⁰ᵃ,ᶜAnd the sister of Tahpenes bore to him Genubath his son, and Genubath lived in Pharaoh's house. *But when he heard that David slept with his fathers, he returned to his land and likewise became an adversary to Solomon.*

Rezon the Aramean ²³God also raised up as an adversary to him, Rezon the son of Eliada, who had fled from his master, Hadadezer king of Zobah. ²⁴And he gathered men about him and became commander of a marauding band,ᵘ and they went to Damascus, and dwelt there and reigned in Damascus. ²⁵ᵃAnd he was an adversary to Israel as long as Solomon lived.

Jeroboam History

Jeroboam's early history ²⁶And Jeroboam the son of Nebat, an Ephraimite of Zeredah, an official of Solomon, whose mother's name was Zeruah, a widow, also lifted up his hand against the king. ²⁷And this was the reason why he lifted up his hand against the king: Solomon built Millo and closed up the exposed place in the city of David his father. ²⁸And Jeroboam was a man of great ability.ᵛ And when Solomon saw that the young man was industrious, he placed him over all the forced levy of the house of Joseph.

Ahijah's prediction that he should rule over ten tribes ²⁹Now it came to pass at that time when Jeroboam went away from Jerusalem, that the prophet Ahijah of Shilo found him in the way and turned him aside from the way. Now Ahijah had clad himself with a new garment;ʷ and they two were alone in the field. ³⁰Then Ahijah took hold of the new garment that was on him, and rent it in twelve pieces. ³¹And he said to Jeroboam, Take for yourself ten pieces; for thus saith Jehovah, the God of Israel, ' Behold, I will rend the kingdom out of the hand of Solomon and will give ten tribes to thee, ³²but he shall have one tribe, for the sake of my servant David and for the sake of Jerusalem, the city which I have chosen out of all the tribes of Israel, ³³because heˣ has forsaken me and worshipped Ashtarte, the goddess of the Sidonians, Chemosh, the god of Moab, and Milcom, the god of the Ammonites, and has not walked in my ways to do that which is pleasing to me, and to act in accordance with my statutes and mine ordinances, as David his father. ³⁴However I will not take the whole kingdom out of his hand; but I will surely uphold him all the days of his life,ᵃ for David my servant's sake whom I chose, who kept my commandments and my statutes. ³⁵But I will take the kingdom out of his son's hands and will give it to thee, even ten tribes. ³⁶And to his son will I give one tribe, that David my servant may have a lamp ever before me in Jerusalem, the city where I have chosen to put my name. ³⁷And I will take thee and thou shalt reign over all that thou desirest, and shalt be king over Israel. ³⁸And if thou wilt hearken to all that I command thee, and wilt walk in my ways and do that which is pleasing to me, in keeping my statutes and my commandments, as David my servant did, then I

ᵗ 11¹⁹ᵇ The Gk. and Luc. in 12²⁴ᵇ, in a closely parallel passage associated with Jeroboam, state that the king gave him Anoth the oldest sister of Tahpenes as wife. It is probable that the two traditions have there been confused and that Anoth was the name of the princess given not to the Hebrew refugee but to the Midianite prince.
ᵘ 11²⁴ So Gk. and Luc. A scribe, reminded by the reference to Zobah in ²³, of David's victory over the king of Zobah (II Sam. 8) added, *when David slew them.*
ᵛ 11²⁸ Cf. I Chr. 9¹³, 26⁸, but also Ruth 2¹ and I Sam. 9¹, where the possession of wealth and reputation rather than personal skill seems to be intended.
ʷ 11²⁹ So Gk. and Luc. This clause is omitted in the Heb. through a scribal error.
ˣ 11³³ So Gk., Luc., Lat., and Syr. Heb. has by mistake introduced a plural in the first part of the verse.
ᵃ 11³⁴ Following the original which appears to have been before the Gk. translators. Heb., *make or appoint him prince,* but Solomon had already long reigned as king.

Jeroboam History

will be with thee and will build thee an enduring house, as I built for David, and will give Israel to thee. ^{39}And I will for this afflict the descendants of David, but not forever.'

^{40}Solomon sought therefore to kill Jeroboam. Then Jeroboam arose and fled to Egypt, to Shishak [Sheshonk I] king of Egypt, and was in Egypt until the death of Solomon. His flight to Egypt

^{41}Now the rest of the acts of Solomon, and all that he did, and his wisdom, are they not already recorded in the History of the Acts of Solomon?^{b} ^{42}And the time during which Solomon reigned in Jerusalem over all Israel was forty years. ^{43}Then Solomon slept with his fathers and was buried in the city of David his father. And Rehoboam his son became king in his place.^{c} Solomon's death

---

b 11^{41} II Chr. 9^{29} gives as additional sources, *the history of Nathan the prophet, the prophecy of Ahijah the Shilonite and the visions of Iddo the seer concerning Jeroboam the son of Nebat.* Cf. Introd., p. 25.

c 11$^{42, 43}$ Paralleled by II Chr. 9$^{30, 31}$.

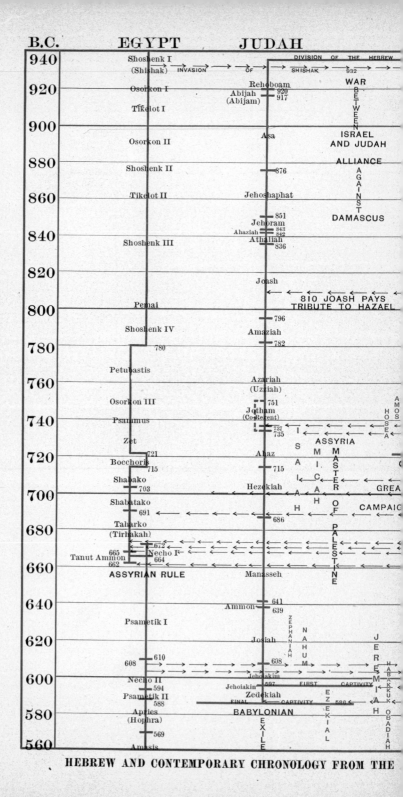

B.C.	EGYPT	JUDAH	
940	Shoshenk I (Shishak)	→ INVASION → → OF → → SHISHAK 932 →	DIVISION OF THE HEBREW / WAR BETWEEN
920	Osorkon I	Rehoboam / Abijah (Abijam) 920 / 917	
	Tikelot I		
900		Asa	ISRAEL AND JUDAH
880	Osorkon II	876	ALLIANCE AGAINST
860	Shoshenk II / Tikelot II	Jehoshaphat	
840	Shoshenk III	851 / Jehoram / Ahaziah 843 842 / Athaliah 836	DAMASCUS
820		Joash	
800	Pemai / Shoshenk IV	810 JOASH PAYS TRIBUTE TO HAZAEL / 796	
780	780	Amaziah 782	
760	Petubastis	Azariah (Uzziah)	
740	Osorkon III / Psammus	751 / Jotham (Co-Regent) / 737 735	AMOS HOSEA / ASSYRIA
720	Zet / 721 / Bocchoris / 715	Ahaz / 715	ISAIAH / MICAH / MASTER OF / GREA
700	Shabako 703 / Shabatako 691	Hezekiah / 686	AHO / CAMPAIG
680	Taharko (Tirhakah) / 672 / 665 Necho I / 664 / Tanut Ammon 662		PALESTINE
660	ASSYRIAN RULE	Manasseh	
640	Psametik I	Ammon 641 / 639	ZEPHANIAH / NAHUM / JE
620	608 610	Josiah / 608	R E
600	Necho II / 594 / Psametik II 588	Jehoiakim / Jehoiakin 597 FIRST CAPTIVITY / Zedekiah / FINAL CAPTIVITY 586	MI JEREMIAH / EZEKIAL / HABAKKUK
580	Apries (Hophra) / 569	BABYLONIAN	EXILE / EZEKIAL / OBADIAH
560	Amasis		

HEBREW AND CONTEMPORARY CHRONOLOGY FROM THE

RAEL	DAMASCUS	ASSYRIA

Rezon I — 930

eroboam I — Hezion — Ashurdan II

ab — 915 913 — Tabrimmon — 911

sha — Adad-nirari II

WARS

— 889 — 891
— 887 — Ben-hadad I — Tiglath-Adar II 885

Omri — 876
— 875 — B E T W E E N — Ashurnaçirpal II

Ahab — 860

iah — 853 851 — Hadadezer (Ben-hadad II) — BATTLE OF KARKAR 854 — 854 849 846 842
Iehoram — 842 — 839 — Shalmaneser II — 825

hu — Hazael — Shamshi-Adad — 812

— 814 — I S R A E L A N D D A M A S C U S — 803

ahaz — 797 — 797 — Adad-nirari III — 783

oash — Ben-hadad III (Mari) — Shalmaneser III — 773

— 781 — Ashurdan III — 755

oam II — Rezon II — Ashurnirari 745

— 740 738 736 734 — FINAL CONQUEST 732 — 738 734 — Tiglath-Pileser III 727 Shalmaneser IV

Hoshea — OF SAMARIA 722

Y OF ISRAEL 721

CAMPAIGN AGAINST ASHDOD 711 Sargon — 705

RN CAMPAIGN OF 701

ST THE ARABIANS AND EGYPTIANS ABOUT 690 Sennacherib — 681

Esarhaddon 675 668 667 662

RE OF THEBES 660

Ashurbanipal

BABYLONIA

REFORMATION OF JOSIAH 621 — 626 Ashuretililí — 626 Sinsharishkem Nabopolassar

BATTLE OF CARCHEMISH 605-4 — 605

QUEST OF JUDAH BY NEBUCHADREZZAR ABOUT 600 — 597

DESTRUCTION OF JERUSALEM 586 — 588

NEBUCHADREZZAR — 562

ON OF THE HEBREW EMPIRE TO THE BABYLONIAN EXILE

HISTORY OF NORTHERN ISRAEL

I Kgs. 12¹–II Kgs. 18¹¹ (*exclusive of data relating to Judah*), II Chr. 10

HISTORY OF NORTHERN ISRAEL FROM THE DIVISION OF THE EMPIRE TO THE FALL OF SAMARIA

I

FROM JEROBOAM TO OMRI, I Kgs. 12^1–14^{20}, 15^{25}–16^{20}, II Chr. 10

§ 59. Rejection of Rehoboam by the Northern Tribes and the Election of Jeroboam, I Kgs. 12$^{1-25}$, II Chr. 10

Jeroboam History

I Kgs. 12 ^{2}Now as soon as Jeroboam the son of Nebat heard [that Solomon was dead]—for he was still in Egypt, whither he had fled from the presence of King Solomon, and he dwelt in Egypt—he returned at once to his native town, Zeredah in Mount Ephraim.^{a} Jeroboam's return from Egypt

^{1}And Rehoboam went to Shechem, for all Israel had come to Shechem to make him king. ^{3}And they sent and called Jeroboam, and he, with all the assembly of Israel, came. And they said to Rehoboam, ^{4}Your father made our yoke intolerable. Now therefore make the intolerable service of your father and the heavy yoke he laid upon us lighter, and we will serve you. ^{5}And he said to them, Go away for three days, then come again to me. So the people went away. Popular demand that Rehoboam define his policy

^{6}And King Rehoboam took counsel with the old men who had stood before Solomon his father during his lifetime, saying, What answer do you advise me to give this people? ^{7}And they replied to him saying, If now you will be a servant to this people, and will serve them, and give them a favorable answer, then they will be your servants forever. ^{8}But he rejected the Counsel of Solomon's advisers

---

From Jeroboam to Omri.—The importance of the division of the kingdom led the editor of Kgs. to quote at length from the source that recorded this. Considerable space is also given to the reign of Jeroboam, the first king of Northern Israel, for to the religious policy inaugurated by him the editor traced the series of calamities that overtook the Northern Kingdom. The remaining reigns of this epoch are dismissed with a few brief citations from the annals of Israel, usually set in the formulas of the editor. For the Chronicler, whose interest was centred in Judah and the temple, events in the North had no significance beyond the fatal act of division.

§ 59 The record of the division of the Hebrew empire was apparently taken from the history of Jeroboam, which the late prophetic editor may have found incorporated as a section in the royal chronicles of Israel. The Gk. and Luc. have preserved a more logical and probably a more original order and reading for the opening verses. The Ephraimite point of view is prominent in $^{1-20}$. Vss. $^{21-24}$ were probably added by a later Judean editor, but otherwise the unity of the section is complete and it is unsurpassed as a vivid piece of early historical writing. It evidently comes from about the same period as the Saul and David narratives of Sam.

^{a} 12^2 So practically Gk. and Luc. The Heb. omits the last clause, substituting ^{3a} for it. But this implies that Jeroboam was summoned from Egypt and arrived at Shechem, ^{20}, before the expiration of the three days, ^{5}, which was an obvious impossibility. The Gk. order followed above removes this and other difficulties. According to the original narrative Jeroboam was not at Shechem until after Rehoboam was rejected, ^{20}.

Jeroboam History

Counsel of the young men

counsel which the old men had given him, and took counsel with the young men who had grown up with him and had stood before him. ⁹And he said to them, What answer do you advise us to give to this people, who have spoken to me, saying, ' Make the yoke that your father put upon us lighter ' ? ¹⁰And the young men who had grown up with him replied to him, saying, Thus must you answer this people who have said to you, ' Your father made our yoke heavy, but you make it lighter for us '; thus must you say to them, ' My little finger is thicker than my father's loins ! ¹¹And now whereas my father loaded you with a heavy yoke, I will make your yoke heavier; my father chastised you with whips, but I will chastise you with scourges.'

Rehoboam's tyrannical reply to the popular demand

¹²So when Jeroboam and all the people came to Rehoboam the third day, as the king bade, saying, Come to me the third day, ¹³the king answered the people harshly, and did not follow the counsel which the old men had given him, ¹⁴but spoke to them according to the counsel of the young men, saying, My father made your yoke heavy, but I also will make your yoke still heavier; my father chastised you with whips, but I will chastise you with scourges. ¹⁵So the king gave no heed to the people; for it was a thing brought about of Jehovah to confirm his word, which Jehovah spoke by Ahijah the Shilonite to Jeroboam the son of Nebat.ᵇ

Rejection of Rehoboam by the northern tribes

¹⁶And when all Israel saw that the king gave no heed to them, the people answered the king, saying,

> What share have we in David?
> We have no claim in the son of Jesse!
> To your tents, O Israel!
> Now care for your own house, O David!

So the Israelites went to their homes. ¹⁷But over the Israelites who dwelt in the cities of Judah, Rehoboam reigned.ᶜ ¹⁸Then King Rehoboam sent Adoniram, who was over the men subject to forced labor; but all Israel stoned him to death. Thereupon King Rehoboam quickly mounted his chariot in order to flee to Jerusalem. ¹⁹So Israel rebelled against the house of David to the present day.

Election of Jeroboam king

²⁰And as soon as all Israel heard that Jeroboam had returned, they sent and called him to the assembly of the people and made him king over all Israel. None remained loyal to the house of David except the tribe of Judah.

The divine approval of the act

²¹Now when Rehoboam had arrived at Jerusalem, he assembled all the house of Judah and the tribe of Benjamin, a hundred and eighty thousand chosen warriors, to fight against the house of Israel in order to restore the kingdom to Rehoboam the son of Solomon. ²²But the word of God came to Shemaiah the man of God, as follows, ²³Speak to Rehoboam the son of Solomon king of Judah, and to all the house of Judah and Benjamin, and to the rest of the people, saying, ²⁴'Thus saith Jehovah, "Ye shall

ᵇ 12⁶⁻¹⁵ The secondary Gk. version in 12 ²⁴ᵃ· ʳ (Swete's text) is briefer, and possibly the original: *And Rehoboam said, Bring the elders in to me that I may take counsel with them as to the answer I should give the people on the third day. And when Rehoboam told them the message that the people had sent to him, the elders of the people replied, So have the people said to you. But Rehoboam cast their counsel to the winds, for it pleased him not. Then he sent and summoned those who had grown up with him, and said the same to them, These terms have the people sent me.*
ᶜ 12¹⁷ Not in the Gk., and evidently not found originally in the present context.

Jeroboam History

not go up to fight against your kinsmen the Israelites; go back home all of you, for this thing has come to pass at my instigation.''' So they listened to the word of Jehovah, and departed according to the word of Jehovah.ᵈ

²⁵Then Jeroboam fortified Shechem in the hill country of Ephraim, and dwelt there. Afterwards he went out from there and fortified Penuel.

Fortification of Shechem

§ 60. Jeroboam's Institution of the Calf Worship at Bethel and Dan, I Kgs. 12²⁶⁻³²

Jeroboam History

I Kgs. 12 ²⁶Then Jeroboam said to himself, Now the sovereignty will revert to the house of David. ²⁷If this people go up to offer sacrifices in the temple of Jehovah at Jerusalem, then will the heart of this people turn again to their lord, even to Rehoboam king of Judah; and they will kill me, and return to Rehoboam king of Judah.ᵉ ²⁸So the king took counsel with himself, and made two calves of gold, and said to the people,ᶠ You have gone up to Jerusalem long enough. Behold your gods, O Israel, which brought you up from the land of Egypt! ²⁹And he set up the one in Bethel, and the other in Dan. ³⁰And this thing became a sin to Israel,ᵍ for the people went to worship before the one, even unto Dan.

Establishment of Bethel and Dan as royal sanctuaries

³¹And he made houses of high places, and made priests from among all the people, who were not of the sons of Levi. ³²And Jeroboam ordained a feast in the eighth month, on the fifteenth day of the month, like the feast that is in Judah, and he went up unto the altar; so he did in Bethel, sacrificing to the calves that he had made; and he placed in Bethel the priests of the high places that he had made.

Appointment of a distinct priesthood and feast-day

§ 61. The Prophecy against the Altar at Bethel, I Kgs. 12³³–13³⁴

Very Late Popular Prophetic Story

I Kgs. 12 ³³And Jeroboam went up to the altar which he had made in Bethel on the fifteenth day of the eighth month,ʰ which he had arbitrarily

Jeroboam's public sacrifice

ᵈ 12²¹⁻²⁴ According to the early source quoted in 14³⁰, *there was constant war between Rehoboam and the son of Rehoboam.* 12¹⁻²⁴ seems to have been the later Judean explanation of why Rehoboam failed to compel the Northerners to submit to his rule. It also introduces the motive of direct divine intervention which characterizes the later narratives. The reference to Benjamin in ²¹ (cf. ²⁰) confirms this conclusion.

§ 60 It is generally held that the material in this passage has been recast by a later editor, but that the main facts are from an older source. There are, however, no strong grounds against regarding it as an extract from the Jeroboam history. In the days of Amos (7⁶⁻¹⁴) Bethel was a royal sanctuary, and Dan was from the days of the judges a famous shrine. Jeroboam in making them royal sanctuaries was but following the example of Gideon and David. Even though the centralization of all sacrificial worship in Jerusalem belongs to a later time, the temple of Solomon with its glories must then have been a dangerous rival to the older local sanctuaries. It is also significant that none of the expressions that characterize all of the work of the late prophetic author is found in the section.

ᵉ 12²⁷ Not found in the Gk. and probably an editorial addition.

ᶠ 12²⁸ So Gk. Owing to a scribal misreading the Heb. has, *to them.*

ᵍ 12³⁰ Following Luc. in adding, *to Israel.*

§ 61 The reference in 13² to the iconoclastic reformation of Josiah recorded in II Kgs. 23 indicates that this strange story is very late. The conception of the prophet as a wonder-worker is also another of the indices of its late origin. Its entire atmosphere is that of post-exilic Judaism. The mission of Amos to Northern Israel during the days of Jeroboam II and his forced departure (Am. 7) may be the nucleus of fact about which it grew up. The point of view is Judean, the date possibly after the days of Nehemiah and Ezra. Cf. the post-exilic conception of Samaria as a province, ³².

ʰ 12³³ So Lat. The Heb. adds *in the month.* The eighth month was Oct.-Nov., while in Judah the corresponding feast of tabernacles was held in the seventh month. Cf. Lev. 23³⁴.

Very Late Popular Prophetic Story

chosen; and he ordained a feast for the Israelites and went up to the altar
to offer sacrifice.

Message
and
sign
of the
un-
known
man
of God

13 ¹At that time a man of God came from Judah at the command of
Jehovah to Bethel. And Jeroboam was standing by the altar to offer sacrifice. ²Then [the man of God] cried against the altar at the command of
Jehovah and said, O altar, altar, thus saith Jehovah: 'Behold, a son shall be
born to the house of David, Josiah by name; and on thee shall he sacrifice
the priests of the high places who offer sacrifices on thee, and heⁱ shall burn
men's bones on thee.' ³And he gave a sign the same day, saying, This is the
sign which Jehovah hath spoken, 'Behold, the altar shall be rent, and the
ashes that are upon it shall be poured out.' ⁴Now when the king heard the
saying of the man of God, which he cried against the altar in Bethel, Jeroboam put forth his hand from the altar, saying, Take hold of him. But
his hand, which he put forth against him, dried up, so that he could not
draw it back again to himself. ⁵The altar also was rent, and the ashes
poured out from the altar, according to the sign which the man of God had
given at the command of Jehovah. ⁶And the king answered and said to
the man of God, Now intercede with Jehovah thy God, and pray for me,
that my hand may be restored me again. So the man of God interceded
with Jehovah, and the king's hand was restored to him again and became
as it was before. ⁷And the king said to the man of God, Come home with
me and refresh yourself, and I will give you a reward. ⁸But the man of
God said to the king, If you were to give me half your house, I would not
go with you, nor would I eat bread nor drink water in this place; ⁹for it was
commanded meʲ by the word of Jehovah, saying, 'Thou shalt eat no bread
nor drink water, nor return by the way that thou camest.' ¹⁰So he went another way, and returned not by the way that he came to Bethel.

The
lying
words
of the
proph-
et of
Bethel

¹¹Now a certain old prophet dwelt in Bethel; and his sonsᵏ came and
told him all the deeds that the man of God had done that day in Bethel;
they also told their father the words which he had spoken to the king. ¹²And
their father said to them, What way did he go? Then his sons showedˡ him
which way the man of God who came from Judah had gone. ¹³And he said
to his sons, Saddle for me an ass. So they saddled for him the ass, and he
rode on it. ¹⁴And he went after the man of God, and found him sitting under
an oak; and he said to him, Are you the man of God who came from Judah?
And he said, I am. ¹⁵Then he said, Come home with me and eat bread.
¹⁶But he said, I may not return with you, nor go in with you,ᵐ neither will
I eat bread nor drink water in this place;ⁿ ¹⁷for it was commanded me by
the word of Jehovah, 'Thou shalt eat no bread nor drink water there, nor

---

ⁱ 13² The Heb. has the plural, but Gk., Luc., Lat., and Syr. presuppose the singular.
Both Gk. and Heb., however, admit of the rendering, *the bones of men shall burn.*
  ʲ 13⁹ An impersonal construction, or with a slight change in Heb., *I was commanded.*
Gk., *he commanded me by the word of Jehovah.*
  ᵏ 13¹¹ Heb., *one of his sons.* But Gk., Luc., Lat., Syr., and ¹¹ᵇ support the plural.
  ˡ 13¹² So Gk., Luc., Lat., Syr., and the Heb. after a slight change in the pointing.
  ᵐ 13¹⁶ Gk. and Luc. omit, *nor go in with you;* Syr., *and enter your house*—a probable
reading, cf. 2¹⁹.
  ⁿ 13¹⁶ So Gk., Luc., Lat., and Syr.

Very Late Popular Prophetic Story

depart by the way that thou camest.' [18]And he said to him, I also am a prophet as you are; and a Messenger spoke to me by the word of Jehovah, saying, 'Bring him back with thee to thy house, that he may eat bread and drink water!' (But he was lying to him.) [19]So he went back with him,[o] and ate bread in his house and drank water.

[20]But while they were sitting at the table, the word of Jehovah came to the prophet who brought him back. [21]And he cried to the man of God who came from Judah, saying, Thus saith Jehovah, 'Since thou hast disobeyed the word of Jehovah, and hast not kept the command[p] which Jehovah thy God commanded thee, [22]but camest back and hast eaten bread and drunk water in the place of which he said to thee, "Eat no bread, and drink no water," thy body shall not come unto the sepulchre of thy fathers.' [23]And after he had eaten bread and drunk water, he saddled for him[q] the ass, and he again departed. [24]But a lion met him by the way and slew him, and his body was cast upon the highway, and the ass stood by it; the lion also stood by the body. [25]And just then men passed by and saw the body cast in the highway, and the lion standing by the body; and they came and told it in the city where the old prophet dwelt.

Death of the unknown prophet as a punishment for his disobedience

[26]And when the prophet who brought him back from the way heard of it, he said, It is the man of God who disobeyed the word of Jehovah; therefore Jehovah hath delivered him to the lion, which has torn him, and slain him, according to the word of Jehovah, which he spoke to him. [27]And he commanded his sons, saying, Saddle for me the ass. And they saddled it.[r] [28]So he went and found his body thrown down in the highway, and the ass and the lion standing by the body; the lion had not eaten the body nor torn the ass. [29]Then the prophet took up the body of the man of God and laid it on the ass, and brought it back to the city[s] to mourn and to bury him. [30]And he laid his body in his own grave; and they mourned over him, saying, Alas, my brother! [31]And when he had buried him, he spoke to his sons, saying, When I die, bury me in the sepulchre in which the man of God is buried; lay my bones beside his bones: [32]for the saying which he cried by the word of Jehovah against the altar in Bethel, and against all the temples of the high places which are in the cities of Samaria, shall surely come to pass.

Burial of the unknown prophet

[33]After this event Jeroboam did not turn from his evil way, but made again from all the people priests of the high places. Whomsoever he would he consecrated[t] to be a priest of the high places.[u] [34]And this thing became a source of sin to the house of Jeroboam, even to cut it off and to destroy it from the face of the earth.

Jeroboam's baneful religious policy

---

o 13[19] Gk. and Luc. suggest, *so he caused him to turn back*, as the original. Cf. [20-26].

p 13[21] Heb., *rebelled against the mouth.* So [26].

q 13[23b, 24a] So Gk. and Luc. Heb., *for the prophets who had brought back.* [24]*And he departed*, which is unintelligible. The sentence is wholly or in part the result of the insertion of a marginal note. This is suggested by Syr., *for the prophet of God, and again he departed.*

r 13[26b, 27] The Gk. omits this sentence.

s 13[29] The cumbersome Heb. is corrected on the basis of the Gk. and Luc.

t 13[33] Heb., *he would fill his hand.*

u 13[33] So Gk., Luc., Lat., Syr. The Heb. is impossible, *and he will be priests of high places.* The above rendering results from a slight change in the Heb.

§ 62. Ahijah's Prophecy against Jeroboam, I Kgs. 14¹⁻¹⁸

Late Prophetic Narrative

The mission of Jeroboam's wife to Ahijah

I Kgs. 14 ¹At that time Abijah the son of Jeroboam fell sick. ²And Jeroboam said to his wife, Arise, I pray you, and disguise yourself, that you may not be known^v to be the wife of Jeroboam, and go to Shiloh. There is Ahijah the prophet who predicted that I should become king^w over this people. ³And take with you ten loaves and cakes and a jar of honey, and go to him; he will tell you what shall become of the child. ⁴And Jeroboam's wife did so; arising, she went to Shiloh and came to the house of Ahijah. Now Ahijah could not see, for his eyes had become dim because of his age. ⁵But Jehovah had said to the aged Ahijah, The wife of Jeroboam cometh now to inquire of thee^x concerning her son, for he is sick; thus and thus shalt thou say to her. And when she came in,^y she pretended to be another woman.

His prediction of the overthrow of Jeroboam's house

⁶But when Ahijah heard the sound of her feet, as she came in at the door, he said, Come in, wife of Jeroboam; why do you pretend to be another? seeing that I am sent to you with heavy tidings. ⁷Go, tell Jeroboam, 'Thus saith Jehovah, the God of Israel: "Because I exalted thee from among the people and made thee prince over my people Israel, ⁸and rent the kingdom away from the house of David and gave it to thee, and yet thou hast not been as my servant David, who kept my command and followed me with all his heart to do that only which was right in mine eyes, ⁹but hast done evil more than all that were before thee, and hast gone and made thee other gods and molten images to provoke me to anger, and hast cast me behind thy back: ¹⁰therefore, behold, I will bring evil upon the house of Jeroboam, and will cut off from Jeroboam every male child—him that is shut up and him that is left at large^a in Israel—and will utterly sweep away the house of Jeroboam, as a man sweepeth away refuse, until it is gone. ¹¹Him that dieth of Jeroboam in the city shall the dogs eat, and him that dieth in the field shall the birds of the heavens eat; for Jehovah hath spoken it."' ¹²Now rise up, go to your house; and when your feet enter the city, the child shall die. ¹³And all Israel shall mourn for him and bury him; for he only of Jeroboam shall come to the grave, because in him there is found some good thing toward Jehovah, the God of Israel, in the house of Jeroboam. ¹⁴Moreover Jehovah will raise up for himself a king over Israel, who shall cut off the house of Jeroboam that day. But even now^b ¹⁵Jehovah will smite Israel, and they shall be shaken^c as a reed is shaken in the water, and he will root

---

§ 62 The language and point of view of this story is that of the late prophetic editor of Kgs. In ¹⁵ the exile of the Northern Israelites is predicted. The data in ¹⁻⁷, ¹⁷, ¹⁸, however, were probably drawn by the editor from older sources to which he had access, and therefore the narrative probably has certain historical as well as religious value.

v 14² Heb., *that they shall not know, i.e.*, the impersonal verb equivalent to a passive.
w 14² Following a pointing suggested by the versions. Heb., *he spoke of me for king*.
x 14⁵ Heb., *to seek an oracle*.
y 14⁵ So the versions. In the Heb. the words are spoken by Jehovah, but they more naturally come from the narrator. The difference in the Heb. is merely one of pointing.
a 14¹⁰ *I.e.*, everyone. The exact application of the phrase is in doubt. *Under and over age, bond and free*, or *married and celibate* have been suggested.
b 14¹⁴ The Heb. is doubtful and the versions are obscure. The above rendering preserves the original thought.
c 14¹⁵ Modern commentators generally agree that Heb. has lost a clause needed as the ground of comparison.

Late Prophetic Narrative

up Israel out of this good land which he gave to their fathers, and will scatter them beyond the River [Euphrates], because they have made their Ashtartes, provoking Jehovah to anger.   [16]And he will give up Israel because of the sins of Jeroboam which he has committed, and with which he has made Israel sin.

[17]Then Jeroboam's wife arose and departed and came to Tirzah. And as she came to the threshold of the house, the child died.   [18]And all Israel buried him and mourned for him, according to the word of Jehovah which he spoke by his servant Ahijah the prophet.

Death of Jeroboam's son

§ 63. Death of Jeroboam and Reign of his Son Nadab, I Kgs. 14[19, 20], 15[25-31]

Annals of Israel

I Kgs. 14 [19]Now the other acts of Jeroboam, how he carried on wars, how he ruled, they are already recorded in the Chronicles of the Kings of Israel.   [20]And the time during which Jeroboam reigned was twenty-two years.   Then he slept with his fathers, and Nadab his son became king in his place.

Jeroboam's reign and death

15 [25]And Nadab the son of Jeroboam became king in the second year of Asa king of Judah, and he reigned over Israel two years.   [26]And he did that which displeased Jehovah, and followed in the way of his father, and in his sin whereby he made Israel sin.   [27]And Baasha the son of Ahijah, of the house of Issachar, conspired against him, and Baasha smote him at Gibbethon, which belonged to the Philistines, while Nadab and all Israel were laying siege to Gibbethon.   [28]So in the third year of Asa king of Judah Baasha slew him, and became king in his place.   [29]But as soon as he became king, he smote all the house of Jeroboam.   He did not leave of Jeroboam's house a single soul which he did not destroy.   According to the word of Jehovah, which he spoke by his servant Ahijah the Shilonite, [30]because of the sins which Jeroboam committed and by which he made Israel to sin, so that he provoked Jehovah,[d] the God of Israel, to anger.   [31]Now the other acts of Nadab and all that he did, are they not recorded in the Chronicles of the Kings of Israel?

Nadab's rule and assassination by Baasha

§ 64. Baasha's Reign, I Kgs. 15[32]–16[7]

Late Prophetic Editorial Summary

I Kgs. 15 [33]In the third year of Asa king of Judah Baasha the son of Ahijah became king over all Israel in Tirzah, and reigned twenty-four years.   [32]And there was war between Asa and Baasha king of Israel all their days.   [34]And he displeased Jehovah, and followed in the way of Jeroboam and in his sin with which he made Israel to sin.   **16** [1]And the following word of Jehovah came to Jehu the son of Hanani against Baasha, [2]Forasmuch as I have raised thee out of the dust, and made thee prince over my people Israel,

Jehovah's disapproval of Baasha's policy

---

§ 63 In 15[27-29a] a brief extract from the annals is found. Otherwise the record is cast in the familiar language of the late prophetic editor.
   d 15[30] A Heb. scribe has added the awkward gloss, *by his provocation.*
   § 64 The fact that Jehu prophesied against Baasha may have been derived from an earlier source, but all of the data in the present section is cast in the language of the late prophetic editor.   15[32] is clearly out of its logical position, which is after [33].

Late Prophetic Editorial Summary

and thou hast walked in the way of Jeroboam and hast made my people Israel to sin, so that they have provoked me to anger with their sins, ³I will utterly sweep away Baasha and his house, and I will make thy house like the house of Jeroboam the son of Nebat. ⁴Whoever belonging to Baasha dies in the city, him shall the dogs eat, and whoever of his dies in the field, him shall the birds of the heavens eat.

His
con-
demna-
tion
and
death

⁵Now the other acts of Baasha, and what he did and his mighty deeds, are they not recorded in the Chronicles of the Kings of Israel? ⁷Moreover, by the prophet Jehu the son of Hanani the word of Jehovah came against Baasha and against his house, both because of the evil that he did in the sight of Jehovah, to provoke him to anger with the work of his hands, in being like the house of Jeroboam, and also because he smote him. ⁶And Baasha slept with his fathers and was buried in Tirzah, and Elah his son became king in his place.

§ 65. Elah's Reign, I Kgs. 16⁸⁻¹⁴

Annals of Israel

Zimri's
con-
spiracy
against
Elah
and his
house

I Kgs. 16 ⁸In the twenty-sixth year of Asa king of Judah Elah the son of Baasha became king over Israel in Tirzah, and reigned two years. ⁹And his servant Zimri, commander of half his chariots, conspired against him. While he was in Tirzah drinking himself drunk in the house of Arza, the royal chamberlain in Tirzah, ¹⁰Zimri went in and smote and killed him, in the twenty-seventh year of Asa king of Judah, and became king in his place. ¹¹But as soon as he became king and had seated himself on the throne, he smote all the house of Baasha; he left him not a single male, either of his kinsfolks or of his friends. ¹²Thus Zimri destroyed all the house of Baasha, according to the word of Jehovah, which he spoke against Baasha by Jehu the prophet, ¹³for all the sins of Baasha and the sins of his son Elah, which they committed and with which they made Israel sin, to provoke Jehovah, the God of Israel, to anger with their vanities. ¹⁴Now the other acts of Elah, and all that he did, are they not recorded in the Chronicles of the Kings of Israel?

§ 66. Brief Reign of Zimri, I Kgs. 16¹⁵⁻²⁰

Annals of Israel

Elec-
tion of
Omri
king
and
over-
throw
of
Zimri

I Kgs. 16 ¹⁵In the twenty-seventh year of Asa king of Judah, Zimri reigned seven days in Tirzah. Now the people were besieging Gibbethon, which belonged to the Philistines. ¹⁶And the people who were engaged in the siege heard the report, Zimri has conspired and has also smitten the king; therefore all Israel made Omri, the commander of the army, king over Israel that day in the camp. ¹⁷So Omri went up from Gibbethon and all Israel with him, and they besieged Tirzah. ¹⁸When Zimri saw that the city was taken, he

---

§ 65 The account of the conspiracy of Zimri, which is taken from a primitive source, well illustrates the orientalism of the age and the civil dissensions which during this epoch wasted the rich resources of the northern kingdom.

§ 66 Although Zimri reigned only seven days, the editor of Kgs. pronounces upon him the same formal condemnation as upon all the kings of Israel. Into his epitome he has introduced a brief quotation telling of the overthrow of the conspirator.

Annals of Israel

went into the castle of the royal palace, and burnt the royal palace over him. Thus he died ¹⁹for his sins which he committed in doing that which displeased Jehovah, in following in the way of Jeroboam and in his sin which he did, to make Israel sin. ²⁰Now the rest of the acts of Zimri, and his conspiracy which he made, are they not recorded in the Chronicles of the Kings of Israel?

II

RULE OF THE HOUSE OF OMRI AND THE WORK OF ELIJAH
I Kgs. 16²¹–22⁴⁰, ⁵¹⁻⁵³, II Kgs. 1, 3¹⁻³

§ 67. Omri's Accession and Reign, I Kgs. 16²¹⁻²⁸

Annals of Israel

I Kgs. 16 ²¹Then the people of Israel were divided.ᵃ Half of the people followed Tibni the son of Ginath and made him king, and the other half followed Omri. ²²But the people with Omri were stronger than the people with Tibni the son of Ginath. So Tibni and his brother Joram died,ᵇ and Omri became king. ²³In the thirty-first year of Asa king of Judah Omri began to reign over Israel, and reigned twelve years; six years he reigned in Tirzah. *Omri's victory over his rival Tibni*

²⁴Then he bought the hill Samaria from Shemer for two talents of silver; and he built on the hill and named the city which he built Samaria, after the name of Shemer, the owner of the hill. *Establishment of Samaria as his capital*

²⁵And Omri did that which displeased Jehovah, and was more wicked than all his predecessors. ²⁶For he followed altogether in the steps of Jeroboam the son of Nebat, and in that with which he made Israel to sin, so that by their heathen practicesᶜ they angered Jehovah the God of Israel. ²⁷Now the rest of the acts of Omri, and all that he did and his mighty deeds, are they not recorded in the Chronicles of the Kings of Israel? ²⁸So Omri slept with his fathers and was buried in Samaria. And Ahab his son became king in his place. *His evil religious policy*

Rule of the House of Omri and the Work of Elijah and Elisha.—Five primary sources are represented in the subsequent sections. From the annals of Israel the editor of Kgs. made a few brief quotations. The longer extracts in I Kgs. 20, 22 he apparently drew from an early Ahab history, and in II Kgs. 9¹⁴–10²⁷ from a Jehu history. These citations he supplemented by the long and valuable extracts from the early Elijah stories, I Kgs. 17-19, 21, II Kgs. 1¹⁻⁸, ¹⁷ᵃ and by the stories taken from the popular Elisha cycles, II Kgs. 2¹–9¹³. Excepting a few notices regarding Judah in I Kgs. 22⁴¹⁻⁵⁰ and II Kgs. 8¹⁶⁻²⁹, the attention of the reader is entirely fixed in these sixteen chapters upon the important events in Northern Israel.

The epoch is chiefly important because in the person of the great Elijah the prophets began to assume an active and commanding position in the social and religious life of the period, and that open struggle with the native religions of Canaan was inaugurated which was destined to end in the complete separation of the Israelitish race and the victory of the exalted ethical conceptions of Jehovah and his demands, which were so courageously advocated by his prophets.

§ 67 The references to the conquest of Moab by Omri in the Mesha inscription (cf. Appendix IV), and the fact that even after his family had ceased to rule over Israel, the Assyrians referred to the northern kingdom as *the house of Omri*, indicate the importance of the man and his reign. What David did for united Israel, Omri appears to have done in a lesser degree for his kingdom. Instead of weakened by war and subject to the Arameans, he left it united and organized, thus preparing the way for the brilliant reign of Ahab.

These facts were either not recorded in the Chronicles of the Kings of Israel or did not seem important to the editor; for, aside from two brief but significant quotations, he simply gives his usual adverse judgment regarding Omri and his reign.

ᵃ 16²¹ So Gk. and Luc. The Heb. through dittography adds, *into two parts.*
ᵇ 16²² So Gk. and Luc. It is so circumstantial that it appears to be original, although not found in the Heb.
ᶜ 16²⁶ Heb., *vanities.*

§ 68. Ahab's Accession and Policy, I Kgs. 16²⁹⁻³⁴

Annals of Israel

Ahab's marriage with Jezebel and his sanction of Baalism

I Kgs. 16 ²⁹Now in the thirty-eighth year of Asa king of Judah Ahab the son of Omri began to reign over Israel; and Ahab the son of Omri reigned over Israel in Samaria twenty-two years. ³⁰And Ahab the son of Omri did that which displeased[d] Jehovah more than all his predecessors. ³¹Furthermore, as if it had been a slight thing for him to walk in the sins of Jeroboam the son of Nebat, he took as wife Jezebel the daughter of Ethbaal king of the Sidonians, and turned them to serve Baal and worshipped him. ³²And he erected an altar for Baal in the temple of Baal, which he had built in Samaria. ³³And Ahab also made the Asherah;[e] and Ahab did yet more to anger Jehovah the God of Israel than all the kings of Israel who preceded him.

Rebuilding of Jericho

³⁴In his days Hiel the Bethelite built Jericho. He laid its foundation with the loss of Abiram his eldest, and set up the gates with the loss of his youngest son Segub, as Jehovah had spoken by Joshua the son of Nun.

§ 69. The Drought Announced by Elijah the Tishbite, I Kgs. 17

Early Ephraimite Elijah Stories

Announcement of the drought

I Kgs. 17 ¹Now Elijah the Tishbite of Tishbe[f] in Gilead, said to Ahab, As Jehovah, the God of Israel, liveth, whom I serve, there shall be neither dew nor rain these years,[g] except according to my word. . . .

Elijah by the Brook Cherith

²Then the word of Jehovah came to him, saying, ³Depart from here and turn eastward and hide thyself by the Brook Cherith, that is east of Jordan. ⁴Then thou shalt drink out of the brook; and I have commanded the ravens to feed thee there. ⁵So he went and obeyed the command of Jehovah and[h] dwelt by the Brook Cherith that is east of Jordan. ⁶And the ravens brought him bread every morning and flesh[i] every evening, and he used to drink out of the brook. ⁷But after a while the brook dried up, because there was no rain in the land.

---

§ 68 The editor introduces the history of Ahab with a review of his reign and two extracts from the Chronicles of the Kings of Israel. Cf. Josh. 6²⁶ for the prediction referred to in ³⁴.

[d] 16³⁰ So Gk. and Luc. and the stereotyped idiom elsewhere. A word has by mistake fallen out of the Heb.

[e] 16³³ Probably a more elaborate representation of the deity than the sacred poles referred to in 14¹⁵ and frequently elsewhere. In II Kgs. 23⁴, as in Judg, 3⁷, *Asherah* seems to be equivalent to the female goddess Ashtarte.

§ 69 The characteristics and approximate date of the early Elijah stories which are here introduced, have already been considered in the Introd., pp. 17, 18. The abruptness with which Elijah is ushered into the history in Kgs. is in perfect keeping with his character, but it is doubtless due to the fact that we have here only a torso. The complete Elijah biography probably localized the opening scene (cf. ³, *from here*) and told of the persecution of the prophets by Jezebel, which is merely alluded to in 18¹³, and of the fulfilment of the divine command to anoint Hazael (19¹⁵).

No critical reader of these stories would maintain that they present a contemporary portrait of the great prophet. They have all the characteristic marks of popular stories. It would be remarkable if oral transmission during seventy or eighty years had not obscured certain facts and introduced some unhistorical elements. Even the latter, however, are significant, for they are the concrete testimony of later generations to the unquestioned greatness of the man and his work. Their courageous, uncompromising spirit, the dramatic incidents, and the vivid, forcible literary style place these stories among the masterpieces of the O.T.

[f] 17¹ So Gk. and Luc. The Heb., *of the sojourners in*, is clearly due to a slight scribal error.

[g] 17¹ Josephus, Ant. VIII, 13², quotes from Meander the statement that this famine occurred during the reign of Ittobaal of Tyre and lasted one full year.

[h] 17⁵ So Gk. The Heb. adds, *and he went*, but this is probably a scribal repetition of the preceding expression.

[i] 17⁶ So Gk. and Luc.

Early Ephraimite Elijah Stories

⁸Then the word of Jehovah came to him, saying, ⁹Arise, go to Zarephath, which belongs to Sidon, and dwell there. Behold, I have commanded a widow there to provide for thee. ¹⁰So he arose and went to Zarephath. And when he came to the gate of the city a widow was there gathering sticks; and calling to her, he said, Bring me, I pray, a little water in a vessel, that I may drink. ¹¹And as she was going to bring it, he called after her, Bring also, I pray, a bit of bread with you. ¹²And she replied, As Jehovah your God liveth, I have nothing^j but a handful of meal in the jar and a little oil in the cruse; and now I am gathering a few^k sticks, that I may go in and prepare it for myself and my son, that we may eat it and then die. ¹³But Elijah said to her, Fear not; go and do as you have said, but first make me from it a little cake, and then make for yourself and your son. ¹⁴For thus saith Jehovah, the God of Israel, 'The jar of meal shall not be used up, neither shall the cruse of oil become empty, until the day that Jehovah sendeth rain upon the earth.' ¹⁵And she went and did as Elijah directed. So she and he and her household had food to eat.¹ ¹⁶From that day the jar of meal was not used up, neither did the cruse of oil become empty, just as Jehovah had said by Elijah.

¹⁷Now after this the son of the mistress of the house fell sick; and his sickness was so severe that there was no breath left in him. ¹⁸Then she said to Elijah, What have I to do with you,^m O man of God? You have come to me to remind me of my sin by slaying my son! ¹⁹And he said to her, Give me your son. And he took him out of her bosom and carried him up into the upper chamber, where he was staying, and laid him upon his own bed. ²⁰And he cried to Jehovah, and said, O Jehovah, my God, hast thou also brought evil upon this widow, whose guest I am, by slaying her son? ²¹And he stretched himself upon the child three times, and cried to Jehovah and said, O Jehovah, my God, I pray thee, let this child's life come back to him again. ²²And Jehovah hearkened to the voice of Elijah; and the life of the child came back to him again, so that he revived. ²³Then Elijah took the child and brought him down from the upper chamber into the house and gave him to his mother. And Elijah said, See, your son lives! ²⁴And the woman said to Elijah, Now I know that you are a man of God, and that the word of Jehovah in your mouth is truth.

§ 70. Jehovah's Vindication on Mount Carmel, I Kgs. 18

Early Ephraimite Elijah Stories

I Kgs. 18 ¹Now a long time after this the word of Jehovah came to Elijah, in the third year, saying, Go, show thyself to Ahab; and I will send rain upon the earth. ²So Elijah went to show himself to Ahab.

Marginal notes: Miraculous provision of food at Zarephath. Restoring the son of the widow. Elijah's call to action.

---

^j 17¹² So Syr. and Targ., supported by the context. The Heb. has a very unusual word possibly meaning, *cake.* Gk., *baked in the ashes.*
^k 17¹² Heb., *two*, the concrete equivalent of *a few.*
¹ 17¹⁵ So Symmachus, Theodotion, and Gk.A. Heb., *some days*, joining it to the preceding sentence.
^m 17¹⁸ *I.e.,* What have you to do with my affairs? Cf. 3¹³, Mt. 8²⁹.
§ 70 This is the direct continuation of the preceding section. The explanatory notes in ³ᵇ·⁴ are probably from the editor and are based on ¹³. Otherwise the section as a whole was apparently quoted without alteration from the original prophetic source.

Early Ephraimite Elijah Stories

Severity of the famine And the famine was severe in Samaria. ³And Ahab had called Obadiah, the prefect of the palace. Now Obadiah revered Jehovah greatly. ⁴For when Jezebel tried to exterminate the prophets of Jehovah Obadiah took a hundred prophets, and hid them by fifty in a cave and fed them continually with bread and water. ⁵And Ahab had said to Obadiah, Up! let us[n] go through the land to all the springs of water and to all the brooks; perhaps we may find grass so that we can save the horses and mules alive and not lose all the beasts.[o] ⁶So they divided the land between them to pass through it: Ahab went in one direction by himself and Obadiah went in another direction by himself,

Elijah's interview with Obadiah ⁷And while Obadiah was on the way, Elijah met him suddenly. When he knew him, he fell on his face and said, Is it you, my lord Elijah? ⁸And he answered him, It is I; go, tell your lord, 'Elijah is here.' ⁹And he said, Wherein have I sinned, that you would deliver your servant into the hand of Ahab, to slay me? ¹⁰As Jehovah your God liveth, there is no nation or kingdom, whither my lord has not sent to seek you; and when they said 'He is not here,' he took an oath of the kingdom and nation, that no one had found you. ¹¹And now you say, 'Go, tell your lord, "Elijah is here."' ¹²And as soon as I am gone from you the spirit of Jehovah will carry you to a place unknown to me, and so when I come and tell Ahab, and he cannot find you, he will put me to death, although I, your servant, have feared Jehovah from my youth. ¹³Was it not told my lord what I did when Jezebel slew the prophets of Jehovah, how I hid a hundred of Jehovah's prophets by fifty in a cave and fed them continually with bread and water? ¹⁴And now you say, 'Go, tell your lord, Elijah is here,' that he may put me to death! ¹⁵But Elijah said, As Jehovah of hosts liveth, before whom I stand, I will surely show myself to him to-day.

His command to Ahab ¹⁶So Obadiah went to meet Ahab, and told him, and Ahab went to meet Elijah. ¹⁷And as soon as Ahab saw Elijah, Ahab said to him, Is it you, you who have brought misfortune to Israel? ¹⁸And he answered, I have not brought misfortune to Israel, but you and your father's house, in that you have forsaken the commands of Jehovah and have run after the Baals. ¹⁹Now therefore send and gather to me all Israel to Mount Carmel, together with the four hundred and fifty prophets of the Baal and the four hundred prophets of the Asherah,[p] who eat at Jezebel's table.

Elijah's address to the people ²⁰So Ahab sent to all the Israelites and gathered the prophets together to Mount Carmel. ²¹Then Elijah came near to all the people and said, How long are you going to limp between the two sides?[q] If Jehovah be God, follow him, but if the Baal, then follow him. But the people gave him no

---

n 18⁵ So Gk. and the implication of succeeding context. Heb., *go through.*
o 18⁵ The context demands and Luc. supports this reading. The Heb. is obscure.
p 18¹⁹ This appears to be a later insertion, for the expression, *prophets of the Asherah*, is late, and in the subsequent context, ²⁰, ⁴⁰, only the prophets of Baal are mentioned. As in II Kgs. 23⁴, *Asherah* probably stands for, *Ashtarte.*
q 18²¹ The word occurs only here. It comes from a root meaning *to divide*, and the phrase may be translated lit., *on two divisions, i.e.*, on two legs or opinions, as unequal as faith in Jehovah and faith in Baal. Gk. and Luc., *knee-cavities.* Slightly emending the text the passage may also be read *leap over two thresholds.* In the light of Zeph. 1⁹ and the common Semitic idioms this would be equivalent to *worship in two sanctuaries, i.e.*, of Jehovah and Baal. This meaning would perfectly fit the context. The saying was evidently a popular proverb current in Elijah's day.

Early Ephraimite Elijah Stories

answer. ²²Then Elijah said to the people, I, even I only, am left as a prophet of Jehovah, but the Baal's prophets are four hundred and fifty men. ²³Let them therefore give us two bullocks, and let them choose one bullock for themselves and cut it in pieces and lay it on the wood without putting on any fire, and I will dress the other bullock and lay it on wood without putting on any fire. ²⁴Then you call on your god and I will call on Jehovah; and the God who answers by fire, he is the God. And all the people answered and said, It is well spoken.

²⁵And Elijah said to the prophets of the Baal, Choose one of the bullocks for yourselves and dress it first, for you are many, and call on your god, without putting on any fire. ²⁶So they took the bullock he gave them and dressed it, and called on the Baal from morning even until noon, saying, O Baal, hear us. But there was no voice nor answer. And they limped about the altar which they had erected.ʳ ²⁷But when it was noon, Elijah mocked them, saying, Cry aloud; for he is a god; either he is musing, or he has gone aside, or he is on a journey, or perhaps he is sleeping and must be awakened! ²⁸Then they cried aloud, and cut themselves after their manner with swords and lances until the blood gushed out upon them. ²⁹And when midday was past, they prophesied until the time of the offering of the evening oblation; but there was neither voice nor answer nor heed paid to their cry. *(margin: Failure of the Baal prophets to meet the test)*

³⁰Then Elijah said to all the people, Come near to me. And all the people came near to him. And he repaired the altar of Jehovah which had been thrown down. ³¹And Elijah took twelve stones corresponding to the number of tribes of the sons of Jacob to whom the word of Jehovah came, saying, Israel shall be thy name. ³²And with the stones he built an altar in the name of Jehovah.ˢ Then he made a trench about the altar of about the capacity of two seahsᵗ of seed. ³³And he laid the pieces of wood in order, cut up the bullock, and laid it on pieces of the wood. And he said, Fill four jars with water and pour it on the burnt-offering and on the pieces of wood. ³⁴And he said, Do it the second time; and they did it the second time. And he said, Do it the third time; and they did it also the third time,ᵘ ³⁵so that the water ran round the altar; and he also filled the trench with water. *(margin: Elijah's preparations for the test)*

³⁶But when it was time to offer the evening oblation, Elijah the prophet came near and said, O Jehovah, God of Abraham, of Isaac, and of Israel, let it be known this day that thou art God in Israel and that I am thy servant, and that I have done all these things at thy command. ³⁷Hear me, O Jehovah, hear me, that this people may know that thou, Jehovah, art God, and that thou hast turned their heart back again. ³⁸Then the fire of Jehovahᵛ fell and consumed the burnt-offering and the wood, the *(margin: The sign from heaven confirming Elijah's words)*

ʳ 18²⁶ So Gk., Luc., Syr., and Lat. Heb., *was erected.*
ˢ 18³¹, ³²ᵃ Vs. ³²ᵇ is the natural sequel of ³⁰. The Gk. translators also recognized that ³¹, ³²ᵃ were awkward after ³⁰ᵃ, and so put ³⁰ᵃ last. The reference to twelve tribes, when only the northern tribes were represented, and the language of ³¹ᵇ, which reflects the priestly passage, Gen. 35¹⁰, confirm the conclusion that these verses are from a late priestly editor.
ᵗ 18³² About five gallons. The ground which would be sown with one and one-fourth bushels of seed, is perhaps intended.
ᵘ 18³⁴ So Gk. The last clause is lacking in the Heb.
ᵛ 18³⁸ Gk. and Luc., *fire from God.*

Early Ephraimite Elijah Stories

stones and the dust, and licked up the water that was in the trench. [39]And when all the people saw it, they fell on their faces, and cried, Jehovah, he is God; Jehovah, he is God. [40]But Elijah commanded them, Take the prophets of the Baal; let not one of them escape! So they took them down to the Brook Kishon and slew them there.

Coming of the rain [41]Then Elijah said to Ahab, Go up, eat and drink; for there is the sound of a heavy downpour of rain. [42]So Ahab went up to eat and drink. But Elijah went up to the top of Carmel, and crouched down upon the earth, with his face between his knees. [43]And he said to his servant, Go up now, look toward the sea. And he went up, and looked and said, There is nothing. And he said, Now go again seven times.[w] So the servant went back seven times.[x] [44]But the seventh time he said, There is a cloud arising out of the sea as small as a man's hand. And he said, Go up, say to Ahab, 'Make ready your chariot, go down, that the rain may not stop you.' [45]And the next instant the heavens grew black with clouds and wind, and there was a great rain. And Ahab rode toward Jezreel. [46]And the hand of Jehovah was on Elijah, so that he girded up his loins and ran before Ahab to the entrance of Jezreel.

§ 71. Revelation to Elijah at Horeb, I Kgs. 19[1-18]

Early Ephraimite Elijah Stories

Elijah's flight to Horeb **I Kgs. 19** [1]Now when Ahab told Jezebel all that Elijah had done, and all the details of his slaying the prophets with the sword, [2]Jezebel sent a messenger to Elijah, saying, As surely as you are Elijah and I am Jezebel,[a] may the gods do to me what they will, if I do not make your life as the life of one of them by to-morrow about this time. [3]Then he was afraid and arose and went for his life. And he came to Beersheba, which belongs to Judah; and there he left his servant. [4]But he himself went a day's journey into the wilderness, and came and sat down under a broom tree,[b] and he asked that he might die, saying, It is enough; now, O Jehovah, take my life, for I am not better than my fathers![c] [5]Then he lay down and slept under the broom tree. Thereupon a divine Messenger touched him and said to him, Rise, eat! [6]And when he looked, he saw there at his head a cake, baked on hot stones, and a jar of water. And he ate and drank and lay

---

[w] 18[43] Slightly reconstructing the text in harmony with a suggestion in the Gk.

[x] 18[43] The Gk. adds the last clause.

§ 71 The passage [9b-11a] appears to be a later expansion of the story. Vs. [10] anticipates [14] and is almost word for word the same. The entire account of the revelation in [9b-11a] also anticipates and weakens the impressiveness of the vision recorded in [11b-14]. Not until in [13] is Elijah represented as coming forth from the cave. Otherwise the graphic narrative is the immediate sequel of the preceding story.

The Assyrian inscriptions record a victory over Hazael of Damascus in 842 B.C. This was probably soon after the revolution whereby Hazael attained to the Aramean throne. The inscriptions also state that in the same year Jehu paid tribute, probably to establish himself on the throne of Israel. Cf. Appendix V.

[a] 19[2] Gk. and Luc. have preserved the characteristic opening words of Jezebel.

[b] 19[4] The *Retama roetam*, a shrub growing from eight to twelve feet high and possessing a dense foliage.

[c] 19[4] *I.e.*, since I must some time die, let it be now.

Early Ephraimite Elijah Stories

down again. ⁷But the Messenger of Jehovah came again the second time and touched him and said, Rise, eat, or else the journey will be too long for you. ⁸So he arose and ate and drank and went in the strength of that food forty days and forty nights to Horeb the Mount of God. ⁹And there he came to a cave and lodged therein.

Thereupon the word of Jehovah came to him. And he said to him, What doest thou here, Elijah? ¹⁰And he said, I have been very jealous for Jehovah, the God of hosts; for the Israelites have forsaken thee,ᵈ thrown down thine altars, and slain thy prophets with the sword; and I only am left, and they seek to take my life from me. ¹¹Then he said, Go forth and stand on the mount before Jehovah. *His complaint*

Thereupon Jehovah passed by, and a great and violent wind rent the mountain and broke in pieces the rocks before Jehovah; but Jehovah was not in the wind. And after the wind an earthquake; but Jehovah was not in the earthquake. ¹²And after the earthquake a fire; but Jehovah was not in the fire. And after the fire the sound of a low, softᵉ whisper.ᶠ ¹³And as soon as Elijah heard it, he wrapped his face in his mantle and went out and stood at the entrance of the cave. And then there came a voice to him and said, What doest thou here, Elijah? ¹⁴And he said, I have been very jealous for Jehovah, the God of hosts, for the Israelites have forsaken thee, thrown down thine altars, and slain thy prophets with the sword, and I only am left, and they seek to take away my life from me. *Revelation of Jehovah's true character*

¹⁵Then Jehovah said to him, Go, return on thy way to the Wilderness of Damascus, and when thou comest anoint Hazael to be king over Aram. ¹⁶And Jehu the son of Nimshi shalt thou anoint to be king over Israel. And Elisha the son of Shaphat of Abel-meholah shalt thou anoint to be prophet in thy place. ¹⁷And it shall be that whoever escapes the sword of Hazael, Jehu shall slay; and whoever escapes the sword of Jehu, Elisha shall slay. ¹⁸Yet will I spare seven thousand in Israel—all the knees which have not bowed to Baal and every mouth which hath not kissed him. *Directions for the overthrow of Baalism*

§ 72. Call of Elisha, I Kgs. 19¹⁹⁻²¹

Early Ephraimite Elijah Stories

I Kgs. 19 ¹⁹Now when he had departed from there he found Elisha the son of Shaphat, as he was plowing with twelve yoke of oxen, and he was with the twelfth. And Elijah went over to him and cast his mantle upon him. ²⁰And he left the oxen and ran after Elijah and said, Let me, I pray you, kiss my father and my mother and then I will follow you. And he said to him, Go back again, for what have I done to you? ²¹So he turned from following him and took the yoke of oxen and slew them and boiled their fleshᵍ with the instruments of the oxen and gave to the people to eat. Then he arose and went after Elijah and entered into his service. *Selection of a disciple and successor*

ᵈ 19¹⁰ So Gk. and Luc. Here and in ¹⁴ a scribe has added, *covenant*, in the Heb.

ᵉ 19¹² Lit., *thin, fine*.

ᶠ 19¹² Cf. Ps. 107²⁹, Job 4¹⁶, a *gentle breeze* or a *low murmur*.

§ 72 Originally ¹⁸ was probably followed by an account of the anointing of Hazael, as commanded in ¹⁵, for Abel-meholah is not on the highway from Horeb to Damascus and the anointing of Hazael was to precede that of Elisha. The omission appears to be due to the fact that it is recounted at length and attributed to Elisha in the later narratives. Cf. II Kgs. 8⁷⁻¹⁵.

ᵍ 19²¹ *Flesh*, which is omitted in Gk. and Luc., may be a scribal addition to the Heb.

§ 73. Murder of Naboth and Elijah's Condemnation of Ahab, I Kgs. 21

Early Ephraimite Elijah Stories

Naboth's refusal to sell his vineyard to Ahab

I Kgs. 21 ¹Now[h] Naboth the Jezreelite had a vineyard beside the palace of Ahab king of Samaria. ²And Ahab spoke to Naboth, saying, Give me your vineyard, that I may have it for a vegetable garden, because it is near my house, and I will give you a better vineyard for it; or, if it is more satisfactory to you, I will give you the value of it in money. ³But Naboth answered Ahab, Jehovah forbid me, that I should give to you the inheritance of my fathers. ⁴And Ahab came into his house in ill-humor[i] because of the word which Naboth the Jezreelite had spoken to him; for he had said, I will not give to you the inheritance of my fathers. And he lay down on his bed and covered[j] his face and would eat no food.

Jezebel's measures to secure Naboth's death

⁵But Jezebel his wife came to him and said to him, Why are you so out of humor that you eat no food? ⁶And he replied to her, Because I made a proposition to Naboth the Jezreelite and said to him, 'Give me your vineyard for money; or else if it is more satisfactory to you I will give you another vineyard for it'; and he answered, 'I will not give you my vineyard.' ⁷Then Jezebel his wife said to him, Is it you who now holds sway in Israel? Arise, eat, and let your heart be cheerful. I will give you the vineyard of Naboth the Jezreelite. ⁸So she wrote letters in Ahab's name and sealed them with his seal, and sent the letters to the elders and to the nobles who were in his city who presided with Naboth. ⁹And she wrote in the letters, Proclaim a fast and also place Naboth in a prominent place among the people. ¹⁰Then place two base men before him and let them bear witness against him, saying, 'You have cursed[k] God and the king.' And then carry him out and stone him to death.

Realization of her designs

¹¹And the men of his city, the elders and the nobles who presided in his city, did as Jezebel had ordered them. As it was prescribed in the letters which she had sent to them, ¹²they proclaimed a fast, and put Naboth in a prominent place among the people. ¹³And two base men came in and sat before him, and the scoundrels bore witness against him (Naboth) in the presence of the people, saying, Naboth cursed God and the king. Then they carried him out of the city and stoned him to death with stones.[l] ¹⁴And they sent to Jezebel, saying, Naboth has been stoned and is dead. ¹⁵And as soon as Jezebel heard that Naboth had been stoned and was dead, Jezebel said to Ahab, Arise, take possession of the vineyard of Naboth the Jezreelite, which he refused to give you for money; for Naboth is not alive but dead. ¹⁶And as soon as Ahab heard that Naboth was dead, Ahab rose up to go down to the vineyard of Naboth the Jezreelite, to take possession of it.

---

§ 73　In introducing 21 immediately after 19 the Gk. has undoubtedly preserved the original order. Not only is the literary style the same here, as in 19, but Elijah occupies the same prominent position, while Ahab appears in a much less favorable light than in 20.

[h] 21¹　So Gk. and Lat. A later scribe has endeavored to connect this story with the incidents in the preceding chapter by adding the introductory phrase *now it came to pass after these things.* This was probably copied from 17¹⁷.

[i] 21⁴　Following the Gk. in reconstructing the Heb.

[j] 21⁴　So Gk. Heb., *turned away.*

[k] 21¹⁰　Lit., *blessed.* The word is apparently used euphemistically with the implication that Naboth had committed an unspeakable crime, probably that of blasphemy.

[l] 21¹³　The later law regarding the punishment of blasphemy is found in Lev. 24¹⁵, ¹⁶.

Early Ephraimite Elijah Stories

Elijah's message of divine condemnation against Ahab and his house

17But the word of Jehovah came to Elijah the Tishbite, saying, 18Arise, go down to meet Ahab the king of Israel, who dwells in Samaria; he is just now in the vineyard of Naboth, whither he has gone down to take possession of it. 19And thou shalt speak to him, saying, 'Thus saith Jehovah, "Hast thou killed and also taken possession?"' Moreover thou shalt speak to him, saying, 'Thus saith Jehovah, "In the place where the dogs licked the blood of Naboth will the dogs lick thy blood also."' 20And Ahab said to Elijah, Have you found me,[m] O mine enemy? And he answered, I have. Because[n] thou hast sold thyself to no purpose,[o] to do that which is displeasing to Jehovah, 21I will bring evil upon thee, and will utterly sweep thee away and will cut off from Ahab every male and him that is shut up and him that is left at large in Israel. 22And I will make thy house like the house of Jeroboam the son of Nebat and like the house of Baasha the son of Ahijah, because of the anger which thou hast aroused and because thou hast made Israel to sin. 23And of Jezebel also Jehovah has spoken, saying, 'The dogs shall eat Jezebel in the district[p] of Jezreel. 24Whoever of Ahab's house dieth in the fields, the birds of the heavens shall eat.'

Ahab's guilt

25There was absolutely none who sold himself to do that which was displeasing to Jehovah, as did Ahab, because Jezebel his wife incited him. 26For he behaved most abominably in following idols, as did all the Amorites, whom Jehovah had driven out before the Israelites.

His repentance

27Now when Ahab heard those words he tore his clothes and put sackcloth on his flesh and fasted, he also slept on sackcloth and went about quietly. 28Then the word of Jehovah came to Elijah the Tishbite, saying, 29Hast thou seen how Ahab has humbled himself before me? Because he has humbled himself before me, I will not bring the evil in his days; but in his son's days will I bring the evil upon his house.[q]

§ 74. Deliverance of Samaria from the Arameans, I Kgs. 20^{1-25}.

Ahab History

Ben-hadad's unreasonable demands

I Kgs. 20 1Then Ben-hadad[r] the king of Aram gathered all his host together, and there were thirty-two kings with him, and horses and chariots. And he went up and besieged Samaria and fought against it. 2And he sent messengers to Ahab king of Israel into the city and said to him, Thus says

---

m 21^{20} *I.e.*, some act to be condemned.

n 21^{20b-22} The original words of Elijah have been here expanded by the late prophetic editor, whose language and ideas are readily recognized. The oracle in $14^{10, 11}$ is repeated almost word for word. Vs. ^{23}, however, may have belonged to the original speech. If not, it was probably added to the text by an early editor, familiar with II Kgs. 9^{36}.

o 21^{20} So Gk. and Luc. The Heb. omits the pregnant phrase, *to no purpose*.

p 21^{23} So Syr., Lat., and Targ. The Heb. is doubtful. RV, *rampart*, but cf. II Kgs. $9^{10, 36, 37}$.

q $21^{28, 29}$ These verses assume, not the older prediction in ^{19}, but the broader judgment in the secondary passage, ^{21}, so that they also are probably secondary. Moreover, they refer to events peculiar to the later Elisha stories.

§ 74 That the incidents recorded in this chapter and its natural sequel, 22^{1-37}, belong to the latter years of Ahab's reign is indicated by 22^{1} and by the fact that Aramean aggressions became especially active at this time.

The evidence that these were not taken from the same source as the preceding Elijah stories is conclusive. Elijah is nowhere mentioned, but instead Micaiah appears as the representative of the true prophets, 22^{8-20}; Ahab is viewed in a much more favorable light, and he is here called *the king of Israel*—not prevailingly by his given name as in the Elijah stories, or as *the king of Samaria*. The narratives also deal with political rather than social and religious questions. The vividness and fidelity with which Ahab's character and acts are portrayed are only paralleled by the early Saul and David histories. He appears as a brave warrior, a wise, patriotic ruler and a gracious conqueror (20^{33}). Nothing is said of his apostasy. Instead he is a ruler who listens to the advice of the prophets of Jehovah, 20^{22-28}; although the victim of the

---

r 20^{1} Ben-hadad II, whose name appears on the Assyrian inscriptions as *Dadda-idri*. The original Heb. transcription was probably, *Hadader* or *Hadadezer*. Cf. chronological chart after p. 199.

Ahab History

Ben-hadad, ³Your silver and your gold are mine; your wives also and your children,ˢ are mine.   ⁴And the king of Israel answered and said, As you say, my lord, O king: I am yours with all that I have.   ⁵And the messengers came again and said, Thus says Ben-hadad, 'I sent to you, saying, "You shall deliver to me your silver and your gold and your wives and your children"; ⁶but to-morrow I will send my servants about this time and they shall search your house and the houses of your servants; and whatever is attractive to them,ᵗ they shall take in their hands and bear it away.'

Ahab's refusal to comply

⁷Then the king of Israel called all the elders of the land and said, Mark, I pray, and see how this man is seeking to make trouble, for he sent to me for my wives and my children and for my silver and gold, and I did not refuse him.   ⁸And all the elders and all the people said to him, Do not hearken nor consent!   ⁹Therefore he said to the messengers of Ben-hadad, Tell my lord the king, 'All that you demanded of your servant at the first I will do, but this I cannot do.'   So the messengers departed and brought him word again.   ¹⁰Then Ben-hadad sent to him and said, Let the gods do to me what they will, if the dust of Samaria shall suffice for handfuls for all the people who follow me!   ¹¹And the king of Israel answered and said, Tell him, ' Let not him who is girding on his sword boast himself as he who is putting it off.'   ¹²Now when Ben-hadadᵘ heard this message—he was drinking together with the kings in the pavilions—he said to his servants, Set yourselves in array.   And they set themselves in array against the city.

His victory over the Arameans

¹³But just then a prophet came near to Ahab king of Israel and said, Thus saith Jehovah, ' Hast thou seen all this great multitude?   Behold, I will deliver it into thy hand to-day, and thou shalt know that I am Jehovah.'   ¹⁴And Ahab said, By whom?   And he said, Thus saith Jehovah, ' By the young men under the provincial commanders.'ᵛ   And he said, Who shall begin the battle?   And he answered, Thou.ʷ   ¹⁵Then he mustered the young men under the provincial commanders, and they were two hundred and thirty-two.   And after them he mustered all the people, even all the Israelitesˣ—seven thousand.   ¹⁶And at noon they made the attack, while

false representatives of the order, 22.   He dies fighting bravely for his people and is buried at Samaria, 22³⁴, ³⁵, ³⁷.   While each history doubtless presents sides of Ahab's character and policy not inconsistent with each other, they cannot possibly be from the same source. Chaps. 20 and 22 may have been included in the Chronicles of the Kings of Israel, but they were probably taken originally from an independent Ahab history, which was written before the early Elijah stories and therefore between 850 and 800 B.C.   This is confirmed by the presence of many linguistic peculiarities found nowhere else.

The historical value of these narratives is very great.   They reveal the political problem of Northern Israel during one of its most important epochs and throw clear light upon the character and work of Ahab.

ˢ 20³ So Gk.   In the Heb. a scribe has awkwardly added after *children, the fairest.*

ᵗ 20⁶ So Gk., Luc., Syr., and Lat.   Heb., *your eyes.*

ᵘ 20¹² Heb., *that one.*

ᵛ 20¹⁴ *I.e.,* not the soldiers of the standing army, but the warriors furnished in time of war by the local feudal lords.   A similar system was in force among the Babylonians and Assyrians. Cf. Johns, *Bab. and Assyr. Laws, Contracts, and Letters,* pp. 76, 77, 200, 201.

ʷ 20¹³, ¹⁴ These verses are not absolutely required by the context and may have been added later—as certain scholars have urged—to show that Ahab's victories as well as disasters were meted out directly by Jehovah; but the rôle assumed by the prophet here is the same as in the oldest narratives and their attitude toward Ahab appears to have been favorable, as is that of the author of the section.   So also ²².

ˣ Gk. and Luc., *all the mighty warriors.*   The reference is evidently to the standing army as contrasted with the militia.

Ahab History

Ben-hadad was drinking himself drunk in the pavilions, together with the thirty-two kings who had come to help him.   [17]And the young men under the provincial commanders went out first.   And Ben-hadad sent out messengers and they reported to him saying, Men have come out from Samaria.   [18]And he said, Whether they have come out with peaceful intent, take them alive; or whether they have come out for war, take them alive.   [19]So these (the young men under the provincial commanders) went out of the city, and the army which followed them.   [20]And they slew each his man, so that the Arameans fled.   And the Israelites pursued them, but Ben-hadad, the king of Aram, escaped on a horse with horsemen.   [21]Then the king of Israel went out and captured[a] horses and chariots, and slew a great number of the Arameans.

[22]And the prophet came near to the king of Israel and said to him, Go, strengthen thyself, and mark and see what thou wilt do, for a year from now the king of Aram will come up against thee.   [23]And the servants of the king of Aram said to him, Their gods are hill-gods, therefore they were too strong for us; but let us fight against them in the plain, and surely we shall be stronger than they.   [24]And do this: take the kings away each from his place, and put commanders in their place, [25]and assemble an army, like the army that you have lost, horse for horse and chariot for chariot; then we will fight against them in the plain, and surely we shall be stronger than they. And he listened to their advice and did so.

Ben-hadad's preparations for a second campaign

§ 75. Ahab's Victory over the Arameans at Aphek, I Kgs. 20[26-34]

Ahab History

I Kgs. 20 [26]Now when the year had come around Ben-hadad mustered the Arameans and went up to Aphek to fight against Israel.   [27]And the Israelites were mustered and provided with provisions,[b] and went against them.   And the Israelites encamped before them like two small flocks of goats, while the Arameans filled the country.   [28]Then a man of God came near and said to the king of Israel, Thus saith Jehovah, 'Because the Arameans think, "Jehovah is a hill-god but not a god of the valleys," therefore I will deliver all this great multitude into thy hand, that ye may know that I am Jehovah.'   [29]So they encamped opposite each other seven days.   But on the seventh day the battle was joined; and the Israelites slew of the Arameans a hundred thousand footmen in one day.   [30]But the rest fled to Aphek, into the city; and the wall fell upon twenty-seven thousand of the men who were left.   Ben-hadad also fled, and came into the city, into an innermost chamber.

Ahab's second great victory

---

[a] 20[21] So Gk. and Luc.   The Heb. has the less probable reading, *slew*.
§ 75 This is the immediate sequel of the preceding narrative.   The story has evidently grown during transmission, *e.g.*, 29[b], 30[b], but these elements may well be from the author who wrote the present narrative.
[b] 20[27] So Gk., Luc., Syr., Lat., and Targ.   The Heb. word is otherwise unknown.

Ahab History

Liberal terms offered to Ben-hadad by Ahab

³¹And his servants said to him, Behold now, we have heard that the kings of the house of Israel are merciful kings; let us therefore put sackcloth about our loins and ropes about our heads and go out to the king of Israel; perhaps he will save your life. ³²So they girded sackcloth about their loins and put ropes about their heads, and came to the king of Israel and said, Your servant Ben-hadad says, 'Let me live.' And he replied, Is he yet alive? He is my brother. ³³Now the men began to divine his thought and quickly caught it up from him^c and said, Ben-hadad is your brother. Then he said, Go, bring him! And when Ben-hadad came out to him he took him up to himself in the chariot. ³⁴And Ben-hadad said to him, The cities which my father took from your father, I will restore, and you may establish streets^d for yourself in Damascus as my father established in Samaria. And Ahab^e said, I will let you go with this agreement. So he made an agreement with him and let him go.

§ 76. Messages of the Unknown Prophet, I Kgs. 20³⁵⁻⁴³

Very Late Popular Prophetic Story

The acted prophecy and its application

I Kgs. 20 ³⁵Now a certain man of the sons of the prophets at the command of Jehovah said to his fellow, Smite me, I pray. But the man refused to smite him. ³⁶Then he said to him, Since you have not obeyed the voice of Jehovah, as soon as you have gone away from me, a lion shall slay you. Accordingly, as soon as he had gone away from him, a lion found him and slew him. ³⁷Then he found another man, and said, Smite me, I pray. And the man smote him so as to wound him. ³⁸Then the prophet departed and waited for the king by the way and disguised himself with a covering over his eyes. ³⁹And as the king was passing by, he cried to the king and said, Your servant had gone out into the midst of the battle, when suddenly a man turned aside, and brought a man to me and said, 'Watch this man; if by any means he be missing, then must your life be for his life, or else you must pay a talent of silver!' ⁴⁰And as your servant was looking here and there,^{f} he was gone. And the king of Israel said to him, Such is your verdict: you yourself have decided it. ⁴¹Then he quickly took the covering away from his eyes, and the king of Israel recognized that he was one of the prophets.

---

^{c} 20³³ The Heb. as it reads is untranslatable. The reading above is based on the text reconstructed with the aid of the Gk. which has, *and they took up the word from his mouth.*

^{d} 20³⁴ *I.e.,* streets with bazaars for the Israelitish traders, who perhaps were under the direct protection and jurisdiction of their native government. This arrangement corresponds to the commercial clause in a modern treaty. In 854 B.C. Ahab and the Aramean king fought against Shalmanezer II.

^{e} 20³⁴ As often in the Heb., the change of subject is probably implied by the context. Otherwise it is necessary radically to change the text so as to read, *You may let me go.*

§ 76 The language and atmosphere of this strange tale are entirely different from the sober narrative to which it is attached. It is closely akin to the very late tradition in 12³³–13³⁴, § 61. The extraordinary and inexplicable appear alike in both. In each a lion is the agent of divine judgment. The conception of the prophets is that of a very late and unhistorical period. The real point of the story is obscure. It seems to be a condemnation of Ahab's lenient policy toward his beaten foe. Like 12³³–13³⁴, it may have been added after the late prophetic compilation of Kgs. had been made.

^{f} 20⁴⁰ So Gk., Luc., and Targ. The Heb., *was a doer of hither and thither,* is an exceedingly awkward, if not impossible construction.

Very Late Popular Prophetic Story

⁴²And he said to him, Thus saith Jehovah, 'Because thou hast let go out of thy hand the man whom I had condemned to destruction,ᵍ therefore thy life shall go for his life and thy people for his people.' ⁴³And the king of Israel went homeward in ill-humor and sullen, and came to Samaria.

§ 77. Predictions of Micaiah and the Four Hundred False Prophets, I Kgs. 22¹⁻²⁸, II Chr. 18¹⁻²⁷

Ahab History

I Kgs. 22 ¹Then for three years they remained at peace, without there being war between Aram and Israel. ²But in the third year, when Jehoshaphat the king of Judah had come down to the king of Israel, ³the king of Israel said to his servants, Do you know that Ramoth in Gilead belongs to us, yet we sit still instead of taking it from the king of Aram?ʰ ⁴And he said to Jehoshaphat, Will you go with me to fight against Ramoth in Gilead? And Jehoshaphat said to the king of Israel, I am as you, my people as your people, my horses as your horses. *The alliance against Aram*

⁵Jehoshaphat also said to the king of Israel, Inquire at this time, I pray, for the word of Jehovah. ⁶Then the king of Israel gathered the prophets together, about four hundred men, and asked them, Shall I go to fight against Ramoth in Gilead or shall I forbear? And they said, Go up; for Jehovahⁱ will deliver it into the hand of the king. ⁷But Jehoshaphat said, Is there no other prophetʲ of Jehovah, that we may inquire of him? ⁸And the king of Israel said, There is another by whom we may inquire of Jehovah, Micaiah the son of Imlah, but I hate him; for he prophesies for me nothing good, but only evil. And Jehoshaphat said, Let not the king say so. *Encouraging message of the official prophets*

⁹Then the king of Israel called an eunuch and said, Bring quickly Micaiah the son of Imlah. ¹⁰Now while the king of Israel and Jehoshaphat the king of Judah were sitting each on his throne, clad in his robes of state at the entranceᵏ of the gate of Samaria, and all the prophets were prophesying before them, ¹¹Zedekiah the son of Chenaanah made for himself horns of iron and said, Thus saith Jehovah, 'With these shalt thou push the Arameans until you have destroyed them!' ¹²And all the prophets prophesied the same saying, Go up to Ramoth in Gilead; for Jehovah will deliver it into the hand of the king. *Their emphatic predictions of victory*

ᵍ 20⁴² Heb., *the man of my ban.*
§ 77 This is the immediate sequel of the victory over the Arameans recorded in 20²⁶⁻³⁴. The portrait which it gives of the early prophets, and especially those associated together in the prophetic guilds and probably in part supported from the royal treasury, is most valuable and explains the indignant declaration of Amos that he was no son of a prophet, 7¹⁴. It also first introduces the idea of a lying spirit which perhaps later developed into the Jewish belief in Satan, the Adversary.
ʰ 22³ The parallel in II Chr. 18³ reads, *and Ahab killed sheep and oxen for him in abundance, and for the people who were with him, and influenced him to go up to Ramoth in Gilead.*
ⁱ 22⁶ So certain codices. Cf. ¹¹, ¹². A scribe has in the received Heb. text substituted, *Lord.*
ʲ 22⁷ Gk., Luc., Syr., and Lat., *Is there not here a prophet of Jehovah?* This implies that the four hundred were not Jehovah prophets. But cf. ¹¹, ¹².
ᵏ 22¹⁰ Making a necessary correction in the Heb.

Ahab History

Mica-
iah's
predic-
tion of
defeat

[13]And the messenger who went to call Micaiah said to him, See, now the prophets have with one consent promised good fortune[1] for the king; therefore speak the same as they all do and prophesy good fortune. [14]But Micaiah said, As Jehovah liveth, I will speak what Jehovah saith to me. [15]And when he came to the king, the king said to him, Micaiah, shall we go to Ramoth in Gilead to fight or shall we forbear? And he answered him, Go up and prosper; and Jehovah will deliver it into the hand of the king! [16]But the king said to him, How many times shall I adjure you that you speak to me nothing but the truth in the name of Jehovah? [17]And he said, I saw all Israel scattered upon the mountains, as sheep that have no shepherd. And Jehovah said, 'These have no master; let each of them go home in peace!'

The
lying
spirit
within
the
official
proph-
ets

[18]And the king of Israel said to Jehoshaphat, Did I not tell you that he would prophesy no good concerning me, but evil? [19]And Micaiah said, Therefore hear the word of Jehovah: I saw Jehovah sitting on his throne and all the host of heaven standing by him on his right hand and on his left. [20]And Jehovah said, 'Who shall delude Ahab so that he will go up and fall at Ramoth in Gilead?' And one proposed one thing and another another, [21]until there came forth a spirit and stood before Jehovah and said, 'I will delude him.' [22]And Jehovah said to him, 'By what means?' And he said, 'I will go forth and become a lying spirit in the mouth of all his prophets.' Thereupon he said, 'Thou shalt delude him and shalt succeed also! Go forth, and do so.' [23]So behold, Jehovah hath now put a lying spirit in the mouth of all these your prophets, since Jehovah hath determined to bring evil upon you.

Mica-
iah's
im-
prison-
ment

[24]Then Zedekiah the son of Chenaanah came near and struck Micaiah on the cheek and said, Which way did the spirit of Jehovah go from me to speak to you?[m] [25]And Micaiah said, Indeed, you shall see on that day, when you shall go from one chamber to another to hide yourself. [26]Then the king of Israel said, Take Micaiah and carry him back to Amon the governor of the city and to Joash the king's son, [27]and say, 'Thus the king commands, "Put this fellow in prison and feed him with a scanty fare of bread and water[n] until I return in peace."' [28]And Micaiah said, If you indeed return in peace, Jehovah hath not spoken by me.[o]

---

[1] 22^13 So Gk. and Luc. Heb., *the words of the prophets are good.*
[m] 22^24 The Gk., partially supported by Luc., has a smoother reading, *where is the spirit of Jehovah that speaks in you?*
[n] 22^27 Heb., *bread-affliction and water-affliction.* As in Is. 30^20, this is the idiomatic designation of prison fare.
[o] 22^28 So Gk. and Luc. In the Heb., a scribe has added from Mi. 1^2, and he said, *Hear O people, all of you,* mistakenly identifying the present prophet with a contemporary of Isaiah.

§ 78. Death of Ahab at Ramoth in Gilead, I Kgs. 22[29-40], II Chr. 18[28-34]

Ahab History

I Kgs. 22 [29]Then the king of Israel and Jehoshaphat the king of Judah went up to Ramoth in Gilead. [30]And the king of Israel said to Jehoshaphat, I will disguise myself and go into the battle, but you can put on your robes. So the king of Israel disguised himself and went into the battle. [31]Now the king of Aram had given orders to the thirty-two commanders of his chariots, saying, Fight with neither small nor great, except only with the king of Israel. [32]Accordingly when the commanders of the chariots saw Jehoshaphat, they said, Surely it is the king of Israel, and they surrounded him to fight against him,[p] but Jehoshaphat cried out. [33]Therefore, as soon as the commanders of the chariots saw that it was not the king of Israel, they turned back from pursuing him. *Ahab's disguise and Jehoshaphat's peril*

[34]But a certain man drew at a venture and smote the king of Israel between the attachments and the coat of mail. Therefore he said to the driver of his chariot, Turn about and carry me out of the army; for I am severely wounded. [35]And the battle increased that day, and the king was propped up in his chariot against the Arameans until evening,[q] and the blood ran out of the wound into the bottom of the chariot. But at evening he died. [36]And toward sunset the cry went throughout the army, Each to his city and each to his land, [37]for the king is dead![r] so they[s] came to Samaria and buried the king in Samaria. [38]And when they washed the chariot by the pool of Samaria, the dogs licked up his blood, and the harlots washed themselves in it,[t] just as Jehovah had declared. *Ahab's fatal wound*

[39]Now the other acts of Ahab, and all that he did and the ivory house which he built and all the cities that he built, are they not recorded in the Chronicles of the Kings of Israel? [40]So Ahab slept with his fathers and Ahaziah his son became king in his place. *Résumé of his reign*

§ 79. Ahaziah's Reign and Fatal Illness, I Kgs. 22[51-53], II Kgs. 1

Early Ephraimite Elijah Stories

I Kgs. 22 [51]Ahaziah the son of Ahab became king over Israel in Samaria in the seventeenth year of Jehoshaphat king of Judah, and he reigned two years over Israel. [52]And he did that which displeased Jehovah, and walked in the way of his father and in the way of his mother and in the way of Jeroboam the son of Nebat, who had led Israel into sin. [53]And he served Baal and worshipped him, and provoked to anger Jehovah, the God of Israel, just as his father had done. *Ahaziah's policy*

---

§ 78 This section contains the conclusion of the Ahab history. To the end of the quotation from the Ahab history some editor has added the note in [38], which reflects an entirely different conception of the king. It is evidently based on the prediction in the Elijah stories, 21[19], although it overlooks the fact that Naboth's vineyard was not in Samaria but in Jezreel. The concluding verses contain a *résumé* of Ahab's reign in the familiar terms of the late prophetic editor.

p 22[32] So Gk., Luc., and the parallel in II Chr. Heb., *They turned aside against him.*

q 22[35] So Gk. and Luc., supported by II Chr. 18[34]. In the Heb. a scribe by mistake has introduced here the phrase, *the king died*, instead of in its logical place at the end of the verse.

r 22[37] So Gk. and Luc. The Heb. connects this first clause with the following.

s 22[37] So Gk. and Luc. Heb., *he came.*

t 22[38] Gk. and Luc., *in his blood.*

§ 79 In addition to his familiar judgment upon the reign of Ahaziah, the editor has introduced in II Kgs. 1[1] (cf. I Kgs. 22[54]) a reference to the rebellion of Mesha, which is well authenticated by the contemporary inscription of that king himself. Cf. Appendix IV. In the older source—probably the Chronicles of the Kings of Israel—from which the editor takes his data

Early Ephraimite Elijah Stories

Moab's rebellion
Ahaziah's embassy to Ekron

II Kgs. 1 ¹And after the death of Ahab Moab rebelled against Israel. . . .
²Now Ahaziah fell out through the lattice in his upper apartment in Samaria, and lay sick. Then he sent messengers and commanded them, Go, inquire of Baal-Zebub, the god of Ekron, whether or not I shall recover of this sickness.

Elijah's message

³But the messenger of Jehovah said to Elijah the Tishbite, Arise, go up to meet the messengers of the king of Samaria and say to them, 'Is it because there is no God in Israel, that ye go to inquire of Baal-Zebub, the god of Ekron?' ⁴Now therefore thus saith Jehovah, 'Thou shalt not come down from the bed whither thou hast gone up, but thou shalt surely die.' Then Elijah went away.

Report of the embassy

⁵And when the messengers came back to him, he said to them, Why have you returned? ⁶And they said to him, A man came up to meet us and said to us, 'Go back again to the king who sent you and say to him, "Thus saith Jehovah: Is it because there is no God in Israel that thou sendest to inquire of Baal-Zebub the god of Ekron? Therefore thou shalt not come down from the bed whither thou hast gone up, but shalt surely die."' ⁷And he said to them, What kind of man was he who told you these things? ⁸And they answered him, A man clad in a skin and girt with a leather girdle about his loins. Then he said, It is Elijah the Tishbite!

Destruction of the later embassies and reiteration of the doom

⁹Thereupon he sent against him a commander of fifty with his fifty. And when he went up to him—for he was sitting on the top of the hill—he said to him, O man of God, the king said, 'Come down.' ¹⁰And Elijah answered and said to the commander of fifty, If I be a man of God, let fire come down from heaven and consume you and your fifty. Then there fell fire from heaven and consumed him and his fifty. ¹¹And again he sent to him another commander of fifty with his fifty. And he answered and said to him, O man of God, thus has the king said, 'Come down quickly.' ¹²And Elijah answered and said to them, If I be a man of God, let fire come down from heaven and consume you and your fifty. And the fire of God fell from heaven and consumed him and his fifty. ¹³And again he sent a third commander of fifty with his fifty. But when the third commander of fifty went up, he came and fell on his knees before Elijah and besought him, saying to him, O man of God, I pray you spare my life and the life of these fifty your servants. ¹⁴Already fire has come down from heaven and consumed the two former commanders of fifty with their fifties; but now spare my life. ¹⁵And the Messenger of Jehovah said to Elijah, Go down with him; do not be afraid of him. So he arose and went down with him to the king. ¹⁶And he said to him, Thus saith Jehovah, 'Because thou hast sent messengers to inquire of Baal-Zebub, the god of Ekron —is it because there is no God in Israel to inquire of his word?ᵘ—therefore thou shalt not come down from the bed whither thou art gone up, but shalt surely die.'

Death of Ahaziah

¹⁷So he died according to the word of Jehovah which Elijah had spoken. And in the second year of Jehoram the son of Jehoshaphat king of Judah, Jehoram his brother became king in his place, because he had no son. ¹⁸Now the other acts which Ahaziah did, are they not recorded in the Chronicles of the Kings of Israel?

---

there may have followed a further account of the rebellion.   3⁵ reiterates the fact and the subsequent verses contain a popular tradition of an unsuccessful attempt to reconquer Moab.

The chief quotation regarding Ahaziah appears to come from the early Elijah stories. As in I Kgs. 17¹, 21¹⁷, the prophet is introduced as Elijah, the Tishbite, ³, ⁸. The forms of the divine address to Elijah in ³, ⁴ recall the corresponding expressions in I Kgs. 21¹⁷, ¹⁹. The Messenger of Jehovah in ³ appears elsewhere in these chapters only in the Elijah stories of I Kgs. 19⁷. Above all the Elijah, who in 1¹⁻⁴ suddenly arises to rebuke Ahaziah, is the same as he who figures in I Kgs. 17-19, 21, and his words reveal the same passionate zeal for Jehovah.

Vss. ⁹⁻¹⁶ are little more than repetitions of the preceding. Cf. ¹⁶ᵃ. The literary style and spirit are radically different. No ethical motive is evident for the wanton destruction of the two companies of fifty. The story strongly recalls the fate of the messengers of Saul in Samuel's presence, I Sam. 19¹⁸⁻²⁴. If not modelled after that late tale, this insertion is closely related to it. It cannot be earlier than the popular Elisha stories (cf. especially 2²³⁻²⁵), and does not reflect the older and nobler conception of the prophet. Cf. Introd., p. 18.

ᵘ 1¹⁶ The interjected question is lacking in the Gk. and Luc.

226

§ 80. Jehoram's Reign, II Kgs. 3¹⁻³

Late Prophetic Summary

II Kgs. 3 ¹Now Jehoram the son of Ahab became king over Israel in
Samaria in the eighteenth year of Jehoshaphat king of Judah, and he reigned
twelve years. ²And he displeased Jehovah, but not as did his father and
mother, for he put away the pillar of Baal that his father had made. ³However he clung to the sins of Jeroboam the son of Nebat with which he made
Israel sin and he did not depart from them.

(margin) Jehoram's religious policy

III

POPULAR TRADITIONS ABOUT ELISHA, II Kgs. 2¹–8¹⁵, 13¹⁴⁻²⁷

§ 81. Translation of Elijah and Consecration of Elisha, II Kgs. 2

Gilgal Cycle of Elisha Stories

II Kgs. 2 ¹Now at the time when Jehovah was about to cause Elijah to
go up by a whirlwind to heaven, Elijah was going with Elisha from Gilgal.
²And Elijah said to Elisha, Remain here, I pray, for Jehovah hath sent me
as far as Bethel. And Elisha said, As Jehovah liveth and as you live, I
will not leave you. So they went down to Bethel. ³And the sons of the
prophets who were at Bethel came out to Elisha and said to him, Do you
know that to-day Jehovah will take away your master from being over you?
And he said, Yes, I know it; only keep silent. ⁴And Elijah said to him,
Elisha, tarry here, I pray, for Jehovah hath sent me to Jericho. And he
said, As Jehovah liveth and as you live, I will not leave you. So they came

(margin) Elisha's persistency in following Elijah

§ 80 This editorial summary of Jehoram's reign naturally follows immediately after 1,
and finds its direct continuation in 8¹⁶ff. Into this editorial framework has been fitted the
large group of Elisha stories, which are written from an entirely different point of view and can
best be studied as a unit. Cf. §§ 81–92.

Popular Traditions about Elisha.—The origin and history of this group of stories have
already been considered in the Introd., pp. 18–20. That they were great favorites with the
common people is demonstrated by their general character. They illustrate that personal and
pastoral side of the prophetic activity which is often overlooked. All the traditions which
gathered about Elisha represent him as a benignant prophet, in close touch with court and people. Their number and striking character testify to the greatness of his personality and work,
for there is never smoke without some fire. Even though popular tradition associates with
Elisha stories which appear originally in connection with Elijah, they contain so many original
and realistic elements that it is impossible to regard their hero as a mere product of the imagination. Unfortunately he lived just before the beginning of Israel's great literary age, so that his
words and acts were first recorded only in the popular memory, but back of the stories stands
the man, identified by birth and training with the agricultural civilization of Northern Israel
and thus fitted personally to direct the life and thought of his people, and to realize in the history of his race the principles and ideals proclaimed by his master Elijah. Differing radically
in character and method from his great predecessor, he appears to have been the first of that
new type of prophets, represented by Amos, Isaiah and their successors, who stood not apart
from but in the midst of the people whom they addressed.

§ 81 This story fittingly introduces those which follow. While it records the close of
Elijah's life, its real purpose is to indicate the source of Elisha's supernatural power. His persistency in following Elijah, his words, and the wonder-working mantle, which fell down upon
his shoulders, are more prominent than the great prophet of Gilead himself. Gilgal is conceived of as Elisha's home. The description of the journey from Gilgal by Bethel down to the
Jordan indicates that the town in question was not the more famous one near Jericho, but the
Gilgal a little southwest of Shiloh, which appears to have early inherited the traditions of that
ancient sanctuary. Cf. Introd., pp. 18, 19. The prominence of the sons of the prophets also
indicates that this story is from the Gilgal cycle.

Gilgal Cycle of Elisha Stories

to Jericho. ⁵Then the sons of the prophets who were at Jericho came near to Elisha and said to him, Do you know that to-day Jehovah will take your master from being over you? And he answered, Yes, I know it; only keep silent. ⁶And Elijah said to him, Remain here, I pray, for Jehovah hath sent me to the Jordan. And he said, As Jehovah liveth and as you live, I will not leave you. So they two went on.

Elisha's request that Elijah's prophetic spirit might rest in fullest measure on him
⁷And fifty men of the sons of the prophets went and stood opposite them at a distance, while they stood by the Jordan. ⁸Then Elijah took his mantle and rolled it up and smote the waters; thereupon they were divided on both sides so that they two could go over on dry ground. ⁹And when they had gone over, Elijah said to Elisha, Ask what I shall do for you before I am taken from you. And Elisha said, I pray, let a double portion of your spirit be upon me.ᵃ ¹⁰And he said, You have asked a hard thing; nevertheless, if you see me when I am taken from you, so shall it be with you; but if not, it shall not be so.

Descent of Elijah's mantle upon Elisha
¹¹Now as they were still going on their way conversing, a chariot of fire with horses of fire suddenly came and separated the two; and Elijah went up by a whirlwind to heaven. ¹²And when Elisha saw it, he cried, My father, my father!ᵇ the chariots of Israel and its horsemen! And he saw him no more, but he took hold of his own robes and tore them in two pieces. ¹³Then he took up the mantle of Elijah that had fallen from him, and went back and stood by the bank of the Jordan. ¹⁴And he took the mantle of Elijah that had fallen from him and smote the waters, and said, Where now is Jehovah, the God of Elijah? And when he had smitten the waters, they were divided on both sides, so that Elisha could go over.

Fruitless search for Elijah
¹⁵And when the sons of the prophets who were at Jerichoᶜ opposite him saw him, they said, The spirit of Elijah rests on Elisha. And they came to meet him and bowed to the ground before him, ¹⁶and said to him, Behold now, there are with your servants fifty strong men; let them go, we pray, and seek your master, lest the spirit of Jehovah has taken him up and cast him on some mountain or into some valley. And he said, Do not send.ᵈ ¹⁷But when they urged him until he was ashamed, he said, Send. They accordingly sent fifty men; and they sought three days, but did not find him. ¹⁸And when they came back to him, while he was still at Jericho, he said to them, Did I not say to you, 'Do not go'?

Elisha's purification of the spring at Jericho
¹⁹And the men of the city said to Elisha, See, the situation of this city is pleasant, as my lord observes; but the water is bad, and the people of the landᵉ have untimely births. ²⁰And he said, Bring me a new flask, and put salt in it. And they brought it to him. ²¹And he went out to the source of

---

ᵃ 2⁹ Lit., *let there be a share of two of your spirit upon me, i.e.,* the especial rights of a first-born son.

ᵇ 2¹² Cf. 13¹⁴. *Father* was probably the term by which the *sons* of the prophets addressed the prophet whom they recognized as their leader. It is equivalent to *master* in ³, ⁵.

ᶜ 2¹⁵ The preceding context suggests that they were not at Jericho, but near the Jordan. The words, *at Jericho,* were probably added from ³, ⁵.

ᵈ 2¹⁶ Gk. adds, *to the Jordan.*

ᵉ 2¹⁹ Lit., *the land casts her young.* But in ²¹ the spring is the cause of this trouble. The only satisfactory explanation is that land, as in I Sam. 14²⁹, 17⁴⁶ and often, is equivalent to the inhabitants.

Gilgal Cycle of Elisha Stories

the waters and cast salt into it and said, Thus saith Jehovah, 'I have made these waters wholesome; death shall no longer come from them nor untimely births.' ²²So the waters were made wholesome to this day, just as Elisha had said.

²³And he went up from there to Bethel. And while he was going up by the way, young lads came out of the city and mocked him with the cry, Go up, you baldhead. ²⁴And he looked behind him, and when he saw them, he cursed them in the name of Jehovah. And there came forth two she-bears out of the wood and tore forty-two of the lads. ²⁵And he went from there to Mount Carmel and from there returned to Samaria. Fate of the boys of Bethel

§ 82. The Widow's Oil, II Kgs. 4¹⁻⁷

Gilgal Cycle of Elisha Stories

II Kgs. 4 ¹Now one of the wives of the sons of the prophets cried to Elisha, saying, Your servant my husband is dead; and you know that your servant feared Jehovah; but now the creditor is come to take my two children to be his slaves. ²And Elisha said to her, What shall I do for you? Tell me; what have you in the house? And she said, Your maid-servant has nothing in the house except a flask of oil.ᶠ ³Then he said, Go, borrow vessels abroad of all your neighbors, even empty vessels, ⁴and you shall go in, shut the door upon yourself and your sons, and pour out into all the vessels, and when one is full, you shall set it aside. Elisha's directions

⁵So she went from him and shut the door upon herself and her sons; and while they brought the vessels to her, she poured out. ⁶When the vessels were full, she said to her son, Give still another. But he said to her, There is not another vessel! Then she ceased. ⁷When she came and told the man of God, he said, Go, sell the oil, and pay your debts, and from what remains you, with your sons, can live. The miraculous flow of oil

§ 83. Miraculous Provision of Food for the Sons of the Prophets, II Kgs. 4³⁸⁻⁴⁴

Gilgal Cycle of Elisha Stories

II Kgs. 4 ³⁸Now Elisha came again to Gilgal while there was a famine in the land. And when the sons of the prophets were sitting before him, he said to his servants, Set on the great pot and boil pottage for the sons of the prophets. ³⁹Then one went out into the field to gather herbs and found a wild vine and gathered from it his lap full of wild gourds and came and cut them up into the dish of pottage, for heᵍ did not know what they were. ⁴⁰So "Death in the pot"

---

§ 82 The prominence of the sons of the prophets, the apparent dependence of this story on the earlier Elijah narrative in I Kgs. 17, and the fact that it relates not to public but to private events, strongly suggest that it was taken from the Gilgal cycle. Cf. Introd., p. 19.

ᶠ 4² Or, *enough oil for anointing.*

§ 83 The reference to Gilgal in ³⁸ and the prominence of the sons of the prophets make clear the classification of this story. The picture which it gives of a prophetic guild is certainly one of the most distinct in the O.T.

ᵍ 4³⁹ So Luc., Syr., and Targ. Heb., *they.*

Gilgal Cycle of Elisha Stories

they poured out for the men to eat. But as they were eating of the pottage, they cried out and said, O man of God, there is death in the pot. And they could not eat of it. ⁴¹Then he said, Bring meal. And he cast it into the pot and said, Pour out for the people, that they may eat. And there was no harm in the pot.

Miracle
of the
bread
and
fruit

⁴²And there came a man from Baal-shalishah and brought the man of God bread of the first-fruits, twenty loaves of barley, and garden fruit[h] in his sack. And he said, Give the people something to eat. ⁴³And his servant said, What, should I set this before a hundred men ? But he said, Give the people that they may eat; for thus saith Jehovah, They shall eat and shall leave some over. ⁴⁴So he set it before them, and they ate and left some over just as Jehovah had said.

§ 84. Recovery of the Lost Axe, II Kgs. 6¹⁻⁷

Gilgal Cycle of Elisha Stories

The
float-
ing
iron

II Kgs. 6 ¹Now the sons of the prophets said to Elisha, See now, the place where we dwell before you is too contracted for us. ²Let us go, we pray, to the Jordan and each take from there a beam and let us make a place for ourselves there, where we may dwell. And he answered, Go. ³And some one said, Consent, I pray, to go with your servants. And he answered, I will go. ⁴So he went with them. And when they came to the Jordan, they cut down wood. ⁵But as one was felling a beam, the axe-head fell into the water. Then he cried, and said, Alas, my master ! for it was borrowed. ⁶And the man of God said, Where did it fall ? And when he showed him the place, he cut down a stick, and threw it in, and made the iron swim. ⁷Then he said, Take it up. So he reached out his hand and took it.

§ 85. Restoration of the Shunammite's Son, II Kgs. 4⁸⁻³⁷

Samaria Cycle of Elisha Stories

The
Shu-
nam-
mite's
hospi-
tality
to Eli-
sha

II Kgs. 4 ⁸Now one day Elisha went over to Shunem, where dwelt a rich woman; and she constrained him to eat food. And afterward, whenever he passed by, he turned in there to eat food. ⁹And she said to her husband, Behold, now I perceive that this is a holy man of God who is continually passing by us. ¹⁰Let us make a little walled-in roof-chamber, and let us

---

h 4⁴² Lat., Syr., and Targ., followed by RV, *fresh ears of corn.*

§ 84 The same geographical setting and point of view appear in this, as in the immediately preceding stories.

§ 85 The probable influence which the early Elijah stories in 17 exerted upon this story have already been noted. Cf. Introd., p. 19. The dependence upon the same early source is also suggested by similarity in language, cf. ³¹ and I Kgs. 18²⁶, ²⁹, ³⁴, ³⁵ and I Kgs. 18⁴². Several phrases found in 2 here recur: cf., *e.g.*, ³⁰ and 2², ⁴, ⁶, indicating possibly that this belongs to the Gilgal cycle. Not Gilgal, however, but Mount Carmel appears to be the home of the prophet, ²⁵. The story and its sequel in 8¹⁻⁶ may be from still a third Mount Carmel cycle, but the familiar references to the king in ¹³ and 8⁴⁻⁶ and the prominence of Gehazi suggest that they probably came from the Samaria cycle.

The story throws much light upon social and domestic life in Northern Israel and justly merits the popularity which it has always enjoyed.

Samaria Cycle of Elisha Stories

place for him there a bed, a table, a seat, and a candlestick, so that, whenever he comes to us, he can turn in.

¹¹Now one day he came there and turned into the chamber and lay there. ¹²And he said to Gehazi his servant, Call this Shunammite. And when he had called her, she stood before him. ¹³And he said to him, Say now to her, 'See, you have been so anxious to care for us; what is to be done for you? Might we commend you to the favor of the king^i or to the commander of the army?' And she answered, I dwell in the midst of my own clan.^j ¹⁴And he said, What then is to be done for her? And Gehazi answered, Verily she has no son, and her husband is old. ¹⁵And he said, Call her. And when he had called her, she stood in the door. ¹⁶And he said, At this time a year hence you shall embrace a son. And she said, No, my lord, O man of God, do not deceive your maid-servant.

His promise that she should have a son

¹⁷But the woman conceived and bore a son about the same time the next year^k as Elisha had said to her. ¹⁸And when the child was grown, he went out one day to his father to the reapers. ¹⁹And he called to his father, My head, my head! And [his father] said to his servant, Carry him to his mother. ²⁰And when he had taken and brought him to his mother, he sat on her lap until noon, and then died. ²¹And she went up and laid him on the bed of the man of God, and shut the door upon him and went out.

Death of the son

²²Then she called to her husband and said, Send me, I pray, one of the servants and one of the asses, that I may go quickly to the man of God and come again. ²³And he said, Why will you go to him to-day since it is neither new moon nor sabbath? And she said, It is well. ²⁴Then she saddled an ass and said to her servant, Drive on fast, do not stop my riding, until I bid you. ²⁵So she went and came to the man of God on Mount Carmel. But when the man of God saw her at a distance, he said to Gehazi his servant, See, there is the Shunammite! ²⁶Run now to meet her and say to her, Is it well with you? Is it well with your husband? Is it well with the child? And she answered, It is well. ²⁷But when she came to the man of God to the mountain, she caught hold of his feet. And when Gehazi came near to thrust her away, the man of God said, Let her alone, for she is deeply troubled and Jehovah hath hidden it from me and hath not told me. ²⁸Then she said, Did I desire a son of my lord? Did I not say, Do not deceive me?

The mother's journey to Elisha

²⁹Then he said to Gehazi, Gird up your loins, take my staff in your hand, and go! If you meet anyone, do not salute him, and if any salute you do not answer him, and lay my staff on the face of the child. ³⁰But the mother of the child said, As Jehovah liveth and as you live, I will not leave. So he arose and went with her. ³¹And Gehazi had gone on before them and had laid the staff upon the face of the child, but there was neither sound nor sign. Therefore he returned to meet him and told him, saying, The child has not awakened.

Gehazi's fruitless mission to the boy

---

i 4¹³ Heb., *Is it to speak for you to the king?*
j 4¹³ Having the support of a powerful clan, she had no need of royal patronage.
k 4¹⁶, ¹⁷ Cf. the close parallel in Gen. 18⁹⁻¹⁴.

Samaria Cycle of Elisha Stories

Resto-
ration
of the
boy to
life

[32]And when Elisha came into the house, there was the child lying dead on his bed. [33]He went in, therefore, and shut the door behind them two, and prayed to Jehovah. [34]And he went up and lay upon the child and put his mouth upon his mouth, and his eyes upon his eyes, and his hands upon his hands, and, as he lay upon[1] him, the flesh of the child became warm. [35]Then he returned and walked backward and forward in the house, and went up and lay upon him, and the child sneezed seven times; thereupon the child opened his eyes. [36]And he called Gehazi, and said, Call this Shunammite. So he called her. And when she came in to him, he said, Take up your son. [37]Then she went in, fell at his feet, and bowed to the ground, after that she took up her son and went out.

§ 86. Restoration of the Shunammite's Land, II Kgs. 8[1-6]

Samaria Cycle of Elisha Stories

The
Shu-
nam-
mite's
resi-
dence
in a
foreign
land at
Elisha's
advice

II Kgs. 8 [1]Now Elisha spoke to the woman, whose son he had restored to life, saying, Arise, go forth with your household, and sojourn wherever you can, for Jehovah hath ordered a famine; and moreover, it shall come upon the land seven years. [2]So the woman arose and acted according to the advice of the man of God: and she went with her household and sojourned in the land of the Philistines seven years. [3]And at the end of seven years the woman returned from the land of the Philistines; and she went forth to petition the king for her house and her land.

Resto-
ration
of her
for-
feited
lands

[4]Now the king happened to be saying to Gehazi the servant of the man of God, Tell me, I pray, all the wonderful things that Elisha has done. [5]And just as he was telling the king how he had restored to life the dead, the woman, whose son he had restored to life, petitioned the king for her house and for her land. And Gehazi said, My lord, O king, this is the woman and this is her son, whom Elisha restored to life. [6]And when the king asked the woman, she told him. So the king appointed for her a court-official,[m] saying, Restore all that was hers, together with the produce of the fields since the day that she left the land until now.

§ 87. Healing of Naaman the Leper, II Kgs. 5

Samaria Cycle of Elisha Stories

De-
mand
of the
king of
Aram

II Kgs. 5 [1]Now Naaman the commander of the army of the king of Aram was a man prosperous and highly esteemed by his master, because by him Jehovah had given victory to Aram;[n] but the man was a leper. [2]And

---

[1] 4[34] Lit., *crouched.* The Heb. verb means not *stretched,* as in the current translations, but rather that he drew up his limbs to correspond to the shorter limbs of the child.
§ 86 Cf. note § 85.
[m] 8[6] Heb., *eunuch.*
§ 87 Here Elisha is the prophet of Samaria, [3], is in close touch with the court and is attended not by the sons of the prophets but by Gehazi. The identification of the story with the Samaria cycle is assured. As in the case of most of these popular stories, it is impossible to determine under whose reigns the events took place.
[n] 5[1] So Luc. Into the Heb. has crept the marginal note, *a man of ability,* intended probably to explain the preceding descriptive adjective.

Samaria Cycle of Elisha Stories

the Arameans had gone forth in marauding bands and had brought away captive out of the land of Israel a little maiden, who became the servant of Naaman's wife. [3]And she said to her mistress, Would that my lord were with the prophet that is in Samaria! Then he would relieve him of his leprosy. [4]And one went in and told his lord, saying, Thus and thus said the maiden from the land of Israel. [5]And the king of Aram said, Go now, and I will send a letter to the king of Israel. So he departed and took with him ten talents of silver and six thousand shekels of gold and ten festal garments. [6]And he brought to the king of Israel the letter which ran: Now when this letter comes to you, be informed that I have sent Naaman my servant to you, that you may relieve him of his leprosy. [7]When, however, the king of Israel read the letter, he tore his clothes and said, Am I a god who can kill and make alive, that this man sends to me to relieve a man of his leprosy? But consider and see how he is seeking a quarrel with me!

Elisha's directions and Naaman's cure

[8]But when Elisha, the man of God, heard that the king of Israel had torn his clothes, he sent to the king, saying, Why have you torn your clothes? Let him come now to me and he shall know that there is a prophet in Israel! [9]So Naaman came with his horses and with his chariots and stood at the door of Elisha's house. [10]And Elisha sent a messenger to him, saying, Go and wash in the Jordan seven times, and your flesh shall again be well and clean. [11]But Naaman went away in a rage and said, I expected that he would come out to me and stand and call on the name of Jehovah his God, and wave his hand over the place, and relieve the leper. [12]Are not Amana[o] and Pharpar, the rivers of Damascus, better than all the waters of Israel? Could I not wash in them and be clean? So he turned and went away in a rage. [13]But his servants came near and spoke to him and said, If[p] the prophet had bidden you do some great thing, would you not have done it? How much rather then, when he says to you, 'Wash and be clean!' [14]Then he went down and dipped himself seven times in the Jordan, according to the command of the man of God, and his flesh became again like the flesh of a little child, and he was clean.

Naaman's gratitude to Elisha and his God

[15]And he returned to the man of God, together with all his retinue. And when he arrived, he stood before him and said, Behold now, I know that there is no God in all the earth, but in Israel; therefore, I pray, take a present from your servant. [16]But he said, As Jehovah liveth, before whom I stand, I will take nothing. And although he urged him to take it, he refused. [17]Then Naaman said, If not, at least let there be given to your servant a load of earth, what two mules can draw, for your servant will hereafter offer neither burnt-offering nor sacrifice to other gods, but to Jehovah. [18]In this thing may Jehovah pardon your servant, when my master goes into the temple of Rimmon to worship there, leaning on my arm, and I bow myself[q] in the temple of Rimmon, when he bows himself in the temple of Rimmon—may

---

[o] 5^{12} So Syr., Targ., and marginal reading of Heb.
[p] 5^{13} The present Heb., *my father*, is in all probability a corruption of, *if*, for the singular does not fit the context and *my father* is omitted in the Gk.
[q] 5^{18} So Gk. and Luc. Heb., *when I bow*.

Samaria Cycle of Elisha Stories

Jehovah pardon your servant in this thing.   ¹⁹And he said to him, Go in peace.

Gehazi's false representations

But when he had gone from him a little way, ²⁰Gehazi, the servant of Elisha the man of God, thought to himself, There my master has spared this Naaman the Aramean without accepting from him what he brought! As Jehovah liveth, I will run after him and take something from him. ²¹So Gehazi followed after Naaman. And when Naaman saw one running after him, he alighted from the chariot to meet him and said, Is all well? ²²And he said, All is well. My master has sent me, saying, 'Just now two young men of the sons of the prophets have come to me from the hill-country of Ephraim. Give them, I pray, a talent of silver and two festal garments.' ²³And Naaman said, Consent to take two talents. And he urged him, and bound two talents of silver in two bags, with two festal garments, and laid them on two of his servants, and they bore them before him. ²⁴But when he came to the hill, he took them from their hand and stored them in the house and let the men go on their way.

His condemnation and punishment

²⁵Then he went in. But when he stood by his master, Elisha said to him, Where do you come from, Gehazi? And he said, Your servant has not been anywhere at all. ²⁶And he said to him, Was I not in spirit with you when the man turned from his chariot to meet you? Is it a time to receive money and to receive garments,^r and oliveyards and vineyards, and sheep and oxen, and men-servants and maid-servants? ²⁷The leprosy therefore of Naaman shall cleave to you and to your descendants forever. Then he went from his presence a leper, as white as snow.

§ 88. The War with Moab, II Kgs. 3^4-27, cf. II Chr. 20^1-30

Samaria Cycle of Elisha Stories

Mesha's rebellion

II Kgs. 3 ⁴Now Mesha king of Moab was a sheepmaster;^s and he rendered regularly to the king of Israel a tribute of a hundred thousand lambs and the wool of a hundred thousand rams. ⁵But after Ahab died, the king of Moab rebelled against the king of Israel.

Perplexity of the invading kings

⁶And King Jehoram went out of Samaria at that time and mustered all Israel. ⁷Then he proceeded at once to send to Jehoshaphat the king of Judah, saying, The king of Moab has rebelled against me; will you go with me to fight against Moab? And he replied, I will come up; I am as you,

---

^r 5²⁶ Gk., Luc., and Lat. suggest as possibly original the reading, *And now you have taken the money and you may take the garments.*

§ 88 The preceding stories illustrate Elisha's activity in private life. These which follow were intended to present his public services. The later Ephraimite conception of the authority and rôle of the prophets, which appears in certain stories regarding Moses (Vol. I, §§ 82, 83) and especially in the closely related Samuel stories (§§ 6–8) is again prominent. Elisha's authority completely overshadows that of the king. By supernatural means he delivers the nation from its great crisis and calls to the kingship, not only Jehu, but also the heathen usurper Hazael. Many of the elements which characterize the Elijah stories reappear, indicating that they are not from the same writer but from a later age and school, strongly influenced by the older prophetic traditions and probably also acquainted with the Ahab history.

The present story is doubtless based on an older historical source from which ⁴⁻⁶ may have

---

^s 3⁴ *I.e.*, breeder of a kind of small sheep, highly esteemed for their wool. Cf. Am. 1¹.

Samaria Cycle of Elisha Stories

my people as your people, my horses as your horses. ⁸And he inquired, Which way shall we go up? And he answered, By the way of the Wilderness of Edom. ⁹So the king of Israel went with the king of Judah and the king of Edom. And when they made a circuit of seven days' journey, the army and the beasts that followed them had no water. ¹⁰And the king of Israel said, Alas! for Jehovah hath called these three kings together to deliver them into the hand of Moab! ¹¹But Jehoshaphat said, Is there no prophet of Jehovah here that through him we may inquire of Jehovah? And one of the king of Israel's servants answered and said, Elisha the son of Shaphat is here, who poured water on the hands of Elijah. ¹²And Jehoshaphat said, The word of Jehovah is with him. So the king of Israel and Jehoshaphat and the king of Edom went down to him.

¹³And Elisha said to the king of Israel, What have I to do with you? Go to the prophets of your father and to the prophets of your mother! But the king of Israel said to him, No; for Jehovah hath called these three kings together to deliver them into the hand of Moab. ¹⁴And Elisha said, As surely as Jehovah of hosts liveth, whose servant I am, were it not that I have regard for the presence of Jehoshaphat the king of Judah, I would pay no attention to you.ᵗ ¹⁵But now bring me a minstrel. And whenever the minstrel played, the powerᵘ of Jehovah came upon him. ¹⁶And he said, Thus saith Jehovah, 'I will make this torrent-bed full of cisterns.'ᵛ ¹⁷For thus saith Jehovah, 'Ye shall not see wind neither shall ye see rain; yet this torrent-bed shall be filled with water, so that ye yourselves together with your armyʷ and your beasts shall drink. ¹⁸But since this is only a slight thing in the sight of Jehovah, he also will deliver the Moabites into your hand. ¹⁹And ye shall smite every fortified cityˣ and fell all the good trees and stop up all the springs of water and destroy with stones all the good cultivated land.' ²⁰Accordingly in the morning, about the time when the offering is presented, water came suddenly from the direction of Edom, so that the country was filled with water.

²¹Now when all the Moabites had heard that the kings had come up to fight against them, they gathered together all who were able to bear arms and upward, and stood on the border. ²²But in the morning early, when the sun had risen on the water, the Moabites saw the water opposite them

(marginal notes:) Elisha's prediction and its realization

The victory over the Moabites

---

been quoted verbatim. The probability that it embodies reliable historical data is strengthened by the testimony of the Moabite stone. Cf. Appendix IV. By many scholars it is assigned to the Ahab history represented in I Kgs. 20, 22, but the evidence is very strong that it comes from the Samaria cycle of the Elisha stories, in the midst of which it is found. The dependence upon I Kgs. 22 is marked, cf. ⁷⁻¹¹ and I Kgs. 22¹⁴⁻⁷. The attitude of Elisha the one true prophet, in ¹³, is very similar to that of Micaiah in I Kgs. 22¹⁴⁻¹⁶. The reference in ¹¹ to Elisha as the disciple of Elijah and in ¹³ to the Baal cult introduced by Jezebel, furthermore indicates dependence upon the Elijah stories. Above all, while in I Kgs. 22 the chief interest is in Ahab and political events, here the house of Ahab is viewed with displeasure and the central figure is Elisha the prophet. Also instead of being a natural historical record, the marvellous element is very prominent, as in the other popular Elisha stories. In II Chr. 20 what appears to have originally been the same story has undergone still further transformation. Cf. § 110.

ᵗ 3¹⁴ Heb., *I would not look toward you nor see you.*

ᵘ 3¹⁵ Heb., *hand,* used here as frequently for power imparted. Luc. adds, *and they took a minstrel for him.* Possibly part of the text has here fallen out through a scribal error. The meaning, however, is clear.

ᵛ 3¹⁶ *I.e.,* every hollow in this dry *wady* shall be filled with water. Another possible reading is, *make this torrent-bed full of trenches.*

ʷ 3¹⁷ So Luc. The Heb., *cattle,* is a scribal variant. Cf. 9ᵇ.

ˣ 3¹⁹ So Gk. and Luc. The Heb. adds, *and every choice city.*

Samaria Cycle of Elisha Stories

as red as blood. ²³And they said, This is blood! The kings have surely
fought together ᵃ and they have smitten one another. Now therefore, Moab,
to the spoil! ²⁴And when they came to the camp of Israel, the Israelites
rose up and smote the Moabites, so that they fled before them; and they
went forward smiting the Moabites as they went.ᵇ ²⁵And they kept on destroying the cities; on all the good cultivated land they cast each his stone,
until they filled it; all the springs of water they stopped up, and felled all
the good trees, and they harried Moab until her sons were left in Kir-hareseth,ᶜ and the slingers surrounded and smote it.

The
desper-
ate
straits
of the
king of
Moab
 ²⁶But when the king of Moab saw that the battle was too fierce for him,
he took with him seven hundred men, armed with swords, to break through
against the king of Edom, but they could not. ²⁷Then he took his eldest
son, who was to reign in his place, and offered him for a burnt-offering upon
the wall. And there came great wrath against Israel, so that they departed
from him and returned to their own land.

§ 89. The Deception of the Arameans, II Kgs. 6⁸⁻²³

Samaria Cycle of Elisha Stories

Elisha's
skill as
a seer
 II Kgs. 6 ⁸Once while the king of Aram was at war with Israel, he took
counsel with his servants, saying, In such and such a place shall we lie in
ambush.ᵈ ⁹And the man of God sent to the king of Israel, saying, Beware
that you do not pass that place, for there the Arameans are concealed.ᵉ ¹⁰So
the king of Israel sent to the place of which the man of God had told him.
Thus he used to warn him, so that he could there be on his guard, not once
merely nor twice.

Resent-
ment
of the
king of
Aram
 ¹¹And the mind of the king of Aram was greatly disturbed by this. And
he called his servants and said to them, Will you not show me who has betrayed us to the king of Israel?ᶠ ¹²Then one of his servants said, No, my
lord, O king! but Elisha, the prophet in Israel, tells the king of Israel the
words that you speak in your bedchamber. ¹³And he said, Go and see
where he is, that I may send and get him. And it was told him, saying,
Behold he is in Dothan.

Elisha's
mirac-
ulous
capt-
ure of
the Ar-
amean
army
 ¹⁴Therefore he sent there horses and chariots and a great army: and they
came by night, and surrounded the city. ¹⁵And when the man of Godᵍ on
the next day rose early in the morning and went forth, there was an army

---

ᵃ 3²³ So Gk., Luc., and Targ., and a possible rendering of the present Heb.
ᵇ 3²⁴ So Gk. and Luc. and corrected Heb. text.
ᶜ 3²⁵ Reconstructing the Heb., with the aid of Luc. The present Heb. reads, *until in
Kir-hareseth they left its stones.*
  § 89 This story bears on its face the evidence that it is a popular tale intended to illustrate
Elisha's miraculous power. Details, such as the name of the kings of Israel and Aram and the
exact place and nature of the war, are conspicuously lacking. The prophet by his potent
prayer leads an army helplessly captive and dictates to the king of Israel, as to a servant, what
shall be done with the captives. Again the story centres about Samaria, so that its classification is reasonably certain. It was, however, probably at first current in a somewhat different
circle from the succeeding tradition.
ᵈ 6⁸ Reconstructing the doubtful Heb., with the aid of Luc., Syr., and Lat.
ᵉ 6⁹ So Gk. and the corrected Heb.
ᶠ 6¹¹ So Gk., Luc., and Old Lat. Present Heb., *who of ours is for the king of Israel.*
ᵍ 6¹⁵ Restoring the confused Heb. text.

Samaria Cycle of Elisha Stories

with horses and chariots about the city, so that his servant said to him, Alas, my master! What shall we do? ¹⁶And he answered, Fear not; for they who are with us are more than they who are with them. ¹⁷And Elisha prayed and said, Jehovah open his eyes, that he may see. Then Jehovah opened the eyes of the young man, and he saw how the mountain around about Elisha was full of horses and chariots of fire. ¹⁸And when they came down to him, Elisha besought Jehovah, saying, Smite this people, I pray, with blindness. And he smote them with blindness according to Elisha's petition. ¹⁹And Elisha said to them, This is not the way nor the city. Follow me, and I will bring you to the man whom you seek! So he led them to Samaria.

²⁰But as soon as they came to Samaria, Elisha said, Jehovah, open the eyes of these men, that they may see. And Jehovah opened their eyes, so that they saw, and there they were in the midst of Samaria. ²¹And the king of Israel said to Elisha, when he saw them, My father, shall I smite them? shall I smite them?ʰ ²²But he answered, You shall not smite them; would you smite those whom you have notⁱ taken captive with your sword and with your bow? Set bread and water before them, that they may eat and drink and go to their master. ²³So he prepared a great feast for them. And when they had eaten and drunk, he sent them back to their master. And the marauding bands of Aram came no more into the land of Israel.

Magnanimous liberation of the captives

§ 90. The Siege and Deliverance of Samaria, II Kgs. 6²⁴–7²⁰

Samaria Cycle of Elisha Stories

II Kgs. 6 ²⁴Now it came to pass after this, that Ben-hadad king of Aram assembled all his army and went up and besieged Samaria. ²⁵Then there was a great famine in Samaria, while they were besieging it, until an ass's head was sold for eighty shekels of silver, and a pintʲ of dove's dungᵏ for five shekels of silver. ²⁶And as the king of Israel was once passing by upon

Horrors of the famine within the city

---

h 6²¹ Or interpreting the Heb., according to Gk., and Syr., *shall I completely cut them down?*

i 6²² So Luc., who inserts the negative demanded by the context.

§ 90 The overshadowing importance of Elisha in this story which records national events, leaves little doubt that it belongs to the group of prophetic stories in which it is embedded. It also centres in Samaria. The statement in 6²³ that the marauding bands of the Arameans came no more into the land of Israel is hardly consistent with the present story, but this fact simply indicates that these stories have little real connection with each other and are topically rather than chronologically arranged. As with the other traditions, however, there are no clear data from which to determine the exact date of the events recorded. The Ben-hadad mentioned in 6²⁴ may either have been the second or the third Aramean ruler bearing that name. The name of the king of Israel also is not given, except by implication, since the story is found in a group which the editor evidently assigned to the reign of Jehoram. The mention of a famine, perhaps, connects it with the one referred to in 4³⁸ and 8¹⁻⁶. At the close of Jehoram's reign the Israelites and Arameans were at war, 9¹⁴, ¹⁵, but hostilities appear to have been confined to the east of Jordan. The two periods, when the Arameans completely overran Israel, were during the earlier years of Ahab and during the years following the revolution of Jehu. If historical, the incident, therefore, probably belongs to the reign of Ben-hadad III and Jehoahaz or Joash of Israel. Or possibly—as has been strongly urged—the tradition has combined the popular version of the famine in the days of Elijah (I Kgs. 17) with that of the defeat of the Arameans in the days of Ahab (I Kgs. 20), and associated both with Elisha.

j 6²⁵ Heb., the *fourth part of a kab*, about a pint.

k 6²⁵ Various emendations have been suggested: *carob pods*, or, *sour wine*.

Samaria Cycle of Elisha Stories

the wall, a woman cried to him, saying, Help, my lord, O king.   ²⁷And he said, Ii Jehovah does not help you, whence can I help you?   Out of the threshing-floor or out of the winepress?   ²⁸However, the king said to her, What is the trouble with you?   And she answered, This woman said to me, 'Give your son, that we may eat him to-day, and we will eat my son to-morrow!'   ²⁹So we boiled my son, and ate him.   And I said to her on the next day, 'Give your son, that we may eat him;' but she has hidden her son.

The king's resolve to kill Elisha

³⁰And when the king heard the words of the woman, he tore his clothes— and as he was passing by upon the wall, the people looked and saw that he wore sackcloth within on his naked flesh—³¹and he said, may God do to me whatever he will, if to-day the head of Elisha the son of Shaphat remains on his shoulders!

Elisha's prediction of plenty

³²Now Elisha was sitting in his house with the elders beside him.   And the king sent a man from before him.   But before the messenger came to him, he said to the elders, See how this murderous villain has sent to take off my head.   Look! when the messenger comes, shut the door and hold the door fast against him; is not the sound of his master's feet behind him?   ³³And while he was still talking with them, the king[1] came down to him and said, See, this is the evil that comes from Jehovah!   Why should I wait for Jehovah any longer?   7 ¹But Elisha said, Hear the word of Jehovah; thus saith Jehovah, 'To-morrow about this time shall a peck[m] of fine meal be sold for a shekel and two pecks of barley for a shekel in the gate of Samaria.'   ²Then the captain on whose hand the king leaned answered the man of God and said, Behold, if Jehovah himself should make windows in heaven, could this thing be?   And he said, You yourself shall see it with your own eyes, but shall not eat of it.

The lepers' discovery that the besieging Arameans had fled

³Now there were four leprous men at the entrance of the gate; and they said one to another, Why do we sit here until we die?   ⁴If we say, 'We will enter into the city,' then famine is in the city, and we shall die there; but if we sit still here, we die also.   Now therefore come and let us go over to the army of the Arameans.   If they save us alive, we shall live; and if they kill us, we shall but die.   ⁵So they rose up at twilight to go over to the camp of the Arameans.   And when they came to the outermost part of the camp of the Arameans, there was no man there, ⁶for the Lord had made the army of the Arameans hear a noise of chariots and of horses and of a great army, so they said to one another, Surely the king of Israel has hired against us the kings of the Hittites and the kings of Muçri[n] to come upon us.   ⁷Therefore they arose and fled in the twilight and left their tents, and their horses and their asses, even the camp as it was, and fled for their life.   ⁸And when these lepers came to the outermost part of the camp, they went into one tent, and ate and drank and carried away silver and gold and clothing and went

---

[1] 6³³ Translating according to the demands of the context.   A scribe has mistaken the original for the very similar Heb. word, *messenger*.

[m] 7¹ Heb., *seah*.

[n] 7⁶ A later scribe has read for *Muçri* the more familiar *Miçraim* (Egypt).   The people of Muçri, however, were near neighbors of the Hittites in Northern Syria, while the Egyptians were too distant for practical alliance.

and hid it. Then they came back and entered into another tent, and carried away its contents also and went and hid it.

Incredulity of the king

9 Then they said to one another, We are not doing right; this day is a day
of good news, while we are keeping still. If we wait until morning light,
punishment will overtake us. Now therefore come, let us go and inform
the palace. 10 So they came and called the watchmen[o] at the city gate and
told them, saying, We came to the camp of the Arameans, and behold there
was no one there and no voice of man, but the horses had been tied and
asses were tied and their[p] tents were as they had been. 11 And the watchmen at the city gate[q] called and announced it to the palace within. 12 And
the king arose in the night, and said to his servants, I will now tell you what
the Arameans have done to us. They know that we are hungry; therefore
they have gone out of the camp to hide themselves in the field, thinking,
'When they come out of the city we shall take them alive and get into the
city.'

Confirmation of the report

13 But one of his servants spoke and said, Let some men take five of the
remaining horses which survive in the city; if they live, they are as all the
multitude of Israel that survive here; if they perish, they are as all the multitude of Israel that are consumed.[r] Therefore let us send and see. 14 So
they took two mounted men,[s] and the king sent them after the army of the
Arameans, saying, Go and see. 15 And they went after them to the Jordan,
and behold all the way was full of garments and vessels which the Arameans
had cast away in their haste. And the messengers returned and told the
king.

Realization of Elisha's prediction

16 And the people went out and plundered the camp of the Arameans.
So a peck of fine meal was sold for a shekel, and two pecks of barley for a
shekel, just as Jehovah had said. 17 And the king appointed the captain
on whose hand he leaned to take charge of the gate; but the people trod
upon him in the gate so that he died, just as the man of God had said, when
the king came down to him. 18 Also it came to pass as the man of God had spoken
to the king, saying, Two pecks of barley will be sold for a shekel and a peck of fine
meal for a shekel, to-morrow about this time at the gate of Samaria; 19 and the captain
answered the man of God, and said, Now, behold, if Jehovah himself should make
windows in heaven, could this thing be? and he said, You yourself shall see it with
your own eyes, but shall not eat of it. 20 So it came to pass to him; for the people trod
upon him at the gate so that he died.[t]

---

o 7[10] Heb., *watchman*, but the plural is demanded by the subsequent context.

p 7[10] So Gk. and Luc. The Heb. has simply, *the*.

q 7[11] So Gk., Luc., Syr., and Targ. Heb., *he called*.

r 7[13] The construction is broken and the sense very obscure. The above reconstruction at least brings out the probable meaning of the passage.

s 7[14] Restoring the original text. The present Heb. is tautological.

t 7[18-20] The original narrative evidently ends with [17]. Vss. [18-20] are later editorial additions, [18, 19] repeating in expanded form what has already been stated in [16], and [20] being but a repetition of [17a].

§ 91. Elisha and Hazael, II Kgs. 8⁷⁻¹⁵

Samaria Cycle of Elisha Stories

Elisha's messages to Ben-hadad and Hazael

II Kgs. 8 ⁷Now Elisha came to Damascus. And Ben-hadadᵘ the king of Aram was sick. And when it was told him, saying, The man of God has come here, ⁸the king said to Hazael, take a present in your hand and go to meet the man of God and inquire of Jehovah through him whether or not I shall recover of this sickness? ⁹So Hazael went to meet him and took a present with him, all kinds of precious things from Damascus, forty camel loads. When he came he stood before him and said, Your son Ben-hadad king of Aram has sent me to you to inquire, ' Shall I recover of this sickness?' ¹⁰And Elisha said to him, Go, say to him, ' You shall surely recover!' but Jehovah hath showed me that he will nevertheless die. ¹¹And he looked intently at him, until he was ashamed;ᵛ and the man of God wept. ¹²And Hazael said, Why does my lord weep? And he answered, Because I know the evil that you will do to the Israelites: their strongholds will you set on fire, their young men will you slay with the sword, their little ones will you dash in pieces, and their women with child will you rip up. ¹³And Hazael said, But what is your servant, the dog, that he should do this great thing? And Elisha answered, Jehovah hath showed me that you shall become king over Aram.

Assassination of Ben-hadad by Hazael

¹⁴And when he departed from Elisha and came to his master, he asked, What did Elisha say to you? And he answered, He told me that you would recover. ¹⁵But the next day he took the coverlet, dipped it in water, and spread it over his face, so that he died. And Hazael became king in his place.

§ 92. Elisha's Farewell Blessing and Death, II Kgs. 13¹⁴⁻²¹

Samaria Cycle of Elisha Stories

Elisha's dying prediction of Israel's victories

II Kgs. 13 ¹⁴Now when Elisha fell sick of the sickness of which he was to die, Joash the king of Israel came down to him, wept over him and said, My father, my father! the chariots of Israel and its horsemen! ¹⁵And Elisha said to him, take bow and arrows; and he took bow and arrows. ¹⁶And he said to the king of Israel, Lay your hand upon the bow. And when he had laid on his hand, Elisha laid his hands upon the king's hands. ¹⁷And he

---

§ 91 Elisha figures here in the same commanding rôle as in the preceding stories. He is represented as in fact, although not in the letter, carrying out the divine command to Elijah, recorded in I Kgs. 19. Cf. note § 71. Like all the Elisha stories this tradition has no real connection with those which precede and follow, and it leaves out many details which an historian would deem important, as for example, a more detailed description of Hazael and the events preceding this incident.

ᵘ 8⁷ Ben-hadad II. Cf. chronological chart after p. 199.

ᵛ 8¹¹ Heb., *And he steadied his countenance and set (it) until he was ashamed.* The meaning apparently is that he stared Hazael out of countenance. Otherwise it may be translated, *And he stared immovably before him and became horrified in the extreme.* In this case the reference would be to the prophet's ecstasy.

§ 92 This section has no real connection with its immediate context in II Kgs., for it is inserted after the death of Joash (who figures in it) has been recorded. It is evidently a passage taken by the editor from the Samaria cycle of Elisha stories, and placed in 13 because of its reference to Joash. Originally it doubtless stood at the end of the group of stories in 2¹⁻8¹⁵, of which it is the natural conclusion.

Samaria Cycle of Elisha Stories

said, Open the window toward the east. And when he opened it, Elisha said, Shoot; and he shot. And he said, Jehovah's arrow of victory, even the arrow of victory over Aram; for you should have smitten the Arameans in Aphek until you had destroyed them. ¹⁸Thereupon he said, Take arrows. And when he had taken them, he said to the king of Israel, Smite on the ground; and he smote three times and then ceased. ¹⁹And the man of God was angry with him and said, You should have smitten five or six times; then you would have smitten Aram until you had destroyed it, but as it is you will smite Aram but three times.

²⁰And when Elisha died they buried him. Now the bands of the Moabites were wont to invade the land each year. ²¹And while they were burying a man, they suddenly spied a marauding band. And they cast the man into the sepulchre of Elisha and went on their way,ʷ but as soon as the man touched the bones of Elisha, he revived and stood on his feet.

[margin: The potency of his healing power]

IV

FROM JEHU TO THE FALL OF SAMARIA, II Kgs. 9, 10, 13²⁻¹³, 22-25, 14⁸⁻²⁹, 15⁸⁻³¹, 17

§ 93. The Prophetic Revolution Led by Jehu, II Kgs. 9¹–10²⁷

Prophetic Jehu History

II Kgs. 9 ¹Now Elisha the prophet called one of the sons of the prophets and said to him, Gird up your loins, take this flask of oil in your hand and go to Ramoth in Gilead. ²And when you arrive there look for Jehuᵃ the son of Jehoshaphat, the son of Nimshi, and go in and make him rise up from among his kinsmen and bring him into an inner chamber. ³Then take the flask of oil and pour it on his head and say, 'Thus saith Jehovah, " I have

[margin: Anointing of Jehu at Elisha's command]

ʷ 13²¹ Making a slight correction demanded by the text.

From Jehu to the Fall of Samaria.—As far as II Kgs. 17 the larger northern kingdom receives the greater attention. The narrative, however, is disjointed and fragmentary. No one source except the Jehu history is quoted at length. For the majority of the reigns the editor only epitomizes the data which he drew from his older source, occasionally expanding or supplementing his summaries with quotations from the state annals, which probably were known to him only through the Chronicles of the Kings of Israel to which he constantly refers his readers for further information. Cf. Introd., pp. 16, 17.

The period is significant because it witnessed the grimly practical application of the principles laid down by Elijah, the appearance of the new school of the prophets represented by Amos and Hosea, the final downfall of the proud northern kingdom, and the amalgamation of those diverse racial elements which later reappeared as the Samaritans.

§ 93 Regarding the classification of this important narrative there is considerable difference of opinion. 9¹⁻¹³ may come from the Elisha stories and constitute a companion piece to the account of Elisha's interview with Hazael, § 91; but the subsequent record of Jehu's revolutionary measures implies that he was supported by the prophets of Jehovah, and Jehu's words in 15ᵇ find their natural preface in 1⁻¹³. It is also characterized by a directness and explicitness regarding details which are lacking in the Elisha stories. On the other hand, there are many points of contact between these chapters and the Elijah stories. The kings are designated in both, not by their

---

ᵃ 9² The *Jaua son of Humri*, twice mentioned on the inscriptions of Shalmaneser II among the Palestinian rulers who brought tribute to the Assyrians. Cf. for the Assyrian record, Appendix V.

Prophetic Jehu History

anointed thee king over Israel."' Then open the door and flee without delay. ⁴So the young man (the servant of the prophet)ᵇ went to Ramoth in Gilead. ⁵And just as he arrived, the commanders of the army were sitting together. And he said, I have a word for you, O commander. And Jehu said, To which of us all? And he said, To you, O commander. ⁶Then he arose and went into the house. And [the young man] poured the oil on his head and said to him, Thus saith Jehovah, the God of Israel, 'I have anointed thee king over Jehovah's people Israel. ⁷And thou shalt cut offᶜ the house of Ahab thy master, that I may avenge the blood of my servants the prophets and the blood of all the servants of Jehovah upon Jezebel. ⁸For the whole house of Ahab must perish; and I will cut off from Ahab every male, and him who is kept in and him who is at large in Israel. ⁹And I will make the house of Ahab like the house of Jeroboam the son of Nebat and like the house of Baasha the son of Ahijah. ¹⁰And the dogs shall eat Jezebel in the field of Jezreel and none shall bury her.'ᵈ Then he opened the door and fled.

Procla-
mation of
Jehu as
king

¹¹When Jehu came out to the servants of his lord, they askedᵉ him, Is all well? Why did this insane fellow come to you? And he said to them, You know the man and his talk. ¹²And they said, It is false! Tell us now. And he said, Thus and thus he spoke to me, saying, 'Thus saith Jehovah, "I have anointed thee king over Israel."' ¹³Then they quickly took each his garment, laid it at his feet and on the bare stairs,ᶠ and blew the trumpet, crying, Jehu is king!

His
plan to
slay
Jeho-
ram

¹⁴So Jehu the son of Jehoshaphat, the son of Nimshi, conspired against Joram. Now Jehu,ᵍ together with all Israel, was defending Ramoth in Gilead against Hazael king of Aram, ¹⁵but King Jehoram had returned to be healed in Jezreel of the wounds which the Arameans had given him, when he fought with Hazael king of Aram.ʰ And Jehu said, If it be in your mind,ⁱ then let none escape from the city to go to tell it in Jezreel. ¹⁶Then Jehu

---

titles, as in the Ahab history, but by their names. The persecutions instigated by Jezebel, the prevalence of Baalism, and the predicted fate of the house of Ahab are alone referred to in the Elijah stories. The events recorded in this section are the natural sequel to I Kgs. 18 and 21.

On the other hand, the interest in II Kgs. 9, 10, is primarily political. Ahab and his house are not viewed as adversely as in I Kgs. 17–19, 21. While there is a prophetic flavor to the present narrative, its point of view resembles most clearly that of the Ahab history in I Kgs. 20 and 22. They also share certain peculiar idioms in common. For these reasons 9¹⁻¹⁰²⁷ are by many classified with I Kgs. 20 and 22. Their many variations, as well as their close relation with the Elijah stories, point, however, to an originally independent source, which may be designated, *the prophetic Jehu history.* The author appears to have been acquainted, either in oral or written form, with both the Ahab history and the Elijah stories. Being a prophet he is in general in sympathy with the movement inaugurated by Jehu, but to all the usurper's bloody acts he does not give his full approval. The revolution proved an important turning-point in Israel's history, for it brought not only the overthrow of Baalism, but a series of political disasters which nearly proved the ruin of the northern kingdom.

ᵇ 9⁴ Evidently an explanatory scribal note.

ᶜ 9⁷ So Gk. and Luc. Heb., *smite.*

ᵈ 9⁸⁻¹⁰ᵃ The characteristic idioms (cf. I Kgs. 21²⁰ᵇ⁻²²) and the variations from the explicit command in ³ indicate that this expansion of the original brief oracle is from the late prophetic editor.

ᵉ 9¹¹ So all the versions except the Heb., which has a singular verb.

ᶠ 9¹³ Cf. Mt. 21⁷. The apparent meaning is that Jehu was standing upon the stairs which probably led to the inner chamber.

ᵍ 9¹⁴ Heb., *Joram,* probably a scribal error for, *Jehu.*

ʰ 9¹⁴ᵃ, ¹⁵ᵇ The contents of this explanatory note are again inserted very awkwardly in 8²⁸, ²⁹. The present context appears to contain the original quotation from what was probably a still older source, as is shown by the name *Jehoram* instead of *Joram.*

ⁱ 9¹⁵ *I.e.,* to make me king, as the anointing by a prophet and their act in acclaiming him king implied.

Prophetic Jehu History

mounted his chariot and went to Jezreel, for Joram lay there. And Ahaziah king of Judah had come down to see Joram.

¹⁷Now the watchman was standing on the tower of Jezreel, when he saw the cloud of dustʲ about Jehu, as he came, and said, I see a cloud of dust. And Joram said, Take a horseman and send him to meet them that he may inquire whether all is well?ᵏ ¹⁸So one went on horseback to meet him and said, Thus saith the king, 'Is all well?' And Jehu replied, What have you to do with welfare? Turn about and follow me. So the watchman reported, The messenger came to them, but comes not back. ¹⁹Then he sent out a second horseman who came to them and said, Thus saith the king, 'Is all well?' And Jehu answered, What have you to do with welfare? Turn about and follow me. ²⁰So the watchman reported, He also came to them but comes not back; however, the driving is like the driving of Jehu the son of Nimshi, for he is wont to drive furiously.

²¹Then Joram said, Make ready. And as soon as they had made ready his chariot, Joram king of Israel and Ahaziah king of Judah set out, each in his chariot, and they went to meet Jehu and found him in the field of Naboth the Jezreelite. ²²And when Joram saw Jehu, he said, Is all well Jehu? And he answered, How can all be well, as long as the whoredoms of your mother Jezebel and her witchcrafts are so many? ²³Then Joram turned about to flee and said to Ahaziah, Treachery, Ahaziah? ²⁴But Jehu, being already armed, shot his bow and struck Joram between his shoulders, so that the arrow went through his heart and he sank down in his chariot. ²⁵Then Jehu said to Bidkar his captain, Take him up and cast him in the field of Naboth the Jezreelite; for I remember how that, when I and you rode together after Ahab his father, Jehovah pronounced this judgment upon him: ²⁶'Surely I saw yesterday the blood of Naboth and his sons,' saith Jehovah; 'and I will requite thee in this plot,' saith Jehovah. Now therefore take and cast him into this plot, according to the word of Jehovah.

²⁷But when Ahaziah the king of Judah saw this, he fled in the direction of Beth-gannin. And Jehu followed after him, with the command, Him also! Smite him in the chariot! And they smoteˡ him at the ascent of Gur, which is by Ibleam. But he fled to Megiddo and died there. ²⁸And his servants carried him in a chariot to Jerusalem, and buried him in his sepulchre with his fathers in the city of David.ᵐ

³⁰Then Jehu came to Jezreel. And as soon as Jezebel heard of it, she painted her eyes,ⁿ attired her head, and looked out at the window. ³¹And as Jehu came in at the gate, she said, Is all well, you Zimri, your master's murderer? ³²But he looked up to the window and said, Who is on my side? who? And two or three eunuchs looked at him. ³³And he said, Throw her down. And they threw her down so that some of her blood

His approach to Jezreel

Joram's death by the hand of Jehu

Ahaziah's death

Jezebel's fate

ʲ 9¹⁷ So Gk. The Heb. is doubtful. The current translation is, *company* or *multitude.*
ᵏ 9¹⁷ Heb., *whether it is peace;* but this was the ordinary Semitic salutation. Cf. 4²⁶ and Johns, *Bab. and Assyr. Laws, Contracts, and Letters,* p. 309.
ˡ 9²⁷ So Syr. In the Heb. the words, *And they smote him,* have fallen out of the text.
ᵐ 9²⁸ The editor here inserts, ²⁹, the synchronism of Ahaziah's succession.
ⁿ 9³⁰ *I.e.,* painted her eyelashes and brows to beautify herself, as do modern Arab women with a pulverized sulphide of antimony, mixed with oil.

Prophetic Jehu History

was spattered on the wall and on the horses, and he[o] trod her under foot.
34 Then he went in and ate and drank. Thereupon he gave the command,
See now to this cursed woman and bury her, for she is a king's daughter.
35 But when they went to bury her, they found no more of her than the skull,
the feet, and the hands. 36 When, therefore, they came back and told him,
he said, This is the word of Jehovah, which he spoke by his servant Elijah
the Tishbite, saying, 'In the plot of Jezreel shall the dogs eat Jezebel's flesh,
37 and the body of Jezebel shall be as dung on the face of the field in the plot
of Jezreel, so that they cannot say, "This is Jezebel."'

Jehu's instructions regarding Ahab's descendants

10 1 Now Ahab had seventy descendants[p] in Samaria. And Jehu wrote
letters and sent to Samaria,[q] to the rulers of the city, to the elders, and those
who had charge of the descendants of Ahab, saying, 2 Now as soon as this
letter comes to you, since you have with you your master's sons, and chariots
and horses, fortified cities[r] and arms; 3 choose the best and most capable of
your master's sons, and set him on his father's throne and fight for your
master's house. 4 But they were exceedingly afraid and said, Behold, the
two kings could not stand before him, how then shall we stand? 5 And he
who was over the household and he who was over the city, together with the
elders and the guardians, sent to Jehu, saying, We are your servants and
we will do all that you bid us; we will not make any one king; do what you
please. 6 Then he wrote a second letter to them, saying, If you are on my
side and if you wish to obey me, then take each of you the head of your
master's son[s] [entrusted to you], and meet me at Jezreel to-morrow at
this time. Now the king's sons, seventy in all, were with the great men of
the city, who brought them up.

Slaughter of all the descendants and friends of Ahab

7 And as soon as the letter came to them, they took the king's sons and
slew them, seventy in all, and put their heads in baskets and sent them to
him to Jezreel. 8 And when the messenger came and told him, saying, They
have brought the heads of the king's sons, he said, Lay them in two heaps
at the entrance of the gate until the morning! 9 And in the morning he went
out and stood and said to all the people, You are fair-minded: to be sure I
conspired against my master and slew him, but who smote all these? 10 Know
now that of the word of Jehovah, which Jehovah spoke against the house of
Ahab by his servant Elijah, nothing shall fail of fulfilment. 11 Thereupon Jehu
smote all who remained of the house of Ahab in Jezreel, together with all his
great men and his kinsmen[t] and his priests, until he left him none remaining.

Slaughter of the Judean princes

12 Then Jehu set out on the way to Samaria. And as he was at Beth-eked[u]
of the shepherds on the way, 13 Jehu met with the kinsmen of Ahaziah king of
Judah, and said, Who are you? And they answered, We are the kinsmen
of Ahaziah, and we have come to visit the children of the king and the chil-

---

[o] 9[33] So Heb., but the other versions read, *they*.

[p] 10[1] Heb., *sons*. Vss. [2, 3] imply that they were sons of Jehoram. Ahab is mentioned because the revolution was directed against practices instituted by him.

[q] 10[1] So Luc. and Lat. Heb., *Jezreel*.

[r] 10[2] So all versions except the Heb., which has, *city*.

[s] 10[6] Slightly reconstructing the text by the aid of Luc.

[t] 10[11] So Luc. Heb., *familiar friends*.

[u] 10[12] Following a slightly corrected text.

Prophetic Jehu History

dren of the queen-mother. ¹⁴And he said, Take them alive. And they took them alive and slew them at the pit of Beth-eked, forty-two men, so that not one of them was left.

¹⁵And when he had departed from there he found Jehonadab the son of Rechab coming to meet him. And he saluted him and said to him, Is your heart in sincere sympathy with my heart,ᵛ as mine is with yours? And Jehonadab answered, It is. *Then Jehu said*, If it be, give me your hand. And he gave him his hand; and he took him up to him into the chariot. ¹⁶And he said, Come with me, and see my zeal for Jehovah. So heʷ made him ride in his chariot. Compact with Jehonadab the Rechabite

¹⁷And when he came to Samaria, he smote all who remained to Ahab in Samaria, until he had destroyed all, according to the word of Jehovah which he spoke to Elijah. ¹⁸Then Jehu gathered all the people together and said to them, Ahab served Baal a little; but Jehu will serve him much. ¹⁹Now therefore call all the prophets of Baal, all his worshippersˣ and all his priests; let none remain behind; for I will make a great sacrifice to Baal; whoever shall remain behind shall not live. But Jehu did it with the secret purpose of destroying the worshippers of Baal. ²⁰Then Jehu said, Proclaim a solemn assembly for Baal. And they proclaimed it. ²¹And Jehu sent through all Israel, and all the worshippers of Baal came, so that there was not a man left who did not come. And when they had come into the temple of Baal, so that the temple of Baal was filled from one end to the other, ²²he said to the one who was in charge of the wardrobe, Bring out garments for all the worshippers of Baal. And he brought out garments for them. ²³Then Jehu, with Jehonadab the son of Rechab, went into the temple of Baal and said to the worshippers of Baal, Search, and look that there may not be here with you any of the servants of Jehovah, but only worshippers of Baal. ²⁴Thereupon heʸ went in to offer sacrifices and burnt-offerings. Now Jehu had appointed eighty men outside with the command, The man who allows any of the men, whom I entrust into your hands, to escape, his life shall be for the life of him. ²⁵And as soon as he had finished offering the burnt-offering, Jehu said to the runners and to the captains, Go in, and slay them, let none come forth. And they put them to the sword, and the runners and the captains cast themᵃ out, and went into the sanctuaryᵇ of the temple of Baal. ²⁶Then they brought out the asherahᶜ from the temple of Baal and burned it, ²⁷and broke down the pillar of Baal and destroyed the temple of Baal and made it a draught-house to this day. Destruction of the worshippers and temple of Baal

---

ᵛ 10¹⁵ Following the Gk. and Luc.

ʷ 10¹⁶ So Gk., Luc., and Syr. Heb., *they.*

ˣ 10¹⁹ Possibly a scribe first added in the margin, *all his worshippers*, for this has been incorporated into the text of the Heb. and Luc., in different order.

ʸ 10²⁴ So Gk. Heb., *they*, evidently referring to Jehu and Jehonadab, but cf. ¹⁶.

ᵃ 10²⁵ The object of the verb is wanting and the construction of the Heb. is awkward. The plausible emendation has been suggested which gives the reading, *and they cast the asherahs to the ground.*

ᵇ 10²⁵ Heb., *into the city.* But this gives no sense. A probable emendation gives the above reading.

ᶜ 10²⁶ Heb., *macceboth, pillars;* but the versions have a singular and the statement that it was burned implies that it was not stone but wood. The reference to the pillars in ²⁷ favors the conclusion that this originally read as above.

§ 94. Jehu's Reign, II Kgs. 10²⁸⁻³⁶

Late Prophetic Summary

Jehu's religious reforms

II Kgs. 10 ²⁸Thus Jehu put an end to Baalism in Israel; ²⁹only from the sins of Jeroboam the son of Nebat with which he led Israel into sin, from these, the golden calves in Bethel and in Dan, Jehu did not depart. ³⁰And Jehovah said to Jehu, Because thou hast done well in carrying out my will, and hast done to the house of Ahab according to all that was in my heart, thy sons even to the fourth generation shall sit on the throne of Israel. ³¹But Jehu took no heed to walk in the law of Jehovah, the God of Israel, with all his heart: he departed not from the sins of Jeroboam with which he led Israel into sin.

Political history

³²In those days Jehovah began to loathe Israel,ᵈ and Hazael smote them in all the territory of Israel, ³³from the Jordan toward the east, all the land of Gilead,ᵉ the Gadites, the Reubenites, and the Manassites, from Aroer by the valley of the Arnon, including Gilead and Bashan. ³⁴Now the other acts of Jehu and all that he did, and all his brave deeds, are they not recorded in the Chronicles of the Kings of Israel? ³⁵And Jehu slept with his fathers, and they buried him in Samaria. And Jehoahaz his son became king in his place. ³⁶And the time that Jehu reigned over Israel in Samaria was twenty-eight years.

§ 95. Jehoahaz's Reign, II Kgs. 13¹⁻⁹

Late Prophetic Summary

The disastrous Aramean invasions

II Kgs. 13 ¹In the twenty-third year of Joash the son of Ahaziah king of Judah, Jehoahaz the son of Jehu became king over Israel in Samaria; and he reigned seventeen years. ²And he did that which displeased Jehovah, and the sins of Jeroboam the son of Nebat with which he led Israel into sin— he did not depart from them. ³And the anger of Jehovah was kindled against Israel and he delivered them continually into the hand of Hazael king of Aram, and into the hand of Ben-hadad the son of Hazael. ⁴Then Jehoahaz besought Jehovah, and Jehovah hearkened to him; for he saw the oppression of Israel, how that the king of Aram oppressed them. ⁵Therefore Jehovah gave Israel a saviour,ᶠ so that they escaped from the hand of the Arameans, and the Israelites could dwell in their homes as formerly. ⁶Nevertheless they did not depart from the sins of the house of Jeroboam, with which he led Israel into sin, but walked therein. Also the asherah in Samaria remained standing. ⁷And he left to Jehoahaz of the people not

---

§ 94 This section throughout is cast in the language and reflects the point of view of the late prophetic editor. The statement in ³² is probably based on information drawn from an earlier source.

ᵈ 10³² So Lat. Heb., *to cut off in Israel.* The error probably arose because of the similarity of the two Heb. words, the scribe adopting the more familiar.

ᵉ 10³² The older source probably read, *all Gilead.* The later editor has added the territory which he conceived of as belonging to Israel, with the result that Gilead is mentioned twice.

§ 95 With the possible exception of ⁷, all of the data in this section are recast in the words of the late prophetic editor. It records in general terms the disastrous period of Aramean dominance to which the prophet Amos refers in his opening address.

ᶠ 13⁵ *I.e.,* the Assyrians, whose attacks from the east broke the power of the Arameans. Cf. chron. chart after p. 199.

Late Prophetic Summary

more than fifty horsemen, ten chariots, and ten thousand footmen; for the
king of Aram destroyed them and made them like the dust in the threshing.ᵍ
⁸Now the other acts of Jehoahaz and all that he did and his brave deeds,
are they not recorded in the Chronicles of the Kings of Israel? ⁹And Jehoahaz slept with his fathers and they buried him in Samaria. And Joash
his son became king in his place.

§ 96. **Events of Jehoash's Reign, II Kgs. 13¹⁰⁻¹³, ²²⁻²⁵, 14⁸⁻¹⁶, II Chr. 25¹⁷⁻²⁴**

Late Prophetic Summary

II Kgs. 13 ¹⁰In the thirty-seventh year of Joash king of Judah, Jehoash *Partial*
the son of Jehoahaz became king over Israel in Samaria, and reigned six- *deliv-*
teen years. ¹¹And he did that which displeased Jehovah; he did not depart *erance*
from all the sins of Jeroboam the son of Nebat with which he led Israel into *the*
sin, but he walked therein. ²²Now Hazael king of Aram oppressed Israel *Ara-*
all the days of Jehoahaz. ²³But Jehovah was gracious to them and had *means*
compassion on them, and turned again to them, because of his covenant
with Abraham, Isaac, and Jacob, and would not destroy them nor as yet cast
them from his presence.

Annals of Israel

²⁴But when Hazael king of Aram died, Ben-hadad his son became king *Recov-*
in his place. ²⁵Then Jehoash the son of Jehoahaz took again from Ben- *ery of*
hadad the son of Hazael the cities which he had taken in war from Jehoahaz *capt-*
his father. Three times Joash smote him and thus recovered the cities of *cities*
Israel.

14 ⁸Then Amaziah sent messengers to Jehoash the son of Jehoahaz, *Ama-*
son of Jehu king of Israel, saying, Come, let us measure strength with each *ziah's*
other.ʰ ⁹But Jehoash the king of Israel sent to Amaziah king of Judah, *upon*
saying, The thistle in Lebanon sent to the cedar on Lebanon, saying, 'Give *Jehoash*
your daughter to my son as wife.' But a wild beast on Lebanon passed by *dis-*
and trod down the thistle. ¹⁰You have indeed smitten Edom and your head *defeat*
has been turned.ⁱ Enjoy your honor and stay at home, for why should
you plunge yourself into trouble, so that you and Judah with you will fall?

ᵍ 13⁷ Lit., *for treading.* The figure is that of the rocky oriental threshing-floor on which
the grain was thrown and then trampled to dust by oxen drawing heavy sledges. Luc. inserts ²³
after ⁷. The deliverance from the Aramean attacks according to ²² did not, however, come until
after the reign of Jehoahaz.

§ 96 The editor's summary appears in 13¹⁰, ¹¹, ²², ²³ and 14¹⁵, ¹⁶. In 13¹², ¹³ (or in Luc.
more appropriately at the end of the chapter) a concluding summary is given of Jehoash's
reign, although important events in which he participated are given in the passages which follow.
Furthermore, in 14¹⁵, ¹⁶ practically the same formulas reappear. The slight variations in the
first passage from the editor's usual form confirm the other indications that it is a repetition due
to the error of a scribe who overlooked the passage 14¹⁵, ¹⁶. In 13²⁴, ²⁵ and 14⁸⁻¹⁴ is found a
brief, direct account of the chief wars in the reign of Jehoash.

The record of Amaziah's unsuccessful attack on Jehoash is written from the Northern
Israelitish point of view and probably comes from the annals of Israel. In his summary, 14¹⁵,
the editor refers to the record, which he found incorporated in the Chronicles of the Kings of
Israel and which he apparently quotes almost in its entirety.

ʰ 14⁸ Heb., *look each other in the face.*
ⁱ 14¹⁰ Heb., *your heart* (or *mind*) *has lifted you up.*

Annals of Israel

¹¹But Amaziah would not hear. So Jehoash king of Israel went up, and he and Amaziah king of Judah measured strength with each other at Bethshemesh, which belongs to Judah. ¹²And Judah was defeated by Israel, so that they fled each to his home. ¹³And Jehoash king of Israel took Amaziah king of Judah, the son of Jehoash, the son of Ahaziah, captive at Bethshemesh. And he brought him downʲ to Jerusalem and tore down the wall of Jerusalem to the distance of four hundred cubits, from the Gate of Ephraim to the Corner Gate. ¹⁴And he took all the gold and silver, and all the vessels that were found in the temple of Jehovah, and in the treasures of the king's palace, the hostages also, and returned to Samaria.

End of Jehoash's reign ¹⁵Now the other acts of Jehoash which he did and his mighty deeds, and how he fought with Amaziah king of Judah, are they not recorded in the Chronicles of the Kings of Israel? ¹⁶And Jehoash slept with his fathers, and was buried in Samaria with the kings of Israel. And Jeroboam his son became king in his place.

§ 97. Jeroboam II's Reign, II Kgs. 14²³⁻²⁹

Late Prophetic Summary

Extension of the boundaries of Israel **II Kgs. 14** ²³In the fifteenth year of Amaziah the son of Joash king of Judah, Jeroboam the son of Joash king of Israel became king in Samaria and reignedᵏ forty-one years. ²⁴And he did that which displeased Jehovah: he did not depart from all the sins of Jeroboam the son of Nebat with which he led Israel into sin. ²⁵He restored the boundary-line of Israel from the entrance to Hamath to the sea of Arabah, according to the word of Jehovah, the God of Israel, which he spoke by his servant Jonah the son of Amittai, the prophet who was of Gath-hepher. ²⁶For Jehovah saw the very bitter affliction of Israel, that none was shut up nor left at large, and that there was no helper for Israel. ²⁷But Jehovah had not determined to blot out the name of Israel from under heaven, so he saved them through Jeroboam the son of Joash.

Conclusion ²⁸Now the other acts of Jeroboam, and all that he did, and his brave deeds, how he carried on war and how he recovered Damascus and Hamath for Israel,¹ are they not recorded in the Chronicles of the Kings of Israel? ²⁹And Jeroboam slept with his fathers, even with the kings of Israel. And Zechariah his son became king in his place.

ʲ 14¹³ So Luc., Lat., and the parallel in II Chr. 25²³. Heb., *came.*

§ 97 Again the editor dismisses an important reign with a brief summary of the chief events. The reign of Jeroboam II was signalized by the appearance of the two prophets Amos and Hosea during the last decade of his long and prosperous rule. In many ways it was the most significant epoch since the days of David and Solomon. The sermons of Amos and Hosea give a vivid picture of its social and religious conditions. Cf. Vol. III *in loco.*

ᵏ 14²³ So Luc. and the usual formula elsewhere. Certain words have fallen out of the Heb.

¹ 14²⁸ So Syr. The Heb., *for Judah by Israel,* makes no sense and is manifestly corrupt. Burney's reconstruction (*Notes on Kings*, p. 320) is simple and gives a good reading, *and how he fought with Damascus and how he turned away the wrath of Jehovah from Israel.*

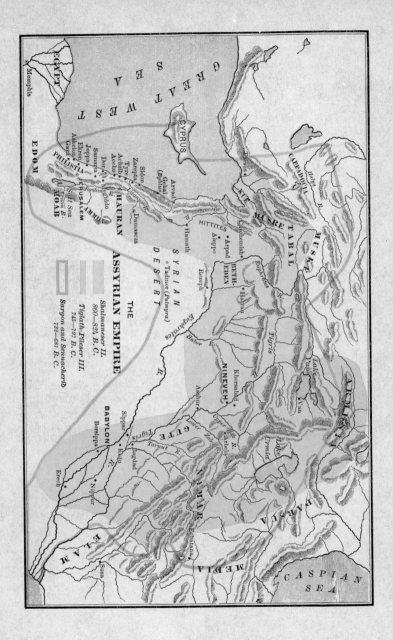

EGYPT

Memphis

GREAT WEST SEA

CYPRUS

EDOM

PHILISTIA
Gaza
Askelon
Ekron
Jopoa
Samaria
Dor
Accho
Tyre
Achzib
Zarephta
Sidon
Gebal (Byblus)
Arvad

JERUSALEM
AMMON
MOAB
Salt Sea
Arnon R.
Jordan R.
HAURAN
Damascus
Litany R.
Orontes R.

Tadmor (Palmyra)

Hamath
Aleppo
Arpad
Carchemish
EDEN
BETH.
Rezeph

HITTITES

SYRIAN DESERT

Euphrates

Euphrates R.

Habor R.

Harran

KUE

MUSRE TABAL

MUSRE

CAPADOCL

Iris R.

Tarsus

Lake Van

Van

ARMENIA

Lake Urmia

Tigris

Khorsabad
NINEVEH
Khorsabad R.
Ashur
Greater Zab R.
Lesser Zab R.

GUTU
MEDIA

PARSUA

SUMMAR

Diala R.

Bagdad
Cutha
Sippar
Tarnut R.
BABYLON
Borsippa
Nipfur
Erech
Tigris R.
Euphrates

ELAM
Susa

CASPIAN SEA

THE
ASSYRIAN EMPIRE

Shalmaneser II.
860—824 B. C.
Tiglath-Pileser III.
745—727 B. C.
Sargon and Sennacherib
722—681 B. C.

§ 98. Reigns of Zechariah, Shallum, Menahem, and Pekahiah, II Kgs. 15[8-26]

Annals of Israel

II Kgs. 15 [8]In the thirty-eighth year of Azariah king of Judah, Zechariah the son of Jeroboam began to reign in Samaria, and he reigned six months. [9]And he did that which displeased Jehovah, as his fathers had done; he did not depart from the sins of Jeroboam the son of Nebat with which he led Israel into sin. [10]And Shallum the son of Jabesh conspired against him, and put him to death in Ibleam[m] and became king in his place. Zechariah's policy and death

[11]Now the other acts of Zechariah are already recorded in the Chronicles of the Kings of Israel. [12]This was the word of Jehovah which he spoke to Jehu, saying, Thy sons to the fourth generation shall sit upon the throne of Israel. And so it came to pass. [13]Shallum the son of Jabesh, began to reign in the thirty-ninth year of Uzziah king of Judah; and he reigned one month in Samaria. [14]Then Menahem the son of Gadi went up from Tirzah and came to Samaria and put Shallum the son of Jabesh to death in Samaria, and became king in his place. [15]Now the other acts of Shallum and his conspiracy which he made, are already recorded in the Chronicles of the Kings of Israel. Realization of prophecy / Menahem's conspiracy

[16]Then Menahem smote Tappuah,[n] and all who were in it and in its entire territory from Tirzah on; because they did not open the gates to him he smote it, and all the women in it with child he ripped up. Cruelty to the citizens of Tappuah

[17]In the thirty-ninth year of Uzziah king of Judah, Menahem the son of Gadi became king over Israel and reigned ten years in Samaria. [18]And he did that which displeased Jehovah: he did not depart from the sins of Jeroboam the son of Nebat with which he led Israel into sin. Evil policy

[19]During his days[o] Pul[p] [Tiglath-Pileser III], the king of Assyria, invaded the land. And Menahem gave Pul a thousand talents of silver, that he might help him to establish his sway over the kingdom.[q] [20]And Menahem commanded[r] all Israel, even all the men of wealth, to give to the king of Assyria each fifty shekels of silver. So the king of Assyria turned back and remained no longer in the land. Tribute to Tiglath-Pileser III

[21]Now the other acts of Menahem and all that he did, are they not recorded in the Chronicles of the Kings of Israel? [22]And Menahem slept with his fathers, and Pekahiah his son became king in his place. Conclusion

[23]In the fiftieth year of Azariah king of Judah, Pekahiah the son of Menahem became king over Israel in Samaria, and reigned two years. [24]And he displeased Jehovah, he did not depart from the sins of Jeroboam the son of Nebat, with which he led Israel into sin. [25]And Pekah the son of Remaliah, his captain,[s] conspired against him and smote him in Samaria in the castle of the royal palace;[t] and with him were fifty Gileadites; and he slew him and became king in his place. [26]Now the other acts of Pekahiah and all that he did are already recorded in the Chronicles of the Kings of Israel. Pekah's conspiracy against Pekahiah

---

§ 98 Into his framework the late prophetic editor has introduced certain brief but important notices which probably came originally from the annals of Israel.

m 15[10] So Luc. The Heb. gives no sense.

n 15[16] So Luc. A town of Manasseh, Josh. 16[8], 17[7, 8]. Heb., *Tipsah* on the Euphrates.

o 15[18, 19] So Gk. and Luc. The Heb. text is corrupt.

p 15[19] The Assyrian king *Pul*, officially known as Tiglath-Pileser III. For his own account of this expedition. cf. Appendix VI.

q 15[19] Heb., *that his hand might be with him to strengthen the kingdom in his hand.*

r 15[20] Slightly correcting the text in conformity with Heb. idiom.

s 15[25] Or, *adjutant.* Cf. I Kgs. 9[22].

t 15[25] The Heb. adds two untranslatable words, possibly proper names, *Argob and Arieh.* The Lat. has, *near Argob and Arie.* It has been plausibly conjectured that they have been introduced by mistake from [29].

§ 99. Reign of Pekah and the Invasion of Tiglath-Pileser III,
II Kgs. 15²⁷⁻³¹

Annals of Israel

Pekah's evil policy

II Kgs. 15 ²⁷In the fifty-second year of Azariah king of Judah, Pekah the son of Remaliah began to reign over Israel in Samaria and reigned twenty years. ²⁸And he displeased Jehovah: he did not depart from the sins of Jeroboam the son of Nebat with which he led Israel into sin.

Conquests of Tiglath-Pileser III

²⁹During the days of Pekah king of Israel Tiglath-Pileser king of Assyria came and captured Ijon, Abel-beth-maacah, Janoah, Kedesh, Hazor, Gilead, and Galilee,ᵘ all the land of Naphtali, and carried their inhabitants captive to Assyria.

Hoshea's conspiracy

³⁰Then Hoshea the son of Elah made a conspiracy against Pekah the son of Remaliah and put him to death and became king in his place in the twentieth year of Jotham the son of Uzziah. ³¹Now the other acts of Pekah and all that he did are already recorded in the Chronicles of the Kings of Israel.

§ 100. Reign of Hoshea and the Fall of Samaria, II Kgs. 17¹⁻⁶, 18⁹⁻¹²

Annals of Israel

Hoshea's submission to Assyria

II Kgs. 17 ¹In the twelfth year of Ahaz king of Judah, Hoshea the son of Elah began to reign in Samaria over Israel and reigned nine years. ²And he displeased Jehovah, yet not as the kings of Israel who were before him. ³Against him came Shalmaneser king of Assyria; and Hoshea became subject to him and brought him tribute.

Later Treason and imprisonment

⁴But when the king of Assyria found Hoshea guilty of conspiracy—for he had sent messengers to Seweᵛ king of Egypt and brought no tribute to the king of Assyria, as he had done each year before—the king of Assyria shut him up and confined him in prison.

Annals of Judah

Final capture of Samaria and deportation of its inhabitants

⁵Then the king of Assyria came up against all the land, and went up to Samaria, and besieged it three years. ⁶In the ninth year of Hoshea, the king of Assyriaʷ took Samaria, and carried the Israelites away captive to Assyria and placed them

II Kgs. 18 ⁹In the fourth year of Hezekiah—that is the seventh year of king Hoshea the son of Elah of Israel—Shalmaneser king of Assyria came up against Samaria and besieged it. ¹⁰At the end of three years they conquered it; in the sixth year of Hezekiah—that is the ninth year of Hoshea king of Israel—was Samaria captured. ¹¹And the king of

---

§ 99 Again the brief account of the campaign of Tiglath-Pileser III was evidently taken by the editor from his older source. For the Assyrian record, cf. Appendix VI. Is. 7³⁻⁹ also supplements the meagre records of this reign.

ᵘ 15²⁹ *Gilead and Galilee* may have been added by a later hand, for they are territorial divisions, while the preceding names are those of towns in Naphtali. Cf. map opp. p. 255.

§ 100 Vss. ³, ⁴ are the direct sequel of 15³⁰. Vss. ⁵, ⁶, however, in view of the statement in ⁶ that Samaria fell in the ninth year of Hoshea and of the parallel in 18⁹ᵇ⁻¹¹, are not the sequel to ³, ⁴, but record different events in the same campaign. Therefore they are probably from different sources. The account of Samaria's capture seems to have been drawn by the editor from the annals of Judah, and slightly recast by him, and then introduced here to supplement the meagre record found in the northern annals. This conclusion is strengthened by the fact that the original parallel to ⁵, ⁶ in 18⁹ᵇ⁻¹¹ was clearly taken from the Judean source. For the Assyrian account of the conquest of Samaria in 722 B.C., cf. Appendix VII.

ᵛ 17⁴ Heb., *So*. Probably to be identified with Shabako or else with an Egyptian general, Sib'u, defeated by Sargon in 720 B.C.

ʷ 17⁶ *I.e.*, Sargon.

Annals of Israel

in Halah and on the Habor, the river of Gozan, and in the cities of the Medes.

Annals of Judah

Assyria carried the Israelites away captive and placed them in Halah and on the Habor, the river of Gozan, and in the cities of the Medes, [12]because they obeyed not the voice of Jehovah their God, but transgressed his covenant, even all that Moses the servant of Jehovah commanded, and would not heed nor do it.

§ 101. Causes of the Downfall of Northern Israel, II Kgs. 17⁷⁻²³

Late Prophetic Summary

II Kgs. 17 [7]Now this came to pass because the Israelites had sinned against Jehovah their God, who had brought them up from the land of Egypt from the power of Pharaoh king of Egypt, and had feared other gods, [8]and followed the customs of the nations whom Jehovah had cast out from before the Israelites, and the kings of Israel, which they had appointed. [9]And the Israelites devised things[x] that were not right against Jehovah their God and built for themselves high places in all their cities, from the watchtower even to the fortified city, [10]and set up for themselves pillars and asherahs on every high hill and under every green tree, [11]and offered sacrifices there (on all the high places) as did the nations whom Jehovah had carried away before them, and they did wicked things to provoke Jehovah to anger. [12]They also served idols, in regard to which Jehovah had said to them, Ye shall not do this thing. [13]Yet Jehovah gave warning to Israel and Judah by all his prophets and seers, saying, Turn from your evil ways and keep my commands and my statutes according to all the law which I commanded your fathers and which I imparted to you by my servants the prophets. [14]However, they would not hear, but were wilful,[a] as were their fathers, who did not believe in Jehovah their God. [15]And they rejected his statutes and his covenant that he had made with their fathers, and his warnings that he had given them, and followed vanity and became vain, and imitated the example of the nations about them, concerning whom Jehovah had charged them that they should not do like them. [16]And they neglected all the commands of Jehovah their God and made for themselves molten images, even two calves and made an asherah and worshipped all the host of heaven and served Baal. [17]And they made their sons and their daughters pass through the fire, and used divination and sorcery, and sold themselves so that they did that which displeased

(marginal note:) Israel's idolatry and apostasy

---

§ 101 To the brief account of Israel's downfall the editors of Kings have appropriately appended an epilogue emphasizing the moral lessons illustrated by that significant event. Vss. ²¹⁻²³ reiterate the familiar judgment of the editor upon the history of Israel as a whole. In ⁷⁻¹⁶ᵃ, ¹⁷ᵇ, ¹⁸, Israel's sins are recapitulated in greater detail. The language throughout is that of the late prophetic school, but it is also strikingly similar at many points to the sermons of Jeremiah, cf. ¹³ and Jer. 18¹¹, 25⁵, 35¹⁵; ¹⁵ and Jer. 2⁵. This perhaps indicates that these opening verses are from a still later hand. At least ¹⁶ᵇ, ¹⁷ᵃ are later additions, for not only do they assign to Israel the sins peculiar to Judah in the days of Manasseh, but they describe types of idolatry different from those already given in ⁹⁻¹². The immediate sequel of ¹⁸ is ²¹. Vss. ¹⁹, ²⁰ are clearly a later addition from the period of the Babylonian exile, when Judah was suffering a like penalty with Israel.

x 17⁹ The RV, *did secretly*, is not tenable. Gk., *clad themselves in*. A change of one letter gives the above reading.

a 17¹⁴ Heb., *hardened their neck like the neck of their fathers*.

Late Prophetic Summary

Jehovah to provoke him to anger. ¹⁸Therefore Jehovah was very angry with Israel and removed them out of his sight; there was nothing left except the tribe of Judah.

Judah's apostasy

¹⁹Also Judah did not keep the commands of Jehovah their God, but followed the customs of Israel which they had introduced, ²⁰so that Jehovah rejected the entire Israelitish race and afflicted them and gave them up to those who plundered them until he had cast them from his sight.

Jeroboam's evil religious policy

²¹And when he had torn Israel from the house of David and they had made Jeroboam the son of Nebat king, Jeroboam drove Israel from following Jehovah and made them commit great sin. ²²Thus the Israelites walked in all the sins of Jeroboam which he committed: they departed not from them, ²³until Jehovah removed Israel from his sight, as he spoke by all his servants the prophets. So Israel was carried away out of their own land to Assyria to this day.

§ 102. Origin and Religion of the Samaritans, II Kgs. 17²⁴⁻⁴¹

Annals of Israel

Foreign colonists

II Kgs. 17 ²⁴Then the king of Assyria brought people from Babylon, Cuthah,[b] Avva,[c] Hamath, and Sepharvaim,[d] and settled them instead of the Israelites in the cities of Samaria. And they took possession of Samaria and dwelt in its cities.

Their religious worship

²⁵Now at the beginning of their dwelling there they did not revere Jehovah. Therefore Jehovah sent lions among them, which were continually killing some of them. ²⁶So when it was told the king of Assyria, saying, The nations which you have carried away and settled in the cities of Samaria do not know the law of the god of the land; therefore he hath sent lions among them, and now they are slaying them because they do not know the law of the god of the land, ²⁷the king of Assyria gave command, Carry thither one of the priests whom I[e] brought from there; and let him[f] go and dwell there and let him teach them the law of the god of the land. ²⁸So one of the priests, whom they had carried away from Samaria, came and dwelt in Bethel and taught them how they should revere Jehovah.

---

§ 102 This section is generally recognized to be composite. Vss. ²⁴⁻²⁸ contain a straightforward statement of the political and religious fortunes of the people transported from different parts of the Assyrian empire to take the place of the exiled Israelites. There is no condemnation of the resulting religious practices. The facts are simply stated as in the annals. The point of view (cf. ², ⁹, ²⁵) is in general that of an early rather than a later age. The same is true of ²⁹⁻³⁴ᵃ, ⁴¹, although by some these verses are assigned to a later editor. At least they embody older data. In ³⁴, however, the statement that they revered Jehovah is reversed, and the thought and literary style of ³⁴ᵇ⁻⁴⁰ are those of an exilic editor. The reference also is not, as in ²⁴⁻³⁴ᵃ, ⁴¹, to the foreign colonists, but apparently to the later Samaritan people, the lineal descendants of the Israelites. The author also alludes to the later written law and is greatly influenced by priestly ideas and language.

b 17²⁴ The Kutu of the Assyrian inscriptions. It is identified with *Tell-Ibrahim*, northeast of Babylon.

c 17²⁴ Not yet definitely identified. Probably a town in Northern Syria. Cf. 19¹³ and the Ivva of 18³⁴.

d 17²⁴ The context suggests that this also was a Syrian town. Cf. 18¹¹. Otherwise it may be the Heb. designation of the two Sippars: Sippar of Shamash and Sippar of Anunitum. The latter hypothesis is supported by ³¹.

e 17²⁷ So Luc. Heb., *you*.

f 17²⁷ So Luc., Syr., and Lat.

Annals of Israel

29But each of the peoples had made gods of their own and set them up in temples of the high places which the Samaritans had made, each people in their cities in which they dwelt: 30the men of Babylon had made an image of Succoth-benoth,[g] and the men of Cuth had made Nergal,[h] and the men of Hamath had made Ashima,[i] 31and the Avvites had made Nibhaz and Tartak; and the Sepharvites burnt their children in the fire to Adrammelech [Adar is king] and Anammelech [Anu is king] the gods of Sepharvaim. 32But when they began to revere Jehovah they made for themselves from their own number priests of the high places, who sacrificed for them in the temples of the high places. 33Thus, while they revered Jehovah, they also served their own gods, after the manner of the nations from which they had been carried away. 34To this day they do according to the earlier custom. They do not revere Jehovah nor do they act according to their statutes or their ordinances or the law or the command which Jehovah commanded the children of Jacob, whom he named Israel, 35with whom Jehovah made a covenant and charged them saying, Ye shall not fear other gods, nor bow yourselves to them, nor serve them, nor sacrifice to them; 36but Jehovah, who brought you up out of the land of Egypt with great power and with an outstretched arm, him shall ye fear, and to him shall ye bow yourselves and to him shall ye sacrifice; 37and the statutes and the ordinances, and the law and the commandment which he wrote for you, ye shall faithfully observe forever, and ye shall not revere other gods; 38and the covenant that I have made with you, ye shall not forget, neither shall ye revere other gods, 39but Jehovah your God shall ye revere; and he will deliver you from all your enemies. 40However, they did not hearken, but rather they did according to their earlier customs. 41So while these peoples revered Jehovah, they also served their graven images; their children likewise, and their children's children—as did their fathers, so do they to this day.

Their mixed heathen and Jehovah religion

---

[g] 17³⁰ Apparently the title of a Babylonian deity. The identification is still uncertain: Marduk, the consort of Marduk, Ishtar, and Saturn (revising the text) have each been suggested.

[h] 17³⁰ The god of war, of pestilence, and of the lower world, especially worshipped at Kutu.

[i] 17³⁰ Marginal reading of the Heb., *god of Sepharvaim*. The expression may be a scribal addition.

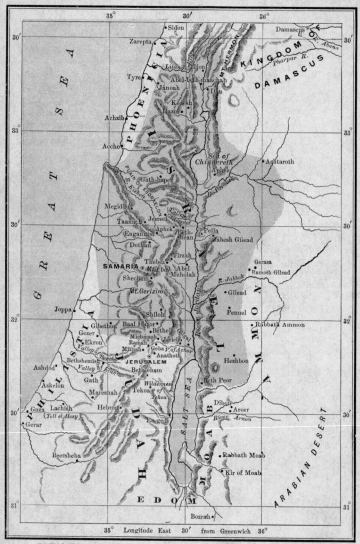

ISRAEL AND JUDAH AFTER THE DIVISION OF
THE HEBREW EMPIRE.

HISTORY OF JUDAH

I KGS. 14[21]—II KGS. 15[37] (*exclusive of data relating to Northern Israel*), II CHR. 11[5]–27[8]

HISTORY OF JUDAH FROM THE DIVISION
OF THE EMPIRE TO THE FALL
OF JERUSALEM

I

FROM REHOBOAM TO AHAZ, I Kgs. 14^{21}–15^{24}, $22^{4,\ 29\text{-}36,\ 41\text{-}50}$, II Kgs. $3^{4\text{-}27}$, $8^{16\text{-}29}$, 9^{29}, 11, 12, $14^{1\text{-}22}$, $15^{1\text{-}7,\ 32\text{-}38}$, II Chr. 11^5–27^9

§ 103. Rehoboam's Reign, I Kgs. $14^{21\text{-}24}$, II Chr. $11^{5\text{-}23}$

Late Prophetic Summary	*Chronicler's Ecclesiastical History*	
ngth	I Kgs. 14	II Chr. 11 ⁵Now Rehoboam dwelt in Jerusalem,	Rehoboam's
ho-am's gn	²¹Now Rehoboam, the son of Solomon, became king in Judah. Rehoboam was forty-one years old when he began to reign, and he reigned seventeen years in Je-	and built cities for defence in Judah. ⁶He built Bethlehem, Etam, Tekoa, ⁷Bethzur, Soco, Adullam, ⁸Gath, Mareshah, Ziph, ⁹Adoraim, Lachish, Azekah, ¹⁰Zorah, Aijalon, and Hebron, which are in Judah and in Benjamin—fortified cities. ¹¹And he fortified the strongholds and put commanders in them and stores of provisions and oil and wine. ¹²Also in each city he put shields and spears and thus made them exceedingly strong. And Judah and Benjamin belonged to him.	boam's fortifications

---

History of Judah.—For two centuries, until the Assyrians came into direct contact with Judah, its national life ran on uneventfully. One dynasty occupied the throne continuously and its crises and religious movements were of secondary magnitude and importance compared with those of the greater Northern Kingdom. The editor of Kgs. simply gives brief epitomes of events, introducing occasionally short quotations from the annals, or from the expanded Chronicles of the Kings of Judah. One event, the revolution and repair of the temple in the days of Joash, receives fuller notice. Here the quotation appears to have been from the temple records.

Since the direct interests of the Chronicler are all centred in Judah, he naturally seeks to supplement the meagre record of Kgs. This he does apparently by drawing from the Midrash of the Kings of Judah and possibly from older annalistic sources which may have been at his command. In general the picture which he gives is traditional rather than historical, didactic rather than exact, although at certain points he seems to have preserved some important facts.

§ 103 The late prophetic editor of Kgs. simply gives in his own language a chronological statement and his usual general estimate of the reign. The Chronicler, however, appears to have quoted at length from some earlier post-exilic source, which, like the book of Kgs. (*e.g.*, I Kgs. 14²¹), represented Rehoboam as king simply of Judah, cf. ⁵, ¹⁴, ¹⁷. The awkward additions of Benjamin in ¹⁰ᵇ, ¹²ᵇ, ²³ᵇ are in accord with the later theory of the Chronicler. The quotation is probably from the Midrash of the Book of the Kings, but in ⁵⁻¹²ᵃ, ¹⁸⁻²³ still older data seem to have been incorporated, which may have been derived from the pre-exilic Chronicles of the Kings of Judah.

*Late Prophetic
Summary*

Chronicler's Ecclesiastical History

rusalem, the city which Jehovah had chosen out of all the tribes of Israel to put his name there. And his mother's name was Naamah the Ammonitess.ᵃ

²²And Judahᵇ did that which displeased Jehovah, and they aroused his anger with the sins which they committed, more than all that their fathers had done. ²³They also built for themselves high places, pillars, and asherahs, on every high hill and under every green tree. ²⁴There were also temple prostitutesᵈ in the land. They did according to all the abominations of the nations which Jehovah drove out before the Israelites.

Heathen practices of the Judeans

¹³And the priests and the Levites who were in all Israel resorted to him out of all their different localities. ¹⁴For the Levites left their common pasture-lands and their possessions and came to Judah and Jerusalem, because Jeroboam and his sons declared them ineligible as priests to Jehovah. ¹⁵And he appointed for himself priests for the high places, for the he-goats, and for the calves which he had made. ¹⁶And after them there came from all the tribes of Israel such as had set their hearts on seeking Jehovah, the God of Israel, to Jerusalem to sacrifice to Jehovah the God of their fathers. ¹⁷So they strengthened the kingdom of Judah, and made Rehoboam the son of Solomon strong for three years, for they walked three years in the way of David and Solomon.

¹⁸And Rehoboam took as wife, Mahalath, the daughter of Jerimoth the son of David, and of Abihailᶜ the daughter of Eliab the son of Jesse. ¹⁹And she bore him sons: Jeush, Shemariah, and Zaham. ²⁰And after her he married Maacah the daughter of Absalom. And she bore him Abijah, Attai, Ziza, and Shelomith. ²¹And Rehoboam loved Maacah the daughter of Absalom more than all his wives and his concubines (for he married eighteen wives and sixtyᵉ concubines and begot twenty-eight sons and sixty daughters). ²²And Rehoboam appointed Abijah the son of Maacah at the head as the crown prince among his brothers, for he purposedᶠ to make him king. ²³He also wisely distributed all his sons throughout the different districts of Judah and Benjamin, to the different cities, and gave them provisions in rich abundance and secured for them many wives.

Popularity of the sanctuary at Jerusalem

Rehoboam's family

ᵃ I Kgs. 14²¹ The Gk. in 12²⁴ᵃ (Swete) reads, *the daughter of Nahash the king of Ammon.*
ᵇ I Kgs. 14²² Gk. and Luc., *Rehoboam.*
ᶜ II Chr. 11¹⁸ So Gk. The Heb. makes Abihail the second wife of Rehoboam, but indicates that but one is intended.
ᵈ I Kgs. 14²⁴ Cf. Vol. I, § 44, note ʲ.
ᵉ II Chr. 11²¹ Gk., Lat., and Jos., *thirty.*
ᶠ II Chr. 11²² So Gk. The verb has fallen out in the Heb.

§ 104. **Shishak's Invasion, I Kgs. 14²⁵⁻³¹, II Chr. 12**

Annals of Judah

Chronicler's Ecclesiastical History

I Kgs. 14 ²⁵Now in the fifth year of King Rehoboam Shishak k i n g of Egypt c a m e up against Jerusalem. ²⁶And he took away the treasures of the temple of Jehovah and the treasures of the royal palace[g]— he took all away. He also took away all the shields of gold which Solomon had made. ²⁷And King R e h o b o a m made in their place shields of brass and gave them into the charge of the com m a n d e r s of the guards, who kept the door of the roy- al palace. ²⁸And as often as the king went into the tem- ple of Jehovah, the guards took them and brought them b a c k i n t o the guard-room. ²⁹Now the other acts of Rehoboam and all that he did, are they not recorded in the Chronicles of the Kings of Judah?

II Chr. 12 ¹Now when the rule of Rehoboam was established and he was strong, he forsook the law of Jehovah and all Israel with him. ²Thereupon Shishak king of Egypt came up against Jerusalem in the fifth year of King Rehoboam, because they had acted falsely toward Jehovah, ³with twelve hundred chariots, and sixty thousand horsemen. And the people were without number, who came with him out of Egypt: Lybians, Sukkites, and Ethiopians. ⁴And he took the fortified cities of Judah, and came to Jerusalem.

⁵Then Shemaiah the prophet came to Rehoboam and to the princes of Judah, who had gathered to- gether to Jerusalem because of Shishak, and said to them, Thus saith Jehovah, 'Ye have abandoned me, therefore I have also abandoned you to Shishak.' ⁶Then the princes of Israel and the king humbled themselves and said, Jehovah is righteous. ⁷And when Jehovah saw that they humbled themselves, the word of Jehovah came to Shemaiah, saying, They have hum- bled themselves. I will not destroy them, but I will grant them a partial deliverance and my wrath shall not be poured out upon Jerusalem through Shishak. ⁸Nevertheless they shall become subject to him, that they may know how to distinguish between my ser- vice and the service of the earthly kingdoms.

⁹So Shishak king of Egypt came up against Jeru- salem and took away the treasures of the temple of Jehovah and the treasures of the royal palace—he took all away. He also took away the shields of gold which Solomon had made. ¹⁰And King Rehoboam made in their place shields of brass, and gave them in- to the charge of the commanders of the guards, who kept the door of the royal palace. ¹¹And as often as the king went into the temple of Jehovah, the guards came and took them and brought them back into the guard-room.

Shi- shak's ad- vance

Shemaiah's proph- ecy

Plunder of the temple

Shishak's plun- der of temple and palace

War with Jero- boam

---

§ 104 The short account of Shishak's invasion in I Kgs. 14²⁵⁻²⁸ and probably the note regard- ing the war with Jeroboam in ³⁰ were clearly taken from an older source which was doubtless the annals of Judah. This brief record has been expanded in II Chr. 12 into a typical midrash, possibly derived by the Chronicler from his midrashic source. The outcome turns not upon the ordinary fortunes of war, but upon the guilt and repentance of Rehoboam and his people and the favor of Jehovah, secured through the mediation of a prophet. For the Egyptian record of Shishak's invasion, cf. Appendix III.

g I Kgs. 14²⁶ Gk. and Luc. add here, *and the golden shields which David took from the ser- vants of Hadadezer king of Zobah and brought to Jerusalem*. It may represent the original text. Cf. II Sam. 8⁷.

Annals of Judah

³⁰And there was war between Rehoboam and Jeroboam continually. ³¹And Rehoboam slept with his fathers and was buried with his fathers in the city of David.[h] And Abijam his son became king in his place.[i]

Chronicler's Ecclesiastical History

¹²But because he humbled himself, the wrath of Jehovah turned from him, so as not to destroy him completely—also in Judah things were found in good condition. ¹³So King Rehoboam strengthened himself in Jerusalem and reigned, for Rehoboam was forty-one years old when he began to reign, and he reigned seventeen years in Jerusalem, the city which Jehovah had chosen out of all the tribes of Israel to put his name there. And his mother's name was Naamah the Ammonitess. ¹⁴And he did that which was evil, because he set not his heart to seek Jehovah.

¹⁵Now the acts of Rehoboam, first and last, are they not written in the histories[j] of Shemaiah the prophet and of Iddo the seer ?[k]

Judah under Reho-boam

§ 105. Abijah's (Abijam's) Reign, I Kgs. 15¹⁻⁸, II Chr. 13¹–14¹ᵃ

Late Prophetic Summary

Abi-jam's evil policy

I Kgs. 15 ¹Now in the eighteenth year of King Jeroboam, the son of Nebat, Abijam began to reign over Judah. ²Three years he reigned in Jerusalem; and his mother's name was Maacah the daughter of Abishalom.[l] ³And he

Chronicler's Ecclesiastical History

II Chr. 13 ¹In the eighteenth year of King Jeroboam Abijah began to reign over Judah. ²He reigned three years in Jerusalem, and his mother's name was Micaiah the daughter of Uriel of Gibeah. And there was war between Abijah and Jeroboam. ³And Abijah began the war with an army of brave warriors, consisting of four hundred thousand picked men, and Jeroboam set the battle in array against him with eight hundred thousand picked men, who were brave warriors.

⁴And Abijah stood up on Mount Zemaraim, which is in the hill-country of Ephraim, and said, Hear me, O Jeroboam and all Israel: ⁵Ought you not to know that Jehovah, the God of Israel, gave the kingdom over Israel to David forever, even to him and to his sons by a covenant of salt ?[m] ⁶Yet Jeroboam the son of Nebat, the servant of

Abi-jah's war with Jero-boam

His con-demna-tion of Jero-boam's relig-ious policy

---

[h] I Kgs. 14³¹ So Gk., Luc., Syr., and Chr. parallel. The Heb. adds from 14²¹, *And his mother's name was Naamah the Ammonitess.*

[i] I Kgs. 14³¹ So 15¹, ⁷. Luc. and Chr., *Abijah.* The latter appears to have been the original form. The alteration may have been made by a scribe to distinguish it from the name of Jero-boam's son. Cf. 14¹.

[j] II Chr. 12¹⁵ Or, *words.*

[k] II Chr. 12¹⁵ The Heb. adds the meaningless phrase, *entered in the genealogies.* The Gk., *and his deeds,* is more intelligible but it perhaps simply indicates that the text was corrupted at an early date.

§ 105 Again the brief facts given by the late prophetic editor of Kgs. have in Chr. been expanded into a long didactic story in which the numbers are astonishingly large and the re-ligious purpose and ritualistic motives are the more prominent. Some of the literary peculiar-ities of the Chronicler are wanting; Judah figures alone, and the priests, not the Levites, play the more important rôle, indicating that this midrash was probably taken from the older source to which he so often refers.

[l] I Kgs. 15² II Chr. 11²⁰, *Absalom.* Maacah was probably daughter of Tamar and there-fore Absalom's granddaughter.

[m] II Chr. 13⁵ Cf. W. R. Smith, *Religion of the Semites,* pp. 206 ff.

ABIJAH'S REIGN

Late Prophetic Summary

walked in all the sins of his father which he had committed before him; and his heart was not perfect with Jehovah his God, as the heart of David his father. [4]Nevertheless for David's sake Jehovah his God gave him a lamp in Jerusalem, in that he raised up his sons[n] after him and preserved Jerusalem, [5]because David did that which pleased Jehovah and turned not aside from anything that he commanded him all the days of his life, except only in the affair of Uriah the Hittite.[o] [7]And the other acts of Abijam and all that he did, are they not recorded in the Chronicles of the Kings of Judah? And there was war between Abijam and Jer-

Chronicler's Ecclesiastical History

Solomon the son of David, rose up and rebelled against his lord, [7]and base scoundrels gathered about him, and worthless men strengthened themselves against Rehoboam the son of Solomon. But Rehoboam was still young and inefficient, and could not withstand them. [8]And now you think you can withstand the rule of Jehovah in the hand of the sons of David, because you are a great multitude, and there are with you golden calves which Jeroboam made for you as gods. [9]Have you not driven out the priests of Jehovah, the sons of Aaron, the Levites, and made for yourselves priests like the heathen peoples? Whoever comes to consecrate himself with a young bullock and seven rams, the same may become a priest of the no-gods! [10]But as for us, Jehovah is our God, and we have not forsaken him, and the sons of Aaron are ministering to Jehovah as priests, and the Levites are doing their work; [11]and they burn to Jehovah every morning and every evening burnt-offerings and sweet incense and the bread is set in order on the clean tables, and the candlestick of gold with its lamps to burn every evening, for we keep the command of Jehovah our God; but you have forsaken him. [12]Yes, and God is with us at our head and his priests with the trumpets of alarm to sound alarm against you. O Israelites, fight not against Jehovah, the God of your fathers; for you will have no success!

[13]But Jeroboam brought around an ambush behind them, so they were before Judah, and the ambush was behind them. [14]And when Judah looked back, there they were being attacked in their front and in their rear. Then the priests sounded with the trumpets, [15]and the men of Judah gave a shout. And as soon as the men of Judah shouted, God smote Jeroboam and all Israel before Abijah and Judah. [16]And when the Israelites fled before Judah, God delivered them into their hand, [17]so that Abijah and his people slew a great many of them, and there fell slain of Israel five hundred thousand picked men. [18]Thus the Israelites were humbled at that time and the Judahites prevailed, because they relied upon Jehovah, the God of their fathers. [19]And Abijah pursued after Jeroboam, and took cities from him, Bethel with its towns, Jeshanah with its towns, and Ephron with

His miraculous victory over Jeroboam

War with Jeroboam

---

[a] I Kgs. 15[4] So Gk. and Luc. Heb., *son.*
[o] I Kgs. 15[5] Not found in Gk. and Luc. Apparently a note added by a later scribe. In the Heb. a scribe has also incorrectly added from 14[30] vs. [6], *Now there was war between Rehoboam and Jeroboam all the days of his life.*

261

Late Prophetic Summary	Chronicler's Ecclesiastical History
oboam. ⁸And Abijam slept with his fathers, and they buried him in the city of David. And Asa his son became king in his place.	its towns. ²⁰Neither did Jeroboam recover his strength again in the days of Abijah, and Jehovah smote him and he died. ²¹But Abijah grew more powerful, and took to himself fourteen wives and begot twenty-two sons and sixteen daughters. ²²And the other acts of Abijah, and his ways and his words, are recorded in the Midrash of the Prophet Iddo.

Abijah's prosperity (margin right)

§ 106. Asa's Piety and Might, II Kgs. 15⁹⁻¹⁵, II Chr. 14¹ᵇ–15¹⁵

Annals of Judah	Chronicler's Ecclesiastical History
I Kgs. 15 ⁹In the twentieth year of Jeroboam king of Israel Asa began to reign over Judah. ¹⁰And he reigned forty-one years in Jerusalem; and his mother's name was Maacah—the daughter of Abishalom.ᴾ ¹¹And Asa pleased Jehovah, as did David his father. ¹²And he put away the sacred prostitutes from the land, and removed all the idols that his fathers had made. ¹³And he also removed Maacah his mother from being queen-mother, because she had made a horrible image as an asherah. And Asa cut down her horrible image, and burnt it in the Kidron Valley. ¹⁴But the high places were not taken away: nevertheless the heart of Asa was perfect with Jehovah all his days. ¹⁵Also he brought into the temple of Jehovah the votive gifts his father consecrated and his own votive gifts—silver, gold, and vessels.	**II Chr. 14** ¹ᵇIn Asa's days the land was quiet ten years. ²And Asa did that which was good and right in the eyes of Jehovah his God, ³for he put away the foreign altars and the high places and broke down the pillars and hewed down the asherahs, ⁴and commanded Judah to seek Jehovah, the God of their fathers, and to fulfil the law and the commandment. ⁵Also he took away from all the cities of Judah the high places and the sun-images, so that the kingdom had rest under his rule. ⁶And he built fortified cities in Judah, for the land was at rest, and he had no war in those years because Jehovah had given him rest. ⁷For he said to Judah, Let us build these cities and make about them walls with towers, gates, and bars; the land is at our disposal because we have sought Jehovah our God; we have sought him, and he hath given us rest on every side. So they built and prospered.

(margins) *Asa's religious reforms* — *Asa's reforms and building enterprises*

---

§ 106 A few facts are taken by the editor of Kgs. from his earlier annalistic source. The Chronicler, however, has substituted a long narrative which has all the characteristics of the midrash: the huge numbers, the supernatural victory and the prophetic exhortation. From 14¹⁴ and a subsequent reference in 21¹⁶ it seems clear that the Cushites were the Arabian peoples bearing that name, not the Ethiopians. The story in 14⁹⁻¹⁵ probably incorporates some earlier historical data. *Judah* is the designation of the southern kingdom, indicating that the midrash is comparatively early. The use of *Judah and Benjamin* in 15¹⁻¹⁵ strongly suggests that this is a later addition from the Chronicler, although it may possibly be from a later midrash of the Book of the Kings.

ᴾ I Kgs. 15¹⁰ Probably a mistaken repetition of ². The error makes it impossible to determine what was the original. Possibly Asa's mother and grandmother both bore the name, *Maacah.*

Chronicler's Ecclesiastical History

^{8}And Asa had an army that carried shields: out of Judah three hundred thousand, and out of Benjamin, that carried shields and drew bows, two hundred and forty thousand—all these were brave warriors. ^{9}But Zerah the Cushite came out against them with an army of a million men and three hundred chariots, and he came to Mareshah. ^{10}Then Asa went out to meet him, and they drew up for battle in the valley of Zephathah at Mareshah. ^{11}And Asa cried to Jehovah his God and said, Jehovah, there are none besides thee to help, between the mighty and him who has no strength. Help us, O Jehovah our God; for we rely on thee and in thy name have we come against this multitude. O Jehovah, thou art our God; let not man prevail against thee. ^{12}Then Jehovah smote the Cushites before Asa and before Judah so that the Cushites fled. ^{13}And Asa and the people who were with him pursued them to Gerar, so that there fell of the Cushites so many that none of them remained alive; for they were shattered before Jehovah and before his army. So they carried away very much booty. ^{14}And they conquered the cities about Gerar, for a terror from Jehovah came upon them, and they plundered all the cities, for there was much spoil in them. ^{15}They smote also the tents of cattle and drove away sheep in abundance and returned to Jerusalem.

15 ^{1}And the spirit of God came upon Azariah the son of Oded, ^{2}so that he went out to meet Asa, and said to him, Hear me, Asa and all Judah and Benjamin: Jehovah is true to you while ye are true to him, and if ye seek him, he will be found of you; but if ye forsake him, he will forsake you. ^{3}Now for a long time Israel has been without the true God and without priestly teaching and without the law; ^{4}but when in their distress they turned to Jehovah, the God of Israel, and sought him, he let himself be found by them. ^{5}And in those times no one could in peace go out or come in; but great disturbances came upon all the inhabitants of the different lands. ^{6}And one nation broke in pieces another nation, and one city another city, for God terrified them with all kinds of adversity. ^{7}But be strong and do not lose courage, for your work shall be rewarded.

^{8}And when Asa heard these words and the prophecy of Oded the prophet,^{q} he took courage, and put away the abominations from all the land of Judah and Benjamin, from the cities which he had taken from the hill-country of Ephraim, and set up again the altar of Jehovah that was before the porch of Jehovah. ^{9}Then he gathered all Judah and Benjamin, together with those who sojourned with them out of Ephraim, Manasseh, and Simeon; for a great number came over to him out of all Israel, when they saw that Jehovah his God was with him. ^{10}So they gathered themselves together at Jerusalem in the third month, in the fifteenth year of the reign of Asa. ^{11}And they sacrificed to Jehovah on that day of the spoil which they had brought, seven hundred oxen and seven thousand sheep. ^{12}Then they entered into a covenant to seek Jehovah, the God of their fathers, with all

Side notes: Victory over Zerah the Cushite — Azariah's prophetic address — The solemn oath to serve Jehovah faithfully

---

^{q} II Chr. 15^8 The impossible Heb. construction shows that these words have crept into the text from a marginal note.

Chronicler's Ecclesiastical History

their heart and with all their soul, ¹³but that whoever would not seek Jehovah, the God of Israel, should be put to death, whether small or great, whether man or woman. ¹⁴And they took an oath to Jehovah with a loud voice and amidst shouting and the blast of trumpet, and rams' horns. ¹⁵And all Judah rejoiced at the oath, for they had sworn with all their heart, and sought him with all their will, so that he let himself be found by them. And Jehovah gave them rest on all sides.

§ 107. Asa's War with Baasha, I Kgs. 15¹⁶⁻²⁴, II Chr. 15¹⁹–16¹⁴

Annals of Judah

Asa's purchase of the aid of Aram

I Kgs. 15 ¹⁶And there was war between Asa and Baasha king of Israel all their days. ¹⁷And Baasha king of Israel went up against Judah and fortified Ramah, so as not to allow anyone to go out or in to Asa king of Judah. ¹⁸Then Asa took all the silver and the gold that were left in the treasures of the temple of Jehovah and the treasures of the royal palace, and entrusted them to his servants. And King Asa sent them to Ben-hadad the son of Tabrimmon, the son of Hezion king of Aram, who dwelt at Damascus, with the statement, ¹⁹There is a league between me and you and between my father and your father; herewith I send you a present of silver and gold. Break your league with Baasha king of Israel, that he may withdraw from me. ²⁰And Ben-hadad listened to King Asa and sent the commanders of his armies against the cities of Israel, and smote Ijon, Dan, Abel-beth-Maacah, and all Chinneroth, together with all the land of Naphtali.

Fortification of Geba and Mizpah

²¹Now as soon as Baasha heard of it, he abandoned the fortifying of Ramah and returned toʳ Tirzah. ²²Thereupon King Asa made a proclamation to all Judah—none was exempted—that they must carry away the stones of Ramah and the timber with which Baasha had fortified it. Then with these King Asa fortified Geba of Benjamin and Mizpah.

Chronicler's Ecclesiastical History

Hanani's condemnation of the Aramean alliance

II Chr. 16 ⁷And at that time Hanani the seer came to Asa king of Judah and said to him, Because you have relied on the king of Aram, and have not relied on Jehovah your God, therefore the army of the king of Aram has escaped from your hand. ⁸Were not the Cushites and the Lybians a great army, with very many chariots and horsemen? Yet, because you relied on Jehovah, he delivered them into your hand. ⁹For the eyes of Jehovah sweep here and there over the whole earth to show his strength in behalf

---

§ 107 The account in Kgs. of Asa's war with Baasha and his short-sighted policy, which brought the Arameans into Palestine, was probably taken originally from the state annals and has the value of a contemporary record. To this account, which the Chronicler reproduces verbatim, he adds what is apparently a quotation from his later source. After the manner of the midrash, the condemnation of Asa's alliance with Aram is put in the mouth of Hanani the seer, doubtless identified in this later tradition with the father of the prophet Jehu, mentioned in I Kgs. 16¹.

ʳ I Kgs. 15²¹ So Gk., Luc., and Lat. Heb., *dwelt in.* The difference in the Heb. is only a question of vocalization.

Chronicler's Ecclesiastical History

of those whose heart is perfect toward him. Herein you have acted foolishly, for from henceforth you shall have wars. ¹⁰Then Asa was angry with the seer and put him in the house of the stocks, for he was in a rage with him because of this thing. And at that time Asa also oppressed some of the people.

Late Prophetic Summary

sa's
ness
eath

I Kgs. 15 ²³Now the other acts of Asa and all his brave deeds and the cities which he built, are they not recorded in the Chronicles of the Kings of Judah? But in his old age he became diseased in his feet. ²⁴And Asa slept with his fathers and was buried with his fathers in the city of David his father. And Jehoshaphat his son became king in his place.

II Chr. 16 ¹¹Now the acts of Asa, the earlier and the later, are already recorded in the Book of the Kings of Judah and Israel. ¹²And Asa became diseased in the feet in the thirty-ninth year of his reign, so that he became very ill. But in his sickness he did not seek help from Jehovah, but from the physician. ¹³And Asa slept with his fathers and died in the forty-first year of his reign. ¹⁴And they buried him in his sepulchre, which he had hewn out in the city of David, and laid him on the bed, which they had filled with all kinds of spices, skilfully mixed; and they burned in his honor an exceedingly great pyre.

§ 108. **The Benign Rule of Jehoshaphat, I Kgs. 22⁴¹⁻⁴⁶, II Chr. 17, 19⁴⁻¹¹, 20³¹⁻³⁴**

Late Prophetic Summary

Chronicler's Ecclesiastical History

ehosh-
phat's
ood
olicy

I Kgs. 22 ⁴¹And Jehoshaphat the son of Asa began to reign over Judah in the fourth year of Ahab king of Israel. ⁴²Jehoshaphat was thirty-five years old when he

II Chr. 17 ¹And Jehoshaphat Asa's son became king in his place and strengthened himself against Israel. ²And he placed troops in all the fortified cities of Judah and set garrisons in the land of Judah and in the cities of Ephraim, which Asa his father had taken. ³And Jehovah was with Jehoshaphat, because he walked in the earlier ways of his ancestor David, and did not resort to the Baals, ⁴but sought

His
fortifi-
cations
and
stand-
ing
army

---

§ 108 I Kgs. 22⁴⁶ was probably taken directly from the annals, but the rest of the passage is from the editor. The parallel in Chr. is expanded and devoted to a didactic end in the spirit of the early midrashes. The earlier designation *Judah* is used throughout instead of *Judah and Benjamin*. 17⁷⁻⁹, like the kindred passage, 19⁴⁻¹¹, however, has none of the characteristics of a midrash. Later institutions are evidently here in part reflected; but the basis of the tradition appears to have been certain definite measures intended to improve the judicial organization.

The existence of brief codes corresponding to those found in Ex. 20–23, 34, and a system of local judges with the central court at Jerusalem is implied by Is. 10¹ and many passages in Dt. Cf. especially Dt. 17. An enterprising king like Jehoshaphat, who was in close alliance with Northern Israel and through it with the high Semitic civilization represented by the Phœnicians, would naturally take the initiative in these reforms. A brief record of this work may have been found in the royal Judean chronicles and later in an exilic Book of the Kings of Judah and Israel which was in turn either quoted directly by the Chronicler or else was already incorporated in the Midrash of the Book of the Kings to which he refers. The noble exhortation to the judges is one of the classical passages in Chr.

Late Prophetic Sum-
mary

began to reign, and he
reigned twenty - five
years in Jerusalem.
A n d his mother's
name was Azubah,
the daughter of Shilhi.
⁴³And he walked alto-
gether in the way of
Asa his father; he did
not turn aside from
it, doing that which
pleased Jehovah. Only
the high places were
not taken away, but
the people still sacri-
ficed and burnt their
offeringsˢ on the high
places. ⁴⁴And Jehosh-
aphat made p e a c e
with the king of Is-
rael.

His
wars
and
re-
forms

⁴⁵Now the other
acts of Jehoshaphat
and his brave deeds,
that he did, and how
he made war, are they
not recorded in the
Chronicles o f t h e
Kings of Judah?ᵗ
⁴⁶Also the rest of the
t e m p l e prostitutes,
who remained in the
days of his father Asa,
he expelled from the
land.

Chronicler's Ecclesiastical History

the God of his ancestor, and walked in his commands and not according to the deeds of Israel.
⁵Therefore Jehovah established the kingdom in
his hand, and all Judah brought Jehoshaphat tribute, so that he had riches and honor in abundance.
⁶Then his heart was exalted in the ways of Jehovah,
so that he also abolished the high places and the
asherahs out of Judah.

¹⁰And the terror of Jehovah fell on all the kingdoms of the lands that were round about Judah,
so that they made no war against Jehoshaphat.
¹¹And some of the Philistines brought Jehoshaphat
presents and a silver tribute; the Arabians also
brought him flocks: seven thousand, seven hundred
rams, and seven thousand, seven hundred he-goats.
¹²So Jehoshaphat gradually grew stronger, so that
he built in Judah castles and store-cities. ¹³He
also had many stores in the cities of Judah, and
soldiers, brave warriors, in Jerusalem. ¹⁴And this
was the number of them according to their families: of Judah, the commanders of thousands, Adnah the commander, and with him three hundred
thousand brave warriors; ¹⁵and next to him Jehohanan the commander, and with him two hundred
and eighty thousand; ¹⁶and next to him Amasiah,
the son of Zichri, who had willingly placed himself
at the command of Jehovah, and with him two hundred thousand brave warriors. ¹⁷And of Benjamin: Eliada a brave warrior, and with him two
hundred thousand armed with bow and shield; ¹⁸and
next to him Jehozabad, and with him a hundred
and eighty thousand, equipped for war. ¹⁹These
were those who were in the service of the king, besides those whom the king put in the fortified cities
throughout Judah.

Jehosh-
aphat's
strength
and
pros-
perity

Public
in-
struc-
tion in
the law

⁷In the third year of his reign he sent his princes, Ben-hail, Obadiah,
Zechariah, Nethanel, Micaiah, to teach in the cities of Judah, ⁸and with
them the Levites, Shemaiah, Nethaniah, Zebadiah, Asahel, Shemiramoth,
Jehonathan, Adonijah, Tobijah, and Tob-adonijah, the Levites; and with
them Elishama and Jehoram, the priests, ⁹that they should teach in Judah,
having the book of the law of Jehovah with them. So they went about
throughout all the cities of Judah and taught among the people.

ˢ I Kgs. 22⁴³ Cf. § 48, noteᵏ.
ᵗ I Kgs. 22⁴⁵ The parallel passage in II Chr. 20³⁴ reads, *in the addresses of Jehu the son of
Hanani, which are incorporated in the history of the kings of Israel.*

Chronicler's Ecclesiastical History

19 ⁴And Jehoshaphat dwelt at Jerusalem.   And he went out again among Ap-
point-
ment
the people from Beersheba to the hill-country of Ephraim and brought them
back to Jehovah, the God of their fathers.   ⁵He also appointed judges in and in-
struc-
the land in all the fortified cities of Judah, city by city, ⁶and said to the judges, tion of
Consider what you do, for you are to render judgment not for man but for local
judges
Jehovah, and he will be with you when you render judgment.   ⁷Now therefore let the fear of Jehovah be upon you.   Take heed in whatever you do, for
with Jehovah our God there is no injustice or partiality or acceptance of
bribes.·

⁸Moreover in Jerusalem Jehoshaphat appointed certain Levites and priests Estab-
lish-
and the heads of the families of Israel to render the judgment of Jehovah ment of
and to decide controversies for the inhabitantsᵘ of Jerusalem.   ⁹And he a su-
preme
charged them saying, Thus shall you do in the fear of Jehovah, faithfully court of
and with sincere purpose.   ¹⁰And whenever any controversy comes to you appeal
at Je-
from your kinsmen who dwell in other cities, between blood and blood,ᵛ rusa-
lem
between law, commandment, statutes, and ordinances, you shall warn them
that they be not guilty toward Jehovah, and so wrath come upon you and
upon your kinsmen; this must you do, that you may not be guilty.   ¹¹And,
behold, Amariah the chief priest shall be at your head in all matters of Jehovah, and Zebadiah the son of Ishmael, the ruler of the house of Judah, in
all the king's matters.   Also the Levites shall be at your disposal as scribes.
Do your work courageously; Jehovah be with those who do what is right.

§ 109. Jehoshaphat's Alliance with Ahab against the Arameans, I Kgs.
22⁴, ²⁹⁻³⁶, II Chr. 18¹–19³

Chronicler's Version of I Kgs. 22⁴, ²⁹⁻³⁶

II Chr. 18 ¹Now when Jehoshaphat had attained riches and honor in The
alli-
abundance, he allied himself by marriage with Ahab.   ²And after some ance
years he went down to Ahab at Samaria.   And Ahab killed sheep and oxen with
Ahab
in abundance for him and for the people who were with him, and influenced
him to go up with him to Ramoth in Gilead.   ³And Ahab king of Israel
said to Jehoshaphat king of Judah, Will you go with me to Ramoth in Gilead ?
And he answered him, I am as you are and my people as your people; and
we will go with you to the war.   .   .   .

²⁸So the king of Israel and Jehoshaphat the king of Judah went up to Ahab's
dis-
Ramoth in Gilead.   ²⁹And the king of Israel said to Jehoshaphat, I will go guise
into the battle disguised, but you put on your robes.   So the king of Israel and
Jehosh-
disguised himself, and they went into the battle.   ³⁰Now the king of Aram aphat's
peril

ᵘ II Chr. 19⁸ So the Gk., which has evidently the original text.   Heb., *And they returned
to Jerusalem.*

ᵛ II Chr. 19¹⁰ *I.e.,* to decide who is guilty and the extent of the guilt in a case of man-
slaughter.

§ 109 At this point the histories of Judah and Israel touch very closely.   Already in con-
nection with the history of the northern kingdom the incident has been given in full in §§ 77, 78.
Here simply the Chronicler's slightly variant version of the events which directly concerned
Judah are reproduced in order to give a complete view of Jehoshaphat's reign.

Chronicler's Version of I Kgs. 22[4, 29-36]

had commanded the captains of his chariots, saying, Fight neither with small nor great, except only with the king of Israel. [31]Therefore when the captains of the chariots saw Jehoshaphat they said, It is the king of Israel, and turned about to fight against him. But Jehoshaphat cried out and Jehovah helped him, in that God lured them from him. [32]And when the captains of the chariots saw that it was not the king of Israel, they turned back from pursuing him.

Ahab's
fatal
wound

[33]And a certain man drew his bow at a venture and smote the king of Israel between the girdle and breastplate; then he cried to the driver of the chariot, Turn about, and carry me out of the army, for I am severely wounded. [34]And the battle increased that day, but the king of Israel held himself up in his chariot against the Arameans until evening; then about sunset he died.

Jehu's
con-
dem-
nation
of the
alli-
ance

19 [1]But Jehoshaphat the king of Judah returned home to Jerusalem in peace. [2]And Jehu the son of Hanani the seer went out to meet him and said to King Jehoshaphat, Should you help the wicked and love those who hate Jehovah? For this wrath has come upon you from Jehovah. [3]Nevertheless some good things are found in you, in that you have put away the asherahs from the land and have set your heart on seeking God.

§ 110. Jehoshaphat's War against the Moabites, the Ammonites, and their Allies, II Chr. 20[1-30], cf. II Kgs. 3[4-27]

Chronicler's Ecclesiastical History

Ad-
vance
of the
invad-
ing foes

II Chr. 20 [1]Now after this the Moabites and the Ammonites and with them some of the Meunites[w] came against Jehoshaphat to battle. [2]Then some came and informed Jehoshaphat, saying, A great multitude is coming against you from the other side of the sea, from Edom;[x] and they are already in Hazazontamar (that is En-gedi). [3]Then Jehoshaphat feared and devoted himself to seeking Jehovah and proclaimed a fast throughout all Judah. [4]And Judah gathered together to seek help of Jehovah, even out of all the cities of Judah they came to seek Jehovah.

Jehosh-
aphat's
prayer
for de-
liver-
ance

[5]And Jehoshaphat stood in the assembly of Judah and Jerusalem in the temple of Jehovah, before the new court, [6]and said, O Jehovah, the God of our fathers, art thou not God of heaven? and art thou not ruler over all the kingdoms of the nations? And in thy hand is power and might, so that none is able to withstand thee? [7]Didst not thou, O our God, drive out the inhabitants of this land before thy people Israel, and give it to the descendants of Abraham thy friend forever? [8]So they dwelt therein and built thee

---

§ 110 Again all the characteristics of the late Jewish midrash reappear. The literary style and the absence of any reference to Benjamin point to an older source rather than to the original work of the Chronicler. The same tradition may possibly be the basis both of the present story and of the Elisha narrative in II Kgs. 3. In the case of both the original has evidently been greatly transformed and embellished during the long process of oral transmission and ultimate adaptation to the final didactic purpose. For the tradition of Jehoshaphat's joint campaign with Jehoram against Moab, cf. § 88.

w 20[1] So Gk. The impossible Heb., *Ammonites*, arose from a transposition of two letters. In [10, 23] and I Chr. 4[41] they are designated as inhabitants of Mount Seir.

x 20[2] As often elsewhere, a scribe has mistaken *Edom* for *Aram*. The sea is the Dead Sea.

Chronicler's Ecclesiastical History

a sanctuary therein for thy name, saying, [9] 'If evil comes upon us, the avenging sword, pestilence, or famine, we will stand before this temple and before thee (for thy name is in this temple) and cry to thee in our affliction and thou wilt hear and save.' [10]And now, behold, the Ammonites and Moabites and the inhabitants of Mount Seir, whom thou wouldest not let Israel attack, when they came out of the land of Egypt, but they turned aside from them without destroying them[a]—[11]now see how they reward us, in that they còme to cast us out of thy possession, which thou hast given us as an inheritance. [12]O our God, wilt thou not judge them? For we have no strength against this great multitude that is coming against us, nor do we know what to do, but our eyes are turned to thee! [13]And all Judah stood before Jehovah, with their children.

[14]Then upon Jahaziel the son of Zechariah, the son of Benaiah, the son of Jeiel, the son of Mattaniah the Levite, of the sons of Asaph, came the spirit of Jehovah in the midst of the assembly; [15]and he said, Hearken, all Judah and ye inhabitants of Jerusalem and thou King Jehoshaphat: Thus saith Jehovah to you, ' Fear not nor be dismayed before this great multitude; for the battle is not yours, but God's. [16]To-morrow go down against them. See they are coming up by the ascent of Ziz, and you shall find them at the end of the valley before the Wilderness of Jeruel. [17]In this battle it is not your part to fight; put yourselves in array, stand still, and see the deliverance which Jehovah will accomplish for you, O Judah and Jerusalem! Fear not, nor be dismayed; to-morrow go out against them, for Jehovah is with you.' [18]And Jehoshaphat bowed his head to the ground, and all Judah and the inhabitants of Jerusalem fell down before Jehovah, worshipping Jehovah. [19]Then the Levites, of the children of the Kohathites and of the children of the Korahites, stood up to praise Jehovah the God of Israel, with an exceeding loud voice.[b]

Jahaziel's encouraging message

[20]And on the following day they rose early and went forth into the Wilderness of Tekoa. And as they went forth, Jehoshaphat stood and said, Hear me, O Judah, and inhabitants of Jerusalem! Believe in Jehovah your God, so shall you live and be established. Believe his prophets, so shall you prosper. [21]And when he had taken counsel with the people, he appointed singers to give praise to Jehovah in holy array, as they went out before the army, and say, Give thanks to Jehovah; for his kindness endureth forever. [22]And as soon as they began to sing and to sing praises, Jehovah sent secret enemies[c] against the Ammonites, Moabites, and the inhabitants of Mount Seir, who had come against Judah, so that they destroyed themselves. [23]For the Ammonites and the Moabites set themselves against the inhabitants of Mount Seir, to root out and completely destroy them. And when they had made an end of the inhabitants of Seir, each helped to destroy the other.

The miraculous victory

---

a 20[10] Cf. Dt. 2[1-19].
b 20[19] Here the Chronicler apparently himself introduces the Levitical singers. In the original narrative the singers seem to be first introduced in [21].
c 20[22] Heb., *Liers-in-wait*. The representation of the story leaves little doubt that angelic messengers are intended and that they stirred up the different hostile nations against each other.

Chronicler's Ecclesiastical History

The great spoil

²⁴And when Judah came to the Watch-tower of the Wilderness and looked toward the multitude, there they were dead bodies fallen to the earth, and none had escaped ! ²⁵And when Jehoshaphat and his people came to take the spoil from them, they found cattle in abundance and personal property,ᵈ garments and precious jewels, which they stripped off for themselves, until they could carry away no more; and they were three days in taking the spoil, it was so much.

Joy and prestige of the people of Judah

²⁶And on the fourth day they assembled in the Valley of Beracah, for there they blessed Jehovah; therefore the name of that place was called The Valley of Beracahᵉ [Blessing] to this day. ²⁷Then they returned, all the men of Judah and Jerusalem, with Jehoshaphat at their head to go again with joy to Jerusalem, for Jehovah had made them rejoice over their enemies. ²⁸And they came to Jerusalem with harps, lyres, and trumpets to the temple of Jehovah. ²⁹And a fear of God came upon all the kingdoms of the earth, when they heard that Jehovah had fought against the enemies of Israel. ³⁰So the realm of Jehoshaphat enjoyed quiet, for his God gave him rest on all sides.

§ 111. Jehoshaphat's Disastrous Commercial Enterprises and Death, I Kgs. 22⁴⁷⁻⁵⁰, II Chr. 20³⁵–21¹

Annals of Judah

The wreck of Jehoshaphat's ships

I Kgs. 22 ⁴⁷Now there was no king in Edom. But the deputy of King Jehoshaphat ⁴⁸made ships of Tarshish to go to Ophir for gold.ᶠ But they did not go; for the ships were wrecked at Ezion-geber. ⁴⁹Then Ahaziah the son of Ahab said to Jehoshaphat, Let my servants go with your servants in the ships. But Jehoshaphat would not. ⁵⁰And Jehoshaphat slept with his fathers, and was buried with his fathers in the city of David his father; and Jehoram his son became king in his place.

Chronicler's Ecclesiastical History

II Chr. 20 ³⁵Now later Jehoshaphat king of Judah allied himself with Ahaziah king of Israel, who did very wickedly. ³⁶And he bound himself by a contract with him to build ships to go to Tarshish, so they made the ships in Ezion-geber. ³⁷But Eliezer the son of Dodavahu of Mareshah prophesied against Jehoshaphat, saying, Because you have allied yourself with Ahaziah, Jehovah will surely tear your work in pieces. Accordingly the ships were broken, so that they were unable to go to Tarshish.

ᵈ 20²⁵ Correcting the Heb. with the aid of the Gk.

ᵉ 20²⁶ Identified with the *Wadi Bereikut* near Tekoa.

§ 111 The citation by the late prophetic editor of Kgs. from this earlier source, is supplemented in the parallel in Chr. by a brief prophetic warning added by the Chronicler or already found in his midrashic source. The descriptive epithet, *Tarshish ship*, was also interpreted to mean that their destination was Tarshish.

ᶠ I Kgs. 22⁴⁷, ⁴⁸ The current translation is untenable. The lucid translation given above is based on a slight emendation of the Heb. text. The Gk., favored by the marginal reading of the Heb., has, *ship*, not *ships*. This may well have been the original text, although the Chronicler's parallel supports the plural.

§ 112. Jehoram's Reign, II Kgs. 8¹⁶⁻²⁴, II Chr. 21²⁻²⁰

Late Prophetic Summary

II Kgs. 8 ¹⁶And in the fifth year of Joram, the son of Ahab king of Israel, Jehoshaphat being then king of Judah, Jehoram the son of Jehoshaphat king of Judah began to reign. ¹⁷He was thirty-two years old when he began to reign, and he reigned eight years in Jerusalem. ¹⁸And he walked in the way of the kings of Israel, as did the house of Ahab, for he had married the daughter of Ahab, and he did that which displeased Jehovah. ¹⁹However, Jehovah would not destroy Judah for the sake of David his servant, since he had promised to give him a lamp before him^g always.

Annals of Judah

²⁰In his days Edom revolted from the rule of Judah and established a king over themselves. ²¹Then Joram passed over to Zair, and all his chariots^h with him.ⁱ And he rose up by night and smote through the Edomites who had surrounded him and the captains of the chariots were with him, but the people fled to their tents. ²²So Edom revolted from under the rule of Judah to this day. Then Libnah revolted at the same time. ²³And the other acts of Joram and all that he did are they not recorded in the Chronicles of the Kings of Judah? ²⁴And Joram slept with his fathers and was buried with his fathers in the city of David, and Ahaziah his son became king in his place.

Chronicler's Ecclesiastical History

II Chr. 21 ²Now Jehoram had brothers, the sons of Jehoshaphat: Azariah, Jehiel, Michael, and Shephatiah; all these were the sons of Jehoshaphat king of Israel. ³And their father gave them great gifts of silver, of gold, and of precious things, with fortified cities in Judah, but the kingdom he gave to Jehoram, because he was the eldest. ⁴Now when Jehoram had taken over the kingdom of his father and had strengthened himself he slew his brothers with the sword, together with certain of the nobles.

⁸In his days Edom revolted from the rule of Judah and established a king over themselves. ⁹Then Jehoram passed over to Zair, and all his chariots^j with him. And he rose up by night and smote through the Edomites who had surrounded him and the captains of the chariots were with him.^k ¹⁰So Edom revolted from the rule of Judah to this day. Then Libnah revolted at the same time from his rule, because he had forsaken **Jehovah**, the God of his fathers.

---

§ 112 To the general statements of the late prophetic editor of Kgs. the Chronicler adds certain facts in 21²⁻⁴, which seem to be authentic and which are apparently derived from one of his older non-canonical sources. Vss. ⁵⁻⁷ are but a verbatim quotation from Kgs. The story in ¹¹⁻²⁰ is evidently a later midrash.
g II Kgs. 8¹⁹ So Luc., Lat., Targ., and the parallel in II Chr. 21⁷. Heb., *for his children;* but they were the *lamp.*
h II Kgs. 8²¹ The Heb. is difficult and the context not complete. Apparently some of the text has been lost, especially the account of the ambush into which the Hebrews fell and which is implied in ²¹ᵇ.
i II Kgs. 8²¹ Supplying, *with him,* from the parallel passage in Chr.
j II Chr. 21⁹ Restoring the original text of Kgs. Heb., *with his captains.*
k II Chr. 21⁹ Restoring, *with him,* from Kgs.

Chronicler's Ecclesiastical History

Elijah's
letter of
con-
demna-
tion

[11]Moreover he made high places in the cities[1] of Judah, and led the inhabitants of Jerusalem into apostasy,[m] and led Judah astray. [12]Then there came a writing to him from Elijah the prophet, saying, Thus saith Jehovah, the God of David your ancestor, ' Because thou hast not walked in the ways of Jehoshaphat thy father, nor in the ways of Asa king of Judah, [13]but hast walked in the way of the kings of Israel and hast led Judah and the inhabitants of Jerusalem into apostasy, as did the house of Ahab, and also hast slain thy brothers of thy father's house, who were better than thyself; [14]now Jehovah will smite with a great plague thy people, thy children, thy wives, and all thy possessions; [15]and thou thyself shalt become very sick with a disease of thy bowels, until, because of the disease, thy bowels shall waste away day by day.

Jeho-
ram's
mis-
fort-
unes
and
loath-
some
end

[16]Then Jehovah stirred up against Jehoram the Philistines and the Arabians, who live beside the Cushites,[n] [17]so that they came up against Judah, and invaded it, and carried away all the possessions that were found in the royal palace, together with his son and his wives. Thus not a single son was left to him, except Jehoahaz his youngest. [18]And after all this Jehovah smote him in the bowels with an incurable disease, [19]so that in process of time, at the end of two years,[o] his bowels wasted away because of his sickness, and he died in great pain. And his people made no such funeral pyre for him as they did for his fathers. [20]He was thirty-two years old when he began to reign, and he reigned in Jerusalem eight years. And he departed without being missed,[p] and they buried him in the city of David, but not in the sepulchre of the kings.

§ 113. Ahaziah's Brief Reign, II Kgs. 8[25-29], 9[27-29], II Chr. 22[1-9]

Late Prophetic Summary

Aha-
ziah's
evil
policy
and al-
liance

II Kgs. 8 [25]In the twelfth year of Joram the son of Ahab king of Israel, Ahaziah the son of Jehoram king of Judah began to reign. [26]Ahaziah was twenty-two years old when he began to reign, and

Chronicler's Ecclesiastical History

II Chr. 22 [1]And the inhabitants of Jerusalem made Ahaziah, his youngest son, king in his place; for the hordes that came with the Arabians to the camp had slain all the older sons. So Ahaziah the son of Jehoram became king of Judah.

---

[1] II Chr. 21[11] So Gk. Heb., *mountains.*
[m] II Chr. 21[11] Heb., *play the harlot.* So also, as in the prophets, it is used primarily in the figurative sense. Cf. Hos. 2[5].
[n] II Chr. 21[16] Probably the Arabian Cushites, although in the O.T. the Heb. word also designates the Ethiopians.
[o] II Chr. 21[19] The Gk., *two days,* makes better sense and may be original.
[p] II Chr. 21[20] Heb., *desired.*
§ 113 Ahaziah's reign of probably less than one year is treated by the editor of Kgs. in the usual manner. Another editor, remembering that Jehoram reigned twelve years and Ahaziah one, and that both died at the same time by the hand of Jehu, reckoned that Ahaziah's accession must have been in the eleventh, not the twelfth (as in 8[25]) year of Jehoram. Accordingly in 8[29], immediately after the account of the death of Ahaziah, he adds, *in the eleventh year of Joram the son of Ahab Ahaziah became king over Judah.* The editor in 8[25] is probably correct, since Ahaziah's reign appears to have been limited to months and reckoned as a year only in round numbers.
The source followed by the Chronicler was in part dependent upon Kgs., but regarding the manner of Ahaziah's death it preserves a variant tradition.

Late Prophetic Summary

he reigned one year in Jerusalem. And his mother's name was Athaliah the granddaughter^q of Omri king of Israel. ²⁷And he walked in the way of the house of Ahab and did that which displeased Jehovah, as did the house of Ahab; for he was related by marriage to the house of Ahab. ²⁸And he went with Joram the son of Ahab to make war against Hazael king of Aram at Ramoth in Gilead. But the Arameans wounded Joram. ²⁹ᵃThen King Joram returned to be healed in Jezreel of the wounds which the Arameans had given him at Ramah, when he fought against Hazael king of Aram.

Chronicler's Ecclesiastical History

²Forty-two years old was Ahaziah, when he began to reign, and he reigned one year in Jerusalem. And his mother's name was Athaliah the granddaughter of Omri. ³He also walked in the ways of the house of Ahab, for his mother was his counsellor to do wickedly. ⁴And he did that which displeased Jehovah, as did the house of Ahab, for they were his counsellors after the death of his father, to his destruction. ⁵He also followed their advice and went with Jehoram the son of Ahab king of Israel, to make war against Hazael king of Aram at Ramoth in Gilead. But the Arameans wounded Joram. ⁶And he returned to be healed of the wounds which they had given him at Ramah, when he fought against Hazael king of Aram.

Prophetic Jehu History

8 ²⁹ᵇAnd Ahaziah the son of Jehoram king of Judah went down to visit Joram the son of Ahab to Jezreel because he was sick. 9 ²⁷*And when Jehu slew Joram*, Ahaziah king of Judah saw it and fled in the direction of Bethgannim. Then Jehu pursued after him with the words, Him also ! Smite him in the chariot. And they smote him in the ascent of Gur, which is by Ibleam. And he escaped to Megiddo and died there. ²⁸But his servants carried him to Jerusalem and buried him there in his sepulchre with his fathers in the city of David.

And Azariah the son of Jehoram king of Judah went down to visit Jehoram the son of Ahab in Jezreel, because he was sick. ⁷Now the destruction of Ahaziah was of God, in that he went to Joram, and after his arrival he went out with Jehoram against Jehu the son of Nimshi, whom Jehovah had anointed to cut off the house of Ahab. ⁸Now when Jehu was executing judgment upon the house of Ahab, he found the princes of Judah and the sons of the brothers of Ahaziah, ministering to Ahaziah, and slew them. ⁹Then he sought Ahaziah. And they caught him while he was hiding in Samaria, and they brought him to Jehu and he slew him. But they buried him, for they said, He is the son of Jehoshaphat, who sought Jehovah with all his heart. And the house of Ahaziah had no one who had the strength necessary to rule.

---

^q II Kgs. 8²⁶ Heb., *daughter*, used in the sense of descendant.

§ 114. Overthrow of Athaliah and Accession of Joash, II Kgs. 11¹⁻²⁰, II Chr. 22¹⁰–23²¹

Temple Records	*Chronicler's Ecclesiastical History*
II Kgs. 11 ¹Now when Athaliah, the mother of Ahaziah, learned that her son was dead she arose and destroyed all the royal family. ²But Jehosheba, the daughter of King Joram and sister of Ahaziah, took Joash, the son of Ahaziah, and stole him away from among the king's sons, who were about to be slain, and put[r] him in the bedchamber. Thus she hid him from Athaliah, so that he was not slain. ³And he was with her, hid in the temple of Jehovah, six years while Athaliah reigned over the land.	**II Chr. 22** ¹⁰Now when Athaliah, the mother of Ahaziah, learned that her son was dead, she arose and destroyed all the royal family of the house of Judah. ¹¹But Jehoshabeath, the daughter of the king, took Joash the son of Ahaziah and stole him away from among the king's sons, who were about to be slain, and put him and his nurse in the bedchamber. Thus Jehoshabeath, the daughter of King Jehoram, the wife of Jehoiada the priest (for she was the sister of Ahaziah), hid him from Athaliah, so that she did not slay him. ¹²And he was with her, hid in the temple of God, six years while Athaliah reigned over the land.
⁴But in the seventh year Jehoiada sent and brought the military commanders[s] of the Carites and of the guards[t] and brought them to him into the temple of Jehovah. Thereupon he showed them the king's son. ⁵And he commanded them saying, This is what you shall do: a third part of you, who go in on the sabbath	**23** ¹But in the seventh year Jehoiada took courage and entered into a covenant with the military commanders, Azariah the son of Jehoram, Ishmael the son of Jehohanan, Azariah the son of Obed, Maaseiah the son of Adaiah, and Elishaphat the son of Zichri. ²And they went about Judah and gathered Levites from all the cities of Judah and the heads of the Israelitish families, and they came to Jerusalem. ³Then all the assembly made a covenant with the king in the house of God. And he said to them, Behold, the king's son

Side notes (left margin):
Athaliah's seizure of the throne

Jehoiada's conspiracy

---

§ 114 The interest in this and its sequel, II Kgs. 12, centres about the temple and the religious revolution effected through the activity of Jehoiada the priest. The narrative is straightforward and circumstantial—evidently from a writer acquainted with the facts and with the details of the sanctuary. Joash plays a secondary rôle. The character and contents of the narrative strongly support the conclusion that it was taken from the temple records and therefore ranks as practically contemporaneous testimony regarding the important events recounted.

By many ¹³⁻¹⁸ᵃ are regarded as a duplicate of ²⁰ and from a different source, but the evidence adduced is far from conclusive. The execution of Athaliah and the priests of Baal and the removal of the symbolism of the cult, fostered within the temple precincts by the queen, were the natural preliminaries to the introduction of the young king to the palace and vacant throne. The care taken that Athaliah shall not be slain in the temple court, ¹⁴, and the prominence given to the covenant and to the overthrow of Baalism, ¹⁷, ¹⁸, all point to the temple records as likewise the source from which these verses were taken. The recapitulation in ²⁰ seems to anticipate ¹⁴ and ¹⁶. It may have been added by the editor, although there is nothing in it to indicate that it is not a concluding summary from the original author of the section.

The Chronicler substitutes the Levites for the captains of the guard and the Carites, thus protecting the temple from all pollution by the common people. He also introduces the singers at the crucial moment, when Athaliah appears; otherwise he follows the narrative of Kgs.

r II Kgs. 11² Restoring the original Heb. by the aid of the parallel in II Chr. 22¹¹.
s II Kgs. 11⁴ Heb., *commanders of hundreds.*
t II Kgs. 11⁴ Heb., *runners.*

Temple Records

and keep guard over the royal palace, ⁶and a third part shall be at the gate Sur; and a third part at the gate behind the guards, that you may keep watch^u over the royal palace.^v ⁷And the two divisions of you, even all who go forth on the sabbath to keep guard over the temple of Jehovah about the king, ⁸shall surround the king, each with his weapons in his hand. And whoever comes within the ranks, let him be slain. Thus you shall be with the king, when he goes out and when he comes in.

⁹And the military commanders did just as Jehoiada the priest had commanded: each brought his men, both those who were to come in on the sabbath and those who were to go out on the sabbath, to Jehoiada the priest. ¹⁰And the priest delivered to the military commanders the spears and shields that had been King David's, which were in the temple of Jehovah.^w ¹¹And the guards stood each with his weapons in his hand, from the south side of the temple to the north side of the temple, before the altar and before the temple, around the king.^x ¹²Then he brought out the king's son and put the crown upon him and the ornaments, and they proclaimed him king and anointed him, and clapped their hands and said, May the king live!

Chronicler's Ecclesiastical History

shall reign, as Jehovah hath spoken concerning the sons of David. ⁴This is what you shall do: A third part of you, the priests and Levites, who come in on the sabbath, shall be porters at the thresholds; ⁵and a third part shall guard the royal palace; and a third part the Gate Jesod; and all the people shall be in the courts of the temple of Jehovah. ⁶But let none come into the temple of Jehovah except the priests and the ministering Levites; they shall come in, for they are ceremonially clean; but all the people shall observe the command of Jehovah. ⁷And the Levites shall surround the king, each with his weapons in his hand; and whoever comes into the temple, let him be slain. Thus you shall be with the king when he comes in and when he goes out.

⁸So the Levites and all Judah did just as Jehoiada the priest commanded: each brought his men, both those who were to come in on the sabbath and those who were to go out on the sabbath; for Jehoiada the priest had dismissed the divisions. ⁹And Jehoiada the priest delivered to the military commanders the spears, bucklers, and shields that had been King David's, which were in the house of God. ¹⁰And he set all the people, each with his weapon in his hand, from the south side of the temple to the north side of the temple, even to the altar and the temple, around the king. ¹¹Then they brought out the king's son and put the crown and the ornaments upon him, and proclaimed him king, and Jehoiada and his sons anointed him, and cried, May the king live!

^u II Kgs. 11⁶ So the free paraphrase in II Chr. 23⁵, supported by a scholia cited by Field. The same is obtained by a simple correction of the present untranslatable Heb.
^v II Kgs. 11⁶ This verse has either been misplaced or else is a gloss, for ⁷ is the direct continuation of ⁵, while ⁶ introduces hopeless confusion.
^w II Kgs. 11¹⁰ But cf. I Kgs. 14^{26, 27}. The temple guards were also doubtless already armed. It is probable that a scribe introduced this verse from II Chr. 23⁹. Its awkward form likewise supports this conclusion. It may also be secondary in Chr.
^x II Kgs. 11¹¹ The awkward form of the Heb. and the fact that Joash was not yet king indicate that these words are also from a later scribe who recalled the command in ⁸.

Temple Records

Death of Queen Athaliah

¹³But when Athaliah heard the cry ᵃ of the people, she came to the people into the temple of Jehovah. **¹⁴**Then she looked and there was the king standing by the pillar, as was the custom, and the commanders and the trumpeters by the king, and all the people of the land rejoicing and blowing trumpets. Then Athaliah tore her clothes and cried, Treason! Treason! **¹⁵**And Jehoiada the priest gave command to the military commanders who were over the army and said to them, Bring her out between the ranks; and whoever follows her, slay with the sword! for the priest said, Let her not be slain in the temple of Jehovah. **¹⁶**So they laid hands on her, and, as she went through the horses' entry to the royal palace, she was slain.

Covenant with Jehovah and overthrow of Baalism

¹⁷And Jehoiada made a covenant between Jehovah and the king and the people, that they should be Jehovah's people; likewise between the king and the people. **¹⁸**And all the people of the land went to the temple of Baal and destroyed it. His altar and his images they broke completely in pieces, and they slew Mattan the priest of Baal before the altars.

Establishment of Joash on the throne

Then the priest appointed watchmen over the temple of Jehovah. **¹⁹**And he took the military commanders and the Carites, and the guards and all the people of the land, and they brought

Chronicler's Ecclesiastical History

¹²But when Athaliah heard the cry of the people running and praising the king, she came to the people into the temple of Jehovah. **¹³**Then she looked and there was the king standing by his pillar at the entrance, and the commanders and the trumpeters by the king, and all the people of the land rejoicing and blowing trumpets, and the singers with musical instruments leading the songs of praise. Then Athaliah tore her clothes, and said, Treason! Treason! **¹⁴**But Jehoiada the priest brought out the military commanders who were over the army, and said to them, Bring her out between the ranks; and whoever follows her, let him be slain with the sword; for the priest said, Slay her not in the temple of Jehovah. **¹⁵**So they laid hands on her, and, as she went to the entrance of the horse-gate which led to the royal palace, they slew her there.

¹⁶And Jehoiada made a covenant between himself and all the people, and the king, that they should be Jehovah's people. **¹⁷**And all the people went to the temple of Baal and destroyed it. And they broke completely in pieces his altars and his images, and Mattan the priest of Baal they slew before the altars.

¹⁸And Jehoiada appointed the watchmen over the temple under the direction of the levitical priests, whom David had distributed in the temple of Jehovah, to offer the burnt-offerings of Jehovah, as it is prescribed in the law of Moses, with rejoicing and with singing, according to the regulation of David. **¹⁹**And he placed the porters at the gates of the temple of Jehovah, that

---

ᵃ II Kgs. 11¹³ A scribe has added, *of the guard.* It is not found in the parallel in Chr.

Temple Records

down the king from the temple of Jehovah and entered through the gate of the guards to the royal palace. And he sat on the royal throne. ²⁰So all the people of the land rejoiced and the city was quiet. Thus they slew Athaliah with the sword in the royal palace.

Chronicler's Ecclesiastical History

none who was at all unclean should enter. ²⁰Then he took the military commanders and the nobles and those who ruled the people of the land, and brought down the king from the temple of Jehovah. And when they had come through the upper gate to the royal palace, they placed the king upon the royal throne. ²¹Then all the people of the land rejoiced and the city was quiet. Thus they slew Athaliah.

§ 115. Joash's Reign and Repair of the Temple, II Kgs. 11²¹–12²¹, II Chr. 24

Temple Records

II Kgs. 11 ²¹Jehoash was seven years old when he began to reign. **12** ¹In the seventh year of Jehu Jehoash began to reign, and he reigned forty years in Jerusalem. And his mother's name was Zibiah of Beersheba. ²And Jehoash did that which pleased Jehovah just as long as Jehoiada the priest instructed him. ³Only the high places were not taken away; the people still sacrificed and burnt their offerings on the high places.

⁴And Jehoash said to the priests, All the money, which in the form of consecration gifts is brought into the temple of Jehovah, the money which comes from each man's assessment, the money from the persons whose value is estimated, and all the money which the people bring of their own free will into the temple of Jehovah,ᵇ

Chronicler's Ecclesiastical History

II Chr. 24 ¹Joash was seven years old when he began to reign, and he reigned forty years in Jerusalem. And his mother's name was Zibiah, of Beersheba. ²And Joash did that which pleased Jehovah all the days of Jehoiada the priest. ³And Jehoiada took for himself two wives, and he begot sons and daughters.

⁴Now after this it occurred to Joash to restore the temple of Jehovah. ⁵And he gathered together the priests and the Levites and said to them, Go out to the cities of Judah and gather of all Israel money to repair the temple of your God from year to year; but you must hasten the matter. However, the Levites did not hasten

(margin, left of first column:) hoila's ise un- l

(margin, left of second paragraph:) ailure the iests e keep e mple re- ir

---

§ 115 The narrative of Kgs. continues the preceding and is clearly from the same source. The editor has introduced it by his usual synchronistic formula. The language of 12¹⁷, ¹⁸ is closely parallel to the citation from the annals of Judah in I Kgs. 16¹⁷, ¹⁸ and they are probably from the same source, although their present connection and the parallel references in II Kgs. 16¹⁷, ¹⁸ and 18¹⁶ to the robbery of the temple in order to pay tribute, both of which are from the temple records, tend to connect them with the latter source. The brief quotation in ²⁰, ²¹ᵃ is evidently from the annals of Judah.

The Chronicler has an expanded and much revised version of the narratives. The Levites appear, as well as the priests, and the Aramean invasion is interpreted as a divine judgment upon Joash for a sin—the murder of the son of Jehoiada—to which no reference is made in Kgs. The parallel passages illustrate most vividly the older and the later conceptions of the history. At the same time it is probable that the later, through the medium of oral priestly tradition, has preserved facts not recorded in the older, although, where there are direct contradictions, the authority is clearly with the older and more natural narrative of Kgs.

ᵇ II Kgs. 12⁴ The passage is exceedingly difficult. The translation aims to bring out the meaning of the text. Three sources of income appear to be suggested: (1) the poll-tax for the temple, (2) the equivalent values for persons consecrated to Jehovah—the later usage is outlined in detail in Lev. 27, (3) the regular vows and freewill offerings. By the majority of scholars (2) is regarded as a scribal note intended to explain (1), but the two peculiar idioms do not appear to be equivalent to each other.

Temple Records

⁵let the priests take that for themselves each from his acquaintances. They must, however, repair the breaches in the temple, wherever any breach is found. ⁶But it transpired that in the twenty-third year of Jehoash the priests had not yet repaired the breaches of the temple. ⁷Then King Jehoash called for Jehoiada the priest and for the other priests and said to them, Why have you not repaired the breaches of the temple? Now therefore take no more money from your acquaintances, but turn it over for the repair of the breaches of the temple. ⁸And the priests agreed that they should take no more money from the people nor repair the breaches of the temple.

Detailed provisions for the expense and repair of the temple ⁹Then Jehoiada the priest took a chest, bored a hole in its cover and placed it beside the doorpost[d] at the right of the entrance of the temple of Jehovah. And the priests, who kept watch at the threshold, put therein all the money that was brought into the temple of Jehovah. ¹⁰And as soon as they saw that there was much money in the chest, the king's scribe and the high[e] priest came up, and they put up in bags and counted the money that was found in the temple of Jehovah. ¹¹Then they gave the money that was weighed out into the hands of those who had the oversight of the temple of Jehovah; and they paid it out to the carpenters and the builders, who worked on the temple of Jehovah, ¹²and to the masons and the stone-cutters, and for the buying of timber and hewn stone to repair the breaches of the temple of

Chronicler's Ecclesiastical History

it. ⁶Then the king summoned Jehoiada the chief and said to him, Why have you not required the Levites to bring in from Judah and Jerusalem the tax of Moses, the servant of Jehovah, and of the assembly of Israel for the tent of the testimony? ⁷For the wicked Athaliah and her sons[c] had wrought devastation in the house of God, and had employed all the objects consecrated to the temple of Jehovah for the Baals.

⁸So the king commanded, that they should prepare a chest and place it outside at the gate of the temple of Jehovah. ⁹And they made a proclamation through Judah and Jerusalem to bring in for Jehovah the tax that Moses, the servant of God, laid upon Israel in the wilderness. ¹⁰And all the princes and all the people rejoiced, and brought in and cast into the chest, until it was full. ¹¹And each time, when the chest was brought to those appointed by the king by the hand of the Levites and they saw that there was much money, the king's scribe and the one appointed by the chief priest came and emptied the chest and took it and carried it again to its place. Thus they did day by day and gathered money in abundance. ¹²And the king and Jehoiada gave it to the master workmen in the construction of the temple of

---

c II Chr. 24⁷ So Gk. and Lat. Heb., *sons of Athaliah that wicked woman.*
d II Kgs. 12⁹ Heb., *altar.* Gk., *maççebah;* but the context indicates that it was beside the entrance. A slight emendation gives the above.
e II Kgs. 12¹⁰ Elsewhere in 11 Jehoiada is called simply, *the priest.* Furthermore he lived in the temple. *High* is evidently from a later scribe; possibly also, *priest.*

Temple Records

Jehovah, and for all for which outlay should be made upon the temple for its repairs. ¹³However, there were not made for the temple of Jehovah silver cups, basins, trumpets, or any vessels of gold or vessels of silver from the money that was brought into the temple of Jehovah, ¹⁴but they gave that to those who did the work and repaired the temple of Jehovah. ¹⁵Moreover they reckoned not with the men, into whose hand they delivered the money to give to those who did the work, for they dealt faithfully. ¹⁶The money from the trespass-offerings and the money from the sin-offerings was not brought into the temple of Jehovah; it belonged to the priests.

Chronicler's Ecclesiastical History

Jehovah. And they hired masons and carpenters to restore the temple of Jehovah, and also those who wrought iron and brass to repair the temple of Jehovah. ¹³So the workmen toiled, and thus the work went forward rapidly in their hands. And they set up the house of God according to the plan, and strengthened it. ¹⁴And when they had finished, they brought the rest of the money before the king and Jehoiada, and he caused to be made from it vessels for the temple of Jehovah, even vessels for the service and for offering the sacrifice, and spoons and vessels of gold and silver. So they offered burnt-offerings in the temple of Jehovah continually as long as Jehoiada lived.

¹⁵But when Jehoiada was old and satisfied with living he died. A hundred and thirty years old was he when he died. ¹⁶And they buried him in the city of David among the kings, because he had done good in Israel and toward God and his temple. Death of Jehoiada

¹⁷But after the death of Jehoiada the princes of Judah came and made obeisance to the king. Then the king gave heed to them. ¹⁸And they forsook the temple of Jehovah, the God of their fathers, and served the asherahs and the idols. But wrath came upon Judah and Jerusalem for their guilt. ¹⁹Yet he sent prophets to them, to bring them back to Jehovah, who testified against them; but they would not heed. Later apostasy of king and people

²⁰Then the spirit of God came upon Zechariah the son of Jehoiada the priest, so that he stood before the temple and said to them, Thus saith God, 'Why do ye transgress the commands of Jehovah, so that ye cannot prosper? Because ye have forsaken Jehovah, he hath also forsaken you.' ²¹But they conspired against him and at the command of the king stoned him to death in the court of the temple of Jehovah. ²²Thus Joash the king did not remember the kindness which Jehoiada his father had done him, but slew his son! And when he died, he said, May Jehovah see and punish! Martyrdom of Zechariah the son of Jehoiada

Annals of Judah

¹⁷Then Hazael king of Aram went up and fought against Gath, and took it. But when Hazael set out to go up to Jerusalem, ¹⁸Jehoash king of Judah took all the consecrated gifts that Jehoshaphat and Jehoram and The Aramean invasion

²³And it came to pass at the end of a year, that the army of the Arameans came up against him. And they came to Judah and Jerusalem and destroyed all the princes of the people from among the people and

Annals of Judah

Chronicler's Ecclesiastical History

Ahaziah, his ancestors the kings of Judah, had dedicated, and his own consecrated gifts, and all the gold that was found in the treasures of the temple of Jehovah and of the royal palace, and sent it to Hazael king of Aram. Then he went away from Jerusalem.

sent all the spoil taken from them to the king of Damascus. ²⁴The army of the Arameans, indeed, came with a small body of men; but Jehovah delivered a very great army into their hand, because the Judeans had forsaken Jehovah the God of their fathers; so that they executed judgment upon Joash.

Fatal conspiracy against Joash
²⁰But his servants arose and made a conspiracy and smote Joash at the house of Millo, that goeth down^g to Silla, ²¹for his servant Jozacar the son of Shimeath and Jehozabad the son of Shomer put him to death. And they buried him with his fathers in the city of David; and Amaziah his son became king in his place. ¹⁹Now the other acts of Joash and all that he did—are they not recorded in the Chronicles of the Kings of Judah?

²⁵And when they departed from him—for they left him very sick—his own servants conspired against him, on account of the bloodguilt of the son^f of Jehoiada the priest, and slew him on his bed. So he died and they buried him in the city of David, but they buried him not in the sepulchres of the kings. ²⁶And these are those who conspired against him: Zacar^h the son of Shimeath the Ammonitess, and Jehozabal the son of Shimrith the Moabitess. ²⁷Now his son and the many divine utterances against him, and the rebuilding of the house of God—they have already been recorded in the Midrash of the Book of the Kings. And Amaziah his son became king in his place.

§ 116. Amaziah's Reign, II Kgs. 14¹⁻²¹, II Chr. 25

Annals of Judah

Summary of Amaziah's reign
II Kgs. 14 ¹In the second year of Joash son of Jehoahaz king of Israel, Amaziah the son of Joash king of Judah began to reign. ²He was twenty years old when he began to reign, and he reigned twenty-nine years in Jerusalem. And his mother's name was Jehoaddin of Jerusalem. ³And he did that which pleased Jehovah, yet not like David his ancestor—he did just as Joash his father had done. ⁴However, he did not take away the high places; the people still sacrificed and burnt their offerings on the high places.

Execution of his father's assassins
⁵Now as soon as the kingdom was firmly established in his hand, he slew his servants who had slain his father. ⁶But the children of the murderers he did not put to death, according to that which is written in the book of the law

---

^f II Chr. 24²⁵ So Gk. and Lat. Heb., *sons.*
^g II Kgs. 12²⁰ The passage is obscure. The original may have read, *as he was going down to the house of Millo.*
^h II Chr. 24²⁶ Heb., *Zabad,* but the original probably had a shortened form of the corresponding, *Jozacar,* cf. II Kgs. 12²¹.

§ 116 Into his usual formulas the editor of Kgs. has introduced two brief citations from the Judean annals, 5, 6a, 7. The reference in 6b is to the late prophetic law-book, Dt. 24¹⁶. The precedent established at this time may well have formed the basis of the later law. As has already been noted, the account of the war with Israel in 8⁻¹⁴ is from the annals of Israel, cf. note § 96.

For the brief account of this war with Edom in II Kgs. 14⁷ the Chronicler has substituted a story probably drawn from his other main source. Possibly ¹⁴⁻¹⁶ are from the same. The account of the war with Joash of Israel is taken from the canonical book of Kgs. (14⁸⁻¹⁶) and is slightly expanded in ¹⁷, ²⁰.

Annals of Judah

of Moses, as Jehovah commanded, saying, The fathers shall not be put to death for the children nor the children be put to death for the fathers, but every man shall die for his own sin.[i]

is
efeat
id
augh-
·r of
ie
dom-
es

⁷He slew of Edom in the valley of Salt ten thousand, and took Sela [the Rock] by storm, and named it Joktheel[j] to this day.

Chronicler's Ecclesiastical History

II Chr. 25 ⁵Moreover Amaziah gathered Judah together, and ordered them according to their families, under commanders of thousands and commanders of hundreds, even all Judah and Benjamin, and numbered them from twenty years old and upward, and found them to be three hundred thousand picked men, able to go forth to war and who could handle spear and shield. ⁶He also hired a hundred thousand brave warriors from Israel for a hundred talents of silver. ⁷But a man of God came to him, saying, O king, let not the army of Israel go with you, for Jehovah is not with Israel, that is, with all the Ephraimites. ⁸But if you think that you will become strong in this way, God will cast you down before the enemy, for God hath power to help and to cast down. ⁹But Amaziah said to the man of God, But what shall I do for the hundred talents I have given to the troops of Israel? And the man of God answered, Jehovah is able to give you much more than this. ¹⁰Then Amaziah separated them (the troops who had come to him out of Ephraim) to go home again. But their anger was greatly aroused against Judah and they returned home in fierce anger. ¹¹Amaziah, however, took courage and led forth his people to the Valley of Salt and smote ten thousand of the children of Seir. ¹²And ten thousand the Judahites carried away alive, brought them to the top of a crag, and cast them down from the top of the crag, so that they all were dashed to pieces. ¹³But the troops whom Amaziah sent back without allowing them to go with him to battle fell upon the cities of Judah, from Samaria to Bethhoron, and smote of them three thousand, and took much spoil.

¹⁴Now after Amaziah returned from the slaughter of the Edomites, he brought the gods of the children of Seir, and set them up to be his gods, and bowed down himself to them, and offered sacrifices to them. ¹⁵Therefore the anger of Jehovah was aroused against Amaziah, and he sent to him a prophet, who said to him, Why have you sought after the gods of the people, which have not delivered their own people out of your hand? ¹⁶And it came to pass, as he talked with him, that the king said to him, Have we appointed you the king's counsellor? Desist; why should you be cut down? Then the prophet desisted and said, I know that God has determined to destroy you, because you have done this and have not hearkened to my counsel.

His idolatry and refusal to listen to Jehovah's prophet

---

[i] II Kgs. 14⁶ Under Ahab the unjust ancient custom was still in force, II Kgs. 9²⁶. The present passage records one of the earliest precedents which in time gave rise to the law of Dt. 24¹⁶ referred to by the late prophetic editor.

[j] II Kgs. 14⁷ The usual identification with Petra, the capital of Edom, is by no means certain. It is nowhere else known as Joktheel. Am. 1¹¹, ¹² implies that Edom was independent.

Chronicler's Ecclesiastical History

His challenge of the king of Israel

¹⁷Then Amaziah king of Judah took advice, and sent to Joash the son of Jehoahaz, the son of Jehu the king of Israel saying, Come, let us meet face to face. ¹⁸But Joash king of Israel sent to Amaziah king of Judah, saying, The thistle that was in Lebanon sent to the cedar that was in Lebanon, saying, ' Give your daughter to my son as wife.' But a wild beast of Lebanon passed by and trod down the thistle. ¹⁹You think, you have indeed smitten Edom; and now your heart impels you to win renown. Remain at home; why should you court misfortune, so that you will fall and Judah with you?

His defeat and humiliation

²⁰But Amaziah would not hear. It was God's doing, that he might deliver them into the hand of their enemies, because they had sought after the gods of Edom. ²¹So Joash king of Israel went up, and he and Amaziah king of Judah met face to face at Bethshemesh, which belongs to Judah. ²²And Judah was defeated by Israel, so that they fled each to his home. ²³And Joash king of Israel took Amaziah king of Judah, the son of Joash, the son of Jehoahaz, at Bethshemesh and brought him down to Jerusalem and broke down the wall of Jerusalem from the Gate of Ephraim to the Corner Gate—four hundred cubits. ²⁴And he took all the gold and silver and all the vessels that were found in the house of God with Obed-edom, together with the treasures of the royal palace and the hostages, and returned to Samaria.

Late Prophetic Summary

His death

II Kgs. 14 ¹⁷And Amaziah the son of Joash king of Judah lived after the death of Jehoash son of Jehoahaz king of Israel fifteen years. ¹⁸Now the other acts of Amaziah, are they not recorded in the Chronicles of the Kings of Judah? ¹⁹And^k they made a conspiracy against him in Jerusalem. And he fled to Lachish, but they sent after him to Lachish and slew him there. ²⁰And they brought him upon horses, and he was buried at Jerusalem with his fathers in the city of David. ²¹And all the people of Judah took Azariah,¹ who was sixteen years old, and made him king in the place of his father Amaziah.

§ 117. Reign of Azariah (Uzziah), II Kgs. 14²², 15¹⁻⁷, II Chr. 26

Late Prophetic Summary	Chronicler's Ecclesiastical History
Summary of Azariah's reign and policy	**II Kgs. 15** ¹In the twenty-seventh year of Jeroboam king of Israel, Azariah son of Amaziah king of Judah began to reign. ²Sixteen years old was he when he began to reign, and	**II Chr. 26** ¹And all the people of Judah took Uzziah, who was sixteen years old, and made him king in the place of his father Amaziah. ²He built Elath, and restored it to Judah

Late Prophetic Summary	*Chronicler's Ecclesiastical History*
he reigned fifty-two years in Jerusalem. And his mother's name was Jecoliah of Jerusalem. ³And he did that which pleased Jehovah, just as his father Amaziah had done. ⁴However the high places were not taken away; the people still sacrificed and burnt their offerings on the high places. 14 ²²He built Elath and restored it to Judah after King Amaziah slept with his fathers.	after the king slept with his fathers. ³Sixteen years old was Uzziah when he began to reign, and he reigned fifty-two years in Jerusalem. And his mother's name was Jechiliah of Jerusalem. ⁴And he did that which pleased Jehovah just as his father Amaziah had done. ⁵And he was ready to seek God during the lifetime of Zechariah, who instructed him in the fear^m of God; and as long as he sought Jehovah, God gave him prosperity.

⁶And he went against the Philistines, and broke down the wall of Gath and the wall of Jabneh and the wall of Ashdod and built cities near Ashdod and among the Philistines. ⁷And God helped him against the Philistines and against the Arabians who dwelt in Gur-baal, and the Meunites.^n ⁸And the Ammonites paid tribute to Uzziah; and his reputation spread abroad even to the entrance of Egypt; for he became exceedingly strong. *His victories*

⁹Moreover Uzziah built towers in Jerusalem at the Corner Gate and at the Valley Gate and at the corner of the wall and fortified them. ¹⁰And he built towers in the wilderness and hewed out many cisterns, for he had many herds, in the lowland and husbandmen in the plain and vinedressers in the mountains and in the fruitful fields, for he loved agriculture. *His building enterprises*

¹¹Moreover Uzziah had an army of fighting men, ready to take the field, divided into companies according to the number of their reckoning made by Jeiel the scribe and Maaseiah the officer, under the direction of Hananiah, one of the king's generals. ¹²The whole number of the heads of families, even the brave warriors, was two thousand, six hundred. ¹³And under their command was an army of three hundred and seven thousand, five hundred, ready for war with complete equipment, to help the king against the enemy. ¹⁴And Uzziah equipped them, even all the army, with coats of mail, bows, and stones for slinging. ¹⁵Also he made in Jerusalem skilfully invented machines, which were set upon the towers and on the battlements, with which to shoot arrows and great stones. *His army and military equipment*

---

are that Azariah restored Elath, which had probably been reconquered by his father Amaziah, and that he was a leper.

The material prosperity of Judah reflected in Is. 2, was due to his constructive aggressive policy. The Chronicler, therefore, doubtless gives not only a fuller, but also a truer picture of this important reign, especially in 26⁶⁻¹⁵ᵃ, where he appears to have quoted from his non-canonical source. Whether in ¹⁵ᵇ⁻²⁰ he simply sought, according to the religious ideas of his age, to explain Uzziah's strange fate, or had earlier data at his command, cannot be definitely determined.

ᵐ II Chr. 26⁵ So the versions and certain Heb. MSS. Received Heb., *vision*.
ⁿ II Chr. 26⁷ Cf. also I Chr. 4⁴¹.

Annals of Judah	*Chronicler's Ecclesiastical History*

His leprosy and death

II Kgs. 15 ⁵And Jehovah smote the king, so that he was a leper to the day of his death. And he dwelt in his house without restraint, while Jotham, the king's son, was at the head of the royal household, ruling the people of the land. ⁶Now the other acts of Azariah and all that he did, are they not recorded in the Chronicles of the Kings of Judah? ⁷And Azariah slept with his fathers; and they buried him with his fathers in the city of David, and Jotham his son became king in his place.

And his name spread far abroad, for he was marvellously helped until he became strong. ¹⁶But when he was strong, his heart was so lifted up, that he acted corruptly. And he trespassed against Jehovah his God by going into the temple of Jehovah to burn incense. ¹⁷And Azariah the priest went in after him, with eighty priests of Jehovah, men of ability. ¹⁸And they withstood Uzziah the king and said to him, It is not your part, Uzziah, to burn incense to Jehovah, but that of the priests, the sons of Aaron, who are consecrated to burn incense. Go out of the sanctuary, for you have trespassed, and that shall not be to your honor in the sight of Jehovah God. ¹⁹Then Uzziah was angry and he had a censer in his hand to burn incense. And while he was angry with the priests, the leprosy broke out on his forehead before the priests in the temple of Jehovah beside the altar of incense. ²⁰And when Azariah the chief priest looked upon him, there he was leprous on his forehead. So they thrust him out quickly from there, and he himself hastened to go out, because Jehovah had smitten him. ²¹And Uzziah the king was a leper to the day of his death, and dwelt in his house without restraint, being a leper, for he was cut off from the temple of Jehovah; while Jotham his son was at the head of the royal household, ruling the people of the land. ²²Now the other acts of Uzziah, first and last, Isaiah the prophet, the son of Amoz, has recorded. ²³So Uzziah slept with his fathers; and they buried him with his fathers in the field of burial which belonged to the kings, for they said, He is a leper. And Jotham, his son, became king in his place.

§ 118. Jotham's Reign, II Kgs. 15³²⁻³⁸, II Chr. 27

Late Prophetic Summary	*Chronicler's Ecclesiastical History*

Jotham's policy, building enterprises and wars

II Kgs. 15 ³²In the second year of Pekah the son of Remaliah king of Israel, Jotham the son of Uzziah king of Judah began to reign. ³³He was twenty-five years old when he began to reign, and he reigned sixteen years in Jerusalem. And his mother's name was Jerusha the

II Chr. 27 ¹Jotham was twenty-five years old when he began to reign, and he reigned sixteen years in Jerusalem. And his mother's name was Jerushah the daughter of Zadok. ²And he did that which pleased Jehovah, just as his father Uzziah had done, only he did not enter into the temple of Jehovah. And the people acted ever more corruptly. ³He built the upper

---

§ 118 In 15³⁵ᵇ, ³⁷ the late prophetic editor of Kgs. has incorporated two brief statements drawn from the annals of Judah. Likewise the Chronicler in 3ᵇ⁻⁵ has also drawn what appears to be authentic data from his non-canonical source. The amount of the tribute, however, in 27⁵, is probably due to the Chronicler's well-known fondness for large numbers.

Late Prophetic Summary	*Chronicler's Ecclesiastical History*
daughter of Zadok. ³⁴And he did that which pleased Jehovah; he did just as his father Uzziah had done. ³⁵However the high places were not taken away; the people still sacrificed and burnt their offerings on the high places. He built the upper gate of the temple of Jehovah. ³⁷In those days Jehovah began to send against Judah Rezin the king of Aram and Pekah the son of Remaliah. ³⁶Now the other acts of Jotham and all that he did, are they not recorded in the Chronicles of the Kings of Judah? ³⁸And Jotham slept with his fathers and was buried with his fathers in the city of David his father; and Ahaz his son became king in his place.	gate of the temple of Jehovah and on the wall of Ophel he built much. ⁴Moreover he built cities in the hill-country of Judah, and in the forests he built castles and towers. ⁵He fought also with the king of the Ammonites and conquered Ammon. And the Ammonites gave him that year a hundred talents of silver and two hundred thousand bushels° of wheat and ten thousand of barley. The same amount did the Ammonites render to him in the second year and in the third. ⁶So Jotham became mighty, because he ordered his ways according to the will of Jehovah his God. ⁷Now the other acts of Jotham and all his wars and his undertakings, they are indeed already recorded in the Book of the Kings of Israel and Judah. ⁸He was twenty-five years old when he began to reign, and he reigned sixteen years in Jerusalem.

II

THE ASSYRIAN PERIOD: FROM AHAZ TO JOSIAH, II Kgs. 16, 18–21, Is. 36–39, II Chr. 28–33

§ 119. The Reign of Ahaz and his Homage to Tiglath-Pileser III, II Kgs. 16, Is. 7¹⁻¹⁷, II Chr. 28

Late Prophetic Summary	*Chronicler's Ecclesiastical History*
II Kgs. 16 ¹In the seventeenth year of Pekah the son of Remaliah Ahaz the son of Jotham became king of Judah. ²Twenty years old was Ahaz when he began to reign, and he reigned sixteen years in Jerusalem.	**II Chr. 28** ¹Ahaz was twenty years old when he began to reign and he reigned sixteen years in Jerusalem. And he did not do that which pleased Jehovah, as did David his ancestor, ²but he walked in the ways of the

(left margin: eac- onary lig- us olicy)

° II Chr. 27⁵ Heb., *ten thousand cors.*
The Assyrian Period.—The folly of Ahaz in seeking aid from Assyria against his northern neighbors gave that strong, ambitious world-power its title to interfere in the politics of Judah. Until Assyria began to fall into decay·in the days of Josiah, it never ceased energetically to maintain that title. The result was that it determined the political history of the surviving

§ 119 Following the usual editorial introduction are two citations, apparently from distinct sources. In ⁵⁻⁹ the designation of the king is simply *Ahaz*, but in ¹⁰⁻¹⁸ it is always *King Ahaz*. Moreover ⁵⁻⁹ recount in the brief annalistic style political facts, but in ¹⁰⁻¹⁸ the important details of Ahaz's journey to Damascus and the far-reaching significance of the act are ignored and the narrative simply tells of the innovations introduced in the temple and its ritual by the king

Late Prophetic Summary

And he did not do that which pleased Jehovah his God, as did David his ancestor, ³but walked in the way of the kings of Israel. He also made his son to pass through fire according to the abominations of the nations, whom Jehovah drove out before the Israelites. ⁴And he sacrificed and burnt their offerings on the high places and on the hills and under every green tree.

Chronicler's Ecclesiastical History

kings of Israel and made molten images for the Baals. ³Moreover he offered sacrifices in the valley of Ben-Hinnom, and burnt his sons in the fire according to the abominations of the nations whom Jehovah drove out from before the Israelites. ⁴And he sacrificed and burnt offerings on the high places and on the hills and under every green tree.

Annals of Judah

Attack of the Arameans and Northern Israelites — ⁵Then Rezin king of Aram and Pekah son of Remaliah came up to attack Jerusalem; and they besieged Ahaz, but could not overcome him. ⁶At that time the king of Edom recovered Elath for Edom[a] and drove the Judahites from Elath; and the Edomites came to Elath and have dwelt there until the present day.

⁵Therefore Jehovah his God delivered him into the hand of the king of Aram, and they smote him and carried away from him a great multitude of captives and brought them to Damascus. And he was also delivered into the power of the king of Israel, who smote him with a great slaughter. ⁶For Pekah the son of Remaliah slew in Judah a hundred and twenty thousand in one day, all of them valiant warriors, because they had forsaken Jehovah the God of their fathers. ⁷And Zichri, a mighty man of Ephraim, slew Maaseiah, the king's son, and Azrikam, the commander of the palace, and Elkanah, who was next to the king.

Hebrew state. Most of its crises came through its relations to Assyria. It was a period of severe political and religious trial.

Fortunately it is possible to view the period from many different sides. The citations from the annals of Judah are brief and few. The late prophetic editor usually adds only the bare facts or else gives his general estimate of each reign; but he also draws at length from what appear to have been three distinct sources: the temple records, a Hezekiah history, and a collection of Isaiah stories. These are richly supplemented by the contemporary addresses of the prophets of the period (cf. Vol. III), which constitute the best possible historical sources. In addition the Assyrian monumental literature contains detailed accounts of the campaigns of the kings who invaded Palestine. Cf. Appendices VI–VIII. At certain points the later Jewish stories in Chr. furnish further data. These combined sources give an unusually clear picture of what was one of the most important periods in the literary and religious history of the Hebrew race.

as the result of his visit to the heathen capital. It seems clear, therefore, that ⁵⁻⁹ are from the annals and ¹⁰⁻¹⁸ from the temple records.

Is. 7¹⁻¹⁷ supplements the meagre records of the annals regarding the early stages of the conflict. The parallel version in II Chr. 28 departs widely from the brief narrative of Kgs. which it incorporates. Again the huge numbers and the rôle of the prophet indicate that the story has been freely adapted to the religious teaching which the author sought thus to impress. It may be the work of the Chronicler, but, more probably was taken from his midrashic source. The data in ⁷ probably came from a still older source. The natural sequel of ¹⁶ is ²⁰. Vss. ²⁶, ²⁷ contain the Chronicler's usual concluding formula. For the contemporary record of the campaigns of Tiglath-Pileser III, cf. Appendix VI.

a II Kgs. 16⁶ So marginal reading of Heb. Clearly *Edom* was mistaken for the very similar Heb. word *Aram*, and *Rezin* was added from ⁵, giving the reading, *Rezin king of Aram recovered Elath for Aram*. But Elath originally belonged not to Aram but to Edom. Cf. map opp. p. 49.

Chronicler's Ecclesiastical History

[8]And the Israelites carried away captive of their kinsmen two hundred thousand, women, sons, and daughters, and also took away much spoil from them and brought it to Samaria. [9]But a prophet of Jehovah was there, by the name of Oded. And he went out to meet the army that came to Samaria, and said to them, See, because Jehovah, the God of your fathers, was wroth with Judah, he hath delivered them into your hand. But ye have slain them in a rage which hath reached up to heaven. [10]And now you purpose to enslave the inhabitants of Judah and Jerusalem that they may be bondmen and bondwomen to you; but are there not even with you crimes of your own against Jehovah your God? [11]Now hear me, therefore, and send back the captives, whom you have taken of your kinsmen, for the fierce wrath of Jehovah is upon you. Prophetic command to return the captives from Judah

[12]Then certain heads of the Ephraimites, Azariah the son of Johanan, Berechiah the son of Meshillemoth, and Jehizikiah the son of Shallum, and Amasa the son of Hadlai, stood up against those who came from the war, [13]and said to them, You shall not bring in the captives here, for you purpose that which will bring us guilt against Jehovah to add to our sins and to our guilt, for our guilt is great, and there is fierce wrath against Israel. [14]So the armed men left the captives and the spoil before the princes and all the assembly. [15]And the men who have been mentioned rose up and took the captives, and with the spoil clothed all who were naked among them, and after they had clothed them, they provided them with sandals and gave them to eat and to drink and anointed them and carried all the feeble among them on asses, and brought them to Jericho, the city of palm-trees, to their kinsmen. Then they returned to Samaria. Return of the captives

Annals of Judah

Ahaz's tribute to secure Assyria's aid against his foes

[7]But Ahaz sent messengers to Tiglath-Pileser king of Assyria, saying, I am your servant and your son; come up and deliver me from the power of the king of Aram and from the power of the king of Israel, who have attacked me. [8]Then Ahaz took the silver and gold that were found in the temple of Jehovah and in the treasures of the royal palace, and sent it as a present to the king of Assyria. [9]And the king of Assyria listened to him. So the king of Assyria went up against Damascus and took it and carried its inhabitants captive to Kir[b] and put Rezin to death.

[16]At that time King Ahaz sent to the kings of Assyria to help him. [17]For the Edomites had come again and smitten Judah and carried away captives. [18]The Philistines also had invaded the cities of the lowland and of the South Country of Judah and had taken Bethshemesh, Aijalon, Gederoth, Soco with its dependent towns, and Timnath with its dependent towns, Gimzo also with its dependent towns, and they dwelt there. [19]For Jehovah brought Judah low because of Ahaz king of Israel, because he had acted wantonly with Judah and had behaved very faithlessly with Jehovah. [20]And Tiglath-Pileser king of Assyria came to him, but proved to be his enemy and did not strengthen him.

---

[b] II Kgs. 16[9] Possibly *Kir* is added from Am. 1[5]. It is not found in the Gk.

Temple Records   *Chronicler's Eccle-*
                                              siastical History

The heathen altar and other innovations introduced by Ahaz ¹⁰Now when King Ahaz went to Damascus to·meet Tiglath-Pileser king of Assyria, he saw there the altar that was at Damascus. Then King Ahaz sent to Urijah the priest a model of the altar and a pattern of all the details of its construction. ¹¹And Urijah the priest built an altar, exactly corresponding to what King Ahaz had sent from Damascus, even thus Urijah the priest made it before King Ahaz returned from Damascus. ¹²And when the king returned from Damascus and saw the altar, the king drew near to the altar, went up on it, ¹³and burnt his burnt-offering and his cereal-offering, and poured out his libation on the altar. ¹⁴And the brazen[d] altar, which stood before Jehovah, he brought from the front of the temple, from between his altar and the temple of Jehovah, and put it on the north side of his altar. ¹⁵And King Ahaz commanded Urijah the priest, saying, On the great altar burn the morning burnt-offering and the evening cereal-offering and the king's burnt-offering and his cereal-offering, with the burnt-offering of all the people of the land,[e] and their cereal-offering and their libations, and sprinkle upon it all the blood of the burnt-offering and all the blood of the sacrifice; but the brazen altar shall be for me to inquire by.[f] ¹⁶Thus did Urijah the priest, just as King Ahaz commanded.

²¹And Ahaz plundered the temple of Jehovah, and the palace of the king and of the princes and gave it to the king of Assyria; but it helped him not. ²²And in the time of his distress[c] he committed still more crimes against Jehovah — this same King Ahaz. ²³For he sacrificed to the gods of Damascus, which smote him, and he thought, Because the gods of the kings of Aram helped them, therefore, I will sacrifice to them, that they may help me. But they were the ruin of him and of all Israel.

Other changes in the temple ¹⁷King Ahaz also cut off the border-frames of the stands and removed the laver from them; he also took down the sea from the brazen oxen that were under it, and put it upon a stone pedestal. ¹⁸And the covered way for the sabbath, that they had built in the temple, and the outer entrance for the king, he sent away from the temple of Jehovah for the sake of the king of Assyria.

²⁴And Ahaz gathered together the vessels of the house of God and shut up the doors of the temple of Jehovah; and he erected altars in every corner of Jerusalem. ²⁵And in every city of Judah he made high places to offer sacrifices to other gods, and thus provoked to anger Jehovah, the God of his fathers.

²⁶Now his other acts, and all his ways, first and last, are already writ-

---

[c] II Chr. 28²² The Gk. corrects the awkward Heb. text by joining ²²ᵃ to the preceding verse, *but distressed him.*
  [d] II Kgs. 16¹⁴ *Brazen* was probably added by mistake from ¹⁵ᵇ.
  [e] II Kgs. 16¹⁵ Gk. and Luc. omit, *of the land*—a later phrase.
  [f] II Kgs. 16¹⁵ *I.e.*, by examining the parts of the sacrifice. The exact meaning of the Heb. is not certain. It may be, *to think of, i.e.*, to decide later what to do with it, but the above interpretation is in closer keeping with the use of the verb elsewhere.

Temple Records

¹⁹Now the other acts of Ahaz which he did, are they not recorded in the Chronicles of the Kings of Judah? ²⁰And Ahaz slept with his fathers and was buried with his fathers in the city of David. And Hezekiah his son became king in his place.

Chronicler's Ecclesiastical History

ten in the Book of the Kings of Judah and Israel. ²⁷And Ahaz slept with his fathers and they buried him in the city, even in Jerusalem; for they brought him not into the sepulchres of the kings of Israel. And Hezekiah his son became king in his place.

§ 120. The Reign of Hezekiah and his Reforms, II Kgs. 18¹⁻⁸, II Chr. 29–31, 32²⁷⁻³¹

Late Prophetic Summary

II Kgs. 18 ¹Now in the third year of Hoshea the son of Elah king of Israel, Hezekiah the son of Ahaz king of Judah began to reign. ²He was twenty-five years old when he began to reign; and he reigned twenty-nine years in Jerusalem. And his mother's name was Abijah^g the daughter of Zechariah. ³And he did that which pleased Jehovah, just as David his ancestor had done.

Heze-kiah's good policy

Chronicler's Ecclesiastical History

II Chr. 29 ³He also in the first year of his reign in the first month opened the doors of the temple of Jehovah and repaired them. ⁴And he brought in the priests and the Levites and gathered them together into the open space on the east, ⁵and said to them, Hear me, O Levites; now sanctify yourselves and make ceremonially clean the temple of Jehovah, the God of your fathers,

His exhor-tation to the Levites

---

§ 120 Hezekiah was approved by later generations because of the reputation that he enjoyed as a religious reformer. That it rested upon a real basis of fact is confirmed by the statement in Jer. 26¹⁷⁻¹⁹ᵃ to the effect that he and all Judah heeded the earnest reform sermons of the prophet Micah. The subsequent reaction under Manasseh also strongly suggests that Hezekiah had introduced certain innovations which struck at popular religious practices. Unless it be a later interpolation, 18²² confirms the general statement in ⁴ and indicates that his reforms were introduced in the earlier part of his reign. Amos and Hosea viewed the high places with disfavor, although they did not demand their abolition. Isaiah attacked tree and idol worship (1²⁹, 2⁸, ¹⁸, ²⁰). There is every reason to believe that the reference to the destruction of the brazen serpent which the tradition, preserved in Num. 21⁸, ⁹, had associated with Moses, is authentic. Certain other heathen symbols still connected with the religion of Jehovah were probably also placed under the ban by the reformers. It is by no means impossible that the movement was inaugurated which later found prominent expression in the Deuteronomic code and application in connection with Josiah's reform, and which resulted in the abolition of all heathen shrines outside of Jerusalem. The account in ⁴ᵃ was, however, probably written by one who had in mind the more sweeping reforms of 621 B.C.

The later tendency to magnify the reforming work of Hezekiah is strikingly illustrated by the parallels in Chr. Later priestly tradition represented him as cleansing the temple, instituting special sacrifices, and celebrating a great passover feast in strict accord with the laws and usages which did not become firmly established until centuries later. These narratives are akin to the priestly precedents in Ex. and Num., associated with Moses and intended to illustrate the ceremonial institutions which grew up about the second temple. Regarded from this point of view their real value becomes apparent.

The account of the great passover in the days of Hezekiah in 30 is not strictly consistent with the one attributed to Josiah in 35 (cf. especially 35¹⁸) and may have been modelled after it by a later midrashist. It seems probable that both were found by the Chronicler in the non-canonical source from which he derived so much of his material. In 29²⁵⁻³⁰ he introduces his favorite levitical singers. Chap. 31 also appears to come from his hand. The important fact in 32³⁰ was probably derived from his non-canonical source.

g II Kgs. 18² So the parallel II Chr. 29¹. The Heb. has the shortened form, *Abi*.

Chronicler's Ecclesiastical History

and carry out the filth from the holy place. ⁶For our fathers have acted faithlessly and done that which displeased Jehovah our God and forsaken him and turned away their faces from the habitation of Jehovah and turned their backs upon him. ⁷Also they have shut up the doors of the porch and put out the lamps, and have not burned incense nor offered burnt-offerings in the holy place to the God of Israel. ⁸Therefore the wrath of Jehovah was upon Judah and Jerusalem, and he hath delivered them to be an object of horror, astonishment, and contempt, as you see with your own eyes. ⁹For now our fathers have fallen by the sword and our sons and our daughters and our wives are in captivity for this. ¹⁰Now it is in my heart to make a covenant with Jehovah, the God of Israel, that his fierce anger may turn away from us. ¹¹My sons, do not now be negligent, for Jehovah hath chosen you to stand before him to minister to him, and that you should be his ministers and offer sacrifices.

Cleansing of the temple ¹²Then the Levites arose, Mahath the son of Amasai, of the sons of the Kohathites; and of the sons of Merari, Kish the son of Abdi and Azariah the son of Jehallelel; and of the Gershonites, Joah the son of Zimmah and Eden the son of Joah; ¹³and of the sons of Elizaphan, Shimri and Jeuel; and of the sons of Asaph, Zechariah and Mattaniah; ¹⁴and of the sons of Heman, Jehuel and Shimei; and of the sons of Jeduthun, Shemaiah and Uzziel. ¹⁵And they gathered their kinsmen and sanctified themselves and went in, according to the commands of the king by the words of Jehovah, to cleanse the temple of Jehovah. ¹⁶And the priests went into the inner part of the temple of Jehovah to cleanse it and brought out all the uncleanness that they found in the temple of Jehovah into the court of the temple of Jehovah. And the Levites took it, in order to carry it out to the Brook Kidron. ¹⁷Now they began on the first day of the first month to make ceremonially clean, and on the eighth day of the month they came to the porch of Jehovah, and they made the temple of Jehovah ceremonially clean in eight days; and on the sixteenth day of the first month they completed their work. ¹⁸Then they went into Hezekiah the king within the palace and said, We have cleansed all the temple of Jehovah and the altar of burnt-offering, with all its vessels, and the table of showbread, with all its vessels. ¹⁹Moreover all the vessels, which King Ahaz in his reign had cast away, when he acted faithlessly, we have again made ceremonially clean, and there they are before the altar of Jehovah.

Offerings in behalf of the temple ²⁰Then Hezekiah the king early in the morning assembled the princes of the city and went up to the temple of Jehovah. ²¹And they brought seven bullocks and seven rams and seven lambs and seven he-goats for a sin-offering in behalf of the king and the sanctuary and Judah. And he commanded the priests, the sons of Aaron, to offer them on the altar of Jehovah. ²²So they killed the bullocks, and the priests received the blood and sprinkled it on the altar, and they killed the rams and sprinkled the blood upon the altar; they also killed the lambs and sprinkled the blood upon the altar. ²³And they brought near the he-goats for the sin-offering before the king and the assembly, that they might lay their hands upon them. ²⁴Then the

Chronicler's Ecclesiastical History

priests killed them and they brought the blood as a sin-offering upon the altar, to make atonement for all Israel; for the king ordered the burnt-offering and the sin-offering for all Israel.

^{25}And he set the Levites in the temple of Jehovah with cymbals, harps, and lutes, according to the command of David and of Gad the king's seer and of Nathan the prophet; for the command was from Jehovah by his prophets. ^{26}And the Levites stood with the instruments of David and the priests with the trumpets. ^{27}And Hezekiah commanded to offer the burnt-offering upon the altar. And when the burnt-offering began, the song in honor of Jehovah also began, and the trumpets, accompanied by the instruments of David king of Israel. ^{28}Then all the assembly worshipped, and the singers sang, and the trumpeters sounded; all this continued until the burnt-offering was finished. ^{29}And when they had made an end of offering, the king and all who were present with him bowed themselves and worshipped. ^{30}Moreover Hezekiah the king and the princes commanded the Levites to sing praises to Jehovah with the words of David and of Asaph the seer. So they sang praises with gladness and bowed their heads and worshipped.

Service of song

^{31}Then Hezekiah spoke up and said, Now you have consecrated yourselves again to Jehovah; come near and bring sacrifices and thank-offerings into the temple of Jehovah. And the assembly brought in sacrifices and thank-offerings, and as many as were of a liberal heart burnt-offerings. ^{32}And the number of the burnt-offerings which the assembly brought was seventy bullocks, a hundred rams, and two hundred lambs; all these were for a burnt-offering to Jehovah. ^{33}And the consecrated things were six hundred oxen and three thousand sheep. ^{34}But the priests were too few to flay all the burnt-offerings. Therefore their kinsmen the Levites helped them, until the work was ended and until the priests had sanctified themselves. The Levites, however, were more faithful in sanctifying themselves than the priests. ^{35}And there were also burnt-offerings in abundance, together with the fat of the peace-offerings and with the drink-offerings for every burnt-offering. So the service of the temple of Jehovah was set in order. ^{3}And Hezekiah and all the people rejoiced because of that which God had prepared for the people, for the thing was done quickly.

Public sacrifices and the restoration of the temple

30 ^{1}And Hezekiah sent to all Israel and Judah and wrote letters also to Ephraim and Manasseh, that they should come to the temple of Jehovah at Jerusalem, to keep the passover to Jehovah, the God of Israel. ^{2}For the king and his princes and all the assembly in Jerusalem had decided to keep the passover in the second month. ^{3}For they could not keep it at that time, because the priests had not sanctified themselves sufficiently, neither had the people gathered themselves together to Jerusalem. ^{4}And the thing seemed right to the king and all the assembly. ^{5}So they determined to make a proclamation throughout all Israel, from Beersheba even to Dan, that they should come to keep the passover to Jehovah, the God of Israel, at Jerusalem; for they had not kept it in such great numbers as is prescribed.

Summons to keep the passover

Chronicler's Ecclesiastical History

The procla-mation
⁶So the couriers went with the letters from the king and his princes through-out all Israel and Judah and proclaimed the command of the king, saying, Israelites! turn again to Jehovah, the God of Abraham, Isaac, and Israel, that he may turn to the remnant which is left of you from the hand of the kings of Assyria. ⁷And be not like your fathers and your kinsmen, who were faithless toward Jehovah, the God of their fathers, so that he gave them up to destruction, as you see. ⁸Now be not obdurate, as were your fathers, but yield yourselves to Jehovah[h] and enter into his sanctuary which he has sanctified forever, and serve Jehovah your God, that his fierce anger may turn away from you. ⁹For through your returning to Jehovah, your kins-men and children shall find compassion in the presence of those who led them captive so that they shall come back into this land; for Jehovah your God is gracious and merciful, and will not turn away his face from you, if you return to him.

Atti-tude of the north-ern tribes
¹⁰So the couriers passed from city to city through the country of Eph-raim and Manasseh, even to Zebulon. But they laughed them to scorn and mocked them. ¹¹Nevertheless some people from Asher and Manasseh and Zebulon humbled themselves and came to Jerusalem. ¹²Also upon Judah came the hand of God to give them one heart to do the command of the king and of the princes by the word of Jehovah.

Cele-bration of the pass-over
¹³So a great crowd of people assembled at Jerusalem to keep the feast of unleavened bread in the second month—a very great assembly. ¹⁴And they arose and took away the altars that were in Jerusalem and all the altars for incense they took away and cast into the Brook Kidron. ¹⁵Then they killed the passover on the fourteenth day of the second month. And the priests and the Levites were ashamed and sanctified themselves and brought burnt-offerings into the temple of Jehovah. ¹⁶And they stood in their place, as was their custom, according to the law of Moses the man of God: the priests sprinkling the blood which they received from the hand of the Levites. ¹⁷For there were many in the assembly who had not sanctified themselves; there-fore the Levites had the charge of killing the passover lambs for every one who was not clean in order to consecrate them to Jehovah. ¹⁸For a ma-jority of the people, most from Ephraim, Manasseh, Issachar, and Zebulon, had not kept themselves ceremonially clean, yet they ate the passover other-wise than is prescribed, for Hezekiah had prayed for them, saying, The good Jehovah pardon every one ¹⁹who setteth his heart to seek God, Jehovah, the God of his fathers, though he be not cleansed according to the purifica-tion of the sanctuary. ²⁰And Jehovah listened to Hezekiah and healed the people. ²¹So the Israelites, who were present at Jerusalem, kept the feast of unleavened bread seven days with great gladness. And the Levites and the priests praised Jehovah day by day with all their might. ²²And Hezekiah spoke reassuringly to all the Levites who had demonstrated their skill in serving Jehovah.[i] So they ate throughout the feast for the seven

---

h II Chr. 30⁸ Heb., *give your hand.*
i II Chr. 30²² Slightly correcting the Heb. text.

Chronicler's Ecclesiastical History

days, offering sacrifices of peace-offerings and making confession to Jehovah, the God of their fathers.

²³Then the whole assembly decided to keep another seven days; and so they kept another seven days with gladness. ²⁴For Hezekiah king of Judah distributed to the assembly a thousand bullocks and seven thousand sheep, and the princes distributed to the assembly a thousand bullocks and ten thousand sheep, and a great number of priests sanctified themselves. ²⁵And all the assembly of Judah, with the priests and the Levites and all the assembly, that came out of Israel, and the sojourners, who came out of the land of Israel and who dwelt in Judah, rejoiced. ²⁶So there was great joy in Jerusalem; for since the time of Solomon the son of David king of Israel there was nothing like it in Jerusalem. ²⁷Then the priests and[j] the Levites arose and blessed the people; and their voice was heard and their prayer came up to this holy habitation, even unto heaven.

The seven days of feasting

Annals of Judah

II Kgs. 18 ⁴He removed the high places and broke in pieces the pillars and cut down the asherah. And he broke in pieces the brazen serpent that Moses had made; for up to that time the Israelites had offered sacrifices to it; and they called it Nehushtan [The Brazen One].[k] ⁵He trusted in Jehovah, the God of Israel; so that after him was none like him among all the kings of Judah, nor among those who were before him. ⁶For he held fast to Jehovah, he departed not from following him, but kept his commands, which Jehovah had commanded Moses.

[margin:] eze-ah's ig-is rms

II Chr. 31 ¹Now when all this was finished, all Israel, who were present, went out to the cities of Judah and broke in pieces the pillars and hewed down the asherahs, and broke down the high places and the altars in all Judah and Benjamin, in Ephraim also and Manasseh, until they had destroyed them all. Then all the Israelites returned to their cities, each to his own possession.

²And Hezekiah appointed divisions of the priests and the Levites after their divisions—each of the priests and the Levites according to his service—for burnt-offerings and for peace-offerings, to minister and to give thanks and praise in the gates of the camp of Jehovah. ³The contribution of the king from his possessions was for burnt-offerings, for the morning and evening burnt-offerings, as well as the burnt-offerings for the sabbaths, for the new moons, and for the set feasts, as it is prescribed in the law of Jehovah. ⁴Moreover he commanded the people who dwelt in Jerusalem to provide the portion of the priests and the Levites, that they might devote themselves to the law of Jehovah. ⁵And as soon as the command was known, the Israelites gave in abundance the first-fruits of grain, new wine, oil, and honey, as well as the increase of the field; and the tithe of all things they also brought in abundantly. ⁶And the Israelites and Judahites who dwelt in the cities of

Provisions for the maintenance of the temple service

---

[j] II Chr. 30²⁷ So the versions and many Heb. manuscripts. The accepted Heb. omits the *and*.

[k] II Kgs. 18⁴ The word may be connected either with the Heb. word for *brass* or for *serpent*. Probably a play on these double meanings was intended.

Chronicler's Ecclesiastical History

Judah, also brought in the tithe of oxen and sheep and the tithe of dedicated things, which were consecrated to Jehovah their God, and laid them by heaps. ⁷In the third month they began to lay the foundation of the heaps and finished them in the seventh month. ⁸And when Hezekiah and the princes saw the heaps, they blessed Jehovah and his people Israel. ⁹Then Hezekiah questioned the priests and the Levites concerning the heaps. ¹⁰And Azariah the chief priest, of the house of Zadok, answered him and said, Since the people began to bring the oblations into the temple of Jehovah, we have eaten and had enough and have left plenty, for Jehovah has blessed his people; and we have left¹ this great store.

Provisions for the support of the Levites ¹¹Then Hezekiah commanded to prepare chambers in the temple of Jehovah; and they prepared them. ¹²Then they conscientiously brought the oblations and the tithes and the dedicated things; and Conaniah the Levite acted as steward in charge of them, and Shimei his brother was second in charge. ¹³And Jehiel, Azaziah, Nahath, Asahel, Jerimoth, Jozabad, Eliel, Ismachiah, Mahath, and Benaiah, were overseers under the direction of Conaniah and Shimei his brother, by the appointment of Hezekiah the king, and Azariah the ruler of the house of God. ¹⁴And Kore the son of Imnah the Levite, the porter at the east gate, was in charge of the freewill offerings of God, to distribute the oblations of Jehovah and the most holy things. ¹⁵And under him were Eden, Miniamin, Jeshua, Shemaiah, Amariah, and Shecaniah, in the cities of the priests, faithfully to distribute to their kinsmen by divisions, to the great and small alike, ¹⁶to each with his male descendants^m from three years old and upward—that is, to every one who entered the temple of Jehovah, as the duty of each day required for their service in their respective offices according to their divisions. ¹⁷And this is the list of the priests, and that of the Levites included the people from twenty years old and upward, in their office by their divisions. ¹⁸And in the list were reckoned all their little ones, their wives, their sons, and their daughters through all the congregation; for they devoted themselves faithfully to the holy things. ¹⁹But for the sons of Aaron, the priests who were in the territory of the common pasture-lands of their cities—in every city there were men who were designated by name to assign portions to all the males among the priests and to all among the Levites who were^n on the lists.^o

His fidelity in the work of reform ²⁰Thus Hezekiah did in all Judah; and he did that which was good and right and faithful before Jehovah his God. ²¹And every work that he began in the service of the house of God and on the basis of the law and commandments, in order to seek his God, he did with all his heart.

Annals of Judah

His material prosperity

II Kgs. 18
⁷And Jehovah was with him; in all that he undertook he prospered; and he rebelled against

32 ²⁷And Hezekiah had riches and honor in fullest measure; and he provided for himself treasuries for silver and gold and precious stones, and for spices and for shields and for all kinds of valuable objects, ²⁸storehouses also for the increase of grain and new wine and

---

¹ II Chr. 31¹⁰ So Gk. The Heb. has an impossible construction.
^m II Chr. 31¹⁶ Restoring the Heb. by the aid of the Gk.
^n II Chr. 31¹⁹ Again following the Gk.
^o II Chr. 31¹⁷⁻¹⁹ This rather obscure note was evidently appended later and was intended to reconcile the statement in ¹⁶ with later current usage and to supply the details which were not furnished in the original record.

Annals of Judah

the king of Assyria and was no longer subject to him. [8]He drove back the Philistines to Gaza and conquered its territory from the watch-tower to the fortified city.

Chronicler's Ecclesiastical History

oil, and stalls for all kinds of animals, and folds for flocks.[p] [29]Moreover he provided for himself cities and abundant possessions of flocks and herds, for God had given him very much property. [30]This same Hezekiah also stopped the upper spring of the waters of Gihon and brought them straight down on the west side of the city of David. And Hezekiah prospered in all his undertakings. [31]However in the matter of the ambassadors of the princes of Babylon, who sent to him to inquire of the wonder that was done in the land, God left him, to try him, that he might know all that was in his heart.

§ 121. Hezekiah's Illness and Recovery, II Kgs. 20[1-11], Is. 38[1-8, 21, 22], II Chr. 32[24-26]

Isaiah Stories

Hezekiah's prayer and Jehovah's message through Isaiah

II Kgs. 20 [1]In those days Hezekiah was mortally ill. And Isaiah the prophet, the son of Amoz, came and said to him, Thus saith Jehovah, 'Set thy house in order; for thou wilt die and not recover.' [2]Then he turned his face to the wall and prayed to Jehovah, saying, [3]Remember now, O Jehovah, I beseech thee, how I have walked before thee in truth and with a perfect heart and have done that which pleaseth thee. And Hezekiah wept loudly. [4]Now before Isaiah had left the courtyard[q] the word of Jehovah came to him, saying, [5]Turn back and say to Hezekiah the prince of my people, 'Thus saith Jehovah, the God of David thy father, "I

Chronicler's Ecclesiastical History

II Chr. 32 [24]In those days Hezekiah was mortally ill, and he prayed to Jehovah. And he answered him and gave him a sign. [25]But Hezekiah rendered not again according to the benefit done to him, for his heart was lifted up with pride, and so wrath came upon him and upon Judah and Jerusalem.

---

[p] II Chr. 32[28] So Gk. Heb., *flocks for folds.*

§ 121 The various events recounted in II Kgs. 20 are practically contemporary, for according to [12] the embassy of Merodach-Baladan was sent at the time of Hezekiah's illness. Its object was evidently to induce Hezekiah to join him in a coalition against Assyria. Three times this Babylonian prince conspired against the common foe: in 721–0, 711–0 and 702 B.C. The third revolt was put down in a few months, but it is possible that the embassy was sent to kindle the general insurrection which broke out in 702 in the east and west. At least it is certain that the events recorded in 20 antedated those in 18[14]–19[37], which belong to the years 701 or 690 B.C. The reference in [6] also implies that Hezekiah's illness antedated the deliverance of 701 B.C. The promise of fifteen more years accords best with the date 702–1 (701–15 = 686, the close of Hezekiah's reign; cf. Appendix, IX).

The chronological note in 18[13a] in its present position dates Hezekiah's accession 715 B.C., while 18[10] distinctly states that it was 727. The former date is best supported by the biblical and contemporary evidence. For a detailed discussion of the problem here presented, cf. Appendix II.

The prophet Isaiah, not Hezekiah, is the hero of these stories. He figures in very much the same rôle as Elijah and Elisha in the cycles of stories that in later generations were associated with their names. They probably come from the same prophetic circles. Cf. Introd., p. 20. Another story from the same cycle is apparently found in [12-19]. Cf. note § 122.

The account of the sign in II Kgs. 20[8-11] has been greatly revised, or else is entirely secondary. The version in Is. 38[7, 8] is briefer and probably original. The insertion in 38[21, 22] appears to be later.

[q] II Kgs. 20[4] Following the marginal reading of the Heb., which is supported by all the versions.

Isaiah Stories

Chronicler's Ecclesiastical History

have heard thy prayer, I have seen thy tears; now I will heal thee: on the day after to-morrow thou canst go up into the temple of Jehovah. ⁶And I will add to the length of thy life fifteen years, and I will deliver thee and this city from the hand of the king of Assyria, and I will defend this city for mine own sake and for the sake of my servant David."ʳ ⁷Then Isaiah said, Let him take a cake of figs, and place it on the boil, that he may recover.ˢ

²⁶Notwithstanding Hezekiah humbled himself as regards the pride of his heart, together with the inhabitants of Jerusalem, so that the wrath of Jehovah came not upon him in the days of Hezekiah.

Secondary Version of Isaiah Stories

The sign that he should be healed

Is. 38 ⁷And this shall be your sign from Jehovah, that Jehovah will do this that he hath promised; ⁸behold, I will bring back the shadow as many steps as the sun has gone downᵗ on the step-clock of Ahaz, even ten steps. So the sun turned back ten steps upon the stepsᵗ by which it had g o n e down.

II Kgs. 20 ⁸And Hezekiah said to Isaiah, What shall be the sign that Jehovah will heal me and that I will go up into the temple of Jehovah the day after to-morrow? ⁹And Isaiah said, This shall be the sign from Jehovah, that Jehovah will do the thing that he has promised: shall the shadow go forward ten steps,ᵘ or back ten steps? ¹⁰And Hezekiah answered, It is an easy thing for the shadow to go ahead ten steps; rather let the shadow turn back ten steps. ¹¹Then Isaiah the prophet cried to Jehovah; and he brought back the shadow ten steps on the steps by which it had gone down on the step-clock of Ahaz.

§ 122. The Embassy of Merodach-Baladan, II Kgs. 20¹²⁻¹⁹, Is. 39

Isaiah Stories

Hezekiah's reception of the embassy

II Kgs. 20 ¹²At that time Merodach-Baladanᵛ the son of Baladan king of Babylon sent eunuchsʷ with a present to Hezekiah; for he had heard that Hezekiah had been sick. ¹³And Hezekiah was gladˣ because of them, and showed them all his treasure-house, the silver, the gold, the spices, the precious oil, and his armory and all that was found among his treasures; there

---

ʳ II Kgs. 20⁶ The parallel in Is. 38⁶ omits, *for mine own sake and for the sake of my servant David.*

ˢ II Kgs. 20⁷ So Gk., Luc., Lat., and the parallel in Is. 38²¹, which was probably originally taken from the Heb.   The present Heb. reads, *and Isaiah said, Take a cake of figs.   And they took and laid it on the boil and he recovered.*

ᵗ Is. 38⁸ Correcting two minor errors in the Heb.

ᵘ II Kgs. 20⁹ Heb., *The shadow has gone forward,* but ¹⁰ implies an alternative, and the Targ. supports the slight emendation of the Heb. which is followed above.

§ 122 This incident is closely connected with the preceding narrative and evidently comes from the later Isaiah stories, for it reflects the age when not the Assyrians but the Babylonians were the world-conquerors.   Cf. Introd., p. 20.

ᵛ 20¹² So Gk., Luc., Syr., Targ., and several Heb. codices.   Received Heb., *Berodach.* The Bab. form of the name is, *Marduk-abal-iddina.*

ʷ 20¹² Heb., *letters.*   But the next vs. indicates that persons were sent, and a probable correction of the Heb. gives the above reading.

ˣ 20¹³ So Gk., Luc., Syr., Lat., several codices, and the parallel, Is. 39².

Isaiah Stories

was nothing, in his palace nor in all his dominion, that Hezekiah did not show them.

¹⁴Then Isaiah the prophet came to King Hezekiah and said to him, What did these men say? and from whence, pray, do they come to you? And Hezekiah said, They have come from a far country, from Babylon. ¹⁵And he said, What have they seen in your palace? And Hezekiah answered, They have seen all that is in my palace; there is nothing among my treasures that I did not show them. ¹⁶Then Isaiah said to Hezekiah, Hear the word of Jehovah: ¹⁷'The days are quickly coming, when all that is in your palace and that which your fathers have stored up to this day shall be carried to Babylon—nothing shall be left,' saith Jehovah. ¹⁸And of your sons who shall issue from you, whom you shall beget, shall they take away, to be eunuchs in the palace of the king of Babylon. ¹⁹Then Hezekiah said to Isaiah, Good is the word of Jehovah which you have spoken. For he thought, As long as I live there shall be peace and stability! ᵃ

Isaiah's prediction of the Babylonian captivity

§ 123. Sennacherib's Invasion of Judah, II Kgs. 18¹³⁻¹⁶, II Chr. 32¹⁻⁸

Annals of Judah

II Kgs. 18 ¹³Now in the fourteenth year of King Hezekiah,ᵇ Sennacherib king of Assyria came up against all the fortified cities of Judah and took them. ¹⁴And Hezekiah king of Judah sent to the king of Assyria to Lachish, saying, I have offended; withdraw from me; whatever you lay on me I will bear. And the king of Assyria made Hezekiah king of Judah pay three hundred talents of silver and thirty talents of

Hezekiah's measures to avert the attack of Sennacherib

Chronicler's Ecclesiastical History

II Chr. 32 ¹After these things and this evidence of fidelity, Sennacherib king of Assyria came, entered into Judah, and besieged the fortified cities and thought to conquer them for himself. ²And when Hezekiah saw that Sennacherib had come and that his purpose was to attack Jerusalem, ³he took counsel with his generals and his mighty warriors to stop up the waters of the fountains which were outside the city. And they helped him, ⁴and many people were detailed to stop up all the fountains and the brooks, that flowed through the midst of the land, for they said, Why should the kings of Assyria come and find much water? ⁵He also took courage and built up all the wall that was broken down and on it reared towers,ᶜ and also outside the second wall, and strengthened Millo in the city of David, and made weapons and shields in abun-

---

ᵃ 20¹⁹ So Gk. and the parallel, Is. 39⁸. The concluding explanatory clause is pryobabl from a later editor.
§ 123 This brief section gives a very different impression of the history during Hezekiah's reign from that presented by the editor in ⁷. In concise, annalistic form it tells of the disastrous effects of Hezekiah's rebellion against Assyria. The representation is in close agreement with the testimony of Sennacherib's inscription. Cf. Appendix IX. It is undoubtedly historical and is in all probability a verbatim quotation from the Judean annals.
The later tradition preserved by the Chronicler transforms this disaster into brave resistance, inspired by the courageous words of Hezekiah. All references to the humiliating tribute are omitted. Evidently it is idealized rather than real history that is here recorded.
ᵇ II Kgs. 18¹³ This chronological note may have been added by the late prophetic editor, but it appears to be based on earlier authentic data. Cf. Appendix II.
ᶜ II Chr. 32⁵ So Lat. Heb., *he went up on the towers.*

Annals of Judah | *Chronicler's Ecclesiastical History*

gold. ¹⁵And Hezekiah gave him all the silver that was found in the temple of Jehovah and in the treasures of the royal palace. ¹⁶At that time Hezekiah stripped the doors of the temple of Jehovah and the pillars, which Hezekiah[d] king of Judah had overlaid, and gave [the gold] to the king of Assyria.

dance. ⁶And he set military officers over the people and gathered them together to him in the broad place at the gate of the city, and spoke reassuringly to them, saying, ⁷Be strong and courageous; do not be afraid nor terrified in the presence of the king of Assyria nor of all the multitude that is with him, for a greater is with us than with him. ⁸With him is an arm of flesh, but with us is Jehovah our God to help us and to fight our battles. And the people rested themselves upon the words of Hezekiah king of Judah.

§ 124. **Sennacherib's Demand and Isaiah's Prophetic Counsel, II Kgs. 18¹⁷–19³⁷, 20²⁰, ²¹, Is. 36, 37, II Chr. 32⁹⁻²³, ³², ³³**

Hezekiah History | *Isaiah Stories* | *Chronicler's Ecclesiastical History*

II Kgs. 18 ¹⁷Then the king of Assyria sent the commander-in-chief, and the chief of the eunuchs, and a high official[e] from Lachish with a great army to King Hezekiah at Jerusalem. And they went up, and when they ar-

II Kgs. 19 ⁹ᵇThen Sennacherib sent messengers again to Hezekiah, saying, ¹⁰Thus shall you speak to Hezekiah king of Judah, ' Let not your God in whom you trust deceive you with the

II Chr. 32 ⁹After this Sennacherib king of Assyria sent his servants to Jerusalem, while he himself with all his forces lay before Lachish, to Hezekiah king of Judah and to all Judah who were at Jerusalem, saying, ¹⁰Thus saith Sennacherib king of As-

Sennacherib's arrogant demand that Jerusalem be surrendered

d II Kgs. 18¹⁶ Probably in the original the name of some other king was found here.
§ 124 II Kgs. 18¹⁷ introduces a quotation from a source distinct from the annals. Not only does another spelling of the king's name appear throughout, but the representation and style are very different. Furthermore the passage, 18¹⁷–19³⁵, contains what seems to be extracts from three sources. The natural sequel to 18¹⁷–19⁹ᵃ is 19³⁶, ³⁷. Sennacherib's letter in 19¹⁰⁻¹³ is simply an epitome of the message already delivered more effectually by the high official, 18²⁸⁻³⁵. His threat, in almost the same terms, is repeated three times in 19⁷, ²⁸ᵇ, ³³. The second extract is found in1 9⁹ᵇ⁻³³, the taunt-song and sign in ²¹⁻³¹ being probably a prophecy of Isaiah inserted here from some other source. The *therefore* at the beginning of ³² finds its natural antecedent in ²⁰ᵇ.
The two narratives of the message of Sennacherib, of Hezekiah's dismay, of Isaiah's inspiring counsel, and of the great deliverance have so many points in common that they are probably duplicate versions of the same incident. It has been urged, however, that they refer to distinct events: 19⁹ᵇ⁻²⁰, ³²⁻³⁵ to Sennacherib's sudden retreat in 701 B.C., and 18¹⁷–19⁹ᵃ, ³⁶, ³⁷ to a later expedition, not long before 681, when he was murdered by his son. The first narrative, however, does not fit naturally into the situation in 701 B.C. A recently discovered inscription confirms the evidence already published that between 691 and 689 Sennacherib made a second western campaign with a view to conquering Egypt, and that these two variant narratives relate to an incident in that expedition. Cf. Appendix IX.
The narrative in 18¹⁷–19⁹ᵃ, ³⁶, ³⁷ has many more details and is in accord with the historical situation implied by the contemporary annals and by the inscriptions of Sennacherib. Hezekiah is the central figure. Isaiah is only introduced briefly at the close. The names of Hezekiah's ministers, in 18³⁷, and of the Assyrian officials and many circumstantial details are given.

e II Kgs. 18¹⁷ Heb., *the tartan and rabsaris and rabshakeh.* The first and third of the titles appear to be of Assyrian origin. The first, *tartanu*, is the regular title of the commander of an Assyrian army. In the parallel in Is. 36 only the *rabshakeh* is mentioned. The other titles may have been added in Kgs. by a later scribe inspired by antiquarian interest, but the parallel in Chr. is evidently based on the present text of Kgs.

Hezekiah History	*Isaiah Stories*	*Chronicler's Ecclesiastical History*
rived[f] at Jerusalem, they came and stood by the conduit of the upper pool, which is on the way to the fuller's field. 18And when they called for the king, Eliakim the son of Hilkiah, who was prefect of the palace, and Shebnah the scribe, and Joah the son of Asaph the chancellor came out to them. 19And the high official said to them, Say now to Hezekiah, 'Thus saith the great king, the king of Assyria, "What confidence is this which you cherish?"' 20You indeed think, "A simple word of the lips is counsel and strength for the war!" Now on whom do you trust, that you have rebelled against me? 21Indeed you trust on the staff of this bruised reed, even upon Egypt which, if a man lean on it, will go into his hand and pierce it. So is Pharaoh king of Egypt to all who trust in him. 22But if you say to me, "We trust in Jehovah our	thought, "Jerusalem shall not be given into the hand of the king of Assyria." 11You have already heard what the kings of Assyria have done to all lands in destroying them completely, and shall you be delivered? 12Have the gods of the nations which my fathers have destroyed delivered them — Gozan, Haran, Rezeph, and the people of Eden who were in Telassar? 13Where is the king of Hamath, and the king of Arpad, and the king of Sepharvaim, of Hena, and Ivvah?'[g] 14And Hezekiah received the letter from the hand of the messengers and read it. Then Hezekiah went up to the temple of Jehovah and spread it out before Jehovah 15and said, O Jehovah the God of Israel who dwellest above the cherubim, thou art the God, even thou	syria, 'On what are you trusting that you are awaiting the siege in Jerusalem? 11Does not Hezekiah mislead you in order to give you over to die by famine and by thirst, saying, "Jehovah our God will deliver us out of the hand of the king of Assyria"? 12Has not the same Hezekiah taken away his high places and his altars and commanded Judah and Jerusalem, saying, "Ye shall worship before one altar and upon it shall you offer sacrifice?" 13Do you not know what I and my fathers have done to all the gods of the peoples of the lands? Were the gods of the nations of the lands at all able to deliver their land out of my hand? 14Who was there among all the gods of those nations on which my fathers laid their ban who could deliver his people out of my hand, that your god should be able to deliver you out of my hand? 15Now therefore let not Hezekiah deceive you in this way nor mislead you nor believe him, for no god of any nation or kingdom

The passage was probably taken from the original Hezekiah history, quoted in the Judean royal chronicles. On the other hand, the spirit of the second narrative, the large numbers in 35 and the prominence of letters and public prayer here and in 20 (cf. 19¹⁴, ¹⁵ and 20¹⁻³) connect it with the cycle of Isaiah stories.

An editor of the book of Isaiah has also taken these passages and introduced them in Chaps. 36 and 37. That they, like the contents of 38, were subsequently inserted into the book of Isaiah is demonstrated by the fact that the late prophetic editorial additions were likewise transferred.

The Chronicler's parallel is a very free paraphrase of the two versions in Kgs. and is adapted to the didactic ends which characterize the midrash.

[f] II Kgs. 18¹⁷ So Gk., Luc., Syr., and Lat. The Heb. adds, *and came up.*
[g] II Kgs. 19¹², ¹³ For the places mentioned, cf. map opp. p. 248.

Hezekiah History	*Isaiah Stories*	*Chronicler's Ecclesiastical History*
God," is not he the one whose high places and altars Hezekiah has taken away and has said to Judah and Jerusalem, " You shall worship before this altar in Jerusalem ? " ²³Now therefore give pledges to my master the king of Assyria and I will give you two thousand horses, if you are able on your part to set riders upon them. ²⁴How then can you repulse one[h] of the least of my master's servants ? And yet you trust in Egypt for chariots and for horsemen ! ²⁵Now have I come up against this place to destroy it without Jehovah's approval ? Jehovah it was who said to me, " Go up against this land and destroy it." '	alone, over all the kingdoms of the earth. ¹⁶Incline thine ear, O Jehovah, and hear; open thine eyes, O Jehovah, and see and hear the words of Sennacherib, which he has sent to defy the living God. ¹⁷It is true, O Jehovah, the kings of Assyria have laid waste the nations and their lands ¹⁸and have cast their gods into the fire; for they were no gods, but the work of men's hands, wood and stone; therefore they have destroyed them. ¹⁹But now, O Jehovah our God, save thou us, that all the kingdoms of the earth may know that thou Jehovah art God alone.	was able to deliver his people from my hand and from the hand of my fathers. How much less shall your gods deliver you out of my hand ? ' ¹⁶And his servants spoke yet more against Jehovah God, and against his servant Hezekiah. ¹⁷He also wrote letters, railing against Jehovah, the God of Israel, and speaking against him to this effect, Just as the gods of the nations of the lands, who have not delivered their people out of my hand, so shall not the God of Hezekiah deliver his people out of my hand. ¹⁸And they cried with a loud voice in the Jewish language to the people of Jerusalem who were on the wall to frighten and terrify them, that they might take the city. ¹⁹And they spoke of the God of Jerusalem, as of the gods of the peoples of the earth, which are the work of men's hands.

Further threats of Sennacherib's official	²⁶Then Eliakim the son of Hilkiah and Shebnah and Joah said to the high official, Speak, I pray thee, to thy servants in the Aramaic language, for we understand it; but do not speak with us in the Jewish language in the hearing of the people who are on the wall. ²⁷But the high official said to them, Has my master sent me to your master and to you to speak these words ? Is it not rather to the men who sit on the wall, that they shall eat their own dung and drink	²⁰Then Isaiah the son of Amoz sent to Hezekiah saying, Thus saith Jehovah, the God of Israel, ' What thou hast asked of me regarding Sennacherib king of Assyria, I have heard.' ²¹This is the word that Jehovah hath spoken concerning him: ' Thee she despises, at thee is laughing— The virgin, daughter of Zion !

(right-margin note) Jehovah's message concerning Assyria

---

[h] II Kgs. 18²⁴ Heb. adds, *satrap*, but the construction is impossible and the word was probably added by a later scribe.

Hezekiah History

their own water together with you ? ²⁸Then the high official stood and cried with a loud voice in the Jewish language and spoke, saying, Hear the message of the great king, the king of Assyria. ²⁹Thus saith the king, ' Let not Hezekiah deceive you; for he will not be able to deliver you out of my^j hand. ³⁰Neither let Hezekiah make you trust in Jehovah, saying, " Jehovah will surely deliver us, and this city shall not be given into the power of the king of Assyria." ' ³¹Hearken not to Hezekiah, for thus says the king of Assyria, ' Make your peace with me and come over to me; thus shall each one of you eat from his own vine and his own fig-tree and drink the waters of his own cistern, ³²until I come and take you away to a land like your own land, a land full of grain and new wine, a land full of bread and vineyards, a land full of olive-trees and honey, that you may live and not die. But hearken not to Hezekiah, when he misleads you, saying, " Jehovah will deliver us." ³³Has any of the gods of the nations ever delivered his land out of the power of the king of Assyria ? ³⁴Where are the gods of Hamath and Arpad ? Where are the gods of Sepharvaim, Hena, and Ivvah ? Where are the gods of the land of Samaria^n that they have delivered Samaria out of my power ? ³⁵Who are they among all the gods of the countries, that have delivered their country out of my power, that Jehovah should deliver Jerusalem out of my power ? '

Isaiah Stories

Behind thee she is wagging her head^i—
The daughter of Jerusalem !
²²Whom hast thou reviled and blasphemed ?
Against whom raised thy voice?
Yea, and lifted up thine eyes on high ?
Against Israel's Holy One !
²³By thy minions hast^k thou reviled the Lord ;
And hast said, " With my many chariots,
I, even I, ascended the mountain heights,
The ravines of Lebanon ;
And I have cut down its tallest cedars,
Its choice cypresses.
And I press into its farthest halting-place,
Into its densest thickets.
²⁴I, even I, dig wells [in the desert],
And drink strange waters,
And with the soles of my feet have I dried up
All the rivers of Egypt."
²⁵Hast thou not heard, I prepared it long ago,
In the days of old I formed it ;
now I have brought it to pass;
Hence thy task is to turn fortified cities into ruined heaps,
²⁶And their inhabitants, helpless, are terrified and put to shame,
They are like the wild plants, the tender grass, and the blades on the roofs and the uplands,^{l}
Before me is thy rising up^m ²⁷and thy lying down, thy going out and thy coming in,
I know thy raging against me^o ²⁸and thine arrogance has come to my ears,
Therefore I will put my ring through thy nose, and my bridle between thy lips,
And will make thee return by the way in which thou hast come.

---

^{i} II Kgs. 19²¹ A gesture of mockery. Cf. Lam. 2¹⁵, Job 16⁴, Ps. 22⁸, 109²⁵.
^{j} II Kgs. 18²⁹ So Luc., Syr., Lat., and Targ. Heb., *his.*
^{k} II Kgs. 19²³ So Gk., Luc., and Lat. Heb. has the tenses of the future.
^{l} II Kgs. 19²⁶ Making a plausible correction. Heb., *blasted corn.*
^{m} II Kgs. 19²⁶ Slightly revising the Heb.
^{n} II Kgs. 18³⁴ So Luc., and demanded by the context. The Heb. has lost the first part of the sentence.
^{o} II Kgs. 19²⁷ Omitting the dittography, *because thou ragest against me.*

301

Hezekiah History

³⁶Then the people were silent and answered him not a word; for the king's command was, Answer him not. ³⁷But Eliakim the son of Hilkiah, the prefect of the palace, and Shebna, the scribe, and Joah the son of Asaph, the chancellor, came to Hezekiah with torn clothes and told him the words of the high official. **19** ¹And as soon as King Hezekiah heard it, he tore his clothes and covered himself with sackcloth and went into the temple of Jehovah. ²And he sent Eliakim, who was prefect of the palace, and Shebna the scribe and the eldest of the priests, covered with sackcloth, to Isaiah the prophet the son of Amoz. ³And they said to him, Thus saith Hezekiah, ' This is a day of trouble and of discipline and of contumely; for the children are come to birth and there is no strength to her who is in travail.ᴾ ⁴It may be Jehovah thy God will hear all the words of the high official, whom his master the king of Assyria has sent to defy the living God, and will rebuke the words which Jehovah your God has heard; therefore lift up your prayer for the remnant that is left.' ⁵And when the servants of King Hezekiah came to Isaiah, ⁶Isaiah said to them, The following answer shall you take to your master, ' Thus saith Jehovah, " Be not afraid of the words that thou hast heard, with which the servants of the king of Assyria have blasphemed me. ⁷Behold I will put a spirit in him so that he shall hear tidings and shall return to his own land, and I will cause him to fall by the sword in his own land." ' ⁸So the high official returned and found the king of Assyria warring against Libnah, for he had heard that he had departed from Lachish. ⁹ªBut that one had heard regarding Tirhakah king of Ethiopia, Behold, he has come out to fight against you. . . . .

Isaiah Stories

²⁹And this shall be your sign: you shall eat this year that which grows of itself, and in the second year that which springs from the same, but in the third year you can sow and reap and plant vineyards and eat the fruit. ³⁰And the remnant that escapes of the house of Judah shall again take root downward and bear fruit upward. ³¹For out of Jerusalem shall go forth a remnant and from Mount Zion a band who shall escape; the zeal of Jehovah of hosts shall accomplish this.' ³²Therefore thus saith Jehovah concerning the king of Assyria, ' He shall not come into this city, nor shoot an arrow therein; neither shall he come before it with shield nor cast up a mound against it. ³³By the same way that he came shall he return, but he shall not come into this city,' saith Jehovah. ³⁴' For I will defend this city to save it for mine own sake, and for the sake of David my servant.'

Chronicler's Ecclesiastical History

³⁶Then Sennacherib king of Assyria went away and returned and dwelt at

³⁵Now that night the Messenger of Jehovah went

II Chr. 32 ²⁰And Hezekiah the king and Isaiah the prophet, the son of Amoz, prayed because of this and cried to heaven. ²¹And Jehovah sent

ᴾ II Kgs. 19³ So Gk., Luc., Syr., and Lat. Heb., *to bring forth.*

Hezekiah History	*Isaiah Stories*	*Chronicler's Ecclesiastical History*

Nineveh. ³⁷And once while he was worshipping in the temple of Nisroch his god, his sons, Adrammelek and Sharezer, smote him with the sword; and they escaped into the land of Ararat. And Esarhaddon his son became king in his place.

forth and smote in the camp of the Assyrians, a hundred and eighty thousand. And when people arose early the next morning, there were only dead bodies.

a Messenger, who cut off all the mighty warriors, with the leaders and generals in the army of the king of Assyria. So he returned with shame to his own land. And when he entered the temple of his god, his own offspring slew him there with the sword. ²²Thus Jehovah saved Hezekiah and the inhabitants of Jerusalem from the hand of Sennacherib the king of Assyria and from the hand of all others and gave them rest^q on every side. ²³And many brought gifts to Jehovah, to Jerusalem and precious things to Hezekiah king of Judah, so that from that time on he was highly esteemed by all peoples.

[*margin:* d of ze- h's gn]

20 ²⁰Now the other acts of Hezekiah, and all his brave deeds and how he made the pool, and the conduit, and brought water into the city, are they not recorded in the Chronicles of the Kings of Judah? ²¹And Hezekiah slept with his fathers; and Manasseh his son became king in his place.

³²Now the other acts of Hezekiah and his good deeds are recorded in the vision of Isaiah the prophet the son of Amoz^r in the Book of the Kings of Judah and Israel. ³³And Hezekiah slept with his fathers and they buried him in the ascent to the sepulchres of the sons of David, and all Judah and the inhabitants of Jerusalem showed him honor at his death. And Manasseh his son became king in his place.

§ 125. Reactionary Reigns of Manasseh and Amon, II Kgs. 21, II Chr. 33

Late Prophetic Narratives

II Kgs. 21 ¹Manasseh was twelve years old when he began to reign, and he reigned fifty-five years in Jerusalem; and his mother's name was Hephzibah. ²And he did that which displeased Jehovah, according to the abominable practices of the nations whom Jehovah cast out before the Israelites. ³For he built again the high places which Hezekiah his father had destroyed, and he erected altars for Baal and made an asherah, as Ahab king of Israel had done, and worshipped all the host of heaven and served them. ⁴And

[*margin:* Heathen symbols and cults introduced by Manasseh]

---

q II Chr. 32²² So Gk. and Lat. Heb., *guided them.*
r II Chr. 32³² The title of Isaiah's prophecies. Cf. Is. 1¹.
§ 125 The allusions to the *Chronicles of Judah* in ¹⁷, ²⁵ indicate that the author of this section had earlier sources before him. The facts in ³⁻⁶ were doubtless taken from them or from the Judean annals. The section ¹⁻⁶, however, as a whole, is clearly from the late prophetic editor. From this time on he stood so near the facts that his testimony is almost equivalent to that of a contemporary witness. Vss. ⁷⁻¹⁵, on the other hand, reflect the exilic point of view. Cf. Introd., p. 21. They were evidently added by the latest editor of Kgs.
The Chronicler quotes the first nine verses practically verbatim. To these he adds a tradition regarding Manasseh's captivity and certain other facts about his building enterprises which appear to be derived from some earlier source.

Late Prophetic Narratives

he built altars in the temple of Jehovah, of which Jehovah said, In Jerusalem will I put my name. ⁵And he built altars for all the host of heaven in the two courts of the temple of Jehovah.ᵃ ⁶And he made his son to pass through the fire and practised augury and witchcraft and appointed mediums and wizards; he did much evil in the sight of Jehovah to provoke him to anger.

Late Prophetic (Exilic) Addition

Desecration of the temple
⁷And he set the graven image of an asherah, that he had made, in the temple of which Jehovah said to David and to Solomon his son, In this house and in Jerusalem, which I have chosen out of all the tribes of Israel, will I put my name forever, ⁸and I will not cause the feet of Israel to wander any more out of the land which I gave their fathers, if only they will faithfully do as I have commanded them, and according to all the law that my servant Moses commanded them. ⁹But they did not hearken, and Manasseh seduced them to do more evil than did the nations which Jehovah destroyed before the Israelites.

Jehovah's announcement of the coming captivity of Judah
¹⁰And Jehovah spoke by his servants the prophets, saying, ¹¹Because Manasseh king of Judah hath done these abominations, and hath done more wickedly than all that the Amorites have done, who were before him, and hath made Judah also sin with his idols; ¹²therefore thus saith Jehovah God of Israel, I am now about to bring such evil on Jerusalem and Judah, that whoever heareth of it, both his ears shall tingle. ¹³And I will stretch over Jerusalem the measuring line, as over Samaria, and the plummet,ᵗ as over the house of Ahab, and I will wipe Jerusalem as a man wipeth a dish, wiping and turning it upside down. ¹⁴And I will cast off the remnant of mine inheritance and deliver them into the hand of their enemies, that they may become a prey and a spoil to all their enemies, ¹⁵because they have done that which is displeasing to me, and have provoked me to anger, since the day their fathers came forth from Egypt, even to the present.

Manasseh's massacres
¹⁶Moreover Manasseh shed much innocent blood until he had filled Jerusalem from one end to the other, besides his sin with which he made Judah sin, in doing that which displeased Jehovah.

Chronicler's Ecclesiastical History

His captivity, repentance, and restoration
II Chr. 33 ¹⁰And Jehovah spoke to Manasseh and to his people, but they gave no heed. ¹¹Therefore Jehovah brought against them the commanders of the army of the king of Assyria, who took Manasseh in chains and bound him with fetters and carried him to Babylon. ¹²But when he was in distress, he besought Jehovah his God, and humbled himself greatly before the God of his fathers. ¹³And he prayed to him, and he was entreated

---

ᵃ II Kgs. 21⁵ Cf. I Kgs. 6³⁶, 20⁴, where the temple appears to have had but one court. Vs. ⁵ is a duplicate of ⁴ and clearly comes from an exilic or post-exilic writer.
ᵗ II Kgs. 21¹³ Symbols of a divine judgment, executed in accord with the strict principles of justice. Cf. Am. 7⁷, ⁸.

Chronicler's Ecclesiastical History

of him and heard his supplication and brought him back to Jerusalem into his kingdom. Then Manasseh knew that Jehovah was indeed God.

^{14}Now after this he built an outer wall to the city of David, on the west side of Gihon in the valley, even to the entrance at the Fish Gate, so that he encircled Ophel; and he made it very high. He also placed valiant commanders in all the fortified cities of Judah. *His building enterprises*

^{15}And he took away the foreign gods and the idol out of the temple of Jehovah and all the altars that he had built in the mount of the temple of Jehovah and in Jerusalem and cast them out of the city. ^{16}And he rebuilt the altar of Jehovah and offered on it sacrifices of peace-offerings and of thank-offering, and commanded Judah to serve Jehovah, the God of Israel. ^{17}Nevertheless the people sacrificed still in the high places, but only to Jehovah their God. *His later religious reforms*

Late Prophetic Summary

II Kgs. 21 ^{17}Now the other acts of Manasseh and all that he did, and his sin that he committed, are they not recorded in the Chronicles of the Kings of Judah? ^{18}And Manasseh slept with his fathers and was buried in the garden of his own palace, in the garden of Uzza; and Amon his son became king in his place.

^{18}Now the other acts^u of Manasseh and his prayer to his God, as well as the words of the seers who spoke in the name of Jehovah, the God of Israel, are already recorded in the history of Israel. ^{19}His prayer also and how it was heard and all his sin and his guilt and the sites on which he built high places and set up the asherahs and the graven images, before he humbled himself, are already recorded in the history of his seers.^{v} ^{20}So Manasseh slept with his fathers and they buried him in the garden of his palace;^{w} and Amon his son became king in his place.

Late Prophetic Narratives

^{19}Amon was twenty-two years old when he began to reign, and he reigned two years in Jerusalem; and his mother's name was Meshullemeth the daughter of Haruz of Jotbah. ^{20}And he did that which displeased Jehovah, as did Manasseh his father. ^{21}And he walked in all the way in which his father had walked and served the idols that his father served, and worshipped them, ^{22}and he forsook Jehovah, the God of his fathers, and walked not in the way of Jehovah. *Amon's evil religious policy*

^{23}And the servants of Amon conspired against him and put the king to death in his palace. ^{24}But the people of the land slew all who had conspired against Amon; and the people of the land made Josiah his son king in his place. ^{25}Now the other acts of Amon which he did, are they not recorded in the Chronicles of the Kings of Judah? ^{26}And he was buried in his sepulchre in the garden of Uzza; and Josiah his son became king in his place. *His assassination*

---

^{u} II Chr. 33^{18} Heb., *among the acts.*
^{v} II Chr. 33^{19} Making a slight correction in the Heb. Gk., *seers.*
^{w} II Chr. 33^{20} So Gk. and the parallel in Kgs.

III

THE BABYLONIAN PERIOD: FROM JOSIAH TO THE RISE OF CYRUS, II Kgs. 22¹–25³⁰, II Chr. 34¹–36²¹, Jer. 26, 34, 36–39¹⁴, 40–44, 52

§ 126. Discovery of the Book of the Law in the Days of Josiah, II Kgs. 22¹⁻²⁰, II Chr. 34¹⁻²⁸

Late Prophetic Summary

Josiah's benign policy

II Kgs. 22 ¹Josiah was eight years old when he began to reign, and he reigned thirty-one years in Jerusalem; and his mother's name was Jedidah the daughter of Adaiah of Bozkath. ²And he did that which pleased Jehovah and walked in all the way of David his father and turned not aside to the right or to the left.

Chronicler's Ecclesiastical History

His early religious reforms

II Chr. 34 ³Now in the eighth year of his reign, while he was yet young, he began to seek after the God of David his father, and in the twelfth year he began to purge Judah and Jerusalem from the high places and the asherahs and the graven and molten images. ⁴And they broke down the altars of the Baals in his presence, and the sun-images that stood above them he hewed down, and the asherahs, and the graven and molten images he broke in pieces and made dust of them and strewed it on the graves of those who had sacrificed to them. ⁵And he burnt the bones of the priests upon their altars

---

The Babylonian Period.—The history of the earlier part of this most important period is recorded in greater detail than that of any other in the life of the Israelitish race. Regarding the great reformation of Josiah, the temple records quoted in Kgs. are the chief source, supplemented by the contemporary sermons of Zephaniah and Jeremiah. For the remainder of the period the citations from the annals of Judah and the historical statements of the late prophetic editor are richly supplemented by the biography of Jeremiah, which has been combined with his prophecies. Many contemporary data are also found in his addresses and those of his younger colleagues, Habakkuk and Ezekiel. Cf. Vol. III. The Babylonian inscriptions, and especially those of Nebuchadrezzar, make it possible for the historian also to study the events from the point of view of the conquerors. Regarding the period of the Babylonian exile Israel's historians are silent, because there were few events and because they were too tragic to be recorded.

§ 126 Vss. ¹, ² are clearly from the late prophetic editor, but with ³ begins a narrative in which the style and interest are very similar to those in the citation from the temple records in 12. The theme, the discovery of the book of the law in connection with certain repairs of the temple, would appeal most naturally and the details in ³⁻⁷ would be familiar to one connected with the temple. Most of the narrative has the characteristics of a practically contemporary record. At the same time the events recorded are so important that it was almost inevitable that the account should be much revised and supplemented by later editors. The character and language of many clauses and verses indicate that this has been done. It must, however, be remembered that the original narrative was also written under the influence of the newly discovered book of the covenant, which powerfully influenced and largely determined the style of the later editors, so that the presence here of late prophetic or Deuteronomic expressions is not conclusive evidence that the passages containing them are later editorial additions. For this reason a definite analysis is especially difficult and there is room for considerable difference of opinion. Fortunately the editorial additions also have almost the value of contemporary authority, so that we may feel confident that we have on the whole a faithful record of the way in which the new law-book, represented by the body of our present book of Dt., was brought to the attention of the king and made the basis of the great reformation. The Chronicler has revised and expanded the original narrative of Kgs. by introducing the Levites as the collectors of the money for the repair of the temple, and also by placing them at the head of the commission which directed the work. He moreover introduces into the eighth year of Josiah's reign the iconoclastic reformation which the narrative of Kgs. places after the discovery of the book of the law in his eighteenth year.

Chronicler's Ecclesiastical History

and purged Judah and Jerusalem. ⁶Also in the cities of Manasseh and Ephraim and Simeon, even to Naphtali, in their ruins round about, ⁷he broke down the altars and beat the asherahs and the graven images into powder, and hewed down all the sun-images throughout all the land of Israel, and then returned to Jerusalem.

Temple Records

II Kgs. 22 ³Now in the eighteenth year of King Josiah, the king sent Shaphan the son of Azaliah, the son of Meshullam, the scribe, to the temple of Jehovah saying, ⁴Go up to Hilkiah the high priest, that he may return the full amount[a] of the money which is brought into the temple of Jehovah, which the keepers of the threshold have gathered from the people ⁵and let them deliver it into the hands of the workmen who have the oversight of the temple of Jehovah; that they may give it to the workmen who are in the temple of Jehovah, to repair the decayed parts of the temple— ⁶to the carpenters and the builders and the masons—as well as to buy timber and hewn stone to repair the temple. ⁷However, there was no reckoning made with them regarding the money that was delivered into their hands, for they dealt faithfully.

⁸Then Hilkiah the high priest said to Shaphan the scribe, I have found the book of the law in the temple of Jehovah. And Hilkiah delivered the book to Shaphan,

⁸Now in the eighteenth year of his reign, in order to purge the land and the temple, he sent Shaphan the son of Azaliah, and Maaseiah the governor of the city, and Joah the son of Joahaz the chancellor to repair the temple of Jehovah his God. ⁹And they came to Hilkiah the high priest, and delivered the money that was brought into the house of God, which the Levites, the keepers of the threshold, had gathered from Manasseh and Ephraim and from the rest of Israel, and from all Judah and Benjamin, and returned to Jerusalem. ¹⁰They in turn delivered it into the hand of the workmen who had the oversight of the temple of Jehovah; and the workmen who worked on the temple of Jehovah gave it to mend and repair the temple—¹¹to the carpenters and to the builders they gave it, that they might buy hewn stone and timber for binders and to make beams for the buildings which the kings of Judah had destroyed. ¹²And the men did the work faithfully; and the overseers over them were Jahath and Obadiah, the Levites, of the sons of Merari, and Zechariah and Meshullam, of the sons of the Kohathites, to direct the work. And the Levites—all who were skilful with instruments of music—¹³were over the burden-bearers, and directed all the workmen who did any kind of service; and some of the Levites were scribes, officers, and porters.

¹⁴And when they brought out the money that had been brought into the temple of Jehovah, Hilkiah the priest found the book of the law of Jehovah given by Moses. ¹⁵And Hilkiah spoke and said to Shaphan the scribe, I have found the book of the law in the tem-

[margin notes: ans : the ɔair the mple]

[margin notes: liv- / of ɛ new ɔk of ɛ law Jo- h]

---

[a] II Kgs. 22⁴ Heb., *bring to an end.*

307

Temple Records

and he read it. ⁹And Shaphan the scribe went to the king and also brought the king word, saying, Your servants have emptied out the money that was found in the temple and have delivered it into the hands of the workmen who have the oversight of the temple of Jehovah. ¹⁰And Shaphan the scribe told the king, saying, Hilkiah the priest has given me a book. And Shaphan read it before the king.

His reception of it

¹¹But when the king had heard the words of the book of the law, he tore his clothes. ¹²And the king commanded Hilkiah the priest and Ahikam the son of Shaphan, and Achbor the son of Micaiah, and Shaphan the scribe, and Asaiah the king's servant, saying, ¹³Go, inquire of Jehovah for me and for the people and for all Judah, concerning the words of this book that is found; for great is the wrath of Jehovah that is kindled against us, because our fathers have not hearkened to the words of this book, to do just as is written in it[c] concerning us.

Chronicler's Ecclesiastical History

ple of Jehovah. And Hilkiah delivered the book to Shaphan. ¹⁶And Shaphan carried the book to the king, and also reported to the king, saying, All that was committed to your servants, they are doing. ¹⁷And they have emptied out the money that was found in the temple of Jehovah, and have delivered it into the hands of the overseers and into the hands of the workmen. ¹⁸And Shaphan the scribe told the king, saying, Hilkiah the priest has delivered to me a book. And Shaphan read out of it before the king.

¹⁹But when the king had heard the words of the law, he tore his clothes. ²⁰Then the king commanded Hilkiah, and Ahikam the son of Shaphan, and Achbor the son of Micaiah,[b] and Shaphan the scribe, and Asaiah the king's servant, saying, ²¹Go, inquire of Jehovah for me and for those who are left in Israel and in Judah concerning the words of the book that has been found; for great is the wrath of Jehovah that is poured out upon us, because our fathers have not kept the word of Jehovah, to do just as is written in this book.

Huldah's prediction regarding Judah and Josiah

¹⁴So Hilkiah the priest and Ahikam and Achbor went to Huldah the prophetess the wife of Shallum, the son of Tikvah, the son of Harhas, keeper of the wardrobe, who dwelt in Jerusalem in the second quarter,[d] and they conversed with her. ¹⁵And she said to them, Thus saith Jehovah, the God of Israel: 'Tell the man who sent you to me, ¹⁶" Thus saith Jehovah: I am now about to bring evil upon this place and upon its inhabitants, even all the threats of the book which the king of Judah hath read. ¹⁷Because they have forsaken me and have offered sacrifices to other gods, that they might provoke me to anger with all the work of their hands; therefore my wrath shall be kindled against this place and it shall not be quenched." '[e]

[b] II Chr. 34²⁰ Restoring the text by the aid of the parallel in Kgs. Heb., *Abdor the son of Micah.*
[c] II Kgs. 22¹³ So Luc. The Heb. omits, *in it.*
[d] II Kgs. 22¹⁴ Cf. Zeph. 1¹⁰ and Neh. 11⁹.
[e] II Kgs. 22¹⁷ This verse abounds in the characteristic expressions of the late prophetic school.

Temple Records

¹⁸But to the king of Judah, who sent you to inquire of Jehovah, this shall you say to him, 'Thus saith Jehovah, the God of Israel, "As regards the words which thou hast heard—¹⁹because thy heart was penitent,ᶠ and thou didst humble thyself before Jehovah, when thou heardest what I spoke against this place and against its inhabitants, that they should become an object of dread and execration, and hast torn thy garments and wept before me, I also have heard thee, saith Jehovah. ²⁰Therefore I will gather thee to thy fathers and thou shalt be borne to thy grave in peace, neither shall thine eyes see all the evil which I will bring upon this place." ' So they brought back word to the king.

§ 127. The **Great Reformation under Josiah**, II Kgs. 23¹⁻²⁷, II Chr. 34²⁹⁻35¹⁹

Temple Records

II Kgs. 23 ¹And the king sent, and they gathered to him all the elders of Judah and of Jerusalem. ²And the king went up to the temple of Jehovah, and with him all the men of Judah and all the inhabitants of Jerusalem, as well as the priests and the prophets and all the people, both small and great; and he read in their hearing all the words of the book of the covenant which was found in the temple of Jehovah. ³And the king stood by the pillar and made a covenant before Jehovah to walk after Jehovah and to keep his commands and his testimonies and his statutes, with all his heart and all his soul,ᵍ to establish the words of this covenant that were written in his book. And all the people confirmed the covenant.ʰ

Public reading and promulgation of the new code

ᶠ II Kgs. 22¹⁸, ¹⁹ Luc. has the more fluent reading, *Because thou hast heard my words and thy heart was penitent* (lit., *tender*).

§ 127 Again there is a great difficulty in distinguishing with assurance between the original narrative and the late prophetic additions. Vss. ²⁶, ²⁷ clearly reflect the exilic point of view and are intended to harmonize the subsequent calamity, which overtook Judah, with the reforming work of Josiah. The allusion in ¹⁶⁻¹⁸ to the very late prophetic tale in I Kgs. 13 is also probably from a later hand. To the late prophetic editor may well be due the succeeding account of the extension of the iconoclastic work of Josiah from Bethel to the high places of Samaria. As in later Jewish times the name of the northern capital has here become the designation of a province. The statement in ²⁰ that Josiah slew the priests of the high places is also not consistent with the general permission in ⁸ for them to come and minister at the Jerusalem sanctuary. The movement, however, was in accord with the spirit of the Deuteronomic code and in keeping with the fierce reforming zeal of Josiah and the reformers who gathered about him. Vss. ⁴, ⁵ anticipate the variant account of the cleansing of the temple in ⁶, ⁷ and the treatment of the priests recorded in ⁸, ⁹. Otherwise the bulk of this important narrative appears to have been taken from the temple records already quoted. It is most fortunate that this event, in many ways the most significant in Judah's religious history, is so fully recorded. Cf. for the character, history, and content of the Deuteronomic code then promulgated, Vol. IV, Introd.

The Chronicler reproduces the account in Kgs. of the public promulgation of the new-found code with practically no changes, except that he expands the account of its formal ratification. Regarding the detailed reforms he makes only a brief general statement, for the picture which the original account gives of the idolatry of the Judahites was repulsive to him.

The brief account in Kgs. of the passover did not satisfy the ritualistic taste of later generations. Therefore the original version was expanded into a midrash, which represents it as having been kept not according to the newly promulgated law of Dt. or the late priestly codes, but much as in the passover described in Ezra 6¹⁹⁻²², in which the Levites also played a very important rôle.

ᵍ II Kgs. 23³ The characteristic expressions of the late prophetic editor.

ʰ II Kgs. 23³ The Chronicler's version is, II Chr. 34³², *And he caused all those who were found in Jerusalem and Benjamin to confirm it; and the inhabitants of Jerusalem did according to the covenant of God, the God of their fathers.*

309

Temple Records

Josiah's
prac-
tical
re-
forms
in Ju-
dah and
Jeru-
salem

⁴And the king commanded Hilkiah the high priest and the second priest[i] and the keepers of the threshold to bring out from the temple of Jehovah all the vessels that were made for Baal and for Asherah[j] and for all the host of heaven; and he burned them without Jerusalem in the lime-kilns[k] by the Kidron, and carried their ashes to Bethel. ⁵He also deposed the idolatrous priests, whom the kings of Judah had ordained to offer sacrifice at the high places in the cities of Judah, and in the places around about Jerusalem; those also who offered sacrifices to Baal, to the sun, the moon, and the planets,[l] and all the host of heaven. ⁶And he brought the asherah from the temple of Jehovah outside Jerusalem to the Prook of Kidron and burned it at the Brook Kidron, beat it to dust, and cast its dust upon the graves of the common people.[m] ⁷And he broke down the houses of the sacred prostitutes who were in the temple of Jehovah, where the women wove tunics[n] for the asherah. ⁸And he brought all the priests out of the cities of Judah and defiled the high places, where the priests had offered sacrifices, from Geba to Beersheba. And he broke down the high places of the satyrs[o], that stood at the entrance of the gate of Joshua the governor of the city, which were on the left as one enters the gate of the city. ⁹Nevertheless the priests of the high places did not come up to the altar of Jehovah in Jerusalem, but ate unleavened bread among their kinsmen. ¹⁰He also defiled Topheth, which is in the valley of Ben-Hinnom, that no man might make his son or his daughter to pass through the fire to Moloch. ¹¹And he took away the horses that the kings of Judah had given to the sun, at the entrance of the temple of Jehovah, by the chamber of Nathan-melech the chamberlain (which was in the Parwarim),[p] and he burned up the chariots of the sun. ¹²And the altars that were on the roof (the upper chamber of Ahaz) which the kings of Judah had made, and the altars which Manasseh had made (in the two courts of the temple of Jehovah)[q] the king broke off and beat down[r] from there and cast the dust from them into the Brook Kidron. ¹³And the high places that were east of Jerusalem, to the south of the hill of the destroyer,[s] which Solomon the king of Israel had built for Ashtarte,[t] the abomination of the Sidonians, and for Chemosh, the abomination of Moab, and for Milcom, the abomination of the Ammonites, the king defiled. ¹⁴And he broke in pieces the pillars, and cut down the asherahs and filled their places with the bones of men.[u]

---

[i] II Kgs. 23⁴ Heb., *priests*, but in the light of 25¹⁸ and the Targs., the reading above seems to have been original.

[j] II Kgs. 23⁴ Here the asherah appears to represent a female deity corresponding to Baal (*i.e., Ashtarte*), but in ⁶ the reference is as usual to the sacred poles.

[k] II Kgs. 23⁴ So Luc., and the corrected Heb. text. The present Heb. has, *fields*, but the word is never used elsewhere in prose.

[l] II Kgs. 23⁵ The word probably means, lit., *heavenly mansions*. The same root is found in the fifth tablet of the Babylonian Creation Epic, *He made mansions of the great gods*. These mansions appear to have been identified with certain planets. The identification accords perfectly with the present context.

[m] II Kgs. 23⁶ Cf. Jer. 26²³.

[n] II Kgs. 23⁷ So Luc., and the transliteration of the Gk. Heb., *houses*.

[o] II Kgs. 23⁸ Slightly emending the Heb.

[p] II Kgs. 23¹¹ Possibly a Persian word meaning, *open kiosk*. It was doubtless identical with the *Parbar*, mentioned in I Chr. 26¹⁸, and located to the west of the temple. Cf. Ezek. 41¹²·¹⁵. The clause is probably a later note.

[q] II Kgs. 23¹² The reference to the two courts rather than the one of the pre-exilic temple, indicates that this also, like the other topographical notes, is a later addition. Cf. § 125, note ⁵.

[r] II Kgs. 23¹² Or, *banished them*. The exact meaning is in doubt.

[s] II Kgs. 23¹³ Or, *destruction*. Possibly the name arose in connection with the incident recorded in II Sam. 24¹⁶. Cf. also I Kgs. 11⁷. It was later identified with the Mount of Olives.

[t] II Kgs. 23¹³ Heb., as elsewhere, *Ashtoreth*.

[u] II Kgs. 23¹⁴ This verse repeats ²·⁷.

Temple Records

¹⁵Moreover the altar that was at Bethel, and the high place which Jero- De-
boam the son of Nebat, who made Israel sin, had made, even that altar and struc-
the high place he tore down, and broke in pieces its stones^v and beat it to the al-
dust and burned the asherah. ¹⁶And when Josiah turned and saw the sepulchres tombs
that were there on the mount, he sent, and took the bones out of the sepulchres, at
burned them upon the altar, and defiled it, according to the word of Jehovah which Bethel
the man of God proclaimed, who proclaimed these things. ¹⁷Then he said, What is
yonder tomb-stone which I see? And the men of the city told him, It is the sepulchre of the man of God, who came from Judah and proclaimed these things that you
have done against the altar of Bethel. ¹⁸And he said, Let him be; let no man move
his bones. So they left his bones undisturbed, together with the bones of the prophet
who came from Samaria.

¹⁹Also all the temples of the high places that were in the cities of Samaria, which the Of the
kings of Israel had made to provoke Jehovah to anger, Josiah took away and did to them north-
just as he had done at Bethel. ²⁰And all the priests of the high places, who were there, ern
he slew upon the altars and burned men's bones upon them. Then he returned to shrines
Jerusalem.

Chronicler's Ecclesiastical History

²¹And the king com- Obser- manded all the people, vation saying, Keep the pass- of the over to Jehovah your Pass- God, as it is prescribed over in this book of the cove- nant. ²²For such a pass- over as this had not been kept from the days of the judges who judged Israel, and during the days of the kings of Is- rael and the kings of Judah; ²³but in the eigh- teenth year of King Jo- siah this passover was kept to Jehovah in Jeru- salem.^x

II Chr. 35 ¹Josiah kept a passover to Jehovah in Jerusalem; and they killed the passover on the fourteenth of the first month. ²And he set the priests in their offices and encouraged them to perform the service of the temple of Jehovah. ³And he said to the Levites who taught all Israel, who were holy to Jehovah, Put the holy ark in the temple which Solomon the son of David king of Israel built. It shall no more be a burden upon your shoulders. Now serve Jehovah your God and his people Israel, ⁴and prepare yourselves after your fathers' houses by your divisions ac- cording to the directions^w of David king of Israel and according to the directions^w of Solomon his son. ⁵And stand in the holy place according to the divisions of the families of your kinsmen, the laity, and let there be for each a part of a levitical family. ⁶Thus kill the passover and keep your- selves holy and prepare it for your kinsmen that they may keep it as Jehovah commanded through Moses.

⁷And Josiah distributed to the laity flocks, lambs and kids—all of them Public
for the passover offerings—to all who were present, to the number of thirty dona-
thousand, and three thousand bullocks—these were from the king's pos- the
sessions. ⁸And his princes distributed as a voluntary gift to the people, and
to the priests, and to the Levites Hilkiah and Zechariah and Jehiel, the rulers princes
of the house of God, gave to the priests for the passover-offerings two thousand
six hundred lambs and three hundred oxen. ⁹Conaniah also and Shemaiah

---

^v II Kgs. 23¹⁵ So Gk. and Luc. The Heb. has the impossible, *burned the high place.*
^w II Chr. 35⁴ Heb., *writing.*
^x II Kgs. 23²², ²³ Possibly these verses are secondary additions, for they seem to reflect a
late point of view.

Chronicler's Ecclesiastical History

and Nethaneel his kinsman, and Hashabiah and Jeiel and Jozabad, the chiefs of the Levites, distributed to the Levites for the passover-offerings five thousand lambs and five hundred oxen.

Preparation of the passover sacrifices

¹⁰So the service was instituted and the priests stood in their place and the Levites by their divisions, according to the king's command. ¹¹And they killed the passover and the priests sprinkled the blood from their hands, while the Levites took off the skins. ¹²And they removed the burnt-offerings, that they might give them according to the divisions of the families of the laity, to offer to Jehovah, as it is prescribed in the book of Moses. And thus they did with the oxen. ¹³And they roasted the passover on the fire according to the ordinance; while they boiled the holy offerings in pots, in caldrons, in pans, and carried them quickly to all the laity. ¹⁴And afterward they prepared for themselves and for the priests, because the priests, the sons of Aaron, were busied in offering the burnt-offerings and the fat pieces until night; therefore the Levites prepared it for themselves and for the priests, the sons of Aaron.

Manner of observing the feast

¹⁵And the singers, the sons of Asaph, were in their place according to the command of David and Asaph and Heman and Jeduthun the king's seer. And the porters were at each gate; they did not need to depart from their service, for their kinsmen the Levites prepared it for them. ¹⁶So all the service of Jehovah was instituted the same day, so that they kept the passover, and offered burnt-offerings on the altar of Jehovah according to the command of King Josiah. ¹⁷And the Israelites who were present kept the passover at that time and the feast of unleavened bread seven days. ¹⁸And there was no passover like that kept in Israel from the days of Samuel the prophet; neither did any of the kings of Israel keep such a passover as Josiah kept; and the priests and the Levites and all Judah and Israel were present, together with the inhabitants of Jerusalem. ¹⁹In the eighteenth year of the reign of Josiah was this passover kept.

Late (Exilic) Prophetic Summary

Josiah's fidelity to the law

II Kgs. 23 ²⁴Moreover the mediums, the wizards, the idols, and all the abominations that were seen in the land of Judah and in Jerusalem, Josiah put away, that he might establish the words of the law which were written in the book that Hilkiah the priest found in the temple of Jehovah. ²⁵And before him there was no king like him who turned to Jehovah with all his heart and with all his soul and with all his might according to all the law of Moses; neither after him did any arise like him.

²⁶Notwithstanding, Jehovah did not turn from the fierceness of his great wrath, since his anger was kindled against Judah, because of all the provocations with which Manasseh had provoked him. ²⁷So Jehovah said, I will remove Judah also out of my sight, as I have removed Israel, and I will cast off this city which I have chosen, even Jerusalem, and the temple of which I said, ' My name shall be there.'ᵃ

ᵃ II Kgs. 23²⁴⁻²⁷ Not only is the general point of view late, but the idioms are those peculiar to the late prophetic school. The references in ²⁷ to the exile indicate that this summary is from the exilic editor of the book of Kgs. Cf. Introd., p. 21.

§ 128. Josiah's Death, II Kgs. 23²⁸⁻³⁰, II Chr. 35²⁰–36¹

Annals of Judah	*Chronicler's Ecclesiastical History*

siah's
cal
tack
on
echo

II Kgs. 23 ²⁹In the days [of Josiah] Pharaoh-necho[b] king of Egypt went up against the king of Assyria to the River Euphrates. And King Josiah went against him; and Pharaoh-necho slew him at Megiddo, as soon as he confronted[e] him. ³⁰And his servants carried him in a chariot from Megiddo and brought him to Jerusalem, and buried him in his own sepulchre.

II Chr. 35 ²⁰After all this, when Josiah had set the temple again in order, Necho king of Egypt went up to fight at Carchemish by the Euphrates. And Josiah went out against him. ²¹But he sent ambassadors to him, saying, What have we to do with each other, king of Judah? I come not against you this day, but against my ancestral enemy,[c] and God has commanded me to make haste; do not interfere with God, who is with me, that he destroy you not. ²²Nevertheless Josiah would not turn away his face from him, but presumed to attack him[d] and gave no heed to the words of Necho from the mouth of God. So he advanced to the attack in the valley of Megiddo. ²³Then the archers shot at King Josiah, so that the king had to say to his servants, Take me away; for I am severely wounded. ²⁴So his servants took him from the chariot and put him in the second chariot that he had and brought him to Jerusalem. There he died and was buried in the sepulchres of his fathers. And all Judah and Jerusalem mourned for Josiah. ²⁵And Jeremiah sang a song of lamentation for Josiah; and all the singing men and singing women speak of Josiah in their lamentations to this day. And they made them a custom in Israel; and now they are written in the lamentations.

ec-
ds of
s
ign

²⁸Now the other acts of Josiah and all that he did, are they not recorded in the Chronicles of the Kings of Judah? ³⁰ᵇAnd the people of the land took Jehoahaz the son of Josiah and anointed him and made him king in place of his father.

²⁶Now the other acts of Josiah and his good deeds, according to that which is prescribed in the law of Jehovah, ²⁷and his earlier, as well as his later acts, are recorded in the Book of the Kings of Israel and Judah.

---

§ 128 The account of the tragic death of Judah's reforming king was doubtless found in the annals of Judah and is quoted by the editor of Kgs. He has prefaced his citation with his usual formula, which, however, logically follows ³⁰ᵃ. The Chronicler's version endeavors to explain why the good king was cut off in his full vigor and gives the earliest trace of the late Jewish traditions that Jeremiah wrote Lamentations. The story is so vividly told and with so many details that it seems probable that it was derived from the oft-quoted source which he mentions in ²⁷. The fact that the death of Josiah was still publicly celebrated also confirms the conclusion that the story took form not long after the events recorded.

ᵇ II Kgs. 23²⁹ Necho II, the second king of the twenty-sixth dynasty. In Kgs. the name is spelled, *Nechoh*. Cf. Chron. chart after p. 199.

ᶜ II Chr. 35²¹ Heb., *the house with which I am at war*. The Heb. text appears to be defective. Possibly the Gk. has the original, *I have come to fight*.

ᵈ II Chr. 35²² So Gk. and many of the versions. The Heb. reading, *disguised himself*, is probably due to the error of a copyist who had in mind Ahab's end, I Kgs. 22.

ᵉ II Kgs. 23²⁹ Heb., *saw*.

§ 129. Jehoahaz's Reign, II Kgs. 23³¹⁻³⁵, II Chr. 36²⁻⁴

Annals of Judah

Evil policy of Jehoahaz

II Kgs. 23 ³¹Jehoahaz was twenty-three years old when he began to reign and he reigned three months in Jerusalem. And his mother's name was Hamutal the daughter of Jeremiah of Libnah. ³²And he did that which displeased Jehovah just as his fathers had done. ³³And Pharaoh-Necho put him in bonds at Riblah in the land of Hamath, that he might not reign in Jerusalem,ᶠ and imposed on the land a tribute of a hundred talents of silver and tenᵍ talents of gold. ³⁴And Pharaoh-Necho made Eliakim the son of Josiah king in place of Josiah his father and changed his name to Jehoiakim. But he took Jehoahaz away with him, and he came to Egypt and died there. ³⁵And Jehoiakim gave the silver and the gold to Pharaoh. He had to tax the land, however, to give the money demanded by Pharaoh: each according to his taxation, exacted the silver and the gold from the people of the landʰ in order to give it to Pharaoh-Necho.

Terms imposed by the conqueror, Necho

§ 130. Jehoiakim's Reign, II Kgs. 23³⁶, ³⁷, 24¹⁻⁷, II Chr. 36⁵⁻⁸

Annals of Judah

Evil policy of Jehoiakim

II Kgs. 23 ³⁶Jehoiakim was twenty-five years old when he became king and he reigned eleven years in Jerusalem. And his mother's name was Zebidahⁱ the daughter of Pedaiah of Rumah. ³⁷And he did that which displeased Jehovah just as his fathers had done.

Conquest of Judah by Nebuchadrezzar

24 ¹ᵃIn his days Nebuchadnezzarʲ king of Babylon came up, and Jehoiakim became subject to him for three years. ⁷And the king of Egypt came no more out of his land; for the king of Babylon had taken, from the Brook of Egypt to the River Euphrates, all that had belonged to the king of Egypt.ᵏ ¹ᵇThen [Jehoiakim] again rebelled against him. ²And Jehovah sent against him guerilla bands of the Chaldeans, of the Arameans, of the Moabites, and of the Ammonites; these he sent against Judah to destroy it, according to the word of Jehovah, which he had spoken by his servants the prophets. ³Surely at the command of Jehovahˡ this came upon Judah that he might remove it out of his sight, because of the sins of Manasseh, according to all that he had done, ⁴and also because of the innocent blood; and Jehovah would not pardon. ⁵Now the other acts of Jehoiakim and all that he did, are they not recorded in the Chronicles of the Kings of Judah? ⁶So Jehoiakim slept with his fathers, and Jehoiachin his son became king in his place.ᵐ

§ 129 As usual the quotations from the state annals are prefaced with the formula of the late prophetic editor. The Chronicler has simply abridged the narrative of Kgs.
ᶠ 23³³ *That he might not reign in Jerusalem* is perhaps a gloss added from the parallel in II Chr. 36³. The first part of ³³ is, however, lacking in Chr.
ᵍ 23³³ So Luc. and Syr. Heb., *one*.
ʰ 23³⁵ The meaning of the Heb. appears to be that the landed proprietors were assessed according to the valuation of their property and then collected it from the peasants who worked their land.
§ 130 In 24² material apparently taken from the state annals is epitomized by the late prophetic editor. The quotation in ⁷ probably originally followed ¹ᵃ. The Chronicler confuses Jehoiakim and his son Jehoiachin, and represents the former as carried away captive to Babylon, II Chr. 36⁶. He also adds in ⁷ that, *Nebuchadnezzar also carried away some of the vessels of the temple of Jehovah and put them in his temple at Babylon.*
ⁱ 23³⁶ Or, *Zebuddah*. Cf. I Kgs. 4⁵.
ʲ 24¹ Heb., in Kgs. and Dan., *Nebuchadnezzar*, but the more exact form, *Nebuchadrezzar*, appears in Jer. The original Bab. is *Nabu-kudur-uçur*.
ᵏ 24⁷ The conquest of all Palestine here recorded was soon after the great victory at Carchemish in 604 B.C. Vs. ⁷ logically follows immediately after ¹ᵃ. The rebellion recorded in ¹ᵇ probably occurred in 600 B.C.
ˡ 24³ Gk., Luc., Syr., and Targ. read, *on account of the anger of.*
ᵐ 24⁶ The Gk. of the parallel in II Chr. 36⁵ adds what may have been struck out of Kgs. because of Jer. 22¹⁹, *and buried him in the garden of Uzza.*

§ 131. Jeremiah's Preaching and Trial, Jer. 26¹⁻¹⁹

Baruch's Biography of Jeremiah

Jer. 26 ¹In the beginning of the reign of Jehoiakim the son of Josiah, Jeremiah's prediction of the destruction of the city and temple

king of Judah, this word came from Jehovah, saying, ²Thus saith Jehovah: ' Stand in the court of Jehovah's house, and speak to all the people[n] of Judah, who come to worship in Jehovah's house, all the words that I command you to speak to them, Do not take away a word. ³Perhaps they will hearken and turn each from his wicked way, that I may repent of the evil which I purpose to do to them because of the wickedness of their deeds. ⁴And thou shalt say to them, " Thus saith Jehovah: If ye will not listen to me, to walk in my law which I have set before you, ⁵to hearken to the words of my servants the prophets, whom I send to you, sending them constantly although you do not heed, ⁶then will I make this temple like Shiloh, and will make this city an object of execration to all the nations of the earth." ' ⁷And the priests and the prophets and all the people heard Jeremiah speaking these words in the temple of Jehovah.

⁸And then when Jeremiah had finished speaking all that Jehovah had commanded him to speak to all the people, the priests and prophets and all the people took hold of him, saying, You must die. ⁹Why have you prophesied in the name of Jehovah, saying, ' This temple shall be like Shiloh, and this city shall be desolate, without habitation ? ' And all the people were gathered about Jeremiah in the temple of Jehovah. *(Popular movement to put him to death)*

¹⁰And when the princes of Judah heard these things, they came up from the king's palace to the temple of Jehovah; and they sat at the entrance of the new gate of the temple of Jehovah. ¹¹Then the priests and the prophets spoke to the princes and to all the people saying, This man is guilty of a capital offence, for he has prophesied against this city as you have heard[o] with your own ears. ¹²Then Jeremiah addressed the princes and all the people, saying, It was Jehovah who sent me to prophesy against this temple, and against this city all the words that you have heard. ¹³Now therefore reform your ways and your acts, and obey the voice of Jehovah your God; and Jehovah will repent of the evil that he has pronounced against you. ¹⁴But as for me, see, I am in your hand; do with me as appears to you to be good and right. ¹⁵Only be assured that, if you put me to death, you will bring innocent blood upon yourselves and upon this city and upon its inhabitants, for assuredly Jehovah hath sent me to you to speak all these things in your ears. *(His response to the public arraignment)*

---

§ 131 This is the first of those important incidents in the life of Jeremiah recorded in the book of Jeremiah, the basis of which probably came directly from the pen of his faithful scribe Baruch. Not only do they clearly and vividly present the experiences and trials of the patriotic prophet, but they also supplement the meagre narrative in Kgs. at certain of the most important epochs in Judah's history. Cf. 7¹⁻¹⁵ for the fuller version of Jeremiah's sermon.

The Gk. has a much briefer version of the extracts from the biography of Jeremiah. In many cases this doubtless approximates more closely to the original than the fuller Heb. Where the Gk. is obviously correct or is strongly supported by the context, it has been followed and the reasons briefly indicated in the notes. Otherwise where the evidence is not conclusive the Heb. text has been adopted. For a fuller discussion of the text of Jer., cf. Vol. III *in loco*.

[n] 26² So Gk. Heb., *cities*, was probably introduced by a scribe familiar with 11⁶.
[o] 26¹¹ So Gk. The Heb. adds, *all*.

Baruch's Biography of Jeremiah

<sup>Cita-
tion of
the
prece-
dent
estab-
lished
by the
prophet
Micah</sup>   ¹⁶Then the princes and all the people said to the priests and to the prophets, This man is not guilty of a capital offence, for he has spoken to us in the name of Jehovah our God.   ¹⁷Thereupon certain of the elders of the land arose and spoke to all the assembly of the people, saying, ¹⁸Micah the Morashite prophesied in the days of Hezekiah king of Judah; and he spoke to all the people of Judah, saying, ' Thus saith Jehovah of hosts:

> " Zion shall be plowed as a field,
> And Jerusalem shall become stone-heaps,
> And the temple-mount wooded heights." 'ᵖ

¹⁹Did Hezekiah�q and all Judah indeed put him to death ?   Did they not fear Jehovah and appease Jehovah, so that Jehovah repented of the evil which he had pronounced against them ?   But we are on the point of doing great injury to ourselves.

§ 132. Martyrdom of the Prophet Uriah, Jer. 26²⁰⁻²⁴

Baruch's Biography of Jeremiah

<sup>Fate of
Uriah
who
proph-
esied
the
same as
Jere-
miah</sup>   **Jer. 26** ²⁰Now there was also a man who prophesied in the name of Jehovah, Uriah the son of Shemaiah of Kiriath-jearim; and he prophesied against this city and against this land in the same terms as did Jeremiah.   ²¹And when Jehoiakim the kingʳ and all the princes heard his words, the king sought to put him to death; but when Uriah heard it he was afraid and fled and went to Egypt.   ²²And Jehoiakim the king sent men to Egypt, Elnathan the son of Achbor and certain men with him to Egypt.ˢ   ²³And they brought Uriah from Egypt, and took him to Jehoiakim the king, and he slew him with the sword and cast his dead body into the graves of the common people.   ²⁴But the influence of Ahikam the son of Shaphan was in favor of Jeremiah that they should not give him into the handsᵗ of the people to put him to death.

§ 133. First and Second Collections of Jeremiah's Sermons, Jer. 36

Baruch's Biography of Jeremiah

<sup>The
divine
com-
mand
to re-
cord his
earlier
proph-
ecies</sup>   **Jer. 36** ¹Now in the fourth year of Jehoiakim the son of Josiah king of Judah, the following message came to Jeremiah from Jehovah, ²Take a book-roll and write on it all the words that I have spoken to thee regarding Jerusalem and Judahᵘ and all the nations, since the day I spoke to thee,

---

ᵖ 26¹⁸ Cf. the prophecy quoted in Mic. 3¹².
q 26¹⁹ So Gk. The Heb. adds the unnecessary, *king of Judah*, probably from ¹⁸.
§ 132 This exceedingly suggestive incidental note was probably also taken from Baruch's biography of Jeremiah, and was intended to illustrate the martyr's fate which Jeremiah so narrowly escaped.
ʳ 26²¹ So Gk. The Heb. adds, *and all his mighty warriors.*
ˢ 26²² Not found in the Gk. and evidently a later addition. In 36¹², ²⁵ Elnathan appears as a friend of Jeremiah.
ᵗ 26²⁴ Heb., *hand.*
§ 133 This valuable account of the origin and fate of the first and second editions of Jeremiah's work is also probably from the pen of his faithful scribe. It is really the only detailed bit of literary history in the O.T., and for that reason is exceedingly illuminating. The immediate motive which influenced the prophet to this act was probably the appearance of the Chaldeans (about 604 B.C.) on the political horizon.
ᵘ 36² So Gk. The Heb. has, *regarding Israel.*

Baruch's Biography of Jeremiah

from the time of Josiah, even to this day. ³Perhaps the house of Judah will give heed to all the evil which I purpose to do to them, so that they will turn each from his evil way, that I may forgive their iniquity and their sin.

⁴Then Jeremiah called Baruch the son of Neriah; and Baruch wrote at the dictation of Jeremiah all the words of Jehovah, which he had spoken to him, upon a roll of a book. ⁵And Jeremiah commanded Baruch, saying, I am prevented, I cannot go to the temple of Jehovah. ⁶Therefore you go and read in the roll, which you have written at my dictation, the words of Jehovah in the hearing of the people in Jehovah's house upon the fast-day. And also you shall read them in the hearing of all the people of Judah who have come from their cities. ⁷Perhaps they will present their supplication before Jehovahᵛ and will turn each from his evil course, for great is the anger and the wrath that Jehovah has pronounced against this people. ⁸And Baruch the son of Neriah did just as Jeremiah the prophet commanded him, reading out of the books the word of Jehovah in the temple of Jehovah.

His command to Baruch to read them before the people

⁹Now in the fifth year of Jehoiakim the son of Josiah king of Judah, in the ninth month, all the people in Jerusalem and all the people who came from the cities of Judah to Jerusalem proclaimed a fast before Jehovah. ¹⁰Then Baruch read in the hearing of all the people out of the book the words of Jeremiah in the temple of Jehovah in the chamber of Gemariah the son of Shaphan, the chancellor in the upper court at the entry of the new gate of Jehovah's house.

The public reading

¹¹And when Micaiah the son of Gemariah, the son of Shaphan, had heard all the words of Jehovah out of the book, ¹²he went down into the royal palace to the chancellor's chamber and there were sitting all the princes, Elishama the chancellor, and Delaiah the son of Shemaiah, Elnathan the son of Achbor, Gemariah the son of Shaphan, Zedekiah the son of Hananiah, and all the princes. ¹³Then Micaiah made known all the words that he had heard, when Baruch read the book in the hearing of the people. ¹⁴Then all the princes sent Jehudi the son of Nethaniah, the son of Shelemiah, the son of Cushi, to Baruch, saying, Take in your hand the roll from which you have read in the hearing of all the people, and come here. So Baruch the son of Neriah took the roll in his hand, and came to them. ¹⁵Then they said to him, Sit down now and read it in our hearing. So Baruch read it in their hearing. ¹⁶But when they had heard all the words, they turned in alarm to one another, and said to Baruch, We must surely tell the king of all these words. ¹⁷And they asked Baruch, saying, Tell us now, ' How did you write all these words?'ʷ ¹⁸Then Baruch answered them, Jeremiah dictatedˣ all these words to me and I wrote them with inkᵃ in the book. ¹⁹Then the princes said to Baruch, Go, hide yourself, you and Jeremiah, and let no man know where you are.

The reading before the nobles in the palace

ᵛ 36⁷ Heb., *their supplication will fall before Jehovah*, i.e., they will approach Jehovah in a penitent, humble attitude.
ʷ 36¹⁷ So Gk. A scribe has added in the Heb., *at his dictation.*
ˣ 36¹⁸ Heb., *called out with his mouth.*
ᵃ 36¹⁸ The exact meaning of the phrase translated, *with ink*, is doubtful. The original text may have read, *with my hand.* The Gk. omits.

Baruch's Biography of Jeremiah

The king's contempt for the prophecies and command to arrest the prophet

²⁰But they went in to the king in his apartment,[b] after they had laid up the roll in the chamber of Elishama the chancellor, and they told all these[c] words in the hearing of the king.   ²¹Then the king sent Jehudi to bring the roll, and he brought it out of the chamber of Elishama the chancellor.   And Jehudi read it in the hearing of the king and of all the princes who stood beside the king.   ²²Now the king was sitting in the winter house[d] with a heated brazier[e] burning before him.   ²³And when Jehudi had read three or four double columns, the king cut it with the paperknife,[f] and threw it into the fire that was on the brazier, until the entire roll was consumed in the fire that was on the brazier.   ²⁴But they were not alarmed nor tore their garments—neither the king nor any of his servants who heard all these words.   ²⁵Moreover, although Elnathan and Delaiah and Gemariah besought the king not to burn the roll, he would not hear them.   ²⁶Then the king commanded Jerahmeel the king's son and Seraiah the son of Azriel and Shelemiah the son of Abdeel to seize Baruch the scribe and Jeremiah the prophet, but Jehovah kept them concealed.

Command to prepare another roll

²⁷Then after the king had burned the roll, that is, all[g] the words which Baruch wrote at the dictation of Jeremiah, the word of Jehovah came to Jeremiah as follows, ²⁸Take again another roll and write in it all the words that were in the first roll, which Jehoiakim the king of Judah burned.

Prophecy of the destruction of Judah and the reigning house

²⁹And concerning Jehoiakim king of Judah thou shalt say, 'Thus saith Jehovah, "Thou hast burned this roll saying: Why hast thou thus written therein: The king of Babylon shall assuredly come and destroy this land and shall remove from there[h] man and beast?" ³⁰Therefore thus saith Jehovah concerning Jehoiakim king of Judah, "He shall have none left to sit upon the throne of David and his dead body shall be exposed to the heat by day and to the frost by night.   ³¹And I will visit upon him and his descendants and his servants their iniquity, and I will bring upon them and the inhabitants of Jerusalem and the men of Judah, all the evil that I have pronounced against them, but which they heeded not."'

Preparation of an enlarged second edition

³²Then Jeremiah took another roll and gave it to Baruch the scribe the son of Neriah, who wrote on it at the dictation of Jeremiah all the words of the book which Jehoiakim king of Judah had burned in the fire.   And there were also added to them many other similar words.

---

§ 134. The First Captivity (597 B.C.), II Kgs. 24⁸⁻¹⁷, II Chr. 36⁹, ¹⁰

Late Prophetic Summary

II Kgs. 24 ⁸Jehoiachin was eighteen years old when he became king, and he reigned in Jerusalem three months. And his mother's name was Nehushta the daughter of Elnathan of Jerusalem. ⁹And he did that which displeased Jehovah just as his father had done.

ⁱ⁰At that time the servants of Nebuchadnezzar king of Babylon came up against Jerusalem, and the city was besieged. ¹¹And Nebuchadnezzar king of Babylon came to the city, while his servants were besieging it; ¹²and Jehoiachin the king of Judah went out to the king of Babylon, together with his mother, and his servants, his princes, and his chamberlains. And the king of Babylon took him captive in the eighth year^i of his reign. ¹³And he carried away from there all the treasures of the house of Jehovah and the treasures of the royal palace and cut in pieces all the vessels of gold which Solomon king of Israel had made in the temple of Jehovah, as Jehovah had said. ¹⁴And he carried away as captives all Jerusalem and all the princes and all the mighty warriors, even ten thousand, and all the craftsmen and the smiths; none remained, except the poorest people of the land. ¹⁵And he carried away Jehoiachin to Babylon; and the king's mother and the king's wives, and his chamberlains, and the chief men of the land, he carried into captivity from Jerusalem to Babylon. ¹⁶And all the men of ability, even seven thousand, and the craftsmen and the smiths a thousand, all of them strong and ready for war; these the king of Babylon took captive to Babylon. ¹⁷And the king of Babylon made Mattaniah, Jehoiachin's uncle, king in his place, and changed his name to Zedekiah.

(marginal notes: Evil policy of Jehoiachin; Capture of Jerusalem and the deportation of Jehoiachin and the ruling classes)

§ 135. Zedekiah's Reign and Rebellion against Babylon, II Kgs. 24¹⁸–25², Jer. 52¹⁻⁵, II Chr. 36¹¹⁻¹⁶

Late Prophetic Summary	*Chronicler's Ecclesiastical History*
II Kgs. 24 ¹⁸Zedekiah was twenty-one years old when he began to reign, and he reigned eleven years in Jerusalem; and his mother's name was Hamutal the daughter of Jeremiah of Libnah. ¹⁹And he did that which displeased Jehovah, just as Jehoiakim had done. ²⁰For through the anger of Jehovah it came over Jerusalem and Judah until he had cast them out of his presence.	**II Chr. 36** ¹¹Zedekiah was twenty-one years old when he began to reign, and he reigned eleven years in Jerusalem. ¹²And he did that which displeased Jehovah his God; he did not humble himself before Jeremiah the prophet who spoke the words^j of Jehovah.

(marginal note: Zedekiah's policy)

§ 134 The remainder of II Kgs. is from the late prophetic historian who was himself probably a witness of many of the events. Vss. ¹³, ¹⁴ and ¹⁵, ¹⁶ contain two variant accounts of the first deportation. The original continuation of ¹² was clearly ¹⁵. The larger round number in ¹⁴ also indicates that this is the later popular version of the event. The event itself was so repugnant to the Chronicler, loyal as he was to Jerusalem and to the temple, that he gives only a very brief summary of the main facts.

^i 24¹² According to Jer. 52²⁸, *in the seventh year of Nebuchadrezzar, i.e.,* 598, instead of 597, B.C.

§ 135 The late prophetic editor's summary in Kgs. has been quoted verbatim by a late editor of Jer. (52¹⁻⁵). The Chronicler again improves the occasion to point out the sins which resulted in the final great national disaster.

^j II Chr. 36¹² Heb., *from the mouth of.*

Late Prophetic Summary | *Chronicler's Ecclesiastical History*

His rebellion against Babylon and the long siege of Jerusalem

And Zedekiah rebelled against the king of Babylon. 25 ¹Then in the ninth year of his reign, in the tenth day of the tenth month, Nebuchadnezzar king of Babylon came, together with all his army, against Jerusalem and b e s i e g e d it and they erected a siege wall about it. ²So the city was besieged to the eleventh year of King Zedekiah.

¹³And he also rebelled against King Nebuchadnezzar, who had made him swear by God. But he stiffened his neck and hardened his heart against turning to Jehovah, the God of Israel. ¹⁴Moreover all the chiefs of the priests and the people proved utterly faithless after the manner of all the abominations of the nations, and they polluted the temple of Jehovah which he had hallowed in Jerusalem. ¹⁵And Jehovah, the God of their fathers, constantly sent to them by his messengers, because he had compassion on his people and on his dwelling-place. ¹⁶But they mocked the messengers of God, despised his words and scoffed at his prophets, until the wrath of Jehovah was aroused against his people so that there was no remedy.

§ 136. Perfidy of the Hebrews During the Siege, Jer. 34

Baruch's Biography of Jeremiah

Prediction that Jerusalem would fall but Zedekiah's life be spared

Jer. 34 ¹The word which came to Jeremiah from Jehovah, while Nebuchadnezzar king of Babylon and all his army and all the kingdoms of the earth that were under his rule and all the peoples were fighting against Jerusalem and against all its cities,ᵏ saying, ²Thus saith Jehovah, the God of Israel, ' Go, and speak to Zedekiah king of Judah and tell him, " Thus saith Jehovah: Behold I will give this city into the power of Babylon that he may burn it with fire. ³And thou shalt not escape out of his hand, but shalt surely be taken and delivered into his hand, and thine eyes shall behold the eyes of the king of Babylon, and he shall speak with thee mouth to mouth, and thou shalt go to Babylon." ' ⁴Yet hear the word of Jehovah, O Zedekiah king of Judah; ' Thus saith Jehovah concerning thee, " Thou shalt not die by the sword. ⁵Peacefully shalt thou die and likeˡ the funeral pyresᵐ for thy fathers, theⁿ kings before thee, so shall they make a funeral pyre for thee; and they shall lament thee, saying: Alas, O Lord! for I have spoken the word," saith Jehovah.' ⁶Then Jeremiah the prophet spoke all these words to Zedekiah king of Judah in Jerusalem, ⁷while the king of Babylon's army was besieging Jerusalem and all the cities of Judah that were left, namely Lachish and Azekah, for these remained among the cities of Judah as fortified cities.

---

§ 136 This chapter was doubtless taken from the biography of Jeremiah which is attributed to Baruch. The original text has probably been expanded at certain points.
ᵏ 34¹ᵇ The original chronological statement is found in ⁷. Vs. ¹ᵇ is a later addition, as the later spelling, *Nebuchadnezzar*, and the inflated style indicate.
ˡ 34⁵ So Gk. and Syr. The Heb., *with*, is clearly an error.
ᵐ 34⁵ Heb., *burnings*.
ⁿ 34⁵ So Gk. The Heb. adds, *former*, which is tautological and evidently due to a later scribe.

320

Baruch's Biography of Jeremiah

Re-enslavement of the liberated Hebrew slaves

8 The word that came to Jeremiah from Jehovah, after King Zedekiah had made a covenant with all the people who were at Jerusalem, to proclaim a general liberation,[o] 9 that each should let his male and female slaves go free in case they were Hebrews or Hebrewesses; that none out of Judah should be a slave.[p] 10 And all the princes and all the people who had entered into the covenant—that each should let his male and female slaves go free, that none should make slaves of them any more—obeyed and let them go. 11 But afterward they changed their minds and made the male and female slaves, whom they had let go free, return, and brought them into subjection as male and female slaves.[q]

The divine judgment awaiting the faithless rulers of Judah

12 Therefore the word of Jehovah came to Jeremiah from Jehovah, saying, 13 Thus saith Jehovah, the God of Israel; 'I made a covenant with your fathers in the day that I brought them forth from the land of Egypt, out of the house of bondage, saying, 14 "At the end of seven years ye shall each set free his brother who is a Hebrew, who has been sold to thee and has served thee six years, and thou shalt let him go free from thee," but your fathers neither hearkened to me nor inclined their ear. 15 And ye had now turned and done that which is pleasing to me, in proclaiming freedom each to his neighbor, and ye made a covenant before me in the temple which is called by my name. 16 But ye have changed your mind and profaned my name, and made each his male and female slaves, whom ye had let go free at their pleasure, return; and have brought them into subjection, to be male and female slaves again.' 17 Therefore thus saith Jehovah, 'Ye have not hearkened to me, to proclaim freedom, each to his brother and to his neighbor—now I proclaim to you a freedom,' saith Jehovah, 'to become the prey of the sword, the pestilence, and the famine; and I will make you an object of terror to all the kingdoms of the earth. 18 And I will deliver over the men who have transgressed my covenant,[r] who have not performed the words of the covenant which they made before the calf which they cut in two and passed between its parts:[s] 19 the princes of Judah, and the princes of Jerusalem, the eunuchs, and the priests, and all the people of the land, who passed between the parts of the calf—20 I will even give them into the hand of their enemies and into the hand of those who seek their life, and their dead bodies shall be food for the birds of the heavens and the beasts of the earth. 21 And I will give Zedekiah king of Judah and his princes into the hand of their enemies and into the hand of those who seek their life, and into the power of the king of Babylon's forces who have gone away from you. 22 Behold, I will command,' saith Jehovah, 'and cause them to return to this city, and they shall besiege it and take it and burn it with fire; and I will make the cities of Judah an uninhabited desolation.'

---

[o] 34^{8} So Gk. The Heb. adds, *to them.* The liberation, as in Ezek. 46^{17}, means the freeing of all slaves after six years of service.

[p] 34^{9} So Gk. The Heb. is very awkward and makes little sense.

[q] $34^{10, 11}$ The Gk. has a much briefer and simpler text, omitting $^{10b, 11a}$. Its brevity appears to be chiefly due to a copyist's error, while the Heb., owing to another mistake, repeats, *obeyed,* in ^{10b}.

[r] 34^{18} This verse is tautological; the second relative clause may well be an addition.

[s] 34^{18} Cf. Gen. 21^{28-30} and especially 15^{9-17}.

§ 137. Jeremiah's Imprisonment and Deliverance, Jer. 37, 38¹⁻²⁸ᵃ, 39¹⁵⁻¹⁸

Baruch's Biography of Jeremiah

Popular disregard of Jeremiah's warnings

Jer. 37 ¹So Zedekiah the son of Josiah became king in the place of Coniah the son of Jehoiakim, whom Nebuchadrezzar king of Babylon made king in the land of Judah; ²but neither he nor his servants nor the people of the land hearkened to the words of Jehovah, which he spoke by the prophet Jeremiah.

Zedekiah's request for Jeremiah's prayers

³And Zedekiah the king sent Jehucal the son of Shelemiah, and Zephaniah the son of Maaseiah, the priest, to the prophet Jeremiah, saying, Pray now to Jehovah our God for us. ⁴Now in that time Jeremiah went in and out among the people, for they had not put him in prison. ⁵And Pharaoh's army had come forth from Egypt, and the Chaldeans who were besieging Jerusalem had received a report regarding them, and had abandoned the siege of Jerusalem.

His prediction of the certainty of Jerusalem's destruction

⁶Then the word of Jehovah came to the prophet Jeremiah, saying, ⁷Thus saith Jehovah the God of Israel, 'Thus shall ye say to the king of Judah, who sent you to me to inquire of me, " Behold, Pharaoh's army, which has come out to help you, shall return to Egypt into their own land. ⁸Then the Chaldeans shall come back and fight against this city and shall take it and burn it with fire." ' ⁹Thus saith Jehovah, ' Do not deceive yourselves with the idea that the Chaldeans will depart from you; for they shall not depart. ¹⁰For though ye had smitten the whole army of the Chaldeans that fight against you, and there remained but wounded men among them, yet would these[t] rise up each in his tent, and burn this city with fire.'

Jeremiah falsely accused of attempting to desert

¹¹But when the army of the Chaldeans had abandoned the siege of Jerusalem for fear of Pharaoh's army, ¹²Jeremiah went forth from Jerusalem to go into the land of Benjamin to receive his inheritance there among the people. ¹³And when he was in the Gate of Benjamin, a captain of the guard was there, by the name of Irijah the son of Shelemiah, the son of Hananiah. And he laid hold on Jeremiah the prophet, saying, You are going over to the Chaldeans. ¹⁴Then Jeremiah said, It is false; I am not going over to the Chaldeans. He, however, paid no heed to Jeremiah but[u] brought him to the princes. ¹⁵And the princes were angry with Jeremiah and smote him and put him[v] in the house of Jonathan the chancellor, for they had made that the prison.

His secret interview with the king

¹⁶And thus Jeremiah came into the house of the cistern and into the cells; and Jeremiah remained there many days. ¹⁷Then Zedekiah the king sent and summoned him; and the king questioned him secretly in his palace and said, Is there any word from Jehovah? And Jeremiah said, There is, and added, You shall be delivered into the hand of the king of Babylon. ¹⁸Moreover Jeremiah said to King Zedekiah, What crime have I commit-

---

§ 137 The chief source of these narratives is the biography already frequently quoted. Possibly the speeches in 37⁶⁻¹⁰ and 39¹⁵⁻¹⁸ are later additions. *Coniah* in 37¹ is the private name of Jehoiachim.

[t] 37¹⁰ So the Gk. The Heb. has lost the, *these.*

[u] 37¹⁴ The Heb. repeats, *took hold of,* by mistake from ¹³.

[v] 37¹⁵ So Gk. A later scribe has added, *in prison,* but this anticipates the latter part of the verse.

Baruch's Biography of Jeremiah

ted against you or your servants or this people, that you have put me in prison? [19]Where now are your prophets, who prophesied to you, saying, 'The king of Babylon shall not come against you nor against this land?' [20]And now hear, O my lord the king; let my petition, I pray, be presented before you, that you may not let me be taken back to the house of Jonathan the chancellor, lest I die there.

[21]Then Zedekiah the king commanded and they committed Jeremiah to the court of the guard, and they gave him daily a loaf of bread from the bakers' street, until all the bread in the city was gone. Thus Jeremiah remained in the court of the guard. In the court of the guard

38 [1]But when Shephatiah the son of Mattan, and Gedaliah the son of Pashhur, and Jucal the son of Shelemiah, and Pashhur the son of Malchijah, heard the words that Jeremiah spoke to all the people, saying, [2]Thus saith Jehovah, 'He that abideth in this city shall die by the sword, by the famine, and by the pestilence; but he who goes over to the Chaldeans shall live and his life shall be to him as booty,[w] and he shall live'; [3]also, Thus saith Jehovah, 'This city shall surely be given into the hand of the army of the king of Babylon and he shall take it,' [4]the princes said to the king, Let this man be put to death, since he weakens the hands of the soldiers who remain in this city and the hands of all the people, in speaking such words to them; for this man seeks not the welfare of this people but the hurt. The charge of the nobles

[5]Then Zedekiah the king said, See, he is in your hands, for the king was not able to do anything against them.[x] [6]Thereupon they took Jeremiah and cast him into the cistern of Malchijah the king's son, that was in the court of the guard, and let Jeremiah down with cords. And in the cistern there was no water, but mire, and Jeremiah sank in the mire. Jeremiah cast into a cistern to die

[7]Now when Ebed-melech the Cushite, a eunuch, who was in the royal palace heard that they had put Jeremiah in the cistern, while the king was sitting in the gate of Benjamin, [8]Ebed-melech went out of the royal palace and spoke to the king, saying, [9]My lord the king, these men have done wrong in all that they have done to Jeremiah the prophet, whom they have cast into the cistern; and he must soon die in the place where he is, because of the famine, for there is no more bread in the city. [10]Then the king commanded Ebed-melech the Cushite, saying, Take from here three[y] men with you and draw up Jeremiah the prophet from the cistern before he dies. [11]So Ebed-melech took the men with him and went into the royal palace below the treasury and took from there rags and worn-out garments, and let them down by cords to Jeremiah in the cistern. [12]And Ebed-melech the Cushite said to Jeremiah, Put now these rags and worn-out garments below your armpits under the cords. And Jeremiah did so. [13]Then they His rescue by Ebed-melech

---

w 38[2] Cf. 21[9], which contains the same prediction.
x 38[5] So Gk. and Luc. The Heb. has, *you*, but the words are very unnatural on the lips of the king.
y 38[10] Heb., *thirty*, but there is no reason why so many should be detailed at a time when the city was greatly in need of defenders. The *thirty*, instead of *three*, is apparently due to a natural copyist's error.

Baruch's Biography of Jeremiah

drew up Jeremiah with the cords and took him out of the cistern. And Jeremiah remained in the court of the guard.

^{The king's inquiries and assurance of protection} ¹⁴Then Zedekiah the king sent and took Jeremiah the prophet to him into the third[z] entry which leads into the temple of Jehovah. And the king said to Jeremiah, I should like to ask you something, conceal nothing from me. ¹⁵Then Jeremiah said to Zedekiah, If I declare it to you, will you promise not to put me to death? And if I give you counsel, you will not hearken to me. ¹⁶Then Zedekiah the king swore secretly to Jeremiah, saying, As Jehovah liveth, who has given us this life, I will not put you to death, neither will I give you into the hand of these men who are seeking your life.

^{Jeremiah's reiterated declaration that surrender alone would save the king and city} ¹⁷Then Jeremiah said to Zedekiah, Thus saith Jehovah, the God of hosts, the God of Israel, 'If thou wilt give thyself up to the princes of the king of Babylon, then thy life shall be preserved and this city shall not be burned with fire, and thou shalt live, together with thy household. ¹⁸But if thou wilt not give thyself up to the princes of the king of Babylon, then this city shall be given into the hand of the Chaldeans, who will burn it with fire, and thou shalt not escape from their hand. ¹⁹Then Zedekiah the king said to Jeremiah, I am afraid of the Jews who have gone over to the Chaldeans, lest they deliver me into their hand and they mock me. ²⁰But Jeremiah said, They shall not deliver you. Obey, I beseech you, the voice of Jehovah, in that which I speak to you; so it shall be well with you. ²¹But if you refuse to give yourself up, this is the revelation that Jehovah has showed me: ²²Behold, all the women who are left in the king of Judah's palace shall be brought forth to the princes of the king of Babylon, singing,

> They have betrayed thee; they have overcome thee,
> Thy familiar friends!
> They have caused thy feet to sink in the mire.
> They turn back![xx]

²³They shall also bring out[yy] all your sons to the Chaldeans. You yourself shall not escape out of their hand, but shall be taken by the hand of the king of Babylon; and this city shall be burned[a] with fire.

^{Secrecy regarding the interview} ²⁴Then said Zedekiah to Jeremiah, Let no man know of these words, or you may die. ²⁵But if the princes hear that I have talked with you, and come to you, and say to you, 'Declare to us now what you have said to the king—hide it not from us, otherwise we will put you to death—also what the king said to you,' ²⁶then say to them, 'I presented my petition before the king, that he would not make me return to Jonathan's house, to die there.' ²⁷Then all the princes came to Jeremiah and inquired of him; and he told them these words just as the king had commanded. So they ceased

---

[z] 38¹⁴ Or slightly revising the text, *of the thirty.* Cf. § 34.
[xx] 38²² This is the song of lamentation which the women are graphically represented as singing over Zedekiah, who was led on by his princes and advisers to rebel against Babylon and then abandoned by them to his tragic fate. The metre is the familiar three beats followed by two, which gives the effect of a final sob.
[yy] 38²³ Heb. adds, *your wives,* but these have already been included in the statement in ²².
[a] 38²³ So Gk., Syr., and Targ. Heb., *you shall cause to be burned.*

Baruch's Biography of Jeremiah

questioning him, for the matter was not reported. ²⁸ᵃBut Jeremiah remained in the court of the guard until the day that Jerusalem was captured.

39 ¹⁵Now the word of Jehovah came to Jeremiah, while he was shut up in the court of the guard, saying, ¹⁶Go, and speak to Ebed-melech the Cushite, saying, 'Thus saith Jehovah of hosts, the God of Israel, "Behold, I will bring my words upon this city for evil and not for good; and they shall be fulfilled before your eyes in that day. ¹⁷But I will deliver thee in that day," saith Jehovah, "and thou shalt not be given into the hand of the men of whom thou art afraid. ¹⁸For I will surely save thee and thou shalt not fall by the sword, but thy life shall be as booty to thee, because thou hast put thy trust in me," saith Jehovah.'

[margin: The reward promised for the services of Ebed-melech]

§ 138. **The Final Capture of Jerusalem and the Deportation of its Inhabitants** (586 B.C.), II Kgs. 25³⁻²¹, Jer. 38²⁸ᵇ–39¹⁰, 52⁶⁻³⁰, II Chr. 36¹⁷⁻²¹

Baruch's Biography of Jeremiah	*Late Prophetic Summary*	*Chronicler's Ecclesiastical History*
Jer. 38 ²⁸ᵇNow when Jerusalem was taken, **39** ¹(in the ninth year of Zedekiah king of Judah, in the tenth month, Nebuchadrezzar king of Babylon and all his army came against Jerusalem and besieged it. ²In the eleventh year of Zedekiah on the ninth day of the fourth month, a breach was made in the city) ³all the princes of the king of Babylon came and sat in the middle gate, Nebushazban the chief of the eunuchs, and Nergal-sharezer the chief of the magicians,ᵈ with all the rest of the	**II Kgs. 25** ³On the ninth day of the fourthᵇ month, when the famine was severe in the city, so that there was no bread for the people of the land, ⁴a breach was made in the city, and the king and all the warriorsᶜ fled by night through the gate between the two walls, which was by the king's garden, while the Chaldeans were besieging	**II Chr. 36** ¹⁷Then [Jehovah] brought against them the king of the Chaldeans, who slew their young men with the sword in their holy temple, and had no compassion on young man or virgin, old man or hoary-headed—he gave them all into his hand. ¹⁸And all

[margin: 'light, capture, and final fate of Zedekiah]

§ 138 The late prophetic editor's account of the final events in the history of Jerusalem is found in II Kgs. 25³⁻²¹. This has been quoted with one or two minor expansions in Jer. 52¹⁻³⁰. Vss. ¹⁶, ¹⁷ of II Kgs. 25 depart from the narrative style, which characterizes the rest of the description, and manifest an interest in the details of the temple ornamentation, which indicates that they were added by a priestly scribe, who had in mind the descriptions of the temple found in I Kgs. 7, and especially ¹⁵⁻²⁰, ⁴⁰⁻⁴⁴. Another scribe has on the basis of the same earlier passages still further expanded the parallel in Jer. 52²⁰⁻²³. The parallel passage in Baruch's biography of Jeremiah has been supplemented by a chronological note in 39¹, ², which interrupts the connection between 38²⁸ᵇ and 39³, and by an abridgment in 39⁴⁻¹⁰ of the parallel narratives of II Kgs. 25³⁻¹² and Jer. 52. To the quotation in Jer. 52 from II Kgs. 25 the editor of the book of Jeremiah has added in ²⁸⁻³⁰ a summary of those carried away in connection with the final captivity. The numbers are given in such detail and the account is so independent of the narrative in Kgs. that it is probable that it represents an authentic, although distinct tradition.

The Chronicler simply makes a general statement which reveals his peculiar interest in the temple and in the moral lessons which this tragic chapter of Israel's history forcibly illustrates.

ᵇ II Kgs. 25³ Restoring, *the fourth,* from the parallel in Jer. 39².

ᶜ II Kgs. 25⁴ Restoring the defective Heb. text by the aid of the parallel in Jer. 39⁴.

ᵈ Jer. 39³ The Heb. text evidently suffered greatly in transmission. Nergal-sharezer is found at the beginning of the list and again at the end. Vs. ¹³ evidently retains the original reading which has been followed above. *Nebosarsechim* is restored to *Nebushazban. Samgar* may be a scribal error for *Rab-mag* (chief of the magicians). The Gk. has, on the whole, a better text than the Heb.

Baruch's Biography of Jeremiah	*Late Prophetic Summary*	*Chronicler's Ecclesiastical History*

princes of the king of Babylon.
⁴And when Zedekiah the king of Judah and all the warriors saw them, they fled and went forth out of the city by night by the way of the king's garden, through the gate between the two walls, and went out toward the Arabah. ⁵But the army of the Chaldeans pursued after them and overtook Zedekiah in the plains of Jericho. Then they took and brought him up to Nebuchadrezzar king of Babylon to Riblah in the land of Hamath; and he passed judgment upon him. ⁶And the king of Babylon slew the sons of Zedekiah in Riblah before his eyes; also the king of Babylon slew all the nobles of Judah. ⁷Moreover he put out Zedekiah's eyes and bound him in chains, to carry him to Babylon.

the city round about, and went in the direction of the Arabah. ⁵But the army of the Chaldeans pursued after the king and overtook him in the plains of Jericho, after all his army had scattered from him. ⁶Then they took the king and carried him up to the king of Babylon to Riblah; and he passed judgment upon him. ⁷And they slew the sons of Zedekiah before his eyes, and put out Zedekiah's eyes and carried him, bound in chains, to Babylon. ᵉ

the vessels of the house of God, great and small, and the treasures of the temple of Jehovah, and the treasures of the king and his princes, all these he brought to Babylon.

Destruction of Jerusalem and deportation of many of its inhabitants

⁸And the Chaldeans burned the royal palace and the houses of the people with fire and tore down the walls of Jerusalem. ⁹Then Nebuzaradan the commander of the body-guard carried away captive to Babylon the rest of the people who remained in the city, the deserters also who had gone over to him, and the rest of the architects.ᶠ ¹⁰But Nebuzaradan the commander of the body-guard left some

⁸But on the seventh day of the month, which was in the nineteenth year of King Nebuchadnezzar king of Babylon, Nebuzaradan the commander of the body-guard, a servant of the king of Babylon, came to Jerusalem. ⁹And he burnt the temple of Jehovah and the royal palace and all the houses of Jerusalem, even every great house he burnt with fire. ¹⁰And all the troops of the Chaldeans, who were with the commander of the body-guard, broke down the walls round about Jerusalem. ¹¹And the rest of the people who were left in the city and the deserters who had gone over to the king of Babylon and the rest of the architects,ᵍ Nebuzaradan the commander of the

¹⁹And they burnt the house of God and tore down the wall of Jerusalem, and burnt the palaces with fire and destroyed all its precious vessels. ²⁰And those who escaped from the sword he carried away captive to Babylon, and they became slaves to him and to his sons until the rule of the kingdom of Persia, ²¹to fulfil the word of Jehovah by the mouth of Jeremiah. Until the land had enjoyed its sabbaths, as long as it lay

---

ᵉ II Kgs. 25⁷ The parallel, Jer. 52¹⁰, reads, *And the king of Babylon slew the sons of Zedekiah before his eyes; he also slew all the princes of Judah.* Cf. Jer. 39⁶.
ᶠ Jer. 39⁹ So the parallel II Kgs. 25¹¹ (Gk., cf. note ᵍ). Heb., *people who remained.*
ᵍ II Kgs. 25¹¹ So the Gk. and the parallel, Jer. 52¹⁵. Heb., *crowd,* or *rabble.*

Baruch's Biography of Jeremiah	*Late Prophetic Summary*	*Chronicler's Ecclesiastical History*
of the poor of the people, who had nothing, in the land of Judah and gave them at that time vineyards and fields.	body-guard carried away captive. ¹²But the commander of the body-guard left some of the poorest of the land as vinedressers and farmers.	desolate, it rested until the seventy years were complete.ʰ

¹³But the pillars of brass that were in the temple of Jevhoah, and the stands and the brazen sea that were in the temple of Jehovah the Chaldeans broke in pieces, and carried the brass from them to Babylon. ¹⁴Also the pots, the shovels, the snuffers, the bowls, and all the vessels of brass, with which the temple service was conducted, they took away. ¹⁵And the fire-pans and the basins, that which was of gold, the commander of the body-guard took away in gold and that which was of silver, in silver. ¹⁶The two pillars, the one sea, and the stands which Solomon had made for the temple of Jehovah— the brass of all these vessels could not be weighed. ¹⁷The height of the one pillar was eighteen cubits, and a capital of brass was above it; and the height of the capital was fiveⁱ cubits, with network and pomegranates round about the capital, all of brass; and like these had the second pillar, with network. *Plunder of the temple*

¹⁸And the commander of the body-guard took Seraiah the chief priest and Zephaniah the second priest, and the three keepers of the threshold. ¹⁹And from the city he took an officerʲ who was set over the troops; and five men who stood close to the king,ᵏ who were found in the city; and the scribe of the commander-in-chief, who mustered the people of the land, and sixty men of the people of the land, who were found in the city. ²⁰And Nebuzaradan the commander of the body-guard took them and brought them to the king of Babylon at Riblah. ²¹And the king of Babylon smote them and put them to death at Riblah in the land of Hamath. So Judah was carried away captive from its native land. *Public execution of certain of the captives*

Editorial Summary

Jer. 52 ²⁸This is the people whom Nebuchadrezzar carried away captive: in the seventeenthˡ year, three thousand and twenty-three Jews; ²⁹in the eighteenth year, of Nebuchadrezzar he carried away captive from Jerusalem eight hundred and thirty-two persons; ³⁰in the twenty-third year of Nebuchadrezzar, Nebuzaradan the commander of the body-guard carried away captive of the Jews seven hundred and forty-five persons.ᵐ The total number of persons was four thousand, six hundred. *Numbers carried away in the three deportations*

ʰ II Chr. 36²¹ The allusion is to Jer. 25¹¹, ¹², 29¹⁰, Lev. 26³⁴, ³⁵. The exact words are not found in Jer. The remaining verses of Chr. are taken from Ezra 1¹⁻³ᵃ.

ⁱ II Kgs. 25¹⁷ Heb., *three*, but the parallel, Jer. 52²², has, *five*. So also I Kgs. 7¹⁶.

ʲ II Kgs. 25¹⁹ Heb., *eunuch*.

ᵏ II Kgs. 25¹⁹ Heb., *who saw the king's face*. Jer. 52²⁵ reads, *seven*, instead of, *five*.

ˡ Jer. 52²⁸ Heb., *seven*. If this is correct this verse would refer to the first captivity recorded in II Kgs. 24¹⁴; but the numbers are so much smaller that it seems probable that ²⁸ refers to a later deportation. The difficulty probably arose because a scribe, having in mind the first captivity, read, *seven*, for an original *seventeen*. The reference would then be to an early deportation in 587 B.C. of the Jews outside Jerusalem.

ᵐ Jer. 52³⁰ Probably this third deportation was after the murder of Gedaliah, § 140.

§ 139. Jeremiah's Liberation, Jer. 39¹¹-40⁶

Midrash Regarding Jeremiah

Special provisions made for Jeremiah

Jer. 39 ¹¹Now Nebuchadrezzar king of Babylon had given the following command concerning Jeremiah to Nebuzaradan the commander of the body-guard, ¹²Take him, and look well to him, and do him no harm; but do to him as he shall direct you. ¹³So Nebuzaradan the commander of the body-guard, and Nebushazban the chief of the eunuchs, and Nergal-sharezer the chief of the magicians, and all the chief officers of the king of Babylon ¹⁴sent and took Jeremiah out of the court of the guard and gave him into the charge of Gedaliah the son of Ahikam, the son of Shaphan, that he should carry him home; so he dwelt among the people.

Set free and allowed to return to Gedaliah

40 ¹The word which came to Jeremiah from Jehovah after Nebuzaradan the commander of the guard had let him go from Ramah, when he had taken him bound in chains among all the captives who were carried away to Babylon. ²And the commander of the guard took Jeremiah and said to him, Jehovah your God pronounced evil upon this place; ³and Jehovah hath brought it and done just as he said, for you have sinned against Jehovah and have not obeyed his voice, therefore this thing is come upon you. ⁴And now behold, I loose you this day from the chains which are upon your hand. If it seem good to you to come with me to Babylon, come, and I will look out for you. But if it seem undesirable to you to come with me to Babylon, do not come;ⁿ ⁵but go back to Gedaliah the son of Ahikam, the son of Shaphan, whom the king of Babylon has made governor over the cities of Judah, and dwell with him among the people, or go wherever it seems right to you to go. So the commander of the body-guard gave him provisions and a present, and sent him away. ⁶So Jeremiah went to Gedaliah the son of Ahikam to Mizpah, and dwelt with him among the people who were left in the land.

§ 140. Brief Rule and Death of Gedaliah, II Kgs. 25²²⁻²⁶, Jer. 40⁷-41¹⁸

Baruch's Biography of Jeremiah

Appointment of Gedaliah

II Kgs. 25 ²²Now over the people who were left in the land of Judah, whom Nebuchadnezzar king of Babylon had left, he made Gedaliah the son of Ahikam, the son of Shaphan, governor.

Gathering of the local chiefs

Jer. 40 ⁷Then all the commanders of the forces that were in the fields, together with their men, heard that the king of Babylon had made Gedaliah the son of Ahikam governor in the land and had committed to him men,

§ 139 39¹⁴ᵃ is the natural sequel of ³, and, as Duhm has acutely noted (*Jeremia*, 313), this was probably originally in Baruch's biography of Jeremiah immediately followed by 40⁶. The rest of the section has the marked characteristics of a later Jewish midrash. It presents quite a different picture from that in 39¹⁴ᵃ, 40⁶. Jeremiah's deliverance is due to a special decree of Nebuchadrezzar, and instead of being placed at once in the care of Gedaliah, he is rescued at Ramah from the midst of the chained captives bound for Babylon. The pious words of the Babylonian general also recall similar speeches in the midrashes of Chr. The midrash was probably originally independent and was later joined to Baruch's brief record.

ⁿ Jer. 40⁴, ⁵ᵃ So the Gk. The Heb. has a gloss at the end of ⁴ which is a practical duplicate of ⁵ᵇ and four words at the beginning of ⁵ which make no sense.

§ 140 This long section in Jer. from the hand of Baruch is one of the best historical passages in the O.T. The parallel passage in II Kgs. 25²³⁻²⁶ is an abridgment of the same. This the editor of Kgs. has prefaced with a statement regarding the appointment of Gedaliah.

Baruch's Biography of Jeremiah

women, and children, and of the poorest of the land, such as were not carried away captive to Babylon. [8]And they came to Gedaliah at Mizpah, Ishmael the son of Nethaniah, and Johanan,[o] the son of Kareah and Seraiah the son of Tanhumeth, and the sons of Ephai the Netophathite, and Jezaniah the son of the Maacathite, together with their men. [9]And Gedaliah the son of Ahikam, the son of Shaphan, swore to them and to their men, saying, Do not be afraid to serve the Chaldeans, settle down and be subject to the king of Babylon, and it shall be well with you. [10]As for me, I will dwell at Mizpah, as your representative to receive[p] the Chaldeans who shall come to us, but you gather for yourselves wine and fruits and oil, and put them in your vessels and dwell in your cities of which you have taken possession. [11]Likewise when all the Jews, who were in Moab and among the Ammonites and in Edom and in all the countries, heard that the king of Babylon had left a remnant of Judah, and that he had set over them Gedaliah the son of Ahikam, the son of Shaphan, [12]all the Jews returned out of all the places whither they had been driven, and came to the land of Judah to Gedaliah at Mizpah, and gathered wine and fruits in great abundance.

His disregard of the conspiracy to take his life

[13]But Johanan the son of Kareah and all the commanders of the forces that were in the fields came to Gedaliah at Mizpah, [14]and said to him, Do you know that Baalis the king of the Ammonites has sent Ishmael the son of Nethaniah to take your life? But Gedaliah the son of Ahikam did not believe them. [15]Then Johanan the son of Kareah spoke to Gedaliah in Mizpah secretly, saying, Let me go and slay Ishmael the son of Nethaniah without any one's knowing it. Why should he take your life with the result that all the Jews who are scattered and the remnant of Judah should perish? [16]But Gedaliah the son of Ahikam said to Johanan the son of Kareah, You shall not do this thing, for you speak falsely regarding Ishmael.

Ishmael's treacherous murder of Gedaliah and his men

41 [1]But afterwards in the seventh month, Ishmael the son of Nethaniah, the son of Elishama, of the royal line,[q] with ten men, came to Gedaliah the son of Ahikam at Mizpah; and there they were eating together in Mizpah. [2]Then Ishmael the son of Nethaniah and the ten men who were with him rose up and smote Gedaliah the son of Ahikam the son of Shaphan with the sword and thus slew him, whom the king of Babylon had made governor over the land. [3]Ishmael also slew all the Jews who were with [Gedaliah] at Mizpah, and the Chaldeans who were found there.[r]

Massacre of the pilgrims

[4]But on the day after he had slain Gedaliah, when no one yet knew it, [5]there came men from Shechem, from Shiloh, and from Samaria, eighty men with shorn beards and with their clothes torn, and with self-inflicted cuts bearing cereal-offerings and frankincense in their hand, to bring them to the temple of Jehovah. [6]And Ishmael the son of Nethaniah went forth from Mizpah to meet them, weeping as he went, and when he met them,

---

[o] Jer. 40[8] So Gk. and the parallel II Kgs. 25[23]. A scribe in the Heb. has rewritten, *Johanan*, in the form, *Jonathan*.

[p] 40[10] So Gk.

[q] 41[1] So Gk. and the parallel in II Kgs. 25[25]. A scribe appears to have added in the Heb., *and the prince of the king*.

[r] 41[3] *I.e.*, the soldiers left as a guard.

Baruch's Biography of Jeremiah

he said to them, Come to Gedaliah the son of Ahikam. ⁷However, when they came into the midst of the city, Ishmael the son of Nethaniah slew them, and cast them into the midst of the cistern with the aid of the men who were with him. ⁸But ten men were found among them who said to Ishmael, Slay us not; for we have stores hidden in the field, of wheat, barley, oil, and honey. So he stopped and did not slay them together with their kinsmen. ⁹Now the cistern into which Ishmael cast all the dead bodies of the men whom he had slainˢ is the great cistern, which Asa the king had made on account of the attack of Baasha king of Israel.ᵗ Ishmael the son of Nethaniah filled it with the slain.

Departure with captives

¹⁰Then Ishmael carried away captive the rest of the people who were in Mizpah, even the king's daughters and all the people in Mizpah, whom Nebuzaradan the commander of the body-guard had placed under the charge of Gedaliah the son of Ahikam. Ishmael the son of Nethaniahᵘ arose and set out to go over to the Ammonites.

Their recapture by Johanan

¹¹But when Johanan the son of Kareah and all the commanders of the forces who were with him heard of all the evil that Ishmael the son of Nethaniah had done, ¹²they took all the men and went to fight with Ishmael the son of Nethaniah, and found him by the great pools that are in Gibeon.ᵛ ¹³And when all the people who were with Ishmael saw Johanan the son of Kareah and all the commanders of the forces who were with him, they were glad. ¹⁴So all the people whom Ishmael had carried away captive from Mizpah turned about and came back and went to Johanan the son of Kareah.ʷ ¹⁵But Ishmael the son of Nethaniah escaped from Johanan with eight men, and went to the Ammonites. ¹⁶Then Johanan the son of Kareah and all the commanders of the forces, who were with him, took the remnant of the people whom he had recovered from Ishmael,ˣ the men (soldiers), the women, the children, and the eunuchs, whom he had brought back from Gibeon.

Preparations for the flight to Egypt

¹⁷And they went further and dwelt in Gedrothª Chimham, which is near Bethlehem, in order to set out on the way to Egypt ¹⁸on account of the Chaldeans, for they were afraid of them, because Ishmael the son of Nethaniah had slain Gedaliah the son of Ahikam, whom the king of Babylon had made governor over the land.

ˢ 41⁹ So Gk. The Heb., *by the side of Gedaliah*, is clearly due to a mistaken reading of a scribe.

ᵗ 41⁹ Cf. I Kgs. 15²².

ᵘ 41¹⁰ So Luc. and certain codices. The Heb., *carried them away captive*, is tautological.

ᵛ 41¹² Cf. II Sam. 2¹⁵.

ʷ 41¹⁴ The Gk. has a much briefer text. The Heb. may well have been expanded.

ˣ 41¹⁶ So Gk. The Heb. adds the awkward phrase, *the son of Nethaniah from Mizpah, after he had slain Gedaliah the son of Ahikam.* It is in all probability a later scribal addition as well as the explanatory word, *soldiers*, which also is not found in the Gk.

ª 41¹⁷ Following the Gk., Heb., *Geruth*.

§ 141. The Jewish Refugees in Egypt, Jer. 42–44

Baruch's Biography of Jeremiah

Jer. 42 ¹Then all the commanders of the forces and Johanan the son of Kareah and Azariah[b] the son of Hoshaiah, and all the people small and great came near, ²and said to Jeremiah the prophet, Permit us to bring our petition before you that you may supplicate Jehovah your God for us, even for all this remnant, for we are left but a few out of many—you yourself see us here—³that Jehovah your God may show us the way wherein we should walk, and the thing that we should do. ⁴Then Jeremiah the prophet said to them, I have heard you; behold I will pray to Jehovah your God according to your words, and whatever Jehovah shall answer you, I will declare it to you; I will keep nothing back from you. ⁵Then they said to Jeremiah, Jehovah be a true and faithful witness against us, if we do not according to all the word with which Jehovah your God shall send you to us. ⁶Whether it be good or whether it be evil, we will obey the voice of Jehovah our God, to whom we send you, that it may be well with us, when we obey the voice of Jehovah our God.

The request of the people

⁷And after ten days the word of Jehovah came to Jeremiah. ⁸And he called together Johanan the son of Kareah and all the commanders of the forces that were with him and all the people small and great, ⁹and said to them, Thus saith Jehovah, the God of Israel, to whom you sent me to present your supplication before him: ¹⁰'If ye will still abide in this land, then will I build you and not pull you down, and I will plant you and not pluck you up; for I am sorry for the evil that I have done to you. ¹¹Be not afraid of the king of Babylon,[c] for I am with you to save you and to deliver you from his hand. ¹²And I will grant you mercy, that he may have mercy upon you and let you return to your own land.' ¹³But if ye say, 'We will not dwell in this land; so that ye obey not the voice of Jehovah your God,' ¹⁴thinking, 'No; but we will go to the land of Egypt, where we shall see no war nor hear the sound of the trumpet nor be hungry, and there will we remain;' ¹⁵then hear the word of Jehovah, O remnant of Judah: Thus saith Jehovah of hosts, the God of Israel, 'If ye have indeed determined to enter into Egypt and go to sojourn there, ¹⁶then shall the sword, which ye fear, overtake you there in the land of Egypt; and the famine, of which ye are afraid, press hard upon you there in Egypt, so that ye shall die there. ¹⁷Thus all the men who have determined to go into Egypt to sojourn there, shall die by the sword, by the famine, and by the pestilence, and none of them shall remain or escape from the evil that I will bring upon them.'

The divine command to remain in the land

¹⁸For thus saith Jehovah of hosts, the God of Israel, 'As mine anger and my wrath have been poured out upon the inhabitants of Jerusalem, so shall my wrath be poured out upon you, when ye shall enter into Egypt; and ye

Certain judgment upon the disobedient people

---

§ 141 This section is the immediate sequel of the preceding and from the same source: 42⁷⁻²² may be due to a later hand, but 43¹⁻⁷ assumes its contents, and the reasons for regarding it and 43⁸⁻¹³ as midrashic expansions of the original are too subjective to be accepted as conclusive. The Gk. has here preserved a briefer and, in some cases, doubtless the original text.
b 42¹ So Gk., confirmed by 43². Heb., *Jezaniah.*
c 42¹¹ Eliminating the repetitive phrase, *of whom ye are afraid; be not afraid of him, saith Jehovah.*

Baruch's Biography of Jeremiah

shall be an object of execration, of astonishment, of cursing, and of reproach, and ye shall never see this place again.' ¹⁹Jehovah hath spoken concerning you, O remnant of Judah, ' Go ye not into Egypt.' Know certainly that I have testified to you this day. ²⁰For you have deceived yourselves, for you sent me to Jehovah your God, saying, ' Pray for us to Jehovah our God, and just as Jehovah our God shall say, so declare to us, and we will do it.' ²¹And I have this day declared it to you, but you have not obeyed the voice of Jehovah your God in anything for which he hath sent me to you. ²²Now therefore know certainly that you shall die by the sword, by famine, and by pestilence, in the place whither you desire to go to sojourn.

Depart-
ure of
all the
people
to
Egypt

43 ¹But when Jeremiah had ceased speaking to the^d people all the words of Jehovah their God, with which Jehovah their God had sent him to them, even all these words, ²Azariah the son of Hoshaiah, and Johanan the son of Kareah, and all the proud men spoke, saying to Jeremiah, You speak falsely; Jehovah our God hath not sent thee to say, ' Ye shall not go into Egypt to sojourn there.' ³But it is Baruch the son of Neriah who stirs you up against us, to deliver us into the hand of the Chaldeans, that they may put us to death, and carry us away captives to Babylon. ⁴So Johanan the son of Kareah and all the commanders of the forces and all the people did not obey the voice of Jehovah, to dwell in the land of Judah. ⁵But Johanan the son of Kareah and all the commanders of the forces took all the remnant of Judah, who had returned from all the nations whither they had been driven to sojourn in the land of Judah, ⁶the men, the women, the children, the king's daughters, and every person whom Nebuzaradan the commander of the body-guard had left with Gedaliah the son of Ahikam, the son of Shaphan, and Jeremiah the prophet and Baruch the son of Neriah, ⁷and they came into the land of Egypt; for they did not obey the voice of Jehovah; and they came to Tahpanhes.

Pre-
diction
of
Egypt's
con-
quest
by
Nebu-
chad-
rezzar

⁸Then the word of Jehovah came to Jeremiah in Tahpanhes, saying, ⁹Take great stones in thy hand, and bury them in the loose foundation^e in the brick-covered place before Pharaoh's palace door in Tahpanhes in the sight of the men of Judah; ¹⁰and say to them, ' Thus saith Jehovah of hosts, the God of Israel, " Behold, I will send and bring Nebuchadrezzar the king of Babylon, my servant, and will set his throne upon these stones that you^f have buried, and he shall spread his royal pavilion over them. ¹¹And he shall come and shall smite the land of Egypt; such as are for death shall be given to death and such as are for captivity shall be given to captivity, and such as are for the sword shall be given to the sword. ¹²And he^g will kindle a fire in the houses of the gods of Egypt, and will burn them and carry them away.^h And he shall wrap himself in the land of Egypt, as a shepherd puts

---

^d 43¹ Omitting the *all* of the Heb. in accord with the Gk.
^e 43⁹ The Heb. word occurs only here. It is apparently connected with the root, *to slip away*. This suggests not the current rendering, *mortar*, which would make Jeremiah's task an almost impossible one, but the loose bed of sand on which was laid the brick pavement, which covered the raised platform which stood before the ancient Egyptian houses and palaces.
^f 43¹⁰ So Gk. Heb., *I*.
^g 43¹² So Gk. and the context. Heb., *I*.
^h 43¹² Or following an emendation suggested by Duhm, *and they will stand desolate*.

Baruch's Biography of Jeremiah

on his mantle, and shall go forth from there in peace. ^{13}He shall also break the obelisks of Heliopolis (that is in the land of Egypt)^i and the temples of the gods of Egypt shall he burn with fire." '

44 ^{1}The word that came to Jeremiah concerning all the Jews who dwelt in the land of Egypt, who dwelt at Migdol, Tahpanhes, Memphis, and in upper Egypt,^{j} saying, ^{2}Thus saith Jehovah of hosts, the God of Israel, ' Ye have seen all the evil that I have brought upon Jerusalem and upon all the cities of Judah; and there they are this day a desolation, and no man dwelleth in them, ^{3}because of their wickedness which they have committed to provoke me to anger in that they went to offer sacrifices^k to other gods, that they knew not, neither they nor ye, nor your fathers. ^{4}However, I constantly sent to them^l all my servants the prophets, saying, " O, do not this abominable thing that I hate." ^{5}But they neither hearkened nor inclined their ear to turn from their wickedness, to offer no sacrifice to other gods. ^{6}And so my wrath and mine anger were poured forth and was kindled against the cities of Judah and the streets of Jerusalem, and they were wasted and desolate, as is now the case.' ^{7}Therefore now thus saith Jehovah, the God of hosts, the God of Israel, ' Why do ye commit a great crime against yourselves to cut off from you man and woman, infant and sucking child, out of the midst of Judah so that ye leave none remaining, ^{8}in that ye provoke me to anger with the work of your hands, offering sacrifice to other gods in the land of Egypt, whither ye have gone to sojourn, that ye may be cut off, and that ye may be an object of cursing and a reproach among all the nations of the earth? ^{9}Have ye forgotten the crimes of your fathers, and the crimes of the kings of Judah, and the crimes of their princes,^{m} which they committed in the land of Judah and in the streets of Jerusalem? ^{10}They are not humbled even to this day, neither have they feared nor walked in my law nor in my statutes that I set before you and before your fathers.'

^{11}Therefore thus saith Jehovah of hosts, the God of Israel: Behold, I set my face against you for evil to cut off ^{12}the remnant of Judah in the land of Egypt, and they shall fall by the sword and by famine; they shall die, small and great, and they shall be an object of execration, of astonishment, of cursing, and of reproach.^{n} ^{13}For I will punish those who dwell in the land of Egypt, as I have punished Jerusalem, by the sword, by famine, and by pestilence, ^{14}so that none of the remnant of Judah, who have gone into the land of Egypt to sojourn there, shall escape or be left to return to the land of Judah, to which they have a desire to return;^{o} for none shall return except fugitives.

Marginal notes: Failure of the Jews to learn the lessons from the past. Fate awaiting the refugees in Egypt.

---

i 43^{13} This explanatory note is not found in the Gk. and is doubtless due to a later scribe.
j 44^1 Heb.,*the country of Pathros.*
k 44^3 So Gk. The Heb. adds the awkward gloss, *to serve.*
l 44^3 So Syr. Heb., *you.*
m 44^9 So Gk. Heb., *wives.* The Heb. also adds, *and your wickedness and the wickedness of your wives.* It is probably due to a scribe who recalled 7$^{17-22}$. It ill accords with the context.
n 44$^{11,\ 12}$ Following the briefer Gk. text, the Heb. is very repetitious.
o 44^{14} Omitting with the Gk. the clause, *to dwell.*

Baruch's Biography of Jeremiah

Their determination to persist in their heathen practices

[15]Then all the men who knew that their wives offered sacrifices to other gods and all the women who stood by, a great assembly (even all the people who dwelt in the land of Egypt and in upper Egypt)[p] answered Jeremiah, saying, [16]In regard to the demand that you have made upon us in the name of Jehovah, we will not hearken to you. [17]But we will rather fulfil every word that is gone forth from our mouth, to offer sacrifices to the queen of heaven and to pour out libations to her, as we have done, along with our fathers, our kings and our princes, in the cities of Judah, and in the streets of Jerusalem; for then we had plenty of food and were well and experienced no misfortune. [18]But since we left off offering sacrifices to the queen of heaven, and pouring out libations to her, we have wanted all things and have been consumed by the sword and by the famine. [19]And when we offered sacrifices to the queen of heaven, and poured out libations to her, did we make cakes[q] and pour out libations to her without the approval of our husbands?[r]

Calamities of the past in punishment of their idolatry

[20]Then Jeremiah said to all the people, to the men and to the women, even to all the people who had given him that answer, saying, [21]Did not Jehovah remember the savor of the sacrifices that you burned in the streets of Jerusalem, you and your fathers, your kings and your princes, and the people of the land, and did it not come to his mind? [22]And so Jehovah could no longer endure, because of the evil of your doings and because of the abominations which you have committed; therefore has your land become a desolation and an object of astonishment, and of cursing, without inhabitant, as it is to-day. [23]Because you have offered sacrifices and because you have sinned against Jehovah and have not obeyed the voice of Jehovah nor walked in his law, nor in his statutes, nor in his testimonies; therefore this calamity has overtaken you, as is now the case.

The judgment upon the defiant people

[24]Moreover Jeremiah said to all the people, and to all the women, Hear the word of Jehovah, all Jews[s] who are in the land of Egypt; [25]' Thus saith Jehovah of hosts, the God of Israel, " You[t] and your wives have spoken with your mouths, and with your hands have carried out this resolution: We will surely perform our vows that we have vowed, to offer sacrifices to the queen of heaven, and to pour out libations to her. Confirm then and perform your vows!"' [26]Therefore hear the word of Jehovah, all Jews who dwell in the land of Egypt, ' I have sworn by my great name,' saith Jehovah, ' that my name shall no more be named in the mouth of any Jew in all the land of Egypt, in the oath, " As the Lord Jehovah liveth." [27]Behold, I will watch over them for evil and not for good, and all the men of Judah who are in the land of Egypt shall be consumed by the sword and by the famine, until there is an end of them. [28]And they that escape the sword shall return from the land of Egypt to the land of Judah, few in number, and all the

---

p 44[15] Apparently a later explanatory note.

q 44[19] So Gk. and Syr. In the Heb. a scribe has added an archæological note which probably means, *to mould them, i.e.*, in some symbolic form.

r 44[19] The verse indicates that the women were the real speakers in [16-18]. Possibly the men were only introduced later in [15].

s 44[24] Heb., *all Judah*. So also in [26].

t 44[25] The Gk. omits, *you*, thus making the wives the speakers in [15].

Baruch's Biography of Jeremiah

remnant of Judah, who have gone into the land of Egypt to sojourn there shall know whose word shall be confirmed, mine or theirs.'

²⁹' And this shall be the sign to you,' saith Jehovah, ' that I will punish you in this place, that ye may know that my words shall surely be confirmed against you for evil.' ³⁰Thus saith Jehovah, ' Behold, I will give Pharaoh-hophra king 'of Egypt into the hand of his enemies and into the hand of those who seek his life, as I gave Zedekiah king of Judah into the hand of Nebuchadrezzar king of Babylon, who was his enemy and sought his life.'

[margin: Hoph-ra's fate to be a sign]

§ 142. Jehoiachin's Liberation, II Kgs. 25²⁷⁻³⁰, Jer. 52³¹⁻³⁴

Late Prophetic Summary

II Kgs. 25 ²⁷Now it came to pass in the thirty-seventh year of the captivity of Jehoiachin king of Judah, in the twenty-seventh day of the twelfth month, Evil-merodach king of Babylon, in the year in which he became king, lifted up Jehoiachin king of Judah from prison to a position of honor. ²⁸And he spoke kindly to him and placed his seat above the seats of the kings who were with him in Babylon, ²⁹and changed his prison garments. And Jehoiachin ate with him continually as long as he lived. ³⁰And for his support^u a continual allowance was given him by the king, each day a portion, as long as he lived.

[margin: Honors conferred upon Jehoiachin in Babylon]

---

§ 142 The one political event during the Babylonian exile deemed worthy of record by the late prophetic editor was the liberation of Jehoiachin in connection with the favors granted his subjects by Amil-marduk on the occasion of his accession in 561 B.C. It is a fitting close to the books of the Kings, for not only does it mark the close of the history of the Hebrew kings, but it also suggests the greater liberation and restoration which awaited the captive people. Jer. 52³¹⁻³⁴ is a verbatim quotation from Kgs.

u 25³⁰ Heb., *allowance*.

THE RE-ESTABLISHMENT OF THE JEWISH COMMUNITY IN PALESTINE

Ezra-Nehemiah

THE RE-ESTABLISHMENT OF THE JEWISH COMMUNITY IN PALESTINE

I

THE REBUILDING OF THE TEMPLE, II Chr. 36$^{22, 23}$, Ezra 1, 3^2– 6^{22}, Hag. 1, I Esdr. (2), 4$^{48-56, 62, 63}$, 5$^{1-6}$ (^{47}–7^{15})

§ 143. **Cyrus's Decree Regarding the Temple at Jerusalem, II Chr. 36$^{22, 23}$, Ezra 1$^{1-4}$, 6$^{3-5}$ (I Esdr. 1$^{1-7}$, 6$^{24-26}$)**

Aramaic Document

Ezra 6 ^{3}In the first year of Cyrus the king, Cyrus the king made a decree: Concerning the house of God in Jerusalem— this house shall be rebuilt, where they offer sacrifices and bring him offerings made by fire.^{a} Its height shall be sixty cubits and its breadth sixty cubits,^{b} ^{4}*It shall be constructed* with three layers of huge stones

Chronicler's Ecclesiastical History

1 ^{1}Now in the first year of Cyrus king of Persia, that the word of Jehovah by the mouth of Jeremiah might be accomplished, Jehovah stirred up the spirit of Cyrus king of Persia, to make a proclamation throughout all his kingdom, and also in writing, as follows, ^{2}Thus saith Cyrus king of Persia: All the kingdoms of the earth hath Jehovah the God of Israel,^{c} the God of heaven, given me; and he hath charged me to build him a temple in Jerusalem, which

---

The Rebuilding of the Temple.—The first six chapters of Ezra cover a period of only twenty-two years from 538–516 B.C. and, with the exception of 2 and 4$^{6-23}$, all relate to the rebuilding of the temple and the restoration of its worship. The centre and nucleus of the whole is the Aramaic account of the experiences of the builders, found in 5^3–6^{13}. This the Chronicler has expanded in 1 and 3. The many vexed problems of these chapters are illuminated by the valuable contemporary testimony found in the books of Hag. and Zech. From these and from the other evidence in Ezra-Neh. it seems clear that there was no general return of Jews from Babylon before 520 B.C., and that the rebuilding of the temple was first seriously begun at that time by the Jews who had remained in Judah and the few who had returned from the lands where they had found temporary refuge. None the less noble and significant was the restoration of the sanctuary and service because accomplished amid great discouragements by the struggling little Judean community. On the other hand, in the light of the subsequent glory and veneration which centred about the temple, it was not strange that this act should be idealized in accord with ideas peculiar to the later age.

§ 143 If the Aramaic temple records in 3^2–6^{15} contained a continuous history of the Judean community, from 6$^{3-5}$ may be inferred what was its version of the decree of Cyrus. It is important because it represents the oldest form of the tradition. This is again given by the Chronicler, with his characteristic modifications in 1$^{1-4}$.

^{a} 6^3 Following the rendering of Haupt (*Ezra-Neh.* SBOT, p. 36). This is supported by I Esdr. 6^{23} and the corresponding expressions of the Chronicler in Ezra 3$^{2-5}$. The Aram. of 6^3 is currently translated, *the place where they offer sacrifices, and let its foundation be strongly laid.* But this is only a conjectural reading. The variations in the Gk. versions indicate that the corruption of the text was early.

^{b} 6^3 The proportions are unusual. The breadth of Solomon's temple was twenty cubits and the height thirty. Nothing is here said of the length. Possibly this is due to textual corruption.

^{c} 1^2 So in 3^2 and the parallel I Esdr. 2^3. The Aram. omits, *the God of Israel.*

339

Aramaic Document	Chronicler's Ecclesiastical History
and one[d] layer of timber. And let the expenses be paid out of the king's treasury.[e] 5Also let the gold and silver vessels of the house of God, which Nebuchadnezzar[g] took from the temple at Jerusalem and brought to Babylon, be restored and brought again to the temple which is at Jerusalem, each to its place, and you shall put them in the house of God.	is in Judah. 3Whoever there is among you of all his people who desires to go,[f] let his God be with him, and let him go up to Jerusalem, which is in Judah, and build the temple of Jehovah, the God of Israel (he is God),[h] which is at Jerusalem. 4And whoever is left, in any place where he now resides as an alien, let the men of his place assist him[i] with silver, with gold, with goods, and with beasts, besides the freewill offering for the house of God which is at Jerusalem.

§ 144. The Return of Certain Jews with the Vessels of the Temple,
Ezra 1⁵⁻¹¹, 5¹⁴, ¹⁵, I Esdr. 4⁴⁷ᵃ, ⁴⁸, ⁵¹⁻⁵⁶, ⁶², ⁶³, 5¹⁻⁶

Chronicler's Ecclesiastical History

The volunteers

Ezra 1 5Then the heads of the fathers' houses of Judah and Benjamin, and the priests and the Levites, even all whose spirit God had stirred to go up to build the temple of Jehovah which is at Jerusalem arose. 6And all those who were about them supplied them[j] with silver vessels, with gold, with goods, and with beasts, and with precious things, besides all that was voluntarily offered.

---

d 6⁴ So Gk. Aram., *new*. The two Aramaic words are easily confused.
e 6⁴ Aram., *house*.
f 1³ So I Esdr. 2⁵, Gk., and Luc.
g 6⁵ The more nearly correct spelling of this word is found in Jer. and Ezek. Cf. § 130, note j. The form *Nebuchadnezzar* is used in Kgs., Ezra-Neh., Dan., and Esther.
h 1³ Apparently a gloss, added by a pious scribe, which has been awkwardly inserted. In Luc. it is found at the end of the verse.
i 1⁴ *I.e.*, to return to Jerusalem.
§ 144 It is significant that, not only do Haggai, Zechariah, and Nehemiah bear testimony that there was no general return of the Jews from Babylon during the earlier part of the Persian period, but even the comparatively late Aramaic temple records are completely silent regarding it. They know only of the return of a certain Sheshbazzar with the vessels of the temple, 5¹⁴, ¹⁵. Their version of the decree of Cyrus speaks only of the rebuilding of the temple, not of the return of the exiles. That a few did come back is shown by the presence of Zerubbabel of the royal house and of Joshua the priest, as well as by the direct reference in Zech. 6¹⁰ to three men who had come from Babylon, bringing the gifts of the Jewish exiles who remained behind.
As has been already recognized, I Esdr. contains the Gk. translation of what is manifestly at many points a superior text of Ezra. Cf. Introd., p. 44. In 3-5 an older account of the return of the Jews under Cyrus has been combined with the later story of the *Three Young Men*. Professor Torrey in the *Jour. of Bib. Lit.*, XXI, pp. 169, 170, has called attention to the fact that the Chronicler's account of the return in Ezra 1 stops abruptly and is obviously incomplete. Also in Ezra 3⁸ it is stated that cedar wood for the temple was brought from Lebanon *according to the command of Cyrus* the king, but our Hebrew book of Ezra contains no such command. This missing conclusion, with the specific command referred to in the Heb. version of Ezra, is found in the composite narrative of I Esdr. 4⁴⁷⁻⁵⁶. It also records the return of Jeshua and Zerubbabel, which is assumed by the Chronicler in Ezra 3² and 5¹, ². The characteristic language of the Chronicler is readily recognized and renders easy its separation from the very different story of the *Three Young Men*. The name *Cyrus*, for which *Darius* has been substituted, as a result of the combination with the later story, must, of course, be restored. This missing fragment was doubtless taken from our present received Heb. text of Ezra when the story of the *Three Young Men*, with which it was closely welded, was removed. The fact that in his Gk. column Origen included I Esdr. (cf. the Syro-Hexaplar) indicates that the present accepted Heb. text was not established until a comparatively late date.
j 1 Heb *strengthened their hands.*

340

Aramaic Temple Records | *Chronicler's Ecclesiastical History*

Ezra 5 [14]Now the gold and silver vessels of the house of God which Nebuchadrezzar took from the temple at Jerusalem and brought to the temple in Babylon, those Cyrus the king took out of the temple in Babylon, and they were delivered to one by the name of Sheshbazzar, whom he had made governor. [15]And he said to him, Take these vessels; go, put them in the temple at Jerusalem, and let the house of God be rebuilt in its place.

[7]Also Cyrus the king brought forth the vessels of the temple of Jehovah, which Nebuchadnezzar had brought from Jerusalem, and had put in the temple of his gods. [8]Those Cyrus king of Persia brought forth under the charge of Mithredath the treasurer, and counted them out to Sheshbazzar, the prince of Judah. [9]And this is the number of them: thirty[k] golden platters, a thousand[l] silver platters, twenty-nine censers, [10]thirty golden bowls, two thousand,[m] four hundred and ten silver bowls, and a thousand other vessels. [11]All the vessels of gold and of silver were five thousand, four hundred and sixty-nine.[n] All these Sheshbazzar brought up, with those of the captivity[o] from Babylon to Jerusalem.

Delivery of the vessels of the temple to them

I Esdr. 4 [47a]And Cyrus the king wrote letters [48]to all the governors of the province beyond the River,[p] and also to those in Lebanon he sent written commands to bring cedar wood from Lebanon to Jerusalem to rebuild the city. [51]And for the rebuilding of the temple he ordered that twenty talents should be given yearly until it should be built; [52]and that ten other talents should be given yearly for the altar,[q] that whole burnt-offerings might be offered day by day, according to the command; [53]further, that all those going up from Babylon to build the city, should have their freedom, both they and their children. And to all the priests who went up, [54]he commanded to give portions, and the priestly garments in which they minister. [55]Furthermore to the Levites he commanded to give portions until the day when the temple should be finished and Jerusalem rebuilt. [56]He also commanded to give to all those guarding the city allotments and wages.

Cyrus's provisions for the re-building and service of the temple

[62]Then they all praised the God of their fathers, because he had given them [63]permission and freedom[r] to go up and rebuild Jerusalem and the temple that is called by his name. And they exulted seven days with music and rejoicing.

Joy of the exiles

5 [1]After this the chief men of the fathers' houses, according to their tribes, were chosen to go up, together with their wives and their son and their daughters and their men-servants and their maid-servants and their cattle.

Their departure for Jerusalem

---

[k] 1[9] So I Esdr. 2[12] (Swete's text). Heb., *thirty.* But compare the total in [11].
[l] 1[9] So I Esdr. 2[12]. Heb., *four hundred and ten.*
[m] 1[10] So I Esdr. 2[12]. The Heb. is unintelligible.
[n] 1[11] The total of the numbers given in the Heb. of [9, 10] is but 2,499, while the Heb. here reads 5,400. I Esdr. 2[12, 13], however, is consistent and doubtless original.
[o] 1[11] Again following I Esdr. 2[13], which has a superior text.
[p] 4[48] This is the translation of the Assyro-Babylonian name of the provinces west of the middle Euphrates. The Gk. equivalent here, as in Ezra 5[3, 6], 6[6, 13], is, *Cœlesyria and Phœnicia.*
[q] 4[52] The Gk. adds what appears to be an obscure gloss, *to bring fifteen.*
[r] 4[62] Torrey suggests, *a remnant and residue.*

Chronicler's Ecclesiastical History

²And Cyrus sent a thousand horsemen to go with them until they had brought them back to Jerusalem in peace.   Then with musical instruments, drums and flutes, ³and loud rejoicing, all their kinsmen sent them on their way,ˢ as they went up.

List of the returning exiles

⁴These are the names of the men who went up, according to their tribes, by their genealogy.   ⁵Of the priests the sons of Phinehas, the son of Aaron: Jeshua the son of Jozadak, the son of Seriah.   And there rose upᵗ with him Zerubbabel the son of Shealtiel of the house of David, of the family of Peres, of the tribe of Judah; ⁶in the second year of Cyrus king of Persia in the first day of the month Nisan.

§ 145. **Re-establishment of Worship at Jerusalem and the Laying of the Foundation of the Temple, Ezra 3²–4⁶, ²⁴ (I Esdr. 5⁴⁸⁻⁷³)**

Chronicler's Ecclesiastical History

Renewal of the altar service and observation of the feasts

Ezra 3 ²Then Jeshua the son of Jozadak, and his kinsmen the priests, and Zerubbabelᵘ the son of Shealtiel and his kinsmen arose and builtᵛ the altar of the God of Israel, to offer burnt-offerings on it, as prescribed in the law of Moses the man of God.   ³And they set up the altar in its place; for fear, because of the peoples dwelling in the land, had come upon them, but they plucked up courageʷ and offered burnt-offerings to Jehovah, even burnt-offerings morning and evening.   ⁴And they kept the feast of booths as it is prescribed, and offered the fixed number of daily burnt-offerings according to the direction for each day;ˣ ⁵and afterward the continual burnt-

---

ˢ 5³ The Gk. text is not grammatical, and is evidently corrupt.   Gk.A ³ᵇ reads, *he (Darius) made them go up with them.*   The above restoration by Torrey at least reproduces the original sense.

ᵗ 5⁵ Following Torrey's restoration of the original Heb., which is mistakenly read, *Joachim*, in the Gk.

§ 145 Ezra 3¹ is but the Chronicler's variant of Neh. 7⁷³ᵇ, 8¹, and was transferred by him from Neh. 7 with the section in Ezra 2.   For the original place of meeting, *the broad space before the Water Gate* (Neh. 8¹), confirmed by the parallel in I Esdr. 5⁴⁷, he substituted, *to Jerusalem*, remembering that the walls had not been rebuilt in 538 B.C.   Also the reference in ¹ to the seventh month and the implication that the Jews were already living in the cities outside Jerusalem have no meaning except in their original context in Neh.   From ³ it is clear that the Chronicler intended to represent the altar as having been erected in 538 B.C., immediately after the return.   From Jer. 41⁵ it would appear that a form of worship was observed at the temple site even after the final destruction of Jerusalem by the Babylonians in 586 B.C.   Hag. 2¹⁴ also implies that sacrifices were offered on the sacred spot.   This section, as a whole, is characterized throughout by the peculiar ideas and expressions of the Chronicler.   Into 4 he has introduced the Aramaic account of the interruption of the building of the city walls, cf. § 149.   Vs. ²⁴ is in Heb., has the Chronicler's usual term, *king of Persia*, and was clearly added by him to connect his quotation in ⁷⁻²³ with the interruption of the rebuilding of the temple.   The Aramaic document evidently had a variant version of the laying of the foundation of the temple, for it states in 5¹⁶, after the account of Cyrus's decree to build the temple, *thereupon this Sheshbazzar came and laid the foundations of the house of God at Jerusalem, and since that time even until now it has been in building and has not yet been completed.*   From the contemporary testimony of Haggai it appears that practically nothing had been done before 520 B.C.   Cf. Hag. 2¹⁵.

ᵘ 3² The mention of Jeshua and Zerubbabel as the leaders in the restoration of the worship of the temple instead of Sheshbazzar, as in the Aramaic records (5¹⁶), suggests that the Chronicler is here simply projecting backward and idealizing the account of the building of the temple recorded in Hag. 1.

ᵛ 3² I Esdr. 5⁴⁸, *made ready.*

ʷ 3³ The Heb. text is evidently corrupt, but the parallel in I Esdr. 5⁵⁰ is not altogether clear and the variations in the Gk. versions of the latter testify that it also is corrupt.   Many conjectural translations have been offered.   The above practically follows the Heb. of Ezra 3³, adding from the Luc. of I Esdr. 5⁵⁰ the evidently original phrase, *plucked up courage.*

ˣ 3⁴ Evidently the Chronicler had in mind the law in Num. 29¹²⁻³⁴.

Chronicler's Ecclesiastical History

offering, and the offerings of the new moons, and of all the sacred feasts of Jehovah,[a] and for every one who offered a freewill offering to Jehovah.[b] [6]From the first day of the seventh month they began to offer burnt-offerings to Jehovah; but the foundation of the temple of Jehovah was not yet laid.

[7]They also gave money to the masons and to the carpenters, and food, and drink, and oil to the Sidonians and the Tyrians to bring cedar-trees from Lebanon on the sea to Joppa,[c] according to the grant that they had from Cyrus king of Persia.

Prepa-rations for the temple

[8]And in the second year of their coming to the house of God at Jerusalem, in the second day of the month, Zerubbabel the son of Shealtiel, and Jeshua the son of Jozadak, and the rest of their kinsmen the priests and the Levites, and all who had come from the captivity to Jerusalem, began and laid the foundation of the house of God on the first day of the second month of the second year[d] after they had come to Judah and Jerusalem. And they appointed the Levites, who were twenty years old and over, to have the oversight of the work of the temple of Jehovah. [9]Then Jeshua arose with his sons and his kinsmen, and Kadmiel his brother and the sons of Judah and the sons of Henadad, with their sons and their kinsmen the Levites, to have together the oversight of the workmen in the house of God.[e] [10]And when the builders had laid the foundation of the temple of Jehovah, the priests stood[f] in their official robes with trumpets, and the Levites, the sons of Asaph, with cymbals to praise Jehovah, according to the directions of David king of Israel. [11]And they sang responsively songs of praise and thanksgiving to Jehovah, saying, For he is good, for his loving-kindness is ever over Israel. And all the people raised a great shout of rejoicing, because the foundation of the temple of Jehovah had been laid. [12]But many of the priests and Levites and heads of fathers' houses and the old men, who had seen the first temple, when the foundation of this temple[g] was laid before their eyes, wept loudly, while many shouted aloud for joy, [13]so that the people could not distinguish the sound of the shout of joy from the sound of the weeping of the people; for the people shouted with a loud shout, and the noise was heard afar off.

Laying of its founda-tion

4 [1]Now when the adversaries of Judah and Benjamin heard that the children of the captivity were building a temple to Jehovah, the God of Israel, [2]they drew near to Zerubbabel and to Jeshua[h] and to the heads of fathers' houses, and said to them, Let us build with you; for we worship your God, as you do, and we have been sacrificing to him since the days of

Inter-ruption of the temple build-ing

---

[a] 3[5] Following the shorter text of I Esdr. 5[52]. The Heb. is exceedingly repetitious.

[b] 3[5] Cf. Lev. 6[1-6], Ex. 29[38-42], Num. 28. I Esdr. 5[52] adds before the offerings of the new moons, that of the sabbath as prescribed in Num. 28[10].

[c] 3[7] The Chronicler here evidently follows the account of the building of Solomon's temple. Cf. I Kgs. 5[7-11], II Chr. 2[8-16].

[d] 3[8] Adding a statement regarding the exact date of the laying of the foundation from I Esdr. 5[56]. Without the statement that the foundation was laid the Heb. is incomplete. Vs. [10] refers to this act.

[e] 3[9] Correcting the Heb., which is obviously corrupt, by the aid of the parallel in I Esdr. 5[58]. Any reconstruction is doubtful.

[f] 3[10] So Gk., I Esdr. 5[59], Lat., and many Heb. manuscripts.

[g] 3[12] I Esdr. 5[63] omits, *temple*.

[h] 4[2] So I Esdr. 5[68] and demanded by [3]. In the Heb. *to Jeshua* has dropped out.

Chronicler's Ecclesiastical History

Esarhaddon[i] king of Assyria, who brought us here. [3]But Zerubbabel and Jeshua and the rest of the fathers' houses said to them, You have nothing to do with us in building a temple to Jehovah our God; but we ourselves will build to Jehovah the God of Israel, as Cyrus the king of Persia has commanded us. [4]Then the peoples of the land continually weakened the energies of the people of Judah, and frightened them out of building, [5]and kept hiring counsellors against them to frustrate their plan, all the days of Cyrus king of Persia, even until the reign of Darius king of Persia.[j] [24]So the work on the house of God at Jerusalem ceased; and it ceased until the second year of the reign of Darius king of Persia.[k]

§ 146. **Beginning of the Rebuilding of the Temple in the Days of Darius,**
Hag. 1, Ezra 5[1, 2] (I Esdr. 6[1, 2])

Prophecy of Haggai

Chronicler's Ecclesiastical History

Jehovah's disapproval of the delay in rebuilding the temple

Hag. 1 [1]In the second year of Darius the king, in the first day of the sixth month, the word of Jehovah came by Haggai the prophet, saying, Speak[l] to Zerubbabel the son of Shealtiel, governor of Judah, and to Joshua the son of Jehozadak the high priest, saying, [2]'Thus saith Jehovah of hosts, "This people say: The time has not yet come[o] to rebuild the temple of Jehovah."' [3]Then the word of Jehovah came by Haggai the prophet, saying, [4]Is it a time for you yourselves to dwell in your own ceiled[p] houses, while this temple lies in ruins?

Ezra 5 [1]Now the prophets, Haggai,[m] and Zechariah, the son of Iddo,[n] prophesied to the Jews who were in Judah and Jerusalem, in the name of the God of Israel who was over them.

[5]Now therefore, thus saith Jehovah of hosts, ' Consider your past experiences.[q] [6]Ye sow

---

[i] 4[2] Neither the O.T. nor the Assyrian inscriptions record a transfer of foreigners into Samaria by Esarhaddon. Of the events in Israelitish history immediately after 690 B.C., the O.T., however, says little, so that it is by no means impossible. Otherwise the event referred to was the deportation in the days of Sargon, II Kgs. 17[24].

[j] 4[5] The Heb. also adds, [6], *And in the beginning of the reign of Xerxes, they wrote an accusation against the inhabitants of Judah and Jerusalem.* Its aim is clearly to trace the Samaritan hostility throughout the Persian period. Whether it was original with the Chronicler or added by a later scribe, as the fact that it is not found in I Esdr. suggests, cannot be definitely determined.

[k] 4[24] I Esdr. 5[73] connects Ezra 4[24] immediately with [5] as above.

§ 146 The brief and fragmentary account of the beginning of the temple building, given by the Chronicler in his introduction to the quotation from the Aramaic document in Ezra 5 and 6 is supplemented by the contemporary sermons of Hag. and Zech. From these it is evident that Haggai by his direct, practical exhortations influenced the Jews to begin the work, and then he and his colleague Zechariah by their repeated addresses kept alive the enthusiasm and devotion of the temple builders. The historical element is so prominent and important in Hag. 1, that this chapter is here given. The first address of Haggai was in September of 520 B.C. when the Persian empire was all aflame with rebellions against the new king Darius. Early in the following October the work was begun. A month later Haggai delivered the message of encouragement in 2[7-9]. In the same month of December Zechariah gave his first address, Zech. 1[1-6]. Just at the close of the year 520 B.C. the foundation of the temple was laid (Hag. 2[18]) and in connection with this ceremony Haggai delivered his last recorded sermon, 2[10-23]. Zechariah's next address was in February of 519 B.C., and the visions in 2-6 appear to come from the period preceding the completion of the temple, which is dated by the Chronicler in 516 B.C.

[l] Hag. 1[1] So Gk. The Heb. omits, *saying, Speak.* But cf. 2[1, 10, 20].

[m] Ezra 5[1] So I Esdr. 6. The Aramaic adds, *the prophet.*

[n] Ezra 5[1] In Zech. 1[1], *the son of Berechiah, the son of Iddo.* Cf. Neh. 12[16].

[o] Hag. 1[2] So Gk. The Heb. text is confused.

[p] Hag. 1[4] Or simply, *covered, roofed.*

[q] Hag. 1[5] Heb., *your ways.*

344

Prophecy of Haggai

much, but bring in little; ye eat, but ye do not have enough; ye drink, but ye are not filled; ye clothe yourselves, but not so as to be warm; and he that earneth wages, earneth wages in a bag with holes.'

Rebuild the temple and prosperity will follow

[7]Thus saith Jehovah of hosts, ' Consider your experiences.[r] [8]Go up to the mountains, and bring wood and rebuild the temple; then I will be pleased with it, and I will reveal my glory,'[s] saith Jehovah. [9]' Ye looked for much, and it came to little;[t] and when ye brought it home, I blew upon it. Why? ' saith Jehovah of hosts. ' Because of my temple that lieth in ruins, while ye are running each to his own house.[u] [10]Therefore[v] the heavens withhold the dew, and the earth withholdeth its fruit. [11]And I have called forth a drought upon the land and upon the mountains, and upon the grain and the new wine and the oil and upon that which the ground bringeth forth, and upon men and animals, and upon all the labor of the hands.'

Chronicler's Ecclesiastical History

Initiation of the work

[12]Then Zerubbabel the son of Shealtiel and Joshua the son of Jehozadak the high priest, with all the rest of the people, obeyed the command of Jehovah their God and the words of Haggai the prophet, as Jehovah their God had sent him to them.[w] The people also feared before Jehovah.[x] [14]And Jehovah stirred up the spirit of Zerubbabel the son of Shealtiel, governor of Judah, and the spirit of Joshua the son of Jehozadak the high priest, and the spirit of all the rest of the people, so that they came and worked on the temple of Jehovah of hosts, their God, [15]in the twenty-fourth day of the sixth month, in the second year of Darius the king.

[2]Then Zerubbabel the son of Shealtiel and Jeshua the son of Jozadak arose and began to build the house of God which is at Jerusalem; a n d with them were the prophets of God, supporting them.

§ 147. Unsuccessful Opposition to the Building of the Temple, Ezra 5³–6¹⁵
(I Esdr. 6³–7⁵)

Aramaic Document

Inquiries of the Persian officials

Ezra 5 [3]At that time Tattenai,[a] the governor of the province beyond the River, and Shethar-bozenai and their associates came to them, and spoke thus to them, Who gave you permission to build this temple and to finish

---

[r] Hag. 1[7] It is possible that this clause has crept into the text through a scribal error from [5]. It certainly interrupts the direct command.
[s] Hag. 1[8] *I.e.*, inaugurate the Messianic era for which they longed.
[t] Hag. 1[9] So Gk. Heb., *behold*.
[u] Hag. 1[9] *I.e.*, solely intent on building.
[v] Hag. 1[10] So Gk. The Heb. adds, *over you.*
[w] Hag. 1[12] So Gk., Syr., and Lat. The Heb. lacks, *to them.*
[x] Hag. 1[12] The literary style and idioms of the first half of [13] are foreign to Hag. and the second has apparently been taken from 2[4b]. Since the context is consistent without it, it has here been omitted. It reads, *Then Haggai, Jehovah's messenger, spoke Jehovah's message to the people, saying, ' I am with you,' saith Jehovah.*
§ 147 Peculiarities in point of view, literary style, and vocabulary, as well as the fact that it is written in Aramaic conclusively demonstrate that this section was quoted by the Chronicler from the earlier Aramaic document, cf. Introd., p. 30. These he has slightly expanded in 6[14], and possibly in 6[9, 10], although a comparison of their contents with [17] and II Chr. 29[21, 22] reveal

---

[a] 5[3] This name appears in various forms in the different versions. Luc., *Thananai*, I Esdr. 6[3], and Josephus, *Sisinnes*.

Aramaic Document

this wall?[b] [4]And[c] who are the builders who are carrying this through? [5]But the eye of their God was upon the elders of the Jews, so that they did not make them cease, until a report should come to Darius and a written decision concerning it be returned.

Their report to Darius
[6]The copy of the letter that Tattenai, the governor of the province beyond the River,[d] and Shethar-bozenai, and his associates the rulers[e] of the province beyond the River, sent to Darius the king:

[7]To Darius the king, greeting. [8]Be it known to the king that we have gone into the province of Judah, to the house of the great God, and this was built with huge stones and timber laid in the walls;[f] and this work is being carefully done and is prospering in their hands. [9]Then we asked those elders, saying,[g] 'Who gave you permission to build this temple and to finish this wall?' [10]We also asked them their names, in order to inform you, that we might record the names of the men who were at their head. [11]And they gave us the following answer, 'We are the servants of the God of heaven and earth and are building the temple that was built many years ago, which a great king of Israel built and finished. [12]But after our fathers had provoked the wrath of the God of heaven, he gave them into the hand of Nebuchadnezzar king of Babylon, the Chaldean, who destroyed this temple and carried the people away to Babylon. [13]But in the first year of Cyrus king of Babylon, Cyrus the king made a decree to build this house of God. [14]And the gold and silver vessels of the house of God, which Nebuchadnezzar took from the temple at Jerusalem and brought to the temple in Babylon, those Cyrus the king took out of the temple in Babylon, and they were delivered to one by the name of Sheshbazzar,[h] whom he had made governor. [15]And he said to him, "Take these vessels, go, put them in the temple at Jerusalem, and let the house of God be rebuilt in its place." [16]Then this Sheshbazzar came, and laid the foundations of the house of God at Jerusalem. And since that time even until now it has been building, and it is not yet completed.' [17]Now therefore if it please the king, let search be made in the king's archives[i] at Babylon,[j] whether it be so, that a decree was made by

---

variations from his usual representation.   While these chapters contain the most reliable and valuable historical data in the book of Ezra, it must be recognized that at least the decrees have, like the others found in Ezra, been recast in Jewish moulds.   Cf., *e.g.*, the distinctively late prophetic expression in 6¹², *God who hath caused his name to dwell there* (in Jerusalem).   On the other hand, the favorable attitude of the Persian kings toward the religions and sanctuaries of subject peoples is well established.   Cf. Appendices XI, XII.   There is excellent ground, therefore, for regarding these decrees as in spirit authentic, although the language and point of view of the Aramaic document in which they were found do not justify us in dating it before the middle or close of the Persian period.

[b] 5³ Or, *sanctuary;* I Esdr. 6⁴, ⁹, *these works.*   Syr. and Targ., *walls.*   Cf., for the same idiom, 4¹².

[c] 5⁴ So I Esdr. 6⁴.   The Heb. has at the beginning a gloss, *and we* (Gk., *they*) *told them as follows,* which was probably originally intended for ⁹, where the same expressions recur.

[d] 5⁶ I Esdr. 6⁷, *of Syria and Phœnicia,* which is a more exact definition of *the province beyond the River Euphrates.*   Cf. § 144, note ᴾ.

[e] 5⁶ Cf. 4⁹.   The exact meaning of the Aram., *Apharsachites,* is unknown.   It is probably a foreign word.   I Esdr. 6⁷ has, *governors* or *rulers.*

[f] 5⁸ Or, *its walls were covered with timber.*

[g] 5⁹ So I Esdr. 6¹¹.   Aram., *and said to them thus.*

[h] 5¹⁴ Slightly correcting the Aram. by the aid of Luc. and I Esdr. 6¹⁷.

[i] 5¹⁷ So I Esdr. 6²¹, and in the parallel to 6¹.   Aram. *treasure-house.*

[j] 5¹⁷ *At Babylon,* here and in 6¹, may be a scribal addition.   Cf. 6².

Aramaic Document

Cyrus to rebuild this house of God at Jerusalem; and let the king send his pleasure to us concerning this matter.

6 [1]Then Darius the king made a decree, and search was made in the archives where the official documents from Babylon had been deposited.[k] [2]And at Ecbatana,[l] the royal palace[m] in the province of Media, a roll[n] was found and in it was thus written: A record:[o] [3]In the first year of Cyrus the king, Cyrus the king made a decree: ' Concerning the house of God at Jerusalem, let the house be rebuilt, where they offer sacrifices and bring him offerings made by fire; its height shall be sixty cubits, and its breadth sixty cubits. [4]*It shall be constructed* with three layers of huge stones and one layer of timber; and let the expenses be paid out of the king's treasury. [5]Also let the gold and silver vessels of the house of God, which Nebuchadnezzar took from the temple at Jerusalem and brought to Babylon, be restored and brought to the temple which is at Jerusalem, each to its place; and you shall put them in the house of God.'

[6]Now therefore,[p] Tattenai, governor of the province beyond the River, Shethar-bozenai, and the rulers of the province beyond the River, go away from there; [7]let the work of this house of God alone; let the governor of the Jews and[q] the elders of the Jews rebuild this house of God in its place. [8]Moreover I make a decree in regard to what you shall do for these elders of the Jews[r] for the building of this house of God: that out of the king's wealth from the tribute of the province beyond the River the expenses be exactly paid to these men, and that without delay.[s] [9]And whatever is needed, both young bullocks and rams and lambs for burnt-offerings to the God of heaven, also wheat, salt, wine, and oil, according to the direction of the priests at Jerusalem, let it be given to them day by day without fail, [10]that they may regularly offer sacrifices of sweet savor to the God of heaven, and pray for the life of the king and of his sons. [11]Also I have made a decree, that whoever shall make this command invalid, a beam shall be pulled out from his house, and he shall be impaled upon it,[t] and his house shall for this be made a refuse-heap. [12]And the God who hath caused his name to dwell there shall overthrow all kings and peoples who shall put forth their

[marginal notes:] Result of the investigation by Darius · His command to aid in the rebuilding of the temple

---

k 6:1 Changing the order of the Aram., which reads, *house of the official documents where the treasures have been deposited at Babylon,* and following the parallel in I Esdr. Cf. 5:17 and note j.

l 6:2 Aram., *Achmetha.* The later equivalent of the old Persian, *Hangmatana,* the Ekbatana of the Greek writers.

m 6:2 *The royal palace,* lit., *castle,* is not found in the parallel in I Esdr. 6:23 and may be a later addition.

n 6:2 The Jewish point of view is here clearly revealed. The document would naturally be a cuneiform tablet.

o 6:2 This appears to have been the title which stood at the head of the memorandum which follows.

p 6:6 I Esdr. 6:27, *But he commanded Sisinnes* (Tattenai). This introduction to the command of Darius, which is introduced abruptly at this point, may be original, but more probably the abruptness is due to the author's desire to present in briefest form the vital facts.

q 6:7 *Governor of the Jews* is probably a later addition from 5:2, for elsewhere simply the elders are mentioned as the builders, 5:5, 8, 9.

r 6:8 I Esdr. 6:27 further adds, *the servant of Jehovah, Zerubbabel, the governor of the Jews.* So also in [14].

s 6:8 I Esdr. 6:28, 29 has what appears to be a later expanded paraphrase of this passage.

t 6:11 Aram., *as one impaled shall be fastened to it.* According to Herodotus (III, 159) this form of punishment was characteristically Persian.

Aramaic Document

hand to make invalid the command or to destroy the house of God at Jerusalem. Exactly will it be executed.

Completion of the temple
[13]Then Tattenai, the governor of the province beyond the River, and
Shethar-bozenai, and their associates did exactly as Darius the king had
given command. [14]And the elders of the Jews built and prospered, through
the prophesying of the prophets[u] Haggai and Zechariah the son of Iddo.[v] And they
finished the building according to the command of the God of Israel and
according to the decree of Cyrus and Darius and Artaxerxes king of Persia.[w]
[15]And this temple was finished on the third day of the month Adar,[x] which was in the
sixth year of the reign of Darius the king.[a]

§ 148. Dedication of the Temple and the Observation of the Passover, Ezra 6[16-22] (I Esdr. 7[6-15])

Chronicler's Ecclesiastical History

Dedication of the temple
Ezra 6 [16]Then the Israelites, the priests, the Levites, and the rest of the
returned exiles,[b] celebrated the dedication of this house of God with joy.
[17]And they offered at the dedication of this house of God a hundred bullocks, two hundred rams, four hundred lambs, and twelve he-goats for a
sin-offering for all Israel, according to the number of the tribes of Israel.
[18]And they set the priests in their divisions and the Levites in their courses,[c]
for the service of God at Jerusalem, as is prescribed in the book of Moses.

The great passover feast
[19]And the returned exiles kept the passover upon the fourteenth day of
the first month. [20]For the priests and the Levites had every one of them
purified themselves; all of them were ceremonially clean. And they killed
the passover for all the returned exiles, and for their brethren the priests,
and for themselves. [21]And the Israelites who had come back from the
captivity, and all those who separated themselves from the uncleanness of
the peoples of the land,[d] to seek Jehovah, the God of Israel, ate [22]and kept
the feast of unleavened bread seven days with joy; for Jehovah had made
them joyful and had turned the heart of the king of Assyria[e] to them, to
strengthen their hands in the work of the house of God, the God of Israel.

---

[u] 6[14] So 5[1] and I Esdr. 7[3].

[v] 6[14] Evidently added by the Chronicler or a later scribe. Cf. 5[1]. The entire verse may
be from the same hand.

[w] 6[14] This error is also probably due to the Chronicler who appears to have regarded Artaxerxes as the predecessor of Darius I, under whom the temple was completed. Cf. § 144.

[x] 6[14] March-April, 516 B.C.

[a] 6[15] This chronological note was probably added by the Chronicler, but he may well have
had authentic data at his command. It is not improbable that he derived it from the Aramaic
document itself. Four years was an ample allowance of time for the rebuilding of the temple.

§ 148 Although the Aram. continues to be used through [18], it is clear that this section is from
the Chronicler. The elders suddenly vanish from the story, and the priests and Levites and a
great assembly made up, as alone seemed to the Chronicler fitting, of the children of the captivity, [16, 19, 21], take their place. In addition to the animal offerings in [9], twelve he-goats are
offered as a sin-offering in accordance with the very late law in Lev. 4[13-21]. The Chronicler's
peculiar ideas and expressions also abound. Cf. [18] and I Chr. 23[1]–27[2], II Chr. 35[4, 5]. As in II
Chr. 35[1-19], he introduces in conclusion a solemn passover feast, observed in accordance with the
ritualistic ideals of his own day.

[b] 6[16, 19] Aram., *children of the captivity.*

[c] 6[18] I Esdr. 7[9] adds, *likewise the porter at each door.* This may possibly be original.

[d] 6[21] Here the Chronicler projects back the work and standards of a later age. These included not proselytes but Jews who had remained in Judah. Cf. § 162.

[e] 6[22] This historical slip is doubtless due to the fact that to students of the earlier prophecies
Assyria figured still as the ancient foe and master of Israel—of course, the Chronicler meant to
say, *king of Persia.*

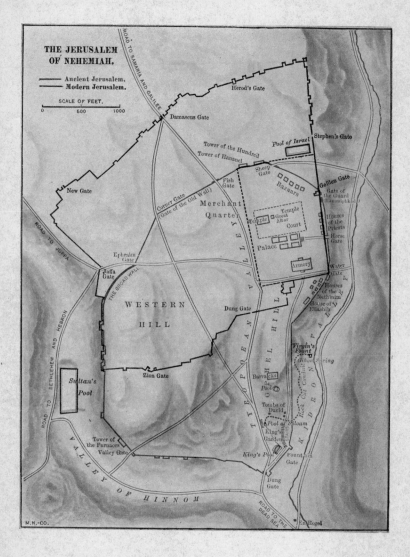

THE JERUSALEM
OF NEHEMIAH.

— — — Ancient Jerusalem.
———— Modern Jerusalem.

SCALE OF FEET.

0   500   1000

ROAD TO SAMARIA AND GALILEE

Herod's Gate

Damascus Gate

Pool of Israel

Stephen's Gate

Tower of the Hundred
Tower of Hananel

Sheep Gate

Golden Gate

New Gate

Fish Gate

Bazaars

Gate of
the Guard
Hammiphkad

Corner Gate
(Gate of the Old Wall)

Merchant Quarter

Temple
Great Altar

Temple
Court

Houses
of the
Priests

ROAD TO JOPPA

Ephraim Gate

Palace

Horse Gate

Jaffa Gate

THE BROAD WALL

Armory

Water Gate

Houses
of the
Nethinim
House of
Eliashib

WESTERN HILL

Dung Gate

TYROPOEAN VALLEY

OPHEL HILL

Virgin's Fount

Gihon Spring

ROAD TO BETHLEHEM AND HEBRON

Zion Gate

Barracks
Pool

Tombs of David

Siloam

ROCK CUT CANAL

KIDRON VALLEY

Sultan's Pool

Pool of Siloam

King's Garden

Tower of
the Furnaces

Valley Gate

King's Pool

Fountain Gate

Dung Gate

VALLEY OF HINNOM

ROAD TO THE DEAD SEA

En Rogel

M.N.-CO.

II

THE WORK OF NEHEMIAH IN RESTORING THE WALLS OF JERUSALEM AND IN REFORMING THE JUDEAN COMMUNITY, Ezra 4$^{7-23}$, Neh. 1^1–7^{5b}, 11$^{1,\ 2}$, 12^{27}–13^{31}
(I Esdr. 2$^{16-30}$, 6$^{1,\ 2}$)

§ 149. Nehemiah's Interest in the Afflicted Judean Community, Neh. 1^{1-11b}

Nehemiah's Memoirs

Neh. 1 [1]Now it transpired in the month of Chislev,[a] in the twentieth year[b] [of Artaxerxes], as I was in Shushan the royal palace,[c] [2]that Hanani,[d] one of my kinsmen came, together with certain men from Judah, and I asked them concerning the Jews who had escaped, who were left from the captivity, and concerning Jerusalem. [3]And they said to me, The survivors who are left from the captivity there in the provinces are in great misfortune and reproach, and the wall of Jerusalem is broken down and its gates have been destroyed by fire.

[4]Now when I heard these statements I sat down and wept and mourned certain days; and I fasted and made supplication before the God of heaven, [5]and I said, I beseech thee, O Jehovah, the God of heaven, the great and terrible God, who keepeth the covenant and showeth kindness to them who love and keep his commands;[e] [6]let thine ears[f] now be attentive and thine eyes open, to hear the supplication of thy servant, which I am now making before thee, day and night, for the Israelites thy servants, while I confess the sins of the Israelites, which we have sinned against thee, as I also and my father's house have sinned. [7]We have dealt very wickedly

(marginal notes:) The bad news from Jerusalem

Nehemiah's prayer for his race and petition for help

The Work of Nehemiah.—For the first time in Israel's history, it is possible to study an important epoch in the light of a contemporary record written by the most prominent man in the life of his age. Cf. Introd., pp. 30, 31. With the first chapter of Neh. the peculiar expression and conceptions of the later Jewish traditions found in Ezra disappear and a straightforward narrative, abounding in exact details, takes their place. That Nehemiah was the pioneer who prepared the way for a general return of the Jews from Babylon and for the institution of the new priestly law in Judah, which is by tradition associated with Ezra, is demonstrated by a great variety of evidence. With Jeremiah, Ezekiel, and the author of Isa. 40–55 he ranks as one of the chief makers of Judaism. Patriotic, energetic, and practical, he was supremely fitted to lift the Judean community out of the slough of corruption and despondency into which it had fallen and to prepare the way for that close union between the religious leaders in Babylon and the Jews of Palestine, which was necessary before there could be any general return, and to blaze the way for those fundamental reforms which transformed the life and religion of the race.

§ 149 The superscription was either added by the Chronicler (cf. 10^2), or else originally stood at the head of Nehemiah's memoirs which are here quoted verbatim, as the vocabulary and literary style, very different from those of the Chronicler, clearly testify. Cf. Introd., p. 30. The chapter well illustrates that rare union of piety and patriotism which was the dominant influence in Nehemiah's life.

a 1^1 November-December.

b 1^1 Probably thoughtlessly added by a scribe from 2^1, for Nisan precedes instead of follows Chislev.

c 1^1 Lit., *castle.* Cf. Dan. 8^2, Esth. 1^1. Susa was the winter residence of the Persian kings.

d 1^2 Cf. 7^2. Probably Hanani was an own brother whose house was in Jerusalem. If so this would explain in part Nehemiah's interest in the Judean community and why the deputation appealed directly to him.

e 1^5 Cf. Dt. 7$^{21,\ 9,\ 12}$.

f 1^6 Luc. reads consistently with the context, *ears.* But cf. ^{11}.

Nehemiah's Memoirs

against thee, and have not kept the commandments, nor the statutes, nor the ordinances, which thou didst command thy servant Moses. [8]Remember, I beseech thee, the word which thou didst command thy servant Moses, saying, "If ye trespass I will scatter you abroad among the peoples;[g] [9]but if ye return to me, and keep my commands and do them, then, though your outcasts were at the ends of the earth,[h] yet will I gather them thence and will bring them to the place that I have chosen, there to cause my name to dwell." [10]Now these are thy servants and thy people, whom thou hast redeemed by thy great power and by thy strong hand. [11a,b]O Lord, I beseech thee, let thine ear be attentive to the supplication of thy servant, and to the supplications of thy servants, who delight to fear thy name; and give success to thy servant this day, and grant him mercy in the sight of this man.[i]

§ 150. Nehemiah's Leave of Absence and Arrival at Jerusalem, Neh. 1¹¹ᶜ-2²⁰

Nehemiah's Memoirs

Nehemiah's request and the king's response

Neh. 1 [11c]Now I was cupbearer to the king. **2** [1]And it came to pass in the month of Nisan, in the twentieth year of Artaxerxes the king, when I had charge of the wine,[j] that I took up the wine and gave it to the king. Now I had not beforetime been sad.[k] [2]And the king said to me, 'Why is your countenance sad, since you are not sick? This is nothing else but sorrow of heart.' Then I was greatly afraid, [3]and I said to the king, 'Let the king live forever: why should not my countenance be sad, when the city, the place of my fathers' sepulchres, lies in ruins, and its gates have been destroyed by fire?' [4]And then the king said to me, 'For what do you make request?' So I prayed to the God of heaven. [5]And I said to the king, 'If it please the king, and if your servant has found favor in your sight, that you would send me to Judah, to the city of my fathers' sepulchres, that I may rebuild it.' [6]And the king said to me (and the queen[l] was also sitting by him), 'For how long will your journey be? And when will you return?' Then it pleased the king to send me; for I set him a time. [7]Moreover I said to the king, If it please the king, let official letters be given me

---

[g] 1⁸ Cf. Dt. 30¹⁻⁵. It is suggestive that this prayer throughout shows great familiarity with Dt. and no acquaintance with the late priestly code and narratives.

[h] 1⁹ So Eng. idiom. Heb., *in the uttermost part of the heavens.* Cf. the corresponding Bab.-Assyr. expression, *the four quarters of the heavens.*

[i] 1¹¹ *I.e.*, Artaxerxes.

§ 150 In determining the exact chronology of this period the most important and also unfortunately the most difficult question to answer is, Which one of the three Persian kings who bore the name of Artaxerxes was Nehemiah's patron? The probabilities lie between Artaxerxes I, 464-424 B.C., and Artaxerxes II, 404-358. If Neh. 12¹⁰ is reliable, the Eliashib, who was high-priest in 432 B.C. (Neh. 13⁴, ²⁸), was the grandson of Joshua, who was high-priest in 520 B.C. This would, therefore, point to the first Artaxerxes. His general character would also favor this conclusion. If the Chronicler or a late scribe had definitely associated Nehemiah with the second or third Artaxerxes, they would probably have noted the fact.

[j] 2¹ So Gk., lit., *wine was before me.* Heb., *wine was before him.*

[k] 2¹ Making a slight correction required to bring out the sense evidently required by the context. The Heb., *I was not sad in his presence*, is contradicted by 7².

[l] 2⁶ The wife of Artaxerxes, Damaspia, was probably here mentioned because of the powerful influence which women were known to exert over the king.

Nehemiah's Memoirs

to the governors of the province beyond the River, that they may let me pass through until I come to Judah, [8]and a letter to Asaph the keeper of the king's park,[m] that he may give me the timber to make beams for the gates of the castle,[n] which belongs to the temple, and for the wall of the city, and for the house that I shall enter. And the king granted me this, according to the hand of my God which kindly cared for me.[o]

[9]Then I came to the governors of the province beyond the River, and gave them the king's official letters.[p] Now the king had sent with me military officers and horsemen. [10]And when Sanballat the Horonite[q] and Tobiah, the Ammonite slave, heard of it, it troubled them exceedingly, that one had come to seek the welfare of the Israelites. [11]So I came to Jerusalem and was there three days. [12]And I arose in the night, together with a few of my followers, and I told no man what my God had put into my heart to do for Jerusalem, neither was there any beast with me, except the beast upon which I rode. [13]And I went out by night through the Valley Gate, toward the Dragon's Well and to the Dung Gate,[r] and investigated carefully the walls of Jerusalem, which were broken down, and where its gates had been destroyed by fire. [14]Then I went on to the Fountain Gate[s] and to the King's Pool, but there was no place for the beast that was under me to pass. [15]Then I went up in the night by the Brook Kidron and investigated carefully the wall, then I turned back and entered by the Valley Gate, and so returned. [16]And the rulers did not know where I went or what I did, neither had I as yet told it to the Jews nor to the priests nor to the nobles nor to the rulers nor to the rest who did the work.

[17]Then I said to them, 'You see the bad condition in which we are, how Jerusalem lies in ruins and its gates are destroyed by fire. Come and let us rebuild the wall of Jerusalem, that we be no more an object of reproach.' [18]And I told them of the hand of my God, which had kindly cared for me, as also of the king's words that he had spoken to me. And they said, 'Let us rise up and build.' So they strengthened their hands[t] for the good work. [19]But when Sanballat, the Horonite and Tobiah, the Ammonite slave, and Geshem the Arabian heard it, they jeered at us and despised us, and said, 'What is this thing that you are doing? Will you rebel against the king?' [20]Then I answered and said to them, 'The God of heaven, he will give us success, for we his servants will proceed to build; but you shall have no portion nor right nor memorial in Jerusalem.'

Margin notes: Nehemiah's arrival in Jerusalem and inspection of conditions. Response of the people to his call and the jeers of their foes.

---

m 2⁸ Probably the so-called, *Garden of Solomon*, south of Jerusalem near Etam. Cf. Josephus, *Ant.*, VIII, 7³.
n 2⁸ Cf. 7² and I Mac. 13⁵², Acts 21³⁷. It was probably erected in connection with the rebuilding of the temple in 520–316 B.C.
o 2⁸ Heb., *the good hand of my God over me.* Cf. also ¹⁸.
p 2⁸, 9ᵃ These verses are not indispensable to the context and contain certain of the Chronicler's idioms which suggest that they may have been added by him.
q 2¹⁰ Probably Bethhoron, northwest of Jerusalem, *Horonaim* in Moab has also been suggested. Cf. Appendix IV.
r 2¹³ For the course of the ride, cf. map opp. p. 349.
s 2¹⁴ Probably the Gate of the King's Garden between the two walls, mentioned in II Kgs. 25⁴, Jer. 39⁴, 52⁷. Cf. map.
t 2¹⁸ *I.e., took courage.*

§ 151. The Rebuilding of the Walls, Neh. 3

Chronicler's Version of the List of Builders

Builders of the northern wall and gate

Neh. 3 ¹Then Eliashib the high priest rose up with his kinsmen the priests and built the Sheep Gate; they laid its beams[u] and set up the doors, even to the Tower of the Hundred,[v] and to the Tower of Hananel. ²And next to him the men of Jericho built. And next to them Zaccur the son of Imri built.

Northwestern wall and gate

³And the Fish Gate the sons of Hassenaah built; they laid its beams, and set up its doors, its bolts, and its bars. ⁴And next to them Meremoth the son of Uriah, the son of Hakkoz, repaired [the wall]. And next to them Meshullam the son of Berechiah, the son of Meshezebel, repaired. And next to them Zadok the son of Baana repaired. ⁵And next to them the Tekoites repaired; but their nobles did not bend their necks in the service of their lord.

Western wall

⁶And the Old Gate, Joida the son of Paseah and Meshullam the son of Besodeiah repaired; they laid its beams, and set up its doors, its bolts, and its bars. ⁷And next to them Melatiah the Gibeonite and Jadon the Meronothite, the men of Gibeon and of Mizpah,[w] which belongs to the jurisdiction of the governor of the province beyond the River, repaired. ⁸Next to him Uzziel the son of Harhaiah, one of the goldsmiths,[x] repaired. And next to him Hananiah, one of those who prepare sweet ointments, repaired. And they[a] fortified[b] Jerusalem even to the broad wall. ⁹And next to them Rephaiah the son of Hur, the ruler of half the district of Jerusalem, repaired. ¹⁰And next to them Jedaiah the son of Harumaph repaired opposite his house. And next to him Hattush the son of Hashabneiah repaired. ¹¹Malchijah the son of Harim and Hasshub the son of Pahath-moab repaired another section even to[c] the Tower of the Furnaces. ¹²And next to him

---

§ 151 In this section a somewhat different style and vocabulary appear. Instead of the vivid narrative of Nehemiah, stereotyped formulas and a long detailed list of names in which the genealogical element is prominent, take their place. The repeated statements that the different builders set up the doors of the city gates, ¹, ³, ⁶, ¹³, ¹⁴, ¹⁵, also anticipate Nehemiah's assertion in 6¹, 7¹ that he himself set them up. In fact, the sudden and complete disappearance of Nehemiah from the narrative and the corresponding prominence of the Chronicler's favorites, the priests, the Levites, and the temple servants, the goldsmiths, and those who prepared sweet ointments, are strongly significant. As Torrey has shown (*Comp. and Hist. Value of Ezra-Neh.*, pp. 37, 38), certain idioms and words of the Chronicler are also prominent.

On the other hand, there is one which naturally calls for a different literary style. 4¹ implies that Nehemiah's memoirs contained some account of the progress of the work. If so, this was doubtless incorporated by the Chronicler. The exact details also favor the conclusion that he drew his facts either from an older written document or from a well-established oral tradition.

In determining the topography of Jerusalem this is the most important chapter in the O.T. For the location of the different places mentioned, cf. map opp. p. 349.

u 3¹ Heb., *sanctified it*, but the sanctifying of a gate is unprecedented. This act is also represented as preceding its completion. The original probably read, *laid its beams*, as in ³, ⁶. The formal act of consecration follows the completion of the walls, 12²⁷⁻⁴³.

v 3¹ Omitting, *sanctified*, which is but a repetition of the preceding scribal error.

w 3⁷ The men of Mizpah are represented by their ruler in ¹⁴. It has been conjectured that instead of *Mizpah*, the original here read, *Merenoth*.

x 3⁸ The Heb. text which reads, *goldsmiths*, has evidently suffered in transmission. Cf. the following, *son of those who prepare sweet ointments*, i.e., one who belonged to the guild, etc. Cf. further ³¹.

a 3⁸ The plural suggests that a proper name has dropped out of the preceding context.

b 3⁸ A technical word, the exact meaning of which is doubtful. It may mean, *plaster* or *complete*.

c 3¹¹ So Gk. Heb., *and*.

Chronicler's Version of the List of Builders

Shallum the son of Hallohesh, the ruler of half the district of Jerusalem, together with its dependencies,^{d} repaired.

^{13}The Valley Gate, Hanun and the inhabitants of Zanoah repaired; they built it, and set up its doors, its bolts, and its bars, and also built a thousand cubits of the wall to the Dung Gate. ^{14}And the Dung Gate, Malchijah the son of Rechab, the ruler of the district of Beth-haccherem, together with his sons^e repaired; they built it, and covered it,^{f} and set up its doors, and its bolts, and its bars. *South-ern wall and gates*

^{15}And the Fountain Gate Shallun the son of Col-hozeh, the ruler of the district of Mizpah, repaired; and he built it, and covered it, and set up its doors, its bolts, and its bars, and he also built the wall of the Pool of Siloam^g by the King's Garden, even to the stairs that go down from the city of David. *South-eastern wall and gates* ^{16}After him Nehemiah the son of Azbuk, the ruler of half the district of Bethzur, repaired to the place opposite the Sepulchres of David, even to the pool that was made and to the House of the Warriors. ^{17}After him the Levites, Rehum the son of Bani repaired. Next to him Hashabiah, the ruler of half the district of Keilah, repaired for his district. ^{18}After him their kinsmen, Bennui^h the son of Henadad the ruler of half the district of Keilah, repaired. ^{19}And next to him Ezer the son of Jeshua, the ruler of Mizpah, repaired another section opposite the ascent to the armory at the bend^i in the wall. ^{20}After him Baruch the son of Zabbai repaired from the bend in the wall to the door of the house of Eliashib the high priest. ^{21}After him Meremoth the son of Uriah, the son of Hakkoz, repaired another section, from the entrance to the house of Eliashib even to the end of the house of Eliashib. ^{22}And after him the priests, the men of the Plain of the Jordan repaired. ^{23}After them Benjamin and Hasshub repaired opposite their house. After them Azariah the son of Maaseiah, the son of Ananiah, repaired beside his own house. ^{24}After him Binnui the son of Henadad repaired another section, from the house of Azariah to the bend in the wall and to the corner. ^{25}After him Palal the son of Uzai repaired^j opposite the bend and the upper tower that stands out from the royal palace of the king, which is toward the court of the guard. After him Pedaiah the son of Parosh repaired, ^{26b}to the place opposite the Water Gate toward the east and the tower that stands out. ^{27}After him the Tekoites repaired another section, opposite the great tower that stands out and to the wall of Ophel. ^{26a}And the temple servants^k dwelt in Ophel.^{l}

---

d 3^{12} Heb., *daughters*. It appears to be equivalent to *dependent villages*, as in 11$^{25, 27}$ and often in the late priestly narratives.

e 3^{14} So Gk. The Heb. omits, *together with his sons*, and has the following verbs in the singular.

f 3^{14} So Gk. The Heb. omits, *and covered it*, but cf. ^{15}.

g 3^{15} Heb., *Shelah*. Cf. Is. 8^6, John 9^7.

h 3^{18} So Gk. and ^{24}. Heb., *Bavvai*.

i 3^{19} The translation of these words is very doubtful.

j 3^{25} Supplying the words which have fallen out of the Hebrew and which are required by the stereotyped idiom.

k 3^{26a} Heb., *Nethinim*.

l 3^{26a} This note interrupts the context and has been restored to its logical position.

Chronicler's Version of the List of Builders

Eastern and north-eastern wall and gates

²⁸Above the Horse Gate the priests repaired, each one opposite his own house. ²⁹After them Zadok the son of Immer repaired opposite his own house. After him Shemaiah the son of Shechaniah, the keeper of the East Gate, repaired. ³⁰After him Hananiah the son of Shelemiah and Hanum the sixth son of Zalaph repaired another section. After him Meshullam the son of Berechiah repaired opposite his chamber. ³¹After him Malchijah one of the goldsmiths repaired as far as the house of the temple servants and of the merchants, opposite the Gate of the Watch Tower and to the ascent of the corner. ³²And between the ascent of the corner and the Sheep Gate the goldsmiths and the merchants repaired.

§ 152. Hostile Opposition and Nehemiah's Precautionary Measures, Neh. 4

Nehemiah's Memoirs

Taunts of the heathen foes of the Jewish community

Neh. 4 ¹Now when Sanballat heard that we were rebuilding the wall, his anger was aroused and he was very indignant, and mocked the Jews.ᵐ ²And he spoke before his kinsmen and the army of Samaria and said, ' What are these feeble Jews doing? Will they leave it to God?ⁿ Will they sacrifice? Will they complete it in a day? Will they revive the stones out of the heaps of rubbish, although they are burned? ' ³Now Tobiah the Ammonite was with him, and he said, ' Even that which they are building, if a fox should go up on it, he would break down their stone wall! ' ⁴Hear, O our God—for we are despised—and turn back their reproach upon their own head and give them up as an object of spoil in a land of captivity, ⁵and cover not their iniquity and let not their sin be blotted out from thy sight, for they have provoked thee to anger before the builders.

Their plots to stop the work

⁶So we built the wall; and all the wall was joined together to half its height, for the people were eager to work. ⁷Butᵒ when Sanballat and Tobiah and the Arabians and the Ammonites and the Ashdodites,ᵖ heard that the restoration of the walls of Jerusalem was progressing,q so that the breaches began to be stopped, they were very angry. ⁸And they all conspired together to come and fight against Jerusalem and to produce a panic therein. ⁹But we made supplication to our God, and set a watch as a protection against them day and night. ¹⁰Then the Judean communityʳ said, ' The strength of the burden-bearers is broken, for there is much rubbish; so that we shall not be able to rebuild the wall. ¹¹And our adversaries have said, " They shall neither know nor see, until we come into their midst and slay them and bring the work to a standstill." ¹²And it came to pass that when the

Fears of the builders and Nehemiah's plan of work

---

§ 152 This section contains a straightforward narrative in the vivid style of Nehemiah. It reveals the discouraging problems which confronted him and the energetic way in which he solved them.

ᵐ 4¹ In the Heb., 3²³.

ⁿ 4² Making a slight change in the Heb. to bring it into harmony with the succeeding context.

ᵒ 4⁷ In the Heb. 4¹, with a corresponding change in the numbering of the remaining verses of the chapter.

ᵖ 4⁷ The Gk. omits, *Ashdodites*, which, perhaps, was taken from 13²³. They are nowhere else mentioned in the present context.

q 4⁷ Heb., *a healing of the walls of Jerusalem went up*.

ʳ 4¹⁰ Heb., *Judah*.

Nehemiah's Memoirs

Jews who dwelt by them came, they said to us ten times, ' From all the places where they dwell they will come up against us.'^{s} ^{13}Therefore I stationed in the lowest parts of the space behind the wall, in the protected places,^{t} I set there the people by their families with their swords, their spears, and their bows. ^{14}And when I saw their fear, I rose up and said to the nobles and to the rulers and to the rest of the people, ' Be not afraid of them. Remember the Lord, who is great and terrible, and fight for your kinsmen, your sons and your daughters, your wives and your homes.'

^{15}And when our enemies heard that their plan was known to us and God had brought it to nought, we all of us returned to the wall, each to his own work. ^{16}And from that time on, while half of my servants were engaged in the work, half of them held the lances, the shields, the bows, and the coats of mail; and the rulers stood behind all the house of Judah.^{u} ^{17}Those who built the wall and those who bore burdens were also armed,^{v} each with one of his hands engaged in the work, and with the other was ready to grasp his spear; ^{18}and each of the builders had his sword girded by his side, and so builded. And he who sounded the trumpet was by me. ^{19}And I said to the nobles and to the rulers and to the rest of the people, ' The work is great and extensive, and we are separated upon the wall far from each other. ^{20}In whatever place you hear the sound of the trumpet, gather there to us; our God will fight for us.' ^{21}So we were active in the work, while half of them held the lances from the appearance of the gray of morning until the stars came out. ^{22}Also I said at that time to the people, Let each man with his servant lodge in Jerusalem, that they may be a guard to us by night and may labor by day. ^{23}So neither I, nor my kinsmen, nor my servants, nor the men of the guard who accompanied me, not one of us took off our clothes, each had his spear in his hand.^{w}

Marginal notes: Rapid progress of the work and the method of defence

§ 153. Nehemiah's Social Reforms, Neh. 5

Nehemiah's Memoirs

Neh. 5 ^{1}Then there was a loud complaint from the common people and their wives against their fellow-countrymen the Jews. ^{2}For there were those who were saying, ' We must give our sons and our daughters in pledge^x to secure grain that we may eat and live.' ^{3}Some also there were who were saying, ' We must mortgage our fields and our vineyards and our houses,

Marginal notes: Complaints of the poor because of the greed of the rich and ruling class

---

^{s} 4^{12} Restoring the corrupt Heb. with the aid of the Gk.
^{t} 4^{13} The translation of the first part of the verse is exceedingly doubtful and the Gk. versions afford little aid.
^{u} 4^{16} The Gk. joins the first word to ^{17} and reads, *the rulers were behind all the house of Judah, who were engaged in the work.*
^{v} 4^{17} So Gk.
^{w} 4^{23} Following a slightly corrected text. The Gk. omits the last clause.
§ 153 As a reformer of special evils, Nehemiah showed himself a true successor of the prophets and a pioneer in establishing precedents which later appear as laws in the priestly code, Lev. 25$^{35-41}$. In the earlier codes the enslaving of a Hebrew for a debt which he was unable to pay was taken for granted. Cf. Ex. 21$^{2-6}$, Dt. 15$^{12-18}$, although the taking of interest or usury was strictly forbidden, at least in loans to the poor, Ex. 22^{25}, Dt. 23$^{19, 20}$. In ^{5} for the first time perhaps in literature the cry of modern socialism finds impassioned expression.
^{x} 5^2 Correcting an obvious error in the Heb. Giving a child in pledge was equivalent to slavery. Cf. ^{5}.

Nehemiah's Memoirs

that we may get grain because of the dearth.' ⁴There were also those who were saying, ' We have borrowed money for the king's tribute.ᵃ ⁵Yet now our flesh is as the flesh of our brothers, our children as their children; but now, we must bring our sons and our daughters into slavery, and some of our daughters have already thus been brought into bondage, neither is it in our power to help it, for our fields and our vineyards belong to the nobles.'ᵇ

Nehe-
miah's
remon-
strance
and
com-
mands ⁶Then I was very angry when I heard their complaint and these statements. ⁷And I took counsel with myself, and contended with the nobles and rulers, and said to them, ' You exact usury each of his brother.' And I held a great assembly against them. ⁸And I said to them, ' We ourselves have, according to our ability redeemed our fellow-countrymen the Jews, who have been sold to the heathen; and would you yourselves sell your fellow-countrymen, and should they sell themselves to us ? ' Then they were silent and could not find a word to say. ⁹Therefore I said, ' The thing that you are doing is not good. Ought you not to walk in the fear of our God, because of the reproach of the heathen our enemies ? ¹⁰For I also, my kinsmen and my servants, lend them money and grain. Let us, therefore, leave off this usury. ¹¹Restore to them this day their fields, their vineyards, their oliveyards, and their houses, also the usuryᶜ of the money and of the grain, the new wine, and the oil, that you exact from them.'

Re-
sponse
and
prom-
ise of
those
who
were
guilty ¹²Then they said, ' We will restore them and will demand nothing from them; we will do just as you say.' Then I called the priests and took an oath of them, that they would do according to this promise. ¹³Also I shook out the fold of my garment,ᵈ and said, ' So may God shake out every man from his house and from the fruit of his labor, who does not fulfil this promise; even thus may he be shaken out and emptied.' And all the assembly said, ' So may it be.' And they praised Jehovah. And the people did according to this promise.

Nehe-
miah's
gener-
osity
while
gov-
ernor ¹⁴Moreover from the time that I was appointed to be their governor in the land of Judah, from the twentieth year even to the thirty-second yearᵉ of Artaxerxes the king, that is for twelve years, I and my brethren had not eaten the bread which was due me as governor. ¹⁵But the former governors who were before me were a source of expense to the people, and took of them bread and wine, and also forty shekels of silver each day; and further-more their servants oppressedᶠ the people. But I did not so, because of the fear of God. ¹⁶I also devoted myself to this work on the wall, and we did not buy any land; and all my servants were gathered there for the work. ¹⁷Also the Jews and the rulers, a hundred and fifty men, besides those who came to us from among the surrounding nations, were at my table. ¹⁸Now that which was prepared for each day was one ox and six choice sheep and

---

ᵃ 5⁴ Through a scribal error in the Heb., *our fields and vineyards*, has been repeated from ³.
ᵇ 5⁵ So Gk. Heb., *to others.* But cf. ⁷.
ᶜ 5¹¹ Heb., *hundredth.* But a scribe has apparently mistaken this for the similar Heb. word for, *usury.*
ᵈ 5¹³ For this characteristic oriental ceremony, cf. Acts 18⁶, also Job 38¹³.
ᵉ 5¹⁴ *I.e.*, if under Artaxerxes I, from 445–433 B.C. Cf. 13⁶.
ᶠ 5¹⁵ So Lat. The Heb. makes no sense.

Nehemiah's Memoirs

fowls. These were prepared at my expense, and once in ten days wine in abundance^g for all the people. Yet with all this I did not demand the bread which was due me as governor, because the public service rested heavily upon this people. ¹⁹Remember to my credit, O my God, all that I have done for this people.

§ 154. Unsuccessful Plots against Nehemiah, Neh. 6

Nehemiah's Memoirs

Neh. 6 ¹Now when it was reported to Sanballat and to Tobiah and to Geshem the Arabian and to the rest of our enemies, that I had rebuilt the wall and that there was no breach left in it—though even to that time I had not set up the doors in the gates—²Sanballat and Geshem sent to me, saying, 'Come, let us meet together in one of the villages on the plain of Ono.' But they planned to do me injury. ³So I sent messengers to them, saying, 'I am doing a great work, so that I cannot come down; why should the work cease, while I leave it and come down to you?' ⁴And they sent to me in this way four times, and I gave them the same answer. ⁵Then Sanballat sent his servant to me in the same way the fifth time with an open letter in his hand, ⁶in which was written, 'It is reported among the nations, and Gashmu confirms it, that you and the Jews plan to rebel, and that this is the reason you are building the wall, and that you would be their king,^h ⁷and that you also have appointed prophets to preach of you at Jerusalem, saying, "There is a king in Judah." And now it will be reported to the king to this effect. Come now, therefore, and let us take counsel together.' ⁸Then I sent to him, saying, 'No such things have been done as you say, but you have devised them in your own mind.' ⁹For they all would have made us afraid, thinking, 'Their hands shall be weakened from the work, that it may not be done.' But now, O God, strengthen thou my hands.

¹⁰And when I went to the house of Shemaiah the son of Delaiah, the son of Mehetabel, who was shut up at home,ⁱ he said, 'Let us meet together in the house of God, within the temple, and let us shut the doors of the temple: for they are coming to slay you in the night; yes, in the night they are coming to slay you!'^j ¹¹And I said, 'Should such a man as I flee? And how could anyone like me [a layman] enter the chief room of the temple and still live? I will not enter.' ¹²Then I perceived and it was clear that God had not sent him; but he pronounced this prophecy against me, because Tobiah and Sanballat had hired him, ¹³that^k I should be alarmed and act accord-

Marginal notes: Charge that Nehemiah was plotting a rebellion / Shemaiah's attempt to frighten Nehemiah

---

g 5¹⁸ So Luc. The Heb. is doubtful. It may possibly mean, *all kinds of wine*.
h 6⁶ So Gk. The Heb. adds, *to this effect* (lit., *to these words*), which has no place in the context. They were probably introduced here by mistake from ⁷.
i 6¹⁰ Perhaps to emphasize his advice to Nehemiah to seek refuge in the temple. His proposal to go to the temple seems to indicate that he was not confined by ceremonial uncleanness.
j 6¹⁰ The Gk. does not repeat the last clause. It is possibly a scribal error, although the repetition may well have been intended to carry conviction.
k 6¹³ Following Luc. in omitting the unintelligible words found in the Heb. at the beginning of this verse. They are evidently due to a scribal repetition of the last words of ¹².

Nehemiah's Memoirs

ingly and sin; and it would have given them occasion for an evil report, that they might reproach me. [14]Remember, O my God, Tobiah and Sanballat according to these their acts, and also the prophetess Noadiah and the rest of the prophets who would have made me afraid.

Completion of the walls

[15]So the wall was finished in the twenty-fifth day of the month Elul,[l] in fifty-two days. [16]And when all our enemies heard, all the surrounding nations feared and fell in their own esteem,[m] for they perceived that this work had been done by our God.

Conspiracies of the friends of Tobiah

[17]Moreover in those days the nobles of Judah sent many letters to Tobiah, and those of Tobiah came to them. [18]For many in Judah had taken oath to him, because he was the son-in-law of Shechaniah the son of Arah and his son Jehohanan had taken the daughter of Meshullam, the son of Berechiah, as wife. [19]Also they praised his good deeds before me and reported my words to him. Then[n] Tobiah sent letters to make me afraid. . . .

§ 155. An Appeal to Artaxerxes to Stop the Rebuilding of Jerusalem, Ezra 4[7-23] (I Esdr. 2[15-22])

Aramaic Document

The accusation of the local Persian officials

Ezra 4 [7]Now in the days of Artaxerxes,[o] Bishlam, Mithredath, Tabeel, and the rest of their associates wrote to Artaxerxes king of Persia.[p] [8a]And Rehum the commander[q] and Shimshai the recorder [9]and the rest of their associates, the judges, the rulers,[r] the scribes,[s] the Archevaites,[t] the Babylonians, the men from Susa, that is[u] the Elamites, [10]and the rest of the peoples whom the great and noble Ashurbanipal[v] transported and settled in the city of Samaria and in the rest of the province beyond the River, [8b]wrote the letter against Jerusalem to Artaxerxes, as follows:

---

[l] 6[15] August-September.
[m] 6[16] Or, *were filled with wonder*.
[n] 6[19] So Gk. and Luc. The Heb. omits the introductory conjunction.
§ 155 Nehemiah 6[15-19] tells of the many letters written by the enemies of the Judean community to frighten Nehemiah and put a stop to the work. After speaking of the letters sent to himself and to other Jews, Nehemiah's account ends abruptly with the statement, *Tobiah sent letters to make me afraid*. It seems probable that the Chronicler has here cut his source short, for in 7[1] the theme is the careful measures instituted to guard the city permanently from attack. Nehemiah also leaves the trusty men in charge of the city, implying that he found it necessary to depart. To whom were Tobiah's letters sent? In their efforts to check the building of the walls, the enemies of the community certainly would not fail to invoke the authority of Persia. In all probability the sequel in Nehemiah's memoirs recorded such an attempt. Nehemiah's extreme haste in pushing the work of rebuilding the walls to completion would suggest that he feared an interruption. His implied departure in 7[1-5a] may well have been because he found it necessary to answer the charge before the king. The Chronicler's omission of this incident is most naturally explained, because he had already introduced the account of it in an entirely different setting. As has already been shown (note § 145), the Aramaic section in Ezra 4[7-23] has no real connection with its context. Not only does it relate solely to the re-

[o] 4[7] Heb., *Arthasastha*.
[p] 4[7] The Heb., but not the Gk., has the explanatory gloss, *the writing of the letter was in Aram. and it was translated into Aramaic* (*Persian?*). It was probably added by a scribe to introduce the Aramaic section which follows.
[q] 4[8a] Probably a Persian title. It was the policy of the Persian rulers to send to each province a military commander and a civil governor, each personally responsible to the king.
[r] 4[9] Cf. § 147, note [e].
[s] 4[9] The exact meaning of these titles can only be conjectured. They apparently designate minor Persian officials.
[t] 4[9] Perhaps the colonists from the southern Babylonian city of *Uruk*.
[u] 4[9] Or, *the Dehaites*.
[v] 4[10] Aram., *Osnappar*.

Aramaic Document

¹¹This is the copy of the letter that they sent to Artaxerxes the king: Thy servants the men of the province beyond the River. And now ¹²be it known to the king, that the Jews who have come up from you to us, have arrived at Jerusalem. This rebellious and bad city they are rebuilding and have finished its walls and repaired the foundations. ¹³And now be it known to the king, that, if this city is rebuilt and its walls finished, they will not pay custom or toll, and it will impair the royal income.ʷ ¹⁴Now because we eat the salt of the palace and it is not proper for us to see the king suffer loss, therefore have we sent and informed the king, ¹⁵that search may be made in the booksˣ of the records of your fathers; then will you find in the books of the records and know that this city is a rebellious city and one that brings harm to kings and provinces and that the Jewsᵃ have been rebellious in it from ancient times, for which cause this city was laid waste. ¹⁶Therefore nowᵇ we declare to the king that, if this city is rebuilt, and itsᶜ walls finished, you will have as a result no portion in the lands beyond the River.

¹⁷Then the king sent a message to Rehum the commander and to Shimshai the scribe and to the rest of their associates who dwelt in Samaria and in the rest of the province beyond the River: Greeting, and as follows:ᵈ ¹⁸The letter which you sent to us has been plainly read before me. ¹⁹And I gave command and search has been made, and it has been found that this city from ancient times has been rebellious against kings and that rebellion and sedition have been stirred up in it. ²⁰There have been mighty kings also over Jerusalem, who have ruled over all the country beyond the River; and tribute, custom, and toll was paid to them. ²¹Now give command

Marginal notes, right side:
Letter containing the formal accusation

The king's command to stop the rebuilding of Jerusalem

---

building of the walls, but it plainly and repeatedly states, 8, 11, 23, that it belongs to the reign of Artaxerxes. If not so stated originally, it is incredible that the Chronicler would have changed it and put it in its present context. Since Nehemiah's words in 1 and 2 strongly suggest that no recent attempt had been made to rebuild the walls, Ezra 4⁷⁻²³ must refer to his own work. This is confirmed by the plain statements in the letter itself, ¹², that the Jews who had come up from Artaxerxes to Jerusalem, had already *finished the walls and repaired the foundations* and were going on to rebuild the city. The king's reply says nothing about the walls, presumably because they had been practically completed, but simply commands that further rebuilding of the city cease until he should issue a decree, ²¹. The first part of the section is in confusion. Vs. ⁷ being in Heb., and, unlike the rest of the section using the term *king of Persia*, is evidently the Chronicler's epitome of the introduction to the Aramaic document.

Many have been the reconstructions offered. The probability is that ⁷ contains the list of local Palestinian officials who appealed to Artaxerxes. Their appeal would naturally be transmitted through the Persian rulers of the province beyond the River. The names of these are given in 8, 9. This conclusion is confirmed by ¹⁷, for the king's reply is addressed to the two officials who wrote the letter and *to the rest of their associates who dwelt at Samaria and in the rest of the province beyond the River*. Of the names of the officials who appealed to Artaxerxes, one, *Bishlam*, is of doubtful derivation. Some have even regarded it as a title. *Mithredath* is a Persian name, probably of the local governor of Samaria. *Tabeel* appears to be the Aram. equivalent of *Tobiah* (*el=jah*), confirming still further the assignment of this chapter to the days of Nehemiah. The parallel in I Esdr. 2¹⁵·¹⁶ is much simpler and combines the names in 7, 8. It certainly indicates that the repetition in 8, 9 of the Heb. is due to the error of a copyist who apparently omitted in ⁸ part of his list of names and then added them in 9, 10, repeating the entire list. Possibly the additional names and lists of officials and peoples in 9, 10 are themselves secondary. A certain formal and repetitious element, however, characterizes the document, and the greater brevity of I Esdr. may be due in part to abridgment.

ʷ 4¹³ Or deriving the word from a Babylonian or Persian root, *in the future* or, *finally*.

ˣ 4¹⁵ So Gk., Luc., and I Esdr. 2²¹.

ᵃ 4¹⁵ I Esdr. 2²³ supplies the subject required in the Aram.

ᵇ 4¹⁶ Restoring the lost introduction found in I Esdr. 2²⁴.

ᶜ 4¹⁶ So I Esdr. 2²⁴ and Syr.

ᵈ 4¹⁷ This represents an epitome of the address and introductory words which is characteristic of every oriental letter.

Aramaic Document

that these men cease and that this city be not rebuilt, until a decree shall be made by me.   ²²And be careful to make no mistake in the matter, that great harm may not be done, to the injury of the kings.

Inter-
ruption
of the
work   ²³Then when the copy of King Artaxerxes's letter had been read to Rehum the commander[e] and Shimshai the scribe and their associates, they went in haste to Jerusalem to the Jews, and by force and might made them cease.

§ 156. Measures to Insure the Protection of Jerusalem, Neh. 7¹⁻⁵ᵃ, 11¹, ²

Nehemiah's Memoirs

The
guard-
ing of
the city
gates   **Neh. 7** ¹Now when the wall had been built and I had set up the doors, and the porters and the singers and the Levites[f] had been appointed, ²I placed my brother Hanani and Hananiah the commander of the castle in charge of[g] Jerusalem; for he was a faithful man, and more God-fearing than many. ³And I said to them, Let not the gates of Jerusalem be opened until the sun is hot;[h] and while watchmen are still on guard, let them shut[i] the doors and bar them.   Also appoint watches consisting of the inhabitants of Jerusalem, every one in his watch and each opposite his own house.

Need of
more
citizens   ⁴Now the city was wide and large; but there were few people in it, and the households were not large.[j]   ⁵ᵃTherefore my God put it into my mind to gather together the nobles and the rulers and the people.

Chronicler's Ecclesiastical History

Meas-
ures to
in-
crease
the
pop-
ulation   **11** ¹And the princes of the people dwelt in Jerusalem, and the rest of the people cast lots, to bring one out of every ten to dwell in Jerusalem the holy city, while nine-tenths remained in the villages.   ²And the people blessed all the men who volunteered to dwell in Jerusalem.

---

e 4²³ So Luc.   *The commander* has been lost from the Aram.

§ 156 Not only does the use of the direct address, but the straightforward nature of the narrative and the presence of Nehemiah's characteristic titles for the leaders of the people in ⁵ᵃ, cf. 2¹⁶, 4¹⁴, indicate that 7¹⁻⁵ᵃ, excepting one or two slight additions, was taken from the memoirs. The assembly of the people, however, and the general theme gave the Chronicler an opportunity to introduce the census which follows in 7⁶⁻⁶⁹.   The reasons why it is not in its original or logical position are given in note § 145.   The immediate and logical sequel to 7¹⁻⁵ᵃ is found in 11¹, ². Its facts were probably taken from Nehemiah's memoirs, but the language is that of the Chronicler.

f 7¹ The context concerns only the provisions for the guarding of the city gates.   The introduction of the singers and Levites is due to the Chronicler or a scribe familiar with his stereotyped formula.

g 7² Torrey, on the basis of ³ and in view of the reference in the Talmud to the officer in charge of the gate-service, has suggested that the words, *gates of*, have fallen out of the present text.

h 7³ The translation of the clause is difficult and doubtful.   The above probably represents the idea.   The original may have read, *while it is still hot.*

i 7³ The Heb. has the imperative form of the verb and the Gk. the passive.

j 7⁴ Usually translated, *the house had not been built,* but this is contradictory to the context and especially to Hag. 1⁴.   The above translation suggested by Haupt is supported by the context and by a similar use of the same idiom in Dt. 25⁹.

§ 157. Dedication of the Walls of Jerusalem, Neh. 12[27-43]

Nehemiah's Memoirs

Assembly of the singers and the consecration of the city

Neh. 12 [27]And at the dedication of the walls of Jerusalem they sought out the Levites
from all their places, to bring them to Jerusalem to celebrate the dedication with gladness, with hymns of thanksgiving, and with singing, with cymbals, harps, and zithers.
[28]And the members of the Levitical guilds,[k] the singers, assembled, both from the Plain
of the Jordan and[l] round about Jerusalem and from the villages of the Netophathites
[29]and from Beth-gilgal and from the fields of Geba and Azmaveth; for the singers had
built themselves villages round about Jerusalem. [30]And the priests and the Levites
purified themselves; and they purified the people and the gates and the wall.

March of the first band along the southern and eastern wall

[31]Then I had the rulers of Judah take their position upon the wall, and I
appointed two great companies that gave thanks, and the first went[m] to the
right hand upon the wall toward the Dung Gate. [32]And behind them went
Hoshaiah and half of the nobles of Judah, [33]and Azariah, Ezra, and Meshullam,
[34]Judah, Benjamin, Shemaiah, Jeremiah, [35]and certain of the priests' sons with trumpets: Zechariah the son of Jonathan, the son of Shemaiah, the son of Mattaniah, the
son of Micaiah, the son of Zaccur, the son of Asaph; [36]and his kinsmen, Shemaiah,
Azarel,[n] Gilalai, Maai, Nethanel, Judah, and Hanani, with the musical instruments
of David the man of God. And Ezra the scribe was before them. [37]And by the
Fountain Gate, they went straight up the stairs of the city of David, at the
ascent of the wall, above the house of David, even to the Water Gate on
the east.

March of the second band along the western and northern wall

[38]And the other company of those who gave thanks went to the left,[o]
and I after them, with the half of the nobles[p] of the people, upon the wall,
above the Tower of the Furnaces, even to the broad wall, [39]and above the
Gate of Ephraim and by the Old Gate and by the Fish Gate and the Tower
of Hananel and the Tower of the Hundred, even to the Sheep Gate; and they
stood in the Gate of the Guard.[q] [40]So the two companies of those who
gave thanks in the house of God took their position, and I, and the half
of the rulers with me;[r] [41]and the priests, Eliakim, Maaseiah, Miniamin, Micaiah,
Elioenai, Zechariah, and Hananiah, with trumpets; [42]and Maaseiah, Shemaiah, Eleazar, Uzzi, Jehohanan, Malchijah, Elam, and Ezer. And the singers sang loudly with

---

§ 157 The dedication of the walls naturally followed soon after their completion, although the Chronicler's supplements to the original Nehemiah memoirs have widely separated the accounts of the two events. The section vividly illustrates the very different points of view of the Chronicler and of Nehemiah. In a definite, detailed narrative in which *the nobles of Judah*, [31, 32], and the rulers, [40] (cf. 2[16], 4[14], 7[5a]), and he himself are the chief actors, Nehemiah in the first person tells his story. Fortunately in [31, 32, 37-40] the Chronicler quotes it almost *in toto*, as would appear from the completeness of the account. At the beginning, at the middle and at the end he supplements it by long sections in which his favorites, the Levites, the singers, and a variety of musical instruments, songs and great sacrifices are introduced that the ceremony might be made to conform to his ideal of the way in which it should have been performed. Cf. II Chr. 5[2-14], 7[4-10], Ezra 3[10-13], 6[16-22], for his accounts of similar ceremonies. The artificiality of his lists is revealed by the fact that Ezra, Judah, and Benjamin are represented as marching in the procession. In [36] he places Ezra the scribe at the head of the first procession.

[k] 12[28] Luc., *sons of Levi*. Cf., *sons of the prophets*. *Levi* appears from [27] and [30] to have dropped out of the Heb. text.

[l] 12[28, 30] So Gk. and Luc. The Heb. has lost, *and*.

[m] 12[31] Slightly correcting the Heb., as [38] demands.

[n] 12[36] Omitting with the Gk. and Luc., *Milalai*, which probably was introduced as the result of a scribal error. This conclusion is confirmed by the number in [42].

[o] 12[38] Slightly correcting the Heb. text in accordance with [31].

[p] 12[38] Cf. [32]. *Nobles* has evidently dropped out of the text.

[q] 12[39] This last sentence is not found in the Gk. It has been urged that it is not original because it represents the second company as extending southward beyond the temple. In the absence of an exact identification of the Gate of the Guard, a final decision is impossible.

[r] 12[40] Originally instead of the Chronicler's addition there probably followed a statement as to what Nehemiah and the princes did.

Nehemiah's Memoirs

Jezrahiah their leader. ⁴³And they offered great sacrifices that day and rejoiced; for God had made them exceeding joyful;ˢ and the women also and the children rejoiced, so that the joy of Jerusalem was heard afar off.

§ 158. Nehemiah's Later Religious Reforms, Neh. 12⁴⁴–13³¹

Nehemiah's Memoirs

Ejection of Tobiah's possessions from the temple chamber

Neh. 13 ⁴Now before my return from the king,ᵗ Eliashib the priest, who was appointed over the chambers of the house of our God, being related to Tobiah, ⁵had prepared for him a great chamber, where formerly they had stored the cereal-offerings, the incense, the vessels, and the tithes of grain, the new wine, and the oil, which were given by command to the Levites, the singers, the porters, and the gifts for the priests. ⁶But during this time I had not been at Jerusalem; for in the thirty-second year of Artaxerxes king of Babylon I went to the king. Then after some time I asked leave of the king, ⁷and I came to Jerusalem and discovered the crime that Eliashib had committed for the sake of Tobiah, in preparing him a chamber in the courtᵘ of the house of God. ⁸And it displeased me greatly; therefore I cast all the household possessions of Tobiah out of the chamber. ⁹Then I gave command that they should cleanse the chambers, and I brought there again the vessels of the house of God, with the cereal-offerings and the incense.

Chronicler's Ecclesiastical History

Providing for the support of the Levites

¹⁰And I perceived that the portions of the Levites had not been given them; so that the Levites and the singers, who performed the service had each fled to his field.ʷ ¹¹Then I contended with the rulers and said, 'Why is the house of God forsaken?' And I gathered them together and placed them at their posts. ¹²And all

Neh. 12 ⁴⁴And in that dayᵛ men were appointed in charge of the chambers for the storehouse, for the gifts, for the first-fruits, and for the tithes, to gather into them, according to the fields of the cities, the portions appointed by the law for the priests and the Levites; for Judah had joy in the priests and the Levites who attended

---

ˢ 12⁴³ For similar characteristic expressions of the Chronicler, cf. Ezra 3¹³, 6²².

§ 158. With 13¹ Nehemiah's vigorous literary style and courageous, assertive spirit reappear. Since the themes treated concern the temple and the ritual, the Chronicler has been led to take greater liberties with his text. As Torrey, who maintains that the entire chapter is from the Chronicler, has pointed out (*Comp. and Hist. Value of Ezra-Nehemiah*, pp. 44–49), it has many phrases and words characteristic of the editor of Ezra-Neh. Since Nehemiah passes for the first time into the latter's peculiar field, more points of similarity are to be anticipated. Certain passages, as for example, ⁵ᵇ, ¹³ᵇ, ²², abound in the Chronicler's expressions and peculiar ideas. Their loose connection with the context confirms the impression that they are later additions. On the other hand, it is almost incredible that the Chronicler could have so far imitated the language and spirit of Nehemiah as to have written the chapter as a whole. A comparison of the Chronicler's parallel in 12⁴⁴–13³ reveals the widely different conception of the course of the history which he entertained. Also it is far more natural to conclude that he here reproduces the older source than that he deliberately made Nehemiah the layman do the work of reform which his school had already attributed to Ezra and the assembly. Cf. further Introd., pp. 31–34.

ᵗ 13⁴ Heb., *after this*, but ⁶ indicates what was probably the event to which reference is made.

ᵘ 13⁷ So Gk. and Luc. Heb., *courts*.

ᵛ 12⁴⁴ The Chronicler's general introductory formula. It would connect the act with the dedication of the temple, cf. ⁴³.

ʷ 13¹⁰ For a similar neglect of the temple service, cf. the Gadatas inscription, Appendix XII.

Nehemiah's Memoirs

Judah brought the tithe of the grain and the new wine and the oil into the store-rooms.ˣ ¹³And I appointed in charge of the store-rooms: Shelemiah the priest and Zadok the scribe, and of the Levites Pedaiah; and next to them was Hanan, the son of Zaccur the son of Mattaniah; for they were considered faithful, and their business was to distribute to their kinsmen. ¹⁴Remember me, O my God, concerning this and forget notᵇ all my good deeds that I have done for the house of my God, and for its services.

Chronicler's Ecclesiastical History

to the service. ⁴⁵And they took charge of the service of their God and of the purification, and so did the singers and the porters, according to the command of David and of Solomon his son. ⁴⁶For in the days of David and Asaph were the leadersᵃ of the singers appointed, and songs of praise and thanksgiving to God. ⁴⁷And all Israel in the days of Zerubbabel and in the days of Nehemiah gave the portions of the singers and the porters, as each required; and they delivered the sacred offerings to the Levites the sons of Aaron.

¹⁵At that time I saw in Judah some men treading wine-presses on the sabbath and bringing in heaps of grain and loading asses, as also wine, grapes, figs, and all kinds of burdens, and that they were bringing them into Jerusalem on the sabbath; and I warned them when they sold provisions. ¹⁶Tyrians also dwelt therein, who brought in fish and all kinds of wares, and sold on the sabbath to the inhabitants of Judah and in Jerusalem. ¹⁷Then I contended with the nobles of Judah and said to them, ' What evil thing is this that you are doing, and thereby profaning the sabbath? ¹⁸Did not your fathers do thus and did not our God bring all this calamity upon them and upon usᶜ and upon this city? Yet you bring more wrath upon Israel by profaning the sabbath.' ¹⁹Accordingly when it began to be dark, the gates of Jerusalem were shut before the sabbath; and I gave command that they should not be opened until after the sabbath. And I placed some of my servants in charge of the gates, and commandedᵈ that no burden should be brought in on the sabbath. ²⁰So the merchants and sellers of all kinds of wares spent the night without Jerusalem once or twice. ²¹Then I warned them and said to them, ' Why do you spend the night before the wall? If ye do so again, I will lay hands on you.' From that time forth they came no more on the sabbath. ²²And I commanded the Levites that they should purify themselves and that they should come and guard the gates, to keep the sabbath holy. Remember, O my God, this also to my credit and show me mercy according to the greatness of thy loving-kindness.

Provisions to guard the observation of the sabbath

ˣ 13¹² So Luc. and Gk.
ᵃ 12⁴⁶ Slightly restoring what is obviously a defective text.
ᵇ 13¹⁴ Heb., *wipe not out [of thy memory]*.
ᶜ 13¹⁸ So Gk. and Luc. Heb. lacks, *upon them and.*
ᵈ 13¹⁹ So Gk. In the Heb., *I gave command*, has been inserted wrongly in the first part of the verse and is lacking in the latter part.

Nehemiah's Memoirs

Chronicler's Ecclesiastical History

Energetic protest against mixed marriages

²³At that time also I saw the Jews who had married women of Ashdod, of Ammon, and of Moab. ²⁴And their children spoke half in the language of Ashdod, but none of them could speak in the Jews' language, but according to the language of each people.ᶠ ²⁵And I contended with them and cursed them and struck some of them and pulled out their hair and made them swear by God, saying, ' You shall not give your daughters to their sons nor take their daughters as wives for your sons or for yourselves. ²⁶Did not Solomon king of Israel sin by these acts? Yet among many nations there was no king like him, and he was beloved by his God, and God made him king over all Israel; nevertheless foreign women led him into sin. ²⁷Shall it also be reported of you that you do all this great evil, to trespass against our God in marrying foreign women? '

13 ¹On that dayᵉ it was read from the book of Moses in the hearing of the people, and it was found written there that an Ammonite and a Moabite should never enter into the assembly of God, ²for they did not meet the Israelites with bread and water but hired Balaamᵍ against them to curse them; but our God turned the curse into a blessing. ³And when they had heard the law, they separated from Israel all the mixed multitude.ʰ

Ejection of a guilty priest

²⁸And one of the sons of Joiada, the son of Eliashib the high priest, was the son-in-law of Sanballat the Horonite; therefore I chased him from me. ²⁹Remember them, O my God, because they have defiled the covenant of the priesthoodⁱ and of the Levites.

Resume of Nehemiah's reforms

³⁰Thus I cleansed them from all foreigners and fixed the duties for the priests and the Levites, each for his appointed task,ʲ ³¹and the bringing of wood for the service at appointed times, and the first-fruits. Remember it, O my God, to my credit.

ᵉ 13¹ Cf. note ᵛ.
ᶠ 13²⁴ This last awkward clause is omitted in the Gk. and perhaps is an explanatory gloss.
ᵍ 13² Cf. Dt. 23³⁻⁶.
ʰ 13³ *I.e.*, all those who had contracted foreign marriages. Cf. Ex. 12³⁸.
ⁱ 13²⁹ So Luc. *The priesthood* has been awkwardly repeated in the Heb.
ʲ 13³⁰ Gk. and Luc., *a man according to his work.*

III

THE WORK OF EZRA AND THE INSTITUTION OF THE PRIESTLY LAW, Ezra 7-10, Neh. 7^{70}-10^{39}

§ 159. Artaxerxes's Commission to Ezra, Ezra 7$^{1-26}$ (I Esdr. 8$^{1-24}$)

Chronicler's Introduction to the Ezra Narrative

Ezra 7 ^{1}Now after these things, in the reign of Artaxerxes king of Persia, there went up^a Ezra the son of Seraiah, the son of Azariah, the son of Hilkiah, ^{2}the son of Shallum, the son of Zadok, the son of Ahitub, ^{3}the son of Amariah, the son of Azariah, the son of Meraioth, ^{4}the son of Zerahiah, the son of Uzzi, the son of Bukki, ^{5}the son of Abishua, the son of Phinehas, the son of Eleazar, the son of Aaron the chief priest. ^{6}This Ezra went up from Babylon; and he was a scribe skilled in the law of Moses, which Jehovah, the God of Israel, had given. And the king granted him all his request, inasmuch as the hand of Jehovah his God was upon him. ^{7}And some of the Israelites, and of the priests, the Levites, the singers, the porters, and the temple servants went up to Jerusalem, in the seventh year of Artaxerxes the king. ^{8}And he came to Jerusalem in the fifth month,^{b} which was in the seventh year of the king. ^{9}For on the first day of the first month he began the journey^c from Babylon, and on the first day of the fifth month he came to Jerusalem, since the good hand of God was with him. ^{10}For Ezra had set his heart to seek the law of Jehovah, and to observe it and to teach in Israel statutes and ordinances.

(margin: The return of Ezra and his band to Jerusalem)

The Work of Ezra and the Institution of the Priestly Law.—Nehemiah's work was that of a pioneer. His unique position at the Persian court opened for him the door by which alone the favor of the absolute despot who ruled the empire could be won. Faithfully improving the rare opportunity thus given him, he prepared the way and established the precedents for the fundamental transformation in the domestic, social, ceremonial, and religious life of the Jews of Palestine. This fruition of Nehemiah's work the later tradition preserved in Ezra 7-10, Neh. 7^{70}-10^{39} associates with Ezra the priest and scribe. As has been shown in the Introd. (pp. 31-34), its language, peculiar idioms, point of view and contents all demonstrate its close relationship with the *midrashes* of Chr. Unlike Nehemiah's memoirs, it is not a mere record of facts, it is idealized history. Probably embodying historical data, it represents, however, the tradition current in the very late priestly school, of which the Chronicler was the final editor, regarding the way in which the law and institutions of his day were put into force in Palestine. It possesses a great and permanent value because it makes concrete and vivid that movement which made the Jewish race what it was in New Testament times. It also reveals most clearly the interests and ideals which henceforth moulded Judaism.

§ 159 Vss. $^{1-10}$ contain the Chronicler's introduction to the Ezra narrative which follows. In $^{6-9}$ he briefly epitomizes the older source which he begins to quote in ^{11}. His love of symmetry led him to state that *on the first day of the first month* Ezra began the journey from Babylon, although the Ezra narrative dates it *on the twelfth day*, 8^{31}. In 8$^{1, 31}$ we also anticipate from all analogies that the year of Artaxerxes's reign in which the events took place will be given. It is almost incredible that they were not found in the original. The simplest explanation is, perhaps, that the Chronicler suppressed them that he might date them in *the seventh year* of Artaxerxes, as he does with great elaboration in $^{7, 8}$, thus giving Ezra the precedence before Nehemiah. Cf. Introd., p. 32. If the date was not found in the original, he was left to his own conjectures. As in the Aram. document in 5^3-6^{15}, the decree is in Aram. It may be from the Chronicler, but more probably belonged to the original Ezra narrative.

^{a} 7^1 So Gk. and I Esdr. 8^1. The verb is lacking in the Heb.
^{b} 7^8 July-August.
^{c} 7^9 Heb., *laid the foundation (of the journey)*.

Ezra Narrative

^{Artax-erxes's decree con-firming Ezra's author-ity}

¹¹Now this is the copy of the letter that King Artaxerxes gave to Ezra the priest, the scribe, who copied the words of the commands of Jehovah^d and of his statutes to Israel: ¹²Artaxerxes, king of kings, to Ezra the priest, the scribe of the law of the God of heaven, greeting.^e ¹³And now I make a decree that anyone of the people of Israel, or their priests or Levites in my realm, who is willing to go to Jerusalem, shall go with you. ¹⁴Because you have been sent by the king and his seven counsellors, to institute an inquiry concerning Judah and Jerusalem on the basis of the law of your God which is in your hand ¹⁵and to carry the silver and gold which the king and his counsellors have freely offered to the God of Israel, whose dwelling is in Jerusalem, ¹⁶with all the silver and gold that you shall receive in all the province of Babylon, with the contributions of the people and priests, who contribute for the house of their God which is in Jerusalem, ¹⁷therefore you shall carefully buy with this money bullocks, rams, lambs, with their cereal-offerings and their libations, and shall offer them on the altar of the house of your God which is in Jerusalem. ¹⁸And whatever shall seem good to you and to your kinsmen to do with the rest of the silver and the gold, so do according to the will of your God. ¹⁹And the vessels that have been given you for the service of the house of your God, deliver them all before your God at Jerusalem.^f ²⁰And whatever more shall be needed for the house of your God, which you shall have occasion to bestow, bestow it out of the king's treasury. ²¹And the decree is given by me, Artaxerxes the king, to all the treasurers of the province beyond the River, that whatever Ezra the priest, the scribe of the law of the God of heaven, shall require of you, let it be carefully done, ²²up to a hundred talents of silver, a thousand bushels^g of wheat, eight hundred gallons^h of wine, eight hundred gallons^h of oil, and salt to any amount. ²³All that is commanded by the God of heaven must be exactly done for the house of the God of heaven; for why should there be wrath against the realm of the king and his sons? ²⁴Also be it known to you that it is not lawful to impose tribute, custom, or toll on any priests, Levites, singers, porters, temple-servants, or servants of this house of God. ²⁵And you, Ezra, according to the wisdom of your God that is in you, appoint magistrates and judges to judge all the people beyond the River, all such as know the laws of your God, and teach such as do know them. ²⁶And whoever will not obey the law of your God, and the law of the king, let strict justice be executed upon him, whether it be death, or banishment, or confiscation of goods, or imprisonment.

---

^d 7¹¹ Gk., *reader of the law of God.*
^e 7¹² So I Esdr. 8⁹. The usual word for, *peace* or *greeting*, has apparently fallen out of the Heb.
^f 7¹⁹ So Luc. Heb., *before the God of Jerusalem.*
^g 7²² Heb., *one hundred cors.*
^h 7²² Heb., *one hundred baths.*

§ 160. **Return of Ezra and his Company, Ezra 7²⁷–8³⁶, Neh. 7⁷⁰⁻⁷³ᵃ**
(I Esdr. 8²⁵⁻⁴⁰, 9³⁷ᵃ)

Ezra Narrative

Ezra 7 ²⁷Blessed be Jehovah the God of our fathers, who hath put such Ezra's
a thing as this into the king's heart, to beautify the temple of Jehovah which grati-
is at Jerusalem, ²⁸and hath granted me favor before the king and his coun- Jeho-
sellors and before all the king's high officials. And I was strengthened, vah
since the hand of Jehovah my God was with me, and I gathered chief men
from Israel to go up with me.

8 ¹Now these are the heads of their fathers' houses, and this is the gene- List of
alogy of those who went up with me from Babylon in the reign of Artaxerxes those
the king: ²Of the sons of Phinehas, Gershom. Of the sons of Ithamar, turned
Daniel. Of the sons of David, Hattush ³the son of Shecaniah.ⁱ Of the Ezra
sons of Parosh, Zechariah, and with him were reckoned by genealogy a
hundred and fifty men.ʲ ⁴Of the sons of Pahath-moab, Eliehoenai the son
of Zerahiah, and with him two hundred men. ⁵Of the sons of Shecaniah,
the son of Jahaziel, and with him three hundred men. ⁶And of the sons
of Adin, Ebed the son of Jonathan, and with him fifty men. ⁷And of the
sons of Elam, Jeshaiah the son of Athaliah, and with him seventy men.
⁸And of the sons of Shephatiah, Zebadiah the son of Michael, and with him
eighty men. ⁹Of the sons of Joab, Obadiah the son of Jehiel, and with
him two hundred and eighteen men. ¹⁰And of the sons of Banias,ᵏ Shelomith the son of Josiphiah, and with him a hundred and sixty men. ¹¹And
of the sons of Bebai, Zechariah the son of Bebai, and with him twenty-eight
men. ¹²And of the sons of Azgad, Johanan the son of Hakkatan, and with
him a hundred and ten men. ¹³And the sons of Adonikam, the last,ˡ and
these are their names: Eliphelet, Jeuel, and Shemaiah, and with them sixty
men. ¹⁴And of the sons of Bigvai, Uthai and Zakkur,ᵐ and with them
seventy men.

¹⁵And I gathered them together to the river that flows toward Ahava.ⁿ Assem-
And there we encamped three days, while I reviewed the people and the bly of
priests; I found there none of the sons of Levi. ¹⁶Then I sent for Eliezer, turning
Ariel, Shemaiah, Elnathan, Jarib, Nathan, Zechariah, and Meshullam, chief exiles
men;ᵒ also for Joiarib, and Elnathan,ᵖ who were teachers. ¹⁷And I sent

§ 160 Nehemiah's memoirs were probably kept in the temple at Jerusalem and were doubtless accessible to the school of the Chronicler. Their tendency to present their teachings in the form of dialogues is amply illustrated in Chr. Cf. Introd., p. 4. It was natural that, influenced by the example of such an epoch-making man as Nehemiah, they should add to their literary equipment, not only the royal decree, but also the personal memoir. That it was merely a literary form is strongly suggested by the abruptness and facility with which the narrative passes from the first person singular to the third, and in Neh. 10 to the first person plural without any apparent reason. The account of the arrival ends abruptly in 8³⁶. On the other hand, Neh. 7⁷⁰⁻⁷³ᵃ has no connection with its context. Joined together, these two torsos, with the sequel of Neh. 7⁷³ᵃ, make a complete and consistent narrative.
ⁱ 8³ Following I Esdr. 8²⁹ in combining and correcting the otherwise unintelligible Heb. text.
ʲ 8³ Lit., *males.*
ᵏ 8¹⁰ Completing the Heb. from the parallel, I Esdr. 8³⁶.
ˡ 8¹³ The text is unintelligible. Possibly it is due to an early scribal error.
ᵐ 8¹⁴ The versions and the marginal reading of the Heb. give but one son of Bigvai, *Zakkur.*
ⁿ 8¹⁵ The identification is unknown.
ᵒ 8¹⁶ I Esdr. 8⁴⁴ completes its list of ten men with, *leaders and men of understanding.*
ᵖ 8¹⁶ In the Heb. *Elnathan* is introduced twice.

Ezra Narrative

them out to[q] Iddo, the chief of the place Casiphia. And I instructed them what they should say to Iddo and his kinsmen at the place Casiphia, namely, that they should bring to us ministers for the house of our God. [18]And since the good hand of our God was with us, they brought us a man of discretion, of the sons of Mahli, the son of Levi, the son of Israel:[r] Shere-biah, with his sons and his kinsmen, eighteen; [19]and Hashabiah and[s] Je-shaiah of the sons of Merari, their[t] kinsmen and their[t] sons, twenty; [20]and of the temple servants, whom David and the princes had given for the service of the Levites, two hundred and twenty; all of them were mentioned by name.[u]

Prelim-
inary
fast
[21]Then I proclaimed a fast there at the River Ahava, that we might humble ourselves before our God to seek of him a fortunate journey[v] for us and for our little ones and for all our possessions. [22]For I was ashamed to ask of the king a band of soldiers and horsemen to protect us against the enemy on the journey, because we had spoken to the king, saying, ' The hand of our God is with all who seek him for good, but his power and his wrath is against all them who forsake him.' [23]So we fasted and besought our God for this, and he was entreated by us.

Depart-
ure
with
the gifts
for the
temple
[24]Then I set apart twelve of the chiefs of the priests, and Sherebiah, Hash-abiah,[w] and ten of their clansmen with them, [25]and weighed to them the silver and the gold and the vessels, even the offering for the house of our God, which the king and his counsellors and his princes and all Israel there present had offered. [26]I weighed into their hands six hundred and fifty talents of silver, and silver vessels, a hundred talents, of gold a hundred talents;[x] [27]and twenty bowls of gold of a thousand darics;[a] and ten[b] vessels of fine bright brass, precious as gold. [28]And I said to them, You are holy to Jehovah, and the vessels are holy, and the silver and the gold are a con-tribution to Jehovah, the God of our[c] fathers. [29]Guard and keep them until you weigh them before the chiefs of the priests and the Levites and the heads[d] of the fathers' houses of Israel at Jerusalem in the chambers of the temple of Jehovah. [30]So the priests and the Levites received the weight of the silver and gold and the vessels, to bring them to Jerusalem to the house of our God. [31]Then we departed from the River Ahava on the twelfth day of the first month to go to Jerusalem.

Arrival
at Je-
rusalem
and the
deliv-
ery of
the
gifts
And the hand of our God was upon us and he delivered us from the hand of the enemy and the lier-in-wait by the way. [32]And when we arrived at Jerusalem, we remained there three days. [33]And on the fourth day the silver and the gold and the vessels were weighed in the house of our God into the

[q] 8¹⁷ Following I Esdr. 8⁴⁶ in restoring the unintelligible Hebrew.
[r] 8¹⁸ So Gk. and I Esdr. 8⁴⁷.
[s] 8¹⁹ Correcting the Heb. by the Gk. and Luc.
[t] 8¹⁹ Heb., *his*, but Luc. in I Esdr. 8⁴⁸ supports the above, which accords with the context.
[u] 8²⁰ This verse is characterized by the expressions and ideas peculiar to the Chronicler. Its construction is also different from that of the preceding verses.
[v] 8²¹ Heb., *straight way.*
[w] 8²⁴ According to ¹⁸, ¹⁹ Sherebiah and Hashabiah were not priests but Levites. Two groups of twelve, therefore, are to be distinguished, following I Esdr. 8⁵⁴.
[x] 8²⁶ Amounting to over a million dollars.
[a] 8²⁷ About five thousand, eight hundred and sixty dollars.
[b] 8²⁷ So I Esdr. 8⁵⁷ (Luc., *twelve*). Heb., *two.*
[c] 8²⁸ So Gk. and I Esdr. 8⁵⁸. Heb., *your.*
[d] 8²⁹ So I Esdr. 8⁵⁹. Heb., *nobles.*

Ezra Narrative

hands of Meremoth the son of Uriah the priest; and with him was Eleazar the son of Phinehas; and with them was Jozabad the son of Jeshua and Noadiah the son of Binnui, the Levites.   ³⁴The whole was delivered by number and by weight, and the weight of everything was recorded.

At that time[e] ³⁵the people who had returned from exile offered burnt-offerings to the God of Israel, twelve bullocks for all Israel, ninety-six rams, seventy-seven lambs, twelve he-goats for a sin-offering; all this was a burnt-offering to Jehovah.   ³⁶And they delivered the king's commissions to the king's satraps and to the governors of the province beyond the River.   And they aided the people and the house of God.   **Neh. 7** ⁷⁰And some from among the heads of fathers' houses gave to the work.[f]   The governor gave to the treasury a thousand darics of gold, fifty basins, five hundred minas of silver and thirty[g] priests' garments.   ⁷¹And some of the heads of fathers' houses gave into the treasury for the work, twenty thousand darics of gold and two thousand, two hundred minas[h] of silver.   ⁷²And that which the rest of the people gave was twenty thousand darics of gold and two thousand minas of silver and sixty-seven priests' garments.

⁷³ªSo the priests and the Levites and the porters and the singers and the common people,[i] and the temple servants, and all Israel dwelt in their cities.[j]

Gifts of the returned exiles to the temple

Location of the temple ministers

§ 161. Public Reading of the Law and the Observation of the Feast of Tabernacles, Neh. 7⁷³ᵇ–8¹⁸ (I Esdr. 9³⁷ᵇ⁻⁵⁵)

Ezra Narrative

Neh. 7 ⁷³ᵇAnd when the seventh month drew near, the Israelites were settled in their cities,[k] **8** ¹all the people gathered themselves together as one man to the broad place that was before the Water Gate.   And they spoke to Ezra the priest[l] and scribe to bring the book of the law of Moses, which Jehovah had commanded Israel.   ²And Ezra the priest brought the law before the assembly of men and women, and all who could hear with understanding, upon the first day of the seventh month.   ³And he read from it before the open place that was before the Water Gate from early morning until mid-day, in the presence of the men and women and of those who could

Reading and explanation of the law to the people

---

e 8³⁴ The Gk. unites these words with ³⁵ as above.

f Neh. 7⁷⁰ The parallel Ezra 2⁶⁸, ⁶⁹ has a variant text which has been adapted to its changed context.   The present text of Neh. is clearly the more original.

g Neh. 7⁷⁰ Following a better reading suggested by the parallel Ezra 2⁶⁹.

h Neh. 7⁷¹ About 1,750 pounds.

i Neh. 7⁷³ª Heb., *sons of the people.*

j Neh. 7⁷³ª Again the distinctive expressions and ideas of the Chronicler indicate that this verse must be from him.

§ 161 Restoring the separated members of the Ezra narrative, its unity is demonstrated. According to Ezra 8³¹ the expedition left the River Ahava on the twelfth day of the first month and arrived in Jerusalem in the fifth month (7⁸).   Two months were devoted to finding homes for the new arrivals.   Then on the seventh month at the feast of the new moon the people assemble for the reading of the law by *Ezra the priest and scribe,* 8¹.   Then follows the earliest extant record of a synagogue service.   Vss. ⁷, ⁸ were probably later added by the Chronicler, for they are not exactly in harmony with the context and duplicate, 9ª.   They also contain one of his favorite lists.

k 7⁷³ᵇ This clause not only disturbs the context but also introduces one of the Chronicler's characteristic conceptions.

l 8¹ So the parallel I Esdr. 9³⁷.   The Heb. omits, *priest,* but cf. ², ⁹, where the title, *priest,* occurs.

Ezra Narrative

understand; and all the people were attentive to the book of the law.   ⁴And Ezra the priest and scribe[m] stood upon a wooden pulpit, which they made for the purpose; and beside him stood Mattithiah, Shema, Anaiah, Azariah,[n] Uriah, Hilkiah, and Maaseiah, on his right hand, and on his left, Pedaiah, Mishael, Malchijah, Hashum, Hashbaddanah, Zechariah, and Meshullam. ⁵And Ezra opened the book in the sight of all the people—for he was above all the people—and when he opened it all the people stood up.   ⁶And Ezra blessed Jehovah, the great God.   And all the people answered, Amen, Amen, while they lifted up their hands and bowed their heads and worshipped Jehovah with their faces to the ground.   ⁷Also Jeshua, Bani, Sherebiah, Jamin, Akkub, Shabbethai, Hodiah, Maaseiah, Kelita, Azariah, Jozabad, Hanan, Pelaiah,[o] the Levites, instructed the people in the law, and the people remained in their place.   ⁸And they read in the book of the law of God by sections,[p] and made the sense so clear that they understood the reading.

Command to rejoice and give gifts to each other

⁹And Nehemiah, who was the governor,[q] and Ezra the priest, the scribe, and the Levites who taught the people said to all the people, This day is holy to Jehovah your God; mourn not, nor weep; for all the people wept when they heard the words of the law.   ¹⁰Then he[r] said to them, Go away, eat the fat, and drink the sweet, and send portions to him for whom nothing is prepared, for this day is holy to our Lord; and do not be troubled, for the joy of Jehovah is your bulwark.   ¹¹So the Levites quieted all the people, saying, Be still, for the day is holy, and do not be troubled.   ¹²And all the people went away to eat and drink and to send portions and to make a great rejoicing, for they had understood the words which had been made known to them.

Celebration of the feast of tabernacles according to the new law

¹³And on the second day the heads of fathers' houses of all the people, the priests and the Levites were gathered together to Ezra the scribe,[s] in order to gain an insight into the words of the law.   ¹⁴And they found written in the law, how Jehovah had commanded by Moses that the Israelites should dwell in booths at the feast in the seventh month; ¹⁵and that they should proclaim aloud in all their cities and in Jerusalem: Go forth to the mount and bring olive branches and branches of wild olive and myrtle and palm branches and branches of thick trees to make booths, as it is prescribed.   ¹⁶So the people went out and brought them, and made themselves booths, each man upon the roof of his house and in their courts and in the courts of the house of God and in the open space at the Water Gate and in the open space at the Ephraim Gate.   ¹⁷And all the assembly of those who had come back from the captivity made booths and lived in the booths; for since the days of Joshua the son of Nun to that day the Israelites had not done so.   And

m 8⁴ I Esdr. 9⁴² reads consistently, *priest and scribe.*
n 8⁴ Adding *Azariah* from the parallel I Esdr. 9⁴³.   This is confirmed by Luc. and the fact that this gives seven on each side.
o 8⁷ Following I Esdr. 9⁴⁸ in omitting, *and,* before Levites.
p 8⁸ So Gk.
q 8⁹ Gk. and I Esdr. 9⁴⁹ do not have *Nehemiah.* The words, *and Nehemiah who was the governor,* were probably added by the Chronicler, who again in 12³⁶ brings Nehemiah and Ezra together.   The absence of Nehemiah in the rest of the narrative, except in another secondary passage, 10¹, confirms this conclusion.
r 8¹⁰ Luc., *they.*
s 8¹³ Following the Gk. in omitting, *and.*

Ezra Narrative

there⁶ was very great gladness. ¹⁸And day by day, from the first to the last day, he read in the book of the law of God. And they celebrated the feast seven days, and on the eighth day, as was the custom, there was a concluding solemn assembly.

§ 162. **Ezra's Crusade against Mixed Marriages, Ezra 9, 10, I Esdr. 8⁶⁸–9³⁶**

Ezra Narrative

Ezra 9 ¹Now when these things had been done, the noblesᵗ drew near to me and said, 'The people of Israel and the nobles and the priests and the Levites have not kept themselves apart from the peoples of the lands, fromᵘ their abominations, even from the Canaanites, the Hittites, the Perizzites, the Jebusites, the Ammonites, the Moabites, the Egyptians, and the Amorites. ²For they have taken of their daughters wives for themselves and their sons, so that they, the holy race, have mixed themselves with the peoples of the lands, and the hand of the noblesᵛ and rulers has been most prominent in this impiety.' ³And when I heard this, I tore my inner-garment and my robe, and pulled the hair from my head and my beard, and sat down dumbfounded. ⁴Then all who trembled at the words of the God of Israel, because of the impiety of those who had returned from the captivity, gathered about me as I sat dumbfounded until the evening oblation.ʷ

⁵And at evening I arose from my self-humiliation, and I tore my inner-garment and my robe, and fell upon my knees and spread out my hands to Jehovahˣ ⁶and said, 'O my God, I am ashamed and blush to lift up my face to thee, my God, for our iniquities have risen higher than our headᵃ and our guilt has grown even to the heavens. ⁷Since the days of our fathers to this day we have been implicated in great guilt; and for our iniquities we, our kings, and our priests, have been delivered into the hands of the kings of the lands, by the sword, captivity, plunder, and confusion of face, as it is this day. ⁸And now for a brief moment grace hath been showed from Jehovah our God, in that he has left us a remnant to escape, and given us a respiteᵇ in his holy place that our God may lighten our eyes,ᶜ and give us a little renewal of life in our bondage. ⁹For we are bondmen; yet our God hath not forsaken us in our bondage, but hath extended to us favor in the sight of the kings of Persia to give us a renewal of life, to set up the house

Discovery of mixed marriages and Ezra's astonishment and grief

His prayer of confession in behalf of the guilty community

---

§ 162 It was only after the preliminary work had been done and the consciences of the people had been touched, as recorded in Neh. 8, that they would be ready for the supreme test imposed in Ezra 9, 10. Neh. 9² also appears to contain a direct reference to the act of separation, the enforcement of which is recorded in Ezra 9, 10.
ᵗ 9¹ Adding, *the nobles*, required by ²ᵇ and found in the parallel I Esdr. 8⁶⁹.
ᵘ 9¹ So I Esdr. 8⁶⁹. Heb., *according to.*
ᵛ 9² The Gk. has only, *rulers.* This may well have been original.
ʷ 9⁴ The parallel I Esdr. 8⁷² reads, *gathered about me, as I mourned for the impiety, and I sat filled with sorrow, until the evening sacrifice.*
ˣ 9⁵ Following I Esdr. 8⁷³ in omitting, *my God*, which has crept in from ⁶.
ᵃ 9⁶ The figure is that of the race engulfed in crime.
ᵇ 9⁸ Heb., *tent-pin.* The figure is taken from the wandering life of the nomad and symbolizes the brief rest which comes when his tent is securely pitched.
ᶜ 9⁸ I Esdr. 8⁷⁹, *that he may uncover for us a light in the house of Jehovah our God.*

Ezra Narrative

of our God, to repair its ruins, and to give us a wall in Judah and in Jerusalem. ¹⁰And now, O our God, what shall we say after all this? For we have forsaken thy commands, ¹¹which thou hast commanded by thy servants the prophets, saying, " The land which we go to possess, is an unclean land because of the uncleanness of the peoples of the land, because of their abominable practices, which have filled it from one to another with their filth. ¹²Now therefore do not give your daughters to their sons, nor take their daughters as wives for your sons, nor seek their peace or their prosperity forever, that ye may be strong, and eat the good of the land and leave it as an inheritance to your children forever." ¹³And after all that is come upon us for our evil deeds and for our great guilt, since thou, our God, hast punished us less than our iniquities deserve, and hast given us such a remnant as this, ¹⁴shall we again break thy commands and intermarry with the peoples who do these abominable acts? Wouldest not thou be angry with us until thou hadst consumed us, so that there would be no remnant nor any to escape? ¹⁵O Jehovah, the God of Israel, thou art righteous; for we are left a remnant that has escaped, as it is this day. Now we are before thee in our guilt, for none can stand before thee because of this.'

Decision of the people to put away all foreign wives

10 ¹Now while Ezra was making supplication and confession, weeping and casting himself down before the house of God, there was gathered together to him out of Israel a very great assembly of men and women and children; for the people wept loudly. ²And Shecaniah the son of Jehiel, one of the sons of Elam, spoke and said to Ezra, We have committed an impiety against our God and have married foreign women of the peoples of the land, yet in this matter there is yet hope for Israel. ³Now therefore let us make a covenant with our God to put away all the foreign wives[d] and those who have been born of them, according to the counsel of my lord[e] and of those who revere the command of our God, and let it be done according to the law. ⁴Arise, carry into execution,[f] for it is your task, and we are with you; be of good courage and act. ⁵Then Ezra arose and made the chiefs of the priests, the Levites, and all Israel take oath that they would do according to this word. So they took oath. ⁶Then Ezra rose up from before the house of God and went into the chamber of Jehonanan the son of Eliashib, and spent the night there, neither eating[g] bread nor drinking water, for he mourned because of the impiety of those who had returned from the captivity. ⁷And they made proclamation throughout Judah and Jerusalem to all the children of the captivity, that they should gather themselves together at Jerusalem. ⁸And that whoever did not come within three days, according to the counsel of the nobles and the elders, all his possessions should be placed under the ban and he should be excluded from the assembly of the captivity.

---

d 10³ So Luc. I Esdr. 8⁹³, *all are our wives from foreigners.*
e 10³ I Esdr. 8⁹⁴, *your counsel.*
f 10⁴ So I Esdr. 8⁹⁵ and Luc.
g 10⁶ Correcting the corrupt Heb. by I Esdr. 9² and the Gk.

Ezra Narrative

⁹Then all the men of Judah and Benjamin gathered themselves to Jerusalem within the three days, that is on the twentieth day of the ninth month.ʰ And all the people sat in the open space before the house of God, trembling on account of the subject itself and also because of the pouring rain. ¹⁰Then Ezra the priest stood up and said to them, You have committed an act of impiety and have married foreign women to increase the guilt of Israel. ¹¹Now therefore make confession to Jehovah, the God of your fathers, and do his will and separate yourselves from the peoples of the land and from the foreign women. ¹²Then all the assembly answered and said with a loud voice, We must do as you have said concerning us. ¹³But the people are many, and it is a time of the autumn rain, and we cannot stand outside, and this is not a work of one day or two, for we have committed great impiety in this matter. ¹⁴Let now our nobles represent all the assemblyⁱ and let all those in our cities who have married foreign women come at appointed times and with them the elders of each city and its judges, until the fierce wrath of our God because of this matter be turned from us. ¹⁵Only Jonathan the son of Asahel and Jazeiah the son of Tikvah opposed this, and Meshullam and Shabbethai the Levite supported them. ¹⁶But those who had returned from the captivity acted according to the will of the assembly.

And Ezra the priest selected certain heads of fathers' houses according to their fathers' houses, and all of them were named by name;ʲ and they held a sitting on the first day of the tenth monthᵏ to examine the matter. ¹⁷And they completed the investigation of all the men who had married foreign women by the first day of the first month.ˡ

¹⁸And among the sons of the priests who had married foreign women were found the sons of Jeshua the son of Jozadak and his clansmen: Maaseiah, Eliezer, Jarib, and Gedaliah. ¹⁹And they gave their handᵐ that they should put away their wives; and their guilt-offering wasⁿ a ram of the flock for their guilt. ²⁰And of the sons of Immer, Hanani and Zebadiah. ²¹And of the sons of Harim: Maaseiah, Elijah, Shemaiah, Jehiel, and Uzziah. ²²And of the sons of Pashhur: Elioenai, Maaseiah, Ishmael, Nethanel, Jozabad, and Elasah. ²³And of the Levites: Jozabad, Shimei, Kelaiah (the same is Kelita), Pethahiah, Judah, and Eliezer. ²⁴And of the singers: Eliashib and Zaccur.ᵒ And of the porters: Shallum, Telem, and Uri.

²⁵And of Israel: Of the sons of Parosh: Ramiah, Izziah, Malchijah, Mijamin, Eleazar, Michaiahᵖ and Benaiah. ²⁶And of the sons of Elam: Mattaniah, Zechariah, Jehiel, Abdi, Jeremoth, and Elijah. ²⁷And of the sons of Zattu: Elioenai, Eliashib, Mattaniah, Jeremoth, Zabad, and Aziza. ²⁸And

Marginal notes:

Decision of the assembly to appoint a special commission to investigate all cases

Work of the commission

List of the priests and Levites who had foreign wives

Of the laymen

ʰ 10⁹ November-December.
ⁱ 10¹⁴ Correcting the meaningless Heb. by the Gk. and I Esdr. 9¹².
ʲ 10¹⁶ So Luc. and I Esdr. 9¹⁶. Heb., *were separated.*
ᵏ 10¹⁶ December-January.
ˡ 10¹⁷ March-April.
ᵐ 10¹⁹ Cf. II Kgs. 10¹⁵, Is. 17¹⁸, for the same form of compact.
ⁿ 10¹⁹ Slightly correcting the difficult Heb.
ᵒ 10²⁴ Added in the Gk. versions and I Esdr. 9²⁴.
ᵖ 10²⁵ Correcting by the aid of Luc. and I Esdr. 9²⁵.

Ezra Narrative

of the sons of Bebai: Jehohanan, Hananiah, Zabbai, Athlai. ²⁹And of the sons of Bani: Meshullam, Malluch, Adaiah, Jashub, Sheal, and Jeremoth. ³⁰And of the sons of Pahath-moab: Adna, Chelal, Benaiah, Maaseiah, Mattaniah, Bezalel, Binnui, and Manasseh. ³¹And of the sons of Harim: Eliezer, Isshijah, Malchijah, Shemaiah, Shimeon, ³²Benjamin, Malluch, Shemariah. ³³Of the sons of Hashum: Mattenai, Mattattah, Zabad, Eliphelet, Jeremai, Manasseh, Shimei. ³⁴Of the sons of Bani: Maadai, Amram, Joel,�q ³⁵Benaiah, Bedeiah, Cheluhi, ³⁶Vaniah, Meremoth, Eliashib, ³⁷Mattaniah, Mattenai, Jaasu, ³⁸And of the sons of Binnui,ʳ Shimei, ³⁹Shelemiah, Nathan Adaiah, ⁴⁰Machnadebai, Shashai, Sharai, ⁴¹Azarel, Shelemiah, Shemariah, ⁴²Shallum, Amariah, Joseph. ⁴³Of the sons of Nebo: Jeiel, Mattithiah, Zabad, Zebina, Iddo, Joel, Benaiah. ⁴⁴All these had taken foreign wives; and they sent them away with their children.ˢ

§ 163. Public Confession of Guilt, Neh. 9¹⁻³⁷

Ezra Narrative

Confession of the people

Neh. 9 ¹Now in the twenty-fourth day of this month the Israelites were assembled with fasting, and with sackcloth and earth upon their heads. ²And the descendants of Israel had separated themselves from all foreigners, and stood and confessed their sins and the iniquities of their fathers. ³And they stood up in their place and read in the book of the law of Jehovah their God a fourth part of the day; and another fourth part they confessed and worshipped Jehovah their God. ⁴Then the Levites, Jeshua, Bani,ᵗ Kadmiel, Shebaniah, Bunni, Sherebiah, and Chenani stood on the raised pulpit and cried with a loud voice to Jehovah their God. ⁵Also the Levites, Jeshua, Kadmiel, Bani,ᵘ Sherebiah, Hodiah, Shebaniah, and Pethahiah, said, Stand up and bless Jehovah ourᵛ God from everlasting to everlasting; and blessed be thy glorious name, which is exalted above all blessing and praise.

Ezra's prayer: Jehovah's supreme rule and promises to Abraham

⁶And Ezraʷ said, Thou art Jehovah, even thou alone; thou hast made heaven andˣ the heavens of heavens with all their host, the earth and all things that are on it, the seas and all that is in them, and thou preservest them all and the host of heavenª worshippeth thee. ⁷Thou art Jehovah

---

q 10³⁴ So Luc. and I Esdr. 9³⁴.

ʳ 10³⁸ So Gk. and I Esdr. 9³⁴.

ˢ 10⁴⁴ The Heb. is hopelessly corrupt. I Esdr. 9³⁶, which has an intelligible text, has therefore been followed.

§ 163 The long prayer in this chapter, like the one in Ezra 9, consists of quotations and allusions to the incidents recorded in the early and especially the late prophetic narratives of the Pentateuch. The didactic principle derived from the survey of the history is that of the late prophetic editor of Judges. Cf. especially ²⁶⁻²⁸ and Judges 2¹¹⁻¹⁹. The prayer ends abruptly without the direct appeal for a national restoration which is implied by ³². Possibly this was not quoted because, according to the Chronicler's theory, the restoration was already complete.

ᵗ 9⁴ The repetition of, *Bani*, and the variations in the versions indicate that the text has suffered in transmission. Correcting the repetition, seven names, as probably in the original text, remain. Cf. the seven in 8⁷.

ᵘ 9⁵ Omitting, *Hashabniah*, which is apparently only a variant of *Shebaniah*. The list here, as the one in ⁴, has doubtless been modified in transmission. Only part of the names agree, although the context suggests that they were originally identical.

ᵛ 9⁵ So Gk. Heb., *your*.

ʷ 9⁶ So Gk. *Ezra* was perhaps removed from the Heb. text because Lev. 16²¹ commands that the public confession be made by the high-priest.

ˣ 9⁶ So Luc.

ª 9⁶ Cf. Ps. 103²¹.

Ezra Narrative

the God, who didst choose Abraham and bring him forth out of Ur of the
Chaldees, and didst give him the name of Abraham, [8]and find his heart
faithful before thee and make a covenant with him to give the land of the
Canaanites, the Hittites, the Amorites, the Perizzites, the Jebusites, and the
Girgashites,[b] to give it to his descendants, and hast performed thy words,
for thou art righteous.

[9]And thou didst see the affliction of our fathers in Egypt and heard their
cry by the Red Sea,[c] [10]and didst show signs and wonders upon Pharaoh and
upon all his servants, and upon all the people of his land; for thou knewest
that they acted extravagantly toward them; and didst get thee a name as it
is this day.[d] [11]And thou didst divide the sea before them, so that they
went through the midst of the sea on the dry land; and thou didst cast their
pursuers into the depths, as a stone into the mighty waters.[e]

Deliverance of his people from Egypt

[12]Moreover by a pillar of cloud thou leddest them by day, and by a pillar
of fire by night, to give them light by the way in which they should go.[f]
[13]Thou camest down also upon Mount Sinai, and spakest with them from
heaven, and gavest them right ordinances and true laws, good statutes and
commandments,[g] [14]and madest known to them thy holy sabbath, and gavest
them commandments and statutes and a law by Moses thy servant, [15]and
gavest them bread from heaven for their hunger, and broughtest forth water
for them out of the rock for their thirst, and commandest them that they
should go in to possess the land which thou hadst sworn to give them.[h] [16]But
they and our father acted arrogantly and hardened their neck and heeded not
thy commands,[i] [17]and refused to obey, neither were mindful of thy wonders
which thou didst among them, but hardened their neck, and set their head
to return to their bondage in Egypt.[j] But thou wast a God ready to pardon,
gracious and merciful, slow to anger, and of great kindness, and didst not
forsake them. [18]Yea, when they made for themselves a molten calf and
said, This is thy God that brought thee up out of Egypt, and acted very
blasphemously,[k] [19]yet thou in thy great mercy didst not forsake them in
the wilderness; the pillar of cloud departed not from over them by day, to
lead them in the way, nor the pillar of fire by night, to give them light on
the way in which[l] they should go. [20]Thou gavest also thy good spirit to
instruct them, and withheldest not thy manna from their mouth, and gavest
them water for their thirst.[m] [21]Yea, forty years didst thou sustain them

Guidance of them in the wilderness

---

b 9⁸ The late priestly form of the Abraham tradition is here most in evidence. This list,
however, is drawn from the later Judean narratives, Gen. 15⁸⁻²¹.

c 9⁹ Cf. Ex. 3⁷, the Judean narrative.

d 9¹⁰ Cf. Dt. 6²², Ex. 18¹¹, 9¹⁶.

e 9¹¹ Cf. Ex. 14²¹, ²², 15⁵, ¹⁹.

f 9¹² Cf. Ex. 13²¹, ²², Num. 14¹⁴, Dt. 1³³.

g 9¹³ Cf. Ex. 19⁸, ²⁰, Dt. 4³⁶.

h 9¹⁵ Cf. Ex. 16⁴, Num. 20⁸.　For the idiom at the end of the vs. cf. Num. 14³⁰.

i 9¹⁶ Cf. Dt. 1⁴³, 10¹⁶.

j 9¹⁷ Cf. Num. 14⁴. The parallel in Num. confirms the reading, *in Egypt*, of the Gk. as
against the Heb.

k 9¹⁸ Cf. Ex. 32⁴, ⁸.

l 9¹⁹ Omitting with the Gk. the awkward, *and.* Cf. ¹².

m 9²⁰ Cf. Num. 11¹⁷, ²³⁻²⁹.

Ezra Narrative

in the wilderness, and they lacked nothing: their clothes waxed not old, and their feet swelled not.[n]

Con-
quest of
their
land

²²Moreover thou gavest them kingdoms and peoples, which thou didst allot,[o] so they possessed the land[p] of Sihon king of Heshbon, and the land of Og king of Bashan.[q] ²³Thou didst also make their children as numerous as the stars of heaven, and broughtest them into the land concerning which thou didst say to their fathers, that they should go in to possess.[r] ²⁴So the children went in and possessed the land,[s] and thou didst subdue before them the Canaanitish inhabitants of the land, and gavest them into their hands, with their kings and the peoples of the land, that they might do with them what they would. ²⁵And they took fortified cities and a fertile land, and possessed houses full of all good things, cisterns hewn out, vineyards, oliveyards, and fruit-trees in abundance. So they ate and were filled, and became fat

Their
disobe-
dience
and
punish-
ment
in the
period
of the
judges

and lived luxuriantly in thy great goodness.[t] ²⁶Nevertheless they were disobedient and rebelled against thee and cast thy law behind their back and slew thy prophets, who testified against them to turn them again to thee, and they acted very blasphemously. ²⁷Therefore thou didst deliver them into the hands of their oppressors, who oppressed them. Then in the time of their trouble, when they cried to thee, thou heardest from heaven, and according to thy great mercy thou didst give them deliverers who saved them out of the power of their adversaries. ²⁸But as soon as they had rest, they did evil again before thee; therefore thou didst leave them in the hands of their enemies, so that they ruled over them; yet when they again cried to thee, thou didst hear from heaven; and many times didst thou deliver them according to thy mercy, ²⁹and testifiedst against them, that thou mightest bring them to thy law. Yet they acted arrogantly and heeded not thy commands, but sinned against thine ordinances—which if a man obey, he shall live[u]—and turned a stubborn shoulder[v] and stiffened their neck and would not hear. ³⁰Yet many years didst thou bear with them, and testify against them by thy spirit through thy prophets, yet they would not heed. Therefore thou gavest them into the hands of the peoples of the lands. ³¹Nevertheless in thy great mercy thou didst not completely destroy nor forsake them, for thou art a gracious and merciful God.

Peti-
tion to
avert
the
merited
judg-
ment
that
rests
upon
the race

³²Now therefore, our God, the great, the mighty, and the terrible God, who keepest covenant and kindness, let not all the affliction seem little before thee, that hath come on us, on our kings, our nobles, our priests, our prophets, our fathers, and on all thy people, since the days of the kings of Assyria to this day. ³³However thou art just in all that has come upon us; for thou

---

n 9²¹ Cf. Dt. 27, 8⁴, 29⁴.

o 9²² So Gk. The Heb. adds a doubtful, *according to their sides.*

p 9²² So Luc. In the Heb., *the land* was evidently here repeated by mistake.

q 9²² Cf. Num. 21²¹⁻³⁵.

r 9²³ Cf. Gen. 22¹⁷, Dt. 1¹⁰.

s 9²⁴ The first half of the verse is lacking in the Gk. texts and may be a gloss, for it anticipates the following context.

t 9²⁵ Cf. Dt. 6¹⁰, ¹¹, 8⁷⁻⁹, 32¹⁵.

u 9²⁹ So Gk. The Heb. adds, *in them.*

v 9²⁹ Cf. for the same figure, Zech. 7¹¹⁻¹⁴.

Ezra Narrative

hast done right, but we have done wickedly, ³⁴neither have our kings, our
nobles, our priests, nor our fathers, kept thy law nor heeded thy commands
and thy testimonies with which thou didst testify against them. ³⁵For they
have not served thee in the time of their kingly rule, and in spite of thy great
goodness that thou gavest them, they have not turned from their wicked
deeds. ³⁶Behold, we this day are slaves, and as for the land that thou gavest
to our fathers to eat its fruit and enjoy its good gifts, see we are only slaves
in it. ³⁷And it yieldeth a great income to the kings whom thou hast set
over us because of our sin; also they have power over our bodies and over
our cattle, at their pleasure, and we are in great distress.

§ 164. The Covenant and its Terms, Neh. 9³⁸–10³⁹

Ezra Narrative

Neh. 9 ³⁸Moreover in addition to all this we made a fixed covenant and *Signers of the written covenant*
wrote it out, and our nobles, our Levites, and our priests were enrolled upon
the sealed document. **10** ¹And those enrolled upon the sealed documentsʷ were:
Nehemiah, the governor,ˣ the son of Hachaliah, and Zedekiah, ²Seraiah, Azariah, Jeremiah, ³Pashur, Amariah, Malchijah, ⁴Hattush, Shebaniah, Malluch, ⁵Harim, Meremoth, Obadiah, ⁶Daniel, Ginnethon, Baruch, ⁷Meshullam, Abijah, Mijamin, ⁸Maaziah,
Bilgai, Shemaiah; these were the priests. ⁹And the Levites, namely, Jeshua the son
of Azaniah, Binnui of the sons of Henadad, Kadmiel; ¹⁰and their kinsmen, Sheka-
niah,ᵃ Hodaviah,ᵇ Kelita, Pelaiah, Hanan, ¹¹Mica, Rehob, Hashabiah, ¹²Zaccur, Sherebiah, Shebaniah, ¹³Hodijah Bani, Beninu. ¹⁴The chiefs of the people: Parosh, Pahath-
moab, Elam, Zattu, Bani, ¹⁵Bunni, Azgad, Bebai, ¹⁶Adonijah, Bigvai, Adin, ¹⁷Ater,
Hezekiah, Azzur, ¹⁸Hodiah, Hashum, Bezai, ¹⁹Hariph, Anathoth, Nobai, ²⁰Magpiash,
Meshullam, Hezir, ²¹Meshezabel, Zadok, Jaddua, ²²Pelatiah, Hanan, Anaiah, ²³Hoshea,
Hananiah, Hasshub, ²⁴Hallohesh, Pilha, Shobek, ²⁵Rehum, Hashabnah, Maaseiah,
²⁶Ahiah, Hanan, Anan, ²⁷Malluch, Harim, Baanah.
²⁸And the rest of the people, the priests, the Levites, the porters, the singers, the *Regula-tions sub-scribed to by the com-munity*
temple servants, and all those who had separated themselves from the peoples
of the lands to the law of God, their wives, their sons, and their daughters,
every one who had knowledge and insight, ²⁹strongly supported their kinsmen,
their nobles, and entered into a solemn obligation and took oath to walk in
God's law, which was given by Moses the servant of God, and to observe and

---

§ 164 That the list in 10¹⁻²⁸ᵃ is not from the same hand as the rest of the chapter is shown
by the order, *Levites, priests,* in 9³⁸, while in 10¹⁻²⁸ᵃ the priests are placed first; in 9³⁸ *sealed document,* but in 10¹ *sealed documents.* Also in 10¹ Nehemiah the governor appears (cf. § 161, note),
indicating that this section was probably added by the editor. A comparison of the list of the
priests with that of the high-priests before Jeshua in 12¹⁻⁷ reveals not only the same number—
twenty-two—but also many of the same names, only arranged in different order, which is further
evidence that this is from the Chronicler whose interest in names and lists is frequently illustrated
in Ezra-Neh. In ²⁸ᵃ his favorites, *the porters, the singers, and the temple servants* also appear.
The close parallelism between Nehemiah's reforms recorded in 13 and the terms of the
covenant, as here stated, has already been noted (Introd., p. 31). The language and point of
view (cf. especially ²⁸ᵇ, ²⁹) of this section are those of the Ezra narratives to which it forms a
natural conclusion. Its importance is great, for it marks the acceptance of the late priestly
law by the Judean community. Five out of its eight regulations were based on that code and
were new to the Jews who still held to the late prophetic code found in Dt.
ʷ 10¹ Possibly this should be changed to the singular to conform with 9³⁸. Two or more
copies may, however, have been made, as among the Babylonians in the case of all important
business documents.
ˣ 10¹ The title is not found in the Gk. and separates the name and the patronymic in an
unprecedented manner, strongly suggesting that it is a later addition.
ᵃ 10¹⁰ So Luc. The *Shebaniah* of the Heb. appears in ¹².
ᵇ 10¹⁰ So Gk. Cf. Ezra 2⁴⁰. The *Hodiah* of the Heb. also appears in ¹³.

Ezra Narrative

do all the commands of Jehovah our Lord, and his ordinances and his statutes;
[30]and that we would neither give our daughters to the peoples of the land nor
take their daughters as wives for our sons;[c] [31]and that, if the peoples of the
land should bring wares or any grain on the sabbath day to sell, we would
not buy of them on the sabbath or on a holy day;[d] and that on the seventh
year we would leave the land uncultivated and would refrain from the ex-
action of any debt.[e]

Obligations assumed for the support of the temple and ritual

[32]We also imposed upon ourselves the obligation to give yearly the third
part of a shekel for the service of the house of our God,[f] [33]for the bread
that was set forth,[g] and for the continual burnt-offering,[h] for the sabbaths,
the new moons, the fixed feasts,[i] and the holy things,[j] and for the sin-offerings to make atonement for Israel,[k] and for all the work of the house of our
God.[l] [34]And we cast lots, the priests, the Levites, and the people, for the
wood-offering, to bring it into the house of our God, according to our father's
houses, at appointed times year by year, to burn upon the altar of Jehovah
our God, as it is prescribed in the law;[m] [35]and to bring the earliest products
of our ground, and the first of all fruit of every kind of tree year by year,
to the temple of Jehovah;[n] [36]also the first-born of our sons and of our cattle,
as is prescribed in the law, and the firstlings of our herds and of our flocks,[o]
to bring to the house of God to the priests who minister in the house of our
God; [37]and that we should bring the first[p] bread baked of our dough,[q]
our gifts,[r] the fruit of every kind of tree, the new wine and the oil,[s] to the
priests, in the chambers of the house of our God;[t] and the tithes of our ground
to the Levites; and that they, the Levites, should receive the tithes in all the
cities of our agricultural districts. [38]And that the priest the son of Aaron
should be with the Levites, when the Levites shall bring up the tithe of the
tithes to the house of our God, to the chambers, into the store-house.[u] [39]For
the Israelites and the sons of Levi shall bring the gifts of grain, of new wine,
and of oil, into the chambers,[v] where are the vessels of the sanctuary, and
the priests who minister and the porters and the singers, and that we would
not neglect the house of our God.

---

[c] 10^{30} Cf. 13^{23} and Ezra 9^{2} and Ex. 34^{6}, Dt. 7^{3}.
[d] 10^{31} Cf. 13^{15-22}, Lev. 23^{3}.
[e] 10^{31} Cf. 5, Ex. $23^{10, 11}$, Dt. 15^{1-3}.
[f] 10^{32} Cf. II Chr. 24^{6-9}, Ex. 30^{11-16}.
[g] 10^{33} Lit., *the bread that was laid in rows* or *piled up*. Cf. Lev. 24^{5-9}.
[h] 10^{33} Cf. Ezra 9^{4}, Ex. 29^{38-42}, Num. 28^{3-8}.
[i] 10^{33} Cf. Num. 28.
[j] 10^{33} Cf. II Chr. 29^{33}, 35^{13}.
[k] 10^{33} Cf. Lev. 4^{13-21}.
[l] 10^{33} Cf. II Chr. 24^{6}.
[m] 10^{34} Cf. 13^{31}. The law referred to is not found in the O.T., but in the Mishnah, *Taanit* 4^{5}. Cf. Jos., *Jewish Wars*, II, 17^{6}.
[n] 10^{35} Cf. Ex. 23^{19}, 34^{26}, Num. $18^{12, 13}$.
[o] 10^{36} Cf. Num. 18^{15-18}, Ex. 13^{13}, 34^{20}.
[p] 10^{37} Or, *best*.
[q] 10^{37} Cf. Num. 15^{20-21}, Dt. $18^{4, 5}$, 26^{1-7}.
[r] 10^{37} Lacking in the Gk. It fits badly in its context and is probably a later addition.
[s] 10^{37} Cf. 13^{5}.
[t] 10^{37} Cf. 13^{12}, Dt. 26^{1-11}.
[u] $10^{37b, 38}$ This may be a later addition. Cf. Num. $18^{21, 24-28}$.
[v] 10^{39} Cf. 13^{12}.

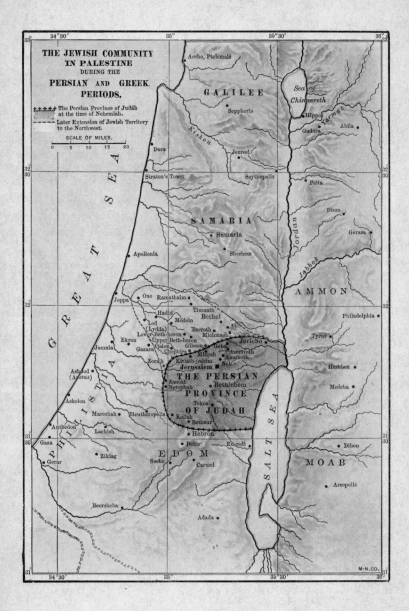

THE JEWISH COMMUNITY
IN PALESTINE
DURING THE
PERSIAN AND GREEK
PERIODS.

+++++ The Persian Province of Judâh
at the time of Nehemiah.
------ Later Extension of Jewish Territory
to the Northwest.

SCALE OF MILES.
0   5   10   15   20

34°30'   35°   35°30'   36°

33   33

Accho, Ptolemais

GALILEE   Sea of
                    Chinnereth

Sephphoris   Hippos
                    Gadara   Abila

Kishon

Jezreel

Dora

32   32
30   30

Straton's Tower   Scythopolis   Pella

SAMARIA   Dium

Samaria   Gerasa

Shechem

Apollonia   Jabbok

32   AMMON   32

Joppa   Ono Ramathaim   Philadelphia

        Hadid   Timnath
        Lod   Modein Bethel   Tyrus
        (Lydda)   Beëroth
Ekron Lower Beth-horon Michmash   Heshbon
        Upper Beth-horon Gibeon Ai
Jamnia Gazara Ajalon Chephirah Jericho
        Zorah Mizpah Anathoth   Medeba
            Kiriath-jearim Nob
            Jerusalem

Ashdod   THE PERSIAN
(Azotus)   Zanoah Bethlehem
            Netophah   PROVINCE
Askelon   OF JUDAH
        Mareshah Eleutheropolis Tekoa
Anthedon   Lachish Keilah Beth-zur
                    Hebron
31   31
30   30
Gaza   Debir'   En-gedi   Dibon

Gerar   Ziklag   EDOM
                Socho   Carmel   MOAB

                                Areopolis

Beersheba

                Adada

M-N.CO.
31   31

34°30'   35°   35°30'   36°

GREAT SEA

PHILISTIA

Jordan

Yarmuk

SALT SEA

IV

ORGANIZATION OF THE RESTORED JUDEAN COMMUNITY,
Ezra 2[1-67], Neh. 7[6-69], 11[3]–12[26]

§ 165. **Census of the Jews in Palestine, Ezra 2[1-67], Neh. 7[6-69] (I Esdr. 5[7-43])**

Chronicler's Ecclesiastical History

Neh. 7 [6]These are the children of the province, who went up out of the The captivity of those who had been carried away, whom Nebuchadnezzar the king of Babylon had carried away to Babylon,[a] and who returned to Jerusalem and Judah, each to his city, [7]who came with Zerubbabel, Jeshua, Nehemiah, Azariah,[b] Raamiah,[c] Nahamani, Mordecai, Bilshan, Mispereth, Bigvai, Rehum,[d] Baanah.[e]

Organization of the Restored Judean Community.—Regarding the history of the Judean community during the last decades of the Persian period the biblical and extra-canonical sources furnish little information. The period appears to have witnessed the expansion of the territory of Judah. This is indicated by a comparison of the comparatively few villages represented by the builders who worked under Nehemiah (Neh. 3), and the lists of Jewish towns in Neh. 7[25-37] and 11[25-35]. The extension was chiefly toward the northwest. Cf. map on the opp. page. Although he stood near enough the events to have written a continuous history on the basis of current information, the Chronicler, guided by his peculiar interests, contents himself with compiling certain lists in which the ideas and traditional claims of the coterie to which he belonged receive especial attention.

§ 165 Nehemiah's statement in Neh. 7[4] that the inhabitants of Jerusalem were few and that he gathered them together apparently gave the Chronicler an opportunity to bring in one of his long genealogical lists. This characteristic tendency has been often illustrated, but perhaps here most strikingly, by the fact that he has introduced the same list in Ezra 2, modifying the concluding words of Neh. 7 in order to fit the different context. Cf. note § 145. He also joins it closely to Nehemiah's memoirs by adding to Nehemiah's statement in [5] that he gathered together the rulers and people (evidently to devise means for increasing the population of Jerusalem), *that they might be reckoned by genealogy. And I found the book of the genealogy of those who came up at the first, and I found written therein:* Then follow the lists. The Heb. word, as well as the idea of reckoning by genealogy, is characteristic of the Chronicler, but not of Nehemiah. The latter also knows nothing of those who came up at the first, while it is one of the leading beliefs of the Chronicler. Cf. Introd., p. 29. Similarly [6, 7] reveal the stamp of the editor and his school. Cf. [6], Ezra 1, 3[8], 6[21], Neh. 11[3]. The exactly twelve leaders in [7] suggest one of his favorite numbers. The concluding section, [61-69], also has several of his characteristic idioms. The method of writing compound numerals in the list is also confined to very late Heb. writings. It is probable that the editor had older lists before him. He purports to give a list of those who returned from Babylon, but such names as the *children of Pahath (governor of) Moab* and the census of the inhabitants of the Judean villages, [25-37], by no means support this implication. On the other hand, the long lists of Levites, porters, singers, temple servants, and Solomon's servants in [43-60] were probably added by him.

The date of this census has been much discussed and is the most important problem connected with the chapter. It is obvious that the position of those who maintain that because of its position in Ezra 2 it represents those who returned in 536 B.C. is untenable. It was placed there simply to support the theory of the Chronicler or possibly that of some still later editor. The evidence of the list of towns in [25-37] points conclusively to the latter part of the Persian period, when, according to the testimony of I Mac. 9[50] and Josephus (*Ant.*, XIII, 1[3]), Judah included Bethel, Bethhoron and Timnath-Parathon. Likewise in the list of leaders *Nehemiah*, and probably originally *Ezra* (cf. note [b]), stood near the head and are followed by the names (some of Persian origin) of later leaders who, following in the wake of Nehemiah's work, probably led back other bands of Jews. Also the large numbers of the *children of Jeshua*, the contemporary of Zerubbabel, and the prominence of the different classes of the temple ministers, all point to a period not long before that of the Chronicler.

[a] 7[6] So Ezra 2[1] and I Esdr. 5[7].
[b] 7[7] Ezra 2[2], *Seraiah.* Cf. Ezra 7[1], where Seraiah is the father of Ezra. After Nehemiah we expect, *Ezra,* and the variant suggests that he was in the mind of the Chronicler. In the Heb., *Azariah* is only slightly different from *Ezra.*
[c] 7[7] Ezra 2[2], *Reelaiah.*
[d] 7[7] So Ezra 2[2] and I Esdr. 5[8].
[e] 7[7] I Esdr. 5[8] adds, *their leaders.*

Chronicler's Ecclesiastical History

THE NUMBER OF MEN OF THE PEOPLE OF ISRAEL

Lay
clans

⁸The children of Parosh, two thousand a hundred and seventy-two. ⁹The children of Shephatiah, three hundred and seventy-two. ¹⁰The children of Arah, six hundred and fifty-two. ¹¹The children of Jeshua and Joab, two thousand eight hundred and eighteen. ¹²The children of Elam, a thousand two hundred and fifty-four. ¹³The children of Zattu, eight hundred and forty-five. ¹⁴The children of Zaccai, seven hundred and sixty. ¹⁵The children of Binnui, six hundred and forty-eight. ¹⁶The children of Bebai, six hundred and twenty-eight. ¹⁷The children of Azgad, two thousand three hundred and twenty-two. ¹⁸The children of Adonikam, six hundred and sixty-seven. ¹⁹The children of Bigvai, two thousand and sixty-seven. ²⁰The children of Adin, six hundred and fifty-five. ²¹The children of Ater, of Hezekiah, ninety-eight. The children of Azzur, four hundred and thirty-two. The children of Hananiah, a hundred and one.ᶠ ²²The children of Hashum, three hundred and twenty-eight.ᵍ ²³The children of Bezai, three hundred and twenty-four. ²⁴The children of Hariph, a hundred and twelve. ³³The childrenʰ of Nebo,ⁱ fifty-two. ³⁴The children of the other Elam, a thousand two hundred and fifty-four. ³⁵The children of Harim, three hundred and twenty. ³⁸The children of Senaah, three thousand nine hundred and thirty.

Inhabi-
tants
of the
differ-
ent
towns

²⁵The menʲ of Gibeon,ᵏ ninety-five. ²⁶The men of Bethlehem and Netophah, a hundred and eighty-eight. ²⁷The men of Anathoth, a hundred and twenty-eight. ²⁸The men of Beth-azmaveth, forty-two. ²⁹The men of Kiriath-jearim, Chephirah, and Beeroth, seven hundred and forty-three. The men of Adasa and Modin, four hundred and twenty-two.ˡ ³⁰The men of Ramah and Geba, six hundred and twenty-one. ³¹The men of Michmas, a hundred and twenty-two. ³²The men of Bethel and Ai, a hundred and twenty-three. ³⁶The menᵐ of Jericho, three hundred and forty-five. The men of Keilah and Azekah, sixty-seven.ⁿ ³⁷The menᵐ of Lod, Hadid, and Ono, seven hundred and twenty-one.

Priestly
clans

³⁹The priests: The children of Jedaiah, of the house of Jeshua, nine hundred and seventy-three. ⁴⁰The children of Immer, a thousand and fifty-two. ⁴¹The children of Pashur, a thousand two hundred and forty-seven. ⁴²The children of Harim, a thousand and seventeen.

Leviti-
cal
clans

⁴³The Levites: The children of Jeshua, namely of Kadmiel, of Benui,ᵒ of Hodevah, seventy-four. ⁴⁴The singers: The children of Asaph, a hundred

---

ᶠ 7²¹ The last two clans are found only in I Esdr. 5¹⁵, ¹⁶. They have evidently been lost from the Heb. in transmission. Cf. Neh. 10¹⁸, ²³.
ᵍ 7²² The order in Ezra is here different.
ʰ 7³³ The original list probably gave the clans first, then the inhabitants of the different towns, and then the groups of temple ministers. This order has been restored.
ⁱ 7³³ So Ezra 2²⁹, which also omits, *other*, before Nebo.
ʲ 7²⁵ So I Esdr. 5¹⁷, supported by the context. Heb., *children*.
ᵏ 7²⁵ I Esdr. 5¹⁷, *Bether*. Cf. Josh. 15²⁹, I Chr. 6⁵⁹ (Gk.). This may be original.
ˡ 7²⁹ I Esdr. 5²⁰ inserts this last group. The exact form and identification of the names cannot be determined. The first may be identified with the place mentioned in Josh. 15³⁷ and I Mac. 7⁴⁰.
ᵐ 7³⁶, ³⁷ So I Esdr. 5²². Heb., *children*.
ⁿ 7³⁶ The last group is found in I Esdr. 5¹⁵.
ᵒ 7⁴³ So I Esdr. 5²⁶.

Chronicler's Ecclesiastical History

and forty-eight. 45The porters: The children of Shallum, the children of
Ater, the children of Talmon, the children of Akkub, the children of Hatita,
the children of Shobai, a hundred and thirty-eight.

Temple-slaves

46The temple servants: The children of Ziha, the children of Hasupa, the
children of Tabbaoth, 47the children of Keros, the children of Sia, the chil-
dren of Padon, 48the children of Lebana, the children of Hagaba, the chil-
dren of Akkub,[p] the children of Salmai, 49the children of Hanan, the
children of Giddel, the children of Gahar, 50the children of Reaiah, the
children of Rezin, the children of Nekoda, 51the children of Gazzam, the
children of Uzza, the children of Paseah, 52the children of Besai, the children
of Asnah,[q] the children of Menunim, the children of Nephsheisim, 53the
children of Bakbuk, the children of Hakupha, the children of Harhur,
54the children of Bazlith, the children of Mehida, the children of Harsha,
55the children of Barkos, the children of Sisera, the children of Temah,
56the children of Neziah, the children of Hatipha.

Clans of Solomon's servants

57The children of Solomon's servants: The children of Sotai, the children
of Sophereth, the children of Perida, 58the children of Jaala, the children of
Darkon, the children of Giddel, 59the children of Shephatiah, the children
of Hattil, the children of Pochereth-hazzebaim, the children of Amon.[r]
60All the temple servants and the children of Solomon's servants were three
hundred and ninety-two.

Clans unable to establish their genealogy

61And these were they who went up from Tel-melah and Tel-harsha:
Cherub,[s] Addon, and Immer; but they could not show their fathers' houses
nor their descent, whether they were of Israel. 62The children of Delaiah,
the children of Tobiah, the children of Nekoda, six hundred and forty-two.
63And of the priests: The children of Hobaiah, the children of Hakkoz,
the children of Barzillai, who took a wife of the daughters of Barzillai the
Gileadite, and was called by their name. 64These sought their register
among those who were reckoned by genealogy, but it was not found; therefore they were excluded from the priesthood, as unclean. 65And the governor commanded them not to eat of the most holy things, until a priest stood
up with the Urim and Thummim.

Total number of persons and animals

66The whole assembly together was forty-two thousand three hundred
and sixty,[t] 67besides their male and female slaves, of whom there were seven
thousand three hundred and thirty-seven. And they had two hundred and
forty-five singing men and singing women. 68Their horses were seven
hundred and thirty-six; their mules, two hundred and forty-five;[u] 69their[v]
camels, four hundred and thirty-five; their[v] asses, six thousand seven hundred
and twenty.

---

[p] 7[48] Supplied from Ezra 2[45].
[q] 7[52] Supplied from Ezra 2[50]. I Esdr. 5[30-32] has a still larger list than Neh. or Ezra.
[r] 7[59] I Esdr. 5[34] adds eight more names, but they cannot all be identified.
[s] 7[61] So I Esdr. 5[36], which adds, *whose leader was Cherub.*
[t] 7[66] I Esdr. 5[41] adds, perhaps preserving in full the original, *Israelites twelve years old and over, apart from the male and female slaves.*
[u] 7[68] This verse is lacking in the standard text and was not reckoned by the Massorites as one of the verses of the book. It and [69], which resembles it, were probably later additions to the list.
[v] 7[69] Adding, *their*, from Ezra 2[67].

§ 166. Population of Jerusalem and the Villages, Neh. 11³⁻³⁶ (cf. I Chr. 9⁴⁻¹⁷)

Chronicler's Ecclesiastical History

Inhabitants of Jerusalem: the Judahites

Neh. 11 ³Now these are the chiefs of the province who dwelt in Jerusalem; but in the cities of Judah every man dwelt in his possession in their cities: Israel, the priests, the Levites, the temple servants, and the children of Solomon's servants. ⁴And in Jerusalem dwelt certain of the children of Judah and of the children of Benjamin. Of the children of Judah: Athaiah the son of Uzziah, the son of Zechariah, the son of Amariah, the son of Shephathiah, the son of Mahalalel, of the children of Perez. ⁶All the sons of Perez who dwelt in Jerusalem were four hundred and sixty-eight valiant men.ʷ And of the sons of Zerah: Jeual and their clansmen, six hundred and ninety.ˣ ⁵And Maaseiah the son of Baruch, the son of Col-hozeh, the son of Hazaiah, the son of Adaiah, the son of Joiarib, the son of Zechariah, the son of the Shelanite.

The Benjamites

⁷And these are the sons of Benjamin: Sallu the son of Meshullam, the son of Joed, the son of Pedaiah, the son of Kolaiah, the son of Maaseiah, the son of Ithiel, the son of Jeshaiah.ᵃ ⁸And his clansmenᵇ were mighty warriors,ᶜ nine hundred and twenty-eight. ⁹And Joel the son of Zichri was appointed over them; and Judah the son of Hassenuah was second in charge of the city.

The priests

¹⁰Of the priests: Jedaiah, Joiarib,ᵈ Jachin, ¹¹and Seraiah the son of Hilkiah, the son of Zadok, the son of Meraioth, the son of Ahitub, the ruler of the house of God, ¹²and their clansmen who did the work of the house, eight hundred and twenty-two; and Adaiah the son of Jeroboam, the son of Pelaliah, the son of Amzi, the son of Zechariah, the son of Pashhur, the son of Malchijah, ¹³and his clansmen, chiefs of fathers' houses, two hundred and forty-two; and Amasai the son of Azarel, the son of Ahzai, the son of Meshillemoth, the son of Immer, ¹⁴and hisᵉ clansmen, mighty warriors, a hundred and twenty-eight; and Zabdiel the son of Haggedolim was appointed over them.

The Levites

¹⁵And of the Levites: Shemaiah the son of Hasshub, the son of Azrikam, the son of Hashabiah, the son of Bunni; ¹⁶and Shabbethai and Jozabad, of the chiefs of the Levites, who had the oversight of the outside work of the house of God; ¹⁷and Mattaniah the son of Mica, the son of Zikri,ᶠ the son of Asaph, who was the leader of the songs of praise, and Bakbukiah was the

---

§ 166 In this section the awkward literary style, the peculiar themes and the prominence of the Levites, the porters, the singers, the temple servants and the children of Solomon's servants, who figure in the Chronicler's other writings, are all in evidence. He has introduced practically the same list in I Chr. 9⁴⁻¹⁷. It is probable that it largely originated with him. It is instructive chiefly as it illustrates the organization of the community which gathered about the temple in the days of the Chronicler and in the half-century immediately preceding.

ʷ 11⁶ Evidently this verse was transposed by mistake.

ˣ 11⁶ Filling in the obvious hiatus from I Chr. 9⁵, ⁶.

ᵃ 11⁷, ⁸ A comparison with the parallel in I Chr. 9⁷, ⁹ indicates that the list is here incomplete.

ᵇ 11⁸ So Luc. and the analogies ¹², ¹³, ¹⁴ and I Chr. 9⁶.

ᶜ 11⁸ The Heb., *Gabbai Sallai*, is due to the corruption of the Heb. words for *mighty warriors.* Cf. ¹⁴.

ᵈ 11¹⁰ So I Chr. 9¹⁰.

ᵉ 11¹⁴ So Gk.

ᶠ 11¹⁷ So Gk. and Lat.

Chronicler's Ecclesiastical History

second among his clansmen; and Abda the son of Shammua, the son of Galal, the son of Jeduthun. ¹⁸All the Levites in the holy city were two hundred and eighty-four.

¹⁹Moreover the porters, Akkub, Talmon, and their kinsmen, who kept watch at the gates, were a hundred and seventy-two. ²¹But the temple servants dwelt in Ophel; and Ziha and Gishpa were over the temple servants. The porters

²²The one appointed over the Levites at Jerusalem was Uzzi the son of Bani, the son of Hashabiah, the son of Mattaniah, the son of Mica, of the sons of Asaph, the singers, over the work of the house of God. ²³For there was a command^g from the king concerning them, and a settled provision for the singers, as each day required. ²⁴And Pethahiah the son of Meshezebel, of the children of Zerah the son of Judah, advised the king^h in all matters concerning the people. Officials appointed by the king

²⁰And the rest of Israel, of the priests, the Levites, were in all the cities of Judah, each in his inheritance. ²⁵And as to the estatesⁱ with their fields, some of the children of Judah dwelt in Kiriath-arba and its dependent villages, in Dibon and its dependent villages, in Jekabzeel and its estates, ²⁶in Jeshua, in Moladah, in Beth-pelet, ²⁷in Hazar-shual, and in Beersheba and its dependent villages, ²⁹in En-rimmon, in Zorah, in Jarmuth, ³⁰Zanoah, Adullam and their estates, Lachish and its fields, Azekah and its dependent villages. So they had their places of temporary abode from Beersheba to the valley of Hinnom. ³¹The children of Benjamin also dwelt at Geba, Michmash, Aija, Bethel, and its dependent villages, ³²at Anathoth, Nob, Ananiah, ³³Hazor, Ramah, Gittaim, ³⁴Hadid, Zeboim, Neballat, ³⁵Lod, and Ono, the valley of the craftsmen. ³⁶And of the Levites, certain divisions in Judah were joined to Benjamin. Inhabitants of the other cities and villages of Palestine

§ 167. Genealogy of the Priests and Levites, Neh. 12¹⁻²⁶

Chronicler's Ecclesiastical History

Neh. 12 ¹Now these are the priests and the Levites who went up with Zerubbabel the son of Shealtiel and Jeshua, Seraiah, Jeremiah, Ezra, ²Amariah, Malluch, Hattush, ³Shecaniah, Harim,^j Meremoth, ⁴Iddo, Ginnethon,^k Abijah, ⁵Mijamin, Maaziah,^l Bilgah, ⁶Shemaiah, and Joiarib, Jedaiah, Heads of the priestly clans

---

^g 11²³ Probably a reference to the decree of Cyrus which comes from the Chronicler and is preserved in I Esdr. 4⁵⁵.   Cf. § 144.
   ^h 11²⁴ Heb., *was at the king's hand.* Cf. I Chr. 18¹⁷.
   ⁱ 11²⁵ Cf. Lev. 25³¹.
   § 167 The difficulties of this section are baffling. In ¹⁻⁶ the names, which have already been assigned by the Chronicler in 10²⁻⁸ to the days of Ezra, are connected with the return under Zerubbabel. These again recur in 12⁻²¹ with many variations; but there they are assigned to the generation immediately following the return under Cyrus. In ¹⁰, ¹¹ the Chronicler gives what appears to be an authentic list of the high-priests of the Persian period. It is probable that these verses and also the names of the Levites were derived from the *Book of the Chronicles* to which he refers in ²³.   Otherwise the rest of the section seems to be from the editor.
   ^j 12³ Cf. ¹⁵ and 10⁵.
   ^k 12⁴ Cf. ¹⁶ and 10⁶.
   ^l 12⁵ Cf. 10⁸ Heb., *Maadiah.* ¹⁷ *Moadiah.*

Chronicler's Ecclesiastical History

[7]Sallu, Amok, Hilkiah, Jedaiah.[m] These were the chiefs of the priests and of
their clansmen in the days of Jeshua.

Heads of the levitical clans

[8]Moreover the Levites: Jeshua, Binnui, Kadmiel, Sherebiah, Judah, and
Mattaniah, he and his clansmen were in charge of the thanksgiving. [9]Also
Bakbukiah and Unno,[n] their brethren, stood over against them in performing
the duties of their office.

High-priests in the Persian period

[10]And Jeshua begat Joiakim, and Joiakim begat Eliashib, and Eliashib
begat Joiada, [11]and Joiada begat Johanan,[o] and Johanan begat Jaddua.

Heads of the priestly fathers' houses

[12]And in the days of Joiakim, the priests, the heads of fathers' houses:
of Seraiah, Meraiah, of Jeremiah, Hananiah; [13]of Ezra, Meshullam; of
Amariah, Jehohanan; [14]of Malluch,[p] Jonathan; of Shecaniah,[q] Joseph; [15]of
Harim, Adna; of Meremoth,[r] Helkai; [16]of Iddo, Zechariah; of Ginnethon,
Meshullam; [17]of Abijah, Zichri; of Miniamin, of Maadiah, Piltai; [18]of
Bilgah, Shammua; of Shemaiah, Jehonathan; [19]and of Joiarib, Mattenai;
of Jedaiah, Uzzi; [20]of Sallu,[s] Kallai; of Amok, Eber; [21]of Hilkiah, Hasha-
biah; of Jedaiah, Nethanel.

Heads of the levitical fathers' houses

[22]Of the Levites, in the days of Eliashib, Joiada, Johanan, and Jaddua,
were recorded the heads of the fathers' houses; also the priests until[t] the reign
of Darius the Persian.[u] [23]The sons of Levi, heads of fathers' houses, were
written in the Book of the Chronicles, even until the days of Johanan the
son of Eliashib. [24]And the chiefs of the Levites: Hashabiah, Sherebiah,
Jeshua, Bennui, and Kadmiel[v] with their clansmen Mattaniah, and Bakbukiah, Obadiah[w] over against them, to praise and give thanks, according
to the command of David the man of God, one division following another.
[25]Meshullam, Talmon, and Akkub, the porters, kept watch over the store-
rooms at the gates. [26]These were in the days of Joiakim the son of Jeshua,
the son of Jozadak, and in the days of Nehemiah the governor, and of Ezra
the priest, the scribe.

---

[m] 12[7] This is found also in [6], but cf. [19-21]. The second may be for Adajah, 11[2], I Chr. 9[12].
[n] 12[9] Wanting in Gk. and Luc. Also in the margin of the Heb. the second name is interpreted as a verb.
[o] 12[11] So [22, 23] and Jos., *Ant.*, XI, 7[1]. Heb., *Jonathan*.
[p] 12[14] So [2].
[q] 12[14] So Gk. and Luc. and [3]. According to [2] *Hattush* has here dropped out.
[r] 12[15] So Luc. and [3].
[s] 12[20] So [7].
[t] 12[22] The verse is obscure. A slight correction supported by the Gk. and Lat. gives the above intelligible reading.
[u] 12[22] Darius II, 335–332 B.C., the last king of Persia.
[v] 12[24] Slightly correcting the text with the aid of Gk. and Luc.
[w] 12[24] According to 11[17] the first three names of [25] in the Heb. are to be connected with [24].

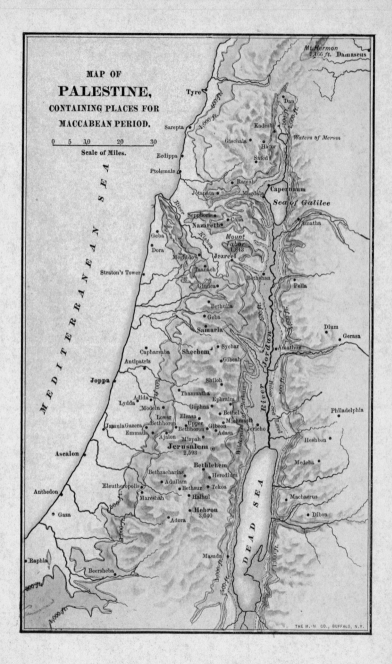

MAP OF
PALESTINE,
CONTAINING PLACES FOR
MACCABEAN PERIOD.

0   5   10   20   30

Scale of Miles.

THE M·N CO., BUFFALO, N.Y.

THE MACCABEAN STRUGGLE

I AND II MACCABEES

THE MACCABEAN STRUGGLE

I

CAUSES OF THE MACCABEAN STRUGGLE, I Mac. 1

§ 168. Alexander the Great and his Successors, I Mac. 1[1-9]

History of the Hasmoneans

I Mac. 1 [1]Now after Alexander the Macedonian, the son of Philip, who Alex-
came from the land of Chittim,[a] had smitten Darius king of the Persians ander's
and Medes, he reigned in his place as the first ruler of the Syrian kingdom.[b] conquests

> [2]He fought many battles,
> And won many strongholds,
> And slew the kings of the earth;[c]
> [3]He went on to the ends of the earth;
> And took spoils from a multitude of nations.
> [4]And when the earth was at peace before him,
> He was exalted and his heart was lifted up;
> He gathered an army exceeding great,
> And ruled over countries and peoples and principalities;
> And they became tributary to him.

[5]Thereupon he fell sick, and when he perceived that he should die, [6]he Divis-
called his most distinguished servants, who had been brought up with him ion
from boyhood; and while he was yet alive, he divided his kingdom among of his empire
them.[d] [7]So Alexander after he had reigned twelve years died. [8]Then after
his
death

Causes of the Maccabean Struggle.—In 198 B.C. Judea passed finally under the control of the Syrian kingdom, with its capital at Antioch. The fusion of Greek and oriental civilizations, which resulted from Alexander's conquests, contained the baser and more degenerate element of both. Luxury, greed, duplicity, and immorality ruled at Antioch and exerted their pernicious influence throughout the kingdom. Its different kings, involved in almost constant wars, compelled after 190 B.C. to pay a heavy annual tribute to Rome, and ambitious to maintain a splendid court, drained the resources of their realm. On the other hand, the Jews were already hated because of their peculiar religious ideas, their exclusive institutions, and their higher morals and superior business ability, which had brought, especially to those of the dispersion, great wealth. As I and II Mac. clearly declare, the Jews were also betrayed by the apostasy and greed of certain of their leaders. Greek ideas and culture were beginning to undermine Judaism. The despotic policy of Antiochus Epiphanes and the immediate events that precipitated the crisis brought the Jewish race its supreme crisis, but also saved it in the end from the deadlier danger of being absorbed by Hellenism. For the analysis and history of I and II Mac., cf. Introd., pp. 35–40.

§ 168 This brief section connects the conquests of Alexander in 333–332 B.C. with the struggle which began a century and a half later.

[a] 1[1] Cf. Jer. 2[10], Ezek. 27[6], the Mediterranean islands and coast lands.

[b] 1[1] Following what was probably the Heb. original. *Hellas* here represents the Syrian kingdom. Cf. 1[10], Dan. 8[21], 10[20], 11[3], and Torrey in Jour. AOS., XXV, pp. 302–311.

[c] 1[2] As in the earlier historical books and elsewhere in I Mac., the author evidently here either quotes from older poems or epics, which recounted the events which he was recording, or else he himself adopts the poetic form.

[d] 1[6] The popular tradition that he divided his empire among his followers before his death was widely circulated, probably by his successors, to substantiate their titles, but it has no historical support.

History of the Hasmoneans

his servants ruled each in his place. ⁹After his death they all put on diadems, and so did their sons after them many years; and they multiplied evils in the earth.

§ 169. Seleucus's Futile Attempt to Rob the Temple, II Mac. 3

Traditional History of the Maccabean Struggle

Simon's malicious report regarding the great wealth in the temple

II Mac. 3 ¹While the holy city lay in perfect peace, and the laws were very well kept because of the piety of Onias the high priest and because of his hatred of wickedness, ²even the kings themselves honored the place, and glorified the temple with the most valuable presents; ³so that even Seleucus the king of Asia from his own revenues bore all the expenses connected with the sacrificial services. ⁴But a certain Simon of the tribe of Benjamin, having been made guardian of the temple, disagreed with the high priest about the management of the city market. ⁵And since he could not overcome Onias, he went to Apollonius the son of Thraseus,ᵉ who at that time was governor of Cœlesyria and Phœnicia; ⁶and reported that the treasury in Jerusalem was so full of untold sums of money, that the amount of the funds was countless, not including the account of the sacrifices, and that it was possible that these should fall into the king's power. ⁷When Apollonius met the king, he informed him of the money of which he had been told; and [the king] appointed Heliodorus his prime minister, and sent him with orders to effect the removal of the aforesaid money. ⁸So Heliodorus at once set out on the journey, ostensibly to visit the cities of Cœlesyria and Phœnicia, but in reality to accomplish the king's purpose.

Heliodorus's demand that the money be given up to the king

⁹When he had arrived at Jerusalem, and had been courteously received by the high priest andᶠ the city, he presented the information which had been given him, and explained why he had come. He also inquired if these things were indeed so. ¹⁰Then the high priest showed him that the money represented the deposits of widows and orphans, ¹¹and also some belonging to Hyrcanus the son of Tobias, a man in very high position, and that it was not as that impious Simon falsely alleged, and that in all there were four hun-

---

§ 169 This story has evidently been greatly expanded and embellished in transmission, but it is probable that there are historical facts at its basis. This probability is strengthened by the discovery of the name of Heliodorus, *who was brought up with King Seleucus Philopater and was prime-minister* (lit., *appointed over the affairs* as in ⁷), on the base of a statue dedicated to Apollo by certain Phœnician shipmasters. Cf. Deissmann, *Bibelstudien*, pp. 173–5. In 187 B.C. Seleucus's predecessor, Antiochus the Great, met his death, according to tradition, while plundering the temple of Elymais. The growing weakness of the kingdom, the expense of its many wars and the necessity of paying heavy tribute to Rome led the unprincipled Syrian rulers to resort to every possible expedient for securing money. The sanctuary at Jerusalem had become, like the ancient Babylonian temples, a place where private as well as public funds were deposited, that they might be under the protection of the Deity. Kings who had already formed the habit of robbing temples would not hesitate to loot the shrine of the Jews. Possibly the basis of the story in its present form was some unusual experience which aroused the superstitious fear of the temple robbers. The tale was one that appealed strongly to the imagination of the painters of the middle ages. Cf. Rafael's presentation of this scene in the Vatican to illustrate the victory of Pope Julius II over his foes.
  ᵉ 3⁵ The identity of this Apollonius the son of Thraseus is doubtful. Cf. 4⁴ and I Mac. 3¹⁰. The original may have read, *of Tarsus.*
  ᶠ 3⁹ So Syr., Lat., and allied MSS. Gk. omits the connective.

Traditional History of the Maccabean Struggle

dred talents of silver and two hundred of gold;ᵍ ¹²and that it was by no means permissible that those should be wronged who had put trust in the sanctity of the place and in the majesty and inviolability of the temple, honored over all the world. ¹³But Heliodorus, because of the orders which he had from the king, said that in any case this money must be confiscated for the king's treasury.

¹⁴When on the day which he had appointed, he entered to direct the inquiry concerning these matters, there was great distress throughout the entire city. ¹⁵The priests, prostrating themselves before the altar in their priestly garments, called to Heaven,ʰ to him who gave the law concerning deposits, that he should preserve these safe for those who had deposited them. ¹⁶And whoever saw the mien of the high priest was wounded in heart, for his countenance and the change in his color betrayed his mental distress. ¹⁷For a terror and a shuddering of the body had come over the man, whereby the pain that was in his heart became manifest to those who looked upon him. ¹⁸The people rushed out of their houses in throngs to make a common supplication because the place was in danger of falling into contempt. ¹⁹And the women, girded with sackcloth under their breasts, filled the streets. The virgins also hurried from their seclusion, some to the gates, others to the walls, and some looked out through the windows. ²⁰And all, stretching out their hands to Heaven, made their supplication. ²¹It was a pitiful sight: the multitude prostrating themselves, all mingled together, and the high priest in extreme distress, but expectant.

²²While therefore they called upon the Almighty Lord to keep the things committed to them safe and secure for those who had intrusted them, ²³Heliodorus went on to execute the decree. ²⁴But just as he with his guard was there at the treasury, the Sovereign of spirits and of all authorityⁱ produced a great apparition, so that all who had presumed to come in with him, smitten with dismay at the power of God, were made faint and fearful. ²⁵For there was seen by them a horse with a terrible rider, and adorned with beautiful trappings, which rushed fiercely and struck at Heliodorus with his forefeet. But he who sat upon the horse appeared to have a complete armor of gold. ²⁶Two other young men also appeared to him, distinguished by their strength and beautiful in their splendor, and gorgeous in their apparel, who stood by him on either side and scourged him unceasingly, inflicting on him many stripes. ²⁷And he fell suddenly to the ground, and great darkness came over him; but he was caught up and put into a litter. ²⁸He who had just entered with a great train and all his guard into the aforesaid treasury was now himself being carried, altogether unable to help himself; and he recognized clearly the sovereignty of God. ²⁹And so through

Marginal notes: Distress and prayers of the priests and people — Overthrow of Heliodorus by the divine messengers

---

ᵍ 3¹¹ If reckoned in Hebrew talents the total gives an almost fabulous sum: about seven hundred thousand dollars in silver and four million two hundred thousand in gold. Probably the smaller Syrian talents (about half as large) were intended.

ʰ 3¹⁵ *Heaven* is here and elsewhere in the book used as the equivalent of *God*, possibly in order to avoid the mention of the divine name. Cf. the use of the term, *kingdom of heaven*, in Mt. as the equivalent of *Kingdom of God.*

ⁱ 3²⁴ Many texts here read, *Lord of the fathers and Sovereign of all authority.*

Traditional History of the Maccabean Struggle

the working of God he lay prostrate, speechless, and bereft of all hope of deliverance. ³⁰But [the Jews] blessed the Lord, who had so miraculously honored his own place; and the temple, which a little before had been full of terror and alarm, was filled with joy and gladness, after the Almighty Lord appeared.

His deliverance and testimony to God's power

³¹But quickly certain of Heliodorus's familiar friends besought Onias to call upon the Most High, and grant life to him who lay at the very point of death.ʲ ³²And the high priest, secretly fearing lest the king might conceive the idea that some treachery toward Heliodorus had been perpetrated by the Jews, brought a sacrifice for the deliverance of the man. ³³But as the high priest was making the propitiation, the same young men appeared again to Heliodorus, arrayed in the same garments; and they stood and said, Give Onias the high priest great thanks, since for his sake the Lord hath granted thee life. ³⁴And do thou, since thou hast been scourged from heaven, make known to all men the mighty power of God. When they had spoken these words, they vanished out of sight. ³⁵So Heliodorus offered a sacrifice to the Lord and vowed very greatᵏ vows to him who had saved his life. Then with a gracious farewell to Onias, he returned with his army to the king. ³⁶And he testified to all men the works of the supreme God which he had beheld with his eyes. ³⁷And when the king asked Heliodorus what kind of a man was fit to be sent yet again to Jerusalem, he said, ³⁸If you have any enemy or conspirator against the state, send him thither, and you will receive him back well scourged, if he escape even with his life; because of a truth there is about the place the power of God. ³⁹For he who has his dwelling in heaven is the watchman and protector of that place; and he smites and destroys those who come to hurt it. ⁴⁰Such was the issue of Heliodorus's attempt and the guarding of the treasury.¹

§ 170. **Atrocities of the Jewish Hellenizing Leaders,** I Mac. 1¹⁰⁻¹⁵, II Mac. 4

Traditional History of the Maccabean Struggle

Onias's mission to Antioch to counteract Simon's slanders

II Mac. 4 ¹Now the Simon already mentioned as having been the betrayer of the funds of his country, slandered Onias, saying that it was he who incited Heliodorus, and had been the author of these evils; ²and this benefactor of the city, and guardian of his fellow-countrymen, and zealot for the laws, he dared to call a conspirator against the state. ³But when

---

ʲ 3³¹ Lit., *at the last gasp.*
ᵏ 3³⁵ Lit., *the greatest.*
¹ 3⁴⁰ Gk., lit., *things concerning Heliodorus and the guarding of the treasury.*
§ 170 Greek culture from 332 B.C. on encircled and pressed the Jews on every side. Greek was the language of commerce, as well as of their conquerors. Even the sacred scriptures had been translated into it. The Jews of the dispersion were enveloped in Hellenic civilization, while those of Palestine met it when they went westward to the rich Greek cities of the Philistine plain, or northward to Samaria, or to the strong Greek cities east of the Jordan, or even to Idumea on the south. Traders and Syrian officials brought it to their very doors; and finally the ruling Syrian party in Judaism itself began to adopt it because it was attractive and the way to preferment at Antioch. Opposed to it were the Puritans who rallied about the law and the ritual of the temple. They undoubtedly still longed for the less exacting rule of Egypt and found strong supporters in their kinsmen at Alexandria, if not in the Egyptian court. Thus the two parties were divided not only on religious, but also on political lines, and this fact undoubtedly throws light upon the attitude of the Syrian court.

Traditional History of the Maccabean Struggle

the enmity reached such a state that murders were committed by one of Simon's trusted followers, ⁴Onias, comprehending how dangerous the contention was and how Apollonius,ᵐ as the governor of Cœlesyria and Phœnicia, by his rage was increasing Simon's malice, ⁵betook himself to that king not to be an accuser of his fellow-citizens, but mindful of both the public and the private welfare; ⁶for he saw that unless the king made some provision the state could not again obtain peace, and that Simon would not cease from his folly.

History of the Hasmoneans

I Mac. 1 ¹⁰Now there came forth from [Alexander's successors] a sinful root, Antiochus Epiphanes, son of Antiochus the king, who had been a hostage at Rome, and he began to reign in the one hundred and thirty-seventh year of the Syrian rule.ⁿ ¹¹In those days there appeared from among the people of Israel those who disregarded the law, who persuaded many, saying, Let us go and make a covenant with the heathen about us; for since we have stood aloof from them many evils have befallen us. ¹²And the proposal met with approval. ¹³And certain of the people acted with promptness, and went to the king who gave them the right to do as the heathen. ¹⁴Then they built a place for gymnastic exercise in

⁷But when Seleucus was dead and Antiochus who was called Epiphanes [Illustrious] succeeded to the kingdom, Jason the brother of Onias surreptitiously obtained the high priesthood⁸ by promising to the king at an audience three hundred and sixty talents of silver and from another fund eighty talents. ⁹Moreover, he undertook to assignᵒ a hundred and fifty more, if he might be allowed by his authority to set up for himself a Greek place for gymnastic exercise and a special place for the youths, and to register the inhabitants of Jerusalem as the citizens of Antioch. ¹⁰With the assent of the king, he secured the office, and at once brought over those of his own race to the Greek fashion. ¹¹And setting aside the privileges settled upon the Jews by the king, through the efforts of John the father of Eupolemus, who went on the embassy to the Romans for friendship and alliance, and abolishing the lawful modes of life, he introduced new customs forbidden by the law; ¹²for he gladly established a Greek place for gymnastic exercise under the citadel itself; and induced the noblest of the young men to wear the Greek cap. ¹³There was such an extreme of Hellenism and a withdrawal to alien customs because of the superlative infamy of Jason, that ungodly man and no high priest, ¹⁴that the priests were no longer zealous for the services of the altar; but despising the sanctuary and neglecting the sacrifices, they hastened to take part in that which was unlawfully provided in the palæstra, after the proclamation of the discus-throwing; ¹⁵de-

Eagerness of certain apostate Jews to adopt Greek customs

ᵐ II Mac. 4⁴ Hort conjectures, but without textual support, that the original read, *Apollonius, the son of Menestheus.* But this Apollonius was probably the same as the one mentioned in 3².
ⁿ I Mac. 1¹⁰ *I.e.*, in 175 B.C. *The Syrian* (lit., *Greek*) *rule* refers to that of the Seleucid Syrian kingdom, established in 312 B.C. Cf. § 168, note ᵇ.
ᵒ II Mac. 4⁹ Following cursive texts.

History of the Hasmo-neans | *Traditional History of the Maccabean Struggle*

Jerusalem according to the customs of the heathen. ¹⁵They also made themselves uncircumcised, and, forsaking the holy covenant, fraternized with the heathen, and sold themselves to do evil.

spising what was esteemed by their fathers and deeming the Greek honors best of all. ¹⁶For these reasons severe calamity overtook them; and the men whose ways they emulated, and whom they wished to be like in every respect, these became their enemies and chastisers. ¹⁷For it is not a light thing to sin against the laws of God. This the course of time will show.

Jason's offering to Hercules

¹⁸When certain games held every fifth[p] year were celebrated at Tyre, and the king was present, ¹⁹the vile Jason sent envoys from Jerusalem, Antiochians, bearing three hundred drachmas of silver[q] for the sacrifice to Hercules. But the bearers requested that they would not use them for sacrifice, since it was not fitting, but reserve them for other expenses. ²⁰So this money intended by the sender for the sacrifice to Hercules, because of the bearers, went for the equipment of the galleys.

Antiochus's visit to Jerusalem

²¹When Apollonius the son of Menestheus was sent into Egypt on account of the enthronement of Philometor[r] as king, Antiochus, discovering that the latter had become hostile to his rule, gave heed to his own security. He therefore came to Joppa and then went on to Jerusalem. ²²Here he was magnificently received by Jason and the city, and was brought in with torches and shoutings. Afterward he led his army down into Phœnicia.

Supplanting of Jason by Menelaus as high priest

²³After an interval of three years Jason sent Menelaus, a brother of the Simon already mentioned, to carry the money to the king and to make reports concerning some necessary matters. ²⁴But he, by commending himself to the king, and extolling him with the mien of a man of influence, secured the high priesthood for himself, outbidding Jason by three hundred talents of silver. ²⁵He returned with the royal mandates, although he was not at all worthy of the high priesthood, but had the passion of a cruel tyrant and the rage of a savage beast. ²⁶Then Jason, who had supplanted his own brother, being supplanted by another, was driven as a fugitive into the country of the Ammonites, ²⁷and Menelaus had possession of the office. But none of the money which had been promised to the king was duly paid, though Sostratus the governor of the citadel demanded it ²⁸(for he had charge over the collection of the revenues). For this cause they were both called by the king to his presence; ²⁹and Menelaus left his own brother Lysimachus as his deputy in the high priesthood; and Sostratus left Crates, the governor of the Cyprians.

Murder of Onias at the instigation of Menelaus

³⁰While such was the state of affairs, it transpired that the citizens of Tarsus and Mallus revolted, because they were to be given as a present to Antiochis the king's concubine. ³¹The king therefore came thither in all

---

p II Mac. 4¹⁸ Really every fourth year, probably in imitation of the Olympic games.
q II Mac. 4¹⁹ The sum is surprisingly small, not more than fifty dollars. The Syr. and certain MSS. read, *three thousand, three hundred.*
r 4²¹ Following the reading of the Lat. and the cursive Gk. MSS.

Traditional History of the Maccabean Struggle

haste to settle matters, leaving for his deputy Andronicus, a man of high rank. ³²Then Menelaus, thinking that he had found a favorable opportunity, presented to Andronicus certain gold vessels of the temple, which he had stolen; others also he had already sold at Tyre and the neighboring cities. ³³And Onias, who had withdrawn into a sanctuary at Daphne,ˢ located near Antioch, when he had positive information of this, sharply reproved him. ³⁴Therefore Menelaus took Andronicus aside and besought him to kill Onias. He, being persuaded to use treachery, came to Onias and swore with uplifted hand and gave him his right handᵗ and so, though he was suspected, persuaded him to come forth from the sanctuary; then he immediately despatched him without regard for justice.

³⁵On account of this not only Jews but also many of the other nations, were provoked and full of indignation over the unjust murder of the man. ³⁶When the king had returned from the places in Cilicia, the Jews who were in the city complained because Onias had been wrongfully slain. ³⁷And the Greeks showed their indignation. Antiochus therefore was heartily sorry, and was moved to pity, and wept, because of the sober and well-ordered life of him who was dead; ³⁸and burning with indignation, he at once stripped Andronicus of his purple robe, tore off his garments and, after leading him round through the whole city to that very place where he had committed the impiety against Onias, he there put the murderer to death. Thus the Lord rendered to him the punishment he deserved. Punishment of the murderer

³⁹Now when many temple thefts had been committed in the city by Lysimachus, with the consent of Menelaus, and a report was circulated outside, the people gathered together against Lysimachus, after many gold vessels had been already carried away. ⁴⁰At the uprising of multitudes who were filled with anger, Lysimachus armed about three thousand men and assumed the offensive. A certain Auranus, a man advanced in years and no less also in wickedness, led the onset. ⁴¹But as soon as they were aware of the attack of Lysimachus, some caught up stones, others logs of wood, and some took handfuls of the ashes that lay near, and flung them all pell-mell upon Lysimachus's men. ⁴²By these means they wounded many of them, some they struck to the ground, and all of them they forced to flee. The temple-thief himself they killed beside the treasury. Death of the temple-robber, Lysimachus

⁴³An accusation regarding these matters was laid against Menelaus. ⁴⁴And when the king arrived at Tyre, the three men, who were sent by the senate, pleaded the cause before him. ⁴⁵But just when he was worsted, Menelaus promised much money to Ptolemy the son of Dorymenes to win over the king. ⁴⁶Thereupon Ptolemy, taking the king aside into a cloister, as it were to take the air, won him over. ⁴⁷And Menelaus, who was the cause of all the evil, he acquitted of the accusations; but those hapless men, who, if they had addressed even Scythians,ᵘ would have been discharged uncon- Unjust acquittal of Menelaus and the execution of the Jewish representatives

---

ˢ 4³³ The more natural Eng. idiom has been adopted.
ᵗ 4³⁴ Lit., *raising right hand with oaths.*
ᵘ 4⁴⁷ Cf. Cicero's oration against Verres II, 5⁵⁸.

Traditional History of the Maccabean Struggle

demned, them he sentenced to death. ⁴⁸Quickly then did those who had pleaded in behalf of the city and the people and the holy vessels suffer unjust punishment. ⁴⁹For this reason even certain Tyrians, aroused to indignation, provided magnificently for their funeral. ⁵⁰But Menelaus through the cupidity of the authorities, remained in his office, where he grew in wickedness and was a great conspirator against his fellow-citizens.

§ 171. Repeated Sackings of Jerusalem by Antiochus Epiphanes, I Mac. 1¹⁶⁻⁴⁰, II Mac. 5¹⁻²⁶

History of the Hasmoneans	Traditional History

Antiochus's successful invasion of Egypt

I Mac. 1 ¹⁶ Now when Antiochus saw that his authority was well established, he thought to reign over Egypt, that he might reign over the two kingdoms. ¹⁷So he invaded Egypt with a great multitude, with chariots and elephants and horsemen, and with a great navy. ¹⁸And he made war against Ptolemy king of Egypt. And Ptolemy was defeated by him and fled, and many fell mortally wounded. ¹⁹And they gained possession of the

II Mac. 5 ¹ Now about this time Antiochus made his second expedition into Egypt. ²It then happened that throughout all the city, for a period of nearly forty days, there were seen horsemen speeding in troopsᵛ through the air, wearing robes inwrought with gold and equipped with full armor and spears; ³also the drawing of swords, and squadrons of horse in array, and repeated encounters and pursuits on both sides, and shaking of shields and multitudes of lances, and casting of darts, and flashing of golden trappings, and girding on of all kinds of armor. ⁴Therefore all men prayed that the vision might portend good. ⁵But when a false rumor arose that Antiochus was deceased, Jason took at least a thousand men, and made a sudden assault upon the city. When those who were on the wall had been routed, and the city was at last on the point of being captured, Menelaus took refuge in the citadel. ⁶But Jason unsparingly slaughtered his own fellow-citizens without considering that success against kinsmen is the greatest ill-success,ʷ but imagining that he was setting up trophies over enemies and not over fellow-countrymen. ⁷However, he did not obtain the office, but only shame as the result of his conspiracy; and he passed again a fugitive into the country of the Ammonites. ⁸At the last therefore he met with a miserable end, after being imprisonedˣ at the court of Aretas the prince of the Arabians,

[margin:] Jason destructive attack upon Jerusalem during the absence of Antiochus

---

§ 171 II Mac. 5 dates the first sacking of Jerusalem in 168 B.C. in connection with Antiochus's second Egyptian campaign. I Mac. 1, however, connects it probably rightly with the first in 170–169 B.C. This is consistent with ²⁹. II Mac. appears to have confused and combined the two events. Later, in June 168 B.C., the Romans succeeded in overcoming the Macedonian Greek Empire and at once made a peremptory demand that Antiochus retire from Egypt, which he was on the point of annexing to his kingdom. His chagrin doubtless intensified the bitterness of his persecution of the Jews.

ᵛ II Mac. 5² The Gk. order puts, *in troops,* after *equipped.*
ʷ II Mac. 5⁶ The Gk. contains a play on the word success: *good success* and *ill-success.*
ˣ II Mac. 5⁸ Following a reading found in several important texts.

History of the Hasmoneans

strong cities in the land of Egypt, and he took the spoils of Egypt.

Traditional History

fleeing from city to city, pursued by all men, hated as an apostate from the laws, and held in abomination as the public executioner of his country and his fellow-citizens, he was driven out into Egypt. ⁹And he who had driven many from their own country perished himself in a strange land, having crossed the sea to the Lacedemonians, expecting to gain protection because they were near of kin.ᵃ ¹⁰Thus he who had cast out a multitude unburied had none to mourn for him, nor had he any funeral at all, or place in the sepulchre of his fathers.

His under the temple at Jerusalem

²⁰Then after Antiochus had conquered Egypt he returned in the hundred and forty-third year,ᵇ and went up against Israel and Jerusalem with a great multitude. ²¹And he insolently went into the sanctuary, and took the golden altar, and the candelabrum, ²²and all that belonged to the table of the showbread, and the cups for libations, and the bowls, and the golden censers, and the curtain and the garlands and decorations which were on the front of the temple—he scaled it all off. ²³And he took the silver and the gold and the precious vessels, and the hidden treasures which he found. ²⁴And taking all, he went away into his own land, having made a great slaughter, and spoken very insolently. ²⁵Thus a great mourning came upon Israel in all their places.

²⁶And the rulers and elders groaned,
The virgins and young men were made feeble.
²⁷And the beauty of the women was changed

¹¹When tidings of what had happened came to the king, he thought that Judea was in revolt. Thereupon setting out from Egypt in a furious temper, he took the city by force of arms, ¹²and commanded his soldiers to cut down without mercy those whom they chanced to meet and to slay those who went up into their houses. ¹³There was killing of young and old, taking away of boys, women and children, slaying of maidens and infants. ¹⁴In the three days alone eighty thousand were lost, forty thousand were put to death, and as many sold as were slain. ¹⁵But not content with this, he presumed to enter the most holy temple of all the earth, guided by Menelaus, who had proved himself a traitor both to the laws and to his country, ¹⁶and with his polluted hands he seized the sacred vessels, and what had been dedicated by other kings for the augmentation of the glory and honor of the place he dragged away with his profane hands. ¹⁷And Antiochus was elated in mind, not perceiving that because of the sins of those who dwelt in the city the Sovereign Lord had been provoked to anger a little while, and that on this account his protection was withdrawn from the place. ¹⁸Had it not been that they were already entangled by many sins, this man, like Heliodorus, who was sent by King Seleucus to view the

His slaughter of the Jews and plunder of the temple

ᵃ II Mac. 5⁹ Cf. I Mac. 12⁷.
ᵇ I Mac. 1²⁰ 169 B.C.

History of the Hasmoneans

Every bridegroom took up a lamentation,
She that sat in the marriage chamber was in heaviness.
²⁸And the land was shaken because of its inhabitants
And all the house of Jacob was clothed with shame.ᵈ

Traditional History

treasury, would, as soon as he pressed forward, have been scourged and turned back from his daring deed. ¹⁹However, the Lord did not choose the nation for the place's sake, but the place for the sake of the nation.ᶜ ²⁰Therefore also the place itself, having shared the calamities which befell the nation, afterward partook of its benefits; and what was forsaken in the wrath of the Almighty was, at the reconciliation of the great Sovereign, restored again with all glory.

Later plundering and dismantling of Jerusalem

²⁹After two years the king sent a chief of collectors of tribute to the cities of Judah, who came to Jerusalem with a great multitude. ³⁰And he spoke words of peace to them in perfidy, and they trusted him so that he attacked the city suddenly, and inflicted a severe blow on it, and destroyed many people from Israel. ³¹And he took the spoils of the city, and set it on fire, and pulled down its houses and walls on every side. ³²They took captive the women and the children, and gained possession of the cattle. ³³Then they walled in the city of David with a great and strong wall, with strong towers, and it served as a citadel. ³⁴And they put there lawless people, impious men, who fortified themselves in it. ³⁵And they stored up weapons and food and, gathering together the spoils of Jerusalem, they stored them there.

³⁶And the citadel became a great trap,
And served as a place of ambush against the sanctuary,
And an evil adversary to Israel continually.
³⁷And they shed innocent blood on every side of the sanctuary
And polluted the sanctuary.
³⁸Then the inhabitants of Jerusalem fled because of this,
And she became the habitation of foreigners;

Successive slaughters of the Jews

²¹As for Antiochus, when he had carried away from the temple a thousand eight hundred talents, he departed in all haste for Antioch, imagining in his arrogance that he could make the land navigable and the sea passable by foot, because his heart was elated. ²²Moreover he left governors to afflict the race: at Jerusalem, Philip, by race a Phrygian, and in character more barbarous than he who set him there; ²³and at Gerizim, Andronicus; and besides these, Menelaus, who, worse than all the rest, bore himself insolentlyᵉ toward his fellow-citizens. And with a spirit hostile to the Jews, ²⁴he sent that arch-villain Apollonius with an army of twenty-two thousand, and commanded him to slay all those who were of mature age, and to sell the women and the younger men. ²⁵And upon his arrival at Jerusalem, he pretended to be a man of peace

---

ᶜ II Mac. 5¹⁹ Cf. Mk. 2¹².
ᵈ I Mac. 1²⁶⁻²⁸ As frequently in descriptive passages of this character the author falls into poetic measures, possibly quoting from a familiar elegy.
ᵉ II Mac. 5²³ Following Gk., Lat., Syr., and Theod.

History of the Hasmoneans

And she became strange to those who were
    born in her,
    And her children forsook her.
³⁹Her sanctuary was laid waste like a wilderness,
    Her feasts were turned into mourning,
    Her sabbaths into a reproach,
    Her honor into contempt,
⁴⁰So great as was once her glory, so now was her
    dishonor,
    And her exaltation was turned into mourning.

Traditional History

and waited until the holy sabbath day. Then finding the Jews at rest from work, he commanded his men to parade in arms. ²⁶And he put to the sword all those who came forth to the spectacle; and running into the city with the armed men, he slew great multitudes.

§ 172. Antiochus's Measures to Root out Judaism, I Mac. 1⁴¹⁻⁶⁴, II Mac. 6¹⁻¹¹

History of the Hasmoneans

[margin: Antiochus's commands to cease worshiping Jehovah]

I Mac. 1 ⁴¹Then King Antiochus wrote to his whole kingdom the command that all should be one people, ⁴²and that each should give up his own laws. And all the nations acceded to the demand of the king. ⁴³Many Israelites too consented to worship him and sacrificed to the idols, and profaned the sabbath. ⁴⁴And the king sent letters by messengers to Jerusalem and the cities of Judah commanding them to follow customs foreign to the land, ⁴⁵and to prevent the making of whole burnt-offerings and sacrifices and libations in the sanctuary, and to profane the sabbaths and feasts, ⁴⁶and pollute the sanctuary and the holy things, ⁴⁷to build altars, temples, and shrines for idols, and to sacrifice swine's flesh and unclean beasts; ⁴⁸also to leave their sons uncircumcised, to stain their souls with all manner of uncleanness and profanation, ⁴⁹so that they might forget the law, and change all the customs. ⁵⁰And that whoever would not do as the king commanded should die. ⁵¹Thus he wrote to his whole kingdom; and appointed overseers over all the people, who commanded the cities of Judah to sacrifice city by city. ⁵²Then many of the people gathered to them, every one who had forsaken the law; and they did evil things in the land, ⁵³and

Traditional History

[margin: Pollution of the temple]

II Mac. 6 ¹Not long after this the king sent an aged Athenian to compel the Jews to depart from the laws of their fathers, and to live no more after the laws of God; ²and also to pollute the sanctuary in Jerusalem, and to call it by the name of Zeus Olympios and the one in Gerizim by the name of Zeus Zenios [the Hospitable],[f] for such were they who dwelt in the place. ³But hard and utterly grievous was the visitation[g] of this evil. ⁴For the temple was filled with debauchery and revellings by the heathen, who dallied with harlots and cohabited with women in the sacred precincts, and moreover brought inside things that were not proper. ⁵The altar, too, was filled with unholy things prohibited by the laws.

[margin: Prohibition of all Jewish religious rites]

⁶And a man could neither keep the sabbath, nor observe the feasts of all the fathers, nor so much as confess himself to

---

[f] II Mac. 6² Here the hospitality of the Samaritans seems to be recognized.
[g] II Mac. 6³ Or, *hard and grievous even for the multitudes.*

History of the Hasmoneans

Pollution of the temple and destruction of the books of the law

Murder of those faithful to the law

caused the Israelites to hide themselves in all their places of refuge.

⁵⁴On the twenty-fifth day of Chisleu, in the one hundred and forty-fifth year,ʰ they built an abomination of desolationⁱ upon the altar; and in the cities of Judah on every side they built idol altars. And at the doors of the houses and in the streets they burnt incense. ⁵⁶And tearing in pieces the books of the law which they found, they set fire to them. ⁵⁷And wherever a book of the covenant was found in the possession of anyone, and if anyone obeyed the law, the king's sentence delivered him to death. ⁵⁸Thus they did in their might month by month to those Israelites who happened to be in the cities. ⁵⁹And on the twenty-fifth day of the month they sacrificed upon the idol altar which was upon the altar [of God]. ⁶⁰And the women who had circumcised their children they put to death according to the command. ⁶¹And they hanged their babes about their necks, and destroyed their households, with those who had circumcised them. ⁶²But many in Israel made strong resolutions not to eat unclean things, ⁶³choosing to die that they might not be defiled with the meats, and might not profane the holy covenant. So they died. And exceedingly great woe came upon Israel.

Traditional History

be a Jew. ⁷But on the king's birthday,ʲ every month, they were led along under bitter constraint to the sacrificial meal, and when the feast of [Bacchus] Dionysia came, they were compelled to go in procession in honor of Dionysos, wearing wreaths of ivy. ⁸A decree was also issued to the neighboring Greek cities, at the suggestion of Ptolemy, that they should act in the same way against the Jews, and should have sacrificial meals, ⁹and should slay those who did not choose to go over to the Greek rites. Anyone then could see what misery had arisen, ¹⁰for two women were brought up for having circumcised their children; and these, when they had led them publicly round about the city, with the babes hung on their breasts, they cast down headlong from the wall. ¹¹And others who had hastily gathered in the caves near by to keep the seventh day secretly, being betrayed to Philip, were all burnt together, because they scrupled to defend themselves, out of regard for the honor of that most holy day.

§ 173. The Martyrs for the Law, II Mac. 6¹²–7⁴²

Traditional History of the Maccabean Struggle

Introduction: the disciplinary value of misfortune

II Mac. 6 ¹²I beseech therefore those who read this book, not to be discouraged because of the misfortunes, but to consider that these punishments were not for the destruction, but for the training of our race. ¹³For it is a sign of great beneficence when the ungodly are not let alone any length of

ʰ I Mac. 1⁵⁴ Dec., 168 B.C. Cf. 4⁵², ⁵⁹. So Josephus.
ⁱ I Mac. 1⁵⁴ Cf. Dan. 11³¹, 12¹¹, 9²⁷, Matt. 24¹⁵, Mk. 13¹⁴. Probably an altar to Zeus, called, *Lord of heaven* (*Shāmtu*), here designated by a play on the title as, *abomination of desolation* (*Shokuç Meshōmēm*).
ʲ II Mac. 6⁷ Grimm suggests that the author has here confused the annual birthday with the monthly sacrifice. Cf. II Mac. 1⁵⁹.
§ 173 While these stories have probably been magnified in transmission and are clearly adapted by the author of the book to his didactic aims, they undoubtedly embody many authentic historical facts and give a vivid idea of the intensity of the crisis and the powerful influences which gave Judaism its final form.

Traditional History of the Maccabean Struggle

time, but quickly meet with retribution. ¹⁴While indeed in the case of the other nations the Sovereign Lord patiently waits, and punishes only when they have attained to the full measure of sins, he decided that it should not be so in our case, ¹⁵that he might not take vengeance on us afterward, when we had reached the limit of our sins. ¹⁶Therefore he never withdraws his mercy from us; though he disciplines with misfortunes, he does not forsake his own people. ¹⁷But let what we have said suffice as a reminder; with this short digression we must proceed to the narrative.

¹⁸Eleazar, one of the principal scribes, a man already advanced in years and of a most noble countenance, was compelled to open his mouth to eat swine's flesh. ¹⁹But he, welcoming death with renown rather than life with pollution, spat it out and advanced of his own accord to the instrument of torture,ᵏ ²⁰as men ought to come who are resolute to repel such things as it is unlawful to taste for the mere love of life. ²¹But those who had charge of the forbidden sacrificial meal, on account of their old-time acquaintance with the man, took him aside and privately besought him to bring flesh of his own providing, such as was proper for him to use, and to pretend to eat of the flesh from the sacrifice, as had been commanded by the king, ²²that by so doing he might be delivered from death, and through his old friendship with them might receive kind treatment. ²³But he, having formed a high resolve, and one that became his years and the dignity of old age and the gray hairs which he had reached with honor, and the noble life which he had livedˡ from his youth, but still more the holy laws of God's ordaining, declared his mind accordingly, promptly bidding them send him to Hades. ²⁴For it becomes not our years to dissemble, *said he*, that thereby many of the young should suppose that Eleazar, a man ninety years old, had gone over to an alien religion, ²⁵and *so* they by reason of my dissimulation and for the sake of this brief and momentary life, should be led astray through me, and I bring a stain and pollution upon my old age. ²⁶For even if for the present I shall be freed from the punishment of men, yet shall I not escape the hands of the Almighty, whether living or dead. ²⁷Therefore, by manfully parting with my life now, I will show myself worthy of my old age, ²⁸and leave behind a noble example to the young to die willingly and nobly a glorious death for the sacred and holy laws. And when he had said these words, he went immediately to the instrument of torture. ²⁹But those who led him changed the good-will they bore him a little while before into ill-will, because these words of his were, as they thought, sheer madness. ³⁰When he was about to die from the blows, he groaned aloud and said, To the Lord, who hath the holy knowledge, it is manifest that, whereas I might have been delivered from death, I endure grievous pains in my body by being scourged; but in my soul I gladly suffer these things for fear of him. ³¹So, then, in such a manner did this man die, leaving his death as an example of nobleness and a memorial of virtue not only to the young but also to the great body of his nation.

Supreme devotion of the aged Eleazar

ᵏ 6¹⁹ The exact nature of the instrument of torture is not known. It was probably some wheel-shaped instrument on which the victim was stretched and then beaten.
ˡ 6²³ Restoring what appears to have been the original text.

Traditional History of the Maccabean Struggle

7 ¹It came to pass also that seven brothers, together with their mother, were at the king's command seized and tortured with scourges and cords, to compel them to taste of the abominable swine's flesh. ²But one of them acting as spokesman said, What would you ask and learn of us? For we are ready to die rather than transgress the laws of our fathers. ³Then the king fell into a rage and gave orders to heat pans and caldrons. ⁴And as soon as these were heated, he gave orders to cut out the tongue of him who had been their spokesman, and to scalp him[m] and to cut off his extremities, while the rest of his brothers and his mother were looking on. ⁵And when he was completely mutilated, but still breathing, [the king] ordered him brought to the fire and fried in the pan. As the vapor from the pan spread far, they and their mother exhorted one another to die nobly, speaking thus: ⁶The Lord God beholdeth, and in truth hath compassion upon us, as Moses declared in his song, which witnessed against them openly, saying, ' And he shall have compassion upon his servants.'[n]

⁷After the first had died in this manner, they brought the second to the mocking;[o] and tearing from his head the skin with the hair, they asked him, Will you eat before your body bears the penalty in every limb? ⁸But he answered in the language of his fathers and said to them, No. Therefore he also, like the first, underwent the torture that followed. ⁹And when he was at the last gasp he said, You, indeed,[o] wretch, release us from this present life, but the King of the world shall raise up us, who have died for his laws, to an eternal renewal of life.

¹⁰After him the third was made an object of mocking. And when bidden, he promptly put out his tongue, and stretched forth his hands courageously, ¹¹and nobly said, From Heaven[p] I have received these, and for the sake of his laws I contemn them, and from him I hope to receive them back again; ¹²so that the king himself and those who were him were astonished at the young man's spirit, for he did not at all regard the pain.

¹³When he too was dead, they maltreated and tortured the fourth in like manner. ¹⁴And as he was at the point of death he spoke thus: It is pleasing to us when we die at the hands of men to look for the hopes which are from God, that we shall be raised up again by him. For you, however, there shall be no resurrection to life.

¹⁵And next after him they brought the fifth, and maltreated him. ¹⁶But he looked at the king[q] and said, Because you have authority among men, though only mortal yourself, you do what you will; yet think not that our race has been forsaken by God. ¹⁷Persist in your course, and you shall behold how his sovereign power will torture you and your descendants!

(marginal notes)
Voluntary martyrdom of seven brothers; death of the first

Of the second

Of the third

Of the fourth

Of the fifth

---

[m] 7⁴ The Greek word means, *to scalp in Scythian fashion* cf. ⁷.

[n] 7⁶ The author here follows the Gk. of Dt. 32³⁶.

[o] 7⁷ The mocking referred to seems to have been a regular practice before execution. Cf. Mt. 27²⁹, Heb. 11³⁶.

[p] 7¹¹ Heaven here as in I Mac. is clearly used as a substitute for the name of the Deity. Cf. § 169, note [h].

[q] 7¹⁶ The Gk. has only, *him*, where *king* must be supplied.

Traditional History of the Maccabean Struggle

¹⁸And after him they brought the sixth. And when he was about to die Of the he said, Be not vainly deceived, for we suffer these things for our own doings, sixth because we have sinned against our own God. On this account are such marvellous things come to pass. ¹⁹But think not that you who have attempted to fight against God shall be unpunished.

²⁰But above all was the mother marvellous and worthy of an honored Brave memory; for when she looked on seven sons perishing within the space of exhor- tation one day, she bore it with a good courage because of her hope in the Lord. of the ²¹She exhorted each one of them in the language of their fathers, filled with mother a noble temper and stirring up her woman's thought with manly passion, saying to them, ²²I know not how you came into my womb, neither was it I who bestowed on you your spirit or your life, and it was not I who brought into order the elementary substance of each of you. ²³Therefore the Creator of the world, by whose fashioning man came into being and by whose devising all things were made, will^r in mercy give back to you again both your spirit and your life, as you now contemn your own selves for the sake of his laws. ²⁴But Antiochus thinking that he was despised, and suspecting the reproachful voice, while the youngest was yet alive, not only urged with words, but also promised with oaths that he would make him rich and to be envied as well, if he would turn from the customs of his fathers, and that he would take him for his Friend and intrust him with affairs. ²⁵But as the young man gave no heed, the king summoned his mother, and exhorted her that she should counsel the lad to save himself. ²⁶After he had exhorted her with many words, she undertook to persuade her son. ²⁷But bending toward him, in mockery of the cruel tyrant, she spoke thus in the language of her fathers: My son, have pity on me who carried you nine months in my womb, and gave you suck three years, and nourishing and training you, reared you up to this age. ²⁸I beseech you, my child, to look upon the heaven and the earth, and see all things which are therein, and recognize that God made them not of things which were, and that so also the race of men has come into being. ²⁹Fear not this executioner, but, proving yourself worthy of your brothers, accept your death, that in the mercy of God I may receive you again with your brothers.

³⁰As soon as she had finished speaking, the young man said, For whom are Fidelity you waiting? I obey not the command of the king, but I hearken to the young- command of the law which was given to our fathers through Moses. ³¹But est son you, who have devised all manner of evil against the Hebrews, shall in no wise escape the hands of God. ³²For we are suffering because of our own sins; ³³and if for reproof and discipline our living Lord hath been angered a little while, yet shall he again be reconciled with his own servants. ³⁴But you, O unholy man and of all men most vile, be not in your wild pride vainly lifted up with uncertain hopes, raising your hand against the children of Heaven; ³⁵for not yet have you escaped the judgment of the Almighty God

---

^r 7²³ Some manuscripts have the present here instead of the future. The context favors the latter.

Traditional History of the Maccabean Struggle

who keepeth watch. [36]For these our brothers having endured a brief agony which brings everlasting life,[s] have now died under God's covenant; but you through the judgment of God, shall receive just punishment for your arrogance. [37]But I, like my brothers, give up both body and soul for the laws of our fathers, calling upon God that he may become speedily gracious to the nation; and that you amidst trials and plagues may confess that he alone is God; [38]and that in me and in my brothers the wrath of the Almighty which has been justly brought upon our whole race may be stayed.[t] [39]Thereupon the king, falling into a rage, treated him worse than all the rest, being exasperated at his mocking. [40]So he also died pure from pollution, putting his whole trust in the Lord. [41]And last of all after her sons the mother died.

Conclusion
[42]Let this now suffice which has been said concerning the sacrificial meals and the extreme tortures.

§ 174. The Uprising of Mattathias and his Sons, I Mac. 2[1-28]

History of the Hasmoneans

Family of Mattathias
I Mac. 2 [1]At that time arose Mattathias the son of John the son of Simeon, a priest of the sons of Joarib,[u] from Jerusalem; and he dwelt in Modein. [2]And he had five sons, John, who was surnamed Gaddis,[v] [3]Simon, who was called Thassi, [4]Judas, who was called Maccabeus,[w] [5]Eleazar, who was called Avaran, Jonathan, who was called Apphus.

His lament over the fate of city and people
[6]When he saw the sacrilegious acts that were being committed in Judah and in Jerusalem, [7]he said,

> Woe to me! Why was I born
> To see the ruin of my people,
> And the ruin of the holy city,[x]
> And to dwell there while it was being given into the hands of the foe,
> The sanctuary into the hands of foreigners?
> [8]The temple has become as though it had no glory,[a]
> Its glorious vessels have been carried into captivity.
> [9]Her children have been slain in the streets,
> Her young men by the sword of the enemy.
> [10]What people has not taken possession of her palace,
> And seized upon her spoils?

---

[s] 7[36] Lit., *agony of everlasting life.* Hort conjectures that the original read, *having endured a short agony, have now drunk of everflowing life.*
[t] 7[38] Following the reading of many important texts. RV, *that thou mayest stay the wrath.*
§ 174 II Mac. says nothing of Mattathias. Possibly his act was recorded in one of the sections in Jason's history omitted by the epitomizer. Judas is introduced abruptly in 5[27].
[u] 2[1] Cf. I Chr. 24[7].
[v] 2[2] The meaning of these secondary names is not clear. Torrey, in *Ency. Bib.,* III, 2851, suggests that they were the names given at birth, while those by which they were commonly known, are the ones which they later received as princes of the Jewish people.
[w] 2[4] The popular interpretation, *Hammer,* is doubtful.
[x] 2[7] The poetic parallelism of this verse and the following is evident. The rhythm seems to have been that commonly used in songs of lamentation: a long line followed by a shorter one, as in Lam., thus giving the effect of a wail. The thought is clearly parallel to that of Lam. and such Pss. as 74 and 79.
[a] 2[8] The Gk. texts have a different reading which is not in accord with the context. The above is based upon a restoration of the Heb. suggested by Torrey. Syr., *The temple was before as a man in glory.*

History of the Hasmoneans

¹¹All her adornments have been taken away,
From freedom she has been reduced to slavery.
¹²And now our holy things, our beauty and our glory have been laid waste,
And the heathen have polluted them.
¹³Why should we still live?

¹⁴And Mattathias and his son tore their clothes, and put on sackcloth, and mourned bitterly.

¹⁵Now the king's officers who were enforcing the apostasy, came into the city of Modein to sacrifice. ¹⁶And many of Israel went over to them, but Mattathias and his sons offered resistance.ᵇ ¹⁷Then the king's officers said to Mattathias, You are a ruler and a man honored in this city and strengthened by sons and brothers. ¹⁸Now therefore come first and do what the king commands, as all the nations have done, the men of Judah too, with those who remain in Jerusalem. Then you and your house shall be in the number of the king's Friends,ᶜ and you and your sons shall be honored with silver and gold and many gifts. ¹⁹But Mattathias replied with a loud voice, If all the nations included in the king's dominionᵈ obey him, in that each is untrue to the worship of his fathers and chooses to follow his command, ²⁰yet I and my sons and my brothers will walk in the covenant made with our fathers. ²¹Heaven forbid that we should forsake the law and the ordinances. ²²We will not listen to the king's words, to go aside from our worship, either to the right hand or to the left. *His refusal to follow the commands of Antiochus*

²³And when he had finished saying these things a Jew came in sight of all to sacrifice on the altar that was in Modein according to the king's command. ²⁴When Mattathias saw it his zeal was kindled and he trembled inwardly. And he let his anger take possession of him, as was right, and he ran and slew him upon the altar. ²⁵Also he killed at that time the king's officer, who was compelling men to sacrifice, and pulled down the altar. ²⁶Thus he showed his zeal for the law, just as Phinehas did in the case of Zimri the son of Salu.ᵉ ²⁷Then Mattathias cried out in the city with a loud voice, saying, Whoever is zealous for the law and will maintain the covenant, ²⁸let him follow me. And he and his sons fled into the mountains, and left behind all that they had in the city. *His hot indignation and open resistance*

§ 175. The Fortunes of the Fugitives, I Mac. 2²⁹⁻⁴⁸, II Mac. 5²⁷, 8¹⁻⁷

History of the Hasmoneans

I Mac. 2 ²⁹Then many who sought justice and right went down into the wilderness, ³⁰to dwell there with their sons and wives and cattle, because the evils were becoming ever harder for them to bear. ³¹And it was reported to the king's officers and to the forces that

Traditional History

II Mac. 5 ²⁷But Judas, who is also *called* Maccabeus, with about nine others withdrew *Hardships and slaughter of the fugitives*

ᵇ 2¹⁶ Gk., *were gathered together*, but a slight emendation gives the above.
ᶜ 2¹⁸ The *king's Friends* constituted a favored class in the state.
ᵈ 2¹⁹ Lit., *in the house of the kingdom.*
ᵉ 2²⁶ Cf. Num. 25⁶⁻⁸.

History of the Hasmoneans

were in Jerusalem, the city of David, that certain men, who had broken the king's command had gone down into the hiding places in the wilderness. 32So many pursued after them, and having overtaken them encamped against them, and drew up the line of battle against them on the sabbath day. 33And they said to them, Things have gone far enough,[g] now come forth and obey the command of the king and you shall live. 34But they said, We will not come forth, neither will we do as the king commands, to profane the sabbath day. 35Then they at once offered them battle. 36But they made no resistance,[h] neither did they cast a stone at them, nor stop up the places of concealment, for they said, Let us all die in our innocency: 37let heaven and earth bear witness for us, that you put us to death unjustly. 38Then they rose up against them in battle on the sabbath, and thus they died with their wives and children and cattle, to the number of a thousand souls.

Traditional History

into the wilderness.[f] He and his companions kept themselves alive in the mountains after the manner of wild beasts. And they subsisted constantly on a diet of herbs to avoid participating in the pollution.

Their later successful armed resistance

39When Mattathias and his friends knew it they mourned bitterly over them. 40And they said to each other, If we all do as our brothers have done, and do not fight against the heathen for our lives and our customs, they will now quickly destroy us from off the earth. 41So they took counsel that day, saying, Whoever shall come against us for battle on the sabbath day, let us fight against him, and we will by no means all die, as our brothers died in the hiding places. 42Then there gathered together to them a company of Hasideans,[i] brave men of Israel, every one who offered himself willingly for the law. 43And all who fled from the evils were added to them, and strengthened them.

44And they mustered a host,
And smote the sinners in their anger
And the lawless in their wrath.

8 1But Judas who is also *called* Maccabeus, and his companions, making their way secretly into the villages summoned their kinsmen and, attaching to themselves those who had continued in the Jewish religion, gathered together as many as six thousand. 2And they called on the Lord, to look mercifully upon the people who were oppressed by all, and to have compassion on the sanctuary which had been profaned by the ungodly men, 3and to have pity on the city which was suffering ruin and would soon be levelled to the ground; also to hearken to the blood which cried to him, 4and to remember the unrighteous slaughter of the innocent children, and the sacrilegious

---

[f] II Mac. 5²⁷ So Gk., Syr., and Lat. *Into the wilderness* is, however, omitted in many Gk. texts.
[g] I Mac. 2³³ Lit., *Thus far, i.e.*, things have gone far enough.
[h] I Mac. 2³⁶ Lit., *answered not.*
[i] I Mac. 2⁴² Or, *Asideans* or, *Chasidim*, the pious, the devotees of the law, who later crystallized into the party of the Pharisees. Cf. also 7¹³.

History of the Hasmoneans

And the rest fled to the heathen for safety. ⁴⁵Also Mattathias and his friends went about and pulled down the altars, ⁴⁶and circumcised by force the children who were uncircumcised, as many as they found in the territory of Israel. ⁴⁷Thus they pursued the sons of arrogance,ʲ and the work prospered in their hand. ⁴⁸They took the direction of affairs out of the hands of the heathen and of the kings, nor did they yield ground to the sinner.

Traditional History

acts that had been committed against his name; and to show his hatred of wickedness. ⁵As soon as Maccabeus had an organized army, the heathen at once found him irresistible, for the wrath of the Lord was changed into mercy. ⁶Coming unawares he set fire to cities and villages. And he won back the most important positions, putting to flight great numbers of the enemy. For such assaults he especially took advantage of the heights.ᵏ And reports of his courage spread abroad everywhere.

§ 176. Death of Mattathias, I Mac. 2⁴⁹⁻⁷⁰

History of the Hasmoneans

I Mac. 2 ⁴⁹When the time approached for Mattathias to die he said to his sons, Now insolence and insult have grown strong, and a period of reversals has come, with flaming wrath.

Farewell exhortation of Mattathias

> ⁵⁰Now, my sons, be zealous for the law,
> And give your lives for the covenant of your fathers.
> ⁵¹And remember the deeds which your forefathers did in their generations;
> And win great glory and everlasting fame.
> ⁵²Was not Abraham found faithful when tested?
> And it was counted to him as righteousness.
> ⁵³Joseph in the time of his distress kept the commandment,
> And became lord of Egypt.
> ⁵⁴Phinehas our father, because he was so zealous,
> Received the covenant of an everlasting priesthood.
> ⁵⁵Joshua for carrying out the word of God,
> Became a judge in Israel.
> ⁵⁶Caleb for bearing witness in the congregation,
> Obtained a heritage in the land.
> ⁵⁷David for being merciful,
> Inherited a kingly throne for ever and ever.
> ⁵⁸Elijah because he was so zealous for the law,
> Was taken up into heaven.
> ⁵⁹Hananiah, Azariah, Mishael believed,
> And were rescued from the flame.
> ⁶⁰Daniel because of his innocence,
> Was delivered from the mouth of lions.

ʲ I Mac. 2⁴⁷ Lit., *sons of pride.*
ᵏ II Mac. 8⁶ Following Gk.A and several MSS. Another reading is, *seized convenient places, i.e.,* those adapted to his strategic plans.

History of the Hasmoneans

⁶¹And thus consider from generation to generation
None who put their trust in him ever want strength.
⁶²Then be not afraid of the words of a sinful man;
For his glory shall be dung and worms.
⁶³To-day he is exalted, but to-morrow he cannot be found,
Because he has returned to dust, and the memory of him has perished.
⁶⁴Then my sons be strong, and show yourselves men in behalf of the law;
So doing you shall obtain glory.

His appointment of Simon and Judas

⁶⁵And, behold, Simon your brother, I know that he is a man of counsel;
Obey him always; let him be your adviser.
⁶⁶Judas Maccabeus, too, he has been a man of war from his youth;
He shall be your captain, and fight the battle of the people.
⁶⁷And take to yourselves all law-abiding men,
And avenge the wrong of your people.
⁶⁸Render a recompense to the heathen,
And give heed to the commands of the law.

His death and burial

⁶⁹Thus he blessed them and was gathered to his fathers. ⁷⁰And he died in the one hundred and forty-sixth year, and his sons buried him in the sepulchres of his fathers at Modein, and all Israel made a great lamentation for him.

II

THE WARS AND ACHIEVEMENTS OF JUDAS MACCABEUS, I Mac. 3–9, II Mac. 8⁸–14³⁶

§ 177. Judas's Victory over Apollonius and Seron, I Mac. 3¹⁻²⁴

History of the Hasmoneans

Courage, prowess, and valiant deeds of Judas

I Mac. 3 ¹Then his son Judas, who was called Maccabeus, rose up in his place. ²And all his brothers helped him, as did all those who had supported his father, and they fought with gladness the battle of Israel.

The Wars and Achievements of Judas.—The brief period from 167 to 161 B.C. was the most active and dramatic in Israelitish history. It witnessed five great victories, in each of which the fortunes of the Jews hung in the balance. Poorly armed, ill-organized, and unaccustomed to war, the Jews faced large armies containing some of the best equipped and trained soldiers of the age. They won because they were banded together in a last desperate struggle for their lives, their homes, and their religion, while their foes were inspired by no patriotic or noble motives, but for the most part were simply mercenaries. Above all, the Jews had at their head one of the bravest, most unselfish, and able leaders of antiquity. He always chose battle-fields in which natural conditions greatly favored the defenders. By an appeal to their faith and patriotism and by his own personal magnetism, Judas welded his followers together as one man and then suddenly, like a thunder-bolt, launched them against their enemies. On the same battle-fields—the deep, narrow valleys which led up from the western coast plain to the Judean highlands—Judas eclipsed the ancient victories of David against the Philistines. History repeated itself. The spirit of that early heroic age was revived. I and II Mac., like I Sam., recount the old inspiring story of right, represented by a few brave, unselfish men, successful against proud, confident injustice and tyranny. In less than a decade Judas and his brothers transformed the weak, yielding Jews into a powerful factor in the politics of the East and laid the foundations of the Maccabean kingdom, which in extent and wealth ultimately equalled that of David. Above all they established the freedom of religious worship, which the heathen never again seriously attempted to take away from the Jews.
§ 177 The panegyric with which the account of Judas's wars opens recalls David's tribute to Saul and Jonathan at their death (cf. especially, *His memory is blessed forever*). The form is highly poetical. It may be from the author of I Mac., whose loyalty and devotion it well expresses, or may come from a popular song of praise and lamentation over the departed hero.

History of the Hasmoneans

³He spread far and wide the fame of his glory,
And put on his breastplate like a giant,
And girded on his weapons of war,
And set battles in array,
Protecting the army with his sword.
⁴He was like a lion in his deeds,
And as a lion's whelp roaring for prey.
⁵He pursued the lawless, seeking them out,
And he burnt up those who troubled his people.
⁶The lawless shrunk for fear of him,
And all the workers of lawlessness were greatly terrified;
And deliverance was attained through him.
⁷He angered many kings,
And made Jacob glad with his acts;
And his memory is blessed forever.
⁸He went about among the cities of Judah,
And destroyed the godless from the land,
And turned away the wrath *of God* from Israel.
⁹And he was renowned to the ends of the earth.ᵃ

¹⁰Then Apollonius gathered the heathen together and a great army from Samaria to fight against Israel. ¹¹And when Judas learned of it, he went out to meet him, and defeated and slew him; and many fell mortally wounded, while the rest fled. ¹²And they captured their spoils, and Judas took the sword of Apollonius, with which he fought all his days. *Defeat and death of Apollonius*

¹³When Seron, the commander of the army of Syria, heard that Judas had gathered a large force of faithful men about him, who went with him to war, ¹⁴he said, I will make myself famous and gain renown in the kingdom; for I will fight with Judas and those with him, who are defying the command of the king. ¹⁵And there went up with him also a mighty army of the godless to help him, to take vengeance on the Israelites. *Seron's advance against Judas*

¹⁶As he approached the ascent of Bethhoron Judas went forth to meet him with a small company. ¹⁷But when they saw the army coming to meet them, they said to Judas, How shall we, few as we are, be able to battle against so great a multitude? and we are faint also, having tasted no food to-day. ¹⁸Then Judas said, It is an easy thing for many to be shut up in the hands of a few; and with Heaven it is equally easy to save by many or by few; ¹⁹for victory in battle does not depend upon the size of an army, but from Heaven comes the strength. ²⁰They come to us full of insolence and lawlessness, to destroy us with our wives and children and to plunder us; ²¹but, as for us, we are fighting for our lives and our laws. ²²And he himself will crush them before our face; so do not be afraid of them. *Judas's address before the battle*

²³Now when he had finished speaking, he leaped suddenly upon them, and Seron and his army were put to flight before him. ²⁴And they pursued them by the descent of Bethhoron to the plain, and there fell of them about eight hundred men; but the rest fled into the land of the Philistines. *Defeat and flight of the Syrians*

ᵃ 3⁹ Vs. ⁹ᵇ, *and he gathered those who were about to perish*, is in the Gk. practically a duplicate of ¹⁰ᵃ. It makes little sense. The evident conclusion of the panegyric is ⁹ᵃ. Vs. ⁹ᵇ is therefore due to a copyist's error.

§ 178. Departure of Antiochus Epiphanes for Persia and his Appointment of Lysias as Regent, I Mac. 3²⁵⁻³⁷

History of the Hasmoneans

Measures to subdue the Jews and to refill the depleted Syrian treasury

I Mac. 3 ²⁵Now the fear of Judas and his brothers and the dread of them began to fall upon the nations round about them. ²⁶And his reputation reached the king, for every nation was telling of the battles of Judas. ²⁷But when King Antiochus heard these things, he was filled with indignation and sent and gathered together all the forces of his realm, a very strong army. ²⁸And he opened his treasury and gave his forces pay for a year, and commanded them to be ready for every emergency. ²⁹And seeing that money was scarce in his treasury and that the tributes of the country were small, because of the dissension and calamity which he had brought upon the land, for the purpose of taking away the laws which had been in force from the earliest days, ³⁰he feared that he should not have enough, as at other times, for the expenses and the gifts which he had formerly given with a liberal hand, in which he had surpassed the kings who had been before him. ³¹And he was exceedingly perplexed in his mind, and determined to go into Persia and to take the tributes of the countries and to gather much money.

Division of the military forces

³²So he left Lysias, an honorable man and one of the royal family, in charge of the affairs of the king from the River Euphrates to the borders of Egypt and to bring up his son Antiochus, until he returned. ³⁴And he delivered to him the half of his forces and the elephants, and gave him charge of all the things that he wished to have done and concerning those who dwelt in Judea and in Jerusalem, ³⁵that he should send a force against them, to root out and destroy the strength of Israel and the remnant of Jerusalem, and to take away their memory from the place, ³⁶and that he should make foreigners dwell in all their territory and should divide their land to them by lot. ³⁷Then the king took the remaining half of the forces and set out from Antioch his capital, in the one hundred and forty-seventh year,[b] and, crossing the Euphrates, he went through the upper countries.

§ 179. Defeat of the Syrian Generals, I Mac. 3³⁸–4²⁵, II Mac. 8⁸⁻³⁶

History of the Hasmoneans	*Traditional History*
The invading Syrian army **I Mac. 3** ³⁸Now Lysias chose Ptolemy the son of Dorymenes, and Nicanor, and Gorgias, influential men among the king's Friends, ³⁹and with them sent forty thousand footmen and seven thousand horsemen to go into the land of Judah to destroy it, as the	**II Mac. 8** ⁸But when Philip saw the man [Judas] little by little gaining ground and advancing more and more in his victories, he wrote to Ptolemy, the governor of Cœlesyria and Phœnicia, that he should support the king's cause. ⁹The latter quickly appointed Nicanor the son of Patroclus, one of the Chief Friends,

b 3³⁷ 165 B.C.
§ 179 I Mac. has a consistent, straightforward narrative, but II Mac., dependent upon popular report (cf. Introd., p. 38), is very confused. In 8³⁰⁻³³ the author gives in the place of the engagement with Gorgias an account of a battle in which Bacchides (mentioned only in I Mac. 7) and Timotheus figure. Apparently he has introduced here in a wrong setting an account of later events.

History of the Hasmoneans	*Traditional History*

king had ordered. ⁴⁰And they set out with all their army and pitched their camp near Emmaus in the plain. ⁴¹And the merchants of the country heard the rumors about them, and taking silver and gold in large quantities, and shackles, they came into the camp to get the Israelites for slaves. There were added to them the forces of Syria and of the Philistines.

and sent him in command of a heathen army of no less than twenty thousand from all nations, to destroy the whole race of Judea. And with him he associated Gorgias, a general and one who had had experience in military affairs. ¹⁰And Nicanor determined to make up for the king from the captive Jews the tribute of two thousand talents which he was to pay to the Romans. ¹¹And immediately he sent to the cities upon the sea coast, inviting them to buy Jewish slaves, promising to allow ninety slaves for a talent, not expecting the judgment which was to overtake him from the Almighty.

Attitude of the Jews and the exhortations of Judas

⁴²Then Judas and his brothers saw that evils were increasing and that the forces were encamping in their territory, and when they learned of the commands which the king had given to destroy the people and make an end of them, ⁴³they said to each other,

Let us raise up the ruin of our people
And let us fight for our people and the
   sanctuary!ᶜ

⁴⁴So the congregation was gathered together, that they might be ready for battle and that they might pray and ask for mercy and compassion.

⁴⁵And Jerusalem was without inhabitant,
   like a wilderness,
There was none of her offspring who
   went in or out,
And the sanctuary was trodden down,
And foreigners were in the citadel,
The city had become a lodging place for
   the heathen,
And joy was taken away from Jacob,
And the pipe and the harp ceased.

⁴⁶Then they gathered together and came to Mizpeh, opposite Jerusalem; for in Mizpehᵈ there was a place of

¹²But tidings came to Judas concerning the sending out of Nicanor; and when he informed his followers of the army's presence, ¹³those who were cowardly and distrustful of the judgment of God ran away and left the country. ¹⁴But the others sold all they had left and likewise besought the Lord to deliver those whom the impious Nicanor had sold before he met them; ¹⁵and if not for their own sakes, yet for the sake of the covenants made with their fathers, and because he had called them by his revered and glorious name. ¹⁶Then Maccabeus gathered his men together, six thousand in number, and exhorted them not to be smitten with dismay at the enemy nor to fear the great multitude of the heathen who were unrighteously coming against them, but to contend nobly. ¹⁷And he pictured before their eyes the outrage which had been wickedly perpetrated upon the sanctuary, and the shameful treatment and mocking of the city, and further the overthrow of their an-

---

ᶜ I Mac. 3⁴³ So Luc.   The Gk. is corrupt.
ᵈ I Mac. 3⁴⁶ Cf. I Sam. 7⁵⁻⁹.

History of the Hasmoneans | *Traditional History*

prayer for Israel. ⁴⁷And they fasted that day, and put sackcloth and ashes on their heads and tore their clothes, ⁴⁸and spread out the book of the law— one of those in which the heathen had been painting images of their idols.[e] ⁴⁹And they brought the priests' garments with the first-fruits, and the tithes, and they cut the hair of the Nazirites who had accomplished their days. ⁵⁰And they cried aloud toward Heaven, saying, What shall we do with these and whither shall we carry them away? ⁵¹For thy sanctuary is trodden down and profaned, and thy priests are in sorrow and humiliation. ⁵²And now the heathen have assembled together against us to destroy us. Thou knowest what plans they are making against us. ⁵³How shall we be able to stand before them, except thou be our help? ⁵⁴And they sounded with the trumpets, and cried with a loud voice.

cestral mode of living. ¹⁸For they, said he, trust to arms and likewise to deeds of daring, but we trust in the Almighty God, who is able with a nod to cast down, not those alone who are coming against us, but the whole world. ¹⁹And he also recounted to them the help given from time to time in the days of their ancestors, both how they were delivered in the time of Sennacherib, when one hundred and eighty-five thousand perished,[f] ²⁰and how in Babylonia at the battle which was fought against the Gauls, only eight thousand in all engaged in battle with four thousand Macedonians, but when the Macedonians were hard pressed, the eight thousand destroyed the one hundred and twenty thousand, because of the succor which they had from Heaven; and how they took great booty.[g]

Preparations for the battle ⁵⁵And after this Judas appointed leaders of the people, commanders over thousands, over hundreds, over fifties, ⁵⁶and over tens. And he told those who were building houses and those who were planting vineyards and those who were afraid, to return, each to his own house, as the law commanded.[h] ⁵⁷Then the army removed and encamped upon the south side of Emmaus. ⁵⁸And Judas said, Gird yourselves and be valiant men; and be ready in the morning to fight with these heathen who are assembled together against us to destroy us and our sanctuary. ⁵⁹For it is better for us to die in battle, than to see the misfortunes of our nation and of the sanctuary. ⁶⁰Nevertheless, let Heaven do whatever be his will.

²¹After he had with these words made them of good courage and ready to die for the laws and their country, he divided his army into four parts. ²²As leaders of the several corps, he appointed his brothers Simon and Joseph and Jonathan, assigning to each fifteen hundred men. ²³ᵃMoreover he also appointed Eleazar to read aloud the sacred book. And he gave as a watchword, The Help of God.

---

e I Mac. 3⁴⁸ Following an acute conjecture of Professor Torrey. The text is obscure.
f II Mac. 8¹⁹ Cf. II Kgs. 19³⁵.
g II Mac. 8²⁰ Perhaps this is a reference to a popular tradition of a battle between Antiochus the Great and Molon, a rebellious governor of Media.
h I Mac. 3⁵⁶ Dt. 20⁵⁻⁹.

History of the Hasmoneans

Traditional History

Gorgias's futile night march

4 ¹And Gorgias took five thousand footmen, and a thousand chosen horsemen, ²and the army set out by night, that it might fall upon the army of the Jews and attack them suddenly. And the men of the citadel were his guides. ³But when Judas heard of it, he broke camp with his valiant men, that he might attack the king's army which was at Emmaus, ⁴while as yet the forces were dispersed from the camp. ⁵And when Gorgias came to the camp of Judas by night, he found no one. Then he looked for them in the mountains, thinking that ⁶the men were fleeing from him.

Judas's exhortation to his men

But as soon as it was day, Judas appeared in the plain with three thousand men; only they had neither armor nor swords as they wished. ⁷When now they saw the camp of the heathen strongly fortified and cavalry about it and experienced warriors there, ⁸Judas said to the men who were with him, Fear not their multitude neither be afraid of their attack. ⁹Remember how our fathers were saved in the Red Sea, when Pharaoh pursued them with a host. ¹⁰And now let us cry to Heaven, if he will show favor to usʲ and will remember the covenant made with our fathers and destroy this army before our face to-day, ¹¹that all the heathen may know that there is one who redeemeth and saveth Israel.

Defeat and pursuit of the Greeks

¹²Then when the foreigners lifted up their eyes and saw them coming toward them, ¹³they went from their camp to battle. And those who were with Judas sounded their trumpets and joined battle; ¹⁴and the heathen were defeated and fled into the plain. ¹⁵But all who were in the rear fell by the sword, and they pursued them to Gazaraᵏ and to the plains of Idu-

²³ᵇThen leading the first corps himself, he joined battle with Nicanor. ²⁴And, since the Almighty fought on their side, they slew of the enemy over nine thousand, wounded and disabled the greater part of Nicanor's army, and compelled all to flee. ²⁵They also took the money of those who had come there to buy them. And after they had pursued them for some distance, they were obliged to return because of the time, ²⁶for it was the day before the sabbath and therefore they made no effort to chase them far. ²⁷When they had gathered the arms of the enemy, and had stripped off their spoils, they gave their attention to the sabbath, blessing and thanking the Lord exceedingly, who had saved them to this day, for his mercy had begun to distil upon them.ⁱ ²⁸After the sabbath, when they had given of the spoils to those who had been tortured, and to the widows and orphans, they distributed the rest among themselves and their children. ²⁹Then when they had completed these things and had made a common supplication, they besought the merciful Lord to be wholly reconciled with his servants.

³⁰And in an encounter with the forces of Timotheus and Bacchides they killed over twenty thousand of them and made themselves masters of exceedingly high strongholds and divided very

Victory over the forces led by Nicanor

Victory over the Greek forces under Timotheus and Bacchides

ⁱ II Mac. 8²⁷ So Lat. and many important Gk. codices. Most MSS. read, *and had begun to show them mercy.*

ʲ I Mac. 4¹⁰ So Luc. and Gk.A.

ᵏ I Mac. 4¹⁵ The O.T. *Gezer.* The following *plains of Idumea* is doubtful, as is also Gk.A, *Judea.*

History of the Hasmoneans

mea and Azotus[l] and Jamnia, and there fell of them about three thousand men.

Flight of the forces under Gorgias

[16]When Judas and his army returned from pursuing them, [17]he said to the people, Do not be greedy for the spoils, since there is a battle before us, [18]and Gorgias and his army are near us in the mountain. But stand now against our enemies and fight them, and afterward you may openly take the spoils. [19]While Judas was still speaking there appeared a part of them, looking out from the mountain; [20]and these saw that their army had been put to flight and that the Jews were burning their camp, for the smoke that was seen showed what had been done. [21]And when they perceived these things, they were thrown into a panic, and seeing the army of Judas also in the plain ready for battle, [22]they all retreated into the land of the Philistines.[n] [23]And Judas returned to sack the camp, and they took much gold and silver and blue and sea-purple[o] and great riches. [24]Then they returned home and sang a song of thanksgiving and gave praise to Heaven, because he is good, because his mercy endureth forever.[p] [25]Thus Israel had a great deliverance that day.

Discouragement of Lysias

[26]But the foreigners, as many as had escaped, came and told Lysias all the things that had happened. [27]And when he heard it, he was astonished and discouraged, because neither had Israel met with reverses as he wished nor had what the king commanded been realized.

Traditional History

much plunder, giving the tortured and orphans and widows and moreover the aged also an equal share with themselves. [31]All the arms of the enemy which they had gathered they stored up carefully in the most suitable places, and the rest of the spoils they carried to Jerusalem. [32]And they killed Phylarches[m] of Timotheus's forces, a most impious man, and one who had done the Jews much harm. [33]As they kept the feast of victory in the city of their fathers, they burned those who had set the sacred gates on fire, and among them Callisthenes, who had fled into a little house; and so they received the suitable reward for their impiety.

Flight and ignominious defeat of Nicanor

[34]Also the thrice-accursed Nicanor, who had brought the thousand merchants to buy the Jews, was through the help of the Lord humbled by those who in his eyes were held to be of least account. [35]Taking off his sumptuous apparel, shunning all company, he came through the midst of the land, like a fugitive slave, to Antioch, supremely unfortunate in the destruction of his army.[q] [36]And he who had taken upon himself successfully to obtain the tribute for the Romans from the captives of Jerusalem declared openly that the Jews had one who fought for them, and that on this account the Jews were invulnerable, because they followed the laws ordained by him.

---

[l] I Mac. 4[15] *Ashdod.*
[m] II Mac. 8[32] It is not clear whether this is a proper name or a title.
[n] I Mac. 4[22] Lit., *strangers.*
[o] I Mac. 4[23] So the Sinaitic text. The reference is to the famous Tyrian purple made from sea-shells.
[p] I Mac. 4[24] Cf. Ps. 118[1-4, 29], 136, and often in Chr.
[q] II Mac. 8[35] Other MSS. read, *having met great misfortune, the destruction of his army.*

§ 180. **Victory over Lysias at Bethsura,** I Mac. 4²⁸⁻³⁵, II Mac. 11¹–12¹

History of the Hasmoneans	*Traditional History*

Bravery of the Jews in meeting and vanquishing the huge army of Lysias

I Mac. 4 ²⁸Now in the next year [Lysias] gathered together sixty thousand picked footmen and five thousand horsemen, that he might subdue [the Jews]. ²⁹When they came to Idumea and encamped at Bethsura, Judas met them with ten thousand men. ³⁰As he saw that the army was strong, he prayed and said, Blessed art thou, O Saviour of Israel, who didst shatter the attacking power of the mighty man by the hand of thy servant David,ʳ and didst deliver the army of the heathen into the hands of Jonathan the son of Saul, and of his armorbearer.ˢ

³¹Shut up this army in the hand of thy people Israel,
And let them be ashamed of their army and their horsemen.
³²Give them faintness of heart,
And let their bold courage melt away,
And let them tremble at their destruction.
³³Cast them down by the sword of those who love thee,
So that all may know thy name who praise thee with thanksgiving.

³⁴Then they joined battle; and there fell of the army of Lysias about five thousand men, and they fell on the spot before them.ᵘ

II Mac. 11 ¹Now a little later Lysias, the king's guardian and kinsman and primeminister, greatly displeased at what had happened, ²collected about eighty thousand footmen and all his horsemen and came against the Jews. He planned to make the city a dwelling-place for Greeks, and to levy tribute on the temple, ³as on the other sacred places of the heathen, and to put up the high priesthood for sale each year. ⁴He had no regard for the might of God, but was puffed up with his ten thousand footmen and his thousands of horsemen and eighty elephants. ⁵As soon as he came into Judea and drew near to Bethsura, which was a strong place distant aboutᵗ three-fifths of a mileᵗ from Jerusalem he pressed it hard. ⁶But when Maccabeus and his men learned that he was besieging the strongholds, with lamentations and tears they and all the people besought

the Lord to send a good messenger to save Israel. ⁷Maccabeus, himself the first, took up arms, and exhorted the others to encounter the danger with him and succor their fellow-countrymen; and very willingly they set forth with him. ⁸But while they were still there, close to Jerusalem, there appeared at their head one on horseback in white apparel, brandishing weapons of gold. ⁹Then all together they praised the merciful God and were strengthened in heart, ready to strike down not men only but the

---

§ 180 Again I Mac. is clearly right in placing the first campaign of Lysias before the death of Antiochus IV. II Mac. dates it a year later, and adds an account of a treaty, the historical basis of which must have been the terms agreed upon after the Jews were defeated by Lysias in his second campaign. Cf. § 185. The author of II Mac., however, has another account of that treaty, 13²³⁻²⁶, and definitely associates with the first campaign the present treaty, and the letters which he appends.
ʳ I Mac. 4³⁰ Cf. I Sam. 17.
ˢ I Mac. 4³⁰ Cf. I Sam. 14.
ᵗ II Mac. 11⁵ Gk., *five stadia*. Some MSS. read, *five schonoi* or *leagues*, which is much nearer the actual distance.
ᵘ I Mac. 4³⁴ Lit., *and they fell over against them.*

Traditional History

wildest beasts and walls of iron, ¹⁰they advanced in array with him who came from Heaven to fight on their side, for the Lord had mercy on them. ¹¹Hurling themselves like lions on the enemy they slew of them eleven thousand footmen and sixteen hundred horsemen ¹²and forced all the rest to flee. But the greater part of them escaped wounded and naked. And Lysias also saved himself by shameful flight.

History of the Hasmoneans :

Lysias's retreat to prepare for another attack

II Mac. 4 ³⁵But when Lysias saw that his army was retreating, and the boldness that had come upon those who were with Judas, and how they were ready either to live or to die nobly, he removed to Antioch and gathered together hired soldiers, that he might come again into Judea with a still greater force.

¹³But as he was a man not without understanding, after reflecting upon the defeat which had befallen him, he considered that the Hebrews could not be overcome, because the Almighty God fought on their side, and so he sent again ¹⁴and persuaded them to come to terms on perfectly just conditions, and promised that he would also constrain the king to become their friend. ¹⁵And Maccabeus gave consent to all that Lysias proposed, for whatever requests Maccabeus delivered in writing to Lysias concerning the Jews the king allowed.

Lysias's treaty with Judas

His letter to the Jews

¹⁶For the letterᵛ written to the Jews from Lysias was to this effect:

Lysias to the people of the Jews, greeting. ¹⁷John and Absalom, your messengers, having delivered the document signed by you,ʷ inquired concerning the things therein. ¹⁸Whatever, therefore, needed also to be brought before the king, these I reported, and whatever was possible he allowed. ¹⁹If then you will preserve your good-will toward the state, henceforth I also will endeavor to contribute to your welfare. ²⁰In regard to the particulars, I have given order, both to these men and to those who are sent from me, to confer with you. ²¹Fare you well. Written in the one hundred and forty-eighth year, on the twenty-fourth day of the month Dioscorinthus.ˣ

Letter of Antiochus V concerning the Jews

²²And the king's letter was to this effect:

King Antiochus to his brother Lysias, greeting. ²³After our father departed to the gods, it was our wish that the subjects of our kingdom should attend to the care of their own affairs undisturbed. ²⁴Having heard that the Jews object to our father's purpose to convert them to the Greek usages, preferring their own manner of living and requesting that their own customs be allowed to them—²⁵we therefore, desiring also that this nation should be free from disturbance, decide that their temple be restored to them, and that they live according to the customs which were in the days of their

---

ᵛ II Mac. 11¹⁶ Or, *letters.*
ʷ 11¹⁷ Or possibly, *the document written below.*
ˣ 11²¹ This word is evidently a corruption, either for the Cretan name of a month (*Dioscuri*) or else of the Macedonian month, *Dius*, November (so Syr.). Probably it is for *March.* 11³³

Traditional History

ancestors. ²⁶You will therefore do well to send to them, and give them the right hand of friendship, that they, knowing our purpose, may be in good spirits and gladly devote themselves to their own affairs.

²⁷And to the nation the king's letter was as follows: His letter to them

King Antiochus to the senate of the Jews and to the other Jews, greeting. ²⁸If you fare well, we have our desire. We ourselves also are in good health. ²⁹Menelaus informed us that you desired to depart and attend to your own business. ³⁰They, therefore, who depart up to the thirtieth day of Xanthicus[a] shall have our friendship, ³¹with full permission to the Jews to use their own laws, even as heretofore; and none of them shall be in any way molested for what was done in ignorance. ³²I have moreover sent Menelaus to encourage you. ³³Fare you well. Written in the hundred and forty-eighth year,[b] on the fifteenth day of Xanthicus. ³⁴And the Romans also sent to them a letter which read thus:

Quintus Memmius and Titus Manlius, ambassadors of the Romans, to the Jewish people, greeting. ³⁵In regard to the concessions which Lysias the king's kinsman granted you, we also give consent. ³⁶But as for the things which he judged should be referred to the king, as soon as you have considered these send some one at once that we may publish such decrees as befit your case, for we are on our way to Antioch. ³⁷Therefore send some one quickly, that we also may learn what is your opinion. ³⁸Farewell. Written in the one hundred and forty-eighth year, on the fifteenth day of Xanthicus.   Letter from the Romans

12 ¹When these agreements had been made Lysias departed to the king, and the Jews attended to their farming.   Lysias's departure

§ 181. Purification of the Temple and Restoration of its Service, I Mac. 4³⁶⁻⁶¹, II Mac. 10¹⁻⁹

History of the Hasmoneans

I Mac. 4 ³⁶Then Judas and his brothers said, Now that our enemies have been defeated, let us go up to cleanse the sanctuary and to dedicate it again; so they went up to Mount Zion. ³⁷And all the army was gathered together and went up to Mount Zion. ³⁸And when they saw the sanctuary laid desolate, the altar profaned, the gates burnt, and shrubs growing in the courts, as in a forest or as on one of the mountains, and the priests' chambers pulled down, ³⁹they tore their garments and made great lamentation, ⁴⁰and putting ashes upon their heads, they fell prone

Traditional History

II Mac. 10 ¹Then Maccabeus and those who were with him, under the guidance of the Lord, recovered the temple and the city. ²And they pulled down the altars which had been built in the marketplace by the for-   Ceremonial cleansing and restoration of the temple

---

[a] 11³⁰ The Macedonian name of the Jewish month *Nisan* (Mar.-Apr.).
[b] 11³³ 165 B.C.
§ 181 I Mac. 10³ makes the period during which the temple was desecrated two years; Josephus three and one-half years; but I Mac. exactly three years, from Dec., 168 (1⁵⁴) to Dec., 165 (4⁵²).

History of the Hasmoneans	*Traditional History*

History of the Hasmoneans

upon the ground. Then they blew a signal on the trumpets and cried to Heaven. ⁴¹And Judas appointed certain men to fight against those who were in the citadel,ᶜ until he should have cleansed the sanctuary. ⁴²And he chose priests who were unimpeachable observers of the law, ⁴³who cleansed the sanctuary and carried out the polluted stones to an unclean place. ⁴⁴And they deliberated as to what they should do with the altar of burnt-offerings which had been profaned. ⁴⁵They finally reached this wise decision: to pull it down lest it should be a reproach to them, because the heathen had defiled it. So they pulled down the altar ⁴⁶and laid the stones on the temple mount in a convenient place, until there should come a prophet to give an oracle concerning them. ⁴⁷Then they took whole stones as the lawᵈ required and built a new altar after the design of the former. ⁴⁸They also rebuilt the sanctuary and the inner parts of the temple and consecrated the courts. ⁴⁹They also made the holy vessels new and brought the candlestick and the altar for burnt-offerings and for incense and the table into the temple. ⁵⁰And they burned incense on the altar and lighted the lamps that were on the candlestick, and they gave light in the temple. ⁵¹Then they set loaves upon the table and spread out the veils. So they finished all the work they had undertaken.

Institution of the feast of dedication

⁵²And they arose early in the morning of the twenty-fifth day of the ninth month, which is the month Chislev, in the one hundred and forty-eighth year,ᵉ ⁵³and offered sacrifice according to the law upon the new altar of burnt-offering which they had made. ⁵⁴About the same time and on the same day, in which the heathen had profaned it, was it dedicated again with songs and harps and lutes and with cymbals. ⁵⁵And all the people prostrated themselves and worshipped and gave praise to Heaven, who had given them good success. ⁵⁶And they celebrated the dedication of the altar eight days, and offered

Traditional History

eigners and also the sacred places. ³And when they had cleansed the sanctuary they made another altar for sacrifice, and they struck sparks from stones and got fire out of them, and offered sacrifices, after an interval of two years, and attended to the incense and lights and the setting-forth of the showbread. ⁴After doing these things, they prostrated themselves and besought the Lord that they might fall no more into such evils; but that, if ever they should sin again, they might be chastened by him with forbearance and not be delivered to blaspheming and barbarous heathen.

⁵Now on the same day that the sanctuary was profaned by foreigners, upon that very day it came to pass that the cleansing of the sanctuary occurred, even on the twenty-fifth day of the same month, which is Chislev. ⁶And they kept eight days with gladness in the manner of the feast of tabernacles, remembering how that not

---

ᶜ I Mac. 4⁴¹ *I.e.*, to distract their attention and thus to anticipate an unexpected sally.
ᵈ I Mac. 4⁴⁷ Ex. 20²⁵, Dt. 27⁶.
ᵉ I Mac. 4⁵² Dec., 165 B.C.

History of the Hasmoneans

burnt-offerings with gladness and sacrificed a sacrifice of deliverance and praise. ⁵⁷And they decorated the front of the temple with crowns of gold and small shields and rededicated the gates and the priests' chambers and made doors for them. ⁵⁸And great joy reigned among the people, because the reproach of the heathen had been removed. ⁵⁹And Judas and his brothers and the whole congregation of Israel decreed that the days of the dedication of the altar should be kept in their seasons from year to year for the period of eight days, from the twenty-fifth day of the month Chislev, with gladness and joy. ⁶⁰At that time also they fortified Mount Zion with high walls and strong towers all round, lest by any chance the heathen should come and tread them down, as they had done before. ⁶¹And he stationed there a force to keep it, and they fortified Bethsura,ᶠ that the people might have a stronghold inᵍ Idumea.

Traditional History

long before, during the feast of tabernacles they were dwelling in the mountains and in the caves like wild beasts. ⁷Therefore bearing wands, wreathed with leaves and fair boughs and palms also, they offered up hymns of thanksgiving to him who had successfully brought to pass the cleansing of his own place. ⁸They ordained also with a common statute and decree, for all the nation of the Jews, that they should observe these days every year.

§ 182. Successful Campaigns against the Surrounding Nations, I Mac. 5, II Mac. 10¹⁴⁻³⁸, 12²⁻⁴⁵

History of the Hasmoneans

I Mac. 5 ¹Now when the heathen round about heard that the altar had been built and the sanctuary dedicated as it was formerly, they were very angry and concluded ²to destroy the race of Jacob that was in the midst of them, and they began to slay and destroy among the people. ³Judas, however, fought against the people of Esau in Idumea

Traditional History

II Mac. 10 ¹⁴But Gorgias, when he became governor of the district, maintained a force of mercenaries and at every turn kept up war with the Jews. ¹⁵And together with him the Idumeans also, being masters of important strongholds, were harassing the Jews; and by receiving the refugees from Jerusalem, were attempting to keep up war. ¹⁶But Maccabeus and his men, having made solemn supplication, and having besought God to fight on their side, rushed upon the strongholds of the Idumeans, ¹⁷and by a vigorous assault made themselves masters of the positions and repulsed all who fought upon the wall and slew those who fell in their way. They

Slaughter of the Idumeans and other foes of the Jews

ᶠ I Mac. 4⁶¹ So Syr. and Codex 55. The other Gk. texts add, *to keep it.*
ᵍ I Mac. 4⁶¹ So Gk. Other Gk. texts, *against.*
§ 182 I Mac. has a much simpler and more consistent narrative. That the account of Timotheus's campaign in II Mac. belongs before the account of his death in 10 is perfectly clear. At certain points both sources are evidently dependent upon popular tradition, and are therefore somewhat vague and confusing. It is also difficult to identify the parallels, for the variations are exceedingly wide.

History of the Hasmoneans	*Traditional History*
at Akrabattine,[h] because they besieged Israel, and he defeated them with a great slaughter and humbled their pride and took their spoils. ⁴He remembered the wickedness of the inhabitants of Baean, who were a source of annoyance and of danger, lying in ambush for them along the roads. ⁵And they were shut up by him in the towers, and he besieged them and destroyed them utterly and burned the towers of the place, with all who were in them.	killed no fewer than twenty thousand. ¹⁸Then, since no less than nine thousand had fled into two exceedingly strong towers, supplied with all things needed for a siege, ¹⁹Maccabeus left Simon and Joseph, and also Zaccheus and those who were with him, a force sufficient to besiege them and himself departed to places where he was most needed. ²⁰But the officers of Simon,[i] yielding to covetousness, were bribed by certain of those who were in the towers, and upon the receipt of seventy thousand drachmas let some of them slip away. ²¹When this act was reported to Maccabeus, he gathered the leaders of the people together, and accused these of having sold their fellow-countrymen for money by setting their enemies free to fight against them. ²²So he slew these men for having turned traitors and forthwith captured the two towers. ²³Succeeding with his arms in all things, he put to death in the two strongholds more than twenty thousand.

Outrage upon the Jews at Joppa

12 ²But certain of the governors of districts, Timotheus and Apollonius the son of Genneus, and Hieronymus also and Demophon, and besides these Nicanor the governor of Cyprus, would not permit them to enjoy tranquillity and live in peace. ³And men of Joppa perpetrated this most impious deed: they invited the Jews who dwelt among them to go with their wives and children into the boats which they had provided, as though they had no ill-will toward them, ⁴but in accordance with the common decree of the city. And when these accepted, because they desired to live in peace and suspected nothing,[j] they took them out to sea and drowned them, not less than two hundred in all.

Judas's vengeance upon Joppa and Jamnia

⁵But as soon as Judas heard of the cruelty done to his fellow-countrymen, he gave command to the men who were with him, and calling upon God the righteous Judge, he came against the murderers of his fellow-countrymen and set the harbor on fire by night and burned the boats and put to the sword those who had fled thither. ⁷As the town was closed against him, he withdrew, intending to come again to root out the whole community of the men of Joppa. ⁸But learning that the men of Jamnia were also disposed to act in the same manner against the Jews who were living among them, ⁹he likewise attacked the Jamnites by night and set fire to the harbor, together with the fleet, so that the glare of the light was seen as far as Jerusalem, twenty-seven and one-half miles away.

---

[h] I Mac. 5³ Probably in the region of the Scorpion Pass at the south of the Salt Sea, cf. Num. 34⁴.

[i] II Mac. 10²⁰ Or, *Simon and those who were with him.*

[j] II Mac. 12⁴ Or, *when these were thinking that they* (the men of Joppa) *desired peace and would awake no suspicion.*

History of the Hasmoneans

I Mac. 5 ⁶Then he passed over to the Ammonites and found a strong force and many people, with Timotheus as their leader. ⁷And he fought many battles with them, and they were defeated before him, and he conquered them. ⁸Then when he had gained possession of Jazer and its villages, he returned again into Judea.

⁹Then the heathen who were in Gilead[k] gathered together against the Israelites who were on the borders to destroy them. ¹⁰And they fled to the stronghold of Dathema and sent letters to Judas and his brothers, saying, The heathen who are about us have gathered together against us to destroy us, ¹¹and they are preparing to come and get possession of the stronghold to which we have fled for refuge, and Timotheus is the leader of their forces. ¹²Now therefore come and rescue us from their power, for many of our men have fallen; ¹³and all our countrymen who dwell in the land of Tob,[l] have been put to death, and they have carried into captivity their wives and children and their possessions. And they destroyed there about a thousand men. ¹⁴While the letters were being read, there came other messengers from Galilee with their garments torn, bringing a message of similar import, ¹⁵saying, That there were gathered together against them men of Ptolemais,[m] of Tyre, of Sidon, and from all heathen Galilee to destroy them completely.

¹⁶Now when Judas and the people heard these things, a great assembly came together to consult what they should do for their kinsmen who were in distress and being attacked by the heathen. ¹⁷And Judas said to Simon his brother, Choose men, and go, rescue your countrymen who are in Galilee, but Jonathan my brother and I will go into the land of Gilead. ¹⁸And he left Joseph the son of Zacharias and Azarias, as leaders of the people, with the rest of the army in Judea, in order to guard it. ¹⁹And he gave orders to them, saying, Take charge of the heathen until we return. ²⁰And to Simon were assigned three thousand men to go to Galilee and to Judas eight thousand men to go into the land of Gilead.

²¹Then Simon went into Galilee and fought many battles with the heathen, and the heathen were defeated by him. ²²And he pursued them to the gate of Ptolemais. And there fell of the heathen about three thousand men, and he took the spoils from them. ²³They took with them those who were in Galilee and in Arbatta, with their wives and their children and all that they had, and brought them into Judea with great rejoicing.

Marginal notes: Defeat of the Ammonites — Reports of outrages in Gilead and Galilee — Preparations for the campaign in Gilead and Galilee — Simon's successes in Galilee

---

Traditional History

²⁴Meanwhile J u d a s Maccabeus and his brother Jonathan crossed the Jordan and went three days' journey in the wilderness. ²⁵T h e n t h e y

II Mac. 12 ¹⁰Now when they had withdrawn a mile from there, as they marched against Timotheus, Arabians attacked him—no fewer than five thousand footmen and five hundred horsemen. ¹¹After a severe battle had been fought and Judas and his followers by the help

Marginal note: Judas's friendly meeting with the nomads and his capture of many strongholds

---

[k] I Mac. 5⁹ Gilead is here a designation of all the east-Jordan region.
[l] I Mac. 5¹³ Cf. Judg. 11³, II Sam. 10⁶. Other MSS. read, *Tubias.*
[m] I Mac. 5¹⁵ The O.T., *Accho.*

419

*History of the Hasmo-
neans*

encountered the Nabate-
ans, who met them in a
peaceable manner a n d
told them all about what
had befallen their kins-
men in the land of Gilead,
²⁶and how many of them
were shut up in Bosora,
Bosor, Alema, Cashphor,
Maked, and Carnaim—
all these cities are strong
and great — ²⁷and how
they were shut up in the
rest of the cities of the
land of Gilead, and that
[their foes] had decided
to encamp against the
strongholds on the next
day and to take them and
destroy all these men in
one day. ²⁸Thereupon
Judas and his a r m y
turned suddenly by the
way of the wilderness to
Bosora; and he took the
city and put all the men
to the sword, and taking
all their spoils, he burned
the city.

Defeat
and
flight
of Ti-
mothe-
us's
forces

²⁹Then he set out from
there b y n i g h t and
marched until he reached
the stronghold.   ³⁰And
when the morning came,
they looked up and there
were people carrying lad-
ders and engines of war
to take the stronghold,
and they were fighting
against them.   ³¹A n d
Judas seeing that the battle had begun and hearing
the alarm of the city ris-

Traditional History

of God had had good success, the defeated nomads
besought Judas to grant them friendship, promising that they would give cattle and in other
ways be a help to them.   ¹²Judas, thinking
that they would indeed be u s e f u l i n m a n y
ways, agreed to live in peace with them; and so,
receiving pledges of friendship, they departed to
their tents.   ¹³He also attacked a certain city,
secured by mounds and fenced about with walls
and inhabited by all sorts of peoples, named
Caspin.   ¹⁴They who were within, trusting to the
strength of the walls and to their store of provisions, behaved rudely toward Judas and his
followers, railing and even blaspheming and
speaking impious words.   ¹⁵But calling upon
the great Sovereign of the world, who without
battering rams or mechanical contrivances hurled
down Jericho in the times of Joshua, Judas and his
followers rushed wildly against the wall, ¹⁶and
took the city by the will of God, and made such
unspeakable slaughter that the adjoining lake,
which was four hundred yards wide, appeared
to be filled with the deluge of blood.

¹⁷From there they withdrew about eighty-four
miles and made their way to Charax, to the
Jews who are called Tubieni.   ¹⁸And they did
not find Timotheus in that district, for he had
departed from the district without accomplishing anything, but had left behind a very strong
garrison in a certain post.   ¹⁹Dositheus and
Sosipater, two of Maccabeus's captains, sallied
forth and destroyed those who had been left by
Timotheus in the stronghold, more than ten
thousand men.   ²⁰Then Maccabeus, having arranged his army into divisions and set them over
one of[n] the divisions, marched in haste against
Timotheus, who had with him a hundred and

---

[n] II Mac. 12²⁰ Most MSS. read, *set these over the divisions.* But in ²⁴ they are over one
division. The word, *one of*, has apparently fallen out of the verse.

*History of the Hasmo-
neans*

Traditional History

ing to heaven with trumpets and great noise, ³²he said to the men of his army, Fight to-day for your kinsmen. ³³Then he went forth behind them in three companies,ᵖ and they sounded with their trumpets and cried out in prayer. ³⁴And the army of Timotheus perceived that it was Maccabeus, and they fled before him. So he defeated them with a great slaughter, and there fell of them on that day about eight thousand men. ³⁵Then he turned aside to Mizpeh and fought against it and captured it and slew all its men and took the spoils from it and burned it. ³⁶From there he departed and took Casphor, Maked, Bosor, and the other cities of the land of Gilead.

³⁷Now after these things Timotheus gathered another army, and encamped opposite Raphon beyond the brook. ³⁸And Judas sent men to spy out the camp. And they brought him word saying, All the heathen who live about us have gathered together to them a very great army. ³⁹They have also hired Ara-

twenty thousand footmen and two thousand five hundred horsemen. ²¹As soon as Timotheus heard of the advance of Judas, he at once sent away the women and the children and also the baggageᵒ into the fortress called Carnion; for the place was hard to besiege and difficult of access because of the narrowness of the approaches on all sides. ²²But when the first division of Judas appeared in sight and terror fell upon the enemy and fear, because the manifestation of him who beholdeth all things came upon them, they rushed headlong in flight, carried this way and that, so that they were often hurt by their own men and pierced with the points of their swords. ²³And Judas continued the pursuit the more hotly, putting the guilty sinners to the sword, and he destroyed as many as thirty thousand men. ²⁴Timotheus himself, falling in with the division of Dositheus and Sosipater, besought them with much deception to let him go in safety, because he had in his power the parents of many and the brothers of some; if he should die little regard would be shown to these. ²⁵After he had with many words confirmed the agreement to restore them without hurt, they let him go that they might save their kinsmen.

10 ²⁴Now Timotheus, who had been before defeated by the Jews, having gathered together foreign forces in great numbers and having collected not a few of the horsemen who were of Asia, came with the avowed purpose of taking Judea by force of arms. ²⁵As he drew near, Maccabeus and his men sprinkled earth upon their heads and girded their loins with sackcloth in supplication to God. ²⁶And falling down upon the step before the altar, they besought him to be gracious to them and to be an enemy to their enemies and an adversary to their adversaries, as the law declares.�q ²⁷Then rising from their prayer they took up their arms and advanced some distance from the city, but

Second defeat of Timotheus and the capture of Carnaim

ᵒ II Mac. 12²¹ Gk., *rest of the baggage.*
ᵖ I Mac. 5³³ For the same tactics cf. Judg. 7¹⁶, I Sam. 11¹¹, II Sam. 18³.
q II Mac. 10²⁶ Cf. Ex. 23³².

History of the Hasmoneans

bians to help them, and they are camping beyond the brook, ready to come against you to battle. Then Judas went to meet them. [40]And Timotheus said to the officers of his army, when Judas with his army was near the brook of water, If he gets over ahead of us, we shall not be able to withstand him, for he will be more than a match for us. [41]But if he is afraid and halts across the river, we will cross to him and overcome him. [42]Now when Judas came near the brook of water, he ordered those who kept the record of the people to remain by the brook and commanded them, saying, Allow no one to halt, but let all come to the battle. [43]And he crossed over ahead of them and all the people after him. And all the heathen were defeated before him, and casting away their weapons, they fled to the temple at Carnaim. [44]And they captured the city and burned the temple, together with all who were in it. Thus Carnaim was subdued, and they were no longer able to offer resistance to Judas.

Traditional History

halted when they drew near to the enemy. [28]Just as the dawn was breaking, both alike charged; the one side having, as a pledge of success and victory—beside their valor—their trust in the Lord, the other making their passion their leader in the strife. [29]But when the battle grew fierce, there appeared from heaven to their adversaries five noble-looking men on horses with bridles of gold and leading on the Jews. And they, taking Maccabeus in the midst of them and covering him with their own armor, guarded him from wounds, while upon their adversaries they shot forth arrows and thunderbolts. Confused, therefore, with blindness, filled with bewilderment, they were cut to pieces. [31]Twenty thousand, five hundred, besides six hundred horsemen, were slain. [32]Timotheus himself fled into a stronghold called Gazara, a very secure fortress, where Chereas was in command. [33]But Maccabeus and his men cheerfully laid siege to the fortress, twenty-four days. [34]And they who were within, trusting in the strength of the place, blasphemed exceedingly and hurled forth impious words. [35]But at the dawn of the twenty-fifth day certain young men of the company of Maccabeus, inflamed with anger because of the blasphemies, assaulted the wall manfully and with furious courage and cut down all who came in their way. [36]And others by a movement on the opposite side, climbing up in like manner against the garrison, set fire to the towers and, kindling pyres, burned the blasphemers alive; while others broke open the gates, and, having given entrance to the rest of the force, occupied the city. [37]And they slew Timotheus, who was hidden in a cistern, and his brother Chereas and also Apollophanes. [38]And when they had accomplished all this, with hymns and thanksgivings they blessed the Lord, who showed such great kindness to Israel and gave them the victory. 12 [26]Judas also went forth against Carnion and the temple of Atergatis and slew twenty-five thousand persons.

History of the Hasmoneans

⁴⁵Then Judas gathered all the Israelites who were in the land of Gilead, from the least to the greatest, with their wives and children and their household possessions, a very great host, that they might go into the land of Judah. ⁴⁶And they came as far as Ephron. This was a large and very strong city situated directly on the pass by which they must go; they could not turn aside from it either to the right or the left, but it was necessary to go through it. ⁴⁷But the inhabitants of the city shut them out, and stopped up the gate with stones. ⁴⁸Then Judas sent a peaceful message to them, saying, We wish to pass through your land to go into our own land, and no one shall do you any harm, we will only march through on foot. But they would not open to him. ⁴⁹Then Judas commanded proclamation to be made in the army, that each man should encamp in the place where he was. ⁵⁰And the men of the army besieged and fought against the city all that day and night, and the city fell into his hands. ⁵¹And then he destroyed all the males with the sword, razed the city, and took the spoils from it, and passed through the city over those who were slain. ⁵²And they crossed the Jordan into the great plain opposite Bethshan. ⁵³And Judas gathered together those who lagged behind and encouraged the people all the way through, until he came into the land of Judah. ⁵⁴And they went up to Mount Zion with gladness and joy and offered whole burnt offerings, because not one of them had been slain, but they had returned safe and sound.

Traditional History

²⁷And after he had put these to flight and destroyed them, he marched against Ephron also, a strong city, in which Lysias[r] had a residence and multitudes of peoples of all nations. And stalwart young men stationed before the w a l l s made a vigorous defence; and there were great stores of engines and darts there. ²⁸But, calling upon the Sovereign who with might breaketh in pieces the strength of the enemy, they gained possession of the city and slew as many as twenty-five thousand of those who were within. ²⁹From there they set out and advanced against Scythopolis,[s] which is distant from Jerusalem sixty-nine miles. ³⁰But when the Jews who were settled there testified of the good-will that the Scythopolitans had shown toward them and of their kindly bearing in the times of their misfortune, ³¹they gave thanks and exhorted them to remain well-disposed toward their race in the future also. Then they went up to Jerusalem, for the feast of weeks was close at hand.

Judas's capture and destruction of Ephron and victorious return to Jerusalem

⁵⁵Now while Judas and Jonathan were in the land of Gilead and Simon his brother in Galilee before Ptolemais, ⁵⁶Joseph the son of Zacharias, and Azarias, commanders of the army, heard of their exploits and the wars which they had carried through, and they said, ⁵⁷Let us also win fame and let us go and fight against the heathen who are around about us. ⁵⁸So they gave

Defeat of Joseph and Azarias before Jamnia

---

[r] II Mac. 12²⁷ *Lysias* is omitted in many MSS., but apparently by mistake.
[s] II Mac. 12²⁹ *Scythopolis* is the Greek name of *Bethshan* mentioned in the parallel, I Mac. 5⁵².

History of the Hasmoneans

command to the men of the army which was with them and went toward Jamnia. ⁵⁹But when Gorgias and his men came out of the city to meet them in battle, ⁶⁰Joseph and Azarias were put to flight and were pursued to the borders of Judea, and there fell on that day of the people of Israel about two thousand men. ⁶¹Thus the people suffered a great disaster because they did not obey Judas and his brothers, thinking to perform some exploit. ⁶²But they were not of the same stock as those men, by whose hand deliverance was given to Israel.

Judas's successful wars against the Idumeans and Philistines

⁶⁵Then Judas and his brothers went out and fought against the people of Esau in the land toward the south. And he smote Hebron and the villages belonging to it and pulled down its citadel and burned the surrounding towers. ⁶⁶Then he set out to go into the land of the Philistines;ᵛ and he went through Marissa. ⁶⁷On that day certain priests, desiring to do exploits there, were slain in battle, when they unwisely went out to fight. ⁶⁸Then Judas turned aside to Azotus, to the land of the Philistines, and pulled down their

---

Traditional History

12 ³²After the feast called Pentecost they advanced against Gorgias, the governor of Idumea. ³³And he came out with three thousand footmen and four hundred horsemen. ³⁴And when they engaged in battle, it transpired that a few of the Jews fell. ³⁵But a certain Dositheus,ᵗ of Bacenor's followers, who rode a horse and was a strong man, laying hold of Gorgias and taking him by his cloak, was drawing him along by main force. But when he purposed to take the accursed man alive, one of the Thracian horsemen bore down upon him and disabled his shoulder so that Gorgias escaped to Marissa. ³⁶After Esdrisᵘ and his followers had fought long and were wearied, Judas called upon the Lord to show himself their ally and the leader of their van of battle. ³⁷And then in the language of his fathers he raised the battle cry, accompanied by hymns, and, rushing unexpectedly upon the troops of Gorgias, he put them to flight. ³⁸Then Judas came with his army to the city of Adullam;ʷ and as the seventh day drew near, according to their custom, they purified themselves and kept the sabbath there. ³⁹On the following day, when it had become necessary, Judas and his men came to take up the bodies of those who had fallen and to bring them back to be with their kinsmen in the sepulchres of their fathers. ⁴⁰Under the garments of each one of the dead they found consecrated tokens of the idols of Jamnia,ˣ with which the law forbids the Jews to have anything to do; and it became clear to all that this was the reason why they had fallen. ⁴¹All therefore blessed the works of the Lord, the righteous Judge, who maketh manifest

---

ᵗ II Mac. 12³⁵ Evidently not the Dositheus mentioned in ¹⁹.
ᵘ II Mac. 12³⁶ Luc., *Gorgias*, but this is evidently an attempt to identify the unexpected proper name, *Esdris* (Heb., *Esri*). The word means, *help* (of Jehovah). Like *Jasher* in the earlier O.T. books, it is probably a title of the chosen people.
ᵛ I Mac. 5⁶⁶ Lit., *strangers*, as in 4²². If it means Philistines, as ⁶⁸ indicates, then *Samaria*, supported by the Gk. MSS., must be changed to, *Marissa*, with Josephus.
ʷ II Mac. 12³⁸ Gk., *Adollam*.
ˣ II Mac. 12⁴⁰ Probably small images used as amulets.

History of the Hasmoneans

altars and burned the carved images of their gods and, taking the spoil of their cities, he returned to the land of Judah. ⁶³And the hero Judas and his brothers were greatly honored by all Israel and by all the heathen wherever their name was heard. ⁶⁴And men gathered to them to sing their praise.ᵃ

Traditional History

the hidden things, and turned to supplication, beseeching that the sin committed might be wholly blotted out. ⁴²And the noble Judas exhorted the multitude to keep themselves from sin, because they had seen before their eyes the consequences of the sin of those who had fallen. ⁴³And when, by a collection among the men, he had gathered as much as two thousand drachmas of silver, he sent it to Jerusalem to offer a sacrifice for sin. In this he acted very well and honorably, in that he was mindful of the resurrection. ⁴⁴For were he not expecting that those who had fallen would rise again, it were superfluous and idle to pray for the dead. ⁴⁵If then he did it, considering that a most excellent gift of grace is laid up for those who sleep in godliness, holy and godly was the thought; therefore he made the propitiation for the dead, that they might be released from their sin.

§ 183. Death of Antiochus Epiphanes and the Accession of Eupator, I Mac. 6¹⁻¹⁷, II Mac. 9¹⁻²⁹, 10⁹⁻¹³

History of the Hasmoneans

I Mac. 6 ¹And as King Antiochus was journeying through the upper countries, he heard that in Elymais,ᵇ in Persia, there was a city renowned for riches, for silver and gold, ²and that the temple there was exceedingly rich and that in it there were golden shields and breastplates and arms, which Alexander son of Philip the Macedonian king, who reigned first over the Syrian Empire, had there left behind. ³Therefore he went and tried to take the city and pillage it, but he was not able because the matter became known to the inhabitants of the city, and they arose against him in battle.

Traditional History

II Mac. 9 ¹About that time it transpired that Antiochus had set out in disgraceᶜ from the region of Persia. ²For he had entered the city called Persepolis and had attempted to rob its templesᵈ and to hold the city. But when in consequence the people ran to defend themselves with their weapons, the attack was repulsed. And Antiochus, put

Antiochus's unsuccessful attempt to plunder a rich Persian city

---

ᵃ I Mac. 5⁶³⁻⁶⁴ These verses belong appropriately at the close of the account of Judas's victorious campaign.

§ 183 I Mac. dates the death of Antiochus in the summer of 164 B.C. (6¹⁶). It is probable, however, that it was not long after the rededication of the temple in Dec., 165. The sudden death of this arch-enemy furnished the historic fact about which grew up the traditions preserved in II Mac. The letter in 9¹⁹⁻²⁷ is contrary not only to probability, but also to his well-known attitude to the Jews and to the testimony of the preceding context, which assumes, ¹⁸, that there was no hope of his recovery. The entire account of his death was evidently written with a didactic purpose and freely elaborated.

ᵇ I Mac. 6¹ The Greek Elumias may represent the original Heb., *Elam.*

ᶜ II Mac. 9¹ Or, *in disorder.*

ᵈ II Mac. 9² Or, *temple.*

History of the Hasmoneans

⁴So he retreated and set out from there in great disappointment to return to Babylon.

Reception of the news of the victories of the Jews

⁵Then one came bringing him tidings into Persia, that the armies which went against the land of Judah had been put to flight, ⁶and that Lysias had gone at the head of a strong host, and had been defeated before them; and that they had grown strong in arms and power, having a store of spoils which they took from the armies which they had cut off; ⁷and that they had pulled down the abomination[e] which he had built upon the altar that was in Jerusalem; and that they had surrounded the sanctuary with high walls as before, and also Bethsura, his city. ⁸And when the king heard these things, he was exceedingly astonished and moved, so that he lay down upon his bed, and fell sick for grief, because his affairs had not prospered as he had expected. ⁹And he was there a long while because great grief was always overcoming him anew.

His repentance and pitiable end

¹⁰And when he saw that his end was near, he called

Traditional History

to flight by the people of the country, had to break up his camp in disgrace.

³While he was at Ecbatana, news came to him of what had happened to Nicanor and the forces of Timotheus. ⁴Then swelling with anger, he thought to make the Jews suffer even for the evil doing of those who had put him to flight. Therefore, as the judgment from heaven was even then following him, he gave orders to his charioteer to drive without ceasing and end the journey. For thus he spoke in his arrogance, I will make Jerusalem a common graveyard of Jews when I come there. ⁵But the all-seeing Lord, the God of Israel, smote him with a fatal and invisible stroke; as soon as he had ceased speaking an incurable pain of the bowels seized him and bitter torments of the inner parts; ⁶and that most justly, for he had tormented other men's bowels with many and strange sufferings. ⁷However he did not at all cease from his insolence, but was still filled with arrogance, breathing fire in his rage against the Jews, and gave orders to hasten the journey. Then it came to pass that he fell from his chariot as it rushed along, and had such a severe fall that all the members of his body were racked. ⁸And he who but recently supposed himself to have the waves of the sea at his bidding, so abnormally[f] vainglorious was he, and who thought to weigh the heights of the mountains in a balance, was now brought to the ground and carried in a litter, showing to all that the power was manifestly God's; ⁹so that even worms swarmed out of the body of the impious man, and, while he was still living in anguish and pain, his flesh fell off piecemeal, and because of the stench his corruption was offensive to the whole army. ¹⁰And the man who a little before supposed himself able to touch the stars of heaven, no one could endure to carry on account of his intolerable stench. ¹¹Then at last sorely stricken he began in great part to cease from his arrogance, and to come to his senses under the scourge of God, for his pains increased

e I Mac. 6⁷ Cf. 1⁵⁴.
f II Mac. 9⁸ Lit., *beyond the condition of a man.*

*History of the
Hasmoneans*

Traditional History

for all his Friends, and said to them, Sleep flees from my eyes and my heart sinks because of bitter grief. ¹¹And I said to myself, To what tribulation have I come, and how great a flood is it in which I now am, although I was gracious and beloved while I still reigned! ¹²But now I remember the evils which I did at Jerusalem, and that I took all the vessels of silver and gold that were in it, and sent to destroy the inhabitants of Judah without a cause. ¹³I perceive that this is why these evils have come upon me, and now I am about to perish through great grief in a foreign land. ¹⁴Then he called for Philip, one of his Friends, and set him over all his kingdom. ¹⁵And gave him his diadem, his robe, and his signet ring, that he should

every moment. ¹²And when he himself could not endure his own smell, he spoke these words: It is right that one should be subject to God and that, being mortal, he should not think himself like God. ¹³Then the vile man vowed to the Sovereign Lord, who now no more would have pity upon him, and said ¹⁴that the holy city which he was hastening to reach, that he might lay it even with the ground and make it a common graveyard, he would declare free. ¹⁵And as for the Jews concerning whom he had decided that they were not even worthy of burial but should be cast out to the beasts with their infants, for the birds to devour, he would make them all equal to citizens of Athens. ¹⁶And the holy sanctuary, which before he had despoiled,[g] he would adorn with goodliest offerings, and would restore all the sacred vessels many times multiplied, and out of his own revenues would defray the charges connected with the sacrifices. ¹⁷And, besides all this, that he would become a Jew and would visit every inhabited place, proclaiming the power of God. ¹⁸But his sufferings did not cease at all, for the judgment of God had come upon him righteously, and so, having given up all hope for himself, he wrote to the Jews the following letter in the nature of a supplication, to this effect:

¹⁹To the worthy Jews, his fellow-citizens, Antiochus, king and general, wishes much joy and health and prosperity. ²⁰If you and your children prosper and your affairs are to your mind, I give God very great thanks,[h] for my hope is in heaven. ²¹I however lie ill.[i] Your esteem and good-will I remembered with affection. On my return from the region of Persia, being seized with a loathsome sickness, I deemed it necessary to take thought for the common safety of all, not despairing of my recovery, ²²but with great hope of escaping from the sickness. ²³But considering that my father also, at the time when he led an army into the upper country, appointed his successor, ²⁴in order that, if anything unexpected occurred, or if any misfortune was merely reported, the people throughout the country, knowing to whom the state had been left,

---

g II Mac. 9¹⁶ Cf. 3³.
h II Mac. 9²⁰ This clause is omitted in many MSS. but is found in others, and is demanded by the context.
i II Mac. 9²¹ *I however lie ill*, is omitted in some MSS., but cf. 11²⁸.

History of the Hasmoneans

carry them[j] to Antiochus, his son, and should bring him up to be king. [16]So K i n g Antiochus died there in the one hundred and forty-ninth year.[k] [17]And when Lysias knew that the king was dead, he set up Antiochus his son to reign, whom he had cared for while he was young, and he called his name Eupator.

Traditional History

might not be troubled; [25]and, besides all this, observing that the bordering princes and the neighbors were looking for opportunities and were awaiting the future event, I have appointed my son Antiochus king. Often, when I was hastening into the upper provinces, I intrusted him and commended him to most of you; and I have written to him what is added below. [26]I exhort you therefore and beseech you to remember the benefits you have received in common and severally, and to preserve each of you your present good-will toward me and my son. [27]For I am persuaded that he in gentleness and kindness, following my policy, will maintain friendly relations with you.

[28]So the murderer and blasphemer having suffered most grievously, as he himself had dealt with other men, died in a strange land, among the mountains, a most pitiable death. [29]And Philip, his foster-brother, conveyed the body home; and then, fearing the son of Antiochus, he betook himself to Ptolemy Philometor in Egypt.[l] **10** [9]Such were the circumstances of the end of Antiochus, who was called Epiphanes.

Eupator's policy toward the Jews

[10]Now will we declare what came to pass under Antiochus Eupator, who was a son of that godless man, and will briefly summarize the evils connected with his wars. [11]For this man, when he succeeded to the kingdom, appointed a certain Lysias prime minister[m] and supreme governor of Cœlesyria and Phœnicia. [12]For Ptolemy, who was called Macron, set an example of observing justice toward the Jews because of the wrong which had been done to them, and endeavored to conduct his dealings with them peaceably. [13]Whereupon he was accused by the Friends before Eupator, and was called traitor in every respect, because he had abandoned Cyprus, which Philometor had entrusted to him, and had withdrawn himself to Antiochus, called Epiphanes. And so, failing to uphold the honor of his office, he took poison and made away with himself.

---

[j] I Mac. 6¹⁵ Following Jos. and Syr.
[k] I Mac. 6¹⁶ Summer of 164.
[l] II Mac. 9²⁹ But cf. 13²³, I Mac. 6⁵⁵⁻⁶³, and Jos., *Ant.*, XII, 9¹, which contradict the statement. Philip on his return was conquered and put to death by Lysias.
[m] II Mac. 10¹¹ Or, *regent*.

§ 184. The Disastrous Battle of Beth-zacharias, I Mac. 6[18-54], II Mac. 13[1-22]

History of the Hasmoneans

ege the tadel nd e appeal of e postates to e yrian ng

I Mac. 6 [18]Now those who were in the citadel were hindering Israel round about the sanctuary and were always seeking to do them harm and were a support to the heathen. [19]But Judas determined to destroy them and called all the people together to besiege them. [20]And they were gathered together and besieged them in the hundred and fiftieth year, and he made mounds from which to shoot and engines of war. [21]Then some of those who were shut up came out and certain apostate Israelites joined them. [22]And they went to the king and said, When will you finally satisfy justice and avenge our brothers? [23]We were willing to serve your father and to live as he enjoined, and to obey his commands; [24]but because of this our own people besieged us in the citadel and were alienated from us; and as many of us as they could find, they killed and despoiled our inheritances. [25]And not against us only have they stretched out their hand, but also against all that bordered on them. [26]And now they are to-day encamped against the citadel at Jerusalem, to take it, and they have fortified the sanctuary and Bethsura. [27]And if you

Traditional History

Advance of Eupator and the well-deserved fate of Menelaus

II Mac. 13 [1]In the one hundred and forty-ninth year news was brought to Judas and his followers that Antiochus Eupator was coming with multitudes against Judea and with him Lysias his guardian and prime minister, [2]each having a Greek force, a hundred and ten thousand footmen and five thousand, three hundred horsemen and twenty-two elephants and three hundred chariots armed with scythes. [3]Menelaus also joined with them and with great dissimulation encouraged Antiochus, not for the deliverance of his country but because he thought he would be established in his office.[n] [4]But the King of kings stirred up the anger of Antiochus against the wicked sinner; and when Lysias informed him that this man was the cause of all the evils, he gave orders to bring him to Berœa[o] and to put him to death according to the custom there. [5]Now in that place is a tower fifty cubits high, full of ashes, with a revolving contrivance[p] from every side of which is an abrupt descent into the ashes. [6]Here they pushed forward to destruction everyone who is guilty of sacrilege[q] or has committed any other conspicuous crime. [7]Such was the death which it befell that law-breaker, Menelaus, to die, without even receiving a portion of the earth for a grave, most justly too,

---

§ 184 II Mac. 13[1] dates the event in 163 B.C., but I Mac. 6[20] without much doubt is correct in placing it one year later. II Mac. also in its zeal to glorify the Jews, or because of the misleading testimony of the popular tradition upon which it is based, turns the virtual defeat into a partial victory. With the reduction of the temple and the victories of Judas, the interest of the epitomizer of II Mac. in the history wanes and his *résumé* of the remaining events is often so compressed that the style is harsh and the meaning at times obscure because of the ellipses.

[n] II Mac. 13[3] The office of the high-priest is meant. Cf. 4[23 ff].

[o] II Mac. 13[4] Located in Syria between Antioch and Hierapolis.

[p] II Mac. 13[5] It is difficult to determine the exact nature of this instrument. It was probably a revolving apparatus which lifted the victim to the top of the tower and dropped him in. As Grimm suggests, the ashes were probably burning.

[q] II Mac. 13[6] The Gk. here reads, *they all push forward whoever is guilty, etc.* A slight change in the Gk. gives the above reading, which was probably the original.

History of the Hasmoneans

do not quickly anticipate them, they will do greater things than these, and you will not be able to check them.

Traditional History

⁸for as he had committed many sins in relation to the altar, the fire and ashes of which were holy, in ashes did he receive his death.

Advance of a powerful Syrian army

²⁸When the king had heard this, he was angry, and gathered together all his Friends, the officers of his army, and those who commanded the cavalry. ²⁹There came to him also from other kingdoms and from isles of the sea, bands of hired soldiers. ³⁰So the number of his forces was a hundred thousand footmen and twenty thousand horsemen and thirty-two elephants trained for war. ³¹Then they went through Idumea and encamped against Bethsura and carried on the siege a long time and made engines of war. The besieged, however, sallied out and burned them and fought valiantly. ³²And Judas departed from the citadel and encamped at Beth-zacharias, opposite the king's camp. ³³Then the king rose early in the morning and had his army set out at full speed along the road to Beth-zacharias and his forces prepared for battle and the trumpets were sounded. ³⁴And they showed the elephants the blood of grapes and mulberries, in order to excite them for the battle. ³⁵Then they distributed the beasts among the phalanxes and stationed by each elephant a thousand men armed with coats of mail and helmets, with brass on their heads; and to each beast five hundred chosen horsemen were appointed. ³⁶These were already there, wherever the beast was, and wherever the beast went, they went with him and did not separate themselves from him. ³⁷And upon them were towers of wood, strong, covered, one girded upon each beast. Upon them were engines and two or three[r] men, who fought upon them, besides the Indian who guided the elephant. ³⁸The rest of the horsemen he stationed on both sides of the two wings of the army to inspire terror and to protect the phalanxes. ³⁹And when the sun struck the golden and bronze shields, the mountain shone with them and blazed like torches of fire. ⁴⁰And a part of the king's army was spread out on the heights, and some on the low ground, and they moved firmly and in good order. ⁴¹And all who heard the noise of their multitude, and the march-

Prayer of the Jews for deliverance from the Syrians

⁹Now the king, in a savage temper, was coming intent upon inflicting on the Jews the very worst of the sufferings which had befallen them in his father's time. ¹⁰But as soon as Judas heard of these things, he charged the multitude to call upon the Lord day and night, that, if ever at any other time, he would now also succor those who were about to be deprived of the law and their country and the holy temple,¹¹and that he would not suffer the people, who had been for only a little while restored, to fall into the hands of those unholy heathen. ¹²When they had all done the same thing together, beseeching the merciful Lord with weeping and fastings and prostration for three days without ceasing, Judas exhorted and commanded them to be ready. ¹³After having gone apart with the elders, he re-

---

[r] I Mac. 6³⁷ The Gk. text reads, *thirty-two*, but the original probably read as above. The error was an easy one.

History of the Hasmoneans   *Traditional History*

ing of the great numbers, and the rattling of the arms, trembled because the army was very great and strong.

solved that, before the king's army should invade Judea and make themselves masters of the city, they should go forth and decide the matter with the help of the Lord.[s]

Brave but futile attack of the Jews

⁴²Then Judas and his army approached for battle, and there fell of the king's army six hundred men. ⁴³Now when Eleazar, who was called Avaran, saw one of the beasts armed with royal breastplates, which was higher than all the beasts, and it looked as though the king was upon it, ⁴⁴he gave himself to save his people and to gain for himself an everlasting fame; ⁴⁵and he ran upon him courageously in the midst of the phalanx and slew on the right hand and on the left, and they scattered from before him on either side. ⁴⁶Then he crept under the elephant, thrust him from beneath, and slew him. And the elephant fell to the earth upon him, and he died there. ⁴⁷But when they saw the strength of the king and the fierce onset of the armies, they turned away from them.

The successful attack

¹⁴Then, after committing the decision to the Creator[t] of the world and exhorting those who were with him to contend nobly even unto death for laws, temple, city, country, and commonwealth, he pitched his camp near Modein. ¹⁵And after giving out to his men the watchword, "Victory is God's," with a chosen body of the bravest young men he fell upon the king's tent by night and slew in the camp[u] as many as two thousand men, and brought down the chief elephant, with all who were[v] in the tower upon him. ¹⁶And at last they filled the camp with terror and alarm and withdrew victorious. ¹⁷And this was accomplished when the day was already dawning, because he had the Lord's helpful protection.

Surrender of Bethsura and the extremities of the Jews in Jerusalem

⁴⁸But those who were in the king's army went up to Jerusalem to meet them, and the king encamped for a struggle with Judea and Mount Sion. ⁴⁹And he made peace with those in Bethsura; for they surrendered the city, because they had no food there to endure the siege, because the land had a sabbath.[w] ⁵⁰So the king took Bethsura and stationed a garrison there to keep it. ⁵¹Then he encamped against the sanctuary for a long time; and he set there mounds from which to shoot and engines of war and instruments for casting stones and fire, and pieces to cast darts and slings. ⁵²And

Siege of Bethsura and final withdrawal of the Syrian army

¹⁸Then the king, having had a taste of the exceeding boldness of the Jews, made attempt by strategy upon their positions, ¹⁹and he advanced upon Bethsura, a strong fortress of the Jews, was turned back, attacked again, was again defeated. ²⁰Then Judas conveyed to those

---

[s] II Mac. 13¹³ Some manuscripts have, *God*, instead of, *the Lord*.
[t] II Mac. 13¹⁴ Some manuscripts have, *God*, instead of, *Creator*.
[u] II Mac. 13¹⁵ Making a slight but necessary correction.
[v] II Mac. 13¹⁵ So the best texts. Others read, *him who was*.
[w] I Mac. 6⁴⁹ Cf. Lev. 25.

History of the Hasmoneans

they also erected engines against those of the be-
siegers and fought for a long time. ⁵³But since
there was no food in the sanctuary, because it
was the seventh year and those who had fled
for safety into Judea from among the heathen
had eaten up what remained of the store of provisions, ⁵⁴there were but a few left in the sanctuary, because the famine became so severe upon
them, and they scattered, each man to his own
home.

Traditional History

within such things as
were necessary. ²¹But
R h o d o c u s, from the
Jewish ranks, m a d e
known to the enemy
their secrets. He was
discovered and taken,
and shut up in prison.
²²The king treated with
those in Bethsura the
second time, exchanged
pledges, departed, at-
tackedˣ the forces of Ju-
das, and was overcome.

§ 185. The Treaty Establishing Religious Freedom, I Mac. 6⁵⁵⁻⁶³, II Mac. 13²³⁻²⁶

History of the Hasmoneans

Compli-
cations
at An-
tioch
and
the
rights
guaran-
teed to
the
Jews

I Mac. 6 ⁵⁵Now Lysias heard that Philip,
whom Antiochus the king, had appointed during his lifetime to bring up his son Antiochus
that he might be king, ⁵⁶had returned from
Persia and Media and with him the forces
that went with the king, and that he was
trying to get control of the government, ⁵⁷he
hastily decided to depart. And he said to the
king, and to the officers of the army and to the
men, We are growing weaker every day, our
supplies are scanty, and the place which we are
besieging is strong, and the welfare of the kingdom depends upon us; ⁵⁸now therefore let us
give the right hand to these men and make peace
with them and with all their nation, ⁵⁹and covenant with them that they may live according
to their own customs as formerly; for because
of their laws, which we abolished, they were
angered and did all these things. ⁶⁰This
counsel pleased the king and the princes, and
he sent to them to make peace. They accepted
it, ⁶¹and when he king and the princes took

Traditional History

II Mac. 13 ²³The king
heard that Philip, who had
been left as prime minis-
ter in Antioch, had become
reckless, was confounded,
made overtures to the
Jews, submitted himself
and accepted on oath all
just conditions, came to
terms with them and
offered sacrifice, honored
the sanctuary and showed
kindness to the place,
²⁴and graciously received
Maccabeus, left Hege-
monides governor from
Ptolemais even to the
Gerrenians,ᵃ *and* came to
Ptolemais. ²⁵The men of
Ptolemais were displeased
at the treaty, for they were
exceedingly   indignant;ᵇ

ˣ II Mac. 13¹⁹⁻²² The unusual frequency of asyndeton is undoubtedly due to the desire of the
epitomizer to condense at this point the contents of his earlier source.
    ᵃ II Mac. 13²⁴ This word is evidently corrupt and appears in a variant form in the codices.
It means, *inhabitants of Gerar*, a city located in the extreme southwestern part of Palestine.
    ᵇ II Mac. 13²⁵ In this extreme condensation of the data in his original, the epitomizer has not
indicated the object of their indignation. It was probably the Jews.

History of the Hasmoneans

oath to them, they came out of the stronghold. ⁶²But when the king entered Mount Sion and saw the strength of the place, he broke the oath which he had sworn and gave orders to pull down the wall round about. ⁶³Then he set out in haste and returned to Antioch and found Philip master of the city; and he fought against him and took the city by force.

Traditional History

they desired to annul the articles of agreement. ²⁶Lysias mounted the rostrum, made the best defence that was possible, persuaded, pacified, made them well disposed, and then departed to Antioch. This was the issue of the invasion and departure of the king.

§ 186. Appointment and Rule of Alcimus as High Priest, I Mac. 7¹⁻²⁶ II Mac. 14¹⁻¹⁴

History of the Hasmoneans

I Mac. 7 ¹In the one hundred and fiftieth year,ᶜ Demetrius the son of Seleucus escaped from Rome and went up with a few men to a city by the sea,ᵈ and there proclaimed himself king. ²And when he entered the palace of his fathers, the army seized Antiochus and Lysias, to bring them to him. ³But when the fact was made known to him, he said, Do not show me their faces. ⁴And the army slew them. So Demetrius sat upon the throne of his kingdom.

⁵And there came to him all the lawless and the apostate men of Israel, with Alcimus,ᶠ their leader, desiring to be high priest. ⁶And they accused the people before the king, saying, Judas and his brethren have destroyed all your friends, and have scattered us from our own land. ⁷Now therefore send a man whom you trust, and let him go and see all the havoc which he has made of us and of the king's country, and

Traditional History

II Mac. 14 ¹Now after an interval of three years, tidings were brought to Judas and his followers that Demetrius, the son of Seleucus, having sailed into the harbor of Tripolis with a strong army and a fleet, ²had taken possession of the country, having made away with Antiochus and Lysias his guardian.

³But one Alcimus, who had formerly been high priest, and had wilfully polluted himself in the period of fusionᵉ with the Greeks, perceiving that there was no deliverance for him in any way nor access any more to the holy altar, ⁴came to King Demetrius in about the hundred and fifty-first yearᵍ and

[side notes: Accession of Demetrius I / Deceitful claims and charges of Alcimus]

---

§ 186 Demetrius, the son of Seleucus, had been carried as a boy of nine years to Rome, where he was held as a hostage. At last escaping the vigilance of the Romans he appeared in Syria to be at once hailed as the rightful king.
ᶜ I Mac. 7¹ 162 B.C.
ᵈ I Mac. 7¹ Cf. II Mac. 14¹, *Tripolis*.
ᵉ II Mac. 14³ Some MSS. read, *of separation*, but this was probably due to later scribes who would admit no period of general fusion. In ³⁸ they have apparently for the same reason changed it in all MSS.
ᶠ I Mac. 7⁵ Alcimus is a Gk. name substituted for the Heb., *Eliakim*.
ᵍ II Mac. 14⁴ Cf. I Mac. 13³⁷, Herod. vii, ²⁷.

History of the Hasmoneans

how he has punished them and all who helped them. ⁸So the king chose Bacchides, one of the king's Friends, who was ruler in the province beyond the River Euphrates, and was a great man in the kingdom, and faithful to the king. ⁹He sent him and also that godless Alcimus, and confirmed him in the high priesthood, and commanded him to take vengeance upon the Israelites. ¹⁰So they set out and came with a great army into the land of Judah, and he sent messengers to Judas and his brothers with words of peace, deceitfully. ¹¹But they paid no attention to their words, for they saw that they had come with a great army. ¹²Then there were gathered together to Alcimus and Bacchides a company of scribes, to seek for justice. ¹³And the Hasidaeans were the first among the Israelites who sought peace with them; ¹⁴for they said, One who is a descendant of Aaron has come with the forces and he will do us no wrong. ¹⁵And he spoke words of peace to them, and took oath to them, saying, We will seek the hurt neither of you nor of your friends. ¹⁶And they put confidence in him. But he seized sixty of them, and slew them in one day, as it is written in the Scriptures,

¹⁷The flesh of thy saints . . .
   And their blood they poured out round about
      Jerusalem;
   And there was no man to bury them.ʲ

¹⁸And the fear and hatred of them fell upon all the people, for they said, There is neither truth nor justice in them; for they have broken the covenant and the oaths which they made.

Traditional History

presented to himʰ a golden chaplet and palm, and moreover some of the festal olive boughs of the temple. And that day he kept quiet; ⁵but he gained opportunity to further his own folly, when he was called by Demetrius to a meeting of his council, and being asked what was the attitude and policy of the Jews, he answered, ⁶Those of the Jews who are called Hasideans,ⁱ whose leader is Judas Maccabeus, keep up the war and are seditious, not allowing the kingdom to obtain peace. ⁷Therefore, having been deprived of my ancestral dignity —I mean the high priesthood —I have now come hither; ⁸first because of the genuine regard I have for the king's interests, and secondly because I am also regardful of my own fellow citizens; for, through the senseless acts of those already mentioned, our whole race is in no slight misfortune. ⁹But do you, O king, inform yourself regarding these things in detail, and take thought both of our country and for our much afflicted race, according to the gracious kindness with which you receive all. ¹⁰For as long as Judas remains alive, it is impossible for the state to obtain peace.

ʰ II Mac. 14⁴ Probably 162 B.C.
ⁱ II Mac. 14⁶ Cf. I Mac. 2⁴², § 175.
ʲ I Mac. 7¹⁷ Ps. 79²˒³:

      They have given the corpses of thy servants
      As food to the birds of the heavens;
      The flesh of thy saints, to the beasts of the earth,
      They have poured out blood like water,
      Round about Jerusalem, and there was none to bury them.

History of the Hasmoneans

¹⁹Then Bacchides departed from Jerusalem and encamped in Bezeth.ᵏ And he sent and took many of the deserters that were with him and certain of the people, and he slew them and cast them into the great well. ²⁰Then he turned over the country to Alcimus and left with him an army to aid him, while Bacchides went away to the king. ²¹Then Alcimus entered the struggle for the high priesthood. ²²And there were gathered to him all who had troubled their people, and they became masters of the land of Judah and caused great consternation in Israel. ²³And when Judas saw that Alcimus and his company had done more mischief among the Israelites than the heathen, ²⁴he went out into the whole territory of Judea round about and took vengeance on the men who had deserted from him, and they were restrained from going forth into the country. ²⁵But when Alcimus saw that Judas and his company were growing strong and knew that he was not able to withstand them, he returned to the king and brought evil charges against them. ²⁶So the king sent Nicanor, one of his honorable princes, a man who hated Israel and was their enemy, and commanded him to destroy the people.

Traditional History

¹¹As soon as he had spoken such words as these, at once, the rest of the king's friends being ill disposed toward Judas, inflamed Demetrius still more. ¹²He straightway summonedˡ Nicanor, who had been master of the elephants, and having made him governor of Judea, sent him forth. ¹³He also gave him written instructions to make way with Judas himself and to scatter those who were with him, and to establish Alcimus as high priest of the very great temple. ¹⁴Then the heathen all over Judea who had fled before Judas thronged to Nicanor in flocks, supposing that the misfortunes and calamities of the Jews would be their own good fortune.

Alcimus's efforts to establish himself as high priest with the aid of the Syrians

§ 187. Defeat and Death of Nicanor, I Mac. 7²⁷⁻⁵⁰, II Mac. 14¹⁵–15³⁶

History of the Hasmoneans

I Mac. 7 ²⁷When Nicanor came to Jerusalem with a great army, he sent to Judas and his brothers a message of peaceful words with deceit-

Traditional History

II Mac. 14 ¹⁵When the Jews heard of Nicanor's advance and the invasion of the heathen, they sprinkled earth upon their heads and made solemn supplication to him who established his own people for all time and who always, making manifest his presence, upholdeth those who are his own portion. ¹⁶Then at the command of their leader theyᵐ immediately set out from there and joined battle with them at a village called Des-

Nicanor's original treaty with Judas and later hostilities

ᵏ I Mac. 7¹⁹ Cf. 9⁴. Probably this was originally, *Beerzith, well of the olive trees*, about a half-day's journey north of Jerusalem.
ˡ II Mac. 14¹² Some MSS. read, *appointing*.
ᵐ II Mac. 14¹⁶ Following the best MSS.

History of the Hasmoneans

ful intent, saying, [28]Let there be no battle between us. I will come with a few men, that I may see your faces in peace. [29]And he came to Judas, and they saluted one another peaceably. But the enemies were prepared to take away Judas, by violence. [30]And when the fact was clear to Judas, that he had come to him with deceit, he was very much afraid of him and would see his face no more. [31]So Nicanor knew that his plan was discovered, and he went out to meet Judas in battle near Capharsalama. [32]And there fell of those with Nicanor about five hundred men. Then they fled into the city of David.

Traditional History

sau.[n] [17]Simon the brother of Judas had encountered Nicanor and had been checked for a time on account of the sudden consternation caused by his adversaries. [18]Nevertheless when Nicanor heard of the manliness of Judas and his followers and of their courage in fighting for their country, he shrank from bringing the matter to a decision by the sword. [19]He therefore sent Posidonius and Theodotus and Mattathias to give and receive pledges of peace. [20]After these proposals had been long under consideration, and the leader had made the troops acquainted with them and they appeared to be all of the same mind, they consented to the agreements. [21]And they appointed a day on which to meet together by themselves. And as he[o] came forward, chairs of state were set for them, one for each. [22]Judas had stationed armed men in convenient places, prepared for the possibility of a sudden and treacherous attempt on the part of the enemy; so they conferred together as was suitable. [23]Nicanor stayed in Jerusalem and did nothing out of place, but dismissed the crowds of people who had gathered together.[p] [24]And he kept Judas always in his presence; he had acquired a hearty affection for the man; [25]he urged him to marry and beget children; so he married, settled quietly, and took part in common life.

[26]But Alcimus, perceiving the good-will between them, and having got possession of the agreements which had been made, came to Demetrius and told him that Nicanor was disaffected toward the state, for he had appointed that conspirator against his kingdom, Judas, to be his successor.[q] [27]Then the king, falling into a rage and being exasperated by the calumnies of that most wicked man, wrote to Nicanor, signifying that he was displeased at the agreements, and commanding him to send Maccabeus prisoner to Antioch in all haste. [28]When this message came to Nicanor, he was perplexed and was much distressed at the thought of annulling the articles which he had agreed upon, when the man had done no wrong. [29]But as he could not act against the king, he watched his time to execute his purpose by stratagem. [30]Maccabeus, however, perceived that Nicanor was behaving

[n] II Mac. 14[16] Some MSS. have confused the Gk. *D* and *L* and read, *Lessau*.

[o] II Mac. 14[21] Probably Nicanor is the one referred to, for Judas is introduced in the next verse. The extreme condensation here makes the meaning obscure.

[p] II Mac. 14[23] Cf. [14].

[q] II Mac. 14[26] *I.e.*, Alcimus's successor in the high-priesthood.

Traditional History

more harshly in his dealings with him, and that he had become ruder in his customary bearing, and understanding that his harshness boded no good, gathered together many of his men, and concealed himself from Nicanor.

History of the Hasmoneans

I Mac. 7

³³Now after these things Nicanor went to Sion. And when some of the priests came out of the sanctuary, and some of the elders of the people, to salute him peaceably and to show him the whole burnt-offering that was being offered for the king, ³⁴he mocked them, and laughed at them, and abused them,ʳ ³⁵and talked insolently. He also swore in a rage, saying, Unless Judas and his army are now delivered into my hands, if I come again in peace, I will burn up this temple. ³⁶He went out in a great rage. Then the priests went in and

³¹But the other, when he became aware that he had been boldly outwitted by the man, came to the great and holy temple, while the priests were offering the usual sacrifices, and commanded them to deliver up the man. ³²Although they declared with oaths that they had no knowledge where the man was whom he sought, ³³he stretched forth his right hand toward the sanctuary, and swore this oath, If you will not deliver up to me Judas as a prisoner, I will level this temple of God to the ground and will break down the altar, and I will erect here a temple to Dionysos for all to see. ³⁴And having said this, he departed. The priests, stretching forth their hands to heaven, called upon him who ever fighteth for our nation, with these words, ³⁵Thou, O Lord, who in thyself hast need of nothing, wast well pleased that a sanctuary for thy habitation should be set among us. ³⁶So now, O holy Lord, from whom all holiness cometh, keep undefiled forever this house which hath been lately cleansed. ³⁷Information was also given to Nicanor against one Razis, an elder of Jerusalem, a lover of his countrymen and a man of very good reputation, and one called Father of the Jews because of his kindliness. ³⁸For in the former period of fusionˢ with the Greeks he had brought forth a defence of Judaism and had hazarded body and life with all earnestness for Judaism. ³⁹Nicanor, wishing to make evident the ill-will which he bore to the Jews, sent over five hundred soldiers to take him prisoner; ⁴⁰for he thought by taking him prisoner to inflict a blow upon them. ⁴¹But when the troops were on the point of taking the tower, and were forcing the door of the court, and giving orders to bring fire and burn the doors, he, surrounded on every side, fell upon his sword, ⁴²preferring to die nobly rather than to fall into the hands of the guilty sinners, and suffer outrage unworthy of his own nobleness. ⁴³But he did not strike true through the excitement of the struggle and, as the crowd were now rushing within the door, he ran boldly up to the wall and cast himself manfully down into the crowds. ⁴⁴They quickly gave way, so a space was made, and he fell in the midst of the empty place. ⁴⁵But still breathing and inflamed with passion,

Nicanor's insolent threats and the prayers and resistance of the faithful Jews

---

ʳ I Mac. 7³⁴ Lit., *polluted.* The context supports the above meaning.
ˢ II Mac. 14³⁸ All MSS. read, *period of preparation,* but cf. ³ where later scribes have also altered the text.

*History of the
Hasmoneans*

Traditional History

s t o o d before
the altar and
the temple; and
they wept and
said, ³⁷Thouᵗ
didst choose this
temple to be
called by thy

he rose up, and though his blood gushed out in streams
and his wounds were severe, he ran through the crowds
and, standing upon a steep rock, ⁴⁶when his blood was
now nearly exhausted, drew forth his bowels and taking
them in both his hands, he shook them at the crowds,
and calling upon him who is the Lord of the life and the
spirit to restore him these again, he thus departed.

name, to be a house of prayer and supplication for thy people. ³⁸Take
vengeance on this man and his army, and let him fall by the sword. Remember their blasphemies, and let them live no longer.

Judas's prayer and great victory over Nicanor

³⁹And Nicanor
set forth from
Jerusalem and en-
camped in Beth-
horon, and there
the army of Syria
met him. ⁴⁰But
Judas encamped
in Adasaᵛ with
three thousand
men. Then Ju-
das prayed and
said, ⁴¹When
they who came
from the king blas-
phemed, thine an-
gel went out and
smote among them
an hundred and
sixty-five t h o u -
sand.ᵘ ⁴²Even so
destroy thou this
army before us to-
day, and let all the
rest know that he
hath spoken wick-
edly against thy
sanctuary, a n d
judge thou him
according to his
wickedness. ⁴³So

Traditional History

15 ¹But Nicanor, hearing that Judas and his followers
were in the region of Samaria, resolved to attack them
without any danger on the day of rest. ²And when
the Jews who were compelled to follow him said, O do
not destroy so savagely and barbarously, but give due
glory to the day which he who beholdeth all things
hath honored above other days, ³the thrice-cursed
wretch asked if there was a Sovereign in heaven who
had commanded to keep the sabbath day. ⁴And when
they openly declared, There is the living Lord, himself
a Sovereign in heaven, who bade us to observe the
seventh day, ⁵the other said, I also am a sovereign upon
the earth, who now command to take up arms and perform the king's service! However he did not succeed
in performing his shocking purpose. ⁶And Nicanor,
bearing himself haughtily with supreme assurance,
had determined to set up a public monument of the
victory over Judas and those who were with him. ⁷But
Maccabeus trusted unceasingly with all hope that he
would obtain help from the Lord. ⁸And he exhorted
those who were with him not to be afraid of the attack
of the heathen, but, keeping in mind the help which
they had often received from heaven, so now also to
look for the victory which would come to them from
the Almighty. ⁹Moreover comforting them out of the
law and prophets, and also reminding them of the
conflicts that they had passed through, he strengthened
their courage. ¹⁰And after he had aroused their spirits,
he gave them his commands, at the same time pointing

ᵗ I Mac. 7³⁷ The characteristic omission of the name of God at the beginning of the prayer.
ᵘ I Mac. 7⁴¹ An allusion to the destruction of Sennacherib's army. Cf. II Kgs. 18²² ᶠᶠ.

History of the Hasmoneans

Traditional History

on the thirteenth day of the month Adar the armies joined battle; and Nicanor's a r m y was defeated, and he himself was the first to fall in the b a t t l e. ⁴⁴And when his army saw that Nicanor had fallen, they threw away their weapons and fled. ⁴⁵And [the Jews] pursued them a d a y ' s journey from Adasaᵛ as far as Gazara, when they sounded the t r u m p e t-s i g n a l f o r t h e return. ⁴⁶Then they came out from all the villages of Judea on every hand and outflanked them; and the one turned them back on the other army, and they all fell by the sword, s o t h a t none of them was left.

out the perfidy of the heathen and their breach of their oath. ¹¹And arming each one of them, not so much with confidence in shields and spears as with the encouragement of good words, he made them all exceeding joyful by relating to them a dream in the highest degree worthy of credence. ¹²And the vision presented by this dream was as follows: he saw Onias, who had been high priest, a noble and good man, reverend in bearing, yet gentle in manner and dignified in all points in speech, and trained from childhood in all the virtues, with outstretched hands invoking blessings on the whole body of the Jews. ¹³Then, in the same way, a man appeared, distinguished by gray hair and noble bearing and surrounded by wonderful and most majestic dignity. ¹⁴And Onias spoke and said, This is the lover of the brothers,ʷ he who prayed much for the people and the holy city, Jeremiah the prophet of God. ¹⁵Then Jeremiah, stretching forth his right hand, delivered to Judas a sword of gold, and in giving it addressed him thus, ¹⁶Take the holy sword, a gift from God, with it shalt thou slay the foes! ¹⁷And being encouraged by these words of Judas, which were of a lofty strain and able to incite to bravery and to stir the souls of the young with manly courage, they determined not to make a fortified camp,ˣ but nobly to make an open attack, and, fighting hand to hand with all courage, to bring the matter to an issue, because the city and the sanctuary and the temple were in danger. ¹⁸For their fear for wives and children, and also for brothers and kinsfolk, had less weight with them; but greatest and first was their fear for the consecrated temple. ¹⁹And they also who were shut up in the city were in no little distress, since they were troubled on account of the engagement in the open field. ²⁰And when all were already waiting for the coming issue, and the enemies had already drawn together, and the army had been set in battle array, and the elephants had taken their place, and the horsemen were drawn up on both flanks, Maccabeus, ²¹perceiving the presence of the great multitudes, and the various arms with which they were equipped, and the ferocity of the elephants, holding up his hands to heaven called upon the Lord who worketh wonders, for he recognized that success comes not by

---

ᵛ I Mac. 7⁴⁰⁻⁴⁵ The original probably read, *Adasa*, for, *Elasa*—a Greek *l* having been mistaken for *d*.
ʷ II Mac. 15¹⁴ Lit., *friend of brothers*.
ˣ II Mac. 15¹⁷ Probably that they might from this vantage-ground attack the advancing enemy.

Traditional History

arms, but that he giveth the victory to those whom he judges worthy of it. ²²And he prayed as follows: Thou, O Sovereign Lord, didst send thine angel in the time of Hezekiah king of Judea, and he slew the army of Sennacherib as many as a hundred and eighty-five thousand. ²³So now also, O Sovereign of the heavens, send a good angel before us to bring terror and trembling. ²⁴Through the greatness of thine arm let those who with blasphemy have come here against thy holy people be smitten with terror. And he concluded with these words, ²⁵while Nicanor and his followers advanced with trumpets and battle songs. ²⁶But Judas and his followers joined battle with the enemy with prayers and supplication. ²⁷And while they fought with their hands and prayed to God with their hearts, they slew no less than thirty-five thousand men, being made exceeding glad by God's visible care.

History of the Hasmoneans

Exultation over the death of Nicanor and the annual festival in commemoration of the victory

I Mac. 7 ⁴⁷And they took the spoils and the booty, and they struck off Nicanor's head and his right hand, which he had stretched out so haughtily, and brought them and hung them ᵃ up in the citadel ᵇ of Jerusalem. ⁴⁸And the people were very glad. ⁴⁹They also enacted an ordinance for the celebration of this day year by year, the thirteenth day of Adar. ⁵⁰So the land of Judah had rest for a brief period.

²⁸And when the engagement was over, and they were returning again with joy, they recognized Nicanor lying dead in full armor. ²⁹Then there arose a great shout and tumult, and they blessed the Sovereign Lord in the language of their fathers. ³⁰And he who in all things was in body and soul the foremost champion of his fellow citizens, he who kept through life the goodwill of his youth toward his countrymen, commanded to cut off Nicanor's head and his hand with the arm and to bring them to Jerusalem. ³¹And when he had arrived there and had called his countrymen together and set the priests before the altar, he sent for those who were in the citadel. ³²Then showing the head of the vile Nicanor and the hand of the profane man, which with loud boasts he had stretched out against the house of the Almighty, ³³and cutting out the tongue of the impious Nicanor, he gave command to give it by pieces to the birds and to hang up the rewards ᶜ of his madness opposite the sanctuary. ³⁴And they all looking up to heaven blessed the Lord who had manifested himself, saying, Blessed be he who hath preserved his own place undefiled. ³⁵And he hung Nicanor's head ᵈ from the citadel, ᵉ a sign, plain to all and visible, of the help of the Lord. ³⁶And they all ordained by a vote of the community, never to let this day pass without being celebrated, but to observe as a feast, the thirteenth day of the twelfth month, which is called Adar in the Assyrian tongue, the day before the day of Mordecai.

ᵃ I Mac. 7⁴⁷ The Gk. translator made here an effective play on words: his right hand, which he had so haughtily *stretched out*, they *stretched out*, i.e., hung up.
ᵇ I Mac. 7⁴⁷ Lit., *by*, but cf. II Mac. 15³⁵.
ᶜ II Mac. 15³³ Or, *penalties*, the reference evidently is to the gory proofs of the consequences of Nicanor's folly in attacking the people of Jehovah.
ᵈ II Mac. 15³⁵ So Luc. and Lat.   Gk., *upper part of the body* (including the head).
ᵉ II Mac. 15³⁵ Contrary to the implication of this verse, the citadel was not captured by the Jews until the days of Simon.

§ 188. The Treaty with Rome, I Mac. 8

History of the Hasmoneans

I Mac. 8 ¹Now Judas had heard of the fame of the Romans, that they are excellent men in dealing[f] with all who ally themselves with them, and make treaties of friendship with all those who come to them, ²and that they are strong in war. And they told him also of their wars and of their valiant deeds which they did among the Galatians,[g] and that they had conquered them and made them pay tribute, ³as well as what they did in the country of Spain, in that they gained possession of the mines of silver and gold which are there; ⁴and that by their cleverness and perseverance they had gained possession of the entire land, although the land was very far from theirs, and of the kings who had come against them from the ends of the earth, until they had defeated and completely overthrown them, while the rest paid them annual tribute. ⁵Further that they had defeated in battle Philip[h] and Perseus, king of the Macedonians,[i] and those who had withstood them, and had overcome them; ⁶and that Antiochus, the great king of Asia, who had come to make war against them with an hundred and twenty elephants, with horsemen and chariots and a very large army, was also defeated by them; ⁷and that they captured him alive, and imposed upon him and those who reigned after him the obligation of paying a heavy tribute, giving hostages and a part of the empire, ⁸even the land of India, Media, and Lydia and a part of their[j] most beautiful territory. When they received these from him they gave them to King Eumenes.[k] ⁹But when the inhabitants of Hellas determined to come and destroy them, ¹⁰and when it became known to them, they sent a general and fought against them, and many of them fell slain. And they carried away their wives and children and plundered them, and they took possession of their land and tore down their fortresses and made them subject to them until the present time.[l] ¹¹They also destroyed and made subject the rest of the kingdoms and as many islands as at any time resisted them. ¹²But with their friends and with those who relied in them, they carefully kept their treaties of friendship, and they have gained possession of the kingdoms far and near. And all who heard of their fame were afraid of them. ¹³All whom they help and wish to have reign, reign; and whomever they wish to depose, they depose, and thus they have attained to great power. ¹⁴But in all this none of them has put on a diadem or clothed himself with purple to be magnified thereby. ¹⁵Rather they have established

[marginal note: Reports current in Judea regarding the victories and noble policy and character of the Romans]

---

§ 188 Although excellently informed regarding the facts in Jewish history, the writer of I Mac. was evidently dependent upon popular traditions for his data regarding contemporary history, as the present section clearly indicates, for many of its statements are disproved by the testimony of the Gk. and Roman historians.

f 8¹ Following the restored Heb. idiom.

g 8² Probably the reference is to the conquest of the Gauls in Northern Italy, by Manlius Bulso in 189 B.C., not to the Galatians in Asia Minor.

h 8⁵ Philip III, son of Demetrius II, defeated in 197 B.C. by Flaminius.

i 8⁵ Gk., *Kittites.* The defeat was at the battle of Pydna, 167 B.C.

j 8⁸ Some MSS. read, *his* or *its.* As a matter of fact, India never belonged to Antiochus. The territory ceded was in Asia Minor, west of the Taurus Mts.

k 8⁸ King of Pergamos, 198–158 B.C.

l 8⁹, ¹⁰ The events referred to are not certain. It is probable that the author has in mind the Achean alliance, 147–146 B.C.

History of the Hasmoneans

a senate, and daily three hundred and twenty counsel together, at all times counselling for the welfare of the whole people that they may be prosperous.[m] [16]And to one man they intrust each year the authority over them and the rulership over all the country, and all are obedient to that one, and there is neither envy nor jealousy among them.

Message of the Jewish ambassadors

[17]And Judas chose Eupolemus the son of John, the son of Accos, and Jason the son of Eleazar, and sent them to Rome to make an alliance offensive and defensive with them, [18]and that they should take the yoke off them, whenever they saw that the Syrian[n] kingdom was enslaving Israel. [19]So they went to Rome (and the journey was exceedingly long) and entered the senate chamber and stated their errand, saying, [20]Judas, who is called Maccabeus, with his brothers and the Jewish people, have sent us to you, to make an alliance and peace with you and that we may be enrolled as your confederates and friends.

Response of the Romans and the terms of the treaty

[21]And the proposal met their approval. [22]Now this is the copy of the writing which they sent to Jerusalem, written on tablets of brass, that it might be with them there as a memorial of peace and alliance:

[23]May it be well with the nation of the Jews by sea and by land forever. May the sword also and the enemy be far from them. [24]But if war first threaten Rome or any of their allies in all their dominion, [25]the Jewish nation shall help them as confederates, heartily as the occasion shall prescribe to them. [26]And to those who make war upon them [the Romans] shall not give supplies, food, arms, money, or ships, as seems best to Rome; and they shall keep their obligations without taking any equivalent. [27]Likewise also, if war come first upon the Jewish nation, the Romans shall help them as allies willingly as the occasion shall prescribe to them; [28]and to those who are allies with their foes there shall not be given food, arms, money, or ships, as seems best to Rome; and they shall keep these obligations, and that without deceit. [29]According to these words have the Romans thus made a treaty with the people of the Jews. [30]But if hereafter the one party and the other should wish to add or withdraw anything, they may do it at their pleasure, and whatever they shall add or take away shall be established. [31]Now in regard to the wrongs which King Demetrius is doing to them, we have written to him, saying, 'Why have you made your yoke heavy upon our friends and confederates, the Jews? [32]If therefore they bring any more complaint against you, we will do them justice and fight with you by sea and by land.'

---

[m] 8[15] Or, *behave properly.*
[n] 8[18] *I.e.*, that the Romans should remove the yoke of the Syrian despot from the neck of the Jews. As in [1] the original has Greeks for Syrians.

§ 189. Death of Judas, I Mac. 9[1-22]

History of the Hasmoneans

I Mac. 9 [1]When Demetrius heard that Nicanor had fallen with his forces in battle, he sent Bacchides and Alcimus again into the land of Judah a second time, and the southern[o] wing of his army with them. [2]And they went by that way that leads to Gilgal,[p] and encamped against Masaloth, which is in Arbela, and gained possession of it and destroyed many people. [3]And the first month of the hundred and fifty-second year[q] they encamped against Jerusalem. [4]Then they set out and went to Berea with twenty thousand footmen and two thousand horsemen. [5]And Judas was encamped at Elasa,[r] and three thousand chosen men with him. [6]And when they saw the multitude of the forces, that they were many, they were greatly frightened, and many slipped away from the army, so that there were left of them not more than eight hundred men. *Advance of the Syrian army and the desertion of Judas by the Jews*

[7]And when Judas saw that his army had dispersed, he was deeply troubled, because he had no time to gather them together, and he grew discouraged. [8]And he said to those who were left, Let us arise and go up against our adversaries, if perhaps we may be able to fight with them. [9]And they would have dissuaded him, saying, We shall not be able; but let us rather save our lives now; let us return again with our fellow-countrymen and fight against them, for we are few. [10]But Judas said, Far be it from me so to do, that I should flee from them. For if our time has come, let us die manfully for the sake of our fellow-countrymen and not leave a cause of reproach against our honor. *His determination to fight*

[11]Then the army set out from the camp and drew up to meet them; and the cavalry drew up into two companies, and the slingers and the archers went before the army, with all the strong, foremost warriors. [12]But Bacchides was in the rear wing. Then the phalanx advanced on both sides, and they sounded their trumpets. [13]And Judas's men also sounded their trumpets, and the earth shook with the shout of the armies; so the battle was begun and continued from morning until evening. [14]And when Judas saw that Bacchides and the strength of his army were on the right side, all who were brave in heart went with him, [15]and the right wing was defeated by them, and he pursued them to the slope of the mountains.[s] [16]And they who were on the left wing, when they saw that the right wing was defeated, turned and followed upon the footsteps of Judas and of those who were with him. [17]And the battle grew fierce, and many on both sides fell mortally wounded. [18]Then Judas fell and the rest fled. *The battle and death of Judas*

[19]And Jonathan and Simon took Judas their brother and buried him in the sepulchre of his fathers at Modein. [20]And they bewailed him, and all Israel made great lamentation for him and mourned many days,[21] and said, *Burial of Judas*

---

[o] 9[1] Lit., *right;* but the Jews always faced the east in determining direction, so that the right was equivalent to the south. Cf. Benjamin, *son of the right hand, i.e.*, the tribe south of Ephraim.

[p] 9[2] Or, *Galgata*. Jos., *Galilee*.

[q] 9[3] March-April, 160 B.C.

[r] 9[5] Or, *Alasa*, so Syr.

[s] 9[15] So Jos. and the slightly corrected text. Revised text, *Azotus*.

History of the Hasmoneans

> How is the hero fallen,
> The saviour of Israel!

**His un-
record-
ed
deeds**
²²And the rest of the valiant acts of Judas, and his wars and the valiant deeds which he did, and his greatness—they have not been recorded, for they were very many.ᵗ

III

THE ATTAINMENT OF POLITICAL INDEPENDENCE UNDER JONATHAN, I Mac. 9²³–13³⁰

§ 190. Jonathan's Contests and Final Treaty with Bacchides, I Mac. 9²³⁻⁷³

History of the Hasmoneans

**Perse-
cution
of the
fol-
lowers
of Ju-
das**
I Mac. 9 ²³Now after the death of Judas, the apostates showed themselves in all the territory of Israel, and all who practised injustice flourished. ²⁴About the same time there was a very severe famine, and the whole people sided with them. ²⁵Then Bacchides selected the godless men and made them rulers of the country. ²⁶And they conducted a thorough search for the friends of Judas and brought them to Bacchides, and he took vengeance on them and tortured them cruelly. ²⁷Then great tribulation came upon Israel, such as had not been since the time that prophets had ceased to appear among them.

**Choice
of Jon-
athan
as
leader**
²⁸Thereupon all the friends of Judas assembled and said to Jonathan, ²⁹Since your brother Judas has died, we have no one like him to go out against our enemies and Bacchides and against those of our own kin who hate us. ³⁰Now therefore we have chosen you this day to be our prince and leader in his place that you may fight our battles. ³¹So Jonathan assumed the leadership at that time and took the place of his brother Judas.

**Pursuit
of Jon-
athan
and
Simon**
³²When Bacchides knew it, he tried to slay him. ³³But Jonathan and Simon his brother and all who were with him learned of it, and they fled into the Wilderness of Tekoa and encamped by the water of the Dead Sea.ª

ᵗ 9²² This closing tribute to Judas is fashioned after the editorial *résumés* in II Kgs.

   The Attainment of Political Independence under Jonathan.—With the restoration of the temple service and the attainment of religious freedom, the ambitions of the Hasideans or party of the pious, who had supported Judas in his earlier struggles and who later appear as the Pharisees, were realized. The withdrawal of their active support alone explains why Judas fell, fighting with only a few men against overwhelming odds. The lack of active support and the loss of prestige which resulted from the death of Judas compelled the national party, which still followed the leadership of the Hasmonean family, to seek refuge in concealment, to await the change in public opinion and in the fortunes of their Syrian masters. At their head was Jonathan, bold, energetic, and crafty, a leader who seized and turned to the advantage of the Jews the civil wars which were undermining the Syrian kingdom. Experience in turn also confirmed the position of the national party, for it became more and more evident that the liberty and purity of worship could be maintained only when defended by the sword from its foes within and without. Hence the cause of political independence gained in popularity, until the bids of rival claimants for the Syrian throne and the bold diplomacy of Jonathan made it virtually a reality. At first a hunted outlaw, Jonathan in 153 B.C. was appointed by Demetrius I high-priest, and until his death reigned practically as king of Judea.

   ª 9³³ Lit., *the cistern* (or pit) *Asphal.*

History of the Hasmoneans

³⁴And Bacchides heard of it on the sabbath day and came with all his army across the Jordan. ³⁵And Jonathan sent his brother, as commander of the baggage-train, to obtain permission from his friends the Nabateans to leave with them their baggage which was cumbersome. ³⁶But the Ambrians[b] came out of Medaba and, seizing John and all that he had, they went their way with it.

³⁷Now after these events they brought word to Jonathan and Simon his brother that the Ambrians were celebrating a great marriage, and were bringing the bride, a daughter of one of the great nobles of Canaan, from Nadabath with a large train. ³⁸Then they remembered John their brother, and going up, hid themselves under the cover of the mountain, ³⁹until they saw them coming with great noise and much baggage, and the bridegroom was coming out with his friends and his relatives to meet them with tambourines and minstrels and many weapons. ⁴⁰Then they started up against them from their ambush and slew them, and many fell mortally wounded, while the survivors fled into the mountain, and they took all their spoils.

Their vengeance upon a hostile Arabian tribe

⁴¹Thus the marriage was turned into mourning,
And the sound of their music into lamentation.

⁴²So they avenged fully the blood of their brother. Then they turned back to the marsh of Jordan.

⁴³When Bacchides heard it, he came on the sabbath day to the banks of Jordan with a great army. ⁴⁴And Jonathan said to his company, Up, now and let us fight for our lives! For it is not to-day as it used to be. ⁴⁵For see, the conflict threatens us behind and before; moreover the water of the Jordan is on this side and that, and marsh and thicket, and there is no chance to escape. ⁴⁶Now therefore cry to Heaven that you may be delivered from the power of your enemies. ⁴⁷When the battle began, Jonathan raised his hand to strike Bacchides, but he recoiled from him.[c] ⁴⁸Then Jonathan and those with him leaped into the Jordan and swam over to the other side, and they did not cross the Jordan against them. ⁴⁹And there fell of Bacchides's company that day about a thousand men; ⁵⁰and he returned to Jerusalem.

Battle with the Syrians at the Jordan

But they[d] built strong cities in Judea, the fortress that was in Jericho and Emmaus, and Bethhoron, Bethel, Timnath, Pharathon, and Tephon,[e] with high walls and gates and bars. ⁵¹And he stationed garrisons in them to harass Israel. ⁵²He also fortified the city Bethsura and Gazara and the citadel, and put forces in them and a store of food. ⁵³And he took the sons of the chief men of the country as hostages, and put them under guard in the citadel in Jerusalem.

Establishment of fortresses by Bacchides

---

b 9³⁶ Jos., *Ant.*, XIII, ¹⁴, *Sons of Ambri*, an Arabian tribe.
c 9⁴⁷ Apparently making a desperate assault upon Bacchides or his forces as a whole, Jonathan and his followers availed themselves of the opportunity furnished by the temporary recoil of the enemy to escape.
d 9⁵⁰ *I.e.*, the Syrians.
e 9⁵⁰ For the location of these fortresses, cf. map opp. p. 385.

History of the Hasmoneans

Death of Alcimus and the departure of Bacchides

⁵⁴And in the second month of the hundred and fifty-third year,[f] Alcimus gave orders to pull down the wall of the inner court of the sanctuary,[g] and so destroyed the works of the prophets. ⁵⁵They were just beginning to pull them down when Alcimus was stricken, and his works were hindered, and his mouth was stopped, and he was seized with a palsy, so that he could no more speak anything or give orders concerning his house. ⁵⁶And Alcimus died at that time in great torment. ⁵⁷And when Bacchides saw that Alcimus was dead, he returned to the king; and the land of Judah was at peace two years.

His return with an army and futile attempts to capture Jonathan and Simon

⁵⁸Then all the apostates took counsel, saying, See, Jonathan and his party are dwelling at ease and in security. Now let us, therefore, bring Bacchides that he may capture them all in one night. ⁵⁹So they went and consulted with him. ⁶⁰And he set out and came with a great army, and sent letters secretly to all his confederates who were in Judea, bidding them seize Jonathan and those who were with him. But they could not because their plan became known to them; ⁶¹and they seized about fifty of the men of the country who were ringleaders in the villainy, and he slew them. ⁶²Then Jonathan and Simon and those who were with him escaped to Bethbasi,[h] which is in the wilderness, and he built up what had been pulled down of it and made it strong. ⁶³And when Bacchides learned it, he gathered all his multitude, and sent word to those who belonged to Judea, ⁶⁴and went and laid siege to Bethbasi, and fought against it for some time, having made engines of war. ⁶⁵And Jonathan left his brother Simon in the city, and went out into the country, going with a few men. ⁶⁶And he slaughtered Odomera and his fellow-countrymen, and the people of Phasiron in their tent, ⁶⁷and began to attack and advance upon the forces. Then Simon and those who were with him went out of the city and set on fire the engines of war. ⁶⁸Thus they fought against Bacchides, and he was defeated by them with heavy loss. Because his plan and invasion were without result, ⁶⁹they were very angry with the apostates who had advised him to come into the country, and they slew many of them. Then he decided to go back to his own country.

Jonathan's treaty with Bacchides and his peaceful rule at Michmash

⁷⁰And Jonathan was informed of it, and sent ambassadors to him in order that they might make peace with him and that he should restore to them the captives. ⁷¹And he accepted and did according to his proposal, and swore to him that he would not seek to harm him all the days of his life. ⁷²And he restored to him the captives whom he had taken on former occasions out of the land of Judah, and returned and departed into his own land, and he came no more into their territory. ⁷³So the sword ceased from Israel. Jonathan then dwelt at Michmash. And Jonathan began to rule the people as judge, and he destroyed the godless out of Israel.

---

f 9⁵⁴ 160 B.C.
g 9⁵⁴ I.e., to throw it open to the heathen.
h 9⁶² Probably Bethhogla at the northern end of the Dead Sea.

§ 191. Concessions by the Syrian Rivals, Demetrius I and Alexander Balas, I Mac. 10¹⁻⁴⁷

History of the Hasmoneans

I Mac. 10 ¹Now in the one hundred and sixtieth year, Alexander the son of[i] Antiochus Epiphanes went up and took possession of Ptolemais, and they received him, and he reigned there. ²When King Demetrius heard of it, he gathered very large forces and went out to meet him in battle. ³Demetrius also sent letters to Jonathan with words of peace, so as to honor him greatly. ⁴For he said, Let us get the start in making peace with them before he makes a compact with Alexander against us. ⁵For he will remember all the wrongs that we have done to him, and to his brothers and his nation. ⁶And he gave him authority to collect forces and to provide arms and to be his ally. Also he commanded that they should deliver up to him the hostages who were in the citadel.

Authority conferred upon Jonathan by Demetrius

⁷Then Jonathan came to Jerusalem, and read the letters in the hearing of all the people, and of those who were in the citadel. ⁸And they were greatly afraid when they heard that the king had given him authority to collect an army. ⁹And the garrison delivered up the hostages to Jonathan, and he restored them to their parents. ¹⁰And Jonathan took up his residence in Jerusalem and began to rebuild and renew the city. ¹¹And he commanded those who did the work to build the walls and Mount Sion round about with square stones for defence; and they did so. ¹²Then the foreigners, who were in the strongholds which Bacchides had built, fled, ¹³and each man left his place and went into his own land. ¹⁴Only some of those who had forsaken the law and the commandments were left at Bethsura, because it was an asylum for them.

Restoration of hostages and rebuilding of Jerusalem

¹⁵And when King Alexander heard all the promises which Demetrius had made to Jonathan and had been told of the battles which he and his brothers had fought and the valiant deeds that they had done and of the hardships which they had endured, ¹⁶he said, Shall we find such another man? Now therefore let us make him our friend and ally. ¹⁷So he wrote letters and sent them to him with contents like these:

Jonathan's appointment as high priest by Alexander Balas

¹⁸King Alexander to his brother Jonathan, greeting: ¹⁹We have heard of you that you are a valiant man and fit to be our friend. ²⁰And now we have appointed you to-day to be high priest of your nation and to be called the king's Friend (and he sent to him a purple robe and a crown of gold), and to take our part and to remain on friendly terms with us.

²¹And Jonathan put on the holy garments in the seventh month of the hundred and sixtieth year[j] at the feast of tabernacles, and he gathered together forces, and provided arms in abundance.

His assumption of his honors

²²When Demetrius heard these things, he was distressed ²³and said, Why have we allowed Alexander to anticipate us in establishing friendship with the Jews to strengthen himself? ²⁴I also will write to them words of

Demetrius's offer to remit all taxes

---

i 10¹ So Syr., and probably the original Heb. Alexander was of low birth, not a son of Antiochus, but was so recognized by Jews and Romans.
j 10²¹ October, 153 B.C.

History of the Hasmoneans

encouragement and regarding honor and gifts, that they may be with me to aid me. ²⁵And so he sent to them the following message:

King Demetrius to the Jewish nation, greeting. ²⁶That you have kept your treaties with us and continued in our friendship and have not allied yourselves with our enemies, we have been delighted to hear. ²⁷Now continue still to keep faith with us, and we will recompense you with good things in return for your dealings with us, ²⁸and will grant you many immunities and give you gifts. ²⁹And now I free you and release all the Jews from the tributes[k] and from the customs of salt and from the crowns.[l] ³⁰And the tax you have paid instead of the third part of the seed and instead of the half of the fruit of the trees, which it is my right to receive, I remit from now on, so that I will not take it from the land of Judah and from the three districts[m] which are added to it from the country of Samaria and Galilee, and from now on even for all time. ³¹And let Jerusalem be holy[n] and untaxed with her territory; the tithes and the tolls shall also be free from royal tax.

To surrender the citadel and release all Jews

³²I yield up also my authority over the citadel at Jerusalem, and give it to the high priest, that he may appoint in it such men as he may choose to garrison it. ³³And every Jew without exception who has been carried captive from the land of Judah into any part of my kingdom, I set at liberty without price. And let all remit the tributes, even for their cattle. ³⁴And all their feasts, and the sabbaths, the new moons, and appointed days, and three days before a feast, and three days after a feast, let all be days of immunity and release for all the Jews who are in my kingdom. ³⁵And no man shall have authority to exact from any of them or to trouble them concerning any matter. ³⁶And let there be enrolled among the king's forces about thirty thousand Jews, and pay shall be given to them as to all the king's troops. ³⁷And some of them shall be placed in the king's great strongholds and some of them shall be placed over the affairs of the kingdom, which are of trust, and let their overseers and officers be of their own race, and let them live according to their own customs, even as the king has commanded in the land of Judah.

To cede certain districts and the city of Ptolemais and to make special grants

³⁸And the three districts which have been added to Judea from the country of Samaria, let them be joined to Judea, that they may be considered to be under one head that they may not obey other authority than the high priest's. ³⁹As for Ptolemais, and the land belonging to it, I have presented it as a gift to the sanctuary which is at Jerusalem for the defraying of expenses incurred by the sanctuary. ⁴⁰And I give every year fifteen shekels of silver from the king's revenues from the proper places. ⁴¹And all the surplus which the king's ministers did not pay in the former years, they shall give

---

k 10²⁹ *I.e.*, poll-tax.
l 10²⁹ Golden crowns originally given as voluntary homage, afterward demanded as a regular tax.
m 10³⁰ Cf. 11³⁴. The three tetrarchies of Apherema, Lydda, and Ramathaim, probably formed a strip across the south of Samaria, so that when they were added to Judea, the borderline of the latter was shifted a little to the north.
n 10³¹ *I.e.*, devoted to the god, and so exempt from taxation.

History of the Hasmoneans

from now on toward the works of the temple. ⁴²And besides this, the five thousand shekels of silver, which they received from the income of the sanctuary in revenue year by year, this also is remitted because it belongs to the priests who minister. ⁴³And whoever shall flee to the temple at Jerusalem and be found inside its precincts, whether one who owes money to the king or any other matter, let them go free, and all that they have in my kingdom. ⁴⁴And for the building and renewing of the works of the sanctuary the expense shall be paid also out of the king's revenue. ⁴⁵And for the building of the walls of Jerusalem and their fortification round about, the expense shall be paid also out of the king's revenue, and for the building of the walls in Judea.

⁴⁶Now when Jonathan and the people heard these words, they put no reliance in them nor did they receive them, because they remembered the great evil which he had done in Israel, and that he had caused them very great distress. ⁴⁷But they were well pleased with Alexander, because he was the first who made overtures of peace to them; so they remained his allies for all time.

Rejection of these offers

§ 192. Honors Bestowed upon Jonathan by Alexander Balas, I Mac. 10⁴⁸⁻⁶⁶

History of the Hasmoneans

I Mac. 10 ⁴⁸Then King Alexander mustered great forces and encamped opposite Demetrius. ⁴⁹But when the two kings joined battle, the army of Alexander retreated, and Demetrius pursued it, and vanquished them. ⁵⁰And he pushed the struggle vigorously until sundown. Demetrius, however, fell that day.

Defeat of Demetrius

⁵¹Then Alexander sent ambassadors to Ptolemy king of Egypt with this message, saying, ⁵²As I have returned to my kingdom, and am seated on the throne of my fathers, and have secured the rulership, and have overthrown Demetrius, and have gotten possession of our country; ⁵³for when I engaged in battle with him, he and his army were defeated by us, we ascended his royal throne; ⁵⁴now, therefore, let us make a treaty with each other, and give me now your daughter as wife and I will become your son-in-law and will give both you and her gifts worthy of her. ⁵⁵And Ptolemy the king answered, Happy the day in which you returned to the land of your fathers and ascended the throne of their kingdom. ⁵⁶And now I will deal with you as you have written. Meet me then at Ptolemais, that we may see each other; and I will make you my son-in-law as you have said. ⁵⁷Then Ptolemy went out of Egypt, with Cleopatra his daughter, and came to Ptolemais in the one hundred and sixty-second year.° ⁵⁸King Alexander met him and he bestowed on him his daughter Cleopatra, and celebrated her marriage at Ptolemais with great pomp, as kings are accustomed to do.

Alexander's alliance with Ptolemy

⁵⁹King Alexander then wrote to Jonathan to come to meet him. ⁶⁰So he went with pomp to Ptolemais and met the two kings and gave them and their Friends silver and gold, and many gifts, and was favorably received by

Honors conferred upon Jonathan

° 10⁵⁷ 150 B.C.

History of the Hasmoneans

them. [61]Then some infamous Israelitish apostates assembled to make accusation against him, but the king paid no attention to them. [62]Rather, the king commanded that they take off Jonathan's garments and clothe him in purple. And thus they did. [63]And the king made him sit with him, and said to his princes, Go forth with him into the midst of the city and make proclamation that none complain against him of any matter, and let none trouble him for any cause. [64]And when those who had accused him saw his glory, as they made proclamation, and saw him clothed in purple, they all took to flight. [65]And the king showed him honor, and inscribed him among his Chief Friends, and made him a commander and governor of a province. [66]And Jonathan returned to Jerusalem with peace and gladness.

§ 193. Jonathan's Victory over Apollonius, I Mac. 10[67-89]

History of the Hasmoneans

Apollonius's challenge to Jonathan

I Mac. 10 [67]Now in the one hundred and sixty-fifth year,[p] Demetrius son of Demetrius, came from Crete into the land of his fathers. [68]Then King Alexander heard of it, and he was exceedingly troubled and returned to Antioch. [69]And Demetrius appointed Apollonius, who was over Cœlesyria,[q] and he collected a great army and encamped in Jamnia, and sent to Jonathan the high priest this message:

[70]You alone are hostile to us, and I have become a laughing-stock and butt of ridicule on account of you. Now why do you flaunt your power against us in the mountains? [71]If, indeed, you trust your forces, come down to us in the plain, and there let us try the matter together, because with me is the power of the cities.[r] [72]Ask and learn who I am and the rest who help us. They will tell you, You cannot make a stand before us, for your troops[s] have been twice put to flight on their own ground. [73]And now you will not be able to withstand the cavalry and such an army as this in the plain, where there is neither stone nor pebble nor place to which to flee.

The battle and defeat of Apollonius

[74]Now when Jonathan heard the words of Apollonius, he was stirred to anger, and he chose ten thousand men and went forth from Jerusalem, and Simon his brother met him to help him. [75]And he encamped against Joppa. The people of the city, however, shut him out, because Apollonius had a garrison in Joppa. [76]So they fought against it. Then the people of the city were afraid and opened to him, and Jonathan became master of Joppa. [77]But when Apollonius heard of it he gathered an army of three thousand horsemen and a great host and marched toward Azotus as though he were going on by [Joppa], and at the same time he advanced into the plain, because he had a large cavalry force and trusted in it. [78]Then [Jonathan] pursued him to Azotus, and the armies joined battle. [79]Now Apollonius

---

[p] 10[67] 147 B.C.

[q] 10[69] Cœlesyria (lit., *the hollow Syria*) was between Lebanon and the Anti-Lebanons, but here as, *e.g.*, in Ezra-Neh., is probably intended to include all Syria.

[r] 10[71] *Yours is the strength of mountains, mine the strength of the cities.* There is a play in Heb. on the words, *mountains and cities*.

[s] 10[72] So in all probability the original Heb. As the result of an error the Gk. reads, *fathers*.

History of the Hasmoneans

had secretly left a thousand horse behind him. ⁸⁰Jonathan, however, knew that there was an ambush laid behind him. So when they surrounded his army, and cast their darts at the people from morning until evening, ⁸¹the people stood still, as Jonathan commanded them, so that their horses became tired out. ⁸²Then Simon led out his army, and joined battle with the phalanx (for the cavalry was exhausted), and they were defeated by him and fled. ⁸³And the horsemen were scattered in the plain and fled to Azotus, where they entered Beth-dagon, their idol's temple, to save themselves. ⁸⁴But Jonathan burned Azotus and the cities about it, and took their spoils; and he burned the temple of Dagon and those who fled into it. ⁸⁵And those who had fallen with the sword, with those who were burned, numbered about eight thousand men. ⁸⁶And Jonathan departed from there and encamped beside Ascalon, and the people of the city came forth to meet him with great pomp. ⁸⁷Then Jonathan, with those who belonged to his party, returned to Jerusalem, having many spoils.

⁸⁸And when King Alexander heard these things, he heaped still more honors on Jonathan, and sent him a buckle of gold, as is customarily given to those who are of royal lineage. He also gave him Ekron with all its territory as a possession.

Additional honors for Jonathan

§ 194. Overthrow of Alexander by Ptolemy and Demetrius II, I Mac. 11¹⁻¹⁹

History of the Hasmoneans

I Mac. 11 ¹Then the king of Egypt collected great forces, as countless as the sands on the seashore, and many ships and treacherously attempted to make himself master of Alexander's kingdom and to add it to his own realm. ²And he went forth into Syria with words of peace, and the peoples of the cities opened to him and received him, for King Alexander's command was that they should receive him because he was his father-in-law. ³But when Ptolemy entered the cities,ᵗ he put his forces as a garrison in each city. ⁴And when he came near Azotus, they showed him the temple of Dagon burned down, and Azotus and its suburbs pulled down, and the bodies cast outside, and those who had been burned, whom Jonathan burned in the war, for they had made heaps of them along the way he was going. ⁵And when they told the king what things Jonathan had done, that they might cast blame on him, the king held his peace. ⁶And Jonathan met the king with pomp at Joppa, and they saluted one another, and they passed the night there. ⁷And Jonathan went with the king as far as the river that is called Eleutherus and then returned to Jerusalem. ⁸But King Ptolemy became master of the cities upon the sea-coast, as far as Seleucia which is by the sea.

And he plotted evil against Alexander. ⁹And he sent ambassadors to King Demetrius, saying, Come, let us make a treaty with each other, and I will give you my daughter whom Alexander has, and you shall reign over your father's kingdom; ¹⁰for I am sorry that I gave my daughter to him,

Ptolemy's invasion of Syria and seizure of the coast cities

Plots against Alexander and the seizure of Antioch

ᵗ 11³ The Gk. adds, *Ptolemais*, but this is an impossible reading, for Ptolemy was still on the march. The original clearly read, *Ptolemy*.

History of the Hasmoneans

for he has attempted to murder me. ¹¹But he was casting blame on him because he coveted his kingdom. ¹²And taking his daughter from him, he gave her to Demetrius, and was estranged from Alexander, so that their enmity was openly seen. ¹³Ptolemy then entered Antioch and assumed the diadem of Asia. And he put two diadems on his head, the diadem of Egypt and that of Asia. ¹⁴But King Alexander was in Cilicia at that time, because the people of that territory were in revolt.

Defeat and death of Alexander and the accession of Demetrius II

¹⁵And when Alexander heard of it, he came to make war against him; and Ptolemy went out to meet him with a strong force, and put him to flight. ¹⁶And Alexander fled into Arabia that he might find asylum there; and so King Ptolemy held the upper hand. ¹⁷Then Zabdiel the Arabian took off Alexander's head and sent it to Ptolemy. ¹⁸King Ptolemy died the third day after, and they who were in his strongholds were slain by those who were in the strongholds,¹⁹ and Demetrius reigned in the hundred and sixty-seventh year.[u]

§ 195. Jonathan's New Honors and Privileges under Demetrius II,
I Mac. 11²⁰⁻⁴⁰

History of the Hasmoneans

Confirmation of Jonathan's authority

I Mac. 11 ²⁰At that time Jonathan gathered together the people of Judea to take the citadel that was at Jerusalem, and he erected many engines of war against it. ²¹Some, however, who hated their own nation, apostates, went to the king, and reported to him that Jonathan was besieging the citadel. ²²And when he heard it, he was angry, and immediately after he heard of it he set out and came to Ptolemais, and wrote to Jonathan that he should not besiege it, and that he should meet him and confer with him at Ptolemais with all speed. ²³But when Jonathan heard this, he gave orders to proceed with the siege, while he chose certain of the elders of Israel and of the priests, and putting himself in peril, ²⁴and taking silver and gold and garments, and various presents besides, he went to the king at Ptolemais. And he was favorably received; ²⁵and although some apostates of the nation made complaints against him, ²⁶the king treated him just as his predecessors had done and exalted him in the presence of all his Friends, ²⁷both confirming to him the high priesthood, and all the other honors that he had before, and giving him pre-eminence among his Chief Friends.

Demetrius's letter proclaiming the integrity and independence of Judea

²⁸And Jonathan requested the king to make Judea free from tribute, together with the three districts of Samaria,[v] and he promised him three hundred talents. ²⁹And the king consented and wrote letters to Jonathan concerning all these things in the following terms:

³⁰King Demetrius to his brother Jonathan and to the nation of the Jews, greeting. ³¹The copy of the letter which we wrote to Lasthenes our kinsman concerning you, we have also written to you, that you may see it. ³²King

u 11¹⁹ 145 B.C.
v 11²⁸ Gk., *the three districts and the country of Samaria*, but it is incredible that Samaria is intended. Probably the original read as above, and a later scribe living after the Jews had conquered Samaria introduced the present error. Cf. ³⁴ and 10³⁰.

History of the Hasmoneans

Demetrius to Lasthenes his father, greeting. ³³To the nation of the Jews who are our friends and observe what is just toward us, we have determined to do good, because of their good-will toward us. ³⁴We have therefore confirmed to them the territory of Judea and also the three districts of Apheremaᵂ and Lydda and Ramathaimˣ—they were added to Judea from the province of Samaria—and all things belonging to them. To all who sacrifice in Jerusalem we remit that which the king formerly received of them yearly instead of the king's dues from the produce of the earth and the fruits of trees. ³⁵And as for the other things that belong to us, henceforth of the tithes and the tolls that belong, and the salt-pits and the crowns that belong to us, all these we will bestow upon them. ³⁶And not one of these things shall be annulled from this time forth and forever. ³⁷Now, therefore, be, careful to make a copy of these things, and let it be given to Jonathan, and let it be set up on the holy mount in a suitable and conspicuous place.

³⁸And when King Demetrius saw that the land was quiet before him and that no resistance was made to him, he sent away all his forces, each one to his own home, except the foreign mercenaries, whom he had enlisted from the isles of the heathen. All the troops, however, who had served his father hated him. ³⁹Now Tryphonᵃ was one of those who had formerly belonged to Alexander's party, and when he saw that all the troops were murmuring against Demetrius, he went to Yamliku,ᵇ the Arabian who was bringing up Antiochus, the young child of Alexander, ⁴⁰and importuned him that he should deliver him to him, that he might reign in his father's place. And he told him all that Demetrius had done, and the hatred which his troops bore him. And he stayed there a long time.

Tryphon's plans to place the son of Alexander on the throne

§ 196. Jonathan's Transfer of Allegiance from Demetrius II to Antiochus, I Mac. 11⁴¹⁻⁷⁴

History of the Hasmoneans

I Mac. 11 ⁴¹Then Jonathan sent a message to King Demetrius requesting him to drive out the garrison at Jerusalem and those who were in the strongholds because they were fighting with Israel continually. ⁴²And Demetrius answered Jonathan, I will not only do this for you and your nation, but I will greatly honor you and your nation, if I find a favorable opportunity. ⁴³Now therefore you will do well if you send me men who shall fight for me, for all my forces have revolted. ⁴⁴So Jonathan sent him three thousand warriors to Antioch, and they came to the king who was glad at their coming. ⁴⁵And the people of the city gathered themselves together at the centre of the city to the number of a hundred and twenty thousand men, and they were eager to slay the king. ⁴⁶But the king fled into the court of the palace, and the men of the city seized the thoroughfares of the city, and began to

Jonathan's great service to Demetrius

ᵂ 11³⁴ See 10³⁰ § 191, noteᵐ. Apherema is probably the Gk. form of Ephraim, the town mentioned in II Sam. 13²³.

ˣ 11³⁴ Following the Syr. and many Gk. MSS. Cf. I Sam. 1¹.

ᵃ 11³⁹ *Tryphon, glutton,* or *debauchee,* instead of his original name, *Diodorus.*

ᵇ 11³⁹ Restoring the original Arabian form. It appears in Diodorus as Jamblichus.

History of the Hasmoneans

fight. ⁴⁷Then the king summoned the Jews to help him, and they came together to him immediately. Thereupon they dispersed themselves about the city, and slew that day as many as a hundred thousand. ⁴⁸And they set the city on fire, and took many spoils that day, and rescued the king. ⁴⁹Now when the men of the city saw that the Jews had made themselves undisputed masters of the city, they lost their courage and cried out to the king in supplication, saying, ⁵⁰Make peace with usᶜ and let the Jews stop fighting against us and the city. ⁵¹So they cast away their weapons and made peace, and the Jews stood high in the estimation of the king and of all who were in his kingdom. And they returned to Jerusalem, having many spoils.

Ingratitude of Demetrius

⁵²But when King Demetrius sat on the throne of his kingdom and the land was quiet, ⁵³he broke all the promises he had made and was hostile to Jonathan, and did not treat him in return as the benefits with which he had befriended him merited, but caused him great trouble.ᵈ

Antiochus as king

⁵⁴Now after this Tryphon returned, and with him the young child Antiochus, and he assumed the sovereignty and put on the diadem. ⁵⁵And there were gathered to him all the forces which Demetrius had sent away in disgrace, and they fought against him, and he fled and was defeated. ⁵⁶And Tryphon took the elephants and became master of Antioch.

Honors conferred upon Jonathan and Simon

⁵⁷Then the young Antiochus wrote to Jonathan, saying, I confirm to you the high priesthood and appoint you over the four districts,ᵉ and to be one of the king's Friends. ⁵⁸He also sent to him golden vessels and table service, and gave him permission to drink from golden vessels, and to be clothed in purple and to have a golden buckle.ᶠ ⁵⁹And his brother Simon he made commander from the Ladder of Tyre to the borders of Egypt.

Jonathan's conquests

⁶⁰Then Jonathan went forth and marched through the territory beyond the river and through the cities. And all the forces of Syriaᵍ gathered themselves to him to be his allies. And when he came to Ascalon, the inhabitants of the city met him with honors. ⁶¹But when he went from there to Gaza, the inhabitants of Gaza shut him out. He therefore laid siege to it and burned its suburbs and plundered them. ⁶²Then the people of Gaza besought Jonathan and he made peace with them and, taking the sons of their princes for hostages, sent them away to Jerusalem, while he passed on through the country as far as Damascus.

Victory of the Syrian forces

⁶³Now when Jonathan heard that the generals of Demetrius had come to Kedesh, which is in Galilee, with a great army, purposing to remove him from his office, ⁶⁴he went to meet them, leaving Simon his brother in the country. ⁶⁵And Simon laid siege to Bethsura, and fought against it a long time and shut it up. ⁶⁶But when they besought him to make peace with them he did so, although he drove them out and took possession of the city, and set a garrison over it. ⁶⁷And Jonathan and his army pitched camp at

---

ᶜ 11⁵⁰ Lit., *give us the right* [hand].
ᵈ 11⁵³ According to Josephus, Demetrius threatened to make war upon him unless he paid the tribute due.
ᵉ 11⁵⁷ Cf. ³⁴.
ᶠ 11⁵⁸ Cf. 10⁸⁹.
ᵍ 11⁶⁰ *I.e.*, according to ⁴³ the troops who had deserted Demetrius.

History of the Hasmoneans

the water of Gennesaret. Then, early in the morning they marched to the plain of Hazor. ⁶⁸And there an army of foreigners met him in the plain and, having laid an ambush for him in the mountains, they themselves met him face to face. ⁶⁹Then those who lay in ambush started up from their places and engaged in the battle, and all who were with Jonathan fled. ⁷⁰Not one of them was left except Mattathias the son of Absalom and Judas the son of Calphi, commander of the forces. ⁷¹Upon this Jonathan tore his garments, and put earth upon his head and prayed. ⁷²Then he turned upon them again in battle and put them to rout, and they fled. ⁷³And when the men of his army who were fleeing saw it, they returned to him, and with him pursued to Kedesh to their camp, and they encamped there. ⁷⁴So there fell of the foreigners on that day about three thousand men. Jonathan then returned to Jerusalem.

§ 197. Jonathan's Alliances, Victories, and Building Operations, I Mac. 12¹⁻³⁸

History of the Hasmoneans

I Mac. 12 ¹When now Jonathan saw that the time was opportune for him, he selected men and sent them to Rome to confirm and renew the treaty which they had with them.ʰ ²Also to the Spartans and other places, he sent letters of similar import. ³And they went to Rome, and entered the senate house, and said, Jonathan the high priest and the Jewish nation have sent us to renew for them the treaty and the alliance on the former conditions. ⁴And [the Romans] gave them letters to the garrisonsⁱ in every place, that they should give them safe conduct on their way to the land of Judah. *Renewal of the alliance with Rome*

⁵And this is the copy of the letter which Jonathan wrote to the Spartans: ⁶Jonathan the high priest, and the senate of the nation, and the priests, and the rest of the Jewish people to their brothers,ʲ the Spartans, greeting. ⁷Even before this time letters were sent to Onias the high priest from Areios,ᵏ who was reigning among you, declaring that you are our brothers, as the copy we have testifies. ⁸And Onias gave an honorable reception to the ambassadors and received the letters, in which there was a plain declaration of alliance and friendship. ⁹Therefore we also, although we need none of these things, having for our encouragement the holy books which are in our hands, ¹⁰have undertaken to send an embassy to you that we may renew our brotherhood and friendship with you in order that we should not become alienated from you altogether, for it is a long time since you sent the embassy to us. ¹¹We therefore at all times continuously, in our feasts and on the other suitable days, remember you in the sacrifices which we offer and in our prayers, as it is right and fitting to be mindful of brothers. ¹²And moreover we rejoice over your fame. ¹³But many adversities and many wars have be- *Jonathan's letter to the Spartans*

ʰ 12¹ Cf. ¹⁶ and 14²².
ⁱ 12⁴ Lit., *to them.*
ʲ 12⁶ For the traditional relationship between the Jews and Spartans, cf. II Mac. 5⁹.
ᵏ 12⁷ So Jos. and Old Lat. All the Gk. MSS. read, *from Dareios.* The Spartan king Areios I (309–265 B.C.) is evidently intended.

History of the Hasmoneans

fallen us from all sides, and the kings who surround us have fought against us. ¹⁴We did not purpose, nevertheless, to be troublesome to you and the rest of our allies and friends in these wars, ¹⁵for we have the help which is from Heaven to aid us, and we have been delivered from our enemies, and our enemies have been humiliated. ¹⁶Now, however, we have chosen Numenius the son of Antiochus and Antipater the son of Jason, and have sent them to the Romans to renew the alliance we had with them and the earlier treaty of friendship. ¹⁷We commanded them at the same time to go also to you and to salute you and to deliver to you our letters concerning the renewing also of our alliance. ¹⁸Now, therefore, you will confer a favor by granting our wish.¹

Earlier letter of the Spartans to Onias
¹⁹And this is a copy of the letter which they sent to Onias:

²⁰Arius king of the Spartans to Onias the chief priest, greeting. ²¹It has been found in writing concerning the Spartans and the Jews, that they are brothers and that they are descendants of Abraham. ²²And now, since this has come to our knowledge, you will confer a favor by writing¹ to us of your welfare. ²³And we moreover write on our part to you, that your cattle and goods are ours and ours are yours. We command therefore that they report to you to this effect.

Jonathan's campaign in Galilee
²⁴And Jonathan heard that Demetrius's generals had returned to fight against him with a greater army than before; ²⁵so he removed from Jerusalem, in order that he might meet them in the country of Hamath, for he did not wish to give them a chance to invade his country. ²⁶And when he sent spies into his camp, they came back and reported to him that they were under orders in such and such a way to fall upon them at night. ²⁷But as soon as the sun went down, Jonathan commanded his men to watch and to be in arms that all night long they might be ready for battle. He also set sentinels around the camp. ²⁸When now the adversaries heard that Jonathan and his men were ready for battle, they were afraid and trembled in their hearts. So they kindled the fires in their camp and withdrew.ᵐ ²⁹Jonathan, however, and his men did not know until morning, for they saw the fire burning. ³⁰Then Jonathan pursued them, but did not overtake them, for they had crossed the river Eleutherus. ³¹Then Jonathan turned aside to the Arabians, who are called Zabadeans, and defeated them and took their spoils. ³²And he set out from there and came to Damascus and journeyed through all the country.

Simon at Joppa
³³And Simon went forth and journeyed as far as Ascalon and the strongholds that were near to it. And he turned aside to Joppa and took possession of it, ³⁴for he had heard that they were plotting to turn the fortress over to the men of Demetrius, and he put a garrison there to keep it.

Jonathan's fortifications in Judea and Jerusalem
³⁵And when Jonathan returned he called the elders of the people together, and he considered plans with them for building strongholds in Judea ³⁶and for making the walls of Jerusalem higher and for raising a great mound between the citadel and the city in order to separate it from the city, that

---

¹ 12¹⁸, ²² Lit., *you shall do well answering us.*
ᵐ 12²⁸ So Luc., Jos., and Syr. The other texts omit the necessary, *and withdrew.*

History of the Hasmoneans

thus it might be isolated that men might neither buy nor sell. ³⁷And they were gathered together to build the city, and they took down part of the wall along the ravine that is on the east side, and from it built up anew the so-called Chaphenatha.ⁿ ³⁸And Simon also built Adida in the lowlandᵒ and made it strong and set up gates and bars.

§ 198. Tryphon's Treacherous Capture and Murder of Jonathan,
I Mac. 12³⁹–13³⁰

History of the Hasmoneans

I Mac. 12 ³⁹Then Tryphon tried to get the sovereignty over Asia and to put on the diadem and to engage in hostilities against Antiochus the king. ⁴⁰But he was afraid lest perhaps Jonathan might not allow him, and that he might fight against him. So he sought a way to take him, that he might destroy him. And he set out and came to Bethshan. ⁴¹Then Jonathan went out to meet him with forty thousand picked soldiers and came to Bethshan. ⁴²And when Tryphon saw that he came with a great army, he was afraid to attack him, ⁴³and he received him honorably and commended him to all his Friends and gave him gifts, and commanded his forces to be obedient to him as to himself. ⁴⁴And he said to Jonathan, Why have you put all this people to trouble, since that there is no war between us? ⁴⁵Now therefore send them away to their homes, retaining for yourself only a few men who shall be with you, and come with me to Ptolemais, and I will give it to you with the rest of the strongholds and the rest of the forces and all the king's officers, and I will set out on my way back, for this is the cause of my coming. ⁴⁶Then he trusted him and did even as he said, and sent away his forces so that they departed into the land of Judah. ⁴⁷But he reserved for himself three thousand men, of whom he left two thousand in Galilee, while one thousand went with him.

⁴⁸Now as soon as Jonathan entered Ptolemais, the people of Ptolemais shut the gates and laid hands on him, and they slew with the sword all who came in with him. ⁴⁹And Tryphon sent forces and horsemen into Galilee, and into the great plain,ᵖ to destroy all of Jonathan's men. ⁵⁰But they perceived that he had been taken and had perished, and those who were with him, and they encouraged one another and marched in closed ranks, prepared to fight. ⁵¹And when those who were pursuing them saw that they were ready to fight for their lives, they turned back again. ⁵²Thus they all came safely into the land of Judah, and they mourned for Jonathan and those who were with him, and they were greatly afraid. And all Israel mourned bitterly. ⁵³Then all the heathen who were round about them sought to destroy them utterly, for they said, They have no ruler nor any to

Marginal notes:
Tryphon's false promises and plot to disarm Jonathan

Seizure of Jonathan and the public mourning for him

ⁿ 12³⁷ Following what was evidently the original Heb., Gk., *fell down*. The meaning of the proper name is unknown.
ᵒ 12³⁸ *I.e.*, the *shephelah*, the lowland west of Judea. Adida is probably to be identified with the O.T. Hadad, east of Lydda.
ᵖ 12⁴⁹ Cf. 5⁵²

History of the Hasmoneans

help them, now therefore let us fight against them and wipe out the memory
of them from among men.

Choice of Simon as leader

13 1Now when Simon heard that Tryphon had collected a vast army to
come into the land of Judah to destroy it utterly, 2and saw that the people
trembled and were greatly afraid, he went up to Jerusalem and gathered
the people together, 3and encouraged them and said to them, You yourselves know all the things that I and my brothers, and my father's house,
have done for the laws and the sanctuary, and the battles and times of distress
through which we have passed. 4In this cause all my brothers have perished
for Israel's sake, and I alone am left. 5And now be it far from me that I
should spare my own life, in any time of affliction; for I am not better than my
brothers.[q] 6Rather I will take revenge for my nation, and for the sanctuary,
and for our wives and children, because all the heathen are gathered to
destroy us out of pure hatred. 7And the courage of the people rose as they
heard these words. 8And they answered with a loud voice, saying, You are
our leader instead of Judas and Jonathan your brother. 9Fight our battles,
and we will do all that you command. 10So he gathered together all the
warriors and made haste to finish the walls of Jerusalem, and fortified the
entire length of it. 11And he sent Jonathan the son of Absalom at the head
of a large army to Joppa, and he drove out those who were in it, and stayed
there in it.

Tryphon's treachery in demanding money and hostages

12And Tryphon set out from Ptolemais with a mighty army to invade the
land of Judah, and Jonathan was with him as a prisoner. 13Then Simon
encamped at Adida on the edge of the plain. 14And when Tryphon knew
that Simon had succeeded to the place of his brother Jonathan and meant to
join battle with him, he sent ambassadors to him, saying, 15It is for money
which Jonathan your brother owed to the king's treasury because of the
offices which he held that we hold him prisoner. 16Now therefore send a
hundred talents of silver and two of his sons as hostages, that, when he is
set at liberty, he will not revolt against us, and we will set him at liberty.
17Although Simon knew that they spoke to him deceitfully, yet he sent the
money and the children, lest perhaps he might incur the great hatred of the
people, who would say, 18Because I did not send him the money and the
children, he perished. 19And when he sent the children and the hundred
talents, [Tryphon] broke his word and did not set Jonathan at liberty.

Failure to invade Judea

20And after this Tryphon came to invade the land and destroy it, and he
went round about by the way that goes to Adora; and Simon and his army
marched opposite and abreast of him to every place wherever he went. 21And
the people of the citadel sent to Tryphon ambassadors urging him to come
by forced marches through the wilderness to them and to send them supplies.
22So Tryphon made ready all his cavalry to go. But that night a very deep
snow fell, so that he did not come because of the snow.

Murder and burial of Jonathan

Then he set out and came to the country of Gilead. 23And when he came
near to Bascama, he slew Jonathan, and he was buried there. 24But when

---

q 13:5 Thinking that his brothers were dead, cf. 12:50.

History of the Hasmoneans

Tryphon went back into his own land. ²⁵Simon sent and took the bones of Jonathan his brother, and buried them at Modein, his ancestral city. ²⁶And all Israel made great lamentation over him and mourned him for many days. ²⁷And Simon built a monument upon the sepulchre of his father and his brothers, and raised it aloft to the sight, with polished stone on the back and front sides. ²⁸He also set up seven pyramids, one opposite another, for his father and his mother and his four brothers.ʳ ²⁹And for these he made artistic designs, setting about them great pillars, and upon the pillars he fashioned different kinds of arms as an everlasting memorial, and beside the arms ships carved, that they should be seen by all who sail on the sea. ³⁰This is the sepulchre which he made at Modein, which stands there at the present time.

IV

SIMON'S PROSPEROUS REIGN, I Mac. 13³¹–16²⁴

§ 199. **Peace with Demetrius and the Capture of Gazara and the Citadel at Jerusalem, I Mac. 13³¹⁻⁵³**

History of the Hasmoneans

I Mac. 13 ³¹Now Tryphon proceeded treacherously with the young king Antiochus, and slew him, ³²and ascended the throne in his place, and put on the diadem of Asia, and brought a great calamity upon the land. Tryphon as king

³³Then Simon built the strongholds of Judea and fenced them about with high towers and great walls and gates and bars, and laid up stores in the strongholds. ³⁴And Simon chose men and sent them to King Demetrius in order to ask that he grant immunity to the country, because all that Tryphon did was to plunder. ³⁵And King Demetrius sent an answer to him in words similar to these, and wrote to him the following letter: Concessions of Demetrius II to the Jew

³⁶King Demetrius to Simon the high priest and Friend of kings, and to the elders and nation of the Jews, greeting: ³⁷the golden crown and the palm branch which you sent, we have received, and we are ready to make a treaty of absolute peace with you, and to write to our officials to grant immunities to you. ³⁸And whatever things we confirmed to you, they are confirmed.

ʳ 13²⁸ The seventh was evidently for himself.

Simon's Prosperous Reign.—After twenty-five years of almost unceasing war, the Jews at last for a brief period, enjoyed the sweet fruits and honors of peace. A wise, benign ruler guarded their interests within and without Palestine. The Syrian kingdom had become so weak as the result of its protracted civil wars and moral corruption that it had ceased to be a serious menace to the existence of the Maccabean state. The protecting influence of Rome was also becoming a powerful factor in the politics of the East. Not suspecting the ulterior designs of that growing world-power, the Jews gloried in its friendship. Although the boundaries of the Jewish kingdom were later extended still further, the reign of Simon marks the height of its internal prosperity. With the reign of his son and successor, John Hyrcanus, the policy of foreign conquest was instituted, which ultimately intensified the hostility of all their heathen neighbors and precipitated the bitter feud between the Pharisees and Sadducees which finally dismembered the Maccabean state. From the succeeding century of struggles and humiliating disasters the Jews looked back upon the bright days of Simon with ever-increasing pride and longing.

History of the Hasmoneans

And the strongholds which you have built, let them be your own.   ³⁹As for any debts you have not acknowledged and acknowledged debts that you have not paid up to the present, we remit them, and the crown which you owed us.   And if there is any other tax which may have been exacted in Jerusalem, let it be exacted no longer.   ⁴⁰And if there are any among you suitable to be enrolled in our court, let them be enrolled, and let there be peace between us.

Simon's independent rule

⁴¹In the hundred and seventieth year^a the yoke of the heathen was taken away from Israel.   ⁴²And the people began to write in their legal documents and contracts, In the first year of Simon the great high priest and commander and leader of the Jews.

Siege and capture of Gazara

⁴³In those days he laid siege to Gazara,^b and surrounded it with armies, and made an engine of siege and brought it up to the city, and smote a tower and captured it.   ⁴⁴And those who were in the engine leaped forth into the city, and there was a great tumult in the city.   ⁴⁵And the people of the city tore their garments, and went up on the walls with their wives and children, and cried with a loud voice, requesting Simon to make peace with them.   ⁴⁶And they said, Do not deal with us according to our wickednesses but according to your mercy.   ⁴⁷So Simon was reconciled to them and did not fight against them.   But he expelled them from the city and cleansed the houses in which the idols were, and so entered into it with singing and praise.   ⁴⁸And when he had put all uncleanness out of it, he placed in it such men as would keep the law and made it stronger than it was before, and built a dwelling place for himself in it.

Capture and fortification of the citadel at Jerusalem

⁴⁹But those who were in the citadel at Jerusalem were prevented from going out and from going into the country, and from buying and selling, so that they suffered exceedingly from hunger, and a great number of them perished through famine.   ⁵⁰Then they cried out to Simon to make peace with them.   He did so, but put them out from there, and cleansed the citadel from its pollutions.   ⁵¹And he entered it on the twenty-third day of the second month in the one hundred and seventy-first year, with praise and palm branches, with harps, with cymbals, with viols, with hymns, and with songs, because a great enemy was destroyed out of Israel.   ⁵²And he ordained that they should observe that day each year with gladness.   And the temple mount, which was beside the citadel, he made stronger than before, and there he dwelt with his men.   ⁵³And Simon saw that John^c his son had grown to manhood, and so he made him commander of all his forces.   And he lived in Gazara.

---

^a 13⁴¹ 142 b.c.
^b 13⁴³ So Jos., *Ant.*, XIII, 6⁷, and *Jewish Wars*, 1, 2². Cf. 4¹⁵. All the Gk. MSS. and the other versions read, *Gaza.*
^c 13⁵³ Who later reigned as John Hyrcanus.

§ 200. Peace and Prosperity under Simon, I Mac. 14¹⁻¹⁵

History of the Hasmoneans

I Mac. 14 ¹And in the one hundred and seventy-second year King Deme- Capt-
trius collected his forces and went into Media to get help that he might fight ure of
against Tryphon.ᵈ ²But when Arsaces the king of Persia and Media heard trius II
that Demetrius had come into his territory, he sent one of his princes to take king of
him alive. ³And he went and defeated the army of Demetrius and capt- and
ured him and brought him to Arsaces, who put him in prison. Media

Captured of Demetrius II by the king of Persia and Media

⁴So the land had rest all the days of Simon,   Benign
  And he sought the good of his nation.   policy
  His authority and his glory were well-pleasing to them all his days.   con-
⁵And amid all his glory he took Joppa for a haven,   quests
  And made it a way to the isles of the sea,   of Si-
⁶And he enlarged the boundaries of his nation,   mon
  And became master of the land.
⁷He also brought many captives together,
  And made himself master of Gazara and Bethsura, and the citadel.
  Moreover he took away from it its uncleannesses;
  And there was none who resisted him.
⁸And they tilled their land in peace,
  And the earth gave her increase,
  And the trees of the plains their fruit.
⁹The old men sat in the streets,   Univer-
  They talked together of the common good,   sal
  And the young men put on glorious, fineᵉ apparel.   peace
¹⁰He provided food for the cities,   and
  And furnished them with means of fortification,   pros-
  Until his famous name was known to the end of the earth.   perity
¹¹He made peace in the land,   under
¹²And Israel rejoiced with great joy,   his
  Everyone sat under his own vine and fig tree,   rule
  And there was no one to make them afraid,ᶠ
¹³And none who warred against them was left upon the earth,
  For the kings were utterly crushed in those days.
¹⁴And he strengthened all the distressed of his people,
  He was full of zeal for the law,
  And every lawless and wicked person he banished.
¹⁵He made the sanctuary glorious,
  And multiplied the vessels of the temple.ᵍ

§ 201. Renewal of the Treaty with Rome and Sparta, I Mac. 14¹⁶⁻²⁴

History of the Hasmoneans

I Mac. 14 ¹⁶Now when they heard at Rome and at Sparta that Jon- Re-
athan was dead, they were very sorry. ¹⁷But as soon as they learned that his newal
brother Simon had been made high priest in his place and ruled the country ances
and its cities, ¹⁸they wrote to him on brass tablets, to renew with him the Rome
    and
    Sparta

Renewal of alliances with Rome and Sparta

ᵈ 14¹ Josephus has little after this point in common with I Mac.
ᵉ 14⁹ So the original Heb. The Gk. mistook it for a similar Heb. word and read, *warlike.*
ᶠ 14¹² Cf. Mi. 4⁴, I Kgs. 4²⁵.
ᵍ 14⁴⁻¹⁵ This poem is in the author's best style. It contains many expressions found in
the earlier prophetic books. Many scholars think the book originally closed with this poem.

History of the Hasmoneans

friendship and the treaty which they had made with Judas and Jonathan his brothers; [19]and these were read before the congregation at Jerusalem.

Letter from the Spartans

[20]And this is the copy of the letters which the Spartans sent:

The rulers of the Spartans, and the city, to Simon the high priest, and to the elders, and the priests, and the rest of the people of the Jews, our brothers, greeting.   [21]The ambassadors who were sent to our people reported to us your glory and honor, and we were glad that they came, [22]and we registered the things that were spoken by them in the public records thus: ' Numenius son of Antiochus and Antipater son of Jason, the Jews' ambassadors, came to us to renew the friendship they had with us.   [23]And it pleased the people to entertain the men honorably, and to put the copy of their words in the public records, in order that the people of the Spartans might have a memorial of them.   Moreover, they wrote a copy of these things to Simon the high priest.'

Simon's present to Rome

[24]After this Simon sent Numenius to Rome with a great shield of gold which weighed a thousand minas,[h] in order to confirm the alliance with them.

§ 202. **Honors Conferred upon Simon by the Jews, I Mac. 14[25-49]**

History of the Hasmoneans

Public recognition of the services of Simon and his brothers

I Mac. 14 [25]Now when the people heard these things, they said, How can we thank Simon and his sons ?   [26]For he and his brothers and the house of his father have shown themselves brave, and have warded off the enemies of Israel from them and made liberty sure.   [27]So they wrote on brass tablets and affixed them to pillars on Mount Sion.   Now this is the copy of the writing:

On the eighteenth day of Elul, in the one hundred and seventy-second year,—and this is the third year of Simon the high priest, the prince of the people of God,[i]—[28]in a great congregation of priests and people and princes of the nation and of the elders of the country, we hereby declare to you:[j] [29]Since there have been frequent wars in the country, Simon the son of Mattathias, the sons of the sons of Joarib, and his brothers have put themselves in peril and withstood the enemies of their nation, that their sanctuary and the law might be established, and won great renown for their nation. [30]And Jonathan assembled the nation together and became their high priest. But when he was gathered to his people, [31]their enemies proposed to invade their country, that they might destroy their country utterly and stretch forth their hand against their sanctuary.   [32]Then Simon rose up and fought for his nation, and spent much of his own property in arming the soldiers of his nation and in giving them wages.   [33]And he fortified the cities of Judea and Bethsura[k] that is situated on the borders of Judea, which was formerly

---

[h] 14[24] Representing a value of about eighteen thousand dollars.
[i] 14[27] Gk., *Asaramel.*   This is evidently a transliteration of the Heb., *prince of the people of God,* or an abbreviation of, *prince of Israel.*   The date was 141 B.C.
[j] 14[28] So Luc. and Syr.   The Gk., *it was notified to us,* makes no sense.
[k] 14[33] Cf. 4[29].

462

History of the Hasmoneans

a depot for the arms of the enemies, and set there a garrison of Jews.   ³⁴He also fortified Joppa[l] which is by the sea and Gazara[m] which is on the borders of Azotus,[n] in which the enemies formerly lived, and placed Jews there and put in it everything needed for repairing it.   ³⁵And when the people saw the worth of Simon and the glory which he aimed to bring to his nation, they made him their governor and high priest, because he had done all these things, and because of the justice and the faith which he showed to his nation, and because he sought by all means to exalt his people.   ³⁶And in his day things prospered in his hands, so that the heathen were taken away from their country, as well as those who were in the city of David, who were in Jerusalem, who had made themselves a citadel from which they were accustomed to sally and pollute everything belonging to the sanctuary, and did great damage to its purity.   ³⁷And he placed Jews in it and fortified it for the safety of the country and the city, and made high the walls of Jerusalem.

³⁸Moreover King Demetrius confirmed to him the high priesthood according to these things, ³⁹and made him one of his Friends, and bestowed great honor upon him, ⁴⁰for he had heard that the Jews had been called friends and allies and brothers by the Romans, and that they had met the ambassadors of Simon with honor, ⁴¹and that the Jews and the priests were well pleased that Simon should be their governor and high priest forever, until there should arise a faithful prophet; ⁴²and that he should be commander over them, and should take charge of the sanctuary,[o] to appoint men on his own authority over their works and over the country and over the arms and over the forts, ⁴³and that he should be obeyed by all, and that all documents drawn up in the country should be written in his name, and that he should be clothed in purple, and wear gold; ⁴⁴and that it should not be lawful for any of the people or of the priests to nullify any of these things, or to resist the commands that he should issue, or to gather an assembly in the country without his permission, or to be clothed in purple or to wear a golden buckle. ⁴⁵But whoever should do otherwise, or act in defiance of any of these things, should be liable to punishment.   ⁴⁶All the people agreed to ordain that Simon should act according to these regulations.   ⁴⁷And Simon accepted and consented to be high priest and to be general and governor of the Jews and of the priests and to be protector of all.

³⁸⁻⁴⁷ *margin:* Confirmation of his authority by Demetrius and the Jewish people

⁴⁸And they gave orders to put this writing on brass tablets and to set them up within the precinct of the sanctuary in a conspicuous[p] place, ⁴⁹and also to put the copies of it in the treasury in order that Simon and his sons might have them.

⁴⁸⁻⁴⁹ *margin:* The public record

---

l 14³⁴ Cf. 12³³.
m 14³⁴ Cf. 4¹⁵, 13⁴³.
n 14³⁴ Cf. 4¹⁵.
o 14⁴² The same clause is repeated by mistake at the end of the verse.
p 14⁴⁸ Gk.A, *safe*.

§ 203. Early Promises and Later Demands of Antiochus Sidetes,
I Mac. 15¹⁻³⁷

History of the Hasmoneans

Antio-
chus's
lavish
prom-
ises

I Mac. 15 ¹And Antiochus son of Demetrius the king sent letters from the isles of the sea to Simon the priest and governor of the Jews, and to all the nation; ²and their contents were as follows:

King Antiochus to Simon the chief priest and governor, and to the Jewish nation, greeting. ³Since certain infamous fellows have made themselves masters of the kingdom of our fathers, my purpose is to claim the kingdom that I may restore it to its former conditions; and moreover I have raised a multitude of troops, and have prepared warships. ⁴And I am planning to land in the country that I may punish those who have destroyed our country and those who have made many cities in the kingdom desolate. ⁵Now, therefore, I confirm to you all the taxes which the kings who were before me remitted to you and whatever gifts beside they remitted to you, ⁶and I give you leave to coin money for your country with your own stamp. ⁷And Jerusalem and the sanctuary shall be free, and all the arms which you have prepared, and the strongholds which you have built, and which you hold in your possession, let them remain yours. ⁸And everything due to the king^q and the things that shall be due the king from now and for evermore, let them be remitted to you. ⁹Moreover, when we shall have established our kingdom, we will bestow great honor upon you and your nation and the temple, so that your glory shall be made manifest in all the earth.

His
pursuit
of Try-
phon
and
siege of
Dor

¹⁰In the one hundred and seventy-fourth year,^r Antiochus went forth into the land of his fathers, and all the forces came together to him, so that there were few men with Tryphon. ¹¹Then King Antiochus pursued him, and he came, as he fled, to Dor, which is on the sea, ¹²for he knew that troubles had come upon him all at once and that his forces had forsaken him. ¹³Then Antiochus laid siege to Dor, and with him were a hundred and twenty thousand infantry and eight thousand cavalry. ¹⁴And he surrounded the city, and the ships joined in the attack from the sea, and he harassed the city by land and sea and allowed no one to go out or in.

Rome's
protec-
tion of
the
Jews

¹⁵Then Numenius and his companions came from Rome, having letters to the kings and to the countries, in which were written these things:

¹⁶Lucius, consul of the Romans, to King Ptolemy, greeting. ¹⁷The ambassadors of the Jews came to us as our friends and confederates, to renew the old treaty of alliance, having been sent from Simon the high priest and from the people of the Jews. ¹⁸Moreover they brought a shield of gold weighing a thousand^s minas. ¹⁹It pleased us therefore to write to the kings and to the countries, that they should not seek their hurt, nor fight against them and their cities and their country, nor be allied with those who fight against them. ²⁰Moreover it seemed good to us to receive the shield from them. ²¹If therefore any seditious fellows have fled from their country to you,

§ 203 Antiochus VII Sidetes was the son of Demetrius I and the brother of Demetrius II, who was held as captive by the Parthians.
q 15⁸ The reference is probably to the contributions of soldiers and support in time of war.
r 15¹⁰ 138 B.C.
s 15¹⁸ So 14²⁴ Gk.A, *five thousand.*

History of the Hasmoneans

give them up to Simon the high priest that he may take vengeance on them according to their law.   ²²And the same things he wrote to Demetrius the king, to Attalus, ²³to Arathes, to Arsaces, and to all the countries, to Sampsames, to the Spartans, to Delos, Myndos, Sicyon, Caria, Samos, Pamphylia, Lycia, Halicarnassus, Rhodes, Phaselis, Cos, Side, Aradus, Gortyna, Cnidus, Cyprus, and Cyrene.ᵗ   ²⁴And the copy of them they sent in writing to Simon the high priest.ᵘ

²⁵And Antiochus the king besieged Dor the second day, continually bringing his forces closer to it and making engines of war, he shut up Tryphon from going in or out.   ²⁶Then Simon sent him two thousand picked men to fight on his side and silver and gold and instruments of war in abundance. ²⁷But he would not accept them, and he broke all the treaties which he had made with him before and was estranged from him.   ²⁸And he sent to him Athenobius, one of his Friends to communicate with him, saying, You hold possession of Joppa and Gazara and the citadel that is in Jerusalem, cities of my kingdom.   ²⁹You have laid waste their territories, and have done great harm in the land and gained the mastery of many places in my kingdom.   ³⁰Now therefore, give up the cities which you have taken and the tributes of the places of which you have gained the mastery outside of the borders of Judea, ³¹or else give me for them five hundred talents of silver, and for the harm that you have done and the tributes of the cities, another five hundred talents, or else we will come and conquer you.

³²And when Athenobius the king's Friend came to Jerusalem and saw the splendor of Simon, and the cupboard of gold and silver vessels, and his great attendance, he was amazed.   Then he reported to him the king's words. ³³And Simon replied to him, We have neither taken other men's land, nor have we possession of that which belongs to others, but of the inheritance of our fathers, which was in the possession of our enemies wrongfully for a certain time.   ³⁴Now we, having opportunity, hold fast the inheritance of our fathers.   ³⁵And with regard to your demand about Joppa and Gazara, they did great harm among the people throughout our country.   We will give a hundred talents for them.

And he answered him not a word, ³⁶but returned in a rage to the king, and reported to him these words, and the splendor of Simon and all that he had seen, and the king was very angry.   ³⁷And Tryphon, embarking on board a ship, fled to Orthosia.

Antiochus's demand that Simon pay a huge tribute

Simon's reply

Rage of Antiochus

§ 204. Defeat of the Syrian Army, I Mac. 15³⁸–16¹⁰

History of the Hasmoneans

I Mac. 15 ³⁸Then the king appointed Cendebaeus commander-in-chief of the sea-coast, and gave him forces of infantry and cavalry, ³⁹and commanded him to encamp before Judea, and ordered him to fortify Kidron

Attacks of the Syrian commander

ᵗ 15²³ This list includes states, islands, and cities.
ᵘ 15¹⁵⁻²⁴ These verses break the close connection between ¹⁴ and ²⁵ and may be later insertions.

465

History of the Hasmoneans

and to make the gates strong, and to fight against the people; but the king pursued Tryphon. ⁴⁰And Cendebaeus came to Jamnia and began to irritate the people, and to invade Judea and to take the people captive and to slay them. ⁴¹And he fortified Kidron, and placed horsemen and infantry there in order that, issuing out, they might make sallies upon the highways of Judea, as the king commanded him.

John's victory over the Syrian forces

16 ¹Then John went up from Gazara and told Simon his father what Cendebaeus was doing. ²And Simon called his two eldest sons, Judas and John, and said to them, I and my brothers and my father's house have fought the battles of Israel from our youth, even to this day and we have repeatedly succeeded in delivering Israel. ³But now I am old, while you, by the mercy of God, are in the prime of life. Take my brother's place and mine and go forth and fight for our nation, and may the help which is from Heaven be with you. ⁴And he chose out of the country twenty thousand infantry and cavalry, and they went against Cendebaeus, passing the night at Modein. ⁵And rising up in the morning, they went into the plain and there a great host came to meet them of footmen and horsemen. And there was a brook between them. ⁶Then he with his people encamped directly opposite them. And when he saw that the people were afraid to cross the brook, he passed over first, and the men saw him and passed over after him. ⁷Then he divided the people, with the horsemen in the midst of the footmen. The enemies' horsemen, however, were very numerous. ⁸And they blew a signal blast with the trumpets, and Cendebaeus and his army were put to flight, and there fell many of them mortally wounded, but those who were left fled to the stronghold.ᵛ ⁹That was the time when Judas, John's brother, was wounded. But John pursued them until he came to the Kidron which Cendebaeus had fortified. ¹⁰Now they fled to the towers which are in the fields of Azotus, and he burned it,ʷ and there fell of them about one thousandˣ men. And he returned into Judea with success.

§ 205. **The Treacherous Murder of Simon, I Mac. 16¹¹⁻²⁴**

History of the Hasmoneans

Ptolemy's dastardly plot

I Mac. 16 ¹¹Now Ptolemy the son of Abubus had been appointed commander over the plain of Jericho. He possessed much silver and gold, ¹²for he was the high priest's son-in-law. ¹³Then he grew ambitious and determined to make himself master of the country. So he formed treacherous plots against Simon and his sons, to make away with them. ¹⁴Now Simon was visiting the cities that were in the country and providing for their good management. And he went down to Jericho with Mattathias and Judas his sons, in the one hundred and seventy-seventh year,ᵃ in the eleventh month, that is the month Sebat. ¹⁵Then the son of Abubus received them

v 16⁸ Cf. 15⁴¹, the fortress Kidron, near Modein, cf. 16⁴.
w 16¹⁰ *I.e.*, Azotus. Cf. 10⁸⁴.
x 16¹⁰ So Gk. B. and A. Other Gk. versions, *two thousand;* Syr. and Luc., *three thousand.*
a 16¹⁴ 135 B.C.

History of the Hasmoneans

treacherously in a little stronghold that is called Dok,[b] which he had built, and made them a great banquet, and his men were there. [16]And when Simon and his sons were drunk, Ptolemy and his men rose up and took their weapons, and rushing in upon Simon in the banquet hall, they slew him and his two sons, and some of his servants. [17]Thus he committed a great act of treachery[c] and paid back evil for good.

[18]Then Ptolemy wrote what had happened, and asked the king to send forces to aid him, and promised to hand over to him their country and the cities. [19]And he sent others to Gazara to make away with John. And to the officers commanding thousands he sent letters to come to him, that he might give them silver and gold and gifts. [20]And others he sent to take possession of Jerusalem and the temple-mount. [21]But some ran before to Gazara and told John that his father and brothers had perished, and they said, He has sent to slay you too. [22]And when he heard, he was dumb with amazement, but he seized the men who came to destroy him, and slew them, for he saw that they were seeking to destroy him.

His failure to murder John Hyrcanus

[23]Now the rest of the acts of John, and the account of his wars, and of the valiant deeds which he did, and of the building of the walls which he rebuilt,[d] and of his achievements, [24]behold, they are recorded in the chronicles of his high priesthood, from the time that he was made high priest after his father.

Record of John's achievements

---

b 16^{15} A little northwest of Jericho.
c 16^{17} Gk.A, *impiety.*
d 16^{23} Cf. Jos. *Ant.* XIII, 8^3. The reference is to the rebuilding of the wall destroyed by Antiochus Sidetes in 134 B.C.

THE LIFE OF THE JEWS OF THE DISPERSION

Esther

THE LIFE OF THE JEWS OF THE DISPERSION

THE STORY OF ESTHER, Esth. 1–10

§ 206. Repudiation of Queen Vashti by Ahasuerus, Esth. 1

Esth. 1 [1]Now it came to pass in the days of Ahasuerus [Xerxes][a]—that is the Ahasuerus who reigned from India even to Ethiopia over a hundred and twenty-seven provinces—[2]in those days when King Ahasuerus sat on the throne of his kingdom, which was in the royal palace[b] at Shushan, [3]in the third year of his reign, he made a feast for all his princes and his servants. And the commanders of the military forces[c] of Persia and Media, the nobles and satraps, were before him, [4]while he showed the riches of his glorious kingdom and the splendor of his great majesty many days, even a hundred and eighty days. [5]And when these days came to an end, the king made for all the people who were present in the royal palace at Shushan, both great and small, a seven days' feast, in the court of the garden of the royal palace. [6]There were fine linen, cotton, and blue hangings, fastened with cords of

(marginal note: Ahasuerus's great feast for his court)

The Life of the Jews of the Dispersion.—Beginning with the fall of Samaria in 722 B.C., the tragic fate of the Israelitish race was to have large numbers of its most prominent and intelligent members carried away in successive deportations and thus scattered throughout the ancient world from northern Africa to central Asia, and from the Black and Caspian seas to the Indian ocean. The result was that from 586 B.C. nearly, if not fully, half of the race were to be found outside Palestine. The importance of the exile in Jewish history is shown by the writings of Ezek., Is. 40–55, and probably a large part of the priestly code, which the exiles contributed to the O.T., and by the work of Joshua, Zerubbabel, and Nehemiah. Of the life of the Jews of the dispersion the O.T. says little. It was a chapter that lacked unity and vital connection with the main current of Israel's history. It is not recorded in the historical writings, but reflected, and for the most part idealized, in the popular stories of the first six chapters of Dan., and in their apocryphal supplements, the History of Susannah, Bel and the Dragon, and the Song of the Three Holy Children. With these belong the story of the *Three Young Men* in I Esdr. 3, 4, the books of Esther and Tobit, and the tales regarding the Jews in Egypt found in III Mac.

It is a striking, suggestive fact that without exception these appear to be the products of the imagination, although possibly in some cases they are based on historical incidents. It would seem, however, that the facts were so few or so unattractive that fancy was called in to invest them with a halo of romance. It is also significant that, while most of the stories are placed in a much earlier age, none of them in their present literary form antedates the beginning of the Maccabean period. That stirring age, with its brilliant achievements, fired the imagination and produced this large group of historical romances. They correspond in many ways to the Sunday-school books of to-day. They were all written with a didactic aim and were intended to arouse the patriotism and inspire their readers to emulate the examples of the heroes and heroines who figure in them.

The book of Esther is the best known of these historical romances. The origin, date, and purpose of the story have already been considered in Chap. V of the Introd. (pp. 39, 40). Its present historical value is due not to the incidents which it purports to record, but to the life of the Jews of the dispersion, which it reflects, and the attitude of the Jews toward their heathen neighbors during the second and first centuries B.C., which it vividly sets forth.

[a] 1[1] The Gk. has, *Artaxerxes*, but Herodotus's pictures of Xerxes (IX, 109), best accords with the present description and the Heb. form of the word, especially the marginal reading in 10[1], represents the Old Persian, *Khshayarsh*, Bab., *Khshiarsha* (Xerxes). The same form also occurs in Ezra 4[6]. Cf. the one hundred and twenty satraps of Dan. 6[1]. Darius I divided the kingdom into twenty satrapies.

[b] 1[2] Heb., *castle*, the winter residence of the Persian kings. Cf. Neh. 1[1].

[c] 1[3] Completing the Hebrew as the context demands.

fine linen and purple to silver rings and pillars of marble; the couches were of gold and silver upon a mosaic pavement of alabaster and white marble and mother-of-pearl and spotted stone.ᵈ ⁷And they gave them drink in vessels of gold, and the vessels were all different from one another, and the royal wine was abundant according to the liberality of the king. ⁸And the drinking was according to the law; none could compel, for so the king had given direction to all the officers of his house, to do according to each man's wishes.

Vash-
ti's re-
fusal to
appear
at the
feast⁹Also Vashti the queen made a feast for the women in the royal palace which belonged to King Ahasuerus. ¹⁰On the seventh day, when the heart of the king was merry with wine, he commanded Mehuman, Biztha, Harbona, Bigtha, and Abagtha, Zethar, and Carcas, the seven eunuchs who ministered in the presence of Ahasuerus the king, ¹¹to bring Vashti the queen before the king with the royal crown, to show the peoples and the princes her beauty, for she was fair to look upon. ¹²But the Queen Vashti refused to come at the king's command by the eunuchs; therefore the king was very angry, and his rage burned within him.

Advice
of the
wise
men
to pun-
ish
Vashti¹³Then the king said to the wise men who knew the timesᵉ—for thus the king was accustomed to consult all who knew the law and precedent; ¹⁴and those next to him were Carshena, Sethar, Admatha, Tarshish, Meres, Marsena, and Memucan, the seven princes of Persia and Media who saw the king's face and occupied the first place in the kingdom, ¹⁵What shall we do to the Queen Vashti according to law, because she has not done the bidding of the King Ahasuerus by the eunuchs? ¹⁶And Memucan answered before the king and the princes, Vashti the queen has not done wrong to the king only, but also to all the princes and to all the peoples, that are in all the provinces of the King Ahasuerus. ¹⁷For this act of the queen will be reported to all women to make their husbands contemptible in their eyes, when it shall be said, ' The King Ahasuerus commanded Vashti the queen to be brought in before him, but she came not.' ¹⁸And this day will the princesses of Persia and Media who have heard of the act of the queen relate it to all the king's princes, and there will be corresponding contempt and rage. ¹⁹If it please the king, let a royal command go forth from him, and let it be written among the laws of the Persians and the Medes, and it cannot be altered, that Vashti may never again come before King Ahasuerus, and that the king will give her royal dignity to another wife who is better than she. ²⁰And when the king's decree which he shall make shall be published throughout all his kingdom—for it is great—all the wives will give to their husbands honor, both to great and small. ²¹And the proposal pleased the king and the princes; and the king did according to the word of Memucan. ²²So the king sent letters to all the provinces, into every province according to its system of writing and to every people according to their language, that every man should be master in his own house, and should speak according to the language of his people.ᶠ

ᵈ 1⁶ Several of these words do not occur elsewhere in the O.T. and their meaning is not certain.

ᵉ 1¹³ The astrologers. Cf. Dan. 2²⁷, 5¹⁵.

ᶠ 1²² The last clause is obscure. The Targs. interpret it to mean in the case of mixed marriages that the language of the husband shall be employed in the household. The Gk. omits it. The Lat. translates, *and this shall be made known among all peoples*—or slightly amending the Hebrew, *and should speak all that seems proper to him.*

§ 207. Choice of Esther as Queen and Mordecai's Service to King Ahasuerus, Esth. 2

Esth. 2 [1]After these things, when the wrath of King Ahasuerus was paci- fied, he remembered Vashti and what she had done and what was decreed against her. [2]Then the king's servants who ministered to him said, Let fair young virgins be sought for the king, [3]and let the king appoint officers in all the provinces of his kingdom, that they may gather together all the fair young virgins to Shushan the palace, to the women's quarters, under the custody of Hegai, the king's eunuch, who has charge of the women; and let the things for their beautifying[g] be given them. [4]And let the maiden who pleases the king be queen instead of Vashti. And the proposal pleased the king, and he did so.

Assembly of fair maidens of the realm

[5]There was a certain Jew in Shushan the palace whose name was Mor- decai the son of Jair, the son of Shimei, the son of Kish, a Benjamite,[h] [6]who had been carried away from Jerusalem with the captives who had been deported with Jeconiah king of Judah, whom Nebuchadnezzar[i] the king of Babylon had carried away. [7]And he brought up Hadassah, that is, Esther, his uncle's daughter, for she had neither father nor mother; and the maiden was fair and beautiful; and when her father and mother died, Mordecai took her as his own daughter.

Mordecai and his cousin Esther

[8]So when the king's command and his decree were made known, and when many maidens were gathered together to Shushan the palace under the custody of Hegai, Esther was also taken into the king's palace under the custody of Hegai, keeper of the women. [9]And the maiden pleased him and she received kindness at his hands, and he quickly gave her things for beau- tifying herself, with her allowance of food, and the seven maidens who were chosen to be given her from the king's palace. And he removed her and her maidens to the best place in the women's quarters. [10]Esther had not made known her people nor her kindred; for Mordecai had charged her that she should not make it known. [11]And Mordecai walked every day before the court of the women's quarters, to know how Esther did and what would become of her.

Her favorable reception in the royal harem

[12]Now when the turn of each maiden came to go in to King Ahasuerus, after it had been done to her according to the regulation for the women twelve months—for so long the days of their beautifying lasted, six months with oil of myrrh, and six months with sweet odors and with the things for the beautifying of the women—[13]then[j] the maiden came to the king; whatever she desired was given her to go with her from the house of the women to the king's palace. [14]In the evening she went and on the following day she re- turned into the second women's apartments[k] to the custody of Shaashgaz, the king's eunuch, who kept the concubines. She came in no more to the king, unless the king delighted in her and she was summoned by name.

The custom in the royal harem

---

[g] 2[3] Lit., *their rubbing off, i.e.,* with oils and cosmetics to enhance their beauty. Cf. [13].
[h] 2[5] A relative therefore of King Saul, cf. Introd., p. 39.
[i] 2[6] This late Jewish spelling of this word is found here as in Ezra and Dan.
[j] 2[13] So Gk., or, *in this way.*
[k] 2[14] Heb., *house.*

Selection of Esther as queen

¹⁵Now when the turn of Esther the daughter of Abihail, the uncle of Mordecai, who had taken her for his daughter, came to go to the king, she required nothing but what Hegai the king's eunuch, the keeper of the women, directed. And Esther obtained favor in the sight of all who saw her. ¹⁶So Esther was taken unto King Ahasuerus into his royal palace in the tenth month, that is, the month Tebeth in the seventh year of his reign. ¹⁷And the king loved Esther more than all the women, and she received favor and kindness from him more than all the virgins; so that he set the royal crown upon her head, and made her queen instead of Vashti. ¹⁸Then the king made a great feast for all his princes and his servants, even a feast in honor of Esther; and he remitted the taxes¹ of the provinces and gave gifts, according to the liberality of the king.

Mordecai's service in saving the life of the king

¹⁹And when the virgins were gathered together the second time, Mordecai was sitting in the king's gate. ²⁰Esther had not yet made known her kindred nor her people, as Mordecai had charged her, for Esther obeyed the command of Mordecai, just as when she was being brought up with him. ²¹In those days, while Mordecai was sitting in the king's gate, two of the king's eunuchs, Bigthan and Teresh, of those who guarded the threshold became enraged and sought to lay hands on King Ahasuerus. ²²And the plan became known to Mordecai, who showed it to Esther the queen; and Esther told the king in Mordecai's name. ²³And when the matter was investigated and it was found to be so, they were both hanged on a tree; and it was recorded in the book of the chronicles for the king.

§ 208. Haman's Purpose and the King's Permission to Put to Death all the Jews in the Empire, Esth. 3

Mordecai's refusal to pay homage to Haman, the royal favorite

Esth. 3 ¹After these things King Ahasuerus promoted Haman the son of Hammedatha the Agagite, and advanced him and gave him a place above all the princes who were with him. ²And all the king's servants who were in the king's gateᵐ bowed down and prostrated themselves before Haman; for the king had so commanded concerning him. But Mordecai did not bow down nor prostrate himself. ³Then the king's servants, who were in the king's gate, said to Mordecai, Why do you transgress the king's command? ⁴Now when they thus spoke daily to him and he paid no heed to them, they told Haman, to see whether Mordecai's acts would stand, for he had told them that he was a Jew. ⁵And when Haman saw that Mordecai did not bow down nor prostrate himself before him, Haman was full of wrath. ⁶But he thought it beneath his dignity to lay hands on Mordecai alone; for they had made known to him Mordecai's race. Therefore Haman sought to destroy all the Jews who were throughout the whole kingdom of Ahasuerus, even the race of Mordecai.

---

¹ 2¹⁸ Or, *release from military service.* So Gk. and Targ. Lat., *holiday.*
ᵐ 3² Cf. the title of the Sultan of Turkey, *Sublime Porte,* or the older Egyptian title, *Pharaoh.*

[7]In the first month, which is the month Nisan,[n] in the twelfth year of King Ahasuerus, they cast Pur,[o] that is, the lot before Haman from day to day and from month to month, to the twelfth month, which is the month Adar. [8]And Haman said to King Ahasuerus, There is a certain people scattered abroad and dispersed among the peoples in all the provinces of your kingdom; and their laws are different from those of every people; neither do they keep the king's laws; therefore there is no advantage to the king in leaving them alone. [9]If it please the king, let an order be given that they be destroyed; and I will pay ten thousand talents of silver into the hands of those who have the charge of the finances, that they may bring it into the king's treasuries. [10]And the king took his ring from his hand and gave it to Haman the son of Hammedatha the Agagite, the Jews' enemy. [11]And the king said to Haman, The silver is given to you, the people also, to do with them as you please. *(The king's consent to have Haman slay all the Jews)*

[12]Then the king's scribes were called in on the thirteenth day of the first month, and it was recorded just as Haman commanded for the kings' satraps and the local governors who were over every province, and the princes of every people, to every province according to its system of writing, and to every people according to their language. In the name of King Ahasuerus was it written, and with the king's ring was it sealed. [13]And letters were sent by runners into all the king's provinces, to destroy, to slay, and to cause to perish all Jews, both young and old, little children, and women in one day, even upon the thirteenth day of the twelfth month, which is the month Adar, and to take the spoil of them as plunder. [14]A copy of the writing, that the decree should be given out in every province, was published to all the peoples, that they should be ready for that day. [15]The runners went forth impelled by the king's command, and the decree was given out in the royal palace at Shushan. And the king and Haman sat down to drink; but the city of Shushan was perplexed. *(Promulgation of the royal decree)*

§ 209. Esther's Successful Efforts to Avert the Calamity and the Ignominious Death of Haman, Esth. 4–7

Esth. 4 [1]Now when Mordecai knew all that was done, Mordecai tore his clothes and put on sackcloth and strewed ashes[p] on his head, and went out into the midst of the city and cried with a loud and bitter cry of lamentation. [2]And he came even before the king's gate; for none might enter the king's gate clothed with sackcloth. [3]And in every province wherever the king's command and his decree came, there was great mourning among the Jews, and fasting, weeping, and wailing; and many lay in sackcloth and ashes.[q] *(Lamentation of Mordecai and the Jews)*

---

n 3⁷ The month Nisan was the month in which the Hebrews came forth from Egypt. For the different months cf. Appendix XIII.
o 3⁷ The casting of the lot was to determine the fortunate day in which to destroy the Jews. The lot was thus used by the Babylonians in determining the date of the great New Year's feast. Cf. Introd., p. 40.
p 4¹ Heb., simply, *with ashes*.
q 4³ Heb., *sackcloth and ashes were spread out under many*

Communi-
cation
of the
sad
news to
Esther ⁴And Esther's maidens and her eunuchs came and told her about it; and the queen was exceedingly pained. And she sent garments to clothe Mordecai that he might take his sackcloth from off him; but he received them not. ⁵Then Esther called for Hathach, one of the king's eunuchs, whom he had appointed to attend upon her, and charged him to go to Mordecai, to know what this was and why it was. ⁶So Hathach went out to Mordecai to the broad place of the city which was before the king's gate. ⁷And Mordecai told him all that had happened to him and the exact sum of the money that Haman had promised to pay to the king's treasuries for the Jews to destroy them. ⁸Also he gave him a copy of the writing of the decree that was given out in Shushan to destroy them, that he might show it to Esther and inform her regarding it and charge her to go in to the king to petition him and to make request before him for her people.

Es-
ther's
reply to
Morde-
cai's
mes-
sage ⁹And Hathach came and told Esther the words of Mordecai. ¹⁰Then Esther spoke to Hathach, and gave him a message to Mordecai, saying, ¹¹All the king's servants and the people of the king's provinces know that whoever, whether man or woman, comes to the king into the inner court without being commanded, there is one law for him, that he be put to death, except those to whom the king shall hold out the golden sceptre, that he may live; but I have not been called to come to the king for thirty days. ¹²And they told Mordecai Esther's words.

Es-
ther's
deci-
sion to
appeal
to the
king ¹³Then Mordecai bade them answer to Esther, Think not that you alone of all the Jews will escape because you belong to the king's household. ¹⁴Rather, if you remain silent at this time, then relief and deliverance will arise for the Jews from another quarter, but you and your father's house will perish; and who knows whether you have not come to the kingdom for such a time as this? ¹⁵Then Esther bade them answer Mordecai, ¹⁶Go, gather together all the Jews that are present in Shushan and fast for me, and neither eat nor drink three days, night or day. I also and my maidens will likewise fast and so will I go in to the king, which is contrary to the law; and if I perish, I perish. ¹⁷So Mordecai went away and did just as Esther had commanded him.

5 ¹Now it came to pass on the third day that Esther put on her royal garments and stood in the inner court of the king's palace directly opposite the king's palace. And the king was sitting upon his royal throne in the royal palace opposite the entrance of the palace. ²And when the king saw Esther the queen standing in the court, she obtained favor in his sight, and the king held out to Esther the golden sceptre that was in his hand. So Esther drew near and touched the top of the sceptre. ³Then the king said to her, What do you wish, Queen Esther, and what is your request? It shall be given you even to the half of the kingdom. ⁴And Esther said, If it seem good to the king, let the king and Haman come this day to the banquet that I have prepared for him.

Her
ban-
quet
for the
king
and
Haman ⁵Then the king said, Bring Haman quickly, that Esther's wish may be fulfilled. So the king and Haman came to the banquet that Esther had prepared. ⁶And the king said to Esther at the banquet of wine, What is your petition? It shall be granted you; and what is your request? Even

to the half of the kingdom shall it be performed. ⁷Then Esther answered and said, My petition and my request is: ⁸'If I have found favor in the sight of the king, and if it please the king to grant my petition and to perform my request, let the king and Haman come to the banquet that I shall prepare for them, and I will do to-morrow as the king has said.'

⁹Then Haman went forth that day joyful and glad of heart. But when Haman saw Mordecai in the king's gate, and he neither stood up nor moved for him, he was filled with wrath against Mordecai. ¹⁰Nevertheless Haman restrained himself and went home, and sent and brought his friends and Zeresh his wife. ¹¹And Haman recounted to them the glory of his riches and the multitude of his children and all the ways in which the king had promoted him and how he had advanced him above the princes and servants of the king. ¹²Haman also said, Yea, Esther the queen let no man come in with the king to the banquet which she had prepared but me, and to-morrow also I am invited by her together with the king. ¹³Yet all this does not satisfy me as long as I see Mordecai the Jew sitting at the king's gate. *Haman's pride and hatred of Mordecai*

¹⁴Then Zeresh his wife and all his friends said to him, Let a gallowsʳ fifty cubits high be erected and in the morning speak to the king that Mordecai may be hanged. Then go in merrily with the king to the banquet. And the thing pleased Haman; and he caused the gallows to be erected. *His wife's advice*

6 ¹On that night sleep fled from the king, and he gave orders to bring the book of records of the chronicles, and they were read before the king. ²And it was found recorded that Mordecai had told of Bigthana and Teresh, two of the king's eunuchs, of those who guarded the threshold, who had sought to lay hands on King Ahasuerus. ³And the king said, What honor and dignity have been bestowed on Mordecai for this? Then the king's servants who ministered to him said, There has been nothing done for him. ⁴And the king said, Who is in the court? Now Haman was come into the outer court of the king's house to speak to the king to hang Mordecai on the gallows that he had prepared for him. ⁵And the king's servants said to him, Behold, Haman is standing in the court. And the king said, Let him come in. ⁶So Haman came in. And the king said to him, What shall be done to the man whom the king delights to honor? Now Haman said to himself, To whom would the king delight to do honor more than to myself? ⁷So Haman said to the king, For the man whom the king delights to honor ⁸let royal garments be brought, which the king is accustomed to wear, and the horse on which the king rides, and on the head of which a crown royal is set. ⁹And let the garments and the horse be delivered to one of the king's most noble princes, and let them therewith clothe the man whom the king delights to honor and cause him to ride on horseback through the street of the city, and proclaim before him, 'Thus shall it be done to the man whom the king delights to honor.' *The plan to reward Mordecai for his service to the king*

¹⁰Then the king said to Haman, Make haste, and take the garments and the horse, as you have said, and do even so to Mordecai the Jew, who sits in the king's gate. Let nothing fail of all that you have said. ¹¹Then Haman took the garments and the horse and clothed Mordecai, and caused him to *Mordecai's honor and Haman's humiliation*

ʳ 5¹⁴ Heb., *wood.*

ride through the street of the city, and proclaimed before him, Thus shall
it be done to the man whom the king delights to honor. ¹²And Mordecai
came again to the king's gate. But Haman hasted to his house, mourning
and with his head covered. ¹³And Haman recounted to Zeresh his wife and
all his friends all that had befallen him. Then his wise men and Zeresh his
wife said to him, If Mordecai before whom you have begun to fall, be of the
Jewish race, you will accomplish nothing against him but will surely fall
before him. ¹⁴While they were still talking with him, the king's eunuchs
came and quickly brought Haman to the banquet that Esther had prepared.

Esther's petition for the life of her people

7 ¹So the king and Haman came to drink with Esther the queen. ²And
the king said again to Esther on the second day of the banquet of wine, What
is your petition, Queen Esther? and it shall be granted to you. And what is
your request? Even to half of the kingdom shall it be performed. ³Then
Esther the queen answered and said, If I have found favor in your sight,
O king, and if it please the king, let my life be given me at my petition and
my people at my request; ⁴for we are sold, I and my people, to be destroyed,
to be slain, and to perish. But if we had been sold as male and female
slaves, I would have remained silent, since for such an affliction it would
not have been worth the while to trouble the king.ˢ

Haman's fate

⁵Then the King Ahasuerus spoke to Esther the queen, saying, Who is he
and where is he who dares presume in his heart to do so? ⁶And Esther said,
An adversary and an enemy, this wicked Haman. Then Haman shrank
before the king and the queen. ⁷And the king arose in his wrath from the
banquet of wine and went into the palace garden. And Haman stood up
to beg for his life of Esther the queen; for he saw that evil was determined
against him by the king. ⁸When the king returned from the palace garden
to the place of the banquet of wine, Haman had fallen upon the couch on
which Esther was. Then said the king, Will he even force the queen before
me in the house? As soon as the word went from the king's mouth, Haman's
face was covered with shame.ᵗ ⁹Then Harbonah, one of the eunuchs who
were before the king said, There are the gallows fifty cubits high, which
Haman has made for Mordecai, who cared for the king's welfare, standing
in the house of Haman. And the king said, Hang him on them. ¹⁰So
they hanged Haman on the gallows that he had prepared for Mordecai.
Then was the king's wrath pacified.

§ 210. The Royal Decrees for the Protection of the Jews, Esth. 8

Transfer of Haman's honors to Mordecai

Esth. 8 ¹At that time the King Ahasuerus gave the house of Haman the
Jews' enemy to Esther the queen. And Mordecai came before the king,
for Esther had told what he was to her. ²And the king took off his ring,
which he had taken from Haman, and gave it to Mordecai. And Esther
set Mordecai over the house of Haman.

ˢ 7⁴ The text is corrupt. A slight correction gives the above. Another possible reconstruction is, *for deliverance is not worth troubling the king, i.e.,* the importance of deliverance
does not justify troubling the king with this request.
ᵗ 7⁸ So Gk. Present Heb., *they covered the face of Haman,* as a sign that he was condemned
to death.

³And Esther spoke yet again before the king, and fell down at his feet, and besought him with tears to avert the evil done by Haman the Agagite, and to frustrate his designs which he had against the Jews. ⁴Then the king held out to Esther the golden sceptre. So Esther arose, and stood before the king. ⁵And she said, If it please the king, and if I have found favor in his sight, and the thing seem right before the king, and I please him, let written orders be given to reverse the letters devised by Haman the son of Hammedatha the Agagite, which he wrote to destroy the Jews who are in all the king's provinces. ⁶For how can I endure to see the evil that will come to my people? Or how can I endure to see the destruction of my kindred?

Esther's entreaty that the decree be reversed

⁷Then the King Ahasuerus said to Esther the queen and to Mordecai the Jew, Behold, I have given Esther the house of Haman, and him they have hanged upon the gallows, because he laid his hands upon the Jews. ⁸Write also concerning the Jews as it pleases you, in the king's name and seal it with the king's ring; for the writing which is written in the king's name and sealed with the king's ring, may no man reverse.

The king's concession

⁹Then were the king's scribes called at that time on the twenty-third day of the third month, which is the month Sivan; and it was written according to all that Mordecai commanded the Jews, and the satraps and the governors and princes of the provinces which are from India to Ethiopia, a hundred and twenty-seven provinces, to every province according to its system of writing, and to every people according to their language, and to the Jews according to their system of writing and according to their language. ¹⁰And he wrote in the name of King Ahasuerus, and sealed it with the king's ring and sent letters by swift messengers on horseback, riding on noble, swift steeds, bred of the royal studs,ᵘ ¹¹wherein the king granted the Jews who were in every city to gather themselves together and to fight for their lives, to destroy, to slay, and to cause to perish all the armed forces of the people and province that would assault them, their little ones and women, and to take the spoil of them as plunder, ¹²upon one day in all the provinces of King Ahasuerus, namely on the thirteenth day of the twelfth month, which is the month Adar. ¹³A copy of the writing, that the decree should be given out in every province, was published to all the peoples, and that the Jews should be ready on that day to avenge themselves upon their enemies. ¹⁴So the swift messengers that rode on the noble, swift steeds went out, being hastened and pressed on by the king's command; and the decree was given out in the royal palace at Shushan.

The royal command that the Jews be empowered to protect themselves

¹⁵And Mordecai went forth from the presence of the king in royal garments of blue and white linen, and with a great crown of gold, and with a robe of fine linen and purple. And the city of Shushan shouted and was glad. ¹⁶The Jews had light and gladness and joy and honor. ¹⁷And in every province and in every city, wherever the king's command and his decree came, the Jews had gladness and joy, a feast and a holiday. And many from among the peoples of the land became Jews; for the fear of the Jews had fallen upon them.

Honors and joy for the Jews

ᵘ 8¹⁰ Here two Persian words are used.

§ 211. Destruction of the Enemies of the Jews, Esth. 9¹⁻¹⁶

Suc-
cessful
resist-
ance of
the
Jews on
the day
ap-
point-
ed for
the
slaugh-
ter

Esth. 9 ¹Now in the twelfth month, which is the month Adar, on the thirteenth day of the same, when the king's command and his decree was about to be put into execution, on the day that the enemies of the Jews hoped to gain the mastery over them, then the tables were turned so that the Jews themselves had the mastery over those who hated them. ²The Jews gathered together in the cities throughout all the provinces of the King Ahasuerus, to lay hand on such as sought their hurt; and none could withstand them, for the fear of them had fallen upon all the peoples. ³And all the princes of the provinces and the satraps and the governors and they who attended to the king's business, helped the Jews, because the fear of Mordecai had fallen upon them. ⁴For Mordecai was great in the king's palace, and his fame went forth throughout all the provinces; for the man Mordecai became constantly more influential. ⁵And the Jews smote all their enemies with the stroke of the sword and with slaughter and destruction, and did what they would to those who hated them. ⁶And in the royal palace at Shushan the Jews slew and destroyed five hundred men. ⁷And they slew Parshandatha, Dalphon, Aspatha, ⁸Poratha, Adalia, Aridatha, ⁹Parmashta, Arisia, Aridai, and Vaizatha, ¹⁰the ten sons of Haman the son of Hammedatha, the Jews' enemy; but they did not put forth the hand to plunder.

Fur-
ther
permis-
sion to
take
ven-
geance
upon
their
enemies

¹¹On that day the number of those that were slain in Shushan the palace was brought before the king. ¹²And the king said to Esther the queen, The Jews have slain and destroyed five hundred men in the royal palace at Shushan, and the ten sons of Haman; what then have they done in the rest of the king's provinces! Now what is your petition, and it shall be granted to you? Or what is your request, and it shall be performed? ¹³Then Esther said, If it please the king, let it be granted to the Jews who are in Shushan to do to-morrow also according to this day's decree, and let Haman's ten sons be hanged upon the gallows. ¹⁴And the king commanded it so to be done. And a decree was given out in Shushan; and they hanged Haman's ten sons. ¹⁵And the Jews who were in Shushan also gathered themselves together on the fourteenth day of the month Adar, and slew three hundred men in Shushan; but they did not put forth their hand to plunder. ¹⁶And the other Jews who were in the king's provinces gathered themselves together and fought for their lives and had relief from their enemies, and slew of those who hated them seventy-five thousand; but they did not put forth their hand to plunder.

§ 212. Institution of the Feast of Purim, Esth. 9¹⁷⁻³²

Obser-
vation
of the
feast of
Purim

Esth. 9 ¹⁷On the thirteenth day of the month Adar and the fourteenth day^v of the same they rested and made a day of feasting and gladness. ¹⁸But the Jews who were in Shushan assembled together on the thirteenth and on the fourteenth, and on the fifteenth day of the same they rested and made

---

v 9¹⁷ Slightly revising the text which is evidently corrupt.

it a day of feasting and gladness. [19]Therefore the Jews of the villages who dwell in the large[w] cities are wont to make the fourteenth day of the month Adar a day of gladness and feasting and a holiday, and a day in which they send portions of food to each other.

[20]And Mordecai wrote these things, and sent letters to all the Jews who were in all the provinces of the King Ahasuerus, both near and far, [21]to enjoin them that they should keep the fourteenth day of the month Adar and the fifteenth day of the same yearly, [22]as the days wherein the Jews had rest from their enemies, and the month which was turned to them from sorrow to gladness and from mourning into a feast day, that they should make them days of feasting and gladness and of sending portions one to another and of gifts to the poor. *(Mordecai's command that the custom be made universal)*

[23]And the Jews adopted as a custom what they had begun and what Mordecai had written to them. [24]For Haman the son of Hammedatha, the Agagite, the enemy of all the Jews, had plotted against the Jews to destroy them, and had cast Pur, that is the lot, to consume them and to destroy them. [25]But when the matter came before the king, he gave orders by letters that his wicked design, which he had planned against the Jews, should come upon his own head, and that he and his sons should be hanged on the gallows. [26]Hence they call these days Purim, after the word Pur. Therefore because of all the words of this letter, as well as because of that which they had seen concerning this matter, and that which had come to them, [27]the Jews ordained and took upon themselves and upon their descendants and upon all those who joined themselves to them, so that it should be unalterable, that they should observe these two days as feasts according to the written command and according to the time appointed every year, [28]and that these days should be remembered and kept throughout every generation, every family, every province, and every city. And these days of Purim should not pass away from among the Jews nor the remembrance of them disappear with their descendants. *(Establishment and occasion of the feast)*

[29]Then Esther the queen, the daughter of Abihail, and Mordecai the Jew, wrote with all authority to confirm this second letter of Purim. [30]And the latter sent letters to all the Jews, to the hundred and twenty-seven provinces of the kingdom of Ahasuerus, with words of peace and truth, [31]to confirm these days of Purim in their appointed times, according as Mordecai the Jew and Esther the queen had enjoined them and as they had ordained for themselves and their descendants, in the matter of the fastings and their cry of lamentation. [32]And the commands of Esther confirmed these matters of Purim; and it was written in the book. *(Confirmation of the custom)*

---

w 9[19] So Gk., which has the antithesis which the context demands. Heb., *who dwell in villages*, a mere repetition.

§ 213. The Greatness of Mordecai, Esth. 10

Morde-
cai's
services
to his
race

Esth. 10 ¹And the King Ahasuerus laid a tribute on the land and the isles of the sea. ²And all the acts of his power and of his might, and the full account of the greatness of Mordecai to which the king advanced him, are they not recorded in the book of the chronicles of the kings of Media and Persia? ³For Mordecai the Jew was next in rank to King Ahasuerus, and great among the Jews, and beloved by all his fellow-countrymen; and he sought the good of his people and consulted the welfare of his entire race.

APPENDIX

APPENDIX

I

SELECTED BIBLIOGRAPHY AND DETAILED REFERENCES

GENERAL INTRODUCTIONS TO THE HISTORICAL BOOKS

André, *Les Apocryphes de l'Ancient Testament*, 1903.
Bennett and Adeney, *Biblical Introduction*, 1899.
Bleek, *Einleitung in das A.T.*,[4] 1878.
Budde, *Bücher Richter und Samuel*, 1890.
Cornill, *Einleitung in das A.T.*,[3] 1896.
Driver, *Introduction to the Literature of the O.T.*,[8] 1901.
Fairweather, *From the Exile to the Advent*, 1895.
Encyclopædia Biblica. Articles, *Samuel, Kings*, etc.
Geissler, *Die literarischen Beziehungen der Esramemoiren*, 1901.
Hastings's *Dictionary of the Bible.* Articles.
Kautzsch, *Literature of the O.T.*, 1899.
König, *Einleitung in das A.T.*, 1893.
Kosters, *Die Wiederherstellung Israels*, 1895.
McFadyen, *Messages of the Prophetic and Priestly Historians*, 1902.
Marquart, *Fundamente israelitischer und jüdischer Geschichte*, 1896.
Niese, *Kritik der beiden Makkabäerbücher*, 1900.
Sacred Books of the O.T. (edited by Haupt).
Smith, W. R., *The O.T. in the Jewish Church*,[2] 1892.
Torrey, *Composition and Historical Value of Ezra-Nehemiah*, 1896.
Wellhausen, *Composition des Hexateuchs und der historischen Bücher des A.T.*,[3] 1899.
    "   *Prolegomena to the History of Israel*, 1895.
Wildeboer, *The Origin of the Canon of the O.T.*, 1891.

HISTORIES OF ISRAEL

Bevan, *Jerusalem under the High-Priests*, 1905.
Budde, *Religion of Israel to the Exile*, 1899.
Cheyne, *Jewish Religious Life after the Exile*, 1898.
Conder, *Judas Maccabeus*, 1894.
Cornill, *History of the People of Israel*, 1898.

Dieulafoy, *Le roi David*, 1897.
Encyclopædia Biblica and Jewish Encylopædia. Article, *Israel*.
Ewald, *History of Israel*, 1869.
Grätz, *Geschichte der Juden*, 1876.
Guthe, *Geschichte des Volkes Israel*, 1899.
Harper, *Commentary on Amos and Hosea*, 1905.
van Hoonacker, *Études sur la Restauration Juive après l'exil de Babylone*,
       1896.
    "   *Néhémie en l'an 20 d'Artaxerxes*, 1892.
    "   *Zorobabel et le second Temple*, 1892.
Hunter, *After the Exile*, I, II, 1890.
Kent, *History of the Hebrew People*, I, *The United Kingdom*,[12] 1905.
  " *History of the Hebrew People*, II, *The Divided Kingdom*,[12] 1905.
  " *History of the Jewish People*,[7] 1905.
Kittel, *History of the Hebrews*, I, II, 1895–96.
Klostermann, *Geschichte des Volkes Israel*, 1896.
Kuenen, *Gesammelte Abhandlungen*, 1894.
Mathews, *History of the New Testament Times in Palestine*, 1899.
Meyer, *Entstehung des Judenthums*, 1896.
Oettli, *Geschichte Israels bis auf Alexander den Grossen*, 1904.
Ottley, *Short History of the Hebrews*, 1896.
Piepenbring, *Histoire du Peuple Israel*, 1898.
Renan, *History of the People of Israel*, 1896.
Riggs, *History of the Jewish People in the Maccabean and Roman Periods*,[4]
       1905.
Sayce, *Early History of the Hebrews*, 1897.
Sellin, *Serubbabel*, 1898; *Studien zur Entstehungsgeschichte der jüdischen
       Gemeinde*, I, II, 1901.
Smend, *Lehrbuch der alttestamentlichen Religionsgeschichte*, 1893.
Smith, H. P., *Old Testament History*, 1903.
Smith, W. R., *Prophets of Israel*,[2] 1895.
Stade, *Geschichte des Volkes Israel*, I, II, 1888.
Streane, *The Age of the Maccabees*, 1898.
Wade, *Old Testament History*, 1903.
Wellhausen, *Israelitische und jüdische Geschichte*,[5] 1904.
    "   *Sketch of the History of Israel and Judah*, 1891.
Willrich, *Juden und Griechen vor der Makkabäischen Erhebung*, 1895.
Winckler, *Geschichte Israels in Einzeldarstellung*, 1900.
    "   *Alttestamentliche Untersuchungen*, 1892.

CONTEMPORARY SEMITIC HISTORY

Archinard, *Israel et ses viosins asiatiques*, 1890.
Ball, *Light from the East*, 1899.
Buhl, *Geschichte der Edomiter*, 1893.
Droysen, *History of Hellenism*, 1895.
Duncker, *Geschichte des Alterthums*,[4] 1880.

CONTEMPORARY SEMITIC HISTORY

Goodspeed, *History of the Babylonians and Assyrians*, 1902.
Hogarth, *Authority and Archæology*, 1899.
Hommel, *Geschichte Babyloniens und Assyriens*, 1885.
Jeremias, *Das A.T. im Lichte des alten Orients*, 1904.
Judeich, *Kleinasiatische Studien*, 1892.
Justi, *Geschichte des alten Persiens*, 1876.
von Landau, *Die Phönizien* in *Das Orient* II, 4, 1901.
Mahaffy, *The Empire of the Ptolemies*, 1895.
"   *History of Egypt Under the Ptolemaic Dynasty*, 1899.
Maspero, *The Struggle of the Nations*, 1897.
"   *The Passing of the Nations*, 1900.
McCurdy, *History, Prophecy, and the Monuments*, I–III, 1884–1901.
Meyer, *Geschichte des alten Aegyptens*, 1887.
Müller, W. M., *Asien und Europa nach altägyptischen Denkmälern*, 1893.
Niese, *Geschichte der griechischen und makedonischen Staaten*, 1893.
Pietschmann, *Geschichte der Phönizier*, 1889.
Rogers, *History of Babylonia and Assyria*, II, 1900.
Schrader, *Cuneiform Inscriptions and the O.T.*, 1885–88.
"   *Die Keilinschriften und das A.T.*,[3] 1901.
"   *Keilinschriftliche Bibliothek*, I–VI, 1891.
Tiele, *Babylonisch-assyrische Geschichte*, 1886–88.
Weber, *Sanherib König von Assyrien*, 705–681, 1905.
Winckler, *Untersuchungen zur altorientalischen Geschichte*, 1889.
"   *Die Völker Vorderasiens*, 1899.

GEOGRAPHY, CHRONOLOGY, AND ARCHÆOLOGY

Benzinger, *Hebräische Archäologie*, 1894.
Buhl, *Geographie des alten Palästina*, 1896.
Cooke, *Palestine in Geography and History*, I, II, 1901.
Döller, *Geographische und ethnographische Studien zum III. und IV. Buche
    der Könige*, 1904.
Hilprecht, *Explorations in Bible Lands During the 19th Century*, 1903.
"   *Recent Research in Bible Lands*, 1896.
Kamphausen, *Die Chronologie der hebräischen Könige*, 1883.
Lederer, *Die biblische Zeitrechnung*, 1888.
Mahler, *Biblische Chronologie und Zeitrechnung der Hebräer*, 1887.
Neteler, *Zusammenhang der A.T. Zeitrechnung mit der Profangeschichte*,
    1879.
Niebuhr, *Die Chronologie der Geschichte Israels, Aegyptiens, Babyloniens
    und Assyriens*, 1896.
Nowack, *Lehrbuch der hebräischen Archäologie*, I, II, 1894.
Perrot and Chipiez, *History of Art in Antiquity*, 1884–92.
Smith, *Historical Geography of the Holy Land*,[6] 1899.
Stewart, *The Land of Israel*,[2] 1900.
Taaks, *Alttestamentliche Chronologie*, 1904.

SELECTED BIBLIOGRAPHY

COMMENTARIES AND TEXTUAL NOTES

Samuel

Budde, *Die Bücher Samuel*, 1902.

" *Sacred Books of the Old Testament, The Books of Samuel*, 1894.

Driver, *Notes on the Hebrew Text of the Books of Samuel*, 1890.

Kirkpatrick, *Books of Samuel* in the *Cambridge Bible*.

Klostermann, *Die Bücher Samuelis und der Könige*, 1887.

Löhr, *Samuel* in *Kurzgefasstes exegetisches Handbuch*, 1898.

Nestle, *Marginalien und Materialien*, 1893.

Nowack, *Richter, Ruth und Bücher Samuelis*, 1902.

Smith, *Critical and Exegetical Commentary on the Books of Samuel*, 1899.

Wellhausen, *Text der Bücher Samuelis*, 1871.

Kings

Benzinger, *Die Bücher der Könige*, 1899.

Burney, *Notes on the Hebrew Text of the Books of Kings*, 1903.

Holzhey, *Das Buch der Könige*, 1899.

Kittel, *Die Bücher der Könige*, 1900.

Chronicles

Barnes, *An Apparatus Criticus to Chronicles in the Peshitta Version*, 1897.

Benzinger, *Die Bücher der Chronik*, 1901.

Bertheau, *Die Bücher der Chronik*,[2] 1873.

Kittel, *Die Bücher der Chronik*, 1902.

" *Sacred Books of the Old Testament, Chronicles*, 1895.

Ezra, Nehemiah, and Esther

Adeney, *Ezra, Nehemiah, and Esther*, 1893.

Bertholet, *Esra und Nehemia*, 1902.

Guthe, *Sacred Books of the Old Testament, Books of Ezra and Nehemiah*, 1896.

Ryle, *Ezra and Nehemiah* in the *Cambridge Bible*, 1893.

Siegfried, *Esra, Nehemia und Esther*, 1901.

I and II Maccabees

Bissell, *Apocrypha* in *Critical, Doctrinal, and Homiletical Commentary*, 1880.

Grimm, *Die Bücher der Maccabäer*, 1858.

Kautzsch, *Apokryphen und Pseudepigraphen des A.T.*, 1900.

DETAILED REFERENCES

The following detailed references have been prepared especially to meet the needs of college and Bible classes and private readers. They do not aim to give a complete bibliography, but rather to call attention to the more

SOURCES FOR THE HISTORY

important books and sections dealing with a given topic. Naturally, greater prominence is given to works written in English, but significant chapters or articles in French or German sources are also referred to and are distinguished by printing the names of the authors in italics, and at the end of each section. To economize space the standard works are represented simply by the names of their authors, followed by the initial letters of the chief words in the titles. Whenever there is any doubt regarding the meaning of the abbreviations, they can be readily identified by referring to the *Selected Bibliography* (pp. 485–88), where each book will be found classified alphabetically according to the name of its author. In the classification of the references the order of the main divisions of this volume has been followed so that they can be used, in connection with the text, as guides in further systematic, comprehensive study.

The History of Israel's Historical and Biographical Narratives

General Introduction: Encyc. Bib. II, 2075–79, 2082–89; Driver LOT 172–200, 516–54; McFadyen MPPH 3–5; Kittel, *Die Anfänge der heb. Geschichtsschreibung im A.T.*

Sources of Samuel-Kings: Hastings DB IV, 382–91; II, 856–70; Encyc. Bib. IV, 4270–80; II, 2664–71; Driver LOT 172–203; Kautzsch LOT 18–45; Smith S XI–XXIX; Cook in AJSL, 1900, pp. 145–77; McFadyen MPPH 139–43, 177–85; *Wellhausen* CHHB 238–302; *Budde* S IX–XXV, BRS 167–276; *Nowack* BS XIV–XXIX; *Benzinger BK* VIII–XV; *Kittel BK.*

Chronicler's Ecclesiastical History: Hastings DB I, 389–97; Encyc. Bib. I, 763–72; Driver LOT 516–40; Kittel, *Chronicles*, in SBOT; Barnes in AJSL Oct., 1896; Wellhausen PHI 171–227; McFadyen MPPH 270–85; Kautzsch LOT 121–28; *Benzinger BC; Kittel BC* III–XVI.

Sources of Ezra-Nehemiah: Hastings DB I, 821–24; Encyc. Bib. II, 1478–87; McFadyen MPPH 314–18; Driver LOT 540–55; Guthe EN in SBOT; Torrey CHVEN; *Bertholet EN* XI–XVI; *Kosters WI; Meyer EJ; Marquart FIJA* 28–66; *Geissler LBE; Siegfried ENE* 1–14.

Records of the Maccabean Age: Hastings III, 187–92; Encyc. Bib. III, 2857–79; *Niese KBM; Geiger, Urschrift Machabee; Willrich, Judaica; Destinon, Die Quellen des Josephus; Schlatter, Jason von Cyrene.*

Recovery of the Original Text: Hastings IV, 726–32; Encyc. Bib. IV, 5011–31; Buhl, *Canon and Text of the O.T.*, §§ 23–99; Driver HTBS IX–LXXXIV; Kenyon, *Our Bible and the Ancient MSS.*; Weir, *A Short History of the Hebrew Text of the O.T.*; Abbot, *Original Texts of the O. and N. T.*, 1–63; Field, *Origen's Hexapla; Bleek EAT,* §§ 275–98; *Nowack BS* V–XIV; *Bertholet ENE* XVI–XVII.

The United Monarchy

Work of Samuel and the Establishment of the Kingdom: Hastings DB IV, 412–15; IV, 381–82; Encyc. Bib. IV, 4302–15; Smith OTH 106–22; Kent HHP I, 113–22; Kittel HH II, 94–104; Smith PI 45, 47, 85, 389–91; *Stade GVI* I, 207–23.

Decline of Saul and the Rise of David: Hastings DB II, 511; I, 560–66; Encyc. Bib. I, 1019–25; II, 2231–32; Smith OTH 122–33; Kent HHP I, 123–35; Kittel HH II, 104–19; *Stade GVI* I, 223–57.

David's Reign over Judah and over all Israel: Hastings DB I, 566–73; Encyc. Bib. I, 1025–35; II, 2232–35; Smith OTH 133–55; Cornill HPI 71–85; Wellhausen PHI 261–72; Kent HHP I, 136–68; Kittel HH II, 120–52; *Stade GVI* I, 223–98; *Dieulafoy RD.*

Solomon's Policy and Reign: Hastings DB IV, 559–69; Encyc. Bib. II, 2235–37; IV, 4680–89; Kent HHP I, 169–88; Kittel HH II, 153–69; Cornill HPI 86–95; Bacon in *New World*, June, 1898, pp. 212 ff.; Smith OTH 156–63, 168–76; *Stade GVI* I, 299–311.

Temple of Solomon: Hastings DB IV, 695–703; Encyc. Bib. IV, 4923–40; Kent HHP I, 189–95; Smith OTH 163–67; Robins, *The Temple of Solomon; Guinard, Monographie du Temple de Solomon; Perrot-Chipiez, Le Temple de Jerusalem; Stade GVI* I, 311–43; *Nowack HA* II, 25–50; *Benzinger HA* 383–8.

History of Northern Israel

From Jeroboam to Omri: Hastings DB II, 516–17; Encyc. Bib. II, 2239–40; Smith OTH 177–82; Kent HHP II, 16–34; Kittel HH II, 207–36; *Stade GVI* I, 344–57.

Rule of the House of Omri: Hastings DB I, 51–53; III, 620–21; Encyc. Bib. I, 89–93; Smith OTH 183–88, 194–97; Kent HHP II, 37–43; Kittel HH II, 240–43; *Stade GVI* I, 519–24, 527–41.

Work of Elijah: Hastings DB I, 687–91; Encyc. Bib. II, 1270–74; Kent HHP II, 46–54; Smith OTH 188–93; Harper AH XXIV–XLI; Kittel HH II, 213–66, 275, 279; Cornill, *Prophets of Israel*, 29–36; Wellhausen HIJ 64–69; *Gunkel* in *Preuss. Jahrbuch*, 1898, pp. 18–51; *Stade GVI* I, 524–27; *Smend LAR* 152–59; *Clemen, Die Wunderberichte über Elia und Elisa.*

Popular Traditions about Elisha and his Real Work: Hastings DB I, 693–96; Encyc. Bib. II, 1275–78; Harper AH XLI–LVIII; *Smend LAR* 158–59; *Benzinger BK* 129–30.

Rule of the House of Jehu: Hastings DB II, 564–66; Encyc. Bib. II, 2241–43; Smith OTH 198–218; Kent HHP II, 61–97; Kittel HH II, 237–78; *Stade GVI* I, 541–85.

Fall of the Northern Kingdom: Smith OTH 219–37; Kent HHP II, 98–110; Kittel HH II, 284–98; *Stade GVI* I, 598–601.

History of Judah

From Rehoboam to Ahaz: Kent HHP II, 35–37, 43–45, 120–26; Kittel HH II, 243–46, 279–84; *Stade GVI* I, 345–49, 566–70.

Assyrian Period: From Ahaz to Josiah: Hastings DB I, 53–54; Encyc. Bib. II, 2243–46; Smith OTH 238–59; Kent HHP II, 127–64; Kittel HH II, 286–321; *Stade GVI* I, 585–641.

The Great Reformation of Josiah: Hastings DB I, 596–603; Smith OTH 260–74; Kent HHP II, 172–82; Kittel HH II, 321–25; *Stade GVI* I, 641–71; *Smend LAR* 641–71.

Babylonian Period: Encyc. Bib. II, 2246–48; Smith OTH 275–87; Kent HHP II, 183–89; Kittel HH II, 325–31; *Stade GVI* I, 671–81.

Work of Jeremiah: Hastings DB II, 569–73; Encyc. Bib. II, 2366–71; Smith OTH 287–94; Kent HHP II, 190–94; Cheyne, *Jeremiah: his Life and Times; Stade GVI* I, 681–94; *Smend LAR* 252–62.

Last Days of the Judean State: Hastings DB II, 513; Smith OTH 294–300; Kent HHP II, 194–204; Kittel HH II, 332–33; *Stade GVI* I, 694–703.

The Babylonian Exile: Smith OTH 301–43; Kent HJP 1–98; *Stade GVI* II, 3–94; *Piepenbring HPI* 438–510.

Rebuilding of the Temple: Hastings II, 514–15; Encyc. Bib. II, 2252–54; IV, 4941–43; Smith OTH 344–81; Kent HJP 120–52; *Stade GVI* II, 98–128; *Piepenbring HPI* 511–28; *Kosters WI* 29–42; *Sellin, Serubbabel.*

Work of Nehemiah: Hastings II, 515; Encyc. Bib. II, 2254–55; III, 3380–87; Smith OTH 382–89; Kent HJP 153–94; Cheyne JRL 36–54, 64–69; *Stade GVI* II, 162–89; *Kosters WI* 42–73.

Work of Ezra and the Institution of the Priestly Law: Encyc. Bib. II, 1473–77; Encyc. Bib. II, 2255–59; Smith OTH 389–412; Kent HJP 195–223; Cheyne JRL 54–64; *Stade GVI* II, 139–60; *Kosters WI* 51–54; *Piepenbring HPI* 536–44.

Causes of the Maccabean Struggle: Encyc. Bib. II, 2259–62; Smith OTH 413–49; Kent HJP 284–330; Riggs HJP 14–28; Streane AM 14–34; Mathews HNTT 1–22; Schürer JPTC II, 186–212; Cornill HPI 175–93; *Stade GVI* II, 311–22, 334–35.

Struggle for Religious Freedom: Encyc. Bib. II, 2263–64; III, 28–50–56; Smith OTH 449–60; Riggs HJP 29–44; Streane AM 35–45; Mathews HNTT 23–35; Cornill HPI 193–97; Schürer JPTC II, 213–24; *Stade GVI* II, 335–43.

Attainment of Political Independence under Jonathan: Encyc. Bib. II, 2264–65; Smith OTH 460–68; Riggs HJP 45–71; Streane AM 46–50; Mathews HNTT 36–46; Cornill HPI 193–205; Schürer JPTC II, 225–57; *Stade GVI* II, 343, 359–75.

Simon's Prosperous Reign: Smith OTH 468–78; Riggs HJP 87–96; Streane AM 50–53; Mathews HNTT 47–58; Cornill HPI 205–208; Schürer JPTC II, 258–71; *Stade GVI* II, 375–85.

The Story of Esther: Hastings DB I, 773–76; V, 91–109; Encyc. Bib. II, 1400–1407; Toy in *New World*, VI, 130–45; Riggs HJP 72–86; Schürer JPTC II, 225–30.

II

HEBREW CHRONOLOGY

Living, as they did, a quiet agricultural life with no very close relations to the great nations of antiquity, it is not strange that the Hebrews developed no chronological system until the Assyrian and Babylonian periods. Even as late as the days of Amos his sermons are simply dated *two years before the earthquake*. No attempt is made in the early sources quoted in Samuel-Kings to fix the absolute dates of events. The result is that all Hebrew chronology before the division of the empire at the death of Solomon is only conjectural.

Early Egyptian chronology is also still equally indeterminate; but fortunately the Babylonians and Assyrians, with their commercial and literary habits and their close connection with universal history, early developed an exact system. The Assyrians gave the name of some high official to each succeeding year. Copies of these eponym lists have been discovered which not only confirm each other, but also connect with the so-called Canon of Ptolemy, which gives the names of the Babylonian, Assyrian, and Persian kings from Nabonassar to Alexander the Great, with records of important eclipses, which make it possible to fix absolutely the given dates and to relate them to later chronological systems. These Assyrian eponym lists begin with the year 893 B.C. The dating of important events in the Assyrian historical inscriptions and chronicles completes the chronological equipment so that, when the Hebrew and Assyrian histories touch each other, a fixed date is at once established. These dates are: 854 B.C., the battle of Karkar at which Ahab fought against Shalmaneser II; 842, when Jehu paid tribute to Tiglath-Pileser III to establish himself on the throne of Israel; 738, when Menahem paid tribute to Assyria; 734, when Pekah was conquered and put to death by the order of Tiglath-Pileser and Hoshea was placed in his stead on the throne of Northern Israel, while Ahaz of Judah paid tribute to the Assyrian king; 722–721, when Samaria was conquered by Sargon; and 701, when Sennacherib first invaded Judah.

The determination of Old Testament chronology is also facilitated by the fact that, after the division, the histories of the two Hebrew kingdoms touched each other at several important points, as, for example, when Jehu, about 842 B.C., slew both Jehoram of Northern Israel and Ahaziah of Judah. Even with these fixed dates, the details of Hebrew chronology would be exceedingly uncertain had not the state annals or tradition preserved the approximate lengths of the reigns of the different kings. Some such data were evidently before the late prophetic editor of I and II Kgs., who has developed the elaborate chronological system which runs through these books. Minor errors have crept in, but they can in most cases be corrected with reasonable assurance. Thus the total number of years assigned to the kings of Israel between the death of Solomon and Jehu's revolution in 842 B.C. is ninety-eight, and to those of Judah during the same period but ninety-five.

The error is evidently in the fourteen years assigned to Ahab's sons Ahaziah and Jehoram, whose reigns were limited by the years 854 B.C., when their father fought at Karkar, and the revolution of Jehu in 842. The error probably arose because Ahaziah suffered the accident recorded in II Kgs. 1[2] soon after his accession, and his reign and that of his brother Jehoram as regent were both counted, although they were contemporary.

Also in the period between 842 and 722 B.C., the additional twenty-two years assigned to the kings of Israel can be traced by the aid of the Assyrian chronology; for in the reckoning of II Kgs. forty-one years are assigned to the kings who reigned between 738 B.C., when Menahem paid tribute to Assyria to establish himself on the throne, and 722–721, when Samaria fell. Evidently the round numbers—ten years attributed to Menahem and the twenty to Pekah—should each be read *two*, for the annals of Tiglath-Pileser III (B, lines [26-29]) record the murder of Pekah in 734 B.C. A few similar errors have crept into the chronology of Judah for the corresponding period. The reigns from Joash to Ahaz yield a total excess of thirty-six years. This is probably in part due to the double counting of the reign of Uzziah and the co-regency of his son Jotham.

Side by side with the length of the reigns, the late prophetic editor of Kings has worked out an elaborate system of synchronisms between the reigns of the kings of Israel and Judah. His model was probably the similar synchronistic chronicles among the Assyrians and Babylonians, illustrated by the Babylonian Chronicle. Cf. Appendix X. There is no evidence, however, that in preparing this system he had any other data than the length of the reigns of the kings. A critical examination of it shows that, in working it out, he fell into many errors. Instead of furnishing additional help in solving the intricate problems of Hebrew chronology, it appears to have influenced the synchronist to introduce certain of the errors which have been noted in connection with the total length of the different reigns. The most striking illustration of the contradictions into which his complex system led him is found in II Kgs. 18. In [13] the simple, definite statement is made that Sennacherib's invasion (of 701 B.C.) fell in the fourteenth year of Hezekiah, which fixes his accession in 715 B.C. This date was probably derived from the early annals; but in [1] the editor states that Hezekiah began to reign in the third year of Hoshea king of Israel and, on the basis of this reckoning, adds in [10] that Samaria was captured in the ninth year of Hoshea and in the sixth of Hezekiah, which would make the date of Hezekiah's accession 727–726 B.C. The recently discovered additional evidence that Sennacherib a second time, about 690, invaded Judah, while Hezekiah was still reigning (cf. Appendix IX), still further establishes 715 B.C. as the date of his accession; for it alone satisfies the older testimony (II Kgs. 18[2]) that he reigned twenty-nine years (715–29 = 686). This would make the reign of Manasseh forty-five instead of the exceedingly improbable fifty-five years, which the editor, or the mistaken reading of a later scribe, assigns to him (II Kgs. 21[1]).

By the close of the seventh century B.C. the Hebrews were so strongly influenced by the spirit and chronological methods of the Assyrians and Babylonians that from this time the Old Testament historians carefully date all important events. During the Babylonian and Persian periods it is indicated by the year of the reigning king of Babylonia or Persia. In I Maccabees the prevailing era began in the spring of 312 B.C. when the Seleucid Empire was established at Antioch.

III

SHISHAK'S LIST OF PALESTINIAN CITIES

On the southern wall of the great temple at Karnak is found a huge relief representing Shishak smiting his conquered foes. Behind him are the names of a hundred and fifty-six districts and towns which he claims to have conquered. A majority of them may be identified as towns of Palestine. Many of them are small and unimportant, but the list as a whole leaves little doubt that the rule of Egypt was acknowledged practically throughout Palestine, while the army of Shishak was present to maintain the ancient title. The list begins with the border city of Gaza, which represented the Philistine cities, and then gives many towns of Northern Israel, among which are Rabbith, Taanach, Shunem, Rehob, Hapharaim, Gibeon, Bethhoron, Aijalon, Megiddo, and east of the Jordan, Mahanaim and probably Penuel. There is no evidence that these towns were besieged and captured. Probably they simply paid tribute. It is also significant that most of them are situated either on the broad plain of Esdraelon or along certain of the great highways of Palestine, and therefore most exposed to attack. The list of Judean towns is longer and the details suggest that the conquest was more complete. Keilah, Socho, Ezem, Arad, and Beth-anoth are among those mentioned. The mutilation of the inscription at the point where it would naturally be expected explains the absence of the name of Jerusalem.

IV

THE MOABITE STONE

In 1868 a German missionary, F. A. Klein, discovered at the ruins of ancient Dibon a monument reared about 825 B.C. by Mesha king of Moab to commemorate his victories over the Israelites. It was of black basalt, about three and one-half feet high and two feet in breadth and thickness, with rounded top. Fortunately in 1869 M. Clermont-Ganneau, by the use of a paper squeeze, secured a rough impression of it, for soon after, as a result of the eager efforts of several competing collectors to gain possession of it, the stone was broken in pieces by the native Arabs in the hope of receiving more profit from the fragments. Twenty of these were soon recovered and put together by the aid of the earlier impression which had been carefully preserved. It is now deposited in the Louvre at Paris, and with the exception of a few words can be completely read. The letters and language are practically identical with those found on the earliest Hebrew inscriptions. The monument itself commemorates the partial reconquest of Moab by Omri and the steps by which Mesha later gradually threw off the Israelitish yoke. The religious ideas and the language are closely parallel to those found in the earliest Old Testament narratives.

MESHA'S INSCRIPTION

I am Mesha son of Chemosh . . . king of Moab the Dibonite. My father was king over Moab thirty years, and I became king after my father. And I made this high place for Chemosh in Karhoh (?)[a] in [gratitude for][b] deliverance, because he saved me from all the assailants (?), and because he made me see my desire upon all those who hated me. Introduction

Omri was king of Israel and he afflicted Moab many days, because Chemosh was angry with his land. And his son succeeded him; and he also said, ' I will afflict Moab.' In my days he said . . . but I saw my desire upon him and upon his house, and Israel perished forever. Omri, however, took possession of the land of Medeba;[c] and he occupied it during his own days and half of his sons' days,[d] forty years; but Chemosh restored it in my days. Omri's rule over Moab

And I fortified Baal-meon; and I made in it the reservoir;[e] and I fortified Kirjathaim.[f] And the men of Gad had occupied the land of Ataroth from of old; and the king of Israel built Ataroth for himself. And I fought against the city and took it. And I slew all the people; the city [became] a gazing-stock to Chemosh and to Moab. And from there I brought the altar-hearth of Dodoh (?);[g] and I dragged it before Chemosh in Kerioth; and I caused the men of Sharon (?)[h] to dwell there, and also the men of . . . Mesha's conquest and destruction of Ataroth

Then Chemosh said to me, 'Go and take Nebo against Israel. So I went by night and fought against it from the break of dawn until noon, and I took it and slew them all—seven thousand men and women and . . . female slaves—for I had devoted it to Ashtar-chemosh. And I took from there the altar-hearths (?) of Jehovah, and dragged them before Chemosh. And the king of Israel had fortified Jahaz,[j] and occupied it while he fought against me. But Chemosh drove him out before me. I took two hundred men of Moab—all its poverty-stricken citizens—and I brought them into Jahaz and took possession of it, to add it to Dibon. Conquest of Nebo Capture of Jahaz

I fortified Karhoh (?), the wall of the forests[k] and the wall of the acropolis.[l] And I built its gates; and I built the royal palace; and I constructed the sluices of the reservoir (?) for the water in the midst of the city. And there was no cistern in the midst of the city, in Karhoh (?); so I said to the people, 'Each of you make a cistern in his own house.' And I cut the trenches (?)[m] for Karhoh (?) with the help of the prisoners of Israel. Building of Karhoh

I built Aroer, and I made the highway by the Arnon. I rebuilt Beth-bamoth, for it had been overthrown. I rebuilt Bezer, for it was in ruins, [with the help of] fifty men of Dibon, for all Dibon was obedient. And I reigned over a hundred [chiefs] (?) in the cities which I added to the land. And I built Medeba and Beth-diblathaim Rebuilding of other Moabite cities

---

a It is not certain what vowels are to be supplied with the consonants in the text. It is probable, however, that the place was identical with the Karhu mentioned in the Karnak list of Rameses II.

b Filling the lacuna according to the implication of the context.

c Cf. Num. 21³⁰, Josh. 13⁹, Is. 15². In the text the form is, *Mehedeba*.

d Omri reigned eighteen and, according to Kgs., his sons thirty-six years. The round number, *forty*, represents the thirty-six of the Heb.

e Or, *pit*.

f Cf. Gen. 14⁵, Jer. 48¹.

g Heb., *David*, Amarna letters, *Dudu*. It is probably the name of a local god.

h Cf. I Chr. 5¹⁶.

i Cf. for the similar Heb. customs, Num. 21², ³, Josh. 6¹⁷⁻¹⁹, Dt. 2³⁴, 3⁶.

j Cf. Num. 21²³, Dt. 2³², Is. 15⁴, Jer. 48²¹.

k Perhaps the wall that ran beside the royal park.

l Heb., *ophel* or *hill*. Cf. Is. 32¹⁴, Neh. 3²⁷.

m Lit., *the cuttings* of some kind.

and Beth-baal-meon. And there I placed [those who bred the small] (?) sheep of the land.

And at Horonaim[n] dwelt the[o] . . . And Chemosh said to me, Go down, fight against Horonaim; so I went down [and fought against the city many days, and] Chemosh [restored it][p] in my days . . .

V

THE WESTERN CAMPAIGNS OF SHALMANESER II

During a long reign of twenty-five years (885–860 B.C.), Ashurnaçirpal III succeeded in thoroughly organizing the Assyrian Empire, and by a series of energetic campaigns in the East, North, and West made it the dominant world-power of the age. For a century his descendants held the throne of Assyria and maintained its supremacy. His son Shalmaneser II reigned for thirty-five years, and by the same unwearied military activity still further expanded the boundaries of the large empire. One monument alone records thirty-three different campaigns. In 854 B.C. he first turned his armies toward Southern Syria, and from this time forward for the next two centuries Assyria became the most important factor in Hebrew history. In succession the three leading states of Syria, Hamath, Damascus, and Israel contested its irresistible advance and, weakened by their wars with each other, fell in turn a prey to its conquering armies.

At first they laid aside their antagonisms and fought together at Karkar on the Orontes, twenty miles north of Hamath, an important battle in which Shalmaneser claims the victory, but the fact that he soon retired without imposing tribute on the local kingdoms indicates that the result was far from decisive. His record of the campaign is found on a monolith now in the British Museum. It is dated in the sixth year of his reign. After telling of his march to the Euphrates and of the tribute presented by the north Syrian states, he adds (lines [97b-102]):a

From Halman (Aleppo) I departed; to the two cities of Irhulini of Hamath I drew near. Adinnu, Mashgâ, Arganâ, his royal cities I conquered. His spoil, his goods, the possessions of his palaces I brought forth; to his palaces I set fire. From Arganâ I departed; to Karkar I drew near. Karkar his royal city, I laid waste, I destroyed, I burned with fire, 1,200 chariots, 1,200 horsemen, 20,000 men of Dad'idri (Hadadezer, Ben-hadad II), of Damascus; 700 chariots, 700 horsemen, 10,000 soldiers of Irhulini of Hamath; 2,000 chariots, 10,000 soldiers of Ahab of Israel; 500 soldiers of Guai,[b] 10,000 soldiers of the land of Muçri; 10 chariots, 10,000 soldiers of the land of Irkanat; 200 soldiers of Matinu-baal, (Mattan-baal) of Arvad; 200 soldiers of the land of Usanata; 30 chariots, 10,000 soldiers of Adnu-bali (Adoni-baal) of Shiana; 1,000 camels of Gindibu of Arba . . . 1,000 soldiers of the Ammonite, Basa son of Ruhubi (Rehob); these twelve kings he (i.e., Irkanat) took to help him; for battle and combat they advanced against me. With the exalted succor, which Asshur, the

---

[n] Cf. Is. 15[5], Jer. 48[3-5].
[o] The end of the inscription is badly mutilated.
[p] Restoring the text in accordance with the preceding idioms, supported by two surviving letters.
  [a] Cf. Schrader KB Pt. I, Vol. I, 177–75; Burney NHTBK 375–77; Hogarth AA 93.
  [b] This is probably identical with the Kuë mentioned in I Kgs. 10[28], together with Muçri. It included the plain of Cilicia.

lord, rendered, with the mighty power, which Nergal, who marched before me, bestowed, I fought with them; from Karkar to Gilzan, I effected their defeat; 14,000 of their troops with weapons I slew; like Adar (the storm-god) I rained down a flood upon them; I scattered their corpses; the surface of the wilderness (?) I filled with their many troops, with weapons I caused their blood to flow. . . . I took possession[c] of the River Orontes. In the midst of that battle I captured their chariots, their horsemen and their teams.

During the lifetime of Ahab, Israel escaped Assyrian attack, but in 849 B.C. and again in 846 Shalmaneser II fought other indecisive battles with the Syrian allies. By 843–842, however, Ben-hadad II of Damascus had been murdered by Hazael and the house of Omri had been overturned by Jehu. In his annals (lines [97b-99b]) and more fully in another inscription from Kalah (lines [1-26]) Shalmaneser describes his campaign in 842 B.C. against Hazael:

In the eighteenth year of my reign for the sixteenth time I crossed the Euphrates. Hazael of Damascus trusted in the multitude of his troops and assembled his innumerable hosts. Senir,[d] a mountain peak in the neighborhood of Lebanon, he made his stronghold. I fought with him, I accomplished his defeat, 6,000 of his soldiers I slew with weapons; 1,121 of his chariots, 470 of his horsemen, together with his stores, I took from him. To save his life, he retreated. I pursued after him. In Damascus, his royal city, I besieged him; his plantations I cut down. To the mountains of Hauran I went; innumerable cities I destroyed, I laid waste, I burned with fire. Their prisoners without number I carried off. I went as far as the mountains of the range Bali-rasi (Baal-rosh)[e], a promontory, I went; there I set up my royal image. At that time I received the tribute of the Tyrians, of the Sidonians, and of Jehu the son of Omri.

On the famous black obelisk containing the annals of Shalmaneser II's reign the tribute which Jehu probably paid to secure the support of Assyria is again mentioned:

Tribute of Jehu son of Omri: silver, gold, a golden bowl, golden goblets, a golden ladle, golden pitchers, bars of lead, a staff for the hand of the king, spear-shafts, I received from him.

Again in 839 B.C. he laid his heavy hand on Syria. The record is found in the annals:

In the twenty-first year of my reign I crossed the Euphrates for the twenty-first time. I went against the cities of Hazael of Damascus. Four of his cities I captured. I received the tribute of the Tyrians, the Sidonians, and the inhabitants of Byblus.

VI

TIGLATH-PILESER III'S CONQUESTS IN PALESTINE

For nearly half a century after the death of Shalmaneser II there were no important Assyrian campaigns in Palestine. In his review of his reign, Adadnirari (812–783 B.C.) claims to have subjected to his yoke, Tyre, Sidon,

---

[c] Or, *dammed*. The meaning of the Assyrian idiom is doubtful.
[d] Cf. Dt. 3[9], where *Senir* is identified as the Amorite name of Mt. Hermon.
[e] Probably the famous headland at the mouth of the Dog River north of Beirut.

the land of Omri, Edom, and Philistia, and to have imposed upon these states the payment of tribute. About 800 B.C. he also forced Damascus to submit. The other peoples probably anticipated attack by at once acknowledging the rule of Assyria.

During the first half of the eighth century B.C. the Assyrian kings were again occupied with problems nearer home. The accession of Tiglath-Pileser III (known in the biblical records by his private name Phul or Pul), in 745 inaugurated a new era in the history of Assyrian conquests in Palestine. The years 742–740 were spent in subjugating Arpad in the north. The conquest of Hamath, which soon followed, is also recorded:

Nineteen districts of the city of Hamath, together with their surrounding towns, which are by the western sea, which in their faithlessness had revolted to Azriyau (Azariah), I annexed to the territory of Assyria. My officers as prefects I appointed over them.

The Azariah mentioned is probably the Azariah or Uzziah of Judah, whose energetic policy and ability may well explain why he had become the head of the coalition that opposed the Assyrian advance. The name, however, is a common one, so that the identification is not absolutely assured. In 738 B.C. Rezon of Damascus, Menahem of Israel and the other Palestinian rulers paid homage to the Assyrian king, but there is no evidence that he invaded their territory.

The great Palestinian campaign of Tiglath-Pileser was in 734 B.C. Its effect upon the politics of Israel and Judah is fully recorded in the Old Testament. Unfortunately the Assyrian record is badly mutilated. The fragments, however, are important. They state that certain cities and territory in the northern part of Israel were annexed to Assyria, and add:

Hanno of Gaza, who fled before my arms, escaped to the land of Egypt. Gaza [I captured]; his possessions and his gods I carried away, and I set up my royal statue. . . . The land of the house of Omri . . . the whole of its inhabitants, together with their possessions I deported to Assyria. Pekah, their king, I slew. Hoshea I appointed over them. Ten [talents of gold, 1,000 talents of silver] . . . I received from them.

Another inscription contains the additional information that, together with certain northern princes, ' Sanibu of Ammon, Salaman of Moab, Mitinti of Ashkelon, Jauhazi (Ahaz) of Judah, Kaushmelek of Edom and Hanno of Gaza,' in 728 B.C. paid tribute to Tiglath-Pileser. Meantime, after a siege of two years, Damascus was finally conquered and its power broken so that the rule of Assyria was established along the eastern Mediterranean.

VII

SARGON'S CAPTURE OF SAMARIA

In 724 B.C. Hoshea, encouraged by the king of Egypt, revolted against Assyria. Shalmaneser IV died before the three years' siege of Samaria was ended, so that the record of its capture in 722–721 is found at the beginning of the annals of his successor, Sargon:

SARGON'S CAPTURE OF SAMARIA

In the beginning of my reign and in the first year of my rule . . . I besieged Samaria and conquered it.[a] . . . Twenty-seven thousand, two hundred and ninety of its inhabitants I carried into captivity; fifty of their chariots I carried away from there [to add to] my royal fighting force.[b] . . . I restored it again and gave it more population than formerly. I settled there people from the lands that I had conquered. I appointed my officers as governors over them. Tribute and customs, like those of the Assyrians, I imposed upon them.

VIII

THE SILOAM INSCRIPTION

In 1880 on an artificial limestone tablet, cut in the rock at the entrance of the Pool of Siloam on the south of the temple-hill at Jerusalem, a brief inscription was accidentally discovered which is known as the Siloam inscription. The Pool of Siloam is the eastern outlet of a rock-cut channel about 1,750 feet in length, which runs from the Virgin's Fount on the eastern side of the southern extension of the temple-hill, under this ridge of rock, to the Tyropœon Valley on the west. Cf. maps opp. pp. 193 and 349. The inscription records the construction of this remarkable piece of ancient engineering, which is generally attributed to the reign of Hezekiah. Cf. II Kgs. 20^{20}, II Chr. 32^{30}. Next to the Moabite stone it is the oldest inscription in the language and writing of the Hebrews thus far discovered with the possible exception of a few words on seals and jars. It is published in Cooke, *North-semitic Inscriptions*, pp. 15–17; Lidzbarski, *Nordsemit epigr.*, p. 439; Driver, *Notes on the Books of Samuel*, p. 16. The translation is as follows:

[Behold] the piercing through! And this was the manner of the piercing through. While yet [the stone-cutters were lifting up] the pick, each toward his fellow, and while yet there were three cubits to be [cut through, there was heard] the voice of each calling to his fellow, for there was a fissure (?) in the rock on the right hand. . . . And on the day of the piercing through, the stone-cutters (lit., hewers) each smote, so as to meet his fellow, pick against pick. And the water flowed from the source to the pool, 1,200 cubits; and the height of the rock above the stone-cutters was one hundred cubits.

Detailed explorations of the tunnel by Warren and Conder have revealed the two shafts which penetrate the rock from either side and nearly meet in the centre. The slight variation in direction is corrected by a connecting shaft precisely as described by the inscription. The water also still flows through it, as it did in early times, from the perennial spring outside the walls to a point inside the ancient city.

IX

SENNACHERIB'S INVASIONS OF JUDAH

In 711 B.C. Judah was partially involved in the rebellion of the Philistine city of Ashdod against Assyria. Sargon also mentions Moab and Edom as parties in the rebellion. The judgment, however, fell chiefly upon Ashdod

---

[a] Three lines are lacking at this point.
[b] A parallel version states, *I allowed the rest of them to retain their possessions.*

and Judah's submission was accepted. But the spirit of revolt continued to smoulder in Judah and blazed into a flame in 705 B.C. when Sargon died and was succeeded by his son Sennacherib. For the first three years he was occupied in Babylon and the East. Under the leadership of Sidon in the north and Askelon and Ekron in the south, most of the states of Palestine were bound together in a coalition against Assyria. Egypt also supported the rebels, and in Judah the Egyptian party gained the ascendancy, notwithstanding the impassioned protests of Isaiah. Cf. Vol. III *in loco.*

Two well-preserved duplicate versions of Sennacherib's account of his early campaign in 701 B.C. are preserved in the British Museum. The references to Judah are found in the Taylor Cylinder, Col. II, 34–III, 41. The king first tells of the subjugation of the northern coast towns, Sidon, Zarepta, Achzib, and Accho. Menahem of Samsimuruna, Tubalu of Sidon, Abdiliti of Arvad, Urumilki of Gebal, Mitinti of Ashdod, Buduilu of Ammon, Chemoshnadab of Moab, Malikram of Edom brought him tribute and took the oath of fealty. The rebellious king of Askelon, Zedek, was carried away captive, together with his family and retainers, to Assyria, and Sharruludari son of Rukibti, the former king, was placed over the people of Askelon. The narrative adds:

Defeat of the Ekronites and their allies at Eltekeh (II, 65–83) In the course of my campaign, Beth-dagon, Joppa, Bene-barak and Azuru, the cities of Zedek, which had not quickly submitted to my rule, I besieged, conquered, carried off their spoil. The leaders, nobles, and people of Ekron, who had cast Padi (their king by virtue of oath and covenant with Assyria) into iron chains, and had delivered him to Hezekiah of Judah, who had imprisoned him in darkness—their heart trembled. They summoned the kings of Egypt, the archers, the chariots, the horses of the king of Miluhhi, forces innumerable, and they came to their aid. Before Eltekeh they drew up in battle array against me; they raised their weapons. In reliance upon Asshur, my lord, I fought with them and effected their defeat. The commander of the chariots and the sons of the king of Egypt, together with the commander of the chariots of the king of Miluhhi I myself took alive as prisoners in the midst of the battle. Eletkeh and Timnath I attacked, conquered, and carried off their spoil.

Their punishment and the reinstatement of Padi (III, 1–11a) I advanced upon Ekron, and the chief officers, the magistrates, who had offended, I slew, and on stakes about the city I impaled their corpses. I counted as prisoners the inhabitants of the town who had done evil and mischief. To the rest of them, who had not practised wickedness and misdeeds, who had not shared in their crime, I proclaimed amnesty. I brought Padi their king from Jerusalem and installed him on the throne of his sovereignty over them. The tribute of my sovereignty I imposed upon him.

Conquest of the cities of Judah (III, 11b–20a) But Hezekiah of Judah who had not submitted to my yoke, forty-six of his fortified towns, together with the innumerable fortresses and small towns in their neighborhood, with assault and battering-rams and approach of siege-engines, with the attack of infantry, of mines . . . I besieged and captured. Two hundred thousand, one hundred and fifty persons, young and old, male and female, horses, mules, asses, camels, oxen and sheep, without number, from their midst I brought out and counted them as spoil.

Siege of Jerusalem (III, 20b–33) I shut him up like a bird in a cage in the midst of Jerusalem, his royal city. I erected fortifications against him and those coming forth from the gates of his city I turned back. His cities which I had plundered I cut off from his domain, and gave them to Mitinti king of Ashdod, to Padi king of Ekron, and to Zilbil king of Gaza, and I diminished his territory. To the former payment of their yearly tribute, the tribute of subjection to my sovereignty I added and laid it upon them. The terror of the glory of my lordship overwhelmed Hezekiah himself, and the Arabians and

THE CAMPAIGN OF 701 B.C.

his trusted soldiers, whom he had introduced for the defence of Jerusalem, his royal city, laid down their arms.

Together with thirty talents of gold and eight hundred talents of silver, I caused to be brought after me to Nineveh, my royal city, precious stones, sparkling . . . stones, great lapislazuli stones, couches of ivory, thrones of state of elephant skins and ivory, . . . wood, whatever there was, an enormous treasure, and his daughters, the women of his palace, his male and female servants (?); and for the payment of tribute and the rendering of homage he despatched his envoy.

Spoil and captives from Jerusalem (III, 34–41)

The event here recorded is evidently the same as the one referred to in II Kgs. 18$^{13-16}$. The exact historical background of the narratives in 18^{17}–20^{37} is not so clear. They are usually assigned to the days immediately following Hezekiah's surrender, on the assumption that Sennacherib, while at Lachish and before departing for Egypt, demanded the unconditional surrender of Jerusalem. But the implication of 18$^{13-16}$, as well as of Sennacherib's inscription, is that Hezekiah had already yielded everything. The reference in 19$^{36, 37}$ to the murder of Sennacherib connects the preceding events, not with the beginning of his reign in 701, but with its close twenty years later. Furthermore Tirhakah, whose expedition is mentioned in 19$^{7-9}$, does not appear to have become master of Egypt until about 691 B.C. A fragmentary text recently discovered by the French Assyriologist P. V. Scheil is claimed to furnish direct proof of a long-suspected western campaign of Sennacherib between 691 and 689 B.C. (Cf. O. Weber, *Sanherib* in *Das Orient*, 3, 1905.) From this and the statement in Esarhaddon's inscription that Sennacherib captured Adumu, an Arabian fortress, it would appear reasonably certain that during the last decade of his reign he made a serious endeavor to bring into complete subjection the rebellious states along the eastern Mediterranean, including the neighboring Arabian tribes, as a preliminary to the conquest of Egypt. It is also significant that the Egyptian tradition regarding his invasion, which is recounted by Herodotus, styles him, *the king of the Arabians and the Assyrians*. The invaders are also called, *the Arabian host*. This would confirm the inference drawn from the inscriptions that the conquest of northern Arabia immediately preceded the invasion of Egypt. Naturally Sennacherib would be desirous of having Jerusalem completely in his control, and yet would be loath to take the time required for its capture by siege. The situation meets fully the conditions implied by the narratives in II Kgs. 18^{17}–19^{37}.

The absence of detailed Assyrian records of this campaign may well be due to the disastrous outcome. Herodotus states that while the Egyptian army lay at Pelusium on the borders of Egypt opposite the invading host,

there came in the night a multitude of field mice, which devoured all the quivers and bow-strings of the enemy and ate the thongs by which they managed their shields. Next morning they commenced their flight, and great multitudes fell, as they had no arms with which to defend themselves. There stands to-day in the temple of Vulcan a stone statue of Sethos, with a mouse in his hand, and an inscription to this effect, Look on me and learn to reverence the gods.

When it is recalled that the mouse was the ancient symbol of pestilence (cf. § 4), it is clear that the Egyptian tradition and the Hebrew narratives in

501

I Kgs. 19[35] both reflect the same story. Both suggest that on the borders of Egypt, the home of contagions, the Assyrian army was overtaken by a virulent plague which forced them to retreat, and that the unexpected deliverance was attributed by Hebrews and Egyptians alike to divine interposition. On the other hand, the Babylonian Chronicle indicates that a rebellion in Babylon made Sennacherib's presence in the East about 690 B.C. absolutely necessary, and in this fact is doubtless one, if not the chief reason, for his sudden abandonment of the Egyptian campaign. These conclusions remove the many difficulties connected with the earlier dating of the incidents recorded in II Kgs. 18[17]–19[37] and accord with the oldest chronological data. Cf. Appendix II. For recent discussions of these problems, cf. Nagel, *Zug des Sanherib gegen Jerusalem*, 1902; Prášek, *Sanherib's Feldzug gegen Juda*, 1903; Weber, *Sanherib König von Assyrien*, 705–681, 1905.

X

THE BABYLONIAN CHRONICLE (B)

Fragments of four distinct Babylonian chronicles have been discovered, which record in brief annalistic form the events of as many different periods. The longest and best preserved is the Babylonian Chronicle (B), a tablet containing one hundred and seventy-six lines, and dated in the twenty-second year of Darius I. It chronicles the chief events of the history of Babylonia and Assyria from the days of Tiglath-Pileser III through the reign of Ashurbanipal, covering the period of over a century when Assyrian history touched that of the Hebrews most closely. Not only is this chronicle of great historical value, but it also suggests the nature of the state annals and the later royal chronicles of Israel and Judah from which the oldest data in the books of Kings were ultimately derived. The formulas of the editor of these books are also closely parallel to those in the Babylonian Chronicle.

The Babylonian Chronicle (B) has been published by Pinches in the *Proceedings of the Society of Biblical Archæology*, VI, pp. 193 ff.; by Winckler, in *Zeitschrift für Assyriologie*, II, pp. 148 ff., and in *Schrader KB*, II, pp. 274–85. The following extracts from the most important section illustrate the general character of this remarkable document:

Tiglath-Pileser's invasion of Babylonia (I, 1–5)

In the third year of Nabonassar king of Babylon, Tiglath-Pileser (III) mounted the throne. In the same year he invaded Babylonia and plundered the cities Rapiku and Hamranu. He carried away the gods of Shapazza. During the reign of Nabonassar, Borsippa rebelled against Babylon. (The successful battle which Nabonassar fought against Borsippa is not mentioned.)[a] In Nabonassar's fifth year Ummanigash mounted the throne of Elam. In the fourteenth year Nabonassar fell sick and died in his palace. Nabonassar reigned fourteen years in Babylon. Nâdinu his son mounted the throne of Babylon.

Events of Nabonassar's reign (I, 6–13)

---

[a] This is evidently a note from the editor of the Chronicle calling attention to an important fact which the earlier source or annals, from which he compiled his data, failed to mention. This reference is exceedingly suggestive.

Reign and assassination of Nâdinu (I, 11–18) Tiglath-Pileser III's rule of Babylonia (I, 19–26) Reign of Sargon and the Elamite invasion (I, 31–37)

In the second year Nâdinu was killed in a rebellion. Two years Nâdinu reigned in Babylon. Shumukin, a governor of a province, who led the revolt, mounted the throne. Two months, . . . days Shumukin reigned in Babylon. Ukinzir . . . seized the throne.

In the third year of Ukinzir, Tiglath-Pileser invaded Babylonia, laid waste Bit-Amukani, and took Ukinzir captive. Three years Ukinzir reigned in Babylonia. Tiglath-Pileser mounted the throne of Babylon. In the second year of Tiglath-Pileser, in the month Tebet he died. . . . years Tiglath-Pileser reigned in Babylonia and Assyria, two years he reigned as the established ruler of Babylonia.

Reign of Shalmaneser IV (I, 27–30)

On the twenty-fifth of Tebet, Shalmaneser mounted the throne of Assyria. The city of Shabarain was destroyed. In the fifth year of his reign, in the month Tebet, Shalmaneser died. Shalmaneser reigned five years in Babylonia and Assyria.

On the twenty-second of Tebet, Sargon mounted the throne of Assyria. In Nisan Merodach-Baladan mounted the throne of Babylonia. In the second year of Merodach-Baladan, Ummanigash king of Elam in the province of Durilu fought a successful battle against Sargon king of Assyria. He devastated Assyria and slew many. Merodach-Baladan and his people, who had come to the help of the king of Elam, did not arrive in time for the battle and followed (?) after him.

Sargon's conquest of Babylonia and Elam (II, 1–9)

In the twelfth year of Merodach-Baladan, Sargon invaded Babylonia and fought a successful battle against Merodach-Baladan. Merodach-Baladan at the head of his nobles fled to Elam. Merodach-Baladan reigned twelve years in Elam. Sargon seated himself on the throne of Elam. In his thirteenth year Sargon seized the land of Bel and conquered Dur-Jakin. In his fourteenth year the king remained in the land [of Babylon]. In the fifteenth year, on the twenty-second of Teshrit, the gods of the coast-lands came back to their place . . . was established in Assyria. In his sixteenth year Sargon marched to Tabal.

Lines 10–18 are lacking, and 19–23 appear to have recorded another attempt of Merodach-Baladan to seize the throne of Babylonia while Sennacherib was king of Assyria. Finally, Belibni became king of Babylonia. The narrative is again well preserved:

In the first year of Belibni, Sennacherib destroyed Hirimma and Hararatu. In the third year of Belibni Sennacherib invaded Babylonia and plundered Babylonia. Belibni and his nobles were carried away to Assyria. Three years Belibni had ruled in Babylon. Sennacherib placed Ashur-nadin-shum his son on the throne in Babylon.

Sennacherib's reconquest of Babylonia (II, 24–31)

XI

CONTEMPORARY ACCOUNTS OF THE CONQUEST OF BABYLON BY CYRUS

The late biblical narrative regarding the conquest of Babylon by Cyrus is richly supplemented by contemporary inscriptions. The brief historical record is found in the chronicle of Nabuna'id and Cyrus or, as it is sometimes called, the Annalistic Tablet of Cyrus. It closely resembles the Babylonian Chronicle. The first part is broken. The chief recorded event of the sixth year of Nabuna'id, the last king of Babylonia, was the revolt of the troops of Astyages, who delivered their king into the hands of Cyrus the king of Anshan. Cyrus then attacked and captured Ecbatana, thus laying the foundations of the Persian empire. In the ninth year, it is recorded that Cyrus king of Persia collected his troops and crossed the Tigris below Arbela, conquering certain adjacent territory. Under the seventeenth year (538 B.C.) is found the account of the final conquest of Babylon:

Conquest of Northern Babylonia (II, 12–15a)

In the month Tammuz (June-July), after Cyrus had fought a successful battle against the troops of Babylonia at the city of Opis, on the banks of the River Zalzallat, he subdued the inhabitants of Babylonia. Whenever they gathered together, he smote them. On the fourteenth of the month, Sippar [a] was taken without a battle. Nabuna'id fled.

Capture of Babylon (III, 15b–18a)

On the sixteenth, Gubaru, governor of the country of Gutium, and the soldiers of Cyrus entered Babylon without a battle. Nabuna'id, since he had been shut in, was taken prisoner in Babylon. To the end of the month Tammuz, the shield-bearers of the country of Gutium guarded the gates of Esagil: [b] no one's spear approached Esagil or came within the sanctuaries, nor was any standard brought therein.

Occupation of the city by Cyrus (II, 18b–24a)

On the third day of Marcheshvan (Oct.-Nov.), Cyrus entered Babylon . . . Peace he established for the city; Cyrus proclaimed peace for all Babylon. Gubaru his governor appointed governors in Babylon. From the month Kislev (Nov.-Dec.) to the month Adar (Feb.-March) the gods of the country of Babylonia, whom Nabuna'id had brought down to Babylon, returned to their own cities. On the eleventh day of Marcheshvan, during the night, Gubaru made an assault (?) and slew the king's son (?). From the twenty-seventh of Adar to the third of Nisan (March-Apr.) there was lamentation in Babylonia: all the people smote their heads.

Further light is shed upon the manner in which Cyrus became master of Babylonia by the proclamation issued by him to his new subjects soon after he entered Babylon. It also clearly indicates his attitude toward the religions of the conquered peoples, and therefore indirectly illuminates the problems presented by the opening chapters of Ezra. The cylinder on which it is inscribed is badly broken, but most of it can still be deciphered. Omitting the fragments of the opening lines, the decree reads:

Marduk's call of Cyrus to the rule of Babylonia (7–19)

The daily offerings [Nabuna'id] suspended . . . He established in the city the worship of Marduk the king of the gods . . . On account of their [the Babylonians'] complaints, the lord of the gods [Marduk] was very wroth. The gods dwelling among them left their abodes in anger, because [Nabuna'id] had brought them to Babylon. Marduk . . . showed compassion. In all lands he looked around and sought a righteous prince, after his own heart, whom he took by his hand. Cyrus king of Anshan he called by name, he proclaimed him by name for the sovereignty of the whole world. He subdued under his feet Kutu (Gutium) and all the Ummanmanda, [c] the black-headed races which [Marduk] had given into his hands; he cared for them justly and righteously. Marduk, the great lord, beheld with joy the protection (?) of his people, [Cyrus's] beneficent deeds, and his upright heart. To his city Babylon he commanded him to march, and made him take his way to Babylon. Like a friend and a helper he went at his side. His great hosts, whose number like the waters of the river could not be known, with their weapons girded on, advanced beside him. Without fighting or battle, he made him enter Babylon. His own city Babylon he spared distress. Nabuna'id the king who did not fear him, he delivered into the hand [of Cyrus]. All the men of Babylonia, the whole land of Sumer and Akkad, the nobles and the governors, bowed before him and kissed his feet, rejoiced at his dominion; their faces beamed. The lord [Marduk] who by his power makes the dead live, who shows favor at all times of distress and need, graciously approached [Cyrus] and honored his name.

---

[a] A town near the Euphrates northwest of Babylon.
[b] The great temple of Babylon.
[c] The northern hordes over which Astyages ruled.

I am Cyrus, the king of hosts, the great king, the mighty king, king of Babylon, king of Sumer and Akkad, king of the four quarters of the earth, the son of Cambyses, the great king, king of the city of Anshan, the great-grandson of Teispes the great king, king of the city of Anshan, the enduring offspring of royalty, whose reign Bel and Nebo love, whose dominion they desired for the gladness of their hearts. *His titles and ancestry (20–22a)*

After I had peacefully entered Babylon, I occupied with rejoicing and festivity the king's palace as my royal residence. Marduk [inclined toward] me the open hearts of the inhabitants of Babylon, and daily I revered him. My vast army spread itself out peacefully in Babylon; the whole land of Sumer and Akkad I freed from every oppressor. In Babylon and all its cities I cared well for their inhabitants . . . Their sighing I stilled, their sorrow I relieved. To [do these] acts Marduk the great lord gave me command. To me, Cyrus, the king who reveres him, and to Cambyses, the son, the offspring of my body, . . . to the whole of my army he graciously inclined and in peace kindly . . . *Establishment of his rule in Babylon (22b–28a)*

All the kings who dwell in royal halls, who in all the world, from the upper [Mediterranean] to the lower sea [Persian Gulf], live inland, together with the kings of the Amorite land [Phœnicia and Philistia], the inhabitants of tents, all of them brought their rich tribute and in Shuannabi [a quarter of Babylon] kissed my feet. To [the cities of Assyria] the gods who abode in them I restored to their place and settled in a permanent abiding place. All their populations I gathered together and restored to their own dwellings. The gods of the land of Sumer and Akkad, whom Nabuna'id, to the displeasure of the lord of the gods had brought to Babylon, at the command of Marduk, the great lord, I caused to take up their abode safely in their own shrines in gladness of heart. *Restoration of the peoples and gods of the land to their homes (28b–34)*

May all the gods, whom I restored to their own cities, daily before Bel and Nebo speak of length of days for me! May they utter words in my favor and to Marduk my lord, may they say: 'Cyrus the king, who revereth thee, and Cambyses his son . . . made them all dwell in a quiet habitation.' *Concluding prayer (25–36)*

XII

THE GADATAS INSCRIPTION

Another interesting contemporary illustration of the attitude of the early Persian kings toward the religions of the peoples subject to them is found in an inscription of Darius, discovered in 1889 in the province of Magnesia and published in *Bulletin de Correspondance Hellénique*, *XIII*, 529:

The king of kings, Darius the son of Hystaspes, speaks to his servant Gadatas as follows: I hear that you have not conformed in all points to my instructions. To be sure you have taken great trouble to cultivate the land which belongs to me, since you have transplanted in the soil of Asia Minor the plants from the trans-Euphrates province. I praise your foresight, and for this you will have great thanks in the royal court. But on the other hand, because you have annulled my arrangement in regard to the gods, in case you do not do differently, I will make you feel the anger which you have aroused in me. For you have compelled the gardeners consecrated to Apollo to pay tribute and to work profane ground, thus failing to appreciate the feeling of my ancestors toward the god who said to the Persians: . . .

Darius here figures as the champion of the great god Apollo against the excessive zeal of one of his agents in Asia Minor, a certain Gadatas, who had evidently compelled those in charge of the gardens connected with a temple of Apollo to pay tribute, probably in money, and to work in the *corvée* or forced labor, which all oriental rulers imposed upon their subjects. The inference is that all connected with the temple were free from taxation.

XIII

THE HEBREW, BABYLONIAN, AND MACEDONIAN MONTHS

The Hebrews, in common with the Canaanites, Babylonians, and Assyrians, divided their year into lunar months of about twenty-nine days, twelve hours and forty-four minutes. The names of only four of the early Canaanite months, which the Hebrews adopted and used until the Babylonian exile, have been preserved. Two of them, *Ethanim* and *Bul* have also been found on Phœnician inscriptions dating from the fourth century B.C. During the exile the Jews ceased to use the old Canaanite names, and the editors of the books of Kings, Jeremiah, and Ezekiel substituted numerals. From the period of the exile the Jews adopted the Babylonian names.

The old Hebrew year began about the middle of September, as did the sacred year even in later times; but with the adoption of the Babylonian names for the months, the Babylonian new year, beginning about the middle of March, was also accepted by the Jews in their secular calendar.

The following table will facilitate the identification of the different months:

Canaanite and Early Hebrew	Exilic Number	Babylonian and Assyrian	Jewish	Macedonian	Modern Equivalents
Abib	1	Nisannu	Nisan	Xanthicos	March-April.
Ziv	2	Airu	Iyyar	Artemisos	April-May.
	3	Sivanu or Simannu	Sivan	Daisios	May-June.
	4	Duzu	Tammuz	Panemos	June-July.
	5	Abu	Ab	Lôos	July-Aug.
	6	Ululu	Elul	Gorpiaios	Aug.-Sept.
Ethanim	7	Tashritum	Tishri	Huperberetaios	Sept.-Oct.
Bul	8	Arah samna	Marcheshvan	Dîos	Oct.-Nov.
	9	Kislimu	Kislev	Apellaios	Nov.-Dec.
	10	Tebitu	Tebeth	Audunaios	Dec.-Jan.
	11	Shabatu	Shebat	Peritios	Jan.-Feb.
	12	Addaru	Adar	Dustros	Feb.-March.
	Intercalary	Arhu mahru ša Addaru	After Adar or Second Adar		

The
Student's Old Testament

*Logically and Chronologically
Arranged and Translated*

BY

CHARLES FOSTER KENT, Ph.D.

WOOLSEY PROFESSOR OF BIBLICAL LITERATURE IN YALE UNIVERSITY

Announcement

**The five essentials for Old Testament study:
(1) A systematic classification of its contents.**

THE Old Testament is a library containing the writings of Israel's inspired teachers, who lived at periods far removed from each other, wrote from widely different points of view, and expressed their thoughts in the language and literary forms peculiar to the primitive Semitic East. Their modern readers, however, live in the very different western world. The result is that, while the combination of early songs, primitive traditions, ethnological tables, tribal stories, genealogical lists, prophetic exhortations, laws, judicial precedents, and historical narratives found, for example, in such a book as Exodus, seems perfectly natural to the intuitive Oriental, it is a fertile source of confusion to the logical Occidental. The obvious solution of the difficulty is to be found in systematic classification. This work was begun by the Greek translators of the Old Testament, to whom is chiefly due the approximately logical arrangement of the books in the English Bible. The confusion may be still further eliminated by grouping together those writings which have the same general theme, aim, and literary form, and then by rearranging them within each group in the approximate order in which they were written.

(2) A comparative presentation of its original sources.

Where there are different versions of the same narrative or where two or more have been combined together—as is often the case in the first twelve books of the Old Testament—it is important that the originally distinct versions be printed side by side, as in a harmony, that they may be studied comparatively and as independent literary units.

(3) A lucid, exact translation. The third essential is a clear, vivid, dignified translation, which will represent not merely the words but also the ideas, the spirit, and the beauty of the original, and which will put the reader, unacquainted with Hebrew, in possession of the latest contributions of philology, exegesis, and theology.

(4) Clear literary analysis. The fourth is a clear literary analysis, which will make it possible readily to trace the logical thought of a story, law, sermon, or poem, and to note the relation of the different parts to each other and to the whole.

(5) Illuminating introductions and foot-notes. Finally concise, lucid notes are demanded, which will at once present the historical background and the critical, geographical, and archæological data required to illuminate the obscurities of the text, without distracting attention from its beauty and thought.

Aims and plan of the Student's Old Testament. These five absolute essentials the *Students' Old Testament* aims to supply in the fullest measure and in the most direct and usable form. The general plan is unique in its simplicity and economy of space. By combining a lucid, scholarly translation, a logical and chronological classification, and a critical and a literary analysis of the text with brief introductions and notes at the foot of the page, the reader is at once placed in command of the practical results of modern biblical research, many of which are otherwise found only in cumbersome technical works, intelligible only to the specialist.

Its origin. The sane, careful scholarship and the reverent constructive spirit of the author are already known to a wide circle of Bible students through his *History of the Hebrew People* and his volumes in the *Messages of the Bible*. The present extensive work is the result of years of preparation, in which he has also been able to profit by the generous suggestions and criticisms of a large number of biblical scholars and practical teachers. The whole has been prepared to meet not theoretical but practical needs and has been tested at each point in university and Bible classes.

Its point of view and method.
The work embodies the positive conclusions of the many hundreds of earnest critical scholars, who have during the past two centuries been grappling with the intricate problems of the Old Testament. For the first time in its history the various versions of its more important stories and historical records are printed throughout in parallel columns so that they can be readily studied in approximately their original form. In the introductions and foot-notes the biblical data upon which these results are based are cogently presented so that the ordinary Bible reader can readily understand and estimate their significance. Where the positions are established the fact is indicated, and where there is still uncertainty this is also frankly stated. When at times the author's conclusions differ from those of the majority of scholars the reasons for the departure are fully outlined.

Its practical value.
To the ordinary conservative biblical student, who rejects or views with alarm the critical positions of modern Old Testament teachers, an opportunity is offered, for the first time, of ascertaining just what those positions are and the chief reasons therefor. To many it will be a genuine relief to find that the foundations of Christian faith, instead of being destroyed, are simply being laid on a deeper and broader historical basis, and that the newer methods of interpretation are supremely helpful in gaining a true knowledge of the eternal messages of the Bible. To the rapidly increasing body of progressive Bible readers, who accept the principles and in general appreciate the practical value of critical biblical research, this clear, definite presentation of its more important fruits cannot fail to be most welcome. It furnishes to the historian the data for the easy reconstruction of biblical history, to the literary student the basis for a new understanding and appreciation of the wonderful literature of the Old Testament, and to the pastor, the Sunday-school teacher, the parent, and the individual reader positive religious facts and teachings, the

want of which is being strongly felt in this age, when destructive conclusions are much in evidence. Above all the *Student's Old Testament* presents those foundations—laid bare through the untiring labors of generations of Christian scholars and by the faithful application of scientific method—upon which Old Testament interpretation and doctrine promise in the future to rest.

No effort or expense has been spared to make this work a complete manual for class-room study, for reading, and for reference. Each volume is complete in itself, embodying all the cognate Old Testament and apocryphal literature in its given field. A detailed table of contents, index, page-headings, and cross-references facilitate its use by primary as well as advanced readers.

Each volume is also fully equipped with thoroughly modern topographical and historical maps, which are introduced in connection with the literature of each period. Comparative chronological charts make it possible to trace readily the growth and approximate dates of the Old Testament and apocryphal writings in connection with the events and movements which determined their form and which in turn they record. Tables of weights and measures and carefully selected and detailed bibliographies, introduced in connection with each epoch, supply both elementary and advanced students with a complete equipment for intelligent reading and fruitful study.

Terms of Subscription

SINGLE VOLUMES. The publishers will supply any single volume of the series for $2.75 net (postage, 15 cents).

ADVANCE SUBSCRIPTIONS. As an inducement to advance subscribers, the publishers will accept subscriptions for the complete set of six volumes for $13.50, payable in instalments on the publication of each volume.

DELIVERY. Each volume will be sent to subscribers as soon as published. Books will be sent by mail or express as requested.

CHARLES SCRIBNER'S SONS
153-157 Fifth Avenue   **NEW YORK**